P9-CRI-435

# TAKING SIDES

Clashing Views on Controversial

# Political Issues

TWELFTH EDITION

Selected, Edited, and with Introductions by

**George McKenna**
*City College, City University of New York*

and

**Stanley Feingold**
*Westchester Community College*

McGraw-Hill/Dushkin
A Division of The McGraw-Hill Companies

Photo Acknowledgment
Cover image: © 2001 by PhotoDisc, Inc.

Cover Art Acknowledgment
Charles Vitelli

Copyright © 2001 by McGraw-Hill/Dushkin,
A Division of The McGraw-Hill Companies, Inc., Guilford, Connecticut 06437

Copyright law prohibits the reproduction, storage, or transmission in any form by any means of any portion of this publication without the express written permission of McGraw-Hill/Dushkin and of the copyright holder (if different) of the part of the publication to be reproduced. The Guidelines for Classroom Copying endorsed by Congress explicitly state that unauthorized copying may not be used to create, to replace, or to substitute for anthologies, compilations, or collective works.

Taking Sides ® is a registered trademark of McGraw-Hill/Dushkin

Manufactured in the United States of America

Twelfth Edition

123456789BAHBAH4321

Library of Congress Cataloging-in-Publication Data
Main entry under title:
Taking sides: clashing views on controversial political issues/selected, edited, and with introductions by George McKenna and Stanley Feingold.—12th ed.
Includes bibliographical references and index.
1. United States—Politics and government—1945–. I. McKenna, George, *comp.*
II. Feingold, Stanley, *comp.*
320'.973
0-07-242251-3
ISSN: 1080-580X

Printed on Recycled Paper

# Dedication

In memory of Hillman M. Bishop and Samuel Hendel, masters of an art often neglected by college teachers: teaching.

# Preface

**D**ialogue means two people talking to the same issue. This is not as easy as it sounds. Play back the next debate between the talking heads you see on television. Listen to them try to persuade each other—actually, the TV audience —of the truth of their own views and of the irrationality of their opponents' views.

What is likely to happen? At the outset, they will probably fail to define the issue with enough clarity and objectivity to make it clear exactly what it is that they are disputing. As the philosopher Alasdair MacIntyre has put it, the most passionate pro and con arguments are often "incommensurable"—they sail past each other because the two sides are talking about different things. As arguments proceed, both sides tend to employ vague, emotion-laden terms without spelling out the uses to which the terms are put. When the heat is on, they may resort to shouting epithets at one another, and the hoped-for meeting of minds will give way to the scoring of political points and the reinforcement of existing prejudices. For example, when the discussion of affirmative action comes down to both sides accusing the other of "racism," or when the controversy over abortion degenerates into taunts and name-calling, then no one really listens and learns from the other side.

It is our conviction that people *can* learn from the other side, no matter how sharply opposed it is to their own cherished viewpoint. Sometimes, after listening to others, we change our view entirely. But in most cases, we either incorporate some elements of the opposing view—thus making our own richer —or else learn how to answer the objections to our viewpoint. Either way, we gain from the experience. For these reasons we believe that encouraging dialogue between opposed positions is the most certain way of enhancing public understanding.

The purpose of this 12th edition of *Taking Sides* is to continue to work toward the revival of political dialogue in America. As we have done in the past 11 editions, we examine leading issues in American politics from the perspective of sharply opposed points of view. We have tried to select authors who argue their points vigorously but in such a way as to enhance our understanding of the issue.

We hope that the reader who confronts lively and thoughtful statements on vital issues will be stimulated to ask some of the critical questions about American politics. What are the highest-priority issues with which government must deal today? What positions should be taken on these issues? What should be the attitude of Americans toward their government? Our conviction is that a healthy, stable democracy requires a citizenry that considers these questions and participates, however indirectly, in answering them. The alternative is apathy, passivity, and, sooner or later, the rule of tyrants.

i

**Plan of the book**    Each issue has an issue *introduction,* which sets the stage for the debate as it is argued in the YES and NO selections. Each issue concludes with a *postscript* that makes some final observations and points the way to other questions related to the issue. In reading the issue and forming your own opinions you should not feel confined to adopt one or the other of the positions presented. There are positions in between the given views or totally outside them, and the *suggestions for further reading* that appear in each issue postscript should help you find resources to continue your study of the subject. We have also provided relevant Internet site addresses (URLs) on the *On the Internet* page that accompanies each part opener. At the back of the book is a listing of all the *contributors to this volume,* which will give you information on the political scientists and commentators whose views are debated here.

**Changes to this edition**    Over the past 22 years *Taking Sides* has undergone extensive changes and improvements, and we are particularly proud of this 12th edition. There are seven new issues in this volume: *Are the Mass Media Dominated by the Powerful Few?* (Issue 4); *Is Congress Limited in Regulating Commerce Within a State?* (Issue 5); *The Presidency: Does the President's Personal Morality Matter?* (Issue 6); *Does the Religious Right Threaten American Freedoms?* (Issue 12); *Would "School Choice" Improve the Quality of U.S. Education?* (Issue 13); *Are Americans Taxed Too Much?* (Issue 18); and *Does China Tend to Threaten World Peace and Stability?* (Issue 19). In addition, for two other issues (capital punishment and welfare reform) we have replaced one of the selections to freshen up the debate. All told, there are 16 new selections in this edition.

We worked hard on what we hope will be a truly memorable 12th edition, and we think you will like the result. Let us know what you think by writing to us care of McGraw-Hill/Dushkin, 530 Old Whitfield Street, Guilford, CT 06437 or e-mailing us at GMcK1320@aol.com or stanleyfeingold@ mindspring.com. Suggestions for further improvements are most welcome!

**A word to the instructor**    An *Instructor's Manual With Test Questions* (multiple-choice and essay) is available through the publisher for the instructor using *Taking Sides* in the classroom. A general guidebook, *Using Taking Sides in the Classroom,* which discusses methods and techniques for integrating the pro-con approach into any classroom setting, is also available. An online version of *Using Taking Sides in the Classroom* and a correspondence service for *Taking Sides* adopters can be found at http://www.dushkin.com/usingts/.

*Taking Sides: Clashing Views on Controversial Political Issues* is only one title in the Taking Sides series. If you are interested in seeing the table of contents for any of the other titles, please visit the Taking Sides Web site at http:// www.dushkin.com/takingsides/.

**Acknowledgments**    We are grateful to Laura McKenna and Jennifer Bornholdt for their researches, which were most helpful to us in preparing this edition. We also received many helpful comments and suggestions from our friends and readers across the United States and Canada. Their suggestions have markedly enhanced the quality of this edition of *Taking Sides* and are reflected in the totally new issues and the updated selections.

Our thanks go to those who responded with suggestions for the 12th edition:

**Michelle Bellini**
*University of Northern Colorado*

**Corlan Carlson**
*Whatcom Community College*

**Gary Donato**
*Three Rivers Community Technical College*

**Gerald Duff**
*Arizona State University*

**Peter Heller**
*Manhattan College*

**Willoughby Jarrell**
*Kennesaw State University*

**Steve Jenks**
*University of Central Oklahoma*

**Mark Kelso**
*Queens College*

**Kenneth Kiser**
*Highland Community College*

**Patrice Mareschal**
*University of Oklahoma*

**Michelle Martin**
*Sierra College*

**Ted R. Mosch**
*University of Tennessee at Martin*

**Marion Moxley**
*El Camino College*

**David S. Myers**
*University of West Florida*

**Susan Rouder**
*City College of San Francisco*

**Harvey Strum**
*Sage Junior College of Albany*

**Paul Tesch**
*Spokane Community College*

We also appreciate the spontaneous letters from instructors and students who wrote to us with comments and observations. Many thanks to Ted Knight, list manager of the Taking Sides series, for his able editorial assistance; to David Brackley, senior developmental editor; and to Rose Gleich, administrative assistant. Needless to say, the responsibility for any errors of fact or judgment rests with us.

**George McKenna**
*City College, City University of New York*

**Stanley Feingold**
*Westchester Community College*

# Contents In Brief

# Contents

Writer Irving Kristol argues that America possesses a rich combination of ingredients that give it strength, resilience, and character. Freelance writer Daniel Lazare contends that America has become paralyzed in a constitutional straitjacket and that it needs radical reform.

Professor of political science Samuel L. Popkin argues that presidential election campaigns perform a unique and essential service in informing and unifying the American people. Political scientist Anthony King contends that American officeholders spend too much time and effort running for office, which detracts from their responsibility to provide good government.

Archibald Cox, a former special prosecutor and a law professor, argues that the increasing amount of money spent in elections corrupts government but that the public's faith in democratic self-government can be restored by campaign finance reform. Bradley A. Smith, an associate

professor at Capital University Law School, asserts that campaign contributions do not corrupt candidates, the biggest spenders do not always
win, and the relatively modest amount that candidates spend is essential
to educate voters and to increase their interest.

Communications research professor Robert W. McChesney fears that
powerful media-owning corporations distort and suppress news and disproportionately favor their corporate interests. Former reporter Steven
Rattner asserts that increasing competition and diversity are ensured by
cable television, the Internet, and the unwillingness of media corporations
to limit expression.

# PART 2  THE INSTITUTIONS OF GOVERNMENT    83

Supreme Court chief justice William H. Rehnquist argues that Congress
cannot regulate activities within a state that are not economic and do not
substantially affect commerce among the states. Supreme Court justice
Stephen G. Breyer upholds the right of Congress to regulate activities
within a state if Congress has a rational basis for believing that it affects
the exercise of congressional power.

William J. Bennett, a former official in the Reagan and Bush administrations, argues that a president's personal morality cannot be divorced from
his job performance, because the latter includes the kind of example he
sets for the youth of the nation. Presidential scholars Thomas E. Cronin
and Michael A. Genovese agree that "character matters" in presidents
but only as it touches on their external behavior; presidents with roguish
private lives, they maintain, can exhibit considerable public integrity.

Law professor Ronald Dworkin contends that judges must read the vaguer
phrases of the Constitution with an eye toward what is best for the nation.
Law professor Mary Ann Glendon warns of the perils of "romantic judging,"
which she argues usurps the role of legislatures and weakens the spirit of
democracy.

Essayist Robert W. Lee argues that capital punishment is the only fair
way for society to respond to certain heinous crimes. Law professor Eric
M. Freedman contends that the death penalty does not reduce crime but
does reduce public safety and carries the risk of innocent people being
executed.

Writer Carl T. Bogus argues that gun control laws will reduce the number
of gun-related crimes. Professor of law Daniel D. Polsby contends that
gun control laws may actually increase the incidence of robbery and other
gun-related crimes.

Journalist Clarence Page argues that although affirmative action is not a
perfect remedy, it has benefited minorities and, in some cases, increased
opportunities for whites as well. Professor of English Shelby Steele argues
that affirmative action demoralizes both blacks and whites and that racial
preferences do not empower blacks.

Economist Paul Krugman maintains that corporate greed, the decline of
organized labor, and changes in production have contributed to a sharp
increase in social and economic inequality in America. Christopher C.
DeMuth, president of the American Enterprise Institute, asserts that Americans have achieved an impressive level of wealth and equality and that a
changing economy ensures even more opportunities.

Legal scholar Robert H. Bork concludes that the semantics of "pro-choice"
cannot hide the fact that aborting a fetus is killing an unborn child and that
most abortions are performed for the woman's convenience. Writer Mary
Gordon maintains that having an abortion is a moral choice that women
are capable of making for themselves, that aborting a fetus is not killing a
person, and that antiabortionists fail to understand female sexuality.

Essayist and editor Andrew Sullivan contends that legalizing gay marriage
would be a profoundly humanizing step because such marriages, with
their honesty, their flexibility, and their equality, could nourish the broader
society as well. Social scientist James Q. Wilson asserts that to legalize homosexual marriage would be to enter an untested area that could
profoundly damage the already-fragile institutions of marriage and family.

*Wall Street Journal* editorial writer Amity Shlaes maintains that the federal
income tax is too high, too complex, and too biased against high-income
earners. Citizens for Tax Justice, a nonprofit research and advocacy association dedicated to fair taxation, concludes that taxes are relatively low,
fair in distributing the tax burden, and necessary.

# Introduction

## Labels and Alignments in American Politics

George McKenna

Stanley Feingold

America's political vocabulary contains a rich variety of terms that have accumulated since the time of the country's founding in the eighteenth century —terms like *liberal, conservative, left wing, right wing, moderate, and extremist.* As we enter the twenty-first century, it is clear that the meanings of these terms have shifted over the past two and a half centuries. Some of the terms— *liberalism* is perhaps the best example—seem almost to have reversed their meaning. It is fair to ask whether these terms have any fixed, core meanings left in them. Are they now anything more than polemical weapons, useful for battering the enemy and rallying the faithful, or is there still something left in them? We believe that there is, but we caution that the terms must be used thoughtfully and with due regard for their origins and usage. Otherwise, the terms may end up obscuring or oversimplifying positions. Our purpose in this introduction is to explore the basic core meanings of these terms in order to make them useful to us as citizens.

## LIBERALS VERSUS CONSERVATIVES: AN OVERVIEW

Let us examine, very briefly, the historical evolution of the terms *liberalism* and *conservatism.* By examining the roots of these terms, we can see how these philosophies have adapted themselves to changing times. In that way, we can avoid using the terms rigidly, without reference to the particular contexts in which liberalism and conservatism have operated over the past two centuries.

### Classical Liberalism

The classical root of the term liberalism is the Latin word *libertas,* meaning "liberty" or "freedom." In the early nineteenth century, liberals dedicated themselves to freeing individuals from all unnecessary and oppressive obligations to authority—whether the authority came from the church or the state. They opposed the licensing and censorship of the press, the punishment of heresy, the establishment of religion, and any attempt to dictate orthodoxy in matters of opinion. In economics, liberals opposed state monopolies and other constraints upon competition between private businesses. At this point in its development, liberalism defined freedom primarily in terms of freedom *from*. It appropriated the French term *laissez-faire,* which literally means "leave to be." Leave people alone! That was the spirit of liberalism in its early days. It wanted government to stay out of people's lives and to play a modest role in general. Thomas Jefferson summed up this concept when he said, "I am no friend of energetic government. It is always oppressive."

Despite their suspicion of government, classical liberals invested high hopes in the political process. By and large, they were great believers in democracy. They believed in widening suffrage to include every white male, and some of them were prepared to enfranchise women and blacks as well. Although liberals occasionally worried about "the tyranny of the majority," they were more prepared to trust the masses than to trust a permanent, entrenched elite. Liberal social policy was dedicated to fulfilling human potential and was based on the assumption that this often-hidden potential is enormous. Human beings, liberals argued, were basically good and reasonable. Evil and irrationality were believed to be caused by "outside" influences; they were the result of a bad social environment. A liberal commonwealth, therefore, was one that would remove the hindrances to the full flowering of the human personality.

The basic vision of liberalism has not changed since the nineteenth century. What has changed is the way it is applied to modern society. In that respect, liberalism has changed dramatically. Today, instead of regarding government with suspicion, liberals welcome government as an instrument to serve the people. The change in philosophy began in the latter years of the nineteenth century, when businesses—once small, independent operations—began to grow into giant structures that overwhelmed individuals and sometimes even overshadowed the state in power and wealth. At that time, liberals began reconsidering their commitment to the *laissez-faire* philosophy. If the state can be an oppressor, asked liberals, can't big business also oppress people? By then, many were convinced that commercial and industrial monopolies were crushing the souls and bodies of the working classes. The state, formerly the villain, now was viewed by liberals as a potential savior. The concept of freedom was transformed into something more than a negative freedom *from;* the term began to take on a positive meaning. It meant "realizing one's full potential." Toward this end, liberals believed, the state could prove to be a valuable instrument. It could educate children, protect the health and safety of workers, help people through hard times, promote a healthy economy, and—when necessary—force business to act more humanely and responsibly. Thus was born the movement that culminated in New Deal liberalism.

## New Deal Liberalism

In the United States, the argument in favor of state intervention did not win an enduring majority constituency until after the Great Depression of the 1930s began to be felt deeply. The disastrous effects of a depression that left a quarter of the workforce unemployed opened the way to a new administration—and a promise. "I pledge you, I pledge myself," Franklin D. Roosevelt said when accepting the Democratic nomination in 1932, "to a new deal for the American people." Roosevelt's New Deal was an attempt to effect relief and recovery from the Depression; it employed a variety of means, including welfare programs, public works, and business regulation—most of which involved government intervention in the economy. The New Deal liberalism relied on government to liberate people from poverty, oppression, and economic exploitation. At the same time, the New Dealers claimed to be as zealous as the classical liberals in defending political and civil liberties.

The common element in *laissez-faire* liberalism and welfare-state liberalism is their dedication to the goal of realizing the full potential of each individual. Some still questioned whether this is best done by minimizing state involvement or whether it sometimes requires an activist state. The New Dealers took the latter view, though they prided themselves on being pragmatic and experimental about their activism. During the heyday of the New Deal, a wide variety of programs were tried and—if found wanting—abandoned. All decent means should be tried, they believed, even if it meant dilution of ideological purity. The Roosevelt administration, for example, denounced bankers and businessmen in campaign rhetoric but worked very closely with them while trying to extricate the nation from the Depression. This set a pattern of pragmatism that New Dealers from Harry Truman to Lyndon Johnson emulated.

## Progressive Liberalism

Progressive liberalism emerged in the late 1960s and early 1970s as a more militant and uncompromising movement than the New Deal had ever been. Its roots go back to the New Left student movement of the early 1960s. New Left students went to the South to participate in civil rights demonstrations, and many of them were bloodied in confrontations with southern police; by the mid-1960s they were confronting the authorities in the North over issues like poverty and the Vietnam War. By the end of the decade, the New Left had fragmented into a variety of factions and had lost much of its vitality, but a somewhat more respectable version of it appeared as the New Politics movement. Many New Politics crusaders were former New Leftists who had traded their jeans for coats and ties; they tried to work within the system instead of always confronting it. Even so, they retained some of the spirit of the New Left. The civil rights slogan "Freedom Now" expressed the mood of the New Politics. The young university graduates who filled its ranks had come from an environment where "nonnegotiable" demands were issued to college deans by leaders of sit-in protests. There was more than youthful arrogance in the New Politics movement, however; there was a pervasive belief that America had lost, had compromised away, much of its idealism. The New Politics liberals sought to recover some of that spirit by linking up with an older tradition of militant reform, which went back to the time of the Revolution. These new liberals saw themselves as the authentic heirs of Thomas Paine and Henry David Thoreau, of the abolitionists, the radical populists, the suffragettes, and the great progressive reformers of the early twentieth century.

While New Deal liberals concentrated almost exclusively on bread-and-butter issues such as unemployment and poverty, the New Politics liberals introduced what came to be known as social issues into the political arena. These included: the repeal of laws against abortion, the liberalization of laws against homosexuality and pornography, the establishment of affirmative action programs to ensure increased hiring of minorities and women, and the passage of the Equal Rights Amendment. In foreign policy, too, New Politics liberals departed from the New Deal agenda. Because they had keener memories of the unpopular and (for them) unjustified war in Vietnam than of World War II, they became doves, in contrast to the general hawkishness of the New Dealers. They were skeptical of any claim that the United States must be the leader of the free world or, indeed, that it had any special mission in the world; some were convinced that America was already in decline and must learn to adjust accordingly. The real danger, they argued, came not from the Soviet Union but from the mad pace of America's arms race with the Soviets, which, as they saw it, could bankrupt the country, starve its social programs, and culminate in a nuclear Armageddon.

New Politics liberals were heavily represented at the 1972 Democratic national convention, which nominated South Dakota senator George McGovern for president. By the 1980s the New Politics movement was no longer new, and many of its adherents preferred to be called progressives. By this time their critics had another name for them: radicals. The critics saw their positions as inimical to the interests of the United States, destructive of the family, and fundamentally at odds with the views of most Americans. The adversaries of the progressives were not only conservatives but many New Deal liberals, who openly scorned the McGovernites.

This split still exists within the Democratic party, though it is now more skillfully managed by party leaders. In 1988 the Democrats paired Michael Dukakis, whose Massachusetts supporters were generally on the progressive side of the party, with New Dealer Lloyd Bentsen as the presidential and vice-presidential candidates, respectively. In 1992 the Democrats won the presidency with Arkansas governor Bill Clinton, whose record as governor seemed to put him in the moderate-to-conservative camp, and Tennessee senator Albert Gore, whose position on environmental issues could probably be considered quite liberal but whose general image was middle-of-the-road. Both candidates had moved toward liberal positions on the issues of gay rights and abortion. By 1994 Clinton was perceived by many Americans as being "too liberal," which some speculate may have been a factor in the defeat of Democrats in the congressional elections that year. Clinton immediately sought to shake off that perception, positioning himself as a "moderate" between extremes and casting the Republicans as an "extremist" party. (These two terms will be examined presently.)

## Conservatism

Like liberalism, conservatism has undergone historical transformation in America. Just as early liberals (represented by Thomas Jefferson) espoused less government, early conservatives (whose earliest leaders were Alexander Hamilton and John Adams) urged government support of economic enterprise and government intervention on behalf of certain groups. But today, in reaction to the growth of the welfare state, conservatives argue strongly that more government means more unjustified interference in citizens' lives, more bureaucratic regulation of private conduct, more inhibiting control of economic enterprise, more material advantage for the less energetic and less able at the expense of those who are prepared to work harder and better, and, of course, more taxes—taxes that will be taken from those who have earned money and given to those who have not.

Contemporary conservatives are not always opposed to state intervention. They may support larger military expenditures in order to protect society against foreign enemies. They may also allow for some intrusion into private life in order to protect society against internal subversion and would pursue criminal prosecution zealously in order to protect society against domestic violence. The fact is that few conservatives, and perhaps fewer liberals, are absolute with respect to their views about the power of the state. Both are quite prepared to use the state in order to further *their* purposes. It is true that activist presidents such as Franklin Roosevelt and John Kennedy were likely to be classified as liberals. However, Richard Nixon was also an activist, and, although he does not easily fit any classification, he was far closer to conservatism than to liberalism. It is too easy to identify liberalism with statism and conservatism with antistatism; it is important to remember that it was liberal Jefferson who counseled against "energetic government" and conservative Alexander Hamilton who designed bold powers for the new central government and wrote, "Energy in the executive is a leading character in the definition of good government."

For a time, a movement calling itself *neoconservatism* occupied a kind of intermediate position between New Deal liberalism and conservatism. Composed for the most part of former New Deal Democrats and drawn largely from academic and publishing circles, neoconservatives supported most of the New Deal programs of federal assistance and regulation, but they felt that state intervention had gotten out of hand during the 1960s. In foreign policy, too, they worried about the directions in which the United States was going. In sharp disagreement with progressive liberals, they wanted a tougher stance toward the Soviet Union, fearing that the quest for détente was leading the nation to unilateral disarmament. After the disappearance of the Soviet Union, neoconcervatism itself disappeared—at least as a distinctive strain of conservatism—and most former neoconservatives either resisted all labels or considered themselves simply to be conservatives.

## The Religious Right

A more enduring category within the conservative movement is what is often referred to as "the religious right." Termed "the new right" when it first appeared more than 20 years, ago, the religious right is composed of conservative Christians who are concerned not so much about high taxes and government spending as they are about the decline of traditional Judeo-Christian morality, a decline that they attribute in part to certain unwise government policies and judicial decisions. They oppose many of the recent judicial decisions on socio-cultural issues such as abortion, school prayer, pornography, and gay rights, and over the past eight years they have been outspoken critics of the Clinton administration, citing everything from President Clinton's views on gays in the military to his sexual behavior while in the White House.

Spokesmen for progressive liberalism and the religous right stand as polar opposites: The former regard abortion as a woman's right; the latter see it as legalized murder. The former tend to regard homosexuality as a lifestyle that needs protection against discrimination; the latter are more likely to see it as a perversion. The former have made an issue of their support for the Equal Rights Amendment; the latter includes large numbers of women who fought against the amendment because they believed it threatened their role identity. The list of issues could go on. The religious right and the progressive liberals are like positive and negative photographs of America's moral landscape. Sociologist James Davison Hunter uses the term *culture wars* to characterize the struggles between these contrary visions of America. For all the differences between progressive liberalism and the religious right, however, their styles are very similar. They are heavily laced with moralistic prose; they tend to equate compromise with selling out; and they claim to represent the best, most authentic traditions of America. This is not to denigrate either movement, for the kinds of issues they address are indeed moral issues, which do not generally admit much compromise. These issues cannot simply be finessed or ignored, despite the efforts of conventional politicians to do so. They must be aired and fought over, which is why we include some of them, such as abortion (Issue 16), in this volume.

# RADICALS, REACTIONARIES, AND MODERATES

The label *reactionary* is almost an insult, and the label *radical* is worn with pride by only a few zealots on the banks of the political mainstream. A reactionary is not a conserver but a backward-mover, dedicated to turning the clock back to better times. Most people suspect that reactionaries would restore us to a time that never was, except in political myth. For many, the repeal of industrialism or universal education (or the entire twentieth century itself) is not a practical, let alone desirable, political program.

Radicalism (literally meaning "from the roots" or "going to the foundation") implies a fundamental reconstruction of the social order. Taken in that sense, it is possible to speak of right-wing radicalism as well as left-wing radicalism—radicalism that would restore or inaugurate a new hierarchical society as well as radicalism that calls for nothing less than an egalitarian society. The term is sometimes used in both of these senses, but most often the word *radicalism* is reserved to characterize more liberal change. While the liberal would effect change through conventional democratic processes, the radical is likely to be skeptical about the ability of the established machinery to bring about the needed change and might be prepared to sacrifice "a little" liberty to bring about a great deal more equality.

*Moderate* is a highly coveted label in America. Its meaning is not precise, but it carries the connotations of sensible, balanced, and practical. A moderate person is not without principles, but he or she does not allow principles to harden into dogma. The opposite of moderate is *extremist,* a label most American political leaders eschew. Yet there have been notable exceptions. When Arizona senator Barry Goldwater, a conservative Republican, was nominated for president in 1964, he declared, "Extremism in defense of liberty is no vice! . . . Moderation in the pursuit of justice is no virtue!" This open embrace of extremism did not help his electoral chances; Goldwater was overwhelmingly defeated. At about the same time, however, another American political leader also embraced a kind of extremism, and with better results. In a famous letter written from a jail cell in Birmingham, Alabama, the Reverend Martin Luther King, Jr., replied to the charge that he was an extremist not by denying it but by distinguishing between different kinds of extremists. The question, he wrote, "is not whether we will be extremist but what kind of extremist will we be. Will we be extremists for hate, or will we be extremists for love?" King aligned himself with the love extremists, in which category he also placed Jesus, St. Paul, and Thomas Jefferson, among others. It was an adroit use of a label that is usually anathema in America.

## PLURALISM

The principle of pluralism espouses diversity in a society containing many interest groups and in a government containing competing units of power. This implies the widest expression of competing ideas, and in this way, pluralism is in sympathy with an important element of liberalism. However, as James Madison and Alexander Hamilton pointed out when they analyzed the sources of pluralism in their *Federalist* commentaries on the Constitution, this philosophy springs from a profoundly pessimistic view of human nature, and in this respect it more closely resembles conservatism. Madison, possibly the single most influential member of the convention that wrote the Constitution, hoped that in a large and varied nation, no single interest group could control the government. Even if there were a majority interest, it would be unlikely to capture all of the national agencies of government—the House of Representatives, the Senate, the presidency, and the federal judiciary—each of which was chosen in a different way by a different constituency for a different term of office. Moreover, to make certain that no one branch exercised excessive power, each was equipped with "checks and balances" that enabled any agency of national government to curb the powers of the others. The clearest statement of Madison's, and the Constitution's, theory can be found in the 51st paper of the *Federalist:*

> It may be a reflection on human nature that such devices should be necessary to control the abuses of government. But what is government itself, but the greatest of all reflections on human nature? If men were angels, no government would be necessary.

This pluralist position may be analyzed from different perspectives. It is conservative insofar as it rejects simple majority rule; yet it is liberal insofar as it rejects rule by a single elite. It is conservative in its pessimistic appraisal of human nature; yet pluralism's pessimism is also a kind of egalitarianism, holding as it does that no one can be trusted with power and that majority interests no less than minority interests will use power for selfish ends. It is possible to suggest that in America pluralism represents an alternative to both liberalism and conservatism. Pluralism is antimajoritarian and antielitist and combines some elements of both.

## SOME APPLICATIONS

Despite our effort to define the principal alignments in American politics, some policy decisions do not fit neatly into these categories. Readers will reach their own conclusions, but we may suggest some alignments to be found here in order to demonstrate the variety of viewpoints.

The conflicts between liberalism and conservatism are expressed in a number of the issues presented in this book. One of the classic splits, and one that revisits an argument famous during the New Deal era, concerns the reach of federal power. The Tenth Amendment states that all powers not delegated to the federal government nor denied to the states "are reserved to the States respectively, or to the people." Yet the federal government passes laws affecting many entities *within* states, from businesses to educational institutions. How can it do that? One of the main "hooks" for federal power within states is the constitutional clause authorizing Congress to regulate commerce "among the several states." The Supreme Court has interpreted the commerce clause to mean that any entity within a state that substantially "affects" interstate commerce can be regulated by the federal government. But how close should the "effect" be? Conservatives insist that the effects on interstate commerce must be quite direct and tangible, while liberals would give Congress more leeway in regulating "intrastate" activities. This liberal/conservative dichotomy is crisply illustrated in the majority opinion versus one of the dissents in the Supreme Court case of *United States v. Lopez* (1995), both of which we present in Issue 5. The immediate question is whether or not the federal government has the authority to ban handguns from the vicinity of public schools, but the larger issue is whether or not the federal government can regulate activities within a state that do not directly and tangibly affect interstate commerce. Liberals say yes, conservatives say no.

The death penalty is another issue dividing liberals and conservatives. Robert Lee's defense of the death penalty (Issue 8) is a classic conservative argument. Like other conservatives, Lee is skeptical of the possibilities of human perfection, and he therefore regards retribution—giving a murderer what he or she "deserves" instead of attempting some sort of "rehabilitation"—as a legitimate goal of punishment. Another classic liberal/conservative split is on welfare. In 1996 Congress passed and President Clinton signed the Family Responsibility Act, which abolished Aid to Families with Dependent Children (AFDC), a New Deal–era welfare program that has been the target of conservatives for at least a quarter of a century. In Issue 14, Daniel Casse contends that the welfare overhaul has gotten people off welfare and into productive jobs, while Christopher Jencks and Joseph Swingle argue that welfare reform will not help the "hard core" unemployed and may throw them and their children into desperate straits. Issue 15, on whether or not the gap between the rich and the poor is increasing, points up another disagreement between liberals and conservatives. Most liberals would agree with Paul Krugman that socioeconomic inequality is increasing and that this undermines the basic tenets of American democracy. Christopher DeMuth, representing the conservative viewpoint, maintains that Americans are becoming more equal and that virtually all people benefit from increased prosperity because it takes place in a free market. Then there is the battle over taxes, the hardiest perennial of all the issues that divide liberals and conservatives. Issue 18 features Amity Shlaes, who advances the conservative argument that "the greedy hand" of government is taking too much from the taxpayer, and Citizens for Tax Justice, which holds that taxes are not too high in America, at least not for the rich. Affirmative action (Issue 10) has become a litmus test of the newer brand of progressive liberalism. The progressives say that it is not enough for the laws of society to be color-blind or gender-blind; they must now reach out to remedy the ills caused by racism and sexism. New Deal liberals, along with conservatives and libertarians, generally oppose affirmative action.

Another progressive/New Deal split occurs between Mary Ann Glendon and Ronald Dworkin in Issue 7. Dworkin, who would not reject the *progressive* label, favors a kind of judicial activism based on judges' views of what outcome "does most credit to the nation." Glendon, echoing the concerns of New Deal liberals during the 1930s, fears that such activism upsurps the legislative function and enervates democracy.

This book contains a few arguments that are not easy to categorize. The issue on hate speech (Issue 11) is one. Liberals traditionally have opposed any curbs on free speech, but Charles Lawrence, who would certainly not call himself a conservative, contends that curbs on speech that abuses minorities may be necessary. Opposing him is Jonathan Rauch, who takes the traditional liberal view that we must protect the speech even of those whose ideas we hate. Issue 21, on whether or not democracy is good for all countries, is also hard to classify. President Woodrow Wilson, a liberal, regarded World War I as a war to "make the world safe for democracy," but some latter-day liberals worry that exporting democracy to the ends of the earth is just as bad as pushing capitalism or other aspects of American life on other peoples. Robert Kaplan, who does not think democracy is the best form of government for all countries, is not necessarily a conservative, then, any more than Robert Kagan is a liberal for thinking that it is. Issue 16, on whether or not abortion should be restricted, also eludes easy classification. The pro-choice position, as argued by Mary Gordon, is not a traditional liberal position. Less than a generation ago legalized abortion was opposed by liberals such as Senator Edward Kennedy (D-Massachusetts) and the Reverend Jesse Jackson, and even recently some liberals, such as the late Pennsylvania governor Robert Casey and columnist Nat Hentoff, have opposed it. Nevertheless, most liberals now adopt some version of Gordon's pro-choice views. Opposing Gordon is former appeals court judge Robert Bork, who is clearly conservative, even if his argument here might be endorsed by liberals like Hentoff. Another issue in this book, that of "school choice" (Issue 13), is also beginning to straddle the traditional lines between liberalism and conservatism. The use of school vouchers, permitting lower-income parents to finance tuition for private and parochial schools, is opposed by liberal groups such as the NAACP and People for the American Way. But it is supported by majorities in black and Hispanic communities, and some prominent black leaders have broken ranks with traditional civil rights groups to support vouchers.

Issues 19 and 20 return us to the liberal/conservative arena of debate. Issue 19 revisits the China debate, which periodically surfaces between liberals and conservatives. In 1972 President Nixon astounded friend and foe alike when he visited China and started melting the ice that had frozen the two countries into postures of confrontation. But Nixon was an exception among conservatives. Most have never stopped regarding "Red China" as a menace to world peace and stability. This is the position taken by Lucian Pye, while David Lampton takes a more liberal view in minimizing the danger posed by today's China. In Issue 20, "Should the United States Put More Restrictions on Immigration?" Daniel James worries about the effect of "newcomers" on the U.S. economy and culture, which is not a surprising view for someone who is deeply committed to stability and continuity of culture, as conservatives are. Stephen Moore, in an argument that could have been made by liberals in the 1930s or the early 1900s, argues that America thrives on the energies brought to its shores by immigrants.

Obviously one's position on the issues in this book will be affected by circumstances. However, we would like to think that the essays in this book are durable enough to last through several seasons of events and controversies. We can be certain that the issues will survive. The search for coherence and consistency in the use of political labels underlines the options open to us and reveals their consequences. The result must be more mature judgments about what is best for America. That, of course, is the ultimate aim of public debate and decision making, and it transcends all labels and categories.

# On the Internet . . .   DUSHKIN ONLINE

## The Federal Web Locator

Use this handy site as a launching pad for the Web sites of U.S. federal agencies, departments, and organizations. It is well organized and easy to use for informational and research purposes.

http://www.infoctr.edu/fwl/

## The Library of Congress

Examine this Web site to learn about the extensive resource tools, library services/resources, exhibitions, and databases available through the Library of Congress in many different subfields of government studies.

http://www.loc.gov

## Scanned Originals of Early American Documents

Through this Emory University site you can view scanned originals of the Declaration of Independence, the Constitution, and the Bill of Rights. The transcribed texts are also available, as are the *Federalist Papers*.

http://www.law.emory.edu/FEDERAL/

## Poynter.org

This research site of the Poynter Institute, a school for journalists, provides extensive links to information and resources about the media, including media ethics and reportage techniques. Many bibliographies and Web sites are included.

http://www.poynter.org/research/index.htm

## The Gallop Organization

Open this Gallup Organization page for links to an extensive archive of public-opinion poll results and special reports on a huge variety of topics related to American society, politics, and government.

http://www.gallup.com

## International Information Programs

This wide-ranging page of the U.S. Department of State provides definitions, related documentation, and a discussion of topics of concern to students of American government. It addresses today's hot topics as well as ongoing issues that form the foundation of the field. Many Web links are provided.

http://usinfo.state.gov

# PART 1

# Democracy and the American Political Process

*D*emocracy *is derived from two Greek words,* démos *and* kratia, *and means "people's rule." The issue today is whether or not the political realities of America conform to the ideal of people's rule. Are the people really running the country? Some contend that the democratic political system has failed. Is that a fair charge, or is it based on simplistic premises? Political campaigns have come under fire in recent years for failing to serve the best interests of American democracy. Is this true, or do campaigns effectively inform and unify the American public? Another issue generating controversy is the increasing amount of money being spent for political campaigns and the effect of this spending on the government. Does the current system of campaign finance need to be reviewed and reformed? Finally, in this section, we address the effects of the news media on the governmental process.*

- Has the American Political System Succeeded?

- Do Political Campaigns Promote Good Government?

- Should Campaign Finance Be Reformed?

- Are the Mass Media Dominated by the Powerful Few?

# ISSUE 1

# Has the American Political System Succeeded?

**YES: Irving Kristol**, from "On the Character of the American Political Order," in Robert L. Utley, Jr., ed., *The Promise of American Politics: Principles and Practice After Two Hundred Years* (University Press of America, 1989)

**NO: Daniel Lazare**, from *The Frozen Republic: How the Constitution Is Paralyzing Democracy* (Harcourt Brace, 1996)

### ISSUE SUMMARY

**YES:** Writer Irving Kristol argues that America possesses a rich combination of ingredients that give it strength, resilience, and character.

**NO:** Freelance writer Daniel Lazare contends that America has become paralyzed in a constitutional straitjacket and that it needs radical reform.

Some men," Thomas Jefferson wrote in 1816, "look at constitutions with sanctimonious reverence, and deem them like the ark of the Covenant, too sacred to be touched." Jefferson made it clear that he was no such person. In his view, "each generation is as independent as the one preceding, as that was of all which had gone before." Jefferson, therefore, put little stock in tradition or continuity, and even less in the Founding Fathers.

Ironically, Jefferson himself has become a sanctified figure, with his own marble memorial near the Capitol and countless tributes quoting his words as if they were scriptural. Indeed, in the popular mind Jefferson is often associated with the Constitution—a document that he played no role in drafting and about which he had some serious reservations.

American political folklore is full of these ironies. America's heroes and their ideas get yanked out of their historical settings and are thrown together into what appears to be a timeless realm of good feelings. Here are Jefferson and Lincoln sitting together, though the former kept slaves and the latter emancipated them. Over there Alexander Hamilton is talking to Teddy Roosevelt, whom the historical Hamilton probably would have regarded as a traitor to his class. Andrew Jackson seems to get along fine with Franklin Roosevelt, though the former hated centralized government and the latter expanded it further than anyone could have dreamed. It is the "Hall of the Presidents" in Disney World, except that the cordial, gesturing statues are not just presidents but also many others who have won their place in the heavenly hall: Malcolm X and Martin Luther King, Jr., Abigail Adams and Eleanor Roosevelt, and Robert LaFollette and Robert Kennedy, for example.

Implicit—sometimes even explicit—in all this is the belief that America has a unique and coherent tradition, an "American way of life" that has carried the American people through a turbulent history and continues to guide them toward whatever lies ahead. It is a creed that celebrates "American exceptionalism," its special heritage; this belief does not rule out change, but it insists that changes are to be made by reaching back into the past and finding new wisdom there. Highest honors are usually reserved for the Founding Fathers, the men who set it going in the first place by their wise craftsmanship. Such talk would have embarrassed Jefferson, but it continues to touch deep chords whenever Americans gather to hear political speech.

The early years of the twentieth century marked a high point of national celebration; in 1909 the American writer Herbert Croly noted that "the faith of Americans in their own country is religious, if not in its intensity, at any rate in its almost absolute and universal authority." Yet a few years later, in 1913, historian Charles A. Beard published *An Economic Interpretation of the Constitution* (Free Press), which, far from portraying the founders as selfless, far-seeing patriots, depicted them as rather venal men bent upon protecting their own mercantile, investment, and manufacturing interests. For decades Beard's book was a favorite among debunkers of the Constitution and American exceptionalism. This current of dissent remained underground during much of the century, but in recent times, particularly since the Vietnam war, it has resurfaced. The last 30 years have seen numerous expressions of discontent with America and its heritage, from revisionist history to flag burning. In 1987 even a Supreme Court justice voiced some of these sentiments. Thurgood Marshall, the first African American to sit on the high court, suggested that the Framers of the Constitution drew up a document based upon "oudated notions of liberty, justice, and equality." In Marshall's view, the Constitution has been saved from obsolescence only by its amendments, particularly those that had been added since the Civil War. The founders themselves, he thought, deserve little credit for wisdom or foresight.

In the following selections, Irving Kristol upholds the celebratory view. America, he contends, possesses a rich mixture of ingredients that make it a successful polity, for which considerable credit should go to its founders. Opposing that view is Daniel Lazare, who suggests that the Constitution is no more suitable to present times than the horse-drawn vehicles that carried the Founding Fathers to Philadelphia in 1787.

Irving Kristol  **YES**

# On the Character of the
# American Political Order

It is an interesting, if rather peculiar, fact about writings on the American political tradition that they are mainly what I would call Manichaean. Manichaeanism was a heresy of the early Christian centuries which held that the world was divided between a good god and a bad god and that the history of the world was the history of their conflict. It was a dualistic vision of reality and human history. Such a dualistic vision seems to be dominant in most interpretations of the American political tradition. Indeed, almost from the beginning, we have perceived the American tradition in terms of aristocrats versus republicans, the people versus the oligarchy, republicanism versus democracy, progressives versus the "special interests." From reading these dualistic interpretations of American history and American politics one would think our history has been particularly bloody, tumultuous, and ambiguous. That is not the case.

Our history has been, by most reasonable, let us say historical, standards not particularly tumultuous; and the American people seem never to have been torn by conflicting interpretations of the American political tradition, though scholars may be. Even our very bloody Civil War had surprisingly little effect on the course of American history. If one were to write an American history textbook with the chapter on the Civil War dropped out, to be replaced by a single sentence to the effect that slavery was abolished by constitutional amendment in 1865, very little in subsequent chapters, as now written, would need revision. The Civil War had even less effect on the American political tradition, since there never really was a distinctively Southern political tradition, nor did the war give rise to one. A textbook on American intellectual history could safely ignore the Civil War, were it not for the fact that one feels it to be almost sacrilegious that so much suffering should be so barren of consequence. The Civil War was and is a most memorable event—but not any kind of turning point in American history.

My thesis, in a nutshell, is that the American people have always understood the American political tradition in an instinctive way, whereas scholarly interpretations inevitably tend to emphasize one aspect of this tradition at the

From Irving Kristol, "On the Character of the American Political Order," in Robert L. Utley, Jr., ed., *The Promise of American Politics: Principles and Practice After Two Hundred Years* (Tocqueville Forum, 1989). Copyright © 1989 by University Press of America. Reprinted by permission.

expense of all others. When I say that I think the American people have an instinctive understanding of the American political tradition, I mean that it is, as
it were, "in their bones." I mean that almost literally. If we transported two or
three thousand Americans to Mars to establish an American colony there and
then left them alone, what would they do? They would do exactly what the original settlers of the West and the South did. They would behave like Americans.
The first thing they would do is build a school. The second thing they would do
is build a church. The third thing they would do is go out and make money. And
the fourth thing they would do is have elections and form political parties—and
fight like hell. They would just clone the American political process out there
on Mars. In fact, if you look at the history of the settling of the West, you find a
group of people—not all of them, by the way, native-born Americans, but it did
not seem to matter—who all behaved in pretty much the same way, who established more or less identical villages which then became more or less identical
cities.

So the question I wish to address is: what is the American political tradition as it is in practice, apart from all the theoretical arguments about it? Of
course these arguments are very valuable. I really do not want to sound philis-
tine; it is very important to study those arguments. But what I want to do is
look at the American political tradition as it exists within American attitudes,
within the American mind, within American habits of behavior, within, to put
it in a cliché, "the American way of life." This is a cliché that has a lot of meaning, one which sums up all of the very different elements that go into making
the American political tradition, as this tradition is apprehended by the American people. It is an extraordinarily mixed tradition. That is why it is possible
for analysts to seize one aspect of it, for instance, the fact that it is capitalist,
or that it is democratic, or that it is republican, and decide that is the basic
aspect. Whereas the truth is that the American political tradition is simultaneously democratic, republican, capitalist, federal, and other things as well. It is,
moreover, a political tradition whose roots are to be found in a Protestantized
version of the Judeo-Christian tradition. I would like to take those elements of
this mixture one by one, and see what they are.

"Democratic" is relatively simple. Ours is a political system and a political
tradition that says that ultimately the will of the people will prevail. Ultimately,
not instantly, because the will that is to prevail is presumed to incorporate
the considered judgment of the people. Hence the separation of powers, the
decentralization of authority, and the slow, cumbersome legislative process.

Moreover, because it is a democratic system, it is a system that prizes
equality. But what does equality mean in the American political tradition? It
means, to begin with, equality before the law. There is no question about that.
It also means social equality; that is to say, a classless society, which we have.
Many of us have studied sociology and have heard that we do not have a classless society. Sociology professors explain that we are really divided into four
classes, seven classes, twenty-two classes, depending on what mode of analysis
they use. But surely if we need a sociologist to tell us whether or not we live in
a class society, then it is certain we do not live in a class society. People who
live in class societies know how many classes there are, and know exactly where

they are within any particular class. There is no secret about it; it is the most obvious and important thing in anyone's life. The simple fact is that American society today is, in any reasonable sense of the term, a society of social equality. This does not mean economic equality. Social equality, not economic equality, is what our version of democracy is about.

Here, again, we can be misled by some learned men. My favorite learned misleader is Thorstein Veblen. He was an enormously gifted man who probably wrote more nonsense about America than any other gifted man in our history. Veblen's best known nonsense, about "conspicuous consumption," is studied soberly in sociology courses. By now the term has passed into the language. But if there is any fact that is obvious about the United States, it is how little conspicuous consumption there really is. I can prove this. Observe any stranger, and guess his income, or how wealthy his family is, or what his social class is. The fact is, you cannot. Almost all students are wearing blue jeans. You cannot tell what their incomes or backgrounds are. As for adults, go out to the parking lot. Can you really tell how much money a person has from his automobile? Professors drive foreign automobiles, businessmen drive American automobiles, and that's about all there is to say. If you see a Cadillac driving down the street, a car ninety feet long, can you tell what kind of person is driving it? Is it a doctor? Is it a pimp? It could be anybody. The truth is that in our kind of democracy there are no social classes by any reasonable definition of that term.

Ours, however, is not simply a democratic political tradition, it is also a republican political tradition. The late Martin Diamond wrote an excellent textbook called *The Democratic Republic.* It is one of the few textbooks I know which takes seriously both of those terms in relation to the American political tradition. What does the word "republic" mean when you say we are a democratic republic? It means that although we are democratic, we have no faith in democracy. Democracy, in the American political tradition, is not, or at least ought not to be, a matter of faith. There are lots of books written called something like "The Democratic Faith." That is the wrong phrase. There is no reason to have faith in democracy, which is simply one form of political government. Faith should be reserved for higher things than any political system. One should not have faith in *any* political system.

One cannot assume that where the will of the people is supreme, the people will do the right things. The republican aspect of our political tradition is the way in which we refine the will of the people through the principle of representation. For instance, it was always assumed, and even is assumed today, that our representatives, though common men, in a sense are also more than common men. Walter Bagehot said of Sir Robert Peel that he was not a common man but a common man could have been cut out of him. That is the way we feel, or should feel, about our representatives. They ought to represent us, be in tune with us, understand us. But they ought to be a little better than we are. They ought to be a little more elevated than we are—because then they elevate us.

We are republicans in that we have a Constitution which curbs the will of the people, forces the people to rethink, forces the people's representatives to debate and consider, and forces the people to be reasonable. In other words, in a democratic republic the republican element is to be perceived when the people put constraints upon themselves because the people do not have any kind of democratic faith. People understand that they are capable of doing foolish things, and people therefore want institutional checks upon their own will, upon their own ultimate power.

Now to consider the federal element of the American political tradition. This is a very important element in the tradition, though often overlooked and, these days, underemphasized. The federal system is important because it institutionalizes the diffusion of power. I do not think anyone who has not experienced centralized power in other nations can understand how diffused power actually is in the United States. I well recall way back in 1970, during the Cambodian business, when some of my students at New York University announced to me that they were going down to Washington to seize power. I said, "How are you going to seize power?" They said, "We're going to take the Pentagon, that's what we're going to do." "Well, let's say the government leaves you the Pentagon," I said, "what are you going to do there?" "Well, we're going to give orders," they said. And I said, "Who's going to listen?"

It had not occurred to them that you cannot seize power in this country, you cannot even locate it. Perhaps in France it is possible to seize power by taking Paris. Suppose we had a revolution in New York City, and on the NBC nightly news broadcast from New York, the rebels proudly announced that a new regime had been established in City Hall. What would happen? The ratings would fall. People would say, "Oh, New York, you know what sort of things go on in New York," and it would not make the faintest bit of difference. It is very important, therefore, to preserve our federal system, so as to make unlikely any undue concentration and usurpation of power.

But there is a much more important aspect to the federal system, namely, the educational aspect. Local government and participation in local institutions is the way in which people learn the most important of all political truths, which is that the world is full of other people. It is a very sad political truth, a very disillusioning political truth. But people who do not understand it are engaged in a kind of utopian politics that is ultimately doomed. That the world is full of other people means that you may have a good idea, but it will often turn out that other people, somehow or other, for reasons which are inexplicable, do not see how good your idea is. It happens, not only does it happen, it is inevitable that it happens. Teaching us to live with other people is the function of the federal structure of our democracy. This kind of self-education can only occur through participation in local institutions, and it does not really matter how small they are. You really do not learn politics until you have the misfortune to be elected to your local school board. *Then* you understand what politics is about. In my own experience—I'm a New Yorker, we don't have local school boards, and if we did I couldn't get elected—I had the misfortune some years ago to be elected to the board of my cooperative apartment house. It was really very interesting to attend the annual meeting of this co-op. The residents were upper-income people, some very prominent socialists among them, some very prominent lawyers, some very wealthy stock brokers. At the annual house meeting the board knew that for the first hour the tenants would get up and denounce the landlord. At the end of the hour it would occur to them that *they* were the landlord and then we would get down to business. It took them about three years before they stopped denouncing us, their elected and unpaid trustees, as the landlord. It was an educational process. Anyone who gets involved in local self-government discovers that the world is full of other people, that there is no point in being dogmatic about what you think is right, that you must come to terms with this world, a world which is what it is and is never going to differ radically from what it is.

One other major virtue of the federal system, which we are only now beginning to appreciate, is that it diffuses some absolutely insoluble problems, so that they fester on a local rather than on a national level. In this sense, I think the decision of the Supreme Court legalizing abortion was a political disaster, never mind the morality of it. It was a disaster because it made abortion a national issue. Until that time abortion had been a state issue and if the states wished, they could always devolve the responsibility for that issue upon local communities (as was and is done with an issue like prohibition). Now, abortion is not an issue you can compromise about. It is one of those issues that is ultimately divisive. Therefore, you are better off diffusing the issue, making it a local issue, rather than importing it as a factor into national politics. As a result of the Supreme Court decision, we have imported a most divisive element into our national politics, one which cannot be compromised, and which we shall just have to live with.

It is deplorable that pornography also has now become nationalized as an issue, as a result of the courts' lack of wisdom. In my day, all the books that were banned in Boston were sold in New York. It was not such a bad system, people in both Boston and New York got what they really wanted and it didn't really matter all that much. Now the issue of pornography has become a matter of national significance, one on which national politicians are forced to make pronouncements, and this raises the question of national censorship. The best way to cope with the problems of pornography and censorship is to let local people solve it any way they want. Some will be permissive, some will not; some will have strict censorship, some will have lax censorship. That is all right. Indeed, that is just the way it is supposed to be. The whole point about federalism and decentralization is to see to it that such controversial issues do not distract national politics from its truly important concerns.

"Capitalist" is perhaps the most controversial of all the terms I have applied to our system. I do not see why it should be, since if anything is obvious, it is that we have been, certainly at least since the enactment of the Constitution, and in fact for many decades prior to that, a capitalist nation. A nation that believes that individual liberty is indissolubly linked to private property— that is what it means to be capitalist. We are a nation that believes that private property, and therefore a market economy (the two go together), are necessary, though not sufficient conditions for a political regime of liberty. Necessary but not sufficient. You can have private property and you can have a market economy in an authoritarian regime. Never in history, however, has there been what we would regard as a free society, or a liberal society, or a regime of liberty that did not have private property and a largely market economy.

Capitalism is important not only because of the support it gives to liberty—it is *the* absolute precondition of liberty—but also because it promises and promotes economic growth. The ancient democracies of classical Greece were full of class strife; the *demos* versus the *aristoi,* the masses versus the oligarchy. If you do not have economic growth, all democracies fall into such class strife. It is economic growth that permits a democracy to avoid class struggles over the distribution of a pie of preestablished size. It does that by always creating a larger pie so that everyone benefits, however unequally, and you do not have to benefit at someone else's expense. You can acquire property without expropriating property. . . .

Our system is democratic, republican, federal, and capitalist. And it is also a system that has a religious basis. Let me explain what I mean. A democratic system where the will of the people rules supreme, and a capitalist system which regards the pursuit of self-interest in the marketplace as legitimate, needs religion to supply certain crucial, missing elements.

Traditional religion is to liberal democratic capitalism as the Old Testament is to the New. Let me explain this puzzling remark. There was a big fight within the Christian church during the first three centuries of its history as to whether or not the Old Testament should be included in Holy Scripture. There were some major movements (subsequently defined as heresies; the Marcionite heresy most notably) that said: "No, let's not bring the Old Testament into Holy Scripture. We have a New Testament, why do we need the Old?" The church fathers, who were very wise men, said: "The New Testament, it's true, completes the Old; but there are things in the old which are not in the New, and which a church needs." The New Testament, after all, was not written with the establishment of the Christian church in mind—there is nothing about an established, authoritative Christian church in the New Testament. Therefore, the church fathers found they needed certain things in the Old Testament that are not in the New such as: the injunction to be fruitful and multiply, the pronouncement that God created the earth and saw it was good. In other words, the fathers needed certain theological premises to create an orthodoxy, to be able to tell its members that they can sanctify God in their daily lives, that they need not be hermits in the desert, they need not all become ascetic or aim at Christian perfection. These have all since been established as crucial affirmations of Christianity but, as it happens, are all to be found in the Old Testament, not in the New, since the people who wrote the New Testament took the Old Testament for granted.

It is not too much to say that the Judeo-Christian tradition, in its Protestantized form, is the Old Testament for liberal capitalism. It supplies things that liberal capitalism, liberal democratic capitalism, cannot itself supply; mainly what we call "values"—a moral code above all—and which the founders of capitalism simply took for granted. Precisely because a capitalist economy is one which does emphasize self-interest, it especially needs a very strong religious element in its culture in order to modify, complement and curb that self-interest.

Adam Smith wrote two books, *The Wealth of Nations* and a lesser known book, *The Theory of Moral Sentiments. The Wealth of Nations* was about how people act in the marketplace. They act in the marketplace out of self-interest, and Adam Smith's great contribution was to show that these actions out of self-interest, nevertheless, in the longer term, served everyone's interest by promoting economic growth. In *The Theory of Moral Sentiments,* however, (a book which, incidentally, he never repudiated—he revised it after publishing *The Wealth of Nations,* but did not change it much) he said, "Fine, what happens when you have created wealth? What will wealthy people do?" He said that in the end, what wealthy people will do is try to earn the good opinion of their fellow citizens by acts of philanthropy, which is just what they are doing. Such acts of philanthropy, in this culture, come out of the Protestantized version of the Judeo-Christian moral tradition with which Adam Smith was familiar....

I want to reassert that without this religious culture, the capitalist economic system becomes rather disgusting. Making money is fun; but, on the other hand, no one ever said it is an ennobling activity, no one ever said it is a heroic activity. It is, at best, a prosaic activity. In a society where most people are involved in commercial activities, you especially need a culture suffused with religious traditions that tell you what you are making money for, that tell you how to conduct yourself when you are making money, and that, above all, answer certain absolutely crucial and inevitable questions about the meaning of life and the meaning of death. It is this religious element that is the final and necessary constituent of the American political tradition.

... There is no point, in my view, in departing radically from that tradition —to socialism, for instance. The most important political fact of the twentieth century has been the death of socialism as an alternative model of society, as an alternative political tradition. There are still socialists to be found, but not in socialist countries. There are no socialists in Eastern Europe, no socialists in the Soviet Union, but there are socialists in American universities, French universities, German universities. The fact is, socialism as a serious political possibility is dead. There are about sixty official socialist countries in the world and not one of them is a place where you and I would want to live. Not one of them is a place where even their own people particularly want to live. They would all immigrate to the United States if given the opportunity. So the socialist ideal is dead. It lives as an academic idea, but as a reality it has been tried, and it does not work. It does not work because it is based upon a utopian vision of human nature, of what human beings are capable of. Because it is utopian it ends up trying to create utopia through coercion, since it cannot be created in any other way. But you cannot create utopia through coercion either; all you do is create a bureaucratic terrorist state.

So there is no alternative but to work within the American tradition. That is the test for the next generation—somehow to renew this tradition, perhaps revitalize it, perhaps amend it, perhaps revise it. But the tradition as I have described it—democratic, capitalist, federal, republican, religious—that is the tradition within which we shall have to work.

# NO

**Daniel Lazare**

# The Frozen Republic: How the Constitution Is Paralyzing Democracy

America is a religious society caught up in a painful contradiction. On one hand, its politics rest on faith in the Founding Fathers—a group of planters, merchants, and political thinkers who gathered in a stuffy tavern in Philadelphia in 1787—and the document they produced during the course of that summer, the Constitution. These are the be-all and end-all of the American system, the alpha and the omega. On the other hand, the faith isn't working. Problems are mushrooming, conflicts are multiplying, and society seems increasingly out of control. As a result, Americans find themselves in the curious position of celebrating the Constitution and Founders, who comprise America's base, yet cursing the system of politics they gave birth to. The more the roof leaks and the beams sag, the more fervent the odes to the original architects and builders seem to grow.

This is curious but not unprecedented. In one form or another, Americans have been simultaneously praising the Constitution and cursing the government since virtually the moment George Washington took office. What is different, however, is the degree. Constitution worship has never been more fervent, while dissatisfaction with constitutional politics has never been greater. Yet rather than attempting to work through the contradiction—rather than wondering, for instance, whether the fact that the house is falling down doesn't reflect poorly on those who set it up—the general tendency over the last two decades or so has been to blame anyone and everyone except the Founders. If the original conception is pure and perfect—and it is an article of faith in America's civic religion that it is—then the fault must lie with the subsequent generations who allowed it to be trampled in the dust. We have betrayed the legacy by permitting politicians, the media, special interests, minorities, etc., to have their way. Therefore, our duty as loyal subjects of the Constitution is to pick it up, dust it off, and somehow restore it to its original purity.

This is the way religious societies think—when confronted with the problems of the modern world, their first instinct is to retreat to some long-lost Eden, where everything was good and clean and honest.... [I]t ain't necessarily so,... Eden was never what it was cracked up to be, and... the Founders

From Daniel Lazare, *The Frozen Republic: How the Constitution Is Paralyzing Democracy* (Harcourt Brace, 1996). Copyright © 1996 by Daniel Lazare. Reprinted by permission of Harcourt, Inc. Notes omitted.

were never as far-seeing and all-wise as their followers allege. The problem with American politics... is not that they are the flawed expression of a perfect plan, but that they are the all too faithful expression of a flawed Constitution. Where the document devised in Philadelphia in 1787 neatly fit the needs of American society at the time, it proved woefully inadequate to the needs of American society in subsequent decades. In 1861, the constitutional system fairly disintegrated under the pressure of seventy years or so of pent-up change, unleashing one of the worst military conflicts of the entire nineteenth century. For approximately the next three-quarters of a century, it proved to be a political straitjacket, in which even the mildest social reform was prohibited on the grounds that it would interfere with the minority rights of bankers and industrialists; then, following a brief golden age after World War II, it has resulted in crippling gridlock and paralysis. The Constitution has performed this way not despite the Founders, but because of them. They created a system in which the three branches of government were suspended in almost perfect equipoise so that a move by one element in any one direction would be almost immediately offset by a countermove by one or both of the others in the opposite direction. The result was a counterdemocratic system dedicated to the virtues of staying put in the face of rising popular pressure. The more the system refused to budge, the more the constitutional sages praised its essential immobility.

The problem with the Constitution lies not with any single clause or paragraph, but rather with the concepts of balance and immutability, indeed with the very idea of a holy, all-powerful Constitution. James Madison, who did more in Philadelphia than anyone else to shepherd the Constitution through to completion, saw the document as an anchor in a flyaway world. An anchor, however, is precisely what is holding American society back. There are times when society needs to fly away and leave the past behind—to cast off old assumptions, to adopt new theories, to forge new frameworks of politics and government. This is precisely what the Madisonian Constitution was designed to prevent and something it has succeeded all too well in doing. As a result, U.S. society is laboring under what is at best an eighteenth-century mode of government as it prepares to enter the twenty-first century.

America must cast off the constraints. At the same time, it has never seemed more unequal to the task. Society has never been more fragmented, politics have never been narrower or more shortsighted, while the extended constitutional priesthood—judges, eminent professors of constitutional law, op-ed columnists, and so forth—has never been more dogmatic. Even as they try to choke each other to death, liberals and conservatives have never been more united in their devotion to the secular religion that supposedly holds society together but is in fact tearing it apart. They are like Catholic and Protestant theologians of the sixteenth and seventeenth centuries, each one claiming to be more faithful to the Word than the other. The outlook for reform seems grim as a consequence, which only makes it all the more *necessary*. What Americans need is less faith and more thought, less willingness to put their trust in a bygone political order and a greater realization that they, the living, are the only ones capable of maneuvering society through the storm. Instead of beginning with the Constitution as the essential building block, they should realize that there are no givens in this world and that all assumptions, beginning with the most basic, must constantly be examined and tested.

This must seem very strange to readers who have been trained from childhood to think of the Constitution as America's rock and foundation, without which it would disintegrate into an unthinking mob. Yet constitutional faith is a form of thoughtlessness, since it means relying on the thought of others rather than on one's own. The alternative is to emancipate oneself from the past, to wake up to the realization that two centuries of struggling and fighting have not been for naught and that we know a few things the Founders didn't as a consequence. Rather than continually deferring to their judgment, it means understanding that we are fully competent to make our way through the modern world on our own. This is not to say we should ignore Madison, Jefferson, et al., merely that there is no reason we should feel bound by their precepts.

... Government in America doesn't work because it's not supposed to work. In their infinite wisdom, the Founders created a deliberately unresponsive system in order to narrow the governmental options and force us to seek alternative routes. Politics were dangerous; therefore, politics had to be limited and constrained. But America cannot expect to survive much longer with a government that is inefficient and none too democratic by design. It is impossible to forge ahead in the late twentieth century using governmental machinery dating from the late eighteenth. Urban conditions can only worsen, race relations can only grow more poisonous, while the middle class can only grow more alienated and embittered. Politics will grow more irrational and self-defeating, while the price of the good life—that is, a nice home, good schools, a quiet street in a safe neighborhood—can only continue its upward climb beyond the reach of all but the most affluent. Rush Limbaugh, Howard Stern, and other demagogues of the airwaves will continue to make out like bandits, while the millions of people who listen to them will only grow angrier and more depressed. Eventually, every other society caught up in such a bind has snapped. Sooner or later, the United States will as well. The stays have already begun to fray....

If they are to emerge from their latest paralysis, Americans will have to resume the job they failed to finish in the 1860s. Rather than mindlessly cursing government and politicians, they will have to get to the bottom of the American predicament and figure out why politics in this country has grown so abysmal. Instead of rallying to this or that favorite son, they will have to figure out why even the best candidates wind up being defeated by the system they have vowed to change. Rather than relying on the Founding Fathers for answers, it means looking to themselves—to their own intelligence, their own analytical powers, their own creative abilities.

... [T]he underlying principle of checks and balances was much subtler than I had imagined. As every schoolchild knows, the Founders had wanted a Constitution that would serve the people as "a safeguard against the tyranny of their own passions." As Supreme Court Justice Louis Brandeis put it in *Myers v. U.S.* (1926), "The doctrine of the separation of powers was adopted ... not to promote efficiency but to preclude the exercise of arbitrary power"—which, put another way, meant that inefficiency was the price Americans had to pay for freedom and democracy. But there was a catch here. How was one to *evaluate* a system that was inefficient by design? What output criteria could one develop? If it was performing well, that is, efficiently, then it was performing in a way that was dangerous and threatening. If it was performing poorly, that is, *in*efficiently, then it was performing well. Bad was good and good was bad—a conundrum designed to stop even the most ardent reformer in his tracks.

Essentially, Madison and his colleagues in Philadelphia had created a puzzle palace in which logic was turned on its head. Or, rather, they had employed a different kind of logic, a pre-industrial version that would prove incomprehensible to citizens of the industrial era.... [N]ot only [is] the Constitution out of date but... by imposing an unchangeable political structure on a generation that has never had an opportunity to vote on the system as a whole, it amounts to a terrible dictatorship by the past over the present. Americans are prisoners, in effect, of one of the most subtle yet powerful systems of restraint in history, one in which it is possible to curse the president, hurl obscenities at Congress, and all but parade naked down Broadway, yet virtually impossible to alter the political structure in any fundamental way. They live in a system not only of limited government, but of limited democracy, which is why politics of late have become so suffocating and destructive. It is like a prison with no guards and no walls, yet from which no one ever escapes.

The answer is not less democracy—which is what term limits, a balanced-budget amendment, and other checks on legislative power represent—but more. Rather than checks and balances, the American people need to cast off constitutional restraints imposed more than two centuries ago and use their power *as a whole* to rebuild society as they see fit. This is not an invitation to lawlessness, but, quite the contrary, a call for the democratic majority to begin refashioning society along more rational and modern lines. Rather than less freedom, it is a plea for more, beginning with the freedom of the popular majority to modify its political circumstances in whatever way it sees fit. Rather than submitting to an immutable Constitution, Americans should cast off their chains and rethink their society from the ground up. They have nothing to lose—except one of the most unresponsive political systems this side of the former Soviet Union.

... Where the malapportioned U.S. Senate was a hot topic in the late nineteenth century, it has been all but forgotten by the late twentieth. Yet the disparities are worse than ever. Nine states account for more than half the total U.S. population, yet they account for less than twenty percent of the Senate vote. By the same token, a Senate majority can be gotten from twenty-six states representing less than one American in five. Twenty-one states, representing as little as one citizen in nine, are enough to filibuster any piece of legislation to death, while thirteen states, representing as little as 4.5 percent of the population, are enough to stop a constitutional amendment in its tracks. This is a minority veto run amok. In other respects, the arrangement is deeply unfair as well. Because they are predominantly rural, the twenty-six smallest states have fewer blacks (in fact, about half the national average), fewer Asians, fewer gays, and, of course, fewer urban dwellers in general. Violations of one person–one vote have been barred at the state or municipal level ever since *Baker v. Carr* in 1962. Yet they are, for the moment, beyond challenge at the federal level.

Disparities like these are not just unfair—they are stupid and lazy. No comparable country puts up with anything like them, yet Americans seem oblivious. On the rare occasion when they do think about them, New Yorkers, Californians, et al. seem to just shrug. Commenting on how the Senate Republican minority had filibustered Clinton's economic-stimulus package in April 1993, the journalist Sidney Blumenthal observed matter-of-factly in the *New Yorker:*

> The Senate, of course, was designed to be unrepresentative; it incorporates the principle of the equality of states, not the equality of citizens. The forty-three Republicans do not represent forty-three percent of the people. Because they are clustered in the smaller states, the Senate Republicans represent less than a third of the population.

That little phrase "of course" sums up all that is fatalistic and unthinking in the American character, as presently constituted, that is. It represents uncritical obedience to the dictates of the Founders—to the notion that if the framers *wanted* the Senate to be unrepresentative, that's the way it shall be forevermore. A conscious decision, on the other hand, to abolish such disparities would mean the opposite. It would signal a determination to think through the problems of government ourselves, to take responsibility for where society is heading, and to put an end to drift and gridlock.

Needless to say, taking control of one's destiny can also be dangerous. Just as there is nothing to stop a young person who gets his own apartment and credit card from behaving irresponsibly, there is nothing to stop a nation either. By abolishing separation of powers and checks and balances, the House would liberate itself from judicial review. Even if the Bill of Rights were to remain in place, citizens would have no assurance that the House would abide by its provisions other than its own pledge to do so. Yet what the House promises one day, it can unpromise the next; it could thus abolish free speech and a free press at a stroke, with little more than a yelp of protest from the courts. The only thing that could stop them would be the people themselves, who would recognize that real majority rule is impossible outside of a framework of free and vigorous criticism and debate. The people would want to preserve democracy not for the sake of various beleaguered minorities, the justification presently cited by the ACLU, but for the sake of the majority, namely, its own. A demos that allowed democracy to be squashed would be a demos no longer, merely a collection of atomized prisoners of the status quo.

For a people who like their guarantees in writing, this may not sound like much. Yet the development of a modern, mass democratic consciousness, of a modern democratic *movement,* is the only assurance that democracy in the United States can even survive. Americans must stop thinking of democracy as a legacy of the Founders and a gift of the gods, something that allows millions of voices to cry, "me! me! me!," while politicians and judges divide up the spoils according to some time-honored formula. Rather, they'll have to think of it as an intellectual framework that *they* create and continuously update, one that allows them to tackle the problems of the modern world not as individuals but as a society. If democracy is to survive, it must grow. And if it is to grow, it must detach itself from pre-democratic eighteenth-century norms and take its place in the modern world.

On the other hand, a young person who does not leave home will be stuck in a stage of attenuated adolescence forever. The same thing is true for Americans as a whole if they fail to emancipate themselves from dependence on a two-century-old legacy. "We're still Jefferson's children," Ronald Reagan once declared in a moment of ersatz piety. And as long as they continue to worship at the shrine of the Founders, Americans will remain in that childlike state indefinitely.

The alternative to taking responsibility and assuming risk is accepting the certainty of decline. There are any number of alternatives that one could imagine to the scenario of a democratic clean sweep sketched out above, none of them very pleasant. Rather than focusing their ire on the federal government, it's all too possible that Californians (not to mention Texans, New Yorkers, Pennsylvanians, etc.) might decide that it is more satisfying to fight among themselves along racial or geographic lines. The vast unfairness of the present arrangement in Washington might all too easily become lost in the mass of petty politics that is life in America, in which a scandal on the local school board often looms larger than the scandalous inequality of the U.S. Senate. Fragmentation, after all, is what has allowed the system to survive the last two centuries, and it may be what allows it to limp along for two centuries more. Not unlike the British, Americans may opt for a variation on the theme of muddling through, in which the devil you know (complacency) is to be preferred over the one you don't (change). Small adjustments may be instituted to keep California from boiling over—a bit of military pork here, a federal boondoggle there, a tacit understanding that even if it is to have only two votes in the Senate, its wishes nonetheless will be accorded extra weight. Perhaps Congress will approve the division of the state into three parts so that residents will wind up electing six senators rather than the present two. It would not eliminate the disparities but would at least make them more tolerable. All the old problems would remain—gridlock, the absence of a coherent, systematic policy to deal with social problems, and so on—yet at least it would keep the ship of state from going to pieces when it is still miles from shore.

On the other hand, it would also mean continued long-term decline, and Americans do not seem to be the sort of people to put up with long-term decline. They are too volatile, too imbued with a sense of their own greatness, too angry with themselves and with each other. Checks and balances may persist in Washington, but, if so, political tension will undoubtedly rise to even more dangerous levels. For those who know their German history, there is already a whiff of Weimar in the air. Just as the prewar German constitution was pulled apart by unresolved tension between the executive and legislative branches, the American system seems to be coming apart in a not-dissimilar way as well. True, the United States is not fragmented among a dozen or so political parties as Weimar was. Rather, thanks to the attenuated two-party system, it is fragmented among some 535 representatives and senators, each of whom recognizes no authority but his or her own. While Newt Gingrich has succeeded in imposing a remarkable degree of discipline on this motley crew, it is at the cost of increasing fragmentation below—between blacks and whites, the federal government and the states, the cities and suburbs, and so forth. H. Ross Perot's bizarre 1992 presidential bid is meanwhile an illustration of the authoritarian potential that has long been latent in the executive branch. "Presidential power is the power to persuade," political scientist Richard Neustadt once proclaimed. But what happens if H. Ross Perot transforms that power into the power to give orders and have Congress snap to attention?

The problem with the Constitution as it has developed over two centuries is that rather than engaging in a fundamental reordering, Americans have tried to democratize a predemocratic structure. As originally conceived, only one ruling institution—the House—was to be popularly elected and even then only by a fraction of what we now regard as the proper electorate (i.e., only, for the most part, by property-owning white males). The other ruling institutions— the Senate, the presidency, and the courts—were to be only indirectly chosen. But then Andrew Johnson helped democratize the presidency, the Seventeenth Amendment democratized the upper chamber to a degree by providing for the direct election of senators, and the furious confirmation battles over Robert Bork and Clarence Thomas have opened up the judiciary to an unprecedented level of popular pressure and inspection as well. The effect of separation of powers under such conditions has been to divide popular democracy against itself in such a way as to send the collective temperature shooting up to the boiling point. The electorate, as a consequence, is locked in a desperate internal struggle, which, as long as Madisonian checks and balances remain in effect, can never end. The results are tortuous, yet ultimately only two outcomes are possible. Either the body politic will keel over from exhaustion or it will explode.

# POSTSCRIPT

# Has the American Political
# System Succeeded?

On one point Kristol and Lazare seem to agree. "What Americans need," writes Lazare, "is less faith and more thought, less willingness to put their trust in a bygone political order and a greater realization that they, the living, are the only ones capable of maneuvering society through the storm." Kristol, too, disparages faith in politics: "Democracy, in the American political tradition, is not, or at least ought not to be, a matter of faith.... One should not have faith in *any* political system." Behind the apparent agreement of the two writers, however, there lies a deeper disagreement. For Lazare himself is not without faith; he shares Jefferson's faith in the ability of today's citizens to govern wisely without the restraints of the past. Of this faith Kristol is profoundly skeptical.

The tension between the two points of view in these arguments is that of continuity versus change. This has been a perennial theme in American thought. In the seventeenth century the Puritans who landed in New England saw themselves as carrying forward a reformation begun a century earlier on the European continent. Yet they also sensed that they were beginning something new. America was to be a brand new experiment, a "city upon a hill," as Puritan leader John Winthrop called it. Today, more than 350 years later, many Americans still regard it in that spirit.

Kristol's *Two Cheers for Capitalism* (Basic Books, 1978) spells out in greater detail some of the points he makes here, particularly that of the role of religion in counterbalancing capitalism. Michael Lind's *The Next American Nation* (Free Press, 1995) analyzes the development of American political thought from Jefferson's time to the present. Like Lazare, Lind believes in constant renewal, but he also stresses that renewal is bound to incorporate elements of the past. Richard Hofstadter's *The American Political Tradition and the Men Who Made It* (Vintage Books, 1989) was originally published in 1948, but it remains readable and provocative. Paul Johnson's massive *History of the American People* (Harper-Collins, 1997) concludes that the American political system is constantly renewing itself, struggling valiantly with the ills that afflict it. "So the ship of state sails on," writes Johnson, "and mankind still continues to watch its progress, with wonder and amazement and sometimes apprehension, as it moves into the unknown waters of the 21st century and the third millenium."

# ISSUE 2

## Do Political Campaigns Promote Good Government?

**YES: Samuel L. Popkin**, from *The Reasoning Voter: Communication and Persuasion in Presidential Campaigns* (University of Chicago Press, 1991)

**NO: Anthony King**, from "Running Scared," *The Atlantic Monthly* (January 1997)

### ISSUE SUMMARY

**YES:** Professor of political science Samuel L. Popkin argues that presidential election campaigns perform a unique and essential service in informing and unifying the American people.

**NO:** Political scientist Anthony King contends that American officeholders spend too much time and effort running for office, which detracts from their responsibility to provide good government.

Americans have the opportunity to vote more often to elect more officeholders than the citizens of any other democracy. Many elected officials serve two-year terms (members of the House of Representatives and many local and state officials), some serve four-year terms (the president, vice president, and other state and local officials), and only a few serve as long as six years (members of the Senate). In addition, voters may participate in primary elections to choose the candidates of the major parties for each of these offices. In the case of the presidential nominee, voters may select national convention delegates, whose election will determine who the party's nominee will be.

As a consequence, Americans are engaged in an almost ceaseless political campaign. No sooner is one congressional election over than another one begins. Given the long period required for organization and delegate-seeking prior to a presidential nomination, those who would be their party's nominee are off and running almost as soon as the last election has been decided.

Does this virtually nonstop campaigning serve the interests of American democracy? It surely makes for the most sustained appeal for public support by would-be candidates and those who finally win their party's support. During the height of the campaign season, lavish amounts of television time are bought for candidates' commercials, speeches, and sound bites on evening news broadcasts. Voters who want to learn more about the candidates and their positions can expose themselves to more information than they can absorb in daily newspapers, the news weeklies, talk radio, and C-SPAN. Less-interested adults cannot entirely escape political campaigns by switching their televisions to sitcoms and dramas, because they will be inundated with 30- and 60-second commercials for the candidates.

Yet despite this surfeit of information and advertisement, a smaller proportion of the eligible American electorate votes in presidential elections than did a century ago, and this proportion is smaller than those of other major democracies throughout the world. Just under 50 percent of the eligible electorate voted for president in 1996. An even smaller percentage votes in congressional, state, and local elections.

Declining voter turnout may derive in part from the reduced role of political parties, which once organized community rallies and door-to-door voter solicitation. In other democracies, party committees choose candidates; in the United States, candidates for national, state, and local office seek nomination by voters in primary elections. This diminishes the influence of parties and increases the amount and cost of campaigning. In presidential campaigns, the national party convention used to be an exciting affair in which the delegates actually chose from among competing candidates. As a result of changes in the method of delegate selection, the winning nominee is now known long before the formal decision, and the convention has been reduced to a carefully scripted show. As a result, the television networks have cut back their coverage, and viewer interest has diminished.

Critics argue that television has not only supplanted traditional campaigning but has placed candidates in contrived settings and reduced issues to slogans. Furthermore, long campaigns become negative and candidates attempt to show their opponents in as bad a light as possible. Examples from recent campaigns abound, including mudslinging, character bashing, and the blatant misrepresentation of opponents' records.

Many supporters of the American electoral system believe that more campaigning is needed in order to educate potential voters and to inspire their participation. The campaign serves the invaluable function of illuminating the common interests of varied economic, social, ethnic, and racial groups in America's heterogeneous society. As for low voter turnout, some maintain that this represents satisfaction with the workings of American democracy. That is, if the two major parties do not represent diametrically opposed positions on the gravest issues, it is precisely because most Americans approve of moderate policies and few would be attracted to extreme views.

In the selections that follow, Samuel L. Popkin maintains that campaigns bring together a diverse population and that voters need to see more campaigning and fuller coverage, not less. Anthony King asserts that short terms, weak parties, and expensive campaigns mean that officeholders spend more time and effort running for office than trying to provide good government.

**Samuel L. Popkin**
 **YES**

# The Reasoning Voter

I believe that voter turnout has declined because campaign stimulation, from the media and from personal interaction, is also low and declining, and there is less interaction between the media and the grass-roots, person-to-person aspects of voter mobilization. The lack of campaign stimulation, I suggest, is also responsible for the large turnout gap in this country between educated and uneducated voters.

The social science research shows clear relations between the turnout and social stimulation. Married people of all ages vote more than people of the same age who live alone. And much of the increase in turnout seen over one's life cycle is due to increases in church attendance and community involvement. I believe that in this age of electronic communities, when more people are living alone and fewer people are involved in churches, PTA's, and other local groups, interpersonal social stimulation must be increased if turnout is to increase....

Political parties used to spend a large portion of their resources bringing people to rallies. By promoting the use of political ideas to bridge the gap between the individual "I" and the party "we," they encouraged people to believe that they were "links in the chain" and that the election outcome would depend on what people like themselves chose to do. Today, less money and fewer resources are available for rallies as a part of national campaigns. And parties cannot compensate for this loss with more door-to-door canvassing; in the neighborhoods where it would be safe to walk door-to-door, no one would be home.

Some of the social stimulation that campaigns used to provide in rallies and door-to-door canvassing can still be provided by extensive canvassing. This is still done in Iowa and New Hampshire. These are the first primary states, and candidates have the time and resources to do extensive personal campaigning, and to use campaign organizations to telephone people and discuss the campaigns. In research reported elsewhere, I have analyzed the effect of the social stimulation that occurs in these states. People contacted by one political candidate pay more attention to all the candidates and to the campaign events reported on television and in the papers. As they watch the campaign they become more aware of differences between the candidates. And as they become more aware of the differences, they become more likely to vote.

From Samuel L. Popkin, *The Reasoning Voter: Communication and Persuasion in Presidential Campaigns* (University of Chicago Press, 1991). Copyright © 1991 by Samuel L. Popkin. Reprinted by permission of University of Chicago Press. Notes omitted.

This suggests a surprising conclusion: The best single way to compensate for the declining use of the party as a cue to voting, and for the declining social stimulation to vote at all, might be to increase our spending on campaign activities that stimulate voter involvement. There are daily complaints about the cost of American elections, and certainly the corrosive effects of corporate fund-raising cannot be denied; but it is not true that American elections are costly by comparison with those in other countries. Comparisons are difficult, especially since most countries have parliamentary systems, but it is worth noting that reelection campaigns to the Japanese Diet—the equivalent of the U.S. House of Representatives—cost over $1.5 million per seat. That would be equivalent to $3.5 million per congressional reelection campaign, instead of the current U.S. average of about $400,000 (given the fact that Japan has one-half the U.S. population and 512 legislators instead of 435). Although the differences in election systems and rules limit the value of such comparisons, it is food for thought that a country with a self-image so different from America's spends so much more on campaigning.

I believe that voters should be given more to "read" from campaigns and television, and that they need more interpersonal reinforcement of what they "read." Considering the good evidence that campaigns work, I believe that the main trouble lies not with American politicians but in the fact that American campaigns are not effective enough to overcome the increasing lack of social stimulation we find in a country of electronic as well as residential communities. This confronts us with some troubling questions. What kinds of electronic and/or social stimulation are possible today? To what extent can newspaper and television coverage provide the kinds of information citizens need to connect their own concerns with the basic party differences that campaigns try to make paramount? Is there a limit to what electronic and print stimulation can accomplish, so that parties must find a way to restore canvassing and rallies, or can electronic rallies suffice? Does watching a rally on television have the same effect as attending a rally? Could a return to bumper stickers and buttons, which have become far less prominent since campaigns began pouring their limited resources into the media, make a difference by reinforcing commitments and encouraging political discussions?

The problem may also be not simply a *lack* of social stimulation, but the growing *diversity* of social stimulation, and a resulting decline in reinforcement. In 1948, Columbia sociologists collected data about the social milieu of each voter and related the effects of the mass media on the voter to the political influences of family, friends, church, etc. They found that a voter's strength of conviction was related to the political homogeneity of the voter's associates. At that time, most voters belonged to politically homogeneous social groups; the social gulf between the parties was so wide that most voters had no close friends or associates voting differently from them. A decline in the political homogeneity of primary groups would lead to less social reinforcement; since the political cleavage patterns which exist today cut more across social groups, voters are in less homogeneous family, church, and work settings and are getting less uniform reinforcement. Whether there is less overall social stimulation today, or whether there is simply less uniformity of social stimulation, the demands on campaigns to pull segments together and create coalitions are vastly greater today than in the past.

## What Television Gives Us

Television is giving us less and less direct communication from our leaders and their political campaigns. Daniel Hallin, examining changes in network news coverage of presidents from 1968 to 1988, has found that the average length of the actual quote from a president on the news has gone from forty-five seconds in 1968 to nine seconds today. Instead of a short introduction from a reporter and a long look at the president, we are given a short introduction from the president and a long look at the reporter.

In the opinion of Peggy Noonan, one of the most distinguished speech-writers of recent years, who wrote many of President Reagan's and President Bush's best speeches, the change from long quotes to sound bites has taken much of the content out of campaigning: "It's a media problem. The young people who do speeches for major politicians, they've heard the whole buzz about sound bites. And now instead of writing... a serious text with serious arguments, they just write sound bite after sound bite." With less serious argument in the news, there is less material for secondary elites and analysts to digest, and less need for candidates to think through their policies.

We also receive less background information about the campaign and less coverage of the day-to-day pageantry—the stump speeches, rallies, and crowds. Moreover, as Paul Weaver has shown, the reporter's analysis concentrates on the horse-race aspect of the campaign and thus downplays the policy stakes involved. To a network reporter, "politics is essentially a game played by individual politicians for personal advancement... the game takes place against a backdrop of governmental institutions, public problems, policy debates, and the like, but these are noteworthy only insofar as they affect, or are used by, players in pursuit of the game's rewards.

As a result of this supposedly critical stance, people are losing the kinds of signals they have always used to read politicians. We see fewer of the kinds of personalized political interactions, including the fun and the pageantry, that help people decide whose side they are on and that help potential leaders assemble coalitions for governing.

Gerald Ford went to a fiesta in San Antonio because he wanted Hispanic voters to see his willingness to visit them on their own ground, and to demonstrate that some of their leaders supported him. He also wanted to remind them of his willingness to deal respectfully with the sovereignty issues raised by the Panama Canal question. But when he bit into an unshucked tamale, these concerns were buried in an avalanche of trivial commentary. Reporters joked that the president was going after the "klutz" vote and talked about "Bozo the Clown." From that moment on, Ford was pictured in the media as laughably uncoordinated. Reporters brought up Lyndon Johnson's contemptuous jibe that Ford "was so dumb he couldn't walk and chew gum at the same time." Jokes circulated that he had played too much football without his helmet. For the rest of the campaign, his every slip was noted on the evening news. Yet the news photos supposedly documenting the president's clumsiness reveal a man of remarkably good balance and body control, given the physical circumstances—not surprising for a man who had been an all-American football player in college and was still, in his sixties, an active downhill skier.

Similarly, during the 1980 campaign, Ronald Reagan visited Dallas and said, in response to a question, that there were "great flaws" in the theory of evolution and that it might be a good idea if the schools taught "creationism" as well. This statement was characterized in the media as the sort of verbal pratfall to be expected from Reagan, and much of the coverage related such gaffes *entirely* to questions about his intellectual capacity, not to the meaning of his appearance or the implications of the appearance for the coalition he was building.

What difference would it have made if press and television reporters had considered these actions by Ford and Reagan as clear and open avowals of sympathy for political causes dear to their hearts? What if Ford's political record on issues dear to Hispanics had been discussed, or if the guest list for the fiesta had been discussed to see which prominent Hispanics were, in fact, endorsing him? The nature of the gathering Reagan attended was noted at the time, but it was never referred to again. It was not until 1984 that Americans uninvolved in religious fundamentalism understood enough about what the Moral Majority stood for to read anything from a politician's embrace of Jerry Falwell, its president, or a religious roundtable such as the one Reagan attended in 1980. By 1988, as more people on the other side of the fundamentalism debates learned what the Moral Majority stood for, the group was disbanded as a political liability.

Television, in other words, is not giving people enough to read about the substance of political coalition building because it ignores many important campaign signals. That rallies and other campaign events are "staged" does not diminish their importance and the legitimate information they can convey to voters. When Richard Nixon met Mao Tse Tung in 1972, the meeting was no less important because it was staged. And when Jesse Jackson praised Lloyd Bentsen by noting the speed with which he could go from biscuits to tacos to caviar, he was acknowledging another fact of great importance: in building coalitions, a candidate must consider the trade-off between offering symbols and making promises.

If politicians cannot show familiarity with people's concerns by properly husking tamales or eating knishes in the right place with the right people, they will have to promise them something. As Jackson noted, the tamales may be better than promises, because promises made to one segment of voters, or one-issue public, will offend other groups and therefore tie the politician's hands in the future policy-making process.

Is it more meaningful when a governor of Georgia hangs a picture of Martin Luther King Jr. in the statehouse, or when a senator or congressman votes for a bill promising full employment? Is it better for a politician to eat a kosher hot dog or to promise never to compromise Israel's borders? When voters are deprived of one shortcut—obvious symbols, for example—obvious promises, for example—instead of turning to more subtle and complicated forms of information.

How good a substitute are electronic tamales for the real thing? Does watching a fiesta provide any of the stimulation to identification and turnout that attendance at a fiesta provides? How long does it take to bring us together, at least in recognizable coalitions? We need not have answers to these questions to see that they speak to the central issue of stimulating turnout and participation in elections in an age of electronic communities. The media *could* provide more of the kinds of information people use to assess candidates and parties. However, I do not know if electronic tamales provide the social stimulation of interacting with others, or the reinforcement of acting with others who agree, and I do not know how much more potent are ideas brought clearly to mind through using them with others. The demands placed on television are greater than the demands ever placed on radio or newspapers because the world is more diverse today and there are more segments which need to be reunited in campaigns.

## Objections and Answers

Two notable objections can be made to my suggestions for increasing campaigning and campaign spending. The first is the "spinmaster" objection: contemporary political campaigns are beyond redemption because campaign strategists have become so adept at manipulation that voters can no longer learn what the candidates really stand for or really intend to do. Significantly, this conclusion is supported by two opposing arguments about voter behavior. One objection is that voters are staying home because they have been turned off by fatuous claims and irrelevant advertising. A variant of this is that voters are being manipulated with great success by unscrupulous campaign advertising, so that their votes reflect more concern with Willie Horton* or school prayer or flag burning than with widespread poverty, the banking crisis, or global warming. The second objection is that popular concern with candidates and with government in general has been trivialized, so that candidates fiddle while America burns. In the various versions of this hypothesis, voter turnout is down because today's political contests are waged over small differences on trivial issues. While Eastern Europe plans a future of freedom under eloquent spokesmen like Vaclav Havel, and while Mikhail Gorbachev declares an end to the cold war, releases Eastern Europe from Soviet control, and tries to free his countrymen from the yoke of doctrinaire communism, in America Tweedledum and Tweedledee argue about who loves the flag more while Japan buys Rockefeller Center, banks collapse, and the deficit grows.

Both of these critiques of the contemporary system argue that campaigns themselves are trivial and irrelevant, that campaign advertising and even the candidates' speeches are nothing but self-serving puffery and distortion. This

---

* [Willie Horton, a convicted murderer, escaped a prison furlough approved by then-governor of Massachusetts Michael Dukakis and committed a violent crime. George Bush exploited the incident in his campaign against Dukakis during the 1988 presidential race.—Eds.]

general argument has an aesthetic appeal, especially to better-educated voters and the power elite; campaign commercials remind no one of the Lincoln-Douglas debates, and today's bumper stickers and posters have none of the resonance of the Goddess of Democracy in Tiananmen Square. But elite aesthetics is not the test of this argument; the test is what voters learn from campaigns.

There is ample evidence that voters *do* learn from campaigns. Of course, each campaign tries hard to make its side look better and the other side worse. Despite that, voter perceptions about the candidates and their positions are more accurate. Furthermore, ... there is no evidence that people learn less from campaigns today than they did in past years. This is a finding to keep in mind at all times, for many of the criticisms of campaigns simplistically assume that because politicians and campaign strategists have manipulative intentions, campaigns necessarily mislead the voter. This assumption is not borne out by the evidence; voters know how to read the media and the politicians better than most media critics acknowledge.

... Voters remember past campaigns and presidents, and past failures of performance to match promises. They have a sense of who is with them and who is against them; they make judgments about unfavorable new editorials and advertisements from hostile sources, ignoring some of what is favorable to those they oppose and some of what is unfavorable to those they support. In managing their personal affairs and making decisions about their work, they collect information that they can use as a reality test for campaign claims and media stories. They notice the difference between behavior that has real consequences, on one hand, and mere talk, on the other.

... The ability of television news to manipulate voters has been vastly overstated, as one extended example will suggest. In television reporting—but not in the academic literature—it was always assumed before 1984 that winning debates and gaining votes are virtually one and the same. But on Sunday, October 7, 1984, in the first debate between Walter Mondale and Ronald Reagan, this assumption was shown to be flawed. Mondale, generally a dry speaker, was unexpectedly relaxed and articulate, and Reagan, known for his genial and relaxed style, was unexpectedly tense and hesitant. Mondale even threw Reagan off guard by using "There you go again," the jibe Reagan had made famous in his 1980 debate with Jimmy Carter. Immediately after the debate, the CBS News/*New York Times* pollsters phoned a sample of registered voters they had interviewed before the debate, to ask which candidate they were going to vote for and which they thought had done a better job in the debate. Mondale was considered to have "done the best job" by 42 percent to 36 percent, and had gained 3 points in the polls. As a result of similar polls in the next twenty-four hours by other networks and news organizations, the media's main story the rest of the week was of Mondale's upset victory over the president in the debate. Two days later, when another CBS News/*New York Times* poll asked voters about the debate and about their intended vote, Mondale was considered to have "done the best job" not by 42 percent to 36 percent margin of Sunday, but by 65 percent to 17 percent. Media reports, then, claimed that millions of voters had changed their minds about what they themselves had just seen days earlier.

Yet in the three days during which millions changed their minds about who had won the debate, the same poll reported, few if any changed their minds about how they would vote.

This example emphasizes just how complex the effects of television can be. Voters now have opinions about opinions. When asked who won the debate, they may say not what they think personally, but what they have heard that the majority of Americans think. It is easier to change their opinions about what their neighbors think than to change their own opinions. And most important of all, it is clear that they understand the difference between a debater and a president, and that they don't easily change their political views about who they want to run the country simply on the basis of debating skills.

Critics of campaign spinmasters and of television in general are fond of noting that campaigners and politicians intend to manipulate and deceive, but they wrongly credit them with more success than they deserve. As Michael Schudson has noted, in the television age, whenever a president's popularity has been high, it has been attributed to unusual talents for using television to sell his image. He notes, for example, that in 1977 the television critic of the *New York Times* called President Carter "a master of controlled images," and that during the 1976 primaries David Halberstam wrote that Carter "more than any other candidate this year has sensed and adapted to modern communications and national mood.... Watching him again and again on television I was impressed by his sense of pacing, his sense of control, very low key, soft." A few years later this master of images still had the same soft, low-key voice, but now it was interpreted as indicating not quiet strength but weakness and indecision. Gerald Rafshoon, the media man for this "master of television," concluded after the 1980 campaign that all the television time bought for Carter wasn't as useful as three more helicopters (and a successful desert rescue) would have been.

As these examples suggest, media critics are generally guilty of using one of the laziest and easiest information shortcuts of all. Assuming that a popular politician is a good manipulator of the media or that a winner won because of his media style is not different from what voters do when they evaluate presidents by reasoning backward from known results. The media need reform, but so do the media critics. One cannot infer, without astonishing hubris, that the American people have been successfully deceived simply because a politician wanted them to believe his or her version of events. But the media critics who analyze political texts without any reference to the actual impact of the messages do just that.

## Negativism and Triviality

Campaigns are often condemned as trivial—as sideshows in which voters amuse themselves by learning about irrelevant differences between candidates who fiddle over minor issues while the country stagnates and inner cities burn—and many assume that the negativism and pettiness of the attacks that candidates make on each other encourage an "a pox on all your houses" attitude. This suggests a plausible hypothesis, which can be given a clean test in a simple experiment. This experiment can be thought of as a "stop and think" experiment because it is a test of what happens if people stop and think about what they know of the candidates and issues in an election and tell someone what they know. First, take a random sample of people across the country and interview them. Ask the people selected what they consider to be the most important issues facing the country, and then ask them where the various candidates stand on these issues. Then ask them to state their likes and dislikes about the candidates' personal qualities and issue stands, and about the state of the country. Second, after the election, find out whether these interviewees were more or less likely to vote than people who were not asked to talk about the campaign. If the people interviewed voted less often than people not interviewed, then there is clear support for the charge that triviality, negativism, and irrelevancy are turning off the American people and suppressing turnout.

In fact, the National Election Studies done by the University of Michigan's Survey Research Center, now the Center for Political Studies, are exactly such an experiment. In every election since 1952, people have been asked what they care about, what the candidates care about, and what they know about the campaign. After the election people have been reinterviewed and asked whether they voted; then the actual voting records have been checked to see whether the respondents did indeed vote.

The results convincingly demolish the triviality and negativism hypothesis. In every election, people who have been interviewed are more likely to vote than other Americans. Indeed, the reason the expensive and difficult procedure of verifying turnout against the voting records was begun in the first place was that the scholars were suspicious because the turnout reported by respondents was so much higher than either the actual turnout of all Americans or the turnout in surveys conducted after the election. So respondents in the national election studies, after seventy minutes of thinking about the candidates, the issues, and the campaign, were both more likely than other people to vote and more likely to try to hide the fact that they did not vote! Further, if people are reinterviewed in later elections, their turnout continues to rise. Still further, while an interview cuts nonvoting in a presidential election by up to 20 percent, an interview in a local primary may cut nonvoting by as much as half.

The rise in no-shows on voting day and the rise of negative campaigning both follow from the rise of candidate-centered elections. When voters do not have information about future policies they extrapolate, or project, from the information they have. As campaigns become more centered on candidates, there is more projection, and hence more negative campaigning. Negative campaigning is designed to provide information that causes voters to stop projecting and to change their beliefs about a candidate's stand on the issues. "Willie Horton . . . was a legitimate issue because it speaks to styles and ways of governance. In that case Dukakis's."

As Noonan has also noted of the 1988 campaign, "There should have been more name-calling, mud slinging and fun. It should have been rock-'em-sock-'em the way great campaigns have been in the past. It was tedious." Campaigns cannot deal with anything substantive if they cannot get the electorate's attention and interest people in listening to their music. Campaigns need to make noise. The tradition of genteel populism in America, and the predictable use of sanitary metaphors to condemn politicians and their modes of communication, says more about the distaste of the people who use the sanitary metaphors for American society than it does about the failing politicians.

The challenge to the future of American campaigns, and hence to American democracy, is how to bring back the excitement and the music in an age of electronic campaigning. Today's campaigns have more to do because an educated, media-centered society is a broadened and segmented electorate which is harder to rally, while today's campaigns have less money and troops with which to fight their battles.

~◈~

When I first began to work in presidential campaigns I had very different ideas about how to change campaigns and their coverage than I have today. Coverage of rallies and fiestas, I used to think, belonged in the back of the paper along with stories about parties, celebrity fund-raisers, and fad diets. Let the society editor cover banquets and rubber chickens, I thought; the reporters in Washington could analyze the speeches and discuss the policy implications of competing proposals.

I still wish that candidates' proposals and speeches were actually analyzed for their content and implications for our future. I still wish that television told us more about how elites evaluate presidential initiatives than what my neighbors said about them in the next day's polls. However, I now appreciate the intimate relationships between the rallies and governance which escaped me in the past. I now appreciate how hard it is to bring a country together, to gather all the many concerns and interests into a single coalition and hold it together in order to govern.

Campaigns are essential in any society, particularly in a society that is culturally, economically, and socially diverse. If voters look for information about candidates under streetlights, then that is where candidates must campaign, and the only way to improve elections is to add streetlights. Reforms can only make sense if they are consistent with the gut rationality of voters. Ask not for more sobriety and piety from citizens, for they are voters, not judges; offer them instead cues and signals which connect their world with the world of politics.

# Running Scared

To an extent that astonishes a foreigner, modern America is *about* the holding of elections. Americans do not merely have elections on the first Tuesday after the first Monday of November in every year divisible by four. They have elections on the first Tuesday after the first Monday of November in every year divisible by two. In addition, five states have elections in odd-numbered years. Indeed, there is no year in the United States—ever—when a major statewide election is not being held somewhere. To this catalogue of general elections has of course to be added an equally long catalogue of primary elections (for example, forty-three presidential primaries [in 1996]). Moreover, not only do elections occur very frequently in the United States but the number of jobs legally required to be filled by them is enormous—from the presidency of the United States to the post of local consumer advocate in New York. It has been estimated that no fewer than half a million elective offices are filled or waiting to be filled in the United States today.

Americans take the existence of their never-ending election campaign for granted. Some like it, some dislike it, and most are simply bored by it. But they are all conscious of it, in the same way that they are conscious of Mobil, McDonald's, *Larry King Live,* Oprah Winfrey, the Dallas Cowboys, the Ford Motor Company, and all the other symbols and institutions that make up the rich tapestry of American life.

To a visitor to America's shores, however, the never-ending campaign presents a largely unfamiliar spectacle. In other countries election campaigns have both beginnings and ends, and there are even periods, often prolonged periods, when no campaigns take place at all. Other features of American elections are also unfamiliar. In few countries do elections and campaigns cost as much as they do in the United States. In no other country is the role of organized political parties so limited.

America's permanent election campaign, together with other aspects of American electoral politics, has one crucial consequence, little noticed but vitally important for the functioning of American democracy. Quite simply, the American electoral system places politicians in a highly vulnerable position. Individually and collectively they are more vulnerable, more of the time, to the vicissitudes of electoral politics than are the politicians of any other democratic

From Anthony King, "Running Scared," *The Atlantic Monthly* (January 1997). Abridged and reprinted from *Running Scared: Why America's Politicians Campaign Too Much and Govern Too Little* by Anthony King (Martin Kessler Books, 1997). Copyright © 1997 by Anthony King. Reprinted by permission of the author.

country. Because they are more vulnerable, they devote more of their time to electioneering, and their conduct in office is more continuously governed by electoral considerations. I will argue that American politicians' constant and unremitting electoral preoccupations have deleterious consequences for the functioning of the American system. They consume time and scarce resources. Worse, they make it harder than it would otherwise be for the system as a whole to deal with some of America's most pressing problems. Americans often complain that their system is not sufficiently democratic. I will argue that, on the contrary, there is a sense in which the system is too democratic and ought to be made less so. . . .

## Fear and Trembling

Politics and government in the United States are marked by the fact that U.S. elected officials in many cases have very short terms of office *and* face the prospect of being defeated in primary elections *and* have to run for office more as individuals than as standard-bearers for their party *and* have continually to raise large sums of money in order to finance their own election campaigns. Some of these factors operate in other countries. There is no other country, however, in which all of them operate, and operate simultaneously. The cumulative consequences, as we shall see, are both pervasive and profound.

The U.S. Constitution sets out in one of its very first sentences that "the House of Representatives shall be composed of members chosen every second year by the people of the several states." When the Founding Fathers decided on such a short term of office for House members, they were setting a precedent that has been followed by no other major democratic country. In Great Britain, France, Italy, and Canada the constitutional or legal maximum for the duration of the lower house of the national legislature is five years. In Germany and Japan the equivalent term is four years. Only in Australia and New Zealand, whose institutions are in some limited respects modeled on those of the United States, are the legal maximums as short as three years. In having two-year terms the United States stands alone.

Members of the Senate are, of course, in a quite different position. Their constitutionally prescribed term of office, six-years, is long by anyone's standards. But senators' six-year terms are not all they seem. In the first place, so pervasive is the electioneering atmosphere that even newly elected senators begin almost at once to lay plans for their re-election campaigns. Senator Daniel Patrick Moynihan, of New York, recalls that when he first came to the Senate, in 1977, his colleagues when they met over lunch or a drink usually talked about politics and policy. Now they talk about almost nothing but the latest opinion polls. In the second place, the fact that under the Constitution the terms of a third of the Senate end every two years means that even if individual senators do not feel themselves to be under continuing electoral pressure, the Senate as a whole does. Despite the Founders' intentions, the Senate's collective electoral sensibilities increasingly resemble those of the House.

Most Americans seem unaware of the fact, but the direct primary—a government-organized popular election to nominate candidates for public office—is, for better or worse, an institution peculiar to the United States. Neither primary elections nor their functional equivalents exist anywhere else in the democratic world. It goes without saying that their effect is to add a further dimension of uncertainty and unpredictability to the world of American elective politicians.

In most other countries the individual holder of public office, so long as he or she is reasonably conscientious and does not gratuitously offend local or regional party opinion, has no real need to worry about renomination. To be sure, cases of parties refusing to renominate incumbent legislators are not unknown in countries such as France, Germany, and Canada, but they are relatively rare and tend to occur under unusual circumstances. The victims are for the most part old, idle, or alcoholic.

The contrast between the rest of the world and the United States could hardly be more striking. In 1979 no fewer than 104 of the 382 incumbent members of the House of Representatives who sought re-election faced primary opposition. In the following three elections the figures were ninety-three out of 398 (1980), ninety-eight out of 393 (1982), and 130 out of 409 (1984). More recently, in 1994, nearly a third of all House incumbents seeking re-election, 121 out of 386, had to face primary opposition, and in the Senate the proportion was even higher: eleven out of twenty-six. Even those incumbents who did not face opposition could seldom be certain in advance that they were not going to. The influence—and the possibility—of primaries is pervasive. As we shall see, the fact that incumbents usually win is neither here nor there.

To frequent elections and primary elections must be added another factor that contributes powerfully to increasing the electoral vulnerability of U.S. politicians: the relative lack of what we might call "party cover." In most democratic countries the fate of most politicians depends not primarily on their own endeavors but on the fate—locally, regionally, or nationally—of their party. If their party does well in an election, so do they. If not, not. The individual politician's interests and those of his party are bound together.

In contrast, America's elective politicians are on their own—not only in relation to politicians in most other countries but also in absolute terms. Party is still a factor in U.S. electoral politics, but it is less so than anywhere else in the democratic world. As a result, American legislators seeking re-election are forced to raise their own profiles, to make their own records, and to fight their own re-election campaigns.

If politicians are so vulnerable electorally, it may be protested, why aren't more of them defeated? In particular, why aren't more incumbent congressmen and senators defeated? The analysis here would seem to imply a very high rate of turnover in Congress, but in fact the rate—at least among incumbents seeking re-election—is notoriously low. How can this argument and the facts of congressional incumbents' electoral success be reconciled?

This objection has to be taken seriously, because the facts on which it is based are substantially correct. The number of incumbent congressmen and

senators defeated in either primary or general elections *is* low. But to say that because incumbent members of Congress are seldom defeated, they are not really
vulnerable electorally is to miss two crucial points. The first is that precisely because they are vulnerable, they go to prodigious lengths to protect themselves.
Like workers in nuclear-power stations, they take the most extreme safety precautions, and the fact that the precautions are almost entirely successful does
not make them any less necessary.

Second, congressmen and senators go to inordinate lengths to secure re-
election because, although they may objectively be safe (in the view of journalists and academic political scientists), they do not *know* they are safe—and
even if they think they are, the price of being wrong is enormous. The probability that anything will go seriously wrong with a nuclear-power station may
approach zero, but the stations tend nevertheless to be built away from the centers of large cities. A congressman or a senator may believe that he is reasonably
safe, but if he wants to be re-elected, he would be a fool to act on that belief.

## How They Came To Be Vulnerable

American politicians run scared—and are right to do so. And they run more
scared than the politicians of any other democratic country—again rightly. How
did this come to be so?

The short answer is that the American people like it that way. They are,
and have been for a very long time, the Western world's hyperdemocrats. They
are keener on democracy than almost anyone else and are more determined
that democratic norms and practices should pervade every aspect of national
life. To explore the implications of this central fact about the United States, and
to see how it came to be, we need to examine two different interpretations of
the term "democracy." Both have been discussed from time to time by political
philosophers, but they have never been codified and they certainly cannot be
found written down in a constitution or any other formal statement of political
principles. Nevertheless, one or the other underpins the political practice of
every democratic country—even if, inevitably, the abstract conception and the
day-to-day practice are never perfectly matched.

One of these interpretations might be labeled "division of labor." In this
view, there are in any democracy two classes of people—the governors and the
governed. The function of the governors is to take decisions on the basis of what
they believe to be in the country's best interests and to act on those decisions. If
public opinion broadly supports the decisions, that is a welcome bonus. If not,
too bad. The views of the people at large are merely one datum among a large
number of data that need to be considered. They are not accorded any special
status. Politicians in countries that operate within this view can frequently be
heard using phrases like "the need for strong leadership" and "the need to take
tough decisions." They often take a certain pride in doing what they believe to
be right even if the opinion of the majority is opposed to it.

The function of the governed in such a system, if it is a genuine democracy, is very important but strictly limited. It is not to determine public policy
or to decide what is the right thing to do. Rather, it is to go to the polls from

time to time to choose those who will determine public policy and decide what the right thing is: namely, the governors. The deciding of issues by the electorate is secondary to the election of the individuals who are to do the deciding. The analogy is with choosing a doctor. The patient certainly chooses which doctor to see but does not normally decide (or even try to decide) on the detailed course of treatment. The division of labor is informal but clearly understood.

It is probably fair to say that most of the world's major democracies—Great Britain, France, Germany, Japan—operate on this basis. The voters go to the polls every few years, and in between times it is up to the government of the day to get on with governing. Electing a government and governing are two different businesses. Electioneering is, if anything, to be deplored if it gets in the way of governing.

This is a simplified picture, of course. Democratically elected politicians are ultimately dependent on the electorate, and if at the end of the day the electorate does not like what they are doing, they are dead. Nevertheless, the central point remains. The existing division of labor is broadly accepted.

The other interpretation of democracy, the one dominant in America, might be called the "agency" view, and it is wholly different. According to this view, those who govern a country should function as no more than the agents of the people. The job of the governors is not to act independently and to take whatever decisions they believe to be in the national interest but, rather, to reflect in all their actions the views of the majority of the people, whatever those views may be. Governors are not really governors at all; they are representatives, in the very narrow sense of being in office solely to represent the views of those who sent them there.

In the agency view, representative government of the kind common throughout the democratic world can only be second-best. The ideal system would be one in which there were no politicians or middlemen of any kind and the people governed themselves directly; the political system would take the form of more or less continuous town meetings or referenda, perhaps conducted by means of interactive television. Most Americans, at bottom, would still like to see their country governed by a town meeting.

## Why Their Vulnerability Matters

In this political ethos, finding themselves inhabiting a turbulent and torrid electoral environment, most American elective officials respond as might be expected: in an almost Darwinian way. They adapt their behavior—their roll-call votes, their introduction of bills, their committee assignments, their phone calls, their direct-mail letters, their speeches, their press releases, their sound bites, whom they see, how they spend their time, their trips abroad, their trips back home, and frequently their private and families' lives—to their environment: that is, to their primary and overriding need for electoral survival. The effects are felt not only in the lives of individual officeholders and their staffs but also in America's political institutions as a whole and the shape and content of U.S. public policy.

It all begins with officeholders' immediate physical environment: with bricks, mortar, leather, and wood paneling. The number of congressional buildings and the size of congressional staffs have ballooned in recent decades. At the start of the 1960s most members of the House of Representatives contented themselves with a small inner office and an outer office; senators' office suites were not significantly larger. Apart from the Capitol itself, Congress was reasonably comfortably housed in four buildings, known to Washington taxi drivers as the Old and New House and Senate Office Buildings. The designations Old and New cannot be used any longer, however, because there are now so many even newer congressional buildings.

Congressional staffs have grown at roughly the same rate, the new buildings having been built mainly to house the staffs. In 1957 the total number of people employed by members of the House and Senate as personal staff was 3,556. By 1991 the figure had grown to 11,572—a more than threefold increase within the political lifetime of many long-serving members. [In 1996] the total number of people employed by Congress in all capacities, including committee staffs and the staffs of support agencies like the Congressional Research Service, was 32,820, making Congress by far the most heavily staffed legislative branch in the world.

Much of the growth of staff in recent decades has been in response to the growth of national government, to Congress's insistence on strengthening its policymaking role in the aftermath of Vietnam and Watergate, and to decentralization within Congress, which has led subcommittee chairmen and the subcommittees themselves to acquire their own staffs. But there is no doubt that the increase is also in response to congressional incumbents' ever-increasing electoral exposure. Congress itself has become an integral part of America's veritable "elections industry."

One useful measure of the changes that have taken place—and also an important consequence of the changes—is the increased proportion of staff and staff time devoted to constituent service. As recently as 1972 only 1,189 House employees—22.5 percent of House members' personal staffs—were based in home-district offices. By 1992 the number had more than doubled, to 3,128, and the proportion had nearly doubled, to 42.1 percent. On the Senate side there were only 303 state-based staffers in 1972, making up 12.5 percent of senators' personal staffs, but the number had more than quadrupled by 1992 to 1,368, for fully 31.6 percent of the total. Since a significant proportion of the time of Washington-based congressional staffs is also devoted to constituent service, it is a fair guess that more than half of the time of all congressional staffs is now given over to nursing the district or state rather than to legislation and policymaking.

Much constituent service is undoubtedly altruistic, inspired by politicians' sense of duty (and constituents' understandable frustration with an unresponsive bureaucracy); but at the same time nobody doubts that a large proportion of it is aimed at securing re-election. The statistics on the outgoing mail of members of Congress and their use of the franking privilege point in that direction too. Congressional mailings grew enormously in volume from some 100 million pieces a year in the early 1960s to more than 900 million in

1984—nearly five pieces of congressional mail for every adult American. New restrictions on franking introduced in the 1990s have made substantial inroads into that figure, but not surprisingly the volume of mail emanating from both houses of Congress is still invariably higher in election years.

The monetary costs of these increases in voter-oriented congressional activities are high: in addition to being the most heavily staffed legislative branch in the world, Congress is also the most expensive. But there is another, nonmonetary cost: the staffs themselves become one of the congressman's or senator's constituencies, requiring management, taking up time, and always being tempted to go into business for themselves. American scholars who have studied the burgeoning of congressional staffs express concern about their cumulative impact on Congress as a deliberative body in which face-to-face communication between members, and between members and their constituents, facilitates both mutual understanding and an understanding of the issues. Largely in response to the requirements of electioneering, more and more congressional business is conducted through dense networks of staffers.

One familiar effect of American politicians' vulnerability is the power it accords to lobbyists and special-interest groups, especially those that can muster large numbers of votes or have large amounts of money to spend on campaigns. Members of Congress walk the electoral world alone. They can be picked off one by one, they know it, and they adjust their behavior accordingly. The power of the American Association of Retired Persons, the National Rifle Association, the banking industry, and the various veterans' lobbies is well known. It derives partly from their routine contributions to campaign funds and the quality of their lobbying activities in Washington, but far more from the votes that the organizations may be able to deliver and from congressmen's and senators' calculations of how the positions they take in the present may affect their chances of re-election in the future—a future that rarely is distant. Might a future challenger be able to use that speech against me? Might I be targeted for defeat by one of the powerful lobbying groups?

A second effect is that American politicians are even more likely than those in other countries to engage in symbolic politics: to use words masquerading as deeds, to take actions that purport to be instrumental but are in fact purely rhetorical. A problem exists; the people demand that it be solved; the politicians cannot solve it and know so; they engage in an elaborate pretense of trying to solve it nevertheless, often at great expense to the taxpayers and almost invariably at a high cost in terms of both the truth and the politicians' own reputations for integrity and effectiveness. The politicians lie in most cases not because they are liars or approve of lying but because the potential electoral costs of not lying are too great.

At one extreme, symbolic politics consists of speechmaking and public position-taking in the absence of any real action or any intention of taking action; casting the right vote is more important than achieving the right outcome. At the other extreme, symbolic politics consists of whole government programs that are ostensibly designed to achieve one set of objectives but are actually designed to achieve other objectives (in some cases simply the re-election of the politicians who can claim credit for them).

Take as an example the crime bills passed by Congress in the 1980s and 1990s, with their mandatory-minimum sentences, their three-strikes-and-you're-out provisions, and their extension of the federal death penalty to fifty new crimes. The anti-drug and anti-crime legislation, by the testimony of judges and legal scholars, has been at best useless and at worst wholly pernicious in its effects, in that it has filled prison cells not with violent criminals but with drug users and low-level drug pushers. As for the death penalty, a simple measure of its sheer irrelevance to the federal government's war on crime is easily provided. The last federal offender to be put to death, Victor H. Feguer, a convicted kidnapper, was hanged in March of 1963. By the end of 1995 no federal offender had been executed for more than thirty years, and hardly any offenders were awaiting execution on death row. The ferocious-seeming federal statutes were almost entirely for show.

The way in which the wars on drugs and crime were fought cannot be understood without taking into account the incessant pressure that elected officeholders felt they were under from the electorate. As one former congressman puts it, "Voters were afraid of criminals, and politicians were afraid of voters." This fear reached panic proportions in election years. Seven of the years from 1981 to 1994 were election years nationwide; seven were not. During those fourteen years Congress passed no fewer than seven major crime bills. Of those seven, six were passed in election years (usually late in the year). That is, there was only one election year in which a major crime bill was *not* passed, and only one nonelection year in which a major crime bill *was* passed.

Another effect of the extreme vulnerability of American politicians is that it is even harder for them than for democratically elected politicians in other countries to take tough decisions: to court unpopularity, to ask for sacrifices, to impose losses, to fly in the face of conventional wisdom—in short, to act in what they believe to be their constituents' interest and the national interest rather than in their own interest. Timothy J. Penny, a Democrat who left the House of Representatives in 1994, put the point starkly, perhaps even too harshly, in *Common Cents* (1995).

> Voters routinely punish lawmakers who try to do unpopular things, who challenge them to face unpleasant truths about the budget, crime, Social Security, or tax policy. Similarly, voters reward politicians for giving them what they want—more spending for popular programs—even if it means wounding the nation in the long run by creating more debt....

## What, If Anything, Might Be Done?

Precisely because American politicians are so exposed electorally, they probably have to display—and do display—more political courage more often than the politicians of any other democratic country. The number of political saints and martyrs in the United States is unusually large.

There is, however, no special virtue in a political system that requires large numbers of politicians to run the risk of martyrdom in order to ensure that tough decisions can be taken in a timely manner in the national interest. The number of such decisions that need to be taken is always likely to be large;

human nature being what it is, the supply of would-be martyrs is always likely to be small. On balance it would seem better not to try to eliminate the electoral risks (it can never be done in a democracy) but to reduce somewhat their scale and intensity. There is no reason why the risks run by American politicians should be so much greater than the risks run by elective politicians in other democratic countries.

How, then, might the risks be reduced? What can be done? A number of reforms to the existing system suggest themselves. It may be that none of them is politically feasible—Americans hold tight to the idea of agency democracy —but in principle there should be no bar to any of them. One of the simplest would also be the most radical: to lengthen the terms of members of the House of Representatives from two years to four. The proposal is by no means a new one: at least 123 resolutions bearing on the subject were introduced in Congress in the eighty years from 1885 to 1965, and President Lyndon B. Johnson advocated the change in his State of the Union address in January of 1966.

A congressman participating in a Brookings Institution round table held at about the time of Johnson's message supported the change, saying, "I think that the four years would help you to be a braver congressman, and I think what you need is bravery. I think you need courage." Another congressman on the same occasion cited the example of another bill that he believed had the support of a majority in the House. "That bill is not going to come up this year. You know why it is not coming up? . . . Because four hundred and thirty-five of us have to face election. . . . If we had a four-year term, I am as confident as I can be the bill would have come to the floor and passed."

A similar case could be made for extending the term of senators to eight years, with half the Senate retiring or running for re-election every four years. If the terms of members of both houses were thus extended and made to co-incide, the effect in reducing America's never-ending election campaign would be dramatic.

There is much to be said, too, for all the reasons mentioned so far, for scaling down the number of primary elections. They absorb extravagant amounts of time, energy, and money; they serve little democratic purpose; few people bother to vote in them; and they place additional and unnecessary pressure on incumbent officeholders. Since the main disadvantage of primaries is the adverse effect they have on incumbents, any reforms probably ought to be concerned with protecting incumbents' interests.

At the moment, the primary laws make no distinction between situations in which a seat in the House or the Senate is already occupied and situations in which the incumbent is, for whatever reason, standing down. The current laws provide for a primary to be held in either case. An incumbent is therefore treated as though the seat in question were open and he or she were merely one of the candidates for it. A relatively simple reform would be to distinguish between the two situations. If a seat was open, primaries would be held in both parties, as now; but if the incumbent announced that he or she intended to run for re-election, then a primary in his or her party would be held only if large numbers of party supporters were determined to have one—that is, were determined that the incumbent should be ousted. The obvious way to ascertain whether such determination existed would be by means of a petition supervised by the relevant state government and requiring a considerable number of signatures. The possibility of a primary would thus be left open, but those who wanted one would have to show that they were both numerous and serious. A primary would not be held simply because an ambitious, possibly demented, possibly wealthy individual decided to throw his or her hat into the ring.

Any steps to strengthen the parties as institutions would be desirable on the same grounds. Lack of party cover in the United States means that elective officeholders find it hard to take tough decisions partly because they lack safety in numbers. They can seldom, if ever, say to an aggrieved constituent or a political-action committee out for revenge, "I had to vote that way because my party told me to," or even "I had to vote that way because we in my party all agreed that we would." Lack of party cohesion, together with American voters' disposition to vote for the individual rather than the party, means that congressmen and senators are always in danger of being picked off one by one.

## Ballot Fatigue

What might be done to give both parties more backbone? Clearly, the parties would be strengthened—and elective officeholders would not need to raise so much money for their own campaigns—if each party organization became a major source of campaign funding. In the unlikely event (against the background of chronic budget deficits) that Congress ever gets around to authorizing the federal funding of congressional election campaigns, a strong case could be made for channeling as much of the money as possible through the parties, and setting aside some of it to cover their administrative and other ongoing costs.

The party organizations and the nexus between parties and their candidates would also be strengthened if it were made easier for ordinary citizens to give money to the parties and for the parties to give money to their candidates. Until 1986, when the program was abolished, tax credits were available for taxpayers who contributed small sums to the political parties. These credits could be restored. Larry J. Sabato, a political scientist at the University of Virginia, has similarly suggested that citizens entitled to a tax refund could be allowed to divert a small part of their refund to the party of their choice. Such measures would not, however, reduce candidates' dependence on donations from wealthy individuals and PACs [political action committees] unless they were accompanied by measures enabling the parties to contribute more generously to their candidates' campaigns. At the moment there are strict legal limits on the amount of money that national or state party organizations can contribute to the campaigns of individual candidates. The limits should be raised (and indexed to inflation). There is even a case for abolishing them altogether.

All that said, there is an even more straightforward way of reducing incumbents' dependence on campaign contributions. At present incumbents have to spend so much time raising funds because the campaigns themselves are so expensive. They could be made cheaper. This, of course, would be one of the effects of making U.S. elections less numerous and less frequent than they are now. Another way to lower the cost of elections would be to provide candidates and parties with free air time on television and radio.

# POSTSCRIPT

## Do Political Campaigns Promote Good Government?

The right of people to choose who governs them is the very essence of democracy. In that spirit Popkin argues that Americans need more democracy—that is, more participation by the people inspired by more campaigning and education of the public. King asserts that America has an excess of democracy and that the burden imposed by so many and so frequent elections is too great and leads to disillusion and more citizens not voting.

In order to stimulate greater voter participation, beginning in 1972 radical reforms were adopted to ensure that the presidential nominees of the two major parties would be those favored by the largest proportion of party members participating in the primaries and caucuses in which the national convention delegates were chosen. The local party organization plays a greatly reduced role because it no longer hand picks the delegates. The national convention plays a greatly reduced role because it no longer engages in any real deliberation regarding the choice of nominee. For better or worse, the electorate gets the presidential candidate endorsed by the largest number of delegates.

More directly, the people vote in primaries in order to designate candidates for all other elective offices. This means that voters are exposed to more and longer campaigns; they should therefore be motivated and informed both in the long primary campaign before the party choices are made and in the months leading up to the election before the officeholders are chosen.

A classic text that provides an overview of presidential campaigns is Nelson W. Polsby and Aaron Wildavsky, *Presidential Elections: Strategies and Structures of American Politics,* 10th ed. (Chatham House, 2000). Ever since Theodore White began his distinguished series of vivid accounts with *The Making of the President 1960* (Atheneum, 1961), each presidential election has produced a spate of books providing insightful analysis and insider revelations regarding the conduct of the campaign. One of the best is Richard Ben Cramer, *What It Takes: The Way to the White House* (Random House, 1992).

In the tradition of White's intimate journalism is Bob Woodward's account of the 1996 presidential campaigns of President Bill Clinton and Senator Bob Dole, *The Choice: How Clinton Won* (Simon & Schuster, 1997). More analytical and less anecdotal are the quadrennial volumes edited by Michael Nelson, *Election of 1996* (Congressional Quarterly Books, 1997), and Gerald M. Pomper, *The Election of 1996: Reports and Interpretations* (Chatham House, 1997). Stephen J. Wayne has updated his study of presidential campaigning in *The Road to the White House 1996: The Politics of Presidential Elections: Post-Election Edition* (St. Martin's Press, 1997).

# ISSUE 3

## Should Campaign Finance Be Reformed?

**YES: Archibald Cox**, from "Ethics, Campaign Finance, and Democracy," *Society* (March/April 1998)

**NO: Bradley A. Smith**, from "The Campaign-Finance Follies," *Commentary* (December 1997)

### ISSUE SUMMARY

**YES:** Archibald Cox, a former special prosecutor and a law professor, argues that the increasing amount of money spent in elections corrupts government but that the public's faith in democratic self-government can be restored by campaign finance reform.

**NO:** Bradley A. Smith, an associate professor at Capital University Law School, asserts that campaign contributions do not corrupt candidates, the biggest spenders do not always win, and the relatively modest amount that candidates spend is essential to educate voters and to increase their interest.

The votes had hardly been counted in President Bill Clinton's successful bid for reelection in 1996 when charges of improper campaign financing began to swirl around the president. It was reported that large contributions could buy a night in the White House's Lincoln bedroom and that smaller contributions could buy coffee with the president in the Roosevelt Room. To many, this fund-raising seemed unseemly; sometimes it appeared sleazy, and when it concerned contributions from foreign nationals and corporations, it could have been illegal. Vice President Al Gore has been sharply criticized for soliciting contributions from the White House and raising money at a Buddhist temple luncheon. Predictably, when the Senate Committee on Governmental Affairs completed hearings early in 1998, the Republican majority castigated President Clinton, his aides, and the Democratic National Committee, while the Democratic minority charged that Republican leaders violated the laws.

Hundreds of millions of dollars are raised during each national campaign cycle, and the amount is increasing. By 1996 the average cost of winning a Senate seat was $4.5 million, while the average cost of winning a House seat was $660,000. In 1994, in the most expensive congressional election ever, Senator

Diane Feinstein (D-California) spent more than $14 million to turn back the challenge of Republican Michael Huffington, who spent $30 million. In her primary, Feinstein spent over $2 million to defeat her opponent, who spent $14,000. In his primary, Huffington spent nearly $6 million to defeat a rival, who spent $800,000.

What is wrong with candidates and parties' raising the large sums of money that are needed to present their messages in the form of television broadcasts and print advertisements? By the same token, what is wrong with voters' putting their money where their mouth is in politics? A great deal, say those who believe that the rampant spending on political campaigns discourages less-wealthy citizens from seeking office, diverts too much of a public officer's attention away from performing his or her duties to raising funds for the next campaign, and turns off voters who believe that money influences public policy more than their votes do. This last concern is exemplified by Roger Tamraz, an oil financier, who gained access to the White House through his $300,000 donation to the Democrats. Testifying before a congressional committee, he said that next time he would give $600,000, in the hope of having more influence.

After the 1996 election, major legislation to change the system of campaign finance was proposed by Senator John McCain (R-Arizona) and Senator Russell Feingold (D-Wisconsin). Perhaps the most prominent feature of the McCain-Feingold Bill was the effort to ban "soft money" contributions to political parties. Soft money is intended for party building and getting out the voters, but it is often closely tied in to particular candidates. Other reform proposals would give free television time to candidates who accept voluntary limits and lower the amounts that political action committees (PACs) can contribute to campaigns.

Critics of these proposed reforms argue that campaign expenditures are really modest. Some suggest that much more should be spent in order to increase public awareness and turnout at the polls. One conservative strategy in opposing radical reforms was to urge a ban on contributions by trade unions without the prior approval of the union members. (A liberal retort was to oppose contributions by corporations without the prior approval of the stockholders.)

The most imposing objection to campaign finance reform is that it abridges the First Amendment's guarantee of freedom of political expression. In 1976 the U.S. Supreme Court considered a challenge to the campaign finance limitations of the Federal Election Campaign Act. In *Buckley v. Valeo* the Court concluded that spending limits violate the constitutional protection of free speech. The Court's reasoning was that to abridge political communication by restricting political expenditures "reduces the quantity of expression by restricting the number of issues discussed, the depth of their exploration, and the size of the audience reached."

In the following selections, Archibald Cox asserts that the present system of campaign finance creates improper political access and contributes to public cynicism regarding the democratic process. Bradley A. Smith maintains that both the cost and impact of campaign financing have been exaggerated and that proposed changes would abridge the people's First Amendment rights.

# Ethics, Campaign Finance, and Democracy

My subject is "Ethics, Campaign Finance, and Democracy." One need hardly argue to a thoughtful audience the general importance of high ethical standards in government. The dollars and cents costs of corruption are obvious. So is the unfairness to competitors. As the moral standards of a community affect the moral standards of political leaders, so do the moral standards of political leaders to an ever greater extent influence the moral standards of the community. But the prime goal is broader. At the beginning James Madison wrote in *The Federalist Papers*:

> The aim of every political constitution is, or ought to be to obtain for rulers men who possess the most wisdom to discern, and the most virtue to pursue, the common good of the society; and in the next place, to take the most effectual precautions for keeping them virtuous whilst they continue to hold their public trust.

How successful have we been in pursuing the second of Madison's aims over the past half century?

In the field normally suggested by the phrase "ethics in government" we seem to have made remarkable progress in writing laws and regulations well designed to set high ethical standards for members of Congress and officers and employees in the executive branch.

The progress began with Senator Douglas' work as chairman of a special subcommittee of the Senate Committee on Labor and Public Welfare. The subcommittee produced one of the first comprehensive reports—the first in the Senate—on the general field of ethical abuses in government. The Senator's Godkin Lectures, delivered at Harvard in 1952, became the classic treatment of the subject. In 1958 Congress enacted a very broad and loosely worded Code of Ethics for Government Service. Watergate gave new impetus to the movement. New Codes of Ethics were adopted by the Senate and House of Representatives in 1977, and a year later Congress enacted the Ethics in Government Act of 1978.

The Ethics in Government Act, as strengthened by amendments, supplies one of the foundation stones for assuring ethics in government: the individual detailed periodic financial reports required of the President and every officer in

From Archibald Cox, "Ethics, Campaign Finance, and Democracy," *Society* (March/April 1998). Copyright © 1998 by Transaction Publishers. Reprinted by permission.

the executive branch and every employee compensated at or above the senior level, and also of Senators and Representatives in Congress and senior congressional staff. The publicity, like sunlight, both deters and corrects. In addition, the reports furnish a wealth of information for the press, reform groups and the public concerning practices tolerated by the current law and codes of ethics but damaging to the public good.

We have made good progress in stopping the flow of money from private interests with axes to grind directly into the personal bank accounts of senior government employees and elected and appointed officials. I refer to once widely accepted practices such as the large earnings for little work done outside one's government position, the honoraria paid in return for a short speech or perhaps simply attendance at a meeting of some trade association or other organization in the private sector. Gifts, transportation, travel expenses, a weekend or perhaps a week at a travel resort in return for a brief appearance at a convention fall in the same category. Senator Douglas explained the cost of such practices much more clearly than I can express it:

> Throughout this whole process, the official will claim—and may indeed believe—that there is no causal connection between the favors he has received and the decisions which he makes. He will assert that the favors were given and received on the basis of pure friendship unsullied by worldly considerations. He will claim that the decisions, on the other hand, will have been made on the basis of the justice and equity of the particular case.

But—Senator Douglas emphasized:

> What happens is a gradual shifting of a man's loyalties from the community to those who have been doing him favors. His final decisions are, therefore, made in response to his private friendships and loyalties rather than to the public good.

Outside earnings have been sharply limited and the receipt of honoraria has been forbidden throughout the government. The Senate put the capstone on such legislation this summer by modifying its rules to forbid acceptance of travel expenses and of any but the most trifling entertainment. The House has not followed suit. On October 1, 1995 the House majority leader, Representative Armey, said that the Republican leadership would not bring a similar measure up for consideration that year. A week later, he reversed himself and said that a bill would be taken up in November. Any failure of the Republican leadership in the House to secure enactment of ethics reforms approved by every other part of the government could only be described as "shameful."

We have also made considerable progress in dealing with the evils of "the revolving door" through which officials, including members of Congress, regularly left government office only to walk back in to the Congress, or their former department or agency to use the friendships, influence and inside information acquired in government service as lobbyists for special interests. Senior personnel in the executive branch, for example, are now barred for one year from participating in any matter that was under their authority within a year prior to leaving the government. Former members of Congress are barred from lobbying any present member of either House or any congressional staff for one year after leaving office. Similar but somewhat narrower limitations are laid upon other employees in both branches.

The measures are not a full remedy for the abuse of the "revolving door." There continues to be serious criticism of the practice of leaving Congress or high executive office and later becoming the lobbyist for a foreign government at any time. Much more important in my opinion, the one-year ban on lobbying is far too short either to eliminate the advantage of "inside information" or to ensure that the individual lobbied will not make his decisions "in response to his private friendships and loyalties [to his former colleagues turned lobbyist] rather than to the public good."

Taking all these reforms as a group, I think that we are thoroughly warranted in saying that, within the field conventionally denominated "ethics in government," we have made good progress in writing rules to keep our rulers virtuous in pursuit of the common good.

## Growing Public Cynicism

Have we succeeded in Madison's aim to keep those chosen to govern virtuous in pursuit of the common good?

Surely, the answer is a resounding "No." Some will respond that the common good of which Madison, Jefferson and the Founding Fathers wrote was always an empty dream, meaningless in actuality, and that Congress has always been a place for striking a balance among the selfish interests of conflicting groups according to their political power. I grant you that pursuit of the common good was an ideal seldom wholly achieved and often submerged in the battle of selfish interests. But I think that the ideal had its force, and that by any measure of achievement we have lost much ground in the past 20 years. Column after column, book after book, by such experienced observers as Elizabeth Drew, Al Hunt, William Greider and Kevin Phillips documents the proposition that "money-driven American politics stinks." A 1992 Gordon S. Black poll found that 75 percent of the registered likely voters agreed that "Congress is largely owned by special interest groups," while 85 percent agreed that "special interest money buys the loyalty of candidates." The 1994 elections resulted in a smashing defeat of the Democratic incumbents. The vote was a rejection of the performance of government and not just of the party in power. One therefore has to ask: What is to blame?

## Influence of Lobbyists

Surely the central cause of the current overwhelming public distrust of government, and of actual subordination of the common good to special interests, is the present system of campaign finance.

A few figures should be sufficient to recall the still swelling torrent of campaign money. In less than 20 years, spending in Senate races has increased more than five-fold. The average expenditure for a Senate winner was $610,026 in 1976 and $4.5 million in 1994, a seven-fold increase. In order to acquire $4.5 million for a campaign, a Senator must raise $14,423 a week each and every week of his six-year term. In 1976 the average spent by successful candidates for the House was $87,280. In 1994 it was $530,031—more than a six-fold increase. In 1994, 45 House candidates spent more than $1 million apiece.

Special interest PAC [political action committee] contributions have become a dominant force in financing congressional campaigns, and consequently in congressional decision making. In 1994, 45 percent of the contributions of incumbent House candidates came from PACs. On the average, an incumbent Senate candidate raised $1.1 million from PACs in the 1994 election cycle. The 1994 elections brought many new members to both Senate and House, a switch to Republican control, and sweeping promises of reform; but the torrent of PAC money is still increasing. The 85 freshman members of the House raised just about $5 million in PAC contributions during the first six months of 1995, 25 percent higher than those of their predecessors in the corresponding first six months of 1993.

Nearly all PACs are affiliated with organizations that are concerned with government decisions and therefore maintain on-going lobbying. And while the law limits to $10,000 the amount any one PAC can contribute to any one member of Congress in a full election cycle, we must remember that large numbers of PACs will often be pressing the same issue. As former Senator Warren Rudman observed while in the House of Representatives:

> I call them wolf packs. Sure, the PACs can only give X amount of dollars, but you can take 10 PACs who are interested in defense or 10 PACs interested in energy or 10 PACs interested in agriculture or 10 PACs interested in trade issues and put them together and you have $100,000 between the primary and general election.

The medical industry PACs invested $45 million in campaign contributions in the decade 1983–1993; $18.6 million (44 percent) went to members of key committees who were still in office in 1993. Similarly, in the decade ending this spring communications industry PACs contributed in excess of $30 million, and communications interests and their executives added $8.6 million in "soft money" given to the Democratic and Republican national committees.

## Campaign Contributions and Political Access

The costs of this system of campaign finance are enormous.

First comes the substitution of money in place of ability to attract votes by character, program and record of public accomplishment as the driving force throughout our political system, ranging from elections to action and inaction by both Congress and the President.

Second, other experienced observers echo Senator Dale Bumpers' observation that "Every Senator knows I speak the truth when I say bill after bill has been defeated in this body because of campaign money."

Former Senator Packwood's diary provides examples. Similarly, outcomes are bound to have been affected by the tens of millions of dollars invested by the medical and communications interests while Congress was working on basic legislation affecting them.

Efforts to analyze the effect of special interest contributions upon key votes point to the same conclusion. Consider the dairy subsidy. Three huge dairy cooperatives had been showering political contributions upon members of Congress. Of those who had received more than $30,000, all voted for the subsidy at the high level. Of those who received from $20,000 to $30,000, 97 percent chose the high level; from $10,000 to $20,000, 81 percent. On the other hand, of those Congressmen who received from $1 to $2,500, only 33 percent voted for the higher subsidy, along with 23 percent of those who received no dairy industry money. The higher subsidy carried the day at a cost of $1 billion to the taxpayers. The effect of the special interest money seems plain whether one infers that it bought votes in Congress or that it made the difference in congressional elections in an age when the key factor is usually the ability to outspend one's opponent in buying skilled campaign managers, pollsters, "packagers" and television spots.

The defenders of large campaign contributions often acknowledge that the contributions buy "access" to Senators and Representatives but deny that they buy votes. But buying and selling access itself changes the very basis of our political system. No one would tolerate a legal system in which the judge heard only the evidence and arguments of one side. Why should the Congress be different? The irresistible forces so well described by Senator Douglas in speaking of gifts and entertainment also come into play:

> What happens is a gradual shifting of man's loyalties from the community to those who have been doing him favors. His final decisions are, therefore, made in response to his private friendships and loyalties rather than to the public good.

The access and the loyalties engendered by large campaign contributions also win innumerable opportunities to advance the special interest in ways less apparent than key votes: the appointment of A rather than B to the staff of a key committee, absence from a hearing, a slight verbal change in a complex 240 page bill, the insertion at midnight of an apparently small, technical exemption into a tax or appropriations bill thus securing some interest in the millions of dollars.

Hand in hand with the torrent of PAC money flowing to the newly elected Republican members of Congress, there has come closer and closer participation by lobbyists in the legislative process. The *Wall Street Journal* reports that while the House Science Committee was writing a regulatory overhaul bill earlier this year, the committee's general counsel was surrounded by lobbyists for businesses vitally interested in the legislation and that one night the majority staff turned its computer over to the business interests. The same account reports that during a House Resources subcommittee hearing on Bureau of Reclamation activities, the lobbyist for a private firm that oversees the Central Arizona project, former Arizona Congressman John Rhodes, actually sat on the dais with the chairman of the subcommittee.

Confronted by these and countless other examples, it is no wonder that a study done for the Kettering Foundation found that:

> People believe two forces have corrupted democracy. The first is that lobbyists have replaced representatives as the primary political actors. The other force seen as more pernicious is that campaign contributions seem to determine political outcomes more than voting.

The third cost of the present system of campaign finance is the shrinking and ultimate loss of faith in democratic self-government. When money and lobbyists are seen to govern, men and women drop out of the political process; they take no interest and cease to vote. Only 55.2 percent of the eligible population voted in 1992, the year of the last presidential election; only 39 percent voted in 1994. Many of those who do vote learn less each year about the issues and candidates. The package gotten up by the professional advertiser, the thirty-second sound bite with its pretested slogans, and the attack message, all received by television, replace informed discussion. The cynicism that accompanies the feeling of powerlessness discourages active citizenship.

Fourth among the costs and first in importance, I would list the loss of faith in a common good of society—of which Madison wrote when he said that one aim of every political constitution should be to keep those elected virtuous in pursuit of the "common good." I return to the point a little later. For the moment it is enough to say that even if the skeptics are right in saying that in a self-governing democracy, elections and the halls of Congress are no more than the places where selfish groups strike an equilibrium of self-interests, still it is a disastrous step back to have money become the sole determinant of where the balance is struck.

# Reforming American Politics

To restore confidence in representative government by turning our elected governors' focus away from special interests and back to the common good, we need first to reform the system of campaign finance. Solid reform would comprise five elements.

1. First, reform must provide viable candidates with substantial public campaign resources in return for their agreement to observe strict spending limits. I couple the two because the U.S. Supreme Court has held that although Congress violates the First Amendment by setting a limit on what one may spend to get elected, Congress may offer public financing to those candidates who subscribe to spending limits, as indeed the present law provides in presidential general elections. There are various forms in which the public financing might be provided: direct grants, matching payments, publicly funded communications vouchers, and so forth. My personal preference is for direct grants large enough to run an effective campaign without becoming indebted to special donors, the kind of plan established in 1974 for presidential general elections.

2. The second essential of campaign finance reform is tighter restriction of PAC contributions. The PAC contributions, unlike many personal contributions, are plainly and simply financial investments made in the hope that they will yield earnings in favorable government decisions. The ceiling on individual PAC contributions to individual candidates should be reduced from the present $5,000 limit to $1,000. The total amount an individual candidate receives from all PACs should also be limited. The influence of the special interest lobbyists would be greatly weakened.

3. Limits upon PAC contributions will be effective only if the reform measure includes as a third component a prohibition against "bundling." Normally a PAC obtains individual contributions to the PAC and then makes PAC contributions to candidates. In the 1980s PACs began to have their contributors write checks to designated individual candidates instead of the PAC but to leave the checks with the PAC. The PAC then bundles together and delivers the checks to each candidate whom it chooses to support. The PAC thus receives the credit and the gratitude from the candidate, and the access and influence that go with it. Nevertheless, today the PAC is held to have made no contribution, and it can thus circumvent even the present $5,000 statutory limit. Closing the bundling loophole is essential to any effective PAC limits.

4. Fourth, it is important to stop the flow of "soft money" from wealthy individuals, corporations, and labor unions into the coffers of the political parties which spend it for the benefit of presidential and congressional candidates outside the existing statutory limits. The present system of funding presidential campaigns worked well until the mid-1980s when the Federal Elections Commission sanctioned the practice whereby a wealthy donor gives unlimited monies to a national political party, normally Democratic or Republican, and the national party then channels those dollars to its state organizations, which spend them for the benefit of the presidential ticket in ways that can be labeled "party building." The whole process escapes federal law.

In the 1991–1992 election cycle George Bush and the Republican National Committee raised $49.6 million in this fashion. Each of 69 contributors gave $100,000 or more. Clinton and the Democratic National Committee raised $35.3 million from 72 contributors, with each giving $100,000 or more. The money was spent in excess of the public funds provided to them on condition that they receive no private contributions. You will have read of the public controversy aroused by President Clinton's offer of personal access to himself and to Vice President Gore and others in return for contributions of $100,000 to the Democratic National Committee. Obviously, no reform of campaign finance can be effective unless it closes this gaping loophole.

5. The last essential major element in any effective reform is reconstitution of the Federal Elections Commission. The present commission has done an admirable job in gathering and publishing information about the financing of election campaigns, but it has done little as an enforcement agency. The requirement that there be six members, three Republicans and three Democrats, means that all too often the commission is deadlocked along party lines. The present practice of appointing members closely linked to the political parties also means that the commission is at best slow to challenge ways of raising and

spending ever larger funds in excess of the statutory limits. Consider the gaping loopholes left by the commission's rulings on bundling and "soft money."

## Restoring Confidence

To outline legislation reforming our present system of financing election campaigns is much easier than to persuade Congress to enact it. On the one hand, the vast majority of the people desires reform: 83 percent according to a *USA Today*/CNN poll. On the other hand, the Senators and Representatives who vote upon a reform bill, the president who must sign it, and the political parties to which they belong, are all beneficiaries of the present system and indebted to the special interests that supply such large proportions of their funds. Most of them cannot know how their personal positions and power and their party's fortunes would be affected by reform. This makes for resistance.

Yet there are also encouraging signs. In 1992 a sound measure was blocked only by a veto by President Bush. In 1993 the Senate and the House passed different measures but the differences were never ironed out in conference. In May 1995 the Senate rebuffed an effort by the Republican leadership to gut the existing system of public financing for presidential campaigns. A strong bipartisan bill sponsored by senators John McCain and Russell Feingold has been filed in the Senate. In July 1995 the Senate, over the strong resistance of the Republican leadership led by Senator Dole, voted its commitment to the consideration of campaign finance reform during the present Congress. The picture in the House was confused. Representatives Linda Smith, Chris Shays and Martin Meehan have introduced a strong bi-partisan bill similar to the McCain-Feingold bill in the Senate. In early October 1995 the Majority Leader said that reform would not be considered by the Congress. Later, he indicated that a reform measure would be brought forward in the spring of 1996. Speaker Gingrich proposed in November 1995 that a large commission be appointed to study not only campaign finance, but the status and future of political parties, the effect of media oligarchies, etc. The minority leader expressed approval. As Representative Linda Smith said, "The old boys and old establishment came together to stall for time."

Our ability to add to the voices and votes for reform and thus obtain reform depends upon exercising the privileges and accompanying duties of true representative government: informing not only ourselves but friends, neighbors, and others in the community, enlisting in or building civic associations for a grass roots movement to lobby for early reform, registering our wills with our chosen representatives and holding them accountable if they do not work for and then accomplish real reform.

Five or six decades ago when the philosopher Alfred North Whitehead was asked how he would explain the extraordinary achievements of the American people, he answered that no other people in the history of mankind had shown such innate qualities of toleration and cooperation. It was the spirit of toleration and cooperation that gave birth to the extraordinary number and variety of associations observed by de Tocqueville during his travels in America. The hardships of the wilderness taught our forebears that, essential though individual liberty might be, they were all fellow voyagers in the same boat; that no one could move very far towards individual goals unless the vessel moved; and that the vessel would not move if some voyagers pulled ahead, others backed water, others demanded a new boat, and more and more dropped out to go ashore. Toleration and cooperation flowed from belief in the value of common enterprise—belief in "the common good of society" of which James Madison wrote.

Today the prevailing style is often confrontational. The language is too often of demand and of "rights," not of cooperation and consensus. By the same token, the old voluntary civic associations are shriveling up: Boy Scouts and Red Cross volunteers, the labor unions, the Lions, the Elks, and even the PTA. Men and women drop out and factions too often seem to press their separate aims, not through general progress, but by taking from each other.

Earlier I counted the people's growing loss of confidence in the government as the most serious cost of the power achieved by lobbyists for special interests under present methods of campaign finance. Confidence in the government is closely related to confidence in representative democracy and to its *sine qua non,* belief in a common good. The link is symbiotic. A marked decline of belief in the working of self-government weakens, and if the decline continues, could destroy, belief in a common good. Happily, the converse is also true. The effective working of government in ways that build confidence in the system, while by no means the only influence, will tend to revive the belief in a common good.

I am confident that our politics, our institutions of self-government, will be purged of the corrupting cancer of today's system of campaign finance. The American people have never resigned themselves to endless corruption. Corruption and reform go in cycles. The ethics measures which I tried briefly to describe were developed over the course of three decades, each in response to evidence of the abuse. The efforts of truly committed Senators and Representatives expressing the will of 83 percent of the people will surely prevail if enough of us care enough not to be deluded by pretenses of reform and to register our wills.

May we also look forward to revival of the belief in the "common good of society" of which Madison and other Founding Fathers so often wrote, and from which flowed the tolerance and cooperation and voluntary civic associations that were hallmarks of the American people? I find guidance in the words of my great teacher, Judge Learned Hand, speaking of the path of mankind from the dark swamp in which our remote ancestors blundered:

> Day breaks forever, and above the eastern horizon the sun is now about to peep. Full light of day? No, perhaps not ever. But yet it grows lighter and the paths that were so blind will, if one watches sharply enough, become hourly plainer. We shall learn to walk straighter. Yes, it is always dawn.

# NO ⬐

**Bradley A. Smith**

# The Campaign-Finance Follies

In 1974, Congress passed amendments to the Federal Elections Campaign Act that, for the first time in our nation's history, seriously undertook to regulate political campaigns. Most states followed suit, and virtually overnight, politics became a heavily regulated industry.

Yet we now see, on videotape and in White House photos, shots of the President of the United States meeting with arms merchants and drug dealers; we learn of money being laundered through Buddhist nuns and Indonesian gardeners; we read that acquaintances of the President are fleeing the country, or threatening to assert Fifth Amendment privileges to avoid testifying before Congress. Regulation, we were told two decades ago, would free our elected officials from the clutches of money, but they now seem to devote more time than ever before to pursuing campaign cash. The 1974 reforms, we were promised, would open up political competition, yet the purely financial advantage enjoyed by incumbents in congressional races has increased almost threefold. Regulation was supposed to restore confidence in government, yet the percentage of Americans who trust their government to "do what is right most of the time" is half what it was before the 1974 act, and campaigns themselves seem nastier and less informative.

Well, say apologists for the law; if we have failed, it is only because our labors have just begun. If our goals seem farther away, we must redouble our efforts. We must ban political action committees (PAC's). We must prevent "bundling," a procedure whereby a group collects contributions from its members and delivers them all at once to a candidate's election committee. We must ban large contributions to political parties ("soft money"). We must, in the words of former Vice President Walter Mondale and former Senator Nancy Kassebaum, learn to distinguish between "campaign endorsements or attacks and [speech] that genuinely debates issues," and we must restrict the former while encouraging the latter. Senators John McCain (R.-Arizona) and Russell Feingold (D.-Wisconsin), the most prominent reformers in today's Washington, have proposed enacting all of these measures at once.

If existing regulation has failed so spectacularly, and existing laws are being broken seemingly at will, is more regulation the solution? Before we rush off on another round, it may be worthwhile to examine the premises on which

From Bradley A. Smith, "The Campaign-Finance Follies," *Commentary* (December 1997). Copyright © 1997 by The American Jewish Committee. Reprinted by permission of *Commentary*.

the impulse to regulate campaign finance is based. Each of them is severely flawed.

❦

The first assumption underlying proposals for campaign-finance regulation is that too much money is being spent on political campaigning. The amounts are often described in near-apocalyptic terms. Candidates, we are informed, amass "huge war chests" from "fat cats" who "pour their millions" into campaigns and "stuff the pockets" of representatives in an "orgy" of contributions. Expenditures "skyrocket," leaving legislators "awash" in "obscene" amounts of cash.

Hyperbole aside, however, the amount spent each year on all political activity in the United States, from every ballot referendum to races for every office from dog catcher to President, is less than the amount spent on potato chips. Total spending of congressional races in 1995–96 was less than what is spent annually on Barbie dolls. Total PAC contributions in federal elections in 1995–96 were just about equal to the amount needed to produce the most recent *Batman* movie.

On a per-voter basis, our expenditures are equally low: less than $2.50 per eligible voter per year, or about the cost of a single video rental, for all congressional races, including all primaries. Looked at as a proportion of gross domestic product, total spending on all political activity in this country amounts to approximately five-hundredths-of-one-percent—less than is spent in nations as varied as Canada, Germany, and Venezuela.

Perhaps more relevant than any of these comparisons are the amounts spent on political campaigning versus other types of advertising. In 1996, the Home Depot corporation alone spent more on advertising than federal law allowed Bill Clinton, Bob Dole, and Ross Perot put together to spend on the general election. Although Michael Huffington was roundly criticized for "exorbitant" spending in his 1994 race for a Senate seat from California, it cost him less than what Sony International spent in the same year to promote a single compact disc by Michael Jackson. Unilever NV, a company most people have never heard of, devotes more money each year to advertising its wares than has ever been spent in any two-year election cycle by all candidates for the House and Senate.

The plain truth is that it costs money to communicate, and there is no reason to expect that political communication should come free. This is the crucial insight of the Supreme Court's 1976 decision in *Buckley* v. *Valeo,* a case issuing from a challenge to the 1974 Federal Elections Campaign Act by a broad coalition of groups ranging from the ACLU to the Conservative and Libertarian parties. There the Court struck down mandatory limits on campaign spending as well as limits on what a candidate could spend from his own personal funds. The Court did not say, as its critics have alleged, that money equals speech; rather, it recognized that limits on spending can restrict speech just as surely as can a direct prohibition. Imagine, for example, if newspapers were limited to $100,000 a year for publishing costs: most would go out of business, and those that remained would become very thin indeed. (This consideration has hardly stopped the *Washington Post,* the *New York Times,* and *USA Today* from ridiculing the *Buckley* decision.)

Spending on political advertisements is important to educate voters, increasing their interest in elections and their knowledge of candidates and issues. Repetition plays an important part in this process: the electorate's hatred of 30-second campaign ads is surpassed only by its desire to get its political information by means of those same ads. And the ads cost money.

Although campaign-finance reformers often appeal to the public's unhappiness with negative ads, negativity has long been a feature of political campaigns, and money is not the source of it. (As long ago as 1796, the presidential candidate Thomas Jefferson was attacked as "an atheist, anarchist, demagogue, coward, mountebank, trickster, and Francomaniac," and his followers as "cut-throats who walk in rags and sleep amidst filth and vermin.") In fact, if the goal is to have positive campaigns, even *more* money would be needed, for the simple reason that positive ads are less memorable than negative ones and hence need to be repeated more frequently. Besides, a limit on spending would mean that candidates would have to depend more on the media to get their message across, and the press is often more negative in its campaign coverage than the contestants themselves.

There is, finally, no objective criterion by which to measure whether "too much" is being spent on political campaigns. But as we have seen, spending in this country is not high. Considering the vital importance of an informed electorate to democratic government, it is hard to discern why it should be lower.

⟨⟩

The hidden premise behind the idea that too much is being spent on campaigns is that money "buys" election results—a second assumption of reformers. It is true that the candidate who spends the most money wins most of the time. But the cause-and-effect relationship between spending and victory is nowhere near so straightforward as this might suggest.

For one thing, the formulation neglects the desire of donors to give to candidates likely to win. In other words, it may be the prospect of victory that attracts money, not the other way around. (What that money does and does not buy is treated below.) Or a candidate's fund-raising edge may simply reflect the relative status of his popularity, later to be confirmed or disconfirmed at the polls.

Even when the ability to raise and spend money actually succeeds in changing the outcome of a race, it is ballots, not dollars, that ultimately decide who wins, and ballots reflect the minds of voters. All that spending can do is attempt to change those minds. It would be a strange First Amendment that cut off protection for speech at the point where speech began to influence people's views, and it reflects a remarkable contempt for the electorate to suggest that it is incapable of weighing the arguments being tendered for its consideration.

Indeed, there is ample evidence that the electorate does so discriminate, and that higher spending in behalf of a losing argument will not necessarily translate into electoral triumph. In the Republican takeover of Congress in 1994, for example, the 34 victorious challengers spent, on average, just two-thirds of the amount spent by their Democratic opponents, who also enjoyed the inherent advantage of incumbency. By contrast, in the 1996 race for the Republican presidential nomination, Phil Gramm, who raised the most money, was the first to have to drop out. As Michael Malbin of the Rockefeller Institute of Government has observed, "Having money means having the ability to be heard; it does not mean that voters will like what they hear."

The key variable in elections is not which candidate spends the most, but whether or not challengers are able to spend enough to overcome the advantage of incumbency and make their names and issues known to voters. Once they reach this threshold, races are up for grabs. For example, in the 1996 House races, 40 percent of challengers who spent over $600,000 won, as opposed to just 3 percent who spent less than $600,000. Once the threshold was crossed, it mattered little whether or not the challenger was outspent, or by how much. The problem, if it can be called that, is not that some candidates "buy" elections by spending too much, but that others spend too little to get their message to the voters.

❦

Still another assumption of reformers is that, if we truly cared about self-government and participatory democracy, we would be better off if campaigns were funded by many small contributors rather than by fewer large ones.

In fact, the burden of financing political campaigns has *always* fallen to a small minority, both in the United States and in other democracies. Nearly eighteen million Americans now make contributions to a political party, candidate, or PAC during an election cycle. Although this figure is higher than at any other time in American history, and represents a broader base of voluntary public support than has been enjoyed by any other system of campaign funding anywhere, it still comes to less than 10 percent of the voting-age population.

Which sorts of candidates are typically able to raise large sums of money in small amounts, as the reformers prefer? In the years prior to federal funding of presidential campaigns, the two most successful in this respect were Barry Goldwater and George McGovern. The former raised $5.8 million from over 400,000 contributors in 1964, only to suffer a landslide defeat, while the latter, who raised almost $15 million from donors making average contributions of about $20, lost in an even bigger landslide eight years later. More recently, Oliver North raised approximately $20 million, almost all from small contributors, for his 1994 U.S. Senate race, outspent his rival by almost four to one, and still lost to a candidate plagued by personal scandal—primarily because the electorate, rightly or wrongly, viewed him as too "extreme."

What these examples suggest is that the ability to raise large sums in small contributions can be a sign less of broad public support, as reformers assert, than of fervent backing by an ideological minority. Other groups positioned to exert influence by this means tend to be those (like unions) in possession of an ongoing structure for mobilizing their constituents or those we usually call "special interests." It is the inchoate, grass-roots public that more often fails to make its interests known, and is therefore frequently reliant on individuals with large fortunes to finance movements that will represent it. Ross Perot forced the deficit to the forefront of attention in 1992, and Steve Forbes brought about a debate on the flat tax in 1996. Both were real issues, but each lacked an organized constituency, a problem Perot and Forbes were able to overcome only by means of their own substantial resources.

Ironically, the banning of large contributions, which means that no single gift is likely to make much difference in a political race, gives potential donors little incentive to become involved. A radical campaign can overcome this difficulty: its supporters tend to be motivated more by ideology than by rational calculations of a candidate's chances of winning. But this just further underscores the way in which banning large contributions can help render the political system more rather than less vulnerable to forces on the fringes of the mainstream—hardly, one presumes, the result the reformers have in mind.

A corollary fallacy entertained by reformers is that the financial resources placed at a candidate's disposal should ideally reflect his level of popular support. But this is to confuse the purpose of elections with the purpose of campaigns. The former do measure popular support. The latter, however, are about something else: persuading voters, and *improving* one's level of support. This, as we have seen, requires monetary expenditures, and it is a sign of health in a democracy when such expenditures are forthcoming.

When Steve Forbes declared his candidacy for the presidency in the fall of 1995, few Americans had heard of him or given much thought to the idea of a flat tax. Forbes's standing in the polls for the Republican nomination was in the vicinity of 2 percent. If his spending had been limited to his preexisting level of support, the flat-tax debate would probably not have occurred. Yet such debates are what campaigns ought to be about, and the more we regulate campaign money, the fewer of them there are likely to be.

❧

Perhaps no belief is more deeply rooted in the psyche of reformers—and of the public at large—than that the money drawn into the system through political campaigns corrupts not only the campaigns themselves but, once a candidate is elected, the entire legislative process. Many officeholders have themselves complained about the influence of money in the legislature. But political scientists and economists who have studied this matter have consistently concluded otherwise. As John Lott and Stephen Bronars, the authors of one such study, conclude: "Our tests strongly reject the notion that campaign contributions buy politicians' votes. . . . Just like voters, contributors appear able to sort [out] politicians who intrinsically value the same things that they do."

The primary factors affecting a legislator's voting record are personal ideology, party affiliation, and constituent wishes—not contributions. Does anybody really think Phil Gramm would suddenly drop his opposition to gun control if the National Rifle Association (NRA) ceased contributing to his campaigns? Of course not: the NRA supports Gramm *because* he opposes gun control, and so, almost certainly, do many if not most of his Texas constituents.

This makes perfect sense. Individuals who enter politics usually do so because they have strong views on political issues; party support is almost always more important to election than any one contribution; and, to repeat, a legislator wins with votes, not dollars. For a politician to adopt an unpopular or unwise position that will cost him voter support in exchange for a $5,000 campaign contribution—the maximum amount allowed under federal law—would be counterproductive, to say the least.

This is not to say that other factors never come into play. A legislator may be concerned about how his vote will be reported in the press, or whether an opponent can easily caricature him in a negative ad. Personal friendships may affect a voting decision, as may the advice of aides and staff, itself often influenced by ideology. Money is another such secondary factor, but it is only one, and not necessarily the political commodity of greatest value. Many of the most influential Washington lobbying groups, including the American Association of Retired Persons, the National Education Association, and the American Bar Association, do not make political contributions. The NRA does have a large PAC, but it also has nearly two million members who care intently about its issues. Although gun-control advocates complain that the NRA outspends them, the more important fact is that it also outvotes them.

Finally, most issues find well-financed lobbies on both sides. A seemingly dull proposal to introduce a one-dollar coin, for example, may line up metal companies, vending-machine manufacturers, and coin laundries on one side, paper and ink companies on the other. Similarly with higher-profile issues like tort reform, where well-financed insurance interests take one position and equally well-financed trial lawyers the other. At least one set of these contributors, and often both, will suffer enormous *losses* in the legislative process, a fact often ignored by reformers.

When push comes to shove, even the most ardent reformers are rarely able to point to a specific instance of corruption. Ask a reformer to name which of our 535 Congressmen and Senators are acting contrary to what they believe to be the public good, or to what their constituents desire, because of campaign contributions, and the answer every time is some variation of "It's the system that's corrupt." But if we cannot name individuals corrupted by the system, on what basis are we to conclude that corruption is a problem intrinsic to the "system"?

⋯⟨⟩⋯

When it came time to fight the American Revolution, the founders of this nation did not go to the king seeking matching funds with which to finance their revolt. Instead, in the Declaration of Independence, they pledged their fortunes as well as their lives and sacred honor.

Today, in order to cure the alleged problem of fortunes in politics, reformers offer a variety of complex schemes aimed at *preventing* private citizens from demonstrating their commitment to democratic political change. Former Senator Bill Bradley and House Minority Leader Richard Gephardt claim that we need a constitutional amendment to overturn the *Buckley* decision. In Gephardt's sweeping formulation, there is a "direct conflict" between "freedom of speech and our desire for healthy campaigns in a healthy democracy," and "you can't have both." Their proposed amendment, if enacted, would grant a greater degree of protection to commercial speech, flag burning, and Internet porn than to the discussion of political candidates and issues.

Meanwhile, "moderate" reformers continue to push the McCain-Feingold bill, lately shorn of a ban on PAC's that even its sponsors admit was "probably" unconstitutional. Even so, this bill would place vast new limits on the freedom of political discussion, ban most contributions to political parties to pay for voter registration, slate cards, rallies, and get-out-the-vote drives, and restrict speech in ways directly prohibited by standing Supreme Court decisions.

If it is not the case that too much money is spent on campaigns, or that money, rather than the character of a handful of elected officials, is the source of political corruption, or that large contributors buy elections or in some way frustrate "true democracy," why should we tolerate such gross infringements of traditional First Amendment freedoms? What would be accomplished by measures like those being proposed by the reformers that would not be better accomplished by minimal disclosure laws that simply require the reporting of all sources of financial support?

Of course, disclosure laws may also be broken, as they appear to have been in the 1996 campaign. Character matters, and the rule has yet to be invented that someone will not succeed in violating. But what all the reformers overlook, from the most extreme to the most moderate, is that we already have, in the First Amendment, a deeply considered response to the problems inherent in democratic elections—and one that is far superior to the supposedly enlightened system of regulation with which we are now saddled.

By assuring freedom of speech and the press, the First Amendment allows for exposure of government corruption and improper favors, whether these consist of White House meetings with drug dealers or huge tax breaks for tobacco companies. By keeping the government out of the electoral arena, it allows for robust criticism of government itself, and prevents incumbents from manipulating the election-law machinery in their own favor. It frees grass-roots activists and everyday speech alike from suffocating state regulation, thereby furthering the democratic aim of political discussion. And it allows candidates to control their own message rather than having to rely on the filters of the press or the vagaries of bureaucrats and judges called upon to decide which forms of speech are to be limited as "endorsements or attacks," and which allowed as "genuine debate."

In the vast muddle that has been made by our decades-old regulatory folly, the only real question concerns whose logic we will now follow: the logic of those who gave us our existing campaign-finance laws and who, despite a disastrous record, now want license to "reform" them still further, or the logic of the founders who gave us the First Amendment. For most Americans, I suspect, the choice would be an easy one.

# POSTSCRIPT

## Should Campaign Finance Be Reformed?

$A$s is often the case when one examines a complex issue, there are several interrelated questions that must be answered in examining campaign finance: Do large contributors have an unfair influence on public policy? Is there a preferable method of raising money, such as through small contributions by less-affluent voters? The problem with this approach is the indifference of much of the electorate, reflected in the failure of the scheme by which voters can make a token contribution to political campaigns through their income tax returns.

Should incentives be created for people of more modest means to run for public office? Just as the U.S. Supreme Court has invalidated poll taxes (the payment of a state fee in order to vote), so too has it struck down high filing fees for primary candidates because "potential office seekers lacking both personal wealth and affluent backers are in every practical sense precluded from seeking the nomination of their chosen party." Beyond this, the U.S. Supreme Court in *Buckley v. Valeo* seemed to preclude any other action to make candidates more financially equal. Upholding limits on contributions, the Court rejected any limits on expenditures by more-affluent candidates.

Does existing campaign finance law give an unfair advantage to the candidate who outspends a rival? Consider that over 85 percent of winners in recent Senate and House elections outspent their rivals. This is partly due to the fact that in less competitive districts, contributors are more likely to give to the incumbent or probable winner. There are, however, conspicuous examples of candidates' winning despite their spending less.

Would free television time create a more level political field? What happens if a trade union, corporation, or other interest wishes to purchase television advertising to support a candidate or an issue? Could such independent expenditures be barred close to the election? What about candidate endorsements in publications or on billboards? Is public financing of congressional elections an alternative? Is there public support for such an expenditure? Would it rule out independent campaigning by individuals who are not formally affiliated with the campaign? When all the knotty political questions have been considered, there remains the constitutional question: Can campaign finance be limited without limiting political speech?

Liberals have found these questions particularly difficult. Numerous articles in *The American Prospect* have approached the issue of campaign reform from different perspectives. The coeditors of this liberal, bimonthly periodical take opposing positions on this question in the January/February 1998 issue: Robert Kuttner favors campaign finance reform in "Rescuing Democracy from 'Speech,' " while Paul Starr argues against limiting campaign spending in "The

Loophole We Can't Close." Similarly, *The Progressive*, another liberal publication, carried a debate on campaign finance in its December 1997 issue, featuring Bob Schiff, "The First Amendment Is Not a Stop Sign Against Reform," and Laura W. Murphy, "We Refuse to Sacrifice the First Amendment in a Desperate Attempt to Adopt Reform Legislation."

Herbert E. Alexander has written for many years on campaign finance, and his judicious treatment is available in *Reform and Reality: The Financing of State and Local Campaigns* (Twentieth Century Fund, 1991). Frank J. Sorauf, in *Inside Campaign Finance: Myths and Realities* (Yale University Press, 1994), provides an excellent introduction. Finally, Thomas Gais, in *Improper Influence: Campaign Finance Law, Political Interest Groups, and the Problem of Equality* (University of Michigan Press, 1996), offers a scholarly critique of the existing rules.

# ISSUE 4

## Are the Mass Media Dominated by the Powerful Few?

**YES: Robert W. McChesney**, from "Oligopoly: The Big Media Game Has Fewer and Fewer Players," *The Progressive* (November 1999)

**NO: Steven Rattner**, from "A Golden Age of Competition," in Nancy J. Woodhull and Robert W. Snyder, eds., *Media Mergers* (Transaction, 1998)

### ISSUE SUMMARY

**YES:** Communications research professor Robert W. McChesney fears that powerful media-owning corporations distort and suppress news and disproportionately favor their corporate interests.

**NO:** Former reporter Steven Rattner asserts that increasing competition and diversity are ensured by cable television, the Internet, and the unwillingness of media corporations to limit expression.

Modern mass communications, especially television, have shaped public perceptions of the most important political events and controversies of the past half-century. This was true during the Watergate scandal that led to President Richard Nixon's resignation and during the sex scandal that led to impeachment proceedings against President Bill Clinton. It was true during the Army-McCarthy hearings, the civil rights movement, the Iran hostage crisis, Iran-Contra, and other issues that found dramatic expression in television coverage. Probably no issue can better illustrate television's impact than the changing attitudes of the American public toward involvement in the Vietnam conflict, largely influenced by the coverage that correspondents and photographers were providing for network television.

The number of radio and television stations, magazines, and newly published books competing for the public's attention is greater than ever. Although most Americans spend many more hours watching television than with other media, the most popular TV programs (other than the World Series, Super Bowl, and Academy Awards ceremony) will be seen or heard in fewer than one-quarter of American households, and in many of those homes some family members will be otherwise occupied.

Despite the appearance of competition, media critics argue that six to eight megacorporations control what is seen on the most-watched television stations and movie theater screens, heard on the most popular radio stations, and read in the most newspapers, magazines, and books. The corporate owners are rarely journalists or individuals whose primary interest is the communication of news, analysis, and diverse opinion. These vast economic empires have no interest in telling us what we need to know to be informed citizens; their sole interest is in selling us their products and those of their advertisers. This, in the view of the media critics, results in slanting some stories and suppressing others in order to protect corporate interests. For example, Rupert Murdoch, whose media ownership is worldwide, cancelled the leading British news service from his Asian satellite system in order to curry favor with China, and HarperCollins, one of Murdoch's publishing houses, canceled publication of a book critical of the Chinese government. Also, CNN, the news cable network, refused to run commercials that expressed fear of higher cable rates.

Those who point to the variety and diversity of media sources contend that such views are alarmist and unfounded. If it is true, as a recent *U.S. News and World Report* poll stated, that "huge majorities believe that TV contributes to social problems like violence, divorce, teen pregnancy and the decline of family values," it is not because too few media owners provide too few choices. It is because many people turn on the programs that dramatize, publicize, or contribute to antisocial behavior. People choose with the click of the remote control that changes the TV channel or with the purchase of a magazine from the large number of publications near the supermarket checkout counter. A corporate conspiracy does not decide what movie we see or what music we hear. All the media and nearly all of the media conglomerates offer serious treatments of serious issues. On television, PBS does much, CNN does more, and C-SPAN and C-SPAN2 offer a surfeit beyond the capacity of a political junkie to absorb. If the networks offer less, it is because they are in the business of appealing to larger audiences in order to gain greater advertising revenue.

Will a few media megacorporations control most news and information? Will independent journalism survive? Will the fear of alienating corporate owners compromise the news media's ability to tell the truth and the public's opportunity to learn it? Will the Internet provide new competition in the marketplace of ideas? Several months after Robert W. McChesney wrote about the purchase of CBS by Viacom, an even larger media merger was announced: America Online (AOL), the most popular Internet service in the world, combined with Time Warner, owner of a major movie studio, television cable stations, and book and magazine publishers. In the following selection, McChesney charges that such concentrated corporate control protects the owners from scrutiny and does not provide informed and unbiased political and economic news coverage and analysis. In the second selection, Steven Rattner contends that competition is alive and flourishing, thanks to the proliferation of media (including the ever-expanding Internet), the nature of the media conglomerates, and their unending competition with one another.

**Robert W. McChesney**

# Oligopoly: The Big Media Game Has Fewer and Fewer Players

**W**hen Viacom announced its offer to gobble up CBS for $37 billion in September, it capped off a decade of unprecedented deal-making and concentration in the media industries. The new Viacom would be one of only nine massive conglomerates—all of which took their present shape in the last fifteen years—that dominate the U.S. media landscape.

These giants—Time Warner, Disney, Rupert Murdoch's News Corp., Viacom, Sony, Seagram, AT&T/Liberty Media, Bertelsmann, and GE—to a large extent furnish your TV programs, movies, videos, radio shows, music, books, and other recreational activities.

They do a superb job of maximizing profit for their shareholders but a dreadful job of providing the basis for a healthy democracy. Their entertainment fare is tailored to the needs of Madison Avenue; their journalism to the needs of the wealthy and powerful.

By any known standard of liberal democracy, such a concentration of media power in a few self-interested firms run by some of the wealthiest people in the world poses an immediate and growing threat to our republic. As James Madison put it in 1822, "A popular government without popular information, or the means of acquiring it, is but a prologue to a farce or a tragedy, or perhaps both."

When the Viacom/CBS deal was announced, *Time* and *Newsweek* lavished attention on the personalities of Viacom's Sumner Redstone and CBS's Mel Karmazin. To the extent that there was analysis, it centered on how the deal would affect Viacom's profits and the strategies of its main competitors.

*The Washington Post's* "Outlook" section featured a lead story entitled, "Clap If You Love Mega-TV! Without the conglomerates, you can wave goodbye to free, high-quality shows." Written by Paul Farhi, a reporter for the *Post's* "Style" section, the article said: "Now is the time to root for the big guys, the conglomerates, the mega-studios."

Aside from some notable reports in *The Boston Globe, Boston Herald, Chicago Tribune,* and *New York Times* that broached the question of whether

From Robert W. McChesney, "Oligopoly: The Big Media Game Has Fewer and Fewer Players," *The Progressive* (November 1999). Copyright © 1999 by *The Progressive*. Reprinted by permission.

this deal might not be good for people, the issue was off-limits. And even those papers that waved at it did not follow up, so the story died.

This paucity of press coverage makes it easier for the federal government to shirk its duties. Far from regulating the media giants, the government has served as the handmaiden to these electronic robber barons.

This oligopoly would never have passed legal muster if the regulators at the Federal Communications Commission and in the antitrust division of the Justice Department were doing their jobs, or if the Telecommunications Act of 1996 were not railroaded through Congress.

The regulators have let these mergers slide, under tremendous pressure from the telecommunications and entertainment industry. And it looks as though the Viacom/CBS merger will sail through, as well. Virtually no one in government is looking out for the public's interest in the media field.

The main defense provided by the government for its laxity is that the Internet upends the rationale for regulating media mergers—or for regulating media at all. It used to be that the major media companies possessed the only access to millions of Americans. Now with the Web, the argument goes, anyone can launch a site at marginal expense and compete directly with the existing media giants. So there is no need to worry about conglomerates. Proponents of the Internet act as though it is a massive comet crashing onto the Earth that will drive media giants into extinction.

This is nonsense.

The Internet is certainly changing the nature of our media system. But after five years, it has not spawned a competitive media marketplace; the giants have too many advantages to be seriously challenged. They have the programming, the brand names, the advertisers, the promotional prowess, and the capital to rule the Internet.

❧❦❧

Media concentration is not a new phenomenon, but it has accelerated dramatically in the last decade, and it is taking a new and dangerous form.

Classically, media concentration was in the form of "horizontal integration," where a handful of firms tried to control as much production in their particular fields as possible. The U.S. film production industry, for instance, has been a tight-knit club effectively controlled by six or seven studios since the 1930s. That remains the case today: The six largest U.S. firms accounted for more than 90 percent of U.S. theater revenues in 1997. All but sixteen of Hollywood's 148 widely distributed films in 1997 were produced by these six firms, and many of those sixteen were produced by companies that had distribution deals with one of the six majors.

The newspaper industry underwent a spectacular consolidation from the 1960s to the 1980s, leaving half a dozen major chains ruling the roost. U.S. book publishing is now dominated by seven firms, the music industry by five, cable TV by six. Nearly all of these are now parts of vast media conglomerates.

That's why looking at specific media sectors fails to convey the extent or the nature of the system today, for no longer are media firms intent on horizontal integration. Today, they seek "vertical integration," not only producing content but also owning distribution. Moreover, they are major players in media sectors not traditionally thought to be related. These conglomerates own some combination of television networks, TV show production, TV stations, movie studios, cable channels, cable systems, music companies, magazines, newspapers, and book publishing firms.

This has all come about seemingly overnight. In 1983, Ben Bagdikian published *The Media Monopoly* (Beacon, 1984), which chronicled how some fifty media conglomerates dominated the entirety of U.S. mass media. By today's standards, that era was downright competitive.

The mega-media firms have enjoyed a staggering rate of growth in the last decade. In 1988, Disney was a $2.9 billion a year amusement park and cartoon company; in 1998, Disney had $22 billion in sales. In 1988, Time was a $4.2 billion publishing company and Warner Communications was a $3.4 billion media conglomerate; in 1998, Time Warner did $26 billion of business. In 1988, Viacom was a measly $600 million syndication and cable outfit; the new Viacom is expected to do $22 billion worth of business in the coming year.

Moreover, each of these firms averages at least one equity joint venture —sharing actual ownership of a company—with six of the eight other media giants. Rupert Murdoch's News Corp. has at least one joint venture with each of them. AT&T Liberty owns nearly 10 percent of both News Corp. and Time Warner. This looks more like a cartel than it does the fabled competitive marketplace.

For decades, U.S. laws and regulations forbade film studios from owning movie theaters, and television networks from producing their own entertainment programs, because it was understood that this sort of vertical integration would effectively prohibit newcomers from entering these production industries. Likewise, regulations forbade companies from owning more than one radio or TV station in the same market and put a strict cap on the total number of stations that could be owned by a single family. Such restrictions have been relaxed or eliminated in these deregulatory times, and, as the Viacom/CBS merger shows, producers and distribution networks are racing to link up with each other.

What these media conglomerates have learned is that the profit whole is greater than the sum of the profit parts. Viacom/CBS, for instance, will now be able to produce a movie at Paramount or a TV show at Spelling studios, air it on Showtime and CBS, advertise it on its thirty-four TV stations, as well as on the 163 Infinity Radio stations, and then sell it at Blockbuster Video—all owned by the same merged company.

Vertical integration enables a company to increase market power by cross-promoting or cross-selling a show.

If a media conglomerate has a successful motion picture, for instance, it can promote the film on its broadcast properties and then use the film to spin off television programs, CDs, books, merchandise, and much else.

"When you can make a movie for an average cost of $10 million and then cross-promote and sell it off of magazines, books, products, television shows out of your own company, the profit potential is enormous," Redstone said, even before he put his money down on CBS.

Take Time Warner. It owns leading film companies (Warner Bros., New Line Cinema, Hanna-Barbera, and Castle Rock), cable TV systems (the second largest in the United States), cable TV channels (CNN, HBO, TBS, TNT), magazines (*Time, People, Sports Illustrated, Fortune*), publishing companies (Little Brown and Warner Books), and music labels (Warner Bros. Records, Elektra, Atlantic, Sire, and Rhino). In the sports field, it owns the Atlanta Braves, the Atlanta Hawks, and World Championship Wrestling.

For its part, Disney has the ABC network, ten TV stations, thirty radio stations, cable programming (ESPN, the Disney Channel, A&E, E!, Lifetime), film studios (Miramax, Walt Disney Pictures, Touchstone, Hollywood), the Hyperion book company, *ESPN* magazine, music labels (Walt Disney Records, Mammoth, Lyric Street), and amusement parks. It also owns the Anaheim Angels and the Mighty Ducks.

Murdoch's News Corp. owns the Fox network and fifteen TV stations. It produces cable programming (Fox News, Fox Sports, Fox Family Channel). Its studios are 20th Century Fox, Fox Animation, and Searchlight. It owns *The New York Post,* along with hundreds of newspapers worldwide. It also owns the conservative *Weekly Standard* and the book company Harper-Collins. Its sports teams are the Los Angeles Dodgers and the National Rugby League in Australia.

These mega-media companies have contributed to the rampant commercialization of U.S. childhood. "More and more companies are realizing," the head of the Fox Family Channel stated, "that if you develop a loyalty with the kids of today, they eventually become the adults of tomorrow." What's more, children age four to twelve are a formidable market in their own right. They spent $2.4 billion in 1997, three times the figure of a decade earlier. And no better medium exists for the delivery of the youth market than television. By age seven, the average American child is watching 1,400 hours of TV and 20,000 TV commercials per year. By age twelve, that child's preferences are stored in massive data banks by marketers of consumer goods.

In the 1990s, commercial television for children may well have been the most rapidly growing and lucrative sector of the U.S. industry, with 1998 ad revenues pegged at approximately $1 billion. Each of the four largest U.S. media giants has a full-time children's cable TV channel to capture the thirty-nine million viewers in the two-to-eleven age group. (Viacom was touted as the "perfect match" for CBS in large part because Viacom's Nickelodeon network, with its young demographic, complements CBS's stodgier audience.)

In 1998, broadcasters even began targeting one-year-olds to get a toehold on the youth market. In a moment of candor, one Time Warner children's television executive conceded that "there's something vaguely evil" about programming to kids that young. Nobody knows what the effects of this unprecedented commercial indoctrination of children will be years down the road. The only thing we know for sure is that the people responsible for it don't care.

Perhaps nowhere is the effect of concentrated corporate control on media more insidious than in journalism, democracy's lifeblood. I do not wish to romanticize the nature of U.S. journalism in the old days. It was highly flawed in key respects, and many of the current problems are only exaggerated forms of those that existed yesterday. But in today's corporate media system, journalism—and by that I mean the rigorous accounting of the powers-that-be and the powers-that-want-to-be, as well as wide-ranging coverage of our most urgent social and political issues—has nearly ceased to exist on the air and has been greatly diminished elsewhere. The reason is simple: Good journalism is bad business, and bad journalism can be very, very good for business.

The corporate assault on journalism assumes many forms. It is bad business, for example, to employ editors and reporters when a small staff can generate the same amount of material, albeit at lower quality. Since the mid-1980s, there has been a 50 percent reduction in the number of broadcast network reporters in Washington. This shifts more power to the P.R. industry and its corporate clients, which are ever eager to provide news fare to the media.

It is bad business, too, to do hard investigative work on corporations and powerful government agencies that primarily serve elite interests, like the Pentagon, the CIA, and the Federal Reserve Board. Such exposés can lead to expensive lawsuits and acrimonious relations with major advertisers, corporate brethren, and political heavyweights.

It is far better business practice to cover trivial stories about celebrities, natural disasters, train wrecks, sensational crimes, the Kennedys, and the royal family, and to limit political reporting to mindless speculation about campaign tactics and the regurgitation of mainstream politicians' soundbites. This is relatively inexpensive and rarely antagonizes anyone in power.

The corporate and commercial pressure of the 1990s has softened news standards. Welcome to the age of fluff.

For network and cable television, news has gone from being a loss-leader and a mark of network prestige to being a major producer of network profit. At present, NBC enjoys what is regarded as "the most profitable broadcast news division in the history of television," according to *Electronic Media,* with annual advertising revenues topping $100 million. NBC is renowned not so much for the quality of its news as for its extraordinary success in squeezing profit from it. NBC uses QNBC, a high-tech statistical service, to analyze its news reports to see exactly how its desired target audience is reacting to different news stories, and to the ads.

The owners of the networks are increasingly hostile to airing reports that may call into question some of their other activities. And, given the reach of those activities, there may be a lot of uncovered territory in the years to come.

In 1998, Disney-owned ABC News killed a *20/20* segment by Brian Ross, its leading investigative reporter, about Disney World in Florida. Ross was prepared to air charges that Disney was so lax in doing background checks on employees that it had hired pedophiles. Although ABC News claimed the cancellation was due to factors other than pressure from above, the stench of conflict-of-interest could not help but fill the air.

The same censorship mentality spills over into programming. This May, NBC heavily advertised a two-part mini-series called *Atomic Train,* which was originally about a runaway train carrying nuclear waste. But just days before broadcast, NBC started to pull the ads for the program and dubbed out all references to nuclear waste, choosing the more generic "hazardous material." Not incidentally, General Electric, which owns NBC, is a major nuclear energy producer.

In 1996, the news story that NBC gave the *most* air time to was the Summer Olympics in Atlanta, an event that did not even rank among the top ten stories covered by CBS, ABC, or CNN. What explains NBC's devotion to this story? It owned the television rights to the Olympics and used its nightly news to pump up the ratings for its prime-time coverage.

NBC is not alone here. "Various shows on ABC, now owned by Disney, have devoted a great deal of time to several movies produced by Disney, although the network has maintained in each instance that there was justified journalistic interest in the films," an article in *The New York Times* noted on July 10, 1998.

Don't expect the new Viacom to be any better. At MTV, it was policy under Redstone to provide editorial coverage—and ample promotional tie-ins—only to those film studios that purchased large amounts of advertising on MTV. The music station even required the studios to pay the production costs for the special shows on MTV about their movies.

The commercial media are increasingly cozy with other wealthy corporations, as well. A News Corp. station in Florida in 1997, for instance, fired two of its on-air reporters, Jane Akre and Steve Wilson, for refusing to water down their investigative story on Monsanto's bovine growth hormone.

And CBS News last year rebuked Roberta Baskin, one of its *48 Hours* correspondents, who was responsible for an acclaimed 1996 exposé of Nike's labor practices in Vietnam. What was her apparent crime? She had protested too loudly when CBS on-camera correspondents wore the Nike logo and Nike gear during the CBS telecasts of the 1998 Winter Olympics, for which Nike was a major sponsor. Baskin said this undermined the network's credibility and detracted from her original story. She also charged that CBS refused to rebroadcast that story for fear of offending Nike, which CBS denied. But the network confirmed that it refused to let Baskin respond to criticisms of her story in *The Wall Street Journal.* And Baskin says CBS would not permit her to do a follow-up story, even though she had uncovered an internal Nike report substantiating her original charges.

In sum, concentrated corporate control of the media has produced a broadcast journalism that is great at generating profit, pleasing advertisers, and protecting powerful institutions from scrutiny, but lousy at what it's supposed to do: informing the citizenry and confronting abusers of power.

If we are serious about democracy, we need decent journalism. And to get decent journalism, we need to make fundamental reforms in our media system.

Even among those who deplore conglomeration, hypercommercialism, and the decline of public interest journalism, there is a fatalistic sense that this is the way it must be. But the U.S. media system is the result of a series of political decisions, not natural law or holy mandate. The U.S. government and the citizens of the United States did not—and do not—have to turn over the broadcast spectrum to nine mega-corporations interested only in maximizing profit.

At any time in the last century, the American people might have chosen to establish a truly nonprofit and noncommercial radio and television system; they have always had the constitutional right to do so. The first major law for U.S. broadcasting was the Communications Act of 1934; the second was the Telecommunications Act of 1996. In 1934, there was considerable opposition to corporate domination of radio broadcasting, but those who led the opposition had barely any influence in Washington. In 1996, there was nowhere near the organized opposition that existed in 1934, and the communications lobbies pushed the law through at breakneck speed.

The striking feature of U.S. media policy-making is how singularly undemocratic it has been—and remains. Crucial decisions are made by the few for the few behind closed doors. Public participation has been minuscule.

That has got to change. We, as citizens, need to let our voices be heard. The airwaves belong to the people. We should demand a democratic media, not one that is controlled by Time Warner, Rupert Murdoch, Disney, GE, and Viacom/CBS.

I'd like to offer four general proposals for media reform. They are by no means blueprints; they are meant only to get the discussion going.

### 1. Shore up nonprofit and noncommercial radio

The starting point for media reform is to shore up a viable nonprofit, noncommercial media sector. Such a sector currently exists in the United States and produces much of value, but it's woefully small and underfunded. This sector is unbeholden to corporations, and its views are undistorted by the profit motive. It thus has the inclination to air stories that run counter to the interests of the huge corporations; it publishes viewpoints on national issues that get short-shrift elsewhere, and it engages in the kind of public-spirited debates that we need more of in our democracy.

Foundations and organized labor could and should contribute far more to nonprofit media. And government itself should foster this sector. It could extend lower mailing costs for a wide range of nonprofit publications. Or it could permit tax deductions for contributions to nonprofit media. To leave the nonprofit, noncommercial sector to starve as the commercial sector gets fatter and fatter makes no sense at all.

### 2. Strengthen public broadcasting

Public broadcasting today is really a system of nonprofit commercial broadcasting, serving a sliver of the population. What we need is a system of real public broadcasting, with no advertising, one that accepts no grants from corporations or private bodies, one that serves the entire population, not merely those who have high-brow tastes and disposable income to contribute during pledge drives.

A new system should include more national networks, local stations, fully utilized and subsidized public access television, and independent community radio stations. Every community should also have a stratum of low-power television and micropower radio stations.

Where will the funds come from to pay for such a service? At present, the federal government provides $260 million annually. The public system I envision—which would put per capita U.S. spending in a league with Britain's and Japan's—may well cost $5 billion to $10 billion annually. I have no qualms about drawing the funds from general revenues. A system of genuinely non-profit, noncommercial, and public broadcasting is essential if we are to be not just consumers but citizens, too.

### 3. Toughen regulation

Media reformers have long been active in this arena, if only because the public ownership of the airwaves gives the Federal Communications Commission a clear legal right to negotiate terms with the chosen few who get broadcast licenses. Still, broadcast regulation has largely been toothless, with the desires of powerful corporations and advertisers rarely challenged.

In my view, commercial broadcasters should be granted licenses only on the following terms: First, they will not air any paid political advertising during electoral campaigns unless every candidate on the ballot is given equal time, free of charge, immediately following the paid spot of a rival. This would go a long way toward clearing up the campaign spending mess that is destroying electoral democracy in the United States.

Second, we should follow the lead of Sweden and ban advertising to children under twelve. Likewise, we should remove advertising from TV news broadcasts.

Third, broadcasters should donate some percentage of their revenues to subsidize several hours per day of noncommercial children's and news/public affairs programming. Educators and artists should control the children's programming; journalists the news programming.

### 4. Antitrust

If ever there was a need for antitrust laws, that need is painfully clear in the area of media conglomerates. Not only do the media giants make a mockery of free competition; they impede the very functioning of democracy. Antitrust laws were put on the books at the turn of the last century to counteract the power of a few huge companies over both our economic and our political system. We should recall those concerns today as we wrestle with the media behemoths.

What is needed is a new media antitrust statute, similar in tone to the Clayton and Sherman Acts, that lays out the general values to be enforced by the Justice Department and the Federal Trade Commission. It would put an emphasis on valuing the importance of ideological diversity and noncommercial content. The objective should be to break up the media conglomerates and smash their vertical integration so that their book publishing, magazine publishing, TV show production, movie production, TV stations, TV networks, cable TV channels, cable TV systems, retail store chains, amusement parks, and so on, all become independent firms. With reduced barriers to entry in these specific markets, new firms could more easily join in, and something resembling fair competition could ensue.

The aim of these combined measures is to produce a media system that is fair and accurate, that scrupulously examines the activities of the powerful, that provides a legitimate accounting of the diverse views and interests of society. It would provide a culture based on artists' interactions with people and ideas, not on the orders from Madison Avenue. The only bias is a fervent commitment to democracy.

There is no reason why we must have a system that gives the wealthy and powerful high-quality information so they may rule the world while the rest of the population is fed a diet of schlock.

*࿈࿈*

The only way to gain some popular control over the communications field is to mobilize a popular movement for it. As the agitator Saul Alinksy noted, to beat organized money, you need organized people. The issue of media reform can attract the enthusiastic support of many citizens who have not been previously active. There's a general disgust with the media and entertainment industry, and there's a wellspring of populist resentment toward media giants.

While the fight for a democratic media is a necessary component—even a cornerstone—of any democratic movement, it cannot be won in isolation. Media reformers need to work with those involved in campaign finance reform, organized labor, civil rights, women's rights, gay and lesbian rights, immigrant rights, environmental protection, health care, and education. We need a broad movement to reshape our society, redeem its democratic promise, and put power in the hands of the many.

It won't be easy. On the media front, the giants are unusually canny, and they have the means at their disposal to get their own views across.

Unless we marshal the forces on our side, we will have no choice but to sit back and watch more mergers like Viacom/CBS—and to hear how good they are for us.

# NO ↩

**Steven Rattner**

# A Golden Age of Competition

It is truly ironic to be assessing the impact of mergers on media competition just as we are entering what may well prove to be the golden age of competition in communications industries.

Look in almost any direction and you see developments that will benefit consumers. In Washington, Congress has just enacted long overdue legislation that will rationalize an outmoded regulatory apparatus and free giant telecommunications and cable companies to battle each other. In New York, an array of news and financial services is being launched by equally giant media companies. Around the country—particularly on the West Coast—smaller, fast-growing companies are fighting to dominate the Internet.

Why is all of this happening now, particularly at a time of such high merger activity? The explanation begins with technological change. Just a couple of decades ago, most Americans had access to only a newspaper or two, some magazines and three or four television stations to provide their information and entertainment. No cable, with its 70–plus channels of programming, no VCRs or video stores, no satellite dishes, no computer on-line services and just a single provider of local and long-distance telephone service. In the television world, as recently as 1984, the three traditional networks—ABC, NBC and CBS—had 69 percent of the viewers (while cable had 14 percent).

The changes since then are familiar but dramatic. Cable now brings us debates about national policy—albeit at various levels of civility—24 hours a day. For news and public affairs, we can now supplement the Big Three networks with Fox, two channels of CNN, C-Span, CNBC and, in many markets, one or more local all-news channels. As a result, by February 1996, the networks' share had dropped to 42 percent and cable's had grown to 27 percent. (For consumers to whom cable is not available, nearly a half-dozen satellite services—which were not around 10 years ago—now provide much of the same programming.)

That's not nearly the end of the story. The cable television companies are busily rewiring to provide not 70 channels or 500 channels or even 1,400 channels but, in effect, an infinite number of channels through video-on-demand. The result will be a vast array of new services, including shopping, games, information retrieval, transactions and much more.

From Steven Rattner, "A Golden Age of Competition," in Nancy J. Woodhull and Robert W. Snyder, eds., *Media Mergers* (Transaction Publishers, 1998). Copyright © 1998 by Transaction Publishers. Reprinted by permission.

Inevitably, these developments will take longer and cost more than many expect. But make no mistake about it, these services are coming. In just the past few months, we have witnessed proposals for a new Dow Jones/ITT financial news network (in addition to CNNfn, which has just been launched) and three news channels (ABC, msNBC and Fox).

All of these developments will give consumers of news and information more quantity and a greater degree of personal choice. For example, as Time Warner's test in Orlando has demonstrated, the cable companies have within reach the ability to provide consumers with the capacity to create their own news programs by instructing a "smart box" to select segments that are of particular interest.

It is difficult to overstate the importance of the Internet in providing a diversity of views. Its arrival brings with it the opportunity for any wannabe publisher to realize that ambition with as little equipment as a personal computer and modem. Thousands of 'zines have sprung up, of varying degrees of sophistication and insight, ranging up to the glossy entry promised by Microsoft when it hired Michael Kinsley of the *New Republic.*

Should you doubt the consequences of this technological change, consider the analogous development of the telephone industry. Only 12 years ago we had a single long-distance telephone company. Today, thanks to technology that allows consumers to change their long-distance carrier almost as easily as they order an item from a catalog, we have 17 major ones. And most significantly, since 1986, the price of long-distance telephone service has gone down 34 percent. (These lower long-distance prices have a further benefit in providing Americans with lower cost access to the Internet and on-line services.)

As for the front-page media mergers, they are certainly taking place. Many of the participants are large, powerful and familiar to all of us. The Disney/Capital Cities/ABC merger brought together two of the world's most respected companies. The Time Warner/Turner deal could create the largest entertainment company in the world. Westinghouse bought CBS, and the sale of MCA brought an important new corporate parent to Hollywood.

While these deals had the highest price tags and generated the most public interest, an equal level of activity has occurred off the front pages. In 1995, more than 160 television stations and more than 1,000 radio stations were sold, and ownership of cable television systems with millions of subscribers has changed hands.

All told in 1995, American media companies set new records in merger-and-acquisition activity, with announced deals reaching $93 billion, 85 percent higher than in 1989, the year many saw as the apex of merger-and-acquisition activity on Wall Street. Media deals have also been rising as a percent of total deals.

As technology continues to change and as we continue to update our regulatory apparatus to take account of these developments, further merger activity is certain to result. In this regard, it is important to appreciate that even after all of the aforementioned activity, the media industry in the United States is not particularly concentrated by any standard.

That is not to say that I do not share in the desire for competition. I do. But in defining competition, it is important to emphasize that size is not the principal issue, although by that standard, even the largest media companies are not among our biggest companies. The market capitalization of the new Disney, for example, will be around $54 billion, only enough to rank it the 15th largest American company. Time Warner's market capitalization after the acquisition of Turner will be around $36 billion. Compare that to Coca-Cola at $102 billion or Philip Morris at $98 billion, to take just two examples.

More relevant to the question of competition are measures such as market share and the barriers to a new company entering the same business. As I argued earlier, the huge increase in the number of cable networks indicates clearly the trend toward fragmenting market shares and lower barriers to entry in this sector, among others. These are true measures of competition.

*Figure 1*

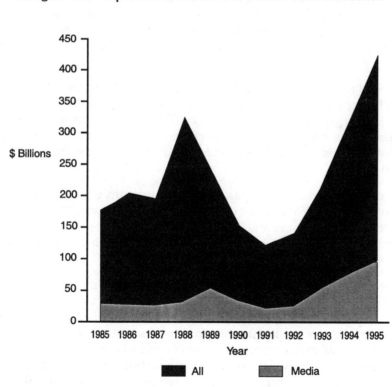

**Mergers and Acquisitions: Media Industries vs. All Industries**

*Source:* Securities Data Corp.

In the cable television industry, Time Warner and TCI have emerged as giant operators, controlling a combined 40 percent of the market. But the 10th largest owner has over 1 million subscribers—an asset value in excess of $2 billion—and the 100th largest owner has 10,000 subscribers. In other words, there is still a long way to go before cable's level of consolidation approaches that of the telephone companies.

Nor do I despair that many of our journalistic enterprises are owned by large corporations. If anything, companies like Cap Cities have demonstrated that the result of corporate ownership can be freer and better journalism than we had when a few press lords controlled many of our newspapers and television networks. And the basic difference between the press lords of yesterday and the media moguls of today is that the press lords often ran their papers as vehicles for their own ideology and personal ambition. Today's moguls, with a few exceptions, seem more interested in making money than in seeing the triumph of their own ideology or personal ambition.

Another fear critics have of these mergers is that the ownership of journalistic organs by large corporations will inhibit the coverage by those journalists of their parent company. First, even if that were the case, so many other outlets would provide unvarnished reportage that the American people would hardly suffer a material loss. Secondly, many examples exist of tough reporting about a journalistic enterprise's parent company. For example, *Time* has published thorough, unbiased coverage of many Time Warner issues, from gangsta rap to the Turner acquisition.

Beyond not diminishing competition or quality, many of the media mergers have brought benefits. In some cases, they have provided the capital needed to launch exciting but expensive new undertakings. For example, the sales of cable companies have in many instances provided the financial resources to upgrade the systems so that all of the aforementioned new services could be provided.

In other cases, different skills have been brought together under a common roof, with the promise of exciting new offerings. Even though their deal hasn't closed, Time Warner and Turner have combined to produce a Time-CNN "AllPolitics" service on the Internet, offering more depth and more data than either entity can provide in its traditional format.

I agree that the nature of the media industry suggests a special need for attentiveness on everyone's part. Maintaining a diversity and plentitude of views —as well as freedom of expression—is critical to our democratic process. There may be a few instances, like the Newspaper Preservation Act, where a special role on the part of government is appropriate in order to maintain the greatest possible diversity of views. But these situations should be few and far between because the more that government views itself as having a special role with regard to the media, the greater the risk of government interference with the free expression of views. In general, the government should approach communications companies as it approaches other companies: with a clear role limited to applying our antitrust laws to ensure that a competitive environment is maintained.

Today, it is often suggested that American journalism has lost too much of its seriousness and too often has become trivialized. For the most part, that is a subject for a separate discussion, although I am convinced that to the extent journalism today is less thoughtful, mergers are not to blame. I am equally certain that, if anything, when the history of media in the latter part of the 20th century is written, it may well be concluded that we are in a golden age of information.

# POSTSCRIPT

## Are the Mass Media Dominated by the Powerful Few?

Some facts of this issue are not in dispute: There are more media of communication. On television, people have more choices. On the Internet, the choice is illimitable. Except for the Internet, there has been a movement toward concentration and consolidation. And fewer than 10 corporations own most of the most popular communications media outlets, although there are numerous independent owners.

Both defenders and critics of the mass media might agree that the trivialization of news and commentary is older and has deeper causes than the diversity or concentration of ownership. When so many choices compete for our attention, we have less time to spend with any of them.

However, media critics argue that the decline in quality is largely the result of concentration in a small number of megamedia corporations that are interested only in profits. When it comes to news, analysis, and thoughtful exchange of opinion, media companies may not have a party line, but they judge by the bottom line: What does it earn? As a consequence, high-rated television talk shows on which guests reveal their most intimate secrets replace low-rated programs on which journalists and scholars debate world affairs. Media defenders point out that this reflects public preference and not a media conspiracy. They also point out that C-SPAN, the impartial full-time network devoted to politics and books, was created and is financed by the networks.

In *What the People Know: Freedom and the Press* (Harvard University Press, 1998), veteran journalist Richard Reeves offers an explanation as to why the print media and television spend less money and space on news and more on entertainment, scandal, health tips, and other non-news features. Reeves states that the amount of time that television networks devote to reporting on foreign news has declined by nearly two-thirds. He concludes that the cause is the success of the Internet in making information instantaneously accessible.

Nevertheless, television remains the most influential source of political news and opinion. The medium of television is the messenger, according to Martin Plissner. In *The Control Room: How Television Calls the Shots in Presidential Elections* (Free Press, 1999), Plissner explains his view that the presidential campaign is a staged television event in which candidates fly from place to place, shake hands, attend festivals, and give speeches, all in the hope that they will generate a broadcast-worthy image or sound bite. As a result, television dominates the presidential selection from the earliest stirrings of would-be candidates to the counting of the votes. The question remains: Do a few powerful corporations dominate the mass media?

# On the Internet ...

DUSHKIN ONLINE

## U.S. House of Representatives

This page of the U.S. House of Representatives will lead you to information about current and past House members and agendas, the legislative process, and so on. You can learn about events on the House floor as they happen.

http://www.house.gov

## The United States Senate

This page of the U.S. Senate will lead you to information about current and past Senate members and agendas, legislative activities, committees, and so on.

http://www.senate.gov

## The White House

Visit the White House page for direct access to information about commonly requested federal services, the White House Briefing Room, and the presidents and vice presidents. The Virtual Library allows you to search White House documents, listen to speeches, and view photos.

http://www.whitehouse.gov/index.html

## Supreme Court Collection

Open this Legal Information Institute (LII) site for current and historical information about the Supreme Court. The LLI archive contains many opinions issued since May 1990 as well as a collection of nearly 600 of the most historic decisions of the Court.

http://supct.law.cornell.edu/supct/index.html

# PART 2

# The Institutions of Government

*T*he Constitution provides for three governing bodies: the president, Congress, and the Supreme Court. Over the years, the American government has generated another organ with a life of its own: the bureaucracy. In this section, we examine issues that concern all the branches of government (executive, legislative, and judicial). Many of these debates are contemporary manifestations of issues that have been argued since the country was founded.

- Is Congress Limited in Regulating Commerce Within a State?

- The Presidency: Does the President's Personal Morality Matter?

- Should Judges Read Their Moral Views into the Constitution?

# ISSUE 5

# Is Congress Limited in Regulating Commerce Within a State?

**YES: William H. Rehnquist**, from Majority Opinion, *United States v. Lopez*, U.S. Supreme Court (April 26, 1995)

**NO: Stephen G. Breyer**, from Dissenting Opinion, *United States v. Lopez*, U.S. Supreme Court (April 26, 1995)

### ISSUE SUMMARY

**YES:** Supreme Court chief justice William H. Rehnquist argues that Congress cannot regulate activities within a state that are not economic and do not substantially affect commerce among the states.

**NO:** Supreme Court justice Stephen G. Breyer upholds the right of Congress to regulate activities within a state if Congress has a rational basis for believing that it affects the exercise of congressional power.

$\mathbf{F}$ederalism—the division of power between the national government and the states—is a central principle of American government. It is evident in the country's name, the United States of America.

The 13 founding states, long separated as British colonies and later cherishing their hard-earned independence, found it necessary to join together for economic stability and military security, but they would not surrender all of their powers to an unknown and untested national government. Many expressed fear of centralized tyranny as well as the loss of state sovereignty.

To reduce those fears, the Framers of the Constitution sought to limit the action of the new government to defined powers. Article I, Section 8, of the Constitution enumerates the powers granted to Congress, implicitly denying any other. The grants of national power were stated in very general terms to enable the new government to act in unforeseen circumstances. Recognizing that they could not anticipate how powers would be exercised, the Framers added that the national government could make all laws that were "necessary and proper" to execute its constitutional powers.

Even after the Constitution was ratified, the surviving fear of the proposed Constitution's critics that a too-powerful national government might undermine the powers of the states led to incorporation of the Tenth Amendment into the Bill of Rights. It states that powers not enumerated in the Constitution as belonging to the national government belong to the states and the people.

In the first important test of federalism, *McCulloch v. Maryland* (1819), Chief Justice John Marshall wrote: "If any one proposition could command the universal assent of mankind, we might expect it to be this—that the government of the Union, though limited in its powers, is supreme within its sphere of action." Forthright as that sounds, precisely what that sphere of action is has never been definitively decided.

For more than two centuries, the constitutional debate between the two levels of government has focused principally on Congress's powers to regulate commerce among the states and to tax and spend for the general welfare. State power has also been challenged when the national government has believed that state law interfered either with a treaty, the executive or judicial power, or the exercise of a valid federal power. The greatest challenges to states' rights developed when the national government, in the administrations of Presidents Woodrow Wilson and Franklin D. Roosevelt, began to regulate activities once thought to be wholly within the power of the states. The U.S. Supreme Court declared unconstitutional laws that they thought exceeded the bounds of national power. In 1918 the Court stated that Congress's power "was not intended to destroy the local power always existing and carefully reserved to the States in the Tenth Amendment to the Constitution."

The Supreme Court did an about-face in 1941 when it unanimously upheld a federal minimum wage law and reduced the Tenth Amendment to "a truism that all is retained which has not been surrendered." For more than 50 years, it appeared that the Supreme Court would sanction no limits on national power except those explicitly stated in the Constitution, as in the Bill of Rights.

In recent years, a more conservative Court has reestablished some limits. In the 1990s it ruled that Congress cannot compel the states to enact and enforce legislation carrying out the will of Congress. More far-reaching is the Supreme Court's 1995 decision in *United States v. Lopez*. In 1990 Congress had outlawed the possession of guns in or near a school. In a five-to-four decision, the Supreme Court concluded that Congress cannot regulate within a state without demonstrating the substantial effect of the regulated activities on commerce among the states. In 2000 the same narrow majority declared unconstitutional a federal law that permitted victims of rape, domestic violence, and other crimes "motivated by gender" to seek remedies in federal courts. Chief Justice William H. Rehnquist declared that "the Constitution requires a distinction between what is truly national and what is truly local."

In the following selections from *United States v. Lopez,* Chief Justice Rehnquist, in his majority opinion, concludes that the law barring guns within the vicinity of a school was too far removed from Congress's commerce power or any other valid national power. Associate Justice Stephen G. Breyer, dissenting with three other justices, argues that reducing the risk of violence in education is a valid exercise of congressional power.

# Majority Opinion

## United States *v.* Lopez

Chief Justice Rehnquist delivered the opinion of the Court.

In the Gun-Free School Zones Act of 1990, Congress made it a federal offense "for any individual knowingly to possess a firearm at a place that the individual knows, or has reasonable cause to believe, is a school zone." The Act neither regulates a commercial activity nor contains a requirement that the possession be connected in any way to interstate commerce. We hold that the Act exceeds the authority of Congress "[t]o regulate Commerce... among the several States...." U.S. Const., Art. I, § 8, cl. 3.

On March 10, 1992, respondent, who was then a 12th-grade student, arrived at Edison High School in San Antonio, Texas, carrying a concealed .38-caliber handgun and five bullets. Acting upon an anonymous tip, school authorities confronted respondent, who admitted that he was carrying the weapon. He was arrested and charged under Texas law with firearm possession on school premises. The next day, the state charges were dismissed after federal agents charged respondent by complaint with violating the Gun-Free School Zones Act of 1990. 18 U.S.C. § 922(q)(1)(A) (1988 ed., Supp. V).[1]

A federal grand jury indicted respondent on one count of knowing possession of a firearm at a school zone, in violation of § 922(q). Respondent moved to dismiss his federal indictment on the ground that § 922(q) "is unconstitutional as it is beyond the power of Congress to legislate control over our public schools." The District Court denied the motion, concluding that § 922(q) "is a constitutional exercise of Congress' well-defined power to regulate activities in and affecting commerce, and the 'business' of elementary, middle and high schools... affects interstate commerce." Respondent waived his right to a jury trial. The District Court conducted a bench trial, found him guilty of violating § 922(q), and sentenced him to six months' imprisonment and two years' supervised release.

On appeal, respondent challenged his conviction based on his claim that § 922(q) exceeded Congress' power to legislate under the Commerce Clause. The Court of Appeals for the Fifth Circuit agreed and reversed respondent's conviction. It held that, in light of what it characterized as insufficient congressional

From *United States v. Lopez,* 514 U.S. 549 (1995). Some notes, references, and case citations omitted.

findings and legislative history, "section § 922(q), in the full reach of its terms, is invalid as beyond the power of Congress under the Commerce Clause." Because of the importance of the issue, we granted certiorari, 511 U.S. 1029 (1994), and we now affirm.

We start with first principles. The Constitution creates a Federal Government of enumerated powers. See Art. I, § 8. As James Madison wrote, "The powers delegated by the proposed Constitution to the federal government are few and defined. Those which are to remain in the State governments are numerous and indefinite." The Federalist No. 45....

The Constitution delegates to Congress the power "[t]o regulate Commerce with foreign Nations, and among the several States, and with the Indian Tribes." Art. I, § 8, cl. 3. The Court, through Chief Justice Marshall, first defined the nature of Congress' commerce power in *Gibbons v. Ogden,* 9 Wheat. 1, 189–190 (1824):

> "Commerce, undoubtedly, is traffic, but it is something more: it is intercourse. It describes the commercial intercourse between nations, and parts of nations, in all its branches, and is regulated by prescribing rules for carrying on that intercourse."

The commerce power "is the power to regulate; that is, to prescribe the rule by which commerce is to be governed. This power, like all others vested in Congress, is complete in itself, may be exercised to its utmost extent, and acknowledges no limitations, other than are prescribed in the constitution." *Id.,* at 196. The *Gibbons* Court, however, acknowledged that limitations on the commerce power are inherent in the very language of the Commerce Clause.

> "It is not intended to say that these words comprehend that commerce, which is completely internal, which is carried on between man and man in a State, or between different parts of the same State, and which does not extend to or affect other States. Such a power would be inconvenient, and is certainly unnecessary.
>
> "Comprehensive as the word 'among' is, it may very properly be restricted to that commerce which concerns more States than one.... The enumeration presupposes something not enumerated; and that something, if we regard the language, or the subject of the sentence, must be the exclusively internal commerce of a State." *Id.,* at 194–195.

For nearly a century thereafter, the Court's Commerce Clause decisions dealt but rarely with the extent of Congress' power, and almost entirely with the Commerce Clause as a limit on state legislation that discriminated against interstate commerce. Under this line of precedent, the Court held that certain categories of activity such as "production," "manufacturing," and "mining" were within the province of state governments, and thus were beyond the power of Congress under the Commerce Clause.

In 1887, Congress enacted the Interstate Commerce Act, and in 1890, Congress enacted the Sherman Antitrust Act. These laws ushered in a new era of federal regulation under the commerce power. When cases involving these laws first reached this Court, we imported from our negative Commerce Clause cases the approach that Congress could not regulate activities such as "production," "manufacturing," and "mining." Simultaneously, however, the Court held that, where the interstate and intrastate aspects of commerce were so mingled together that full regulation of interstate commerce required incidental regulation of intrastate commerce, the Commerce Clause authorized such regulation.

In *A. L. A. Schecter Poultry Corp. v. United States,* 295 U.S. 495, 550 (1935), the Court struck down regulations that fixed the hours and wages of individuals employed by an intrastate business because the activity being regulated related to interstate commerce only indirectly. In doing so, the Court characterized the distinction between direct and indirect effects of intrastate transactions upon interstate commerce as "a fundamental one, essential to the maintenance of our constitutional system." Activities that affected interstate commerce directly were within Congress' power; activities that affected interstate commerce indirectly were beyond Congress' reach. The justification for this formal distinction was rooted in the fear that otherwise "there would be virtually no limit to the federal power and for all practical purposes we should have a completely centralized government."

Two years later, in the watershed case of *NLRB v. Jones & Laughlin Steel Corp.,* 301 U.S. 1 (1937), the Court upheld the National Labor Relations Act against a Commerce Clause challenge, and in the process, departed from the distinction between "direct" and "indirect" effects on interstate commerce. The Court held that intrastate activities that "have such a close and substantial relation to interstate commerce that their control is essential or appropriate to protect that commerce from burdens and obstructions" are within Congress' power to regulate.

In *United States v. Darby,* 312 U.S. 100 (1941), the Court upheld the Fair Labor Standards Act, stating:

> "The power of Congress over interstate commerce is not confined to the regulation of commerce among the states. It extends to those activities intrastate which so affect interstate commerce or the exercise of the power of Congress over it as to make regulation of them appropriate means to the attainment of a legitimate end, the exercise of the granted power of Congress to regulate interstate commerce."

In *Wickard v. Filburn,* the Court upheld the application of amendments to the Agricultural Adjustment Act of 1938 to the production and consumption of home-grown wheat. 317 U.S., at 128–129. The *Wickard* Court explicitly rejected earlier distinctions between direct and indirect effects on interstate commerce, stating:

> "[E]ven if appellee's activity be local and though it may not be regarded as commerce, it may still, whatever its nature, be reached by Congress if it exerts a substantial economic effect on interstate commerce, and this irrespective of whether such effect is what might at some earlier time have been defined as 'direct' or 'indirect.'" *Id.,* at 125.

The *Wickard* Court emphasized that although Filburn's own contribution to the demand for wheat may have been trivial by itself, that was not "enough to remove him from the scope of federal regulation where, as here, his contribution, taken together with that of many others similarly situated, is far from trivial."

*Jones & Laughlin Steel, Darby,* and *Wickard* ushered in an era of Commerce Clause jurisprudence that greatly expanded the previously defined authority of Congress under that Clause. In part, this was a recognition of the great changes that had occurred in the way business was carried on in this country. Enterprises that had once been local or at most regional in nature had become national in scope. But the doctrinal change also reflected a view that earlier Commerce Clause cases artificially had constrained the authority of Congress to regulate interstate commerce.

But even these modern-era precedents which have expanded congressional power under the Commerce Clause confirm that this power is subject to outer limits. In *Jones & Laughlin Steel,* the Court warned that the scope of the interstate commerce power "must be considered in the light of our dual system of government and may not be extended so as to embrace effects upon interstate commerce so indirect and remote that to embrace them, in view of our complex society, would effectually obliterate the distinction between what is national and what is local and create a completely centralized government." Since that time, the Court has heeded that warning and undertaken to decide whether a rational basis existed for concluding that a regulated activity sufficiently affected interstate commerce.

Similarly, in *Maryland v. Wirtz,* 392 U.S. 183 (1968), the Court reaffirmed that "the power to regulate commerce, though broad indeed, has limits" that "[t]he Court has ample power" to enforce. In response to the dissent's warnings that the Court was powerless to enforce the limitations on Congress' commerce powers because "[a]ll activities affecting commerce, even in the minutest degree, may be regulated and controlled by Congress," the *Wirtz* Court replied that the dissent had misread precedent as "[n]either here nor in *Wickard* has the Court declared that Congress may use a relatively trivial impact on commerce as an excuse for broad general regulation of state or private activities." Rather, "[t]he Court has said only that where *a general regulatory statute bears a substantial relation to commerce,* the *de minimis* character of individual instances arising under that statute is of no consequence." (emphasis added).

Consistent with this structure, we have identified three broad categories of activity that Congress may regulate under its commerce power. First, Congress may regulate the use of the channels of interstate commerce. Second, Congress is empowered to regulate and protect the instrumentalities of interstate commerce, or persons or things in interstate commerce, even though the threat may come only from intrastate activities. Finally, Congress' commerce authority includes the power to regulate those activities having a substantial relation to interstate commerce, *Jones & Laughlin Steel,* 301 U.S., at 37 , i.e., those activities that substantially affect interstate commerce.

Within this final category, admittedly, our case law has not been clear whether an activity must "affect" or "substantially affect" interstate commerce in order to be within Congress' power to regulate it under the Commerce Clause. We conclude, consistent with the great weight of our case law, that the proper test requires an analysis of whether the regulated activity "substantially affects" interstate commerce.

We now turn to consider the power of Congress, in the light of this framework, to enact § 922(q). The first two categories of authority may be quickly disposed of: § 922(q) is not a regulation of the use of the channels of interstate commerce, nor is it an attempt to prohibit the interstate transportation of a commodity through the channels of commerce; nor can § 922(q) be justified as a regulation by which Congress has sought to protect an instrumentality of interstate commerce or a thing in interstate commerce. Thus, if § 922(q) is to be sustained, it must be under the third category as a regulation of an activity that substantially affects interstate commerce.

First, we have upheld a wide variety of congressional Acts regulating intrastate economic activity where we have concluded that the activity substantially affected interstate commerce. Examples include the regulation of intrastate coal mining, intrastate extortionate credit transactions, restaurants utilizing substantial interstate supplies, inns and hotels catering to interstate guests, and production and consumption of home-grown wheat. These examples are by no means exhaustive, but the pattern is clear. Where economic activity substantially affects interstate commerce, legislation regulating that activity will be sustained.

Even *Wickard*, which is perhaps the most far reaching example of Commerce Clause authority over intrastate activity, involved economic activity in a way that the possession of a gun in a school zone does not. Roscoe Filburn operated a small farm in Ohio, on which, in the year involved, he raised 23 acres of wheat. It was his practice to sow winter wheat in the fall, and after harvesting it in July to sell a portion of the crop, to feed part of it to poultry and livestock on the farm, to use some in making flour for home consumption, and to keep the remainder for seeding future crops. The Secretary of Agriculture assessed a penalty against him under the Agricultural Adjustment Act of 1938 because he harvested about 12 acres more wheat than his allotment under the Act permitted. The Act was designed to regulate the volume of wheat moving in interstate and foreign commerce in order to avoid surpluses and shortages, and concomitant fluctuation in wheat prices, which had previously obtained. . . .

Section § 922(q) is a criminal statute that by its terms has nothing to do with "commerce" or any sort of economic enterprise, however broadly one might define those terms. Section § 922(q) is not an essential part of a larger regulation of economic activity, in which the regulatory scheme could be undercut unless the intrastate activity were regulated. It cannot, therefore, be sustained under our cases upholding regulations of activities that arise out of or are connected with a commercial transaction, which viewed in the aggregate, substantially affects interstate commerce.

. . . The Government argues that possession of a firearm in a school zone may result in violent crime and that violent crime can be expected to affect the functioning of the national economy in two ways. First, the costs of violent crime are substantial, and, through the mechanism of insurance, those costs are spread throughout the population. Second, violent crime reduces the willingness of individuals to travel to areas within the country that are perceived to be unsafe. The Government also argues that the presence of guns in schools poses a substantial threat to the educational process by threatening the learning environment. A handicapped educational process, in turn, will result in a less productive citizenry. That, in turn, would have an adverse effect on the Nation's economic well-being. As a result, the Government argues that Congress could rationally have concluded that § 922(q) substantially affects interstate commerce.

We pause to consider the implications of the Government's arguments. The Government admits, under its "costs of crime" reasoning, that Congress could regulate not only all violent crime, but all activities that might lead to violent crime, regardless of how tenuously they relate to interstate commerce. Similarly, under the Government's "national productivity" reasoning, Congress could regulate any activity that it found was related to the economic productivity of individual citizens: family law (including marriage, divorce, and child custody), for example. Under the theories that the Government presents in support of § 922(q), it is difficult to perceive any limitation on federal power, even in areas such as criminal law enforcement or education where States historically have been sovereign. Thus, if we were to accept the Government's arguments, we are hard-pressed to posit any activity by an individual that Congress is without power to regulate.

Although Justice Breyer argues that acceptance of the Government's rationales would not authorize a general federal police power, he is unable to identify any activity that the States may regulate but Congress may not. Justice Breyer posits that there might be some limitations on Congress' commerce power, such as family law or certain aspects of education. These suggested limitations, when viewed in light of the dissent's expansive analysis, are devoid of substance.

Justice Breyer focuses, for the most part, on the threat that firearm possession in and near schools poses to the educational process and the potential economic consequences flowing from that threat. Specifically, the dissent reasons that (1) gun-related violence is a serious problem; (2) that problem, in turn, has an adverse effect on classroom learning; and (3) that adverse effect on classroom learning, in turn, represents a substantial threat to trade and commerce. This analysis would be equally applicable, if not more so, to subjects such as family law and direct regulation of education.

For instance, if Congress can, pursuant to its Commerce Clause power, regulate activities that adversely affect the learning environment, then, *a fortiori*, it also can regulate the educational process directly. Congress could determine that a school's curriculum has a "significant" effect on the extent of classroom learning. As a result, Congress could mandate a federal curriculum for local elementary and secondary schools because what is taught in local schools has a significant "effect on classroom learning," and that, in turn, has a substantial effect on interstate commerce.

Justice Breyer rejects our reading of precedent and argues that "Congress ... could rationally conclude that schools fall on the commercial side of the line." Justice Breyer's rationale lacks any real limits because, depending on the level of generality, any activity can be looked upon as commercial. Under the dissent's rationale, Congress could just as easily look at child rearing as "fall[ing] on the commercial side of the line" because it provides a "valuable service—namely, to equip [children] with the skills they need to survive in life and, more specifically, in the workplace." ...

The possession of a gun in a local school zone is in no sense an economic activity that might, through repetition elsewhere, substantially affect any sort of interstate commerce. Respondent was a local student at a local school; there is no indication that he had recently moved in interstate commerce, and there is no requirement that his possession of the firearm have any concrete tie to interstate commerce.

To uphold the Government's contentions here, we would have to pile inference upon inference in a manner that would bid fair to convert congressional authority under the Commerce Clause to a general police power of the sort retained by the States. Admittedly, some of our prior cases have taken long steps down that road, giving great deference to congressional action. The broad language in these opinions has suggested the possibility of additional expansion, but we decline here to proceed any further. To do so would require us to conclude that the Constitution's enumeration of powers does not presuppose something not enumerated, and that there never will be a distinction between what is truly national and what is truly local. This we are unwilling to do.

## Note

1. The term "school zone" is defined as "in, or on the grounds of, a public, parochial or private school" or "within a distance of 1,000 feet from the grounds of a public, parochial or private school." § 921(a)(25).

# NO ☜

Stephen G. Breyer

# Dissenting Opinion of Stephen G. Breyer

Justice Breyer, with whom Justice Stevens, Justice Souter, and Justice Ginsburg join, dissenting.

The issue in this case is whether the Commerce Clause authorizes Congress to enact a statute that makes it a crime to possess a gun in, or near, a school. 18 U.S.C. § 922(q)(1)(A) (1988 ed., Supp. V). In my view, the statute falls well within the scope of the commerce power as this Court has understood that power over the last half century.

## I

In reaching this conclusion, I apply three basic principles of Commerce Clause interpretation. First, the power to "regulate Commerce... among the several States," U.S. Const., Art. I, § 8, cl. 3, encompasses the power to regulate local activities insofar as they significantly affect interstate commerce. As the majority points out, the Court, in describing how much of an effect the Clause requires, sometimes has used the word "substantial" and sometimes has not.... And, as the majority also recognizes... the question of degree (how *much* effect) requires an estimate of the "size" of the effect that no verbal formulation can capture with precision. I use the word "significant" because the word "substantial" implies a somewhat narrower power than recent precedent suggests. But to speak of "substantial effect" rather than "significant effect" would make no difference in this case.

Second, in determining whether a local activity will likely have a significant effect upon interstate commerce, a court must consider, not the effect of an individual act (a single instance of gun possession), but rather the cumulative effect of all similar instances (*i.e.,* the effect of all guns possessed in or near schools). As this Court put the matter almost 50 years ago:

> "[I]t is enough that the individual activity when multiplied into a general practice... contains a threat to the interstate economy that requires preventative regulation."

From *United States v. Lopez,* 514 U.S. 549 (1995). Some references and case citations omitted.

Third, the Constitution requires us to judge the connection between a regulated activity and interstate commerce, not directly, but at one remove. Courts must give Congress a degree of leeway in determining the existence of a significant factual connection between the regulated activity and interstate commerce—both because the Constitution delegates the commerce power directly to Congress and because the determination requires an empirical judgment of a kind that a legislature is more likely than a court to make with accuracy. The traditional words "rational basis" capture this leeway. Thus, the specific question before us, as the Court recognizes, is not whether the "regulated activity sufficiently affected interstate commerce," but, rather, whether Congress could have had *"a rational basis"* for so concluding.

I recognize that we must judge this matter independently. "[S]imply because Congress may conclude that a particular activity substantially affects interstate commerce does not necessarily make it so." And, I also recognize that Congress did not write specific "interstate commerce" findings into the law under which Lopez was convicted. Nonetheless, as I have already noted, the matter that we review independently (*i.e.,* whether there is a "rational basis") already has considerable leeway built into it. And, the absence of findings, at most, deprives a statute of the benefit of some *extra* leeway. This extra deference, in principle, might change the result in a close case, though, in practice, it has not made a critical legal difference. It would seem particularly unfortunate to make the validity of the statute at hand turn on the presence or absence of findings. Because Congress did make findings (though not until after Lopez was prosecuted), doing so would appear to elevate form over substance. . . .

# II

Applying these principles to the case at hand, we must ask whether Congress could have had a *rational basis* for finding a significant (or substantial) connection between gun-related school violence and interstate commerce. Or, to put the question in the language of the *explicit* finding that Congress made when it amended this law in 1994: Could Congress rationally have found that "violent crime in school zones," through its effect on the "quality of education," significantly (or substantially) affects "interstate" or "foreign commerce"? As long as one views the commerce connection, not as a "technical legal conception," but as "a practical one," the answer to this question must be yes. Numerous reports and studies—generated both inside and outside government—make clear that Congress could reasonably have found the empirical connection that its law, implicitly or explicitly, asserts.

For one thing, reports, hearings, and other readily available literature make clear that the problem of guns in and around schools is widespread and extremely serious. These materials report, for example, that four percent of American high school students (and six percent of inner-city high school students) carry a gun to school at least occasionally; that 12 percent of urban high school students have had guns fired at them; that 20 percent of those students have been threatened with guns; and that, in any 6-month period, several hundred thousand schoolchildren are victims of violent crimes in or near their schools. And, they report that this widespread violence in schools throughout the Nation significantly interferes with the quality of education in those schools. Based on reports such as these, Congress obviously could have thought that guns and learning are mutually exclusive. Congress could therefore have found a substantial educational problem—teachers unable to teach, students unable to learn—and concluded that guns near schools contribute substantially to the size and scope of that problem.

Having found that guns in schools significantly undermine the quality of education in our Nation's classrooms, Congress could also have found, given the effect of education upon interstate and foreign commerce, that gun-related violence in and around schools is a commercial, as well as a human, problem. Education, although far more than a matter of economics, has long been inextricably intertwined with the Nation's economy. When this Nation began, most workers received their education in the workplace, typically (like Benjamin Franklin) as apprentices. As late as the 1920's, many workers still received general education directly from their employers—from large corporations, such as General Electric, Ford, and Goodyear, which created schools within their firms to help both the worker and the firm. As public school enrollment grew in the early 20th century, the need for industry to teach basic educational skills diminished. But, the direct economic link between basic education and industrial productivity remained. Scholars estimate that nearly a quarter of America's economic growth in the early years of this century is traceable directly to increased schooling; that investment in "human capital" (through spending on education) exceeded investment in "physical capital" by a ratio of almost two to one); and that the economic returns to this investment in education exceeded the returns to conventional capital investment.

In recent years the link between secondary education and business has strengthened, becoming both more direct and more important. Scholars on the subject report that technological changes and innovations in management techniques have altered the nature of the workplace so that more jobs now demand greater educational skills. . . .

Increasing global competition also has made primary and secondary education economically more important. The portion of the American economy attributable to international trade nearly tripled between 1950 and 1980, and more than 70 percent of American-made goods now compete with imports. Yet, lagging worker productivity has contributed to negative trade balances and to real hourly compensation that has fallen below wages in 10 other industrialized nations. At least some significant part of this serious productivity problem is attributable to students who emerge from classrooms without the reading or mathematical skills necessary to compete with their European or Asian counterparts. . . .

Finally, there is evidence that, today more than ever, many firms base their location decisions upon the presence, or absence, of a work force with a basic education. . . . In light of this increased importance of education to individual firms, it is no surprise that half of the Nation's manufacturers have become involved with setting standards and shaping curricula for local schools, that 88 percent think this kind of involvement is important, that more than 20

States have recently passed educational reforms to attract new business, and that business magazines have begun to rank cities according to the quality of their schools.

The economic links I have just sketched seem fairly obvious. Why then is it not equally obvious, in light of those links, that a widespread, serious, and substantial physical threat to teaching and learning *also* substantially threatens the commerce to which that teaching and learning is inextricably tied? That is to say, guns in the hands of six percent of inner-city high school students and gun-related violence throughout a city's schools must threaten the trade and commerce that those schools support. The only question, then, is whether the latter threat is (to use the majority's terminology) "substantial." The evidence of (1) the *extent* of the gun-related violence problem, (2) the *extent* of the resulting negative effect on classroom learning, and (3) the *extent* of the consequent negative commercial effects, when taken together, indicate a threat to trade and commerce that is "substantial." At the very least, Congress could rationally have concluded that the links are "substantial." ...

To hold this statute constitutional is not to "obliterate" the "distinction between what is national and what is local," nor is it to hold that the Commerce Clause permits the Federal Government to "regulate any activity that it found was related to the economic productivity of individual citizens," to regulate "marriage, divorce, and child custody," or to regulate any and all aspects of education. First, this statute is aimed at curbing a particularly acute threat to the educational process—the possession (and use) of life-threatening firearms in, or near, the classroom. The empirical evidence that I have discussed above unmistakably documents the special way in which guns and education are incompatible. This Court has previously recognized the singularly disruptive potential on interstate commerce that acts of violence may have. Second, the immediacy of the connection between education and the national economic well-being is documented by scholars and accepted by society at large in a way and to a degree that may not hold true for other social institutions. It must surely be the rare case, then, that a statute strikes at conduct that (when considered in the abstract) seems so removed from commerce, but which (practically speaking) has so significant an impact upon commerce.

In sum, a holding that the particular statute before us falls within the commerce power would not expand the scope of that Clause. Rather, it simply would apply pre-existing law to changing economic circumstances. It would recognize that, in today's economic world, gun-related violence near the classroom makes a significant difference to our economic, as well as our social, well-being. In accordance with well-accepted precedent, such a holding would permit Congress "to act in terms of economic... realities," would interpret the commerce power as "an affirmative power commensurate with the national needs," and would acknowledge that the "commerce clause does not operate so as to render the nation powerless to defend itself against economic forces that Congress decrees inimical or destructive of the national economy." ...

# IV

In sum, to find this legislation within the scope of the Commerce Clause would permit "Congress... to act in terms of economic... realities." It would interpret the Clause as this Court has traditionally interpreted it, with the exception of one wrong turn subsequently corrected. Upholding this legislation would do no more than simply recognize that Congress had a "rational basis" for finding a significant connection between guns in or near schools and (through their effect on education) the interstate and foreign commerce they threaten. For these reasons, I would reverse the judgment of the Court of Appeals. Respectfully, I dissent.

# POSTSCRIPT

## Is Congress Limited in Regulating Commerce Within a State?

The difference of views on today's divided Supreme Court may be defined (concededly too simply and neatly) in terms of whether the powers of the states are *reserved*, that is, secure against encroachment or abridgement by Congress or the president, or whether state powers are *residual*, that is, the powers that are left after upholding valid claims of national power.

On the one hand, the historical evidence leaves no doubt that the Constitution was designed to create a national government powerful enough to deal with areas that the states believed required unified action (such as commerce, coinage, and national defense) but not so powerful as to diminish the authority of the states in all other areas. The Constitution's authors went to some pains to define and confine the powers of the new central government.

On the other hand, Chief Justice John Marshall stated the logic of delegated national power: "Let the end be legitimate, let it be within the scope of the constitution, and all means which are appropriate, which are plainly adapted to that end, which are not prohibited, but consist with the letter and spirit of the constitution, are constitutional." If Congress's exercise of power is valid, no matter how far it extends, the power of the states is reduced by that much.

Congressional hearings have provided a public forum for airing opposing views on the boundaries of national and state power. The U.S. Senate Committee on Governmental Affairs heard testimony on the state of federalism in 1999. In *The Delicate Balance: Federalism, Interstate Commerce and Economic Freedom in the Technological Age* (Heritage Foundation, 1998), Adam D. Thierer seeks to redefine and defend federalism in the modern world. Edward B. McLean and other scholars deplore what they call *Derailing the Constitution: The Undermining of American Federalism* (Doubleday, 1997). In *Disunited States* (Basic Books, 1997), John D. Donahue expresses skepticism of the judicial movement toward reducing the exercise of national power.

Despite the learned constitutional and historical arguments, one may harbor the suspicion that where one stands on the balance of power in American federalism often depends less on abstract theory than on practical considerations of public policy. Perhaps there is a more than a coincidental correspondence between positions on civil rights or national welfare legislation and the defense of either the principle of national supremacy or that of states' rights. As long as political differences exist as to whether we should have "more" or "less" national government, the constitutional debate will continue.

# ISSUE 6

## The Presidency: Does the President's Personal Morality Matter?

**YES: William J. Bennett**, from *The Death of Outrage: Bill Clinton and the Assault on American Ideals* (Free Press, 1998)

**NO: Thomas E. Cronin and Michael A. Genovese**, from "President Clinton and Character Questions," *Presidential Studies Quarterly* (Fall 1998)

### ISSUE SUMMARY

**YES:** William J. Bennett, a former official in the Reagan and Bush administrations, argues that a president's personal morality cannot be divorced from his job performance, because the latter includes the kind of example he sets for the youth of the nation.

**NO:** Presidential scholars Thomas E. Cronin and Michael A. Genovese agree that "character matters" in presidents but only as it touches on their external behavior; presidents with roguish private lives, they maintain, can exhibit considerable public integrity.

In an address written aboard the *Arbella*, one of the ships that first carried the Puritans to America in 1630, their leader, John Winthrop, issued a stern admonition to those who were to found the first Puritan commonwealth in America. "We must consider," he wrote, "that we shall be as a city upon a hill, the eyes of all people are upon us." If the Puritans were to prove unfaithful to their holy covenant, Winthrop warned, "we shall shame the faces of many of God's worthy servants, and cause their prayers to be turned to curses upon us, till we be consumed out of the good land whither we are going." Despite all the changes that have occurred in America since Puritan times, many Americans still regard their country as having a special moral mission, and they worry about what will happen to their country if that mission is abandoned.

Many of these hopes and fears center upon the American presidency. The president, after all, is more than a politician or a government leader. He is the chief of state, the symbolic head of the nation. As such, the presidency has become, in the words of President Theodore Roosevelt, a "bully pulpit." Roosevelt's cousin, Franklin Roosevelt, later put it more explicitly by announcing that the presidency "is preeminently a place of moral leadership."

But what does "moral leadership" mean? Does it mean that the president has a special responsibility to execute the laws faithfully, to lead the nation with a coherent program, and to communicate the highest ideals to the nation? Our greatest presidents, including both Roosevelts, have excelled in these areas. But does it also involve a responsibility to live by a code of personal morality generally accepted by most Americans? If moral leadership in that sense is the litmus test, then some of our most esteemed presidents might fail. For example, Franklin Roosevelt himself carried on a long-term affair with his wife's former social secretary, and John F. Kennedy was repeatedly unfaithful to his wife.

Examples such as these were often cited by defenders of President Bill Clinton during his impeachment hearings in 1998–1999. Yes, they conceded, this president's personal behavior in the White House was not exemplary, but if sexual morality is relevant to judging a president's fitness for office, what would happen to Jefferson, Roosevelt, and the others? In reply, Clinton's accusers noted two differences between the Clinton presidency and that of previous White House occupants. First, in the past, the public did not know about the indiscretions until years later. The second difference is that Clinton was accused of more than personal misbehavior; the charges against him included perjury and obstruction of justice.

To the first point, the rejoinder of the president's defenders was that this time the American people did know about a president's personal misbehavior —and did not care. Clinton's job performance ratings in public opinion polls actually increased during the impeachment hearings, while public approval of Congress declined. To the second point, the reply was usually that, even assuming that President Clinton had committed perjury and obstruction of justice (which neither he nor most of his defenders conceded), the alleged offenses were committed in an effort to prevent public exposure of private behavior— behavior that was none of the public's business anyway.

Beyond the interminable impeachment debate there still remains the larger question: what sort of "moral leadership" do Americans have a right to expect of their president? Does his personal behavior matter as long as his public demeanor and actions are acceptable? Some observers have suggested that America should adopt as its own the easygoing attitude of France and some other European countries, where not only the wives but the mistresses of national leaders are sometimes given places of honor at their funerals. But America is not Europe. For better or worse, American culture still owes much to its Puritan foundations, including the belief that the United States is "a city upon a hill," keenly watched by the rest of the world to see whether or not its leaders follow standards higher than those of the Old World. That seems to be the belief of William J. Bennett, who argues in the following selection that a president's personal morality cannot be divorced from his job performance. Opposing Bennett's philosophy in the second selection are Thomas E. Cronin and Michael A. Genovese, who agree that "character matters" in presidents but only as it touches their public behavior.

**William J. Bennett**

 **YES**

# The Death of Outrage

In America, morality is central to our politics and attitudes in a way that is not the case in Europe, and precisely this moral streak is what is best about us. It is a moral streak that has made America uncommonly generous in its dealings with foreign nations (in matters ranging from the Marshall Plan, to the sending of peacekeeping troops, to disaster relief, to much else); liberated Europe from the Nazi threat and the Iron Curtain; and prevented noxious political movements like fascism from taking root at home. Europeans may have some things to teach us about, say, wine or haute couture. But on the matter of morality in politics, America has much to teach Europe....

⁓◈⁓

"Moral authority is when a president deals with the issues that affect [people's] families, when he deals with educating their children, when he deals with jobs, when he deals with the economy." Thus Leon Panetta [White House chief of staff, 1994–1997]. But there is much more to moral authority than that. We— all of us, but especially the young—need around us individuals who possess a certain nobility, a largeness of soul, and qualities of human excellence worth imitating and striving for. Every parent knows this, which is why parents are concerned with both the company their children keep, and the role models they choose. Children watch what we do as well as what we say, and if we expect them to take morality seriously, they must see adults taking it seriously.

The extraordinary political appeal of General Colin Powell is rooted in his rock-solid character, his wartime valor, his faithfulness as a husband and father. He is the type of man that mothers can point to and say to their children, "Here is a man who fought for his country, honors his wife, loves his family. Be like that man." Thus it was said of General Washington: "His example was as edifying to all around him as were the effects of that example lasting."

Character education depends not only on the articulation of ideals and convictions, but on the behavior of those in authority. This is why the president is a role model, whether he likes it or not, and why Wendy Kaminer is dead wrong when she writes that there is something "childlike and potentially

From William J. Bennett, *The Death of Outrage: Bill Clinton and the Assault on American Ideals* (Free Press, 1998). Copyright © 1998 by William J. Bennett. Reprinted and edited by permission of The Free Press, a Division of Simon & Schuster, Inc.

dangerous" in expecting a president to have high moral standards. That is obviously not his only responsibility. Nor is it his first responsibility. But it *is* a responsibility he cannot shirk.

The basketball star Charles Barkley insists that sports figures ought not be role models for children. I believe Barkley is wrong—but even if he is right, the one public figure who cannot dodge his responsibility as a role model is the president. It is worth noting that the president—whoever he is—is almost always voted the most admired man in America, not just because he is so well-known, but because of the prestige of the office itself. What he does, and who he is, matter.

It is true that the bond of trust between a president and the American people matters most when times require some measure of sacrifice or hardship; it is then that we most need someone who is reliable, dependable, believable. But the implicit argument that a president can compromise his moral authority in a time of peace and prosperity is more than a misunderstanding; it is absurd. Moral authority once having been compromised, who can with confidence expect it to be magically available in a time when sacrifice is needed? . . .

In general, if the president's word cannot be trusted—an issue of character —voters cannot take seriously his election platform or his campaign promises— an issue of public duty. Words are deconstructed, promises emptied of meaning. Politics is reduced to a mere game. It is all very straightforward: if a man's word means nothing, it means nothing. It is folly to believe otherwise. . . .

❧

In living memory, the chief threats to American democracy have come from without: first, Nazism and Japanese imperialism, and, later, Soviet communism. But these wars, hot and cold, ended in spectacular American victories. The threats we now face are from within. They are far different, more difficult to detect, more insidious: decadence, cynicism, and boredom.

Writing about corruption in democratic government, Alexis de Tocqueville warned about "not so much the immorality of the great as the fact that immorality may lead to greatness." When private citizens impute a ruler's success "mainly to some of his vices . . . an odious connection is thus formed between the ideas of turpitude and power, unworthiness and success, utility and dishonor." The rulers of democratic nations, Tocqueville said, "lend the authority of the government to the base practices of which they are accused. They afford dangerous examples, which discourage the struggles of virtuous independence."

Tocqueville recognized, too, that democratic citizens wouldn't be conscious of this tendency, and in fact would probably disagree that it even existed. This is what makes it all the more dangerous; the corrupt actions of democratic leaders influence the public in subtle ways which often go unnoticed among citizens. This sort of decay is gradual, difficult to perceive over a short period of time, and terribly dangerous. . . .

...[I]f the arguments made in defense of Bill Clinton become the coin of the public realm, we will have committed an unthinking act of moral and intellectual disarmament. Here is one specific example of what is now becoming a thoroughly mainstream, perfectly respectable point of view: in order to cover up an adulterous relationship between the president and a young White House intern, acts of perjury and obstruction of justice should be considered inconsequential. That this matter is even the subject of a serious national debate is revealing and alarming. It was the *New York Times* which offered this eloquent reminder of what was once a common, elementary-grade civics lesson:

"Law is the keystone of American society and political culture. If it does not apply to small matters concerning this President, the day will come when the public will be asked to believe that it should be ignored in large matters concerning some other President. Neither Mr. Clinton's political convenience nor Mr. Starr's clumsiness must tempt us into paying so high a price. The rule of law, whether applied to matters trivial or grand, is the central magic of the American governmental experience. To abandon it today will lead to peril tomorrow."

Perhaps the history books will describe the Clinton era as a time during which (to recall the words of John Adams) the president of the United States insidiously betrayed, and wantonly trifled away, public trust. When, rocked with serious, credible allegations of grave misconduct and violations of law, the president retreated for as long as he could to a gilded bunker, obstinately and "absolutely" unwilling to rebut troubling allegations made against him. And the history books may describe how a diffident public, when confronted with all the evidence of wrongdoing and all the squalor, simply shrugged its shoulders. And, finally, that William Jefferson Clinton really was the representative man of our time, when the overwhelming majority of Americans no longer believed that presidential character mattered, and that no man, not even a president, was accountable to the law.

Perhaps this is what it will all come to. But we do not yet know. More acts must be played out in this manifestly sordid, but now manifestly important, national drama. We shall see. As a self-governing nation, it is finally up to us. Not a court of law. Not Ken Starr. Us.

# NO ↵

**Thomas E. Cronin and
Michael A. Genovese**

# President Clinton and
# Character Questions

P resident Clinton's critics relentlessly attack him on the character issue. His supporters no longer even bother to put up much of a defense of the president, shrugging their shoulders and saying, "Well, at least he is doing a good job." It is now all but universally accepted that President Clinton is "character challenged," that he has certain character weaknesses, and yet, in spite of these flaws, he has been at least a good president.

The gap between Bill Clinton's polling ratings of his job performance and his personal character has been persistent and wide. In June 1998, for example, a CNN-*Time* poll reported that while 63 percent of those surveyed gave Clinton a favorable rating for being an effective president, only 33 percent approved of his personal character, thus creating a 30 percent "character gap."

Poll data indicate that many people approve of Clinton's presidency who do not necessarily approve of him and his widely discussed social life. As the editors of the April/May issue of *The Public Perspective* put it, "Lots Who Say They Approve Clinton's Handling of the Presidency Don't Approve of Clinton."[1]

Those who voted for Clinton in 1992 and 1996 were aware Clinton was a flirt and possibly even a rogue. But those who generally identified with his domestic and foreign policy proposals made what amounted to a Faustian bargain. "We overlooked Mr. Clinton's past indiscretions—he was hardly the first politician with testosterone overload," writes *New York Times* columnist Thomas Friedman,

> on the condition that he pursue his agenda and postpone his next dalliance until after he left the White House. But he broke the bargain. I knew he was a charming rogue with an appealing agenda, but I didn't think he was a reckless idiot with an appealing agenda.[2]

A generation ago, political scientist James David Barber urged us to pay more attention to presidential character. He encouraged voters to support candidates who liked people, liked politics, had high self-esteem, and had high energy. These active-positive types were far less likely than others, claimed Barber, to become rigid, dogmatic, petty, and paranoid.[3] But Barber, writing more

From Thomas E. Cronin and Michael A. Genovese, "President Clinton and Character Questions," *Presidential Studies Quarterly*, vol. 28, no. 4 (Fall 1998). Copyright © 1998 by Sage Publications, Inc. Reprinted by permission.

than twenty-five years ago, did not dwell on sexual indiscretions or the sexual habits of would-be presidents.

Other writers have often ignored or even dismissed sexual behavior in explaining presidential effectiveness or lack thereof. Thus, historian Stephen Ambrose differentiates between two presidents about whom he has written. Dwight Eisenhower may have had a wartime dalliance with an aide yet was a man with impeccable integrity. He believed his word was his bond and had an abiding respect for other people. Nixon was a model family man. But "Richard Nixon, by contrast, respected almost no one and had contempt for so many. This, not any personal pecadillos, is what Mr. Ambrose argues" is the difference between Eisenhower's and Nixon's characters.[4]

Character counts, yet not as much nor in the same way most scholars probably have believed. Americans tell pollsters every four years they would like presidential candidates who are honest and who have character. The Clinton experience encourages a reconsideration. He has had a reasonably effective presidency, and, despite his well publicized flaws, most Americans approve of the way he has handled the job.

We speculate there are several reasons why Clinton has not been crucified on the cross of character. First, most people most of the time, especially between presidential elections, are more likely to judge a president on the basis of the economy's performance (stock market, inflation, unemployment, interest rates, economic growth, etc.) than on personal character traits. And the economy has been Clinton's best ally.

Second, Clinton had the ironic good fortune of having Judge Starr as his legal antagonist. Starr repeatedly made mistakes that allowed Clinton's friends to raise compelling questions about Starr and his tactics.

Third, the American people, while caring about character and moral virtue, do not believe adultery should disqualify a political leader from holding office. There is a bit of a paradox here; Americans do not favor adultery, yet they are more tolerant than they used to be about leaders who have extramarital affairs. Moreover, they know that even people of good character are not perfect.

Fourth, Clinton is a gifted politician. He not only "feels people's pain," he has an upbeat, positive, caring attitude about people, politics, and his job. He is, as we noted, an active-positive, in James David Barber's analytical typology. His political skills have allowed him to emphasize his policy agenda and his vision of America. (And he clearly exudes a love of people, sometimes, perhaps, a bit too much.) Finally, and clearly related to this last point, Clinton's presidential efforts usually suggest a public morality or at least an arguable use of presidential power in favor of the common man and woman. And this public morality, to the degree it is perceived as positive, effectively blunts some, although not all, of the criticism of Clinton's personal character deficiencies. People believe Bill Clinton is on their side, working for them, and are thus somewhat forgiving concerning some of the president's "private flaws."

One of the enduring paradoxes about presidential character is that many of those we judged to possess high levels of personal character (Hoover, Ford, and Carter come to mind) often are judged to have had low effectiveness as presents. In contrast, some of the personally flawed presidents, such as Roosevelt, Kennedy, and Nixon, are viewed as having been influential or effective.[5]

When examining the connection between character and leadership, we are confronted with this paradox: we want our leaders to be of high integrity and virtuous yet want our presidents to be adroit, tough, and even at times ruthless. We are, after all, electing a president, not a pope or a Mother Teresa. At times, we ask presidents to do things, especially in dealing with foreign adversaries, that are difficult from a moral standpoint. Could a completely moral leader order a bombing raid on Iraq?

Would a Mother Teresa have made a good president? Certainly, the moral example she would have set could serve as a model of individual goodness. But would she have been tough enough to stand up to foreign dictators and international terrorists? Would she have been tough enough to reform welfare? Would she have been tough enough to even get elected? The word *character* comes from the Greek *charakter*, meaning the mark of a coin or seal. Euripides defined character as "a stamp of good repute on a person." Some of our most highly regarded presidents were men of checkered personal character in their private relations. Recent press attention has focused on extramarital relations presidents and candidates may have had, implying that such affairs might disqualify a candidate from the presidency. Yet, had that long been the standard of judgement, several of our popular presidents—Jefferson, Roosevelt, Eisenhower, Kennedy, Clinton, and others—would have been disqualified from office.

While the president represents the nation and serves as a symbol of who we are, and while logic tells us that character is important, in terms of presidential performance, there is little correlation between "high" personal moral character and performance in office. As already noted, some of our presidents with checkered backgrounds performed well, and others of the highest character were political failures.

Sometimes it appears we demand a double-faced personality. We demand the sinister as well as the sincere, the cunning as well as the compassionate, President Mean and President Nice, the president as Clint Eastwood and the president as Mr. Rogers—tough and hard enough to stand up to Khrushchev and North Korea, to Saddam Hussein and the Ayatollah, or to press the nuclear button, yet compassionate enough to care for the ill-fed, ill-clad, and ill-housed. In this case, the public seems to want a kindhearted s.o.b., hard roles to cast and an even harder role to perform over eight years.

Former President Nixon, in writing about leaders he worked with, said a modern-day leader has to employ a variety of unattractive qualities on occasion to be effective or at least appear effective. Nixon may have carried these practices too far when he was in office, but his retirement writings are, nonetheless, instructive:

> In evaluating a leader, the key question about his behavior traits is not whether they are attractive or unattractive, but whether they are useful. Guile, vanity, dissembling—in other circumstances these might be unattractive habits, but to the leader they can be essential. He needs guile in order to hold together the shifting coalitions of often bitterly opposed interest groups that governing requires. He needs a certain measure of vanity in

order to create the right kind of public impression. He sometimes has to dissemble in order to prevail on crucial issues.[6]

Nixon should know. Despite other failings, he was often an effective foreign affairs president.

We want decency and compassion at home yet often demand toughness and guile when presidents have to deal with foreign adversaries. We want presidents to be fierce or compassionate, nice or mean, sensitive or ruthless depending on what we want done, on the situation, and, to some extent, on the role models of the recent past. But woe to a president who is too much or too little possessed of these characteristics!

Americans severely criticize would-be leaders who are viewed as soft or afraid to make decisions, use power, or fire anyone. Carter and Ford were faulted for indecision, timidity, or failure to be pragmatic. Journalists said they merely did not know how to play "hardball." "He must know when to dissemble, when to be frank. He must pose as a servant of the public in order to become its master," wrote Charles de Gaulle in his book on leadership, *The Edge of the Sword*. De Gaulle also said leaders need strong doses of egotism, pride, and hardness.[7]

Leaders plainly need to balance their competing impulses. Because leadership is wholly contextual, what works in one setting may fail in another. Thus, to be effective across issues and time, leaders must be flexible in matching style to circumstance. Plainly, however, ambition is essential if a leader is to make a major difference. And, to gain power and retain it, one must have a love of power, and this love is often incompatible with moral goodness. In fact, it is often more linked to qualities of hubris and duplicity.

To what extent are questions of private character relevant to presidential politics? While the president is, in many ways, a moral or symbolic spokesperson for the nation, must the person who fills the office be personally above reproach to be a good president? Probably not. The public may want its presidents to be of the highest character, but any examination of the private lives of our great presidents reveals an array of personal foibles.

Some people with roguish private lives exhibit considerable public integrity. Others of spotless private life exhibit public qualities of treachery and duplicity. Journalists and rival candidates nowadays search the backgrounds of candidates, looking for indiscretions. If found, as it was with Gary Hart and almost with Clinton, that candidate is scrutinized, criticized, and often forced from the race. Is it fair to base our judgments of character on events that may have occurred years ago and from which the candidate may have drawn useful lessons? Is it fair to judge a potential president mainly on his or her personal life?

Questions about presidential character are as old as the office itself. In 1800, ministers denounced Thomas Jefferson from their pulpits as "godless," and Andrew Jackson was pilloried as a barbarian and adulterer. The election of 1884 provides a fascinating case study of character in politics. In that election, Democratic candidate Grover Cleveland was charged with fathering a child out of wedlock. Cleveland took responsibility and agreed to pay for the child's up-bringing. Understandably, this became a prime issue for his opponent James G. Blaine. The dilemma was that while Cleveland's private life did indeed raise doubts, he was highly responsible in his political and professional life. Blaine, on the other hand, had an "upright" private life yet was far less well regarded for his political integrity. The voters selected Cleveland.

Presidents, like the rest of us, are human; they make mistakes. Some learn from their mistakes, others do not. The perfect person does not exist. Our presidents come with a wide array of strengths and weaknesses. To disqualify candidates because it is revealed they made mistakes years ago or because of certain questions about their personal lifestyle seems shortsighted.

Presidents—both good and bad—have lied to us. But is there a difference between the behavior of Roosevelt prior to U.S. entry into World War II and Nixon's lies about Watergate? The essential difference is that Roosevelt misled with the public good in mind, and Nixon misled to save himself. In the long run, historians judge Roosevelt's methods as questionable but his goals and outcome as honorable. Historians see Nixon's actions as self-serving and dishonorable. Clinton appears to have occasionally misled the American public about his dating and flirting habits. His lies appear to be self-serving rather than intended to further the public good. And this has most assuredly damaged his reputation and lessened our trust in him, even if it has not lowered his presidential job-approval ratings.

While no single definition of character adequately covers all our needs, the following qualities are desirable in a person who becomes president: courage of conviction, an internal moral compass, respect for others, commitment to the public good, respect for democratic standards, trustworthiness, generosity of spirit, compassion, optimism, a sense of decency and fair play, and inner strength and confidence.

Is there a useful model for judging character in presidents? The following tests could serve as a beginning: (1) Does the behavior in question exceed the boundaries of what most reasonable people would think of as acceptable in those circumstances? (2) Is there a clear pattern of this behavior and not an isolated act or event? (3) Does it affect job performance? Clinton may well be faulted both by the public and historians on questions 1 and 2, yet he and his defenders may well be able to claim these incidents did not seriously affect job performance. In the end, the real tests of presidential character may well be, "Did this president bring out the best in all of us?" And, "Did this president effectively serve the best interests of the nation as a whole?"

Franklin Roosevelt suggested that the presidency "is preeminently a place of moral leadership." But Roosevelt plainly was talking about the capacity to do good, the capacity of presidents to liberate the forces of good in the country.

There are a few things we "know" about the relationship between character and leadership: first, private character is not necessarily the best guide or predictor of public character or performance. Second, public character—that is, how well one had behaved in previous offices and public tasks—is a better, although still imperfect, guide to future behavior. Third, our preoccupation with scandal doubtless chases away some fine candidates who understandably refuse to put themselves and their families through the ugliness of public scandal hunts. Fourth, do not look for saints. We are all human; we all make mistakes. The Zen parable, "Water which is too pure has no fish," might be our guide.

We should judge presidents more by what they do than who they are. While both are important, we must remember we elect a president to govern, not preach. And while the ceremonial, symbolic, and even priestly functions of the presidency are important, we are a weaker people if we let our presidents, television celebrities, or sports stars set the moral tone for the nation.

Perhaps the most useful test of presidential character, the one that most closely applies to the task of presidential leadership, is to ask the question Abraham Lincoln raised. Did the president, as Lincoln suggested, "appeal to the better angels within us?" Did he try to bring out what was best in us and our nation, or did he pander to our weaknesses, prejudices, and hatreds? In the long run, Clinton and his successors will be judged far more on what they did on behalf of the average American than what they did in what little private or personal life we let presidents have.

President Clinton has, in several ways, dishonored himself and the office of president. In future years, historians who evaluate Clinton's presidency will certainly take these failures into consideration in judging his administration. These negatives obviously made it more difficult for Clinton to provide needed leadership. Historian Robert Dallek appropriately suggests:

> Successful presidential leadership has always relied on moral authority: a president's conviction that he is battling for the national good and public perception that he is a credible chief committed to advancing the national well-being. Few things are more destructive to a president's influence than the belief that he is a deceitful manipulator more intent on serving his personal needs than those of the public.[8]

Still, as important as any president's character failures may be, they are not the whole picture. And doubtless also it will be decades before biographers and historians can take the full measure of Clinton's successes and failures.

## Notes

1. *The Public Perspective*, April/May, 1998, p. 20.
2. Thomas L. Friedman, "Character Suicide," *New York Times*, January 27, 1998, p. A23.
3. James David Barber, *The Presidential Character* (Englewood Cliffs, NJ: Prentice Hall, 1972).
4. Albert R. Hunt, "The Real Stuff of Character," *Wall Street Journal*, February 5, 1998, p. A23.
5. See poll data in *The Public Perspective*, April/May, 1998, p. 19.
6. Richard M. Nixon, *Leaders* (New York: Warner Books, 1983), p. 341.
7. Charles de Gaulle, *The Edge of the Sword* (New York: Criterion, 1960).
8. Robert Dallek, "Can Clinton Still Govern?," *Washington Post National Weekly Edition*, October 5, 1998, p. 22.

# POSTSCRIPT

## The Presidency: Does the President's Personal Morality Matter?

**P**erhaps the difference between these two perspectives on presidential character comes down to this: Cronin and Genevose believe that a president's personal behavior can remain on a different track from his public behavior, whereas Bennett thinks that what a president does in private eventually runs into the public realm and into the public's consciousness. For Bennett, then, the public's seeming indifference to the Monica Lewinsky affair suggests that America's moral standards have been lowered, while for Cronin and Genovese it means that the public has become discerning and nuanced in its moral judgments.

As Cronin and Genovese note, one of the pioneer books on presidential character was that of political scientist James David Barber, *The Presidential Character* (Prentice Hall, 1972). A more general book on the character of public leaders, Gail Sheehy's *Character: America's Search for Leadership* (William Morrow, 1988) also tackles the subject, arguing that "we have suffered repeated disillusionment with recent presidents because we failed to enter into the compact aware of even the most obvious patterns of behavior." A more recent book by political scientist Stephen Skowronek suggests that the success or failure of a presidency depends in part on the president's personality but also on the time and circumstances in which he comes to power. See *The Politics Presidents Make: Leadership from John Adams to George Bush* (Belknap Press, 1993).

The American people have become increasingly tolerant of the marital behavior of officeholders and candidates. Back in 1964 one of the factors that doomed the presidential candidacy of New York governor Nelson Rockefeller was his pending divorce. As late as 1984 Colorado senator Gary Hart felt compelled to drop out of the race for the Democratic presidential nomination after reports came out of his tryst with a woman aboard a yacht named *Monkey Business*. But in spring 2000 reports of a liaison between New York mayor (and senatorial candidate) Rudolph Giuliani and a divorced woman left the public unfazed; more than 80 percent of New Yorkers said that the reports would have no effect at all on their vote. As it turned out, Giuliani dropped out of the race anyway, but that may have been, as he asserted, because of problems related to his health (prostate cancer) rather than his personal behavior.

# ISSUE 7

## Should Judges Read Their Moral Views into the Constitution?

**YES: Ronald Dworkin**, from "The Moral Reading of the Constitution," *New York Review of Books* (March 21, 1996)

**NO: Mary Ann Glendon**, from "Partial Justice," *Commentary* (August 1994)

### ISSUE SUMMARY

**YES:** Law professor Ronald Dworkin contends that judges must read the vaguer phrases of the Constitution with an eye toward what is best for the nation.

**NO:** Law professor Mary Ann Glendon warns of the perils of "romantic judging," which she argues usurps the role of legislatures and weakens the spirit of democracy.

I t is emphatically, the province and duty of the judicial department, to say what the law is." This assertion lay at the heart of Chief Justice John Marshall's opinion for the U.S. Supreme Court in the landmark case *Marbury v. Madison* (1803). Marshall was building a case for judicial review—the authority of federal courts to strike down congressional laws or presidential rulings that, in their view, violate the Constitution. Most lawmakers at that time accepted the supremacy of the Constitution, but, many asked, why should courts have the last say in interpreting the Constitution?

The answer, said Marshall, is that judges have no choice: they *cannot* blind their eyes to the Constitution when somebody before the court is accused of a federal crime. Suppose someone is condemned to death for treason on the basis of an unconstitutional statute, such as a law that said that the testimony of one witness is enough for conviction (the Constitution says that there must be two). Now suppose he appeals to the courts. Should the courts ignore his appeal and let him be hanged for violating an unconstitutional statute?

Marshall's argument for judicial review would be unanswerable if every case of unconstitutionality were as clear-cut as the one just mentioned. Where Marshall's argument becomes problematic is in cases where the language of the Constitution is not clear-cut but fuzzy. For example, what is an "establishment of religion," which is prohibited by the First Amendment? Does it mean an established church, such as they have in England, or is it broad enough to include nondenominational prayers in public schools? And what of the Fourteenth Amendment's guarantee of "equal protection of the laws"? How broad should that protection be? Does it encompass not only blacks but women, homosexuals, disabled people, and unborn children? The Constitution itself does not say. Why, then, should a court's interpretation be preferred over the interpretation of Congress or the president?

Chief Justice Marshall implied that there are objective legal principles for interpreting the Constitution in such disputed cases, though he never spelled them out. Down through the years, other jurists and commentators have tried to devise guiding principles. Appeals court judge Learned Hand (1872–1961) thought that the Supreme Court should assume final authority to interpret the Constitution only when it was absolutely necessary to resolve competing claims of the other two branches of the federal government. In a somewhat similar mode, Justice Felix Frankfurter (1882–1965), who served on the Supreme Court from 1939 to 1962, preached a doctrine that he called "judicial self-restraint." Only if a federal law is clearly unconstitutional, Frankfurther believed, should it be struck down; in doubtful cases the Court should defer to the elected branches of government and presume that the law is constitutional.

During the Reagan administration in the 1980s, former appeals court judge Robert H. Bork became embroiled in controversy because of his doctrine of "original intent." Bork believes that the most objective way of interpreting some of the vaguer and fuzzier clauses in the Constitution is to go back and examine the intent of those who originally wrote those clauses. Bork's views offended many feminists and civil rights activists, and when President Ronald Reagan nominated him to the Supreme Court in 1987, they feared that he would roll back abortion rights and affirmative action. His nomination was therefore defeated in the Senate.

In the following selections, Ronald Dworkin rejects Bork's "originalism" as well as the "self-restraint" approach of Hand and Frankfurter. Dworkin's view is that judges, in interpreting some of the vaguer phrases in the Constitution, must ultimately decide "which conception does most credit to the nation." This broadly moralistic approach to constitutional interpretation worries Mary Ann Glendon. Characterizing it as "romantic judging," she argues that it usurps the function of legislatures and weakens the spirit of democracy.

**Ronald Dworkin**

 **YES**

# The Moral Reading of the Constitution

It is patent that judges' own views about political morality influence their constitutional decisions, and though they might easily explain that influence by insisting that the Constitution demands a moral reading, they never do. Instead, against all evidence, they deny the influence and try to explain their decisions in other—embarrassingly unsatisfactory—ways. They say they are just giving effect to obscure historical "intentions," for example, or just expressing an overall but unexplained constitutional "structure" that is supposedly explicable in nonmoral terms.

This mismatch between role and reputation is easily explained. The moral reading is so thoroughly embedded in constitutional practice and is so much more attractive, on both legal and political grounds, than the only coherent alternatives, that it cannot readily be abandoned, particularly when important constitutional issues are in play. But the moral reading nevertheless seems intellectually and politically discreditable. It seems to erode the crucial distinction between law and morality by making law only a matter of which moral principles happen to appeal to the judges of a particular era. It seems grotesquely to constrict the moral sovereignty of the people themselves—to take out of their hands, and remit to a professional elite, exactly the great and defining issues of political morality that the people have the right and the responsibility to decide for themselves.

That is the source of the paradoxical contrast between mainstream constitutional practice in the United States, which relies heavily on the moral reading of the Constitution, and mainstream constitutional theory, which wholly rejects that reading. The confusion has had serious political costs. Conservative politicians try to convince the public that the great constitutional cases turn not on deep issues of political principle, which they do, but on the simpler question of whether judges should change the Constitution by fiat or leave it alone. For a time this view of the constitutional argument was apparently accepted even by some liberals. They called the Constitution a "living" document and said that it must be "brought up to date" to match new circumstances and sensibilities. They said they took an "active" approach to the Constitution, which seemed to suggest reform, and they accepted John Ely's characterization

From Ronald Dworkin, "The Moral Reading of the Constitution," *New York Review of Books* (March 21, 1996). Copyright © 1996 by NYREV, Inc. Reprinted by permission of *New York Review of Books*. Notes omitted.

of their position as a "noninterpretive" one, which seemed to suggest invent-ing a new document rather than interpreting the old one. In fact, this account of the argument was never accurate. The theoretical debate was never about whether judges should interpret the Constitution or change it—almost no one really thought the latter—rather it was about how it should be interpreted. But conservative politicians exploited the simpler description, and they were not effectively answered.

The confusion engulfs the politicians as well. They promise to appoint and confirm judges who will respect the proper limits of their authority and leave the Constitution alone, but since this misrepresents the choices judges actually face, the politicians are often disappointed. When Dwight Eisenhower, who denounced what he called judicial activism, retired from office in 1961, he told a reporter that he had made only two big mistakes as President—and that they were both on the Supreme Court. He meant Chief Justice Earl Warren, who had been a Republican politician when Eisenhower appointed him to head the Supreme Court, but who then presided over one of the most "activist" periods in the Court's history, and Justice William Brennan, another politician who had been a state court judge when Eisenhower appointed him, and who became one of the most liberal and explicit practitioners of the moral reading of the Constitution in modern times.

⌒⟨◉⟩⌒

Presidents Ronald Reagan and George Bush were both intense in their outrage at the Supreme Court's "usurpation" of the people's privileges. They said they were determined to appoint judges who would respect rather than defy the people's will. In particular, they (and the platform on which they ran for the presidency) denounced the Court's 1973 *Roe* v. *Wade* decision protecting abor-tion rights, and promised that their appointees would reverse it. But when the opportunity to do so came, three of the justices Reagan and Bush had appointed between them voted, surprisingly, not only to retain that decision in force, but to provide a legal basis for it that much more explicitly adopted and relied on a moral reading of the Constitution. The expectations of politicians who appoint judges are often defeated in that way, because the politicians fail to appreciate how thoroughly the moral reading, which they say they deplore, is actually em-bedded in constitutional practice. Its role remains hidden when a judge's own convictions support the legislation whose constitutionality is in doubt—when a justice thinks it morally permissible for the majority to criminalize abortion, for example. But the ubiquity of the moral reading becomes evident when some judge's convictions of principle—identified, tested, and perhaps altered by ex-perience and argument—bend in an opposite direction, because then enforcing the Constitution must mean, for that judge, telling the majority that it cannot have what it wants....

# The Moral Reading

The clauses of the American Constitution that protect individuals and minorities from government are found mainly in the so-called Bill of Rights—the first ten amendments to the document—and the further amendments added after the Civil War. (I shall sometimes use the phrase "Bill of Rights," inaccurately, to refer to all the provisions of the Constitution that establish individual rights, including the Fourteenth Amendment's protection of citizens' privileges and immunities and its guarantee of due process and equal protection of the laws.) Many of these clauses are drafted in exceedingly abstract moral language. The First Amendment refers to the "right" of free speech, for example, the Fifth Amendment to the process that is "due" to citizens, and the Fourteenth to protection that is "equal." According to the moral reading, these clauses must be understood in the way their language most naturally suggests: they refer to abstract moral principles and incorporate these by reference, as limits on government's power.

There is of course room for disagreement about the right way to restate these abstract moral principles, so as to make their force clearer to us, and to help us to apply them to more concrete political controversies. I favor a particular way of stating the constitutional principles at the most general possible level. I believe that the principles set out in the Bill of Rights, taken together, commit the United States to the following political and legal ideas: government must treat all those subject to its dominion as having equal moral and political status; it must attempt, in good faith, to treat them all with concern; and it must respect whatever individual freedoms are indispensable to those ends, including but not limited to the freedoms more specifically designated in the document, such as the freedoms of speech and religion. Other lawyers and scholars who also endorse the moral reading might well formulate the constitutional principles, even at a very general level, differently and less expansively than I just have, however, and though here I want to explain and defend the moral reading, not my own interpretations under it, I should say something about how the choice among competing formulations should be made.

Of course the moral reading is not appropriate to everything a constitution contains. The American Constitution includes a great many clauses that are neither particularly abstract nor drafted in the language of moral principle. Article II specifies, for example, that the President must be at least thirty-five years old, and the Third Amendment insists that government may not quarter soldiers in citizens' houses in peacetime. The latter may have been inspired by a moral principle: those who wrote and enacted it might have been anxious to give effect to some principle protecting citizens' rights to privacy, for example. But the Third Amendment is not itself a moral principle: its *content* is not a general principle of privacy. So the first challenge to my own interpretation of the abstract clauses might be put this way. What argument or evidence do I have that the equal protection clause of the Fourteenth Amendment (for example), which declares that no state may deny any person equal protection of the laws, has a moral principle as *its* content though the Third Amendment does not?

This is a question of interpretation or, if you prefer, translation. We must try to find language of our own that best captures, in terms we find clear, the content of what the "framers" intended it to say. (Constitutional scholars use the word "framers" to describe, somewhat ambiguously, the various people who drafted and enacted a constitutional provision.) History is crucial to that project, because we must know something about the circumstances in which a person spoke to have any good idea of what he meant to say in speaking as he did. We find nothing in history, however, to cause us any doubt about what the framers of the Third Amendment meant to say. Given the words they used, we cannot sensibly interpret them as laying down any moral principle at all, even if we believe they were inspired by one. They said what the words they used would normally be used to say: not that privacy must be protected, but that soldiers must not be quartered in houses in peacetime.

***

The same process of reasoning—about what the framers presumably intended to say when they used the words they did—yields an opposite conclusion about the framers of the equal protection clause, however. Most of them no doubt had fairly clear expectations about what legal consequences the Fourteenth Amendment would have. They expected it to end certain of the most egregious Jim Crow practices of the Reconstruction period. They plainly did not expect it to outlaw official racial segregation in school—on the contrary, the Congress that adopted the equal protection clause itself maintained segregation in the District of Columbia school system. But they did not *say* anything about Jim Crow laws or school segregation or homosexuality or gender equality, one way or the other. They said that "equal protection of the laws" is required, which plainly describes a very general principle, not any concrete application of it.

The framers meant, then, to enact a general principle. But which general principle? That further question must be answered by constructing different elaborations of the phrase "equal protection of the laws," each of which we can recognize as a principle of political morality that might have won their respect, and then by asking which of these it makes most sense to attribute to them, given everything else we know. The qualification that each of these possibilities must be recognizable as a political *principle* is absolutely crucial. We cannot capture a statesman's efforts to lay down a general constitutional principle by attributing to him something neither he nor we could recognize as a candidate for that role. But the qualification will typically leave many possibilities open. It was once debated, for example, whether the framers intended to stipulate, in the equal protection clause, only the relatively weak political principle that laws must be enforced in accordance with their terms, so that legal benefits conferred on everyone, including blacks, must not be denied, in practice, to anyone.

History seems decisive that the framers of the Fourteenth Amendment did not mean to lay down only so weak a principle as that one, however, which would have left states free to discriminate against blacks in any way they wished so long as they did so openly. Congressmen of the victorious nation, trying to capture the achievements and lessons of a terrible war, would be very unlikely to settle for anything so limited and insipid, and we should not take them to have done so unless the language leaves no other interpretation plausible. In any case, constitutional interpretation must take into account past legal and political practice as well as what the framers themselves intended to say, and it has now been settled by unchallengeable precedent that the political principle incorporated in the Fourteenth Amendment is not that very weak one, but something more robust. Once that is conceded, however, then the principle must be something *much* more robust, because the only alternative, as a translation of what the framers actually *said* in the equal protection clause, is that they declared a principle of quite breathtaking scope and power: the principle that government must treat everyone as of equal status and with equal concern.

⤜❦⤏

Two important restraints sharply limit the latitude the moral reading gives to individual judges. First, under that reading constitutional interpretation must begin in what the framers said, and, just as our judgment about what friends and strangers say relies on specific information about them and the context in which they speak, so does our understanding of what the framers said. History is therefore plainly relevant. But only in a particular way. We turn to history to answer the question of what they intended to *say*, not the different question of what *other* intentions they had. We have no need to decide what they expected to happen, or hoped would happen, in consequence of their having said what they did, for example; their purpose, in that sense, is not part of our study. That is a crucial distinction. We are governed by what our lawmakers said—by the principles they laid down—not by any information we might have about how they themselves would have interpreted those principles or applied them in concrete cases.

Second, and equally important, constitutional interpretation is disciplined, under the moral reading, by the requirement of constitutional *integrity*. Judges may not read their own convictions into the Constitution. They may not read the abstract moral clauses as expressing any particular moral judgment, no matter how much that judgment appeals to them, unless they find it consistent in principle with the structural design of the Constitution as a whole, and also with the dominant lines of past constitutional interpretation by other judges. They must regard themselves as partners with other officials, past and future, who together elaborate a coherent constitutional morality, and they must take care to see that what they contribute fits with the rest. (I have elsewhere said that judges are like authors jointly creating a chain novel in which each writes a chapter that makes sense as part of the story as a whole.) Even a judge who believes that abstract justice requires economic equality cannot interpret the equal protection clause as making equality of wealth, or collective ownership of productive resources, a constitutional requirement, because that interpretation simply does not fit American history or practice, or the rest of the Constitution.

Nor could he plausibly think that the constitutional structure commits any other than basic, structural political rights to his care. He might think that a society truly committed to equal concern would award people with handicaps special resources, or would secure convenient access to recreational parks for everyone, or would provide heroic and experimental medical treatment, no matter how expensive or speculative, for anyone whose life might possibly be saved. But it would violate constitutional integrity for him to treat these mandates as part of constitutional law. Judges must defer to general, settled understandings about the character of the power the Constitution assigns them. The moral reading asks them to find the best conception of constitutional moral principles—the best understanding of what equal moral status for men and women really requires, for example—that fits the broad story of America's historical record. It does not ask them to follow the whisperings of their own consciences or the traditions of their own class or sect if these cannot be seen as embedded in that record. Of course judges can abuse their power—they can pretend to observe the important restraint of integrity while really ignoring it. But generals and presidents and priests can abuse their powers, too. The moral reading is a strategy for lawyers and judges acting in good faith, which is all any interpretive strategy can be.

I emphasize these constraints of history and integrity, because they show how exaggerated is the common complaint that the moral reading gives judges absolute power to impose their own moral convictions on the rest of us. [English historian Thomas Babington] Macaulay was wrong when he said that the American Constitution is all sail and no anchor, and so are the other critics who say that the moral reading turns judges into philosopher-kings. Our constitution is law, and like all law it is anchored in history, practice, and integrity. Still, we must not exaggerate the drag of that anchor. Very different, even contrary, conceptions of a constitutional principle—of what treating men and women as equals really means, for example—will often fit language, precedent, and practice well enough to pass these tests, and thoughtful judges must then decide on their own which conception does most credit to the nation. So though the familiar complaint that the moral reading gives judges unlimited power is hyperbolic, it contains enough truth to alarm those who believe that such judicial power is inconsistent with a republican form of government. The constitutional sail is a broad one, and many people do fear that it is too big for a democratic boat.

## What Is the Alternative?

Constitutional lawyers and scholars have therefore been anxious to find other strategies for constitutional interpretation, strategies that give judges less power. They have explored two different possibilities. The first, and most forthright, concedes that the moral reading is right—that the Bill of Rights can only be understood as a set of moral principles. But it denies that judges should have the final authority themselves to conduct the moral reading—that they should have the last word about, for example, whether women have a constitutional right to choose abortion or whether affirmative action treats all races with equal concern. It reserves that interpretive authority to the people. That is by no means a contradictory combination of views. The moral reading, as I said, is a theory about what the Constitution means, not a theory about whose view of what it means must be accepted by the rest of us.

This first alternative offers a way of understanding the arguments of a great American judge, Learned Hand. Hand thought that the courts should take final authority to interpret the Constitution only when this is absolutely necessary to the survival of government—only when the courts must be referees between the other departments of government because the alternative would be a chaos of competing claims to jurisdiction. No such necessity compels courts to test legislative acts against the Constitution's moral principles, and Hand therefore thought it wrong for judges to claim that authority. Though his view was once an open possibility, history has long excluded it; practice has now settled that courts do have a responsibility to declare and act on their best understanding of what the Constitution forbids. If Hand's view had been accepted, the Supreme Court could not have decided, as it did in its famous *Brown* decision in 1954, that the equal protection clause outlaws racial segregation in public schools. In 1958 Hand said, with evident regret, that he had to regard the *Brown* decision as wrong, and he would have had to take the same view about later Supreme Court decisions that expanded racial equality, religious independence, and personal freedoms such as the freedom to buy and use contraceptives. These decisions are now almost universally thought not only sound but shining examples of our constitutional structure working at its best.

The first alternative strategy, as I said, accepts the moral reading. The second alternative, which is called the "originalist" or "original intention" strategy, does not. The moral reading insists that the Constitution means what the framers intended to say. Originalism insists that it means what they expected their language to *do*, which as I said is a very different matter. (Though some originalists, including one of the most conservative justices now on the Supreme Court, Antonin Scalia, are unclear about the distinction.) According to originalism, the great clauses of the Bill of Rights should be interpreted not as laying down the abstract moral principles they actually describe, but instead as referring, in a kind of code or disguise, to the framers' own assumptions and expectations about the correct application of those principles. So the equal protection clause is to be understood as commanding not equal status but what the framers themselves thought was equal status, in spite of the fact that, as I said, the framers clearly meant to lay down the former standard not the latter one.

The *Brown* decision I just mentioned crisply illustrates the distinction. The Court's decision was plainly required by the moral reading, because it is obvious now that official school segregation is not consistent with equal status and equal concern for all races. The originalist strategy, consistently applied, would have demanded the opposite conclusion, because, as I said, the authors of the equal protection clause did not believe that school segregation, which they practiced themselves, was a denial of equal status, and did not expect that it would one day be deemed to be so. The moral reading insists that they misunderstood the moral principle that they themselves enacted into law. The originalist strategy would translate that mistake into enduring constitutional law.

That strategy, like the first alternative, would condemn not only the *Brown* decision but many other Supreme Court decisions that are now widely regarded as paradigms of good constitutional interpretation. For that reason, almost no one now embraces the originalist strategy in anything like a pure form. Even Robert Bork, who remains one of its strongest defenders, qualified his support in the Senate hearings following his nomination to the Supreme Court—he conceded that the *Brown* decision was right, and said that even the Court's 1965 decision guaranteeing a right to use contraceptives, which we have no reason to think the authors of any pertinent constitutional clause either expected or would have approved, was right in its result. The originalist strategy is as indefensible in principle as it is unpalatable in result, moreover. It is as illegitimate to substitute a concrete, detailed provision for the abstract language of the equal protection clause as it would be to substitute some abstract principle of privacy for the concrete terms of the Third Amendment, or to treat the clause imposing a minimum age for a President as enacting some general principle of disability for persons under that age.

ↄ⦿ↄ

So though many conservative politicians and judges have endorsed originalism, and some, like Hand, have been tempted to reconsider whether judges should have the last word about what the Constitution requires, there is in fact very little practical support for either of these strategies. Yet the moral reading is almost never explicitly endorsed, and is often explicitly condemned. If neither of the two alternatives I described is actually embraced by those who disparage the moral reading, what interpretive strategy do they have in mind? The surprising answer is: none. Constitutional scholars often say that we must avoid the mistakes of both the moral reading, which gives too much power to judges, and of originalism, which makes the contemporary Constitution too much the dead hand of the past. The right method, they say, is something in between which strikes the right balance between protecting essential individual rights and deferring to popular will. But they do not indicate what the right balance is, or even what kind of scale we should use to find it. They say that constitutional interpretation must take both history and the general structure of the Constitution into account as well as moral or political philosophy. But they do not say why history or structure, both of which, as I said, figure in the moral reading, should figure in some further or different way, or what that different way is, or what general goal or standard of constitutional interpretation should guide us in seeking a different interpretive strategy.

So though the call for an intermediate constitutional strategy is often heard, it has not been answered, except in unhelpful metaphors about balance and structure. That is extraordinary, particularly given the enormous and growing literature in American constitutional theory. If it is so hard to produce an alternative to the moral reading, why struggle to do so? One distinguished constitutional lawyer who insists that there must be an interpretive strategy somewhere between originalism and the moral reading recently announced, at a conference, that although he had not discovered it, he would spend the rest of his life looking. Why?

I have already answered the question. Lawyers assume that the disabilities that a constitution imposes on majoritarian political processes are antidemocratic, at least if these disabilities are enforced by judges, and the moral reading seems to exacerbate the insult. If there is no genuine alternative to the moral reading in practice, however, and if efforts to find even a theoretical statement of an acceptable alternative have failed, we would do well to look again at that assumption.

# NO ↩

**Mary Ann Glendon**

# Partial Justice

$A$s late as the early 1960's, Justice William O. Douglas was widely regarded as a disgrace to the bench even by many lawyers who shared his social and economic views. Douglas's contempt for legal craftsmanship was seen as sloppiness; his visionary opinions were taken as evidence that he was angling for the presidency; and his solicitude for those he considered underdogs was perceived as favoritism.

By the end of the 1960's, however, a new and very romantic ideal of judging had begun to take shape. In eulogies, tributes, law-review articles, and legal journalism, judges began to be praised for qualities that would once have been considered problematic: compassion rather than impartiality, boldness rather than restraint, creativity rather than craftsmanship, and specific results regardless of the effect on the legal order as a whole. In the 1990's, Douglas would surely have basked in the "Greenhouse Effect"—a term (named after the *New York Times*'s Linda Greenhouse) for the warm reciprocity between activist journalists and judges who meet their approval.

This great change was set into motion by the appointment of Earl Warren as Chief Justice in 1953. President Eisenhower's choice of Warren was an unusual move, for the new Chief Justice had spent almost all his professional life in electoral politics. After serving as California's attorney general, he became a power in the state Republican party and then a popular governor. He was Thomas E. Dewey's running mate in 1948, and a serious contender for the Republican presidential nomination himself in 1952.

Nothing in Warren's background had prepared him for the fine-gauge work of opinion writing. He was impatient with the need to ground a desired outcome in constitutional text or tradition. As described by an admirer, Warren was a man who brushed off legal and historical impediments to the results he felt were right; he was not a "look-it-up-in-the-library" type.

What he was, above all, was a statesman, and although scholars may argue about its foundations in constitutional text and tradition, the Warren Court's decision in *Brown* v. *Board of Education* was indeed a great act of statesmanship. Those academics who downplay the importance of *Brown* in the struggle for racial justice have underrated its effects on attitudes about race relations —effects that in turn helped to bring about important political changes like

From Mary Ann Glendon, "Partial Justice," *Commentary* (August 1994). Copyright © 1994 by The American Jewish Committee. Reprinted by permission of *Commentary*.

the Civil Rights Act of 1964 and voting-rights legislation. The Warren Court laid its prestige on the line in a bid not only to dismantle official segregation, but to delegitimate racially discriminatory attitudes. That wager was successful. Though racial prejudice has not been eradicated, it has no respectability at all in contemporary American society.

The effects of *Brown* on the legal profession and on the legal order as a whole were another matter. And here it was not Warren but William Brennan, appointed to the Supreme Court by Eisenhower in 1956, who came to incarnate those less salutary effects most fully.

⋅◆⋅

Brennan was of humble origins. The son of Irish immigrants, he made his way to Harvard Law School—encouraged by his trade-unionist father who told him that a lawyer could do a lot for working people. Brennan did go into labor law, but enlisted on the other side of the cause that had meant so much to his father. After some years as a successful corporate practitioner in New Jersey, he became a trial judge and rose in time to the New Jersey Supreme Court. On the U.S. Supreme Court, he became a towering hero to those who shared his view that the Court had not only the power but the duty to promote social and political change.

Described by his biographer, Kim Eisler, as neither the most brilliant nor the best writer on the Court, Brennan during his long tenure may nevertheless have had the most influence on the general direction of its decisions. Few lawyers would disagree with the *New Yorker*'s evaluation, on Brennan's retirement in 1990, that he had come "to personify the expansion of the role of the judiciary in American life."

Even toward the end of his career, as the composition and mood of the Court changed, Brennan was often able to beat the odds and further his vision. As portrayed by Bob Woodward and Scott Armstrong in *The Brethren,* Brennan "cajoled in conference, walked the halls constantly and worked the phones, polling and plotting strategy with his allies." In later years, when his colleagues declined to follow him on such excursions as judicially banning capital punishment or abolishing the custom of prayer at the opening of legislative sessions, Brennan went out on the hustings, calling on state courts to take up the cudgels.

In speeches and writings, Brennan encouraged state judges to exercise their powers of constitutional review in new and creative ways. State courts, he pointed out, could interpret their own constitutions so as to provide even more rights than are afforded under the federal Constitution. Like the fox in Aesop's fable, the wily Brennan cajoled whole flocks of jurists into dropping their reserve. "State courts cannot rest," he wrote, "when they have afforded their citizens the full protections of the federal Constitution. State constitutions, too, are a font of individual liberties, their protections often extending beyond those afforded by the Supreme Court's interpretation of federal law."

Unlike many adventurous judges, Brennan had well-developed views of judging and did not mind discussing them. Here he is in a 1988 essay:

> The Constitution is fundamentally a public text—the monumental charter of a government and a people—and a Justice of the Supreme Court must apply it to resolve public controversies. For, from our beginnings, a most important consequence of the constitutionally created separation of powers has been the American habit, extraordinary to other democracies, of casting social, economic, philosophical, and political questions in the form of lawsuits, in an attempt to secure ultimate resolution by the Supreme Court.... Not infrequently, these are the issues on which contemporary society is most deeply divided. They arouse our deepest emotions. The main burden of my 29 years on the Supreme Court has thus been to wrestle with the Constitution in this heightened public context, to draw meaning from the text in order to resolve public controversies.

⇜⊙⇝

That passage can instructively be compared with views often expressed in the past by Justices Oliver Wendell Holmes and Louis D. Brandeis. Holmes insisted that legislatures, no less than courts, were the ultimate guardians of the liberties and welfare of the people. "About 75 years ago," he said as a very old man, "I learned that I was not God. And so, when the people want to do something I can't find anything in the Constitution expressly forbidding them to do, I say, whether I like it or not, 'Goddammit, let 'em do it.'"

Brandeis for his part emphasized that, where vexing social problems were concerned, it would often be more advantageous to leave state and local governments free to experiment than to impose uniform and untested federal mandates upon the entire country. The states, he said, were like "laboratories" where innovative approaches to novel problems could be tested and refined or rejected.

Although one of the opinions of which Brennan was proudest was on legislative reapportionment, he maintained an uncharacteristic silence on the role of the elected branches in resolving the issues on which "society is most deeply divided." The reason must be that the way he saw his own life's work, as indicated in the above passage, put him in direct competition with the popular branches. Quoting Justice Robert Jackson, he made no bones about his position that, right or wrong, the Court was to have the last word: "The Justices are certainly aware that we are not final because we are infallible; we know that we are infallible because we are final."

Brennan's approach to judging could not be more remote in spirit from Holmes's structural restraint. Nor did Brennan have much use for the prudent avoidance of the appearance of judicial imperialism that was characteristic of the first great shaper of the Court, John Marshall. Brennan did not hesitate to claim, regarding the Court's powers: "The course of vital social, economic, and political currents may be directed."

Energized and prodded to no small degree by Brennan, majorities on the Warren and Burger Courts actively pursued a high-minded vision of empowering those individuals and groups they perceived as disadvantaged. When deference to the elected branches served those ends, as in many affirmative-action cases, Brennan deferred as humbly as any classical judge. When the decisions of councils or legislatures got in his way, he invoked expansive interpretations of constitutional language to brush them aside.

While Brennan was not one to let text or tradition stand in the way of a desired result, he knew how to turn his corners squarely. But he did not share the devotion to judicial craftsmanship that characterized the work of colleagues like John Marshall Harlan or Byron White. Nor did he show much concern about the probable side-effects of a desired result in a particular case on the separation of powers, federal-state relations, or the long-term health of political processes and institutions. With respect to such matters, he was impatient with what he considered to be abstractions and technicalities.

When it came to compassion, Brennan had plenty for those he made (or wished to make) winners, but he showed little sensitivity toward those he ruled against. His heart went out to Native Americans when a Court majority permitted the federal government to build a road through sacred Indian places on public land. But in striking down a longstanding and successful New York City program providing remedial math and reading teachers to poor, special-needs children in religious schools, Brennan was pitiless. It took a dissent by Justice Sandra Day O'Connor to point out that the majority ruling, written by Brennan, had sacrificed the needs and prospects of 20,000 children from the poorest families in New York, and thousands more disadvantaged children across the country, for the sake of a maximalist version of the principle of separation of church and state.

*❧*

The new model of bold, assertive judging has also had its exemplars in the lower courts. One federal appellate judge famed for his crusading decisions was the late J. Skelley Wright. Looking back on his role in expanding landlords' liability for the condition of leased premises, he wrote in 1982:

> I didn't like what I saw, and I did what I could to ameliorate, if not eliminate, the injustice involved in the way many of the poor were required to live in the nation's capital. I offer no apology for not following more closely the legal precedents which had cooperated in creating the conditions that I found unjust.

The romantic ideal also fired the imaginations of judges in the capillaries of the legal system, the sites of the everyday administration of justice described in *The Federalist* as "the great cement of society." A longtime District of Columbia Superior Court judge, Sylvia Bacon, told the American Society for Public Administration that "There is a sense among judges that there are wrongs to be righted and that it is their responsibility to do it." As for the role of the Constitution and the law in guiding the judge's sense of right and wrong, Judge Bacon brusquely remarked: "Legal reasons are often just a cover for a ruling in equity (basic fairness)."

By "fairness," Judge Bacon apparently did not mean anything so prosaic as keeping an open mind to the arguments, and applying the relevant law without regard to the identity of the litigants and without regard to a particular outcome. Her notion was more visceral: "Plain and simple sense of outrage by the judge." Such views were no impediment to Judge Bacon's election to a seat on the American Bar Association's board of governors in the 1980's.

Yet they would have been anathema to the Founders, for whom impartiality was the *sine qua non* of judicial justice. Massachusetts, adopting John Adams's words, built the concept into its Bill of Rights:

> It is essential to the preservation of the rights of every individual, his life, liberty, property, and character, that there be an impartial interpretation of the laws, and administration of justice. It is the right of every citizen to be tried by judges as free, impartial, and independent as the lot of humanity will admit.

From the early years of the Republic to the present day, every American judge has taken a vow to carry out his duties without fear or favor:

> I do solemnly swear that I will administer justice without respect to persons, do equal right to the poor and to the rich, and that I will impartially discharge and perform all the duties incumbent upon me, according to the best of my abilities and understanding agreeably to the Constitution and laws of the United States, so help me God.

Some critics of the world view implicit in this oath say that judging "without respect to persons" can lead to inhumane results by ignoring important differences—between men and women, rich and poor, black and white, strong and weak. If the critics had their way, the oath would be revised to read something like this:

> I affirm that I will administer justice with careful attention to the individual characteristics of the parties, that I will show compassion to those I deem disadvantaged, and that I will discharge my duties according to my personal understanding of the Constitution, the laws of the United States, and such higher laws as may be revealed to me.

Besides, the critics observe, impartiality is often just a mask covering various sorts of bias. They point to historical research that has found more than a little clay on the feet of classical idols. It may well have been Holmes's obnoxious eugenic views, for example, rather than his vaunted restraint, that prompted him to uphold a state statute providing for the forced sterilization of mental patients—with the cruel comment that "three generations of imbeciles are enough."

But are judicial compassion and responsiveness viable substitutes for the elusive ideal of impartiality? Few would dispute that judges should be able to empathize with the people who come before them. But in the early years of this century, adventurous judges were extremely tender-hearted toward big business, while showing little compassion for women and children working long hours in factories.

❧❦❧

Let us acknowledge that until someone figures out how to make judges from other than human material, neither classical nor romantic feet will be a pretty sight. The real question, then, is which judicial attributes, systematically culti-vated, offer the most protection against arbitrariness and bias.

Whatever one may conclude about the right mix of qualities for the spe-cial circumstances of the Supreme Court, it is hard to imagine that the routine administration of justice can benefit from an increase of compassion at the expense of impartiality. A close-knit, relatively homogeneous community can perhaps get along with a system where village elders reach decisions on the ba-sis of their personal sense of fairness and their informed concern for the parties and the community. But that pastoral model cannot serve for an ethnically and ideologically diverse nation where litigants are strangers to the judge and often to each other. Under such conditions, the liberties and fortunes of citizens can-not be left to the mercy of each judge's personal sense of what procedures are fair, what outcome is just, who needs protection, and who deserves compassion.

In constitutional cases, romantic judging also exacts a toll on the demo-cratic elements in our form of government. When Warren and Burger Court majorities converted the Constitution's safety valves (the Bill of Rights, due process, equal protection) into engines with judges at the controls, they wreaked havoc with grass-roots politics. The dismal failures of many local authorities in dealing with racial issues became pretexts for depriving citizens everywhere of the power to experiment with new approaches to a wide range of problems that often take different forms in different parts of the coun-try. Constitutional provisions designed to protect individuals and minorities against majoritarian excesses were increasingly used to block the normal pro-cesses through which citizens build coalitions, develop consensus, hammer out compromises, try out new ideas, learn from mistakes, and try again.

Elected officials have offered little resistance to judicial inroads on their powers. On hot issues, they often are only too happy to be taken off the hook by the courts. But each time a court sets aside an action of the polit-ical branches through free-wheeling interpretation, self-government suffers a setback. Political skills atrophy. People cease to take citizenship seriously. Citi-zens with diverse points of view lose the habit of cooperating to set conditions under which all can flourish. Adversarial legalism supplants the sober legalistic spirit that, in the 19th century, Alexis de Tocqueville admired in the American people. For, as Abraham Lincoln warned,

> if the policy of the government, upon vital questions, affecting the whole people, is to be irrevocably fixed by decisions of the Supreme Court, ... the people will have ceased to be their own rulers, having, to that extent, practically resigned their government into the hands of that eminent tribunal.

❧

In retrospect, one can see that the rise of bold judging proceeded for the most part with good intentions. Earlier in the century, state-court judges often had to take the initiative to keep judge-made law abreast of social and economic changes. In the wake of the New Deal, federal judges had to improvise techniques for dealing with regulatory law. Then in *Brown*—and also in the one-man, one-vote cases—the Supreme Court had to exercise statesmanship in addressing legal aspects of the country's most pressing social problems.

The achievements of gifted judges in meeting those challenges made it difficult for some of them—as well as for their less capable colleagues—to resist the impulse to keep on doing justice by their own lights. That those lights were not always powered by authoritative sources was easy to disguise, even from themselves. It was a case of successes leading to temptations, of a good thing taken to extremes.

In finding our way back from these extremes, the beginning of wisdom is to recognize that, whatever the pros and cons of adventurous judging by the Supreme Court on momentous occasions, romantic ideals are a poor guide to how judges throughout the system should comport themselves as a general matter. The unique political role of the nation's highest court may require its members at times to show the sorts of excellence that are traditionally associated with executives or legislators—energy, leadership, boldness. But, day in and day out, those qualities are no substitute for the ordinary heroism of sticking to one's last, of demonstrating impartiality, interpretive skill, and responsibility toward authoritative sources in the regular administration of justice.

As things now stand in the topsy-turvy world of legal journalism, however, a judge will win no plaudits for such heroism, and may even earn contempt for not being interesting enough. When Byron White stepped down from the Supreme Court in 1993, the *New Republic*'s cover story called him "a perfect cipher." Admitting that White was "a first-rate legal technician," a writer for that magazine sneered at him for being "uninterested in articulating a constitutional vision." To this writer, it was evidence of White's "mediocrity" that he was hard to classify as a liberal or a conservative.

What made White hard to classify, of course, were the very qualities that made him an able and conscientious judge—his independence and his faithfulness to a modest conception of the judicial role. His "vision," implicit in nearly every one of his opinions, was not that difficult to discern. As summed up by a former clerk, it was one

> in which the democratic process predominates over the judicial; [and] the role of the Court or any individual Justice is not to promote particular ide-ologies, but to decide cases in a pragmatic way that permits the political branches to shoulder primary responsibility for governing our society.... The purpose of an opinion... is quite simply to decide the case in an intel-lectually and analytically sound manner.

Though White's competence, independence, and integrity did not make for lively copy, he was a model of modern neoclassical judging. As for the fu-ture, it is heartening that White's replacement, Ruth Bader Ginsburg, took the occasion of a speech shortly after her appointment to embrace the model of the "good judge" as represented by Learned Hand. Quoting Hand's biographer, Justice Ginsburg said:

> The good judge is "open-minded and detached... heedful of limitations stemming from the judge's own competence and, above all, from the pre-suppositions of our constitutional scheme; [the good] judge... recognizes that a felt need to act only interstitially does not mean relegation of judges to a trivial or mechanical role, but rather affords the most responsible room for creative, important judicial contributions."

As Justice Ginsburg's former colleague Robert Bork has observed, the key check on judicial authoritarianism will always be the judge's own understand-ing of the scope and limits of judicial power—and the insistence of a vigilant citizenry on having judges who will resist the temptation to remake the consti-tutional design for government and who will wholeheartedly comply with the judicial oath's promise to do equal justice without respect to persons.

# POSTSCRIPT

## Should Judges Read Their Moral Views into the Constitution?

$A$t some point, every critic of the moralistic judicial activism advocated by Dworkin must take a stand on the case *Brown v. Board of Education* (1954), which struck down state-imposed racial discrimination. The *Brown* Court did so by taking an extremely broad interpretation of the Fourteenth Amendment's "equal protection" clause, an interpretation that (as Dworkin concedes) far exceeded the apparent intentions of the Framers. Yet who today would say that the *Brown* decision was wrong? Glendon herself admits that it greatly advanced the cause of racial justice. Her concern is that it may have tempted jurists to go even further, continually stretching the Constitution to make it fit their own moral views.

Glendon argues some of her points at greater length in *A Nation Under Lawyers: How the Crisis in the Legal Profession Is Transforming American Society* (Farrar, Straus, & Giroux, 1994), as does Dworkin in *Freedom's Law: The Moral Reading of the American Constitution* (Harvard University Press, 1996). Three recent books provide accounts of factional and personal fights inside the Supreme Court: Phillip J. Cooper's *Battles on the Bench: Conflict Inside the Supreme Court* (University of Kansas Press, 1995) illuminates battles behind the scenes in the Court since John Marshall's time; James F. Simon's *The Center Holds: The Power Struggle Inside the Rehnquist Court* (Simon & Schuster, 1995) celebrates the defeat of "conservatives" on the Rehnquist Court; and Bernard Schwartz, in *Decision: How the Supreme Court Decides Cases* (Oxford University Press, 1996), relies on cases and anecdotes to reveal what goes on behind the scenes when the Supreme Court justices deliberate.

Glendon quotes with approval this famous quip of Justice Oliver Wendell Holmes: "About 75 years ago I learned that I was not God." Yet, for better or worse, Supreme Court justices have to act as if they *were* mortal gods. They have come to be designated the final interpreters of the Constitution's meaning. Even if the Court decides to leave a decision to one of the other branches or levels of government, that itself is a decision, one with possibly momentous consequences. The justices, then, cannot escape their responsibility by renouncing it.

# On the Internet ...

## American Studies Web

This eclectic site provides links to a wealth of Internet resources for research in American studies, including agriculture and rural development, government, and race and ethnicity.

http://www.georgetown.edu/crossroads/asw/

## The Written Word

This is an online journal of economic, political, and social commentary, primarily from a center or left-of-center viewpoint. The site provides links to governmental and political Web resources.

http://www.mdle.com/WrittenWord/

## Policy Digest Archives

Through this site of the National Center for Policy Analysis, access discussions on an array of topics that are of major interest in the study of American government, from regulatory policy and privatization to economy and income.

http://www.public-policy.org/~ncpa/pd/pdindex.html

## The Henry L. Stimson Center

The Henry L. Stimson Center, a nonprofit and (self-described) nonpartisan organization, focuses on issues where policy, technology, and politics intersect. Use this site to find assessments of U.S. foreign and domestic policy and other topics.

http://www.stimson.org

## RAND

RAND is a nonprofit institution that works to improve public policy through research and analysis. Links offered on this home page provide for keyword searches of certain topics and descriptions of RAND activities and major research areas.

http://www.rand.org

# PART 3

# Social Change and Public Policy

*F*ew topics are more emotional and divisive than those that involve so-cial morality. Whatever consensus once existed on such issues as capital punishment, abortion, and equality of opportunity, that consensus has been shattered in recent years as Americans have lined up very clearly on opposing sides—and what is more important, they have taken those competing views into Congress, state legislatures, and the courts.

The issues in this section generate intense emotions because they ask us to clarify our values on a number of very personal concerns.

- Is Capital Punishment Justified?

- Do We Need Tougher Gun Control Laws?

- Does Affirmative Action Advance the Cause of Racial Equality?

- Should Hate Speech Be Punished?

- Does the Religious Right Threaten American Freedoms?

- Would "School Choice" Improve the Quality of U.S. Education?

- Is Welfare Reform Succeeding?

- Is Socioeconomic Inequality Increasing in America?

- Should Abortion Be Restricted?

- Should Gay Marriage Be Legalized?

- Are Americans Taxed Too Much?

# ISSUE 8

# Is Capital Punishment Justified?

**YES: Robert W. Lee**, from "Deserving to Die," *The New American* (August 13, 1990)

**NO: Eric M. Freedman**, from "The Case Against the Death Penalty," *USA Today Magazine* (March 1997)

### ISSUE SUMMARY

**YES:** Essayist Robert W. Lee argues that capital punishment is the only fair way for society to respond to certain heinous crimes.

**NO:** Law professor Eric M. Freedman contends that the death penalty does not reduce crime but does reduce public safety and carries the risk of innocent people being executed.

From 1995 through 1999, 373 inmates were executed in the United States, and at the beginning of 2000, 3,652 more were on death row. The numbers are small relative to the murder rate during those years, but the issue of capital punishment remains bitterly divisive.

Polls have shown that somewhat more than half of all Americans approve of capital punishment. If a shift in opinion is taking place, it is in response to the concern that innocent people may be executed in error. In 2000 Illinois governor George Ryan, who supports the death penalty, announced a moratorium on executions because he believed that the state's criminal justice system, in which 13 death row inmates had been exonerated since 1987, was "fraught with error." In Texas, where one-third of the executions in America have taken place in recent years (127 from 1995 through 1999), Governor George W. Bush expressed confidence that every person executed in that state was guilty.

Capital punishment is an ancient penalty, but both the definition of a capital crime and the methods used to put convicted persons to death have changed dramatically. In eighteenth-century Massachusetts, for example, capital crimes included blasphemy and the worship of false gods. Slave states often imposed the death penalty upon blacks for crimes that were punished by only two or three years' imprisonment when committed by whites. It has been estimated that in the twentieth century approximately 10 percent of all legal executions

134

have been for the crime of rape, 1 percent for all other crimes except murder (robbery, burglary, attempted murder, etc.), and nearly 90 percent for the commission of murder.

Long before the Supreme Court severely limited the use of the death penalty, executions in the United States were becoming increasingly rare. In the 1930s there were 1,667; the total for the 1950s was 717. In the 1960s the numbers fell even more dramatically. For example, seven persons were executed in 1965, one in 1966, and two in 1967.

Then came the Supreme Court case *Furman v. Georgia* (1972), which many thought—mistakenly—"abolished" capital punishment in America. Actually, only two members of the *Furman* majority thought that capital punishment *per se* violates the Eighth Amendment's injunction against "cruel and unusual punishment." The other three members of the majority took the view that capital punishment is unconstitutional only when applied in an arbitrary or racially discriminatory manner, as they believed it was in this case. The four dissenters in the *Furman* case were prepared to uphold capital punishment both in general and in this particular instance. Not surprisingly, then, with a slight change of Court personnel—and with a different case before the Court—a few years later, the majority vote went the other way.

In the latter case, *Gregg v. Georgia* (1976), the majority upheld capital punishment under certain circumstances. In his majority opinion in the case, Justice Potter Stewart noted that the law in question (a new Georgia capital punishment statute) went to some lengths to avoid arbitrary procedures in capital cases. For example, Georgia courts were not given complete discretion in handing out death sentences to convicted murderers but had to consult a series of guidelines spelling out "aggravating circumstances," such as if the murder had been committed by someone already convicted of murder, if the murder endangered the lives of bystanders, and if the murder was committed in the course of a major felony. These guidelines, Stewart said, together with other safeguards against arbitrariness included in the new statute, preserved it against Eighth Amendment challenges.

Although the Court has upheld the constitutionality of the death penalty, it can always be abolished by state legislatures. However, that seems unlikely to happen in many states. If anything, the opposite is occurring. Almost immediately after the *Furman* decision of 1972, state legislatures began enacting new death penalty statutes designed to meet the objections raised in the case. By the time of the *Gregg* decision, 35 new death penalty statutes had been enacted.

In response to the public mood, Congress has put its own death penalty provisions into federal legislation. In 1988 Congress sanctioned the death penalty for drug kingpins convicted of intentionally killing or ordering anyone's death. More recently, in the 1994 crime bill, Congress authorized the death penalty for dozens of existing or new federal crimes, such as treason or the murder of a federal law enforcement agent.

In the following selections, Robert W. Lee argues that capital punishment is an appropriate form of retribution for certain types of heinous offenses, while Eric M. Freedman asserts that the practice of capital punishment fails every practical and moral test that may be applied to it.

**Robert W. Lee**

 **YES**

# Deserving to Die

$A$key issue in the debate over capital punishment is whether or not it is an effective deterrent to violent crime. In at least one important respect, it un-questionably is: It simply cannot be contested that a killer, once executed, is forever deterred from killing again. The deterrent effect on others, however, depends largely on how swiftly and surely the penalty is applied. Since capital punishment has not been used with any consistency over the years, it is vir-tually impossible to evaluate its deterrent effect accurately. Abolitionists claim that a lack of significant difference between the murder rates for states with and without capital punishment proves that the death penalty does not deter. But the states with the death penalty on their books have used it so little over the years as to preclude any meaningful comparison between states. Through July 18, 1990 there had been 134 executions since 1976. Only 14 states (less than 40 percent of those that authorize the death penalty) were involved. Any punish-ment, including death, will cease to be an effective deterrent if it is recognized as mostly bluff. Due to costly delays and endless appeals, the death penalty has been largely turned into a paper tiger by the same crowd that calls for its abolition on the grounds that it is not an effective deterrent!

To allege that capital punishment, if imposed consistently and without undue delay, would not be a deterrent to crime is, in essence, to say that people are not afraid of dying. If so, as columnist Jenkin Lloyd Jones once observed, then warning signs reading "Slow Down," "Bridge Out," and "Danger—40,000 Volts" are futile relics of an age gone by when men feared death. To be sure, the death penalty could never become a 100-percent deterrent to heinous crime, because the fear of death varies among individuals. Some race automobiles, climb mountains, parachute jump, walk circus high-wires, ride Brahma bulls in rodeos, and otherwise engage in endeavors that are more than normally haz-ardous. But, as author Bernard Cohen notes in his book *Law and Order*, "there are even more people who refrain from participating in these activities mainly because risking their lives is not to their taste."

From Robert W. Lee, "Deserving to Die," *The New American* (August 13, 1990). Copyright © 1990 by *The New American*. Reprinted by permission.

# Merit System

On occasion, circumstances *have* led to meaningful statistical evaluations of the death penalty's deterrent effect. In Utah, for instance, there have been three executions since the Supreme Court's 1976 ruling:

- Gary Gilmore faced a firing squad at the Utah State Prison on January 17, 1977. There had been 55 murders in the Beehive State during 1976 (4.5 per 100,000 population). During 1977, in the wake of the Gilmore execution, there were 44 murders (3.5 per 100,000), a 20 percent decrease.

- More than a decade later, on August 28, 1987, Pierre Dale Selby (one of the two infamous "hi-fi killers" who in 1974 forced five persons in an Ogden hi-fi shop to drink liquid drain cleaner, kicked a ballpoint pen into the ear of one, then killed three) was executed. During all of 1987, there were 54 murders (3.2 per 100,000). The count for January through August was 38 (a monthly average of 4.75). For September–December (in the aftermath of the Selby execution) there were 16 (4.0 per month, a nearly 16 percent decrease). For July and August there were six and seven murders, respectively. In September (the first month following Selby's demise) there were three.

- Arthur Gary Bishop, who sodomized and killed a number of young boys, was executed on June 10, 1988. For all of 1988 there were 47 murders (2.7 per 100,000, the fewest since 1977). During January–June, there were 26; for July–December (after the Bishop execution) the tally was 21 (a 19 percent difference).

In the wake of all three Utah executions, there have been notable decreases in both the number and the rate of murders within the state. To be sure, there are other variables that could have influenced the results, but the figures are there and abolitionists to date have tended simply to ignore them.

Deterrence should never be considered the *primary* reason for administering the death penalty. It would be both immoral and unjust to punish one man merely as an example to others. The basic consideration should be: Is the punishment deserved? If not, it should not be administered regardless of what its deterrent impact might be. After all, once deterrence supersedes justice as the basis for a criminal sanction, the guilt or innocence of the accused becomes largely irrelevant. Deterrence can be achieved as effectively by executing an innocent person as a guilty one (something that communists and other totalitarians discovered long ago). If a punishment administered to one person deters someone else from committing a crime, fine. But that result should be viewed as a bonus of justice properly applied, not as a reason for the punishment. The decisive consideration should be: Has the accused *earned* the penalty?

# The Cost of Execution

The exorbitant financial expense of death penalty cases is regularly cited by abolitionists as a reason for abolishing capital punishment altogether. They prefer to ignore, however, the extent to which they themselves are responsible for the interminable legal maneuvers that run up the costs....

As presently pursued, death-penalty prosecutions *are* outrageously expensive. But, again, the cost is primarily due to redundant appeals, time-consuming delays, bizarre court rulings, and legal histrionics by defense attorneys:

> Willie Darden, who had already survived three death warrants, was scheduled to die in Florida's electric chair on September 4, 1985 for a murder he had committed in 1973. Darden's lawyer made a last-minute emergency appeal to the Supreme Court, which voted against postponing the execution until a formal appeal could be filed. So the attorney (in what he later described as "last-minute ingenuity") then requested that the emergency appeal be technically transformed into a formal appeal. Four Justices agreed (enough to force the full court to review the appeal) and the execution was stayed. After additional years of delay and expense, Darden was eventually put out of our misery on March 15, 1988.

> Ronald Gene Simmons killed 14 members of his family during Christmas week in 1987. He was sentenced to death, said he was willing to die, and refused to appeal. But his scheduled March 16, 1989 execution was delayed when a fellow inmate, also on death row, persuaded the Supreme Court to block it (while Simmons was having what he expected to be his last meal) on the grounds that the execution could have repercussions for other death-row inmates. It took the Court until April 24th of [1990] to reject that challenge. Simmons was executed on June 25th.

> Robert Alton Harris was convicted in California of the 1978 murders of two San Diego teenagers whose car he wanted for a bank robbery. Following a seemingly interminable series of appeals, he was at last sentenced to die on April 3rd of [1990]. Four days earlier, a 9th U.S. Circuit Court of Appeals judge stayed the execution, largely on the claim that Harris was brain-damaged and therefore may possibly have been unable to "premeditate" the murders (as required under California law for the death penalty). On April 10th, the *Washington Times* reported that the series of tests used to evaluate Harris's condition had been described by some experts as inaccurate and "a hoax."

The psychiatric game is being played for all it is worth. On May 14th, Harris's attorneys argued before the 9th Circuit Court that he should be spared the death penalty because he received "inadequate" psychiatric advice during his original trial. In 1985, the Supreme Court had ruled that a defendant has a constitutional right to "a competent psychiatrist who will conduct an appropriate examination." Harris had access to a licensed psychiatrist, but now argues that—since the recent (highly questionable) evaluations indicated brain damage and other alleged disorders that the original psychiatrist failed to detect (and which may have influenced the jury not to impose the death sentence)—a new trial (or at least a re-sentencing) is in order. If the courts buy this argument, hundreds (perhaps thousands) of cases could be reopened for psychiatric challenge.

On April 2, 1974 William Neal Moore shot and killed a man in Georgia. Following his arrest, he pleaded guilty to armed robbery and murder and was convicted and sentenced to death. On July 20, 1975 the Georgia Supreme Court denied his petition for review. On July 16, 1976 the U.S. Supreme Court denied his petition for review. On May 13, 1977 the Jefferson County Superior Court turned down a petition for a new sentencing hearing (the state Supreme Court affirmed the denial, and the U.S. Supreme Court again denied a review). On March 30, 1978 a Tattnall County Superior Court judge held a hearing on a petition alleging sundry grounds for a writ of *habeas corpus,* but declined on July 13, 1978 to issue a writ. On October 17, 1978 the state Supreme Court declined to review that ruling. Moore petitioned the U.S. District Court for Southern Georgia. After a delay of more than two years, a U.S. District Court judge granted the writ on April 29, 1981. After another two-year delay, the 11th U.S. Circuit Court of Appeals upheld the writ on June 23, 1983. On September 30, 1983 the Circuit Court reversed itself and ruled that the writ should be denied. On March 5, 1984 the Supreme Court rejected the case for the third time.

Moore's execution was set for May 24, 1984. On May 11, 1984 his attorneys filed a petition in Butts County Superior Court, but a writ was denied. The same petition was filed in the U.S. District Court for Georgia's Southern District on May 18th, but both a writ and a stay of execution were denied. Then, on May 23rd (the day before the scheduled execution) the 11th Circuit Court of Appeals granted a stay. On June 4, 1984 a three-judge panel of the Circuit Court voted to deny a writ. After another delay of more than three years, the Circuit Court voted 7 to 4 to override its three-judge panel and rule in Moore's favor. On April 18, 1988, the Supreme Court accepted the case. On April 17, 1989 it sent the case back to the 11th Circuit Court for review in light of new restrictions that the High Court had placed on *habeas corpus.* On September 28, 1989 the Circuit Court ruled 6 to 5 that Moore had abused the writ process. On December 18, 1989 Moore's attorneys again appealed to the Supreme Court.

Moore's case was described in detail in *Insight* magazine for February 12, 1990. By the end of [1989] his case had gone through 20 separate court reviews, involving some 118 state and federal judges. It had been to the Supreme Court and back four times. There had been a substantial turnover of his attorneys, creating an excuse for one team of lawyers to file a petition claiming that all of the prior attorneys had given ineffective representation. No wonder capital cases cost so much!

Meanwhile, the American Bar Association proposes to make matters even worse by requiring states (as summarized by *Insight*) "to appoint two lawyers for every stage of the proceeding, require them to have past death penalty experience and pay them at 'reasonable' rates to be set by the court."

During an address to the American Law Institute on May 16, 1990, Chief Justice Rehnquist asserted that the "system at present verges on the chaotic" and "cries out for reform." The time expended between sentencing and execution, he declared, "is consumed not by structured review ... but in fits of frantic action followed by periods of inaction." He urged that death row inmates be given one chance to challenge their sentences in state courts, and one challenge in federal courts, period.

# Lifetime to Escape

Is life imprisonment an adequate substitute for the death penalty? Presently, according to the polls, approximately three-fourths of the American people favor capital punishment. But abolitionists try to discount that figure by claiming that support for the death penalty weakens when life imprisonment without the possibility of parole is offered as an alternative. (At other times, abolitionists argue that parole is imperative to give "lifers" some hope for the future and deter their violent acts in prison.)

Life imprisonment is a flawed alternative to the death penalty, if for no other reason than that so many "lifers" escape. Many innocent persons have died at the hands of men previously convicted and imprisoned for murder, supposedly for "life." The ways in which flaws in our justice system, combined with criminal ingenuity, have worked to allow "lifers" to escape include these recent examples:

- On June 10, 1977, James Earl Ray, who was serving a 99-year term for killing Dr. Martin Luther King Jr., escaped with six other inmates from the Brushy Mountain State Prison in Tennessee (he was captured three days later).
- Brothers Linwood and James Briley were executed in Virginia on October 12, 1984 and April 18, 1985, respectively. Linwood had murdered a disc jockey in 1979 during a crime spree. During the same spree, James raped and killed a woman (who was eight months pregnant) and killed her five-year-old son. On May 31, 1984, the Briley brothers organized and led an escape of five death-row inmates (the largest death-row breakout in U.S. history). They were at large for 19 days.

- On August 1, 1984 convicted murderers Wesley Allen Tuttle and Walter Wood, along with another inmate, escaped from the Utah State Prison. All were eventually apprehended. Wood subsequently sued the state for $2 million for violating his rights by allowing him to escape. In his complaint, he charged that, by allowing him to escape, prison officials had subjected him to several life-threatening situations: "Because of extreme fear of being shot to death, I was forced to swim several irrigation canals, attempt to swim a 'raging' Jordan River and expose myself to innumerable bites by many insects. At one point I heard a volley of shotgun blasts and this completed my anxiety."

- On April 3, 1988 three murderers serving life sentences without the chance of parole escaped from the maximum-security West Virginia Penitentiary. One, Bobby Stacy, had killed a Huntington police officer in 1981. At the time, he had been free on bail after having been arrested for shooting an Ohio patrolman.

- On November 21, 1988 Gonzalo Marrero, who had been convicted of two murders and sentenced to two life terms, escaped from New Jersey's Trenton state prison by burrowing through a three-foot-thick cell wall, then scaling a 20-foot outer wall with a makeshift ladder.

- In August 1989 Arthur Carroll, a self-proclaimed enforcer for an East Oakland street gang, was convicted of murdering a man. On September 28th, he was sentenced to serve 27-years-to-life in prison. On October 10th he was transferred to San Quentin prison. On October 25th he was set free after a paperwork snafu led officials to believe that he had served enough time. An all-points bulletin was promptly issued.

- On February 11, 1990 six convicts, including three murderers, escaped from their segregation cells in the maximum security Joliet Correctional Center in Illinois by cutting through bars on their cells, breaking a window, and crossing a fence. In what may be the understatement of the year, a prison spokesman told reporters: "Obviously, this is a breach of security."

Clearly, life sentences do not adequately protect society, whereas the death penalty properly applied does so with certainty.

# Equal Opportunity Execution

Abolitionists often cite statistics indicating that capital punishment has been administered in a discriminatory manner, so that the poor, the black, the friendless, etc., have suffered a disproportionate share of executions. Even if true, such discrimination would not be a valid reason for abandoning the death penalty unless it could be shown that it was responsible for the execution of *innocent* persons (which it has not been, to date). Most attempts to pin the "discrimination" label on capital convictions are similar to one conducted at Stanford University a few years ago, which found that murderers of white people (whether white or black) are more likely to be punished with death than are killers of black people (whether white or black). But the study also concluded that blacks who murdered whites were somewhat *less* likely to receive death sentences than were whites who killed whites.

Using such data, the ACLU attempted to halt the execution of Chester Lee Wicker in Texas on August 26, 1986. Wicker, who was white, had killed a white person. The ACLU contended that Texas unfairly imposes the death penalty because a white is more likely than a black to be sentenced to death for killing a white. The Supreme Court rejected the argument. On the other hand, the execution of Willie Darden in Florida attracted worldwide pleas for amnesty from sundry abolitionists who, ignoring the Stanford study, claimed that Darden had been "railroaded" because he was black and his victim was white.

All criminal laws—in all countries, throughout all human history—have tended to be administered in an imperfect and uneven manner. As a result, some elements in society have been able to evade justice more consistently than others. But why should the imperfect administration of justice persuade us to abandon any attempt to attain it?

The most flagrant example of discrimination in the administration of the death penalty does not involve race, income, or social status, but gender. Women commit around 13 percent of the murders in America, yet, from 1930 to June 30, 1990, only 33 of the 3991 executions (less than 1 percent) involved women. Only one of the 134 persons executed since 1976 (through July 18th [1990]) has been a woman (Velma Barfield in North Carolina on November 2, 1984). One state governor commuted the death sentence of a woman because "humanity does not apply to women the inexorable law that it does to men."

According to L. Kay Gillespie, professor of sociology at Weber State College in Utah, evidence indicates that women who cried during their trials had a better chance of getting away with murder and avoiding the death penalty. Perhaps the National Organization for Women can do something about this glaring example of sexist "inequality" and "injustice." In the meantime, we shall continue to support the death penalty despite the disproportionate number of men who have been required to pay a just penalty for their heinous crimes.

## Forgive and Forget?

Another aspect of the death penalty debate is the extent to which justice should be tempered by mercy in the case of killers. After all, abolitionists argue, is it not the duty of Christians to forgive those who trespass against them? In Biblical terms, the most responsible sources to extend mercy and forgiveness are (1) God and (2) the victim of the injustice. In the case of murder, so far as *this* world is concerned, the victim is no longer here to extend mercy and forgiveness. Does the state or any other earthly party have the right or authority to intervene and tender mercy on behalf of a murder victim? In the anthology *Essays on the Death Penalty,* the Reverend E. L. H. Taylor clarifies the answer this way: "Now it is quite natural and proper for a man to forgive something you do to *him.* Thus if somebody cheats me out of $20.00 it is quite possible and reasonable for me to say, 'Well, I forgive him, we will say no more about it.' But what would you say if somebody had done you out of $20.00 and I said, 'That's all right. I forgive him on your behalf'?"

The point is simply that there is no way, in *this* life, for a murderer to be reconciled to his victim, and secure the victim's forgiveness. This leaves the civil authority with no other responsible alternative but to adopt *justice* as the standard for assigning punishment in such cases.

Author Bernard Cohen raises an interesting point: " ... if it is allowable to deprive a would-be murderer of his life, in order to forestall his attack, why is it wrong to take away his life after he has successfully carried out his dastardly business?" Does anyone question the right of an individual to kill an assailant should it be necessary to preserve his or her life or that of a loved one?

Happily, however, both scripture and our legal system uphold the morality and legality of taking the life of an assailant, if necessary, *before* he kills us. How, then, can it be deemed immoral for civil authority to take his life *after* he kills us?

## Intolerant Victims?

Sometimes those who defend the death penalty are portrayed as being "intolerant." But isn't one of our real problems today that Americans are *too tolerant* of evil? Are we not accepting acts of violence, cruelty, lying, and immorality with all too little righteous indignation? Such indignation is not, as some would have us believe, a form of "hatred." In *Reflections on the Psalms,* C. S. Lewis discussed the supposed spirit of "hatred" that some critics claimed to see in parts of the Psalms: "Such hatreds are the kind of thing that cruelty and injustice, by a sort of natural law, produce.... Not to perceive it at all—not even to be tempted to resentment—to accept it as the most ordinary thing in the world—argues a terrifying insensibility. Thus the absence of anger, especially that sort of anger which we call indignation, can, in my opinion, be a most alarming symptom."

When mass murderer Ted Bundy was executed in Florida on January 24, 1989, a crowd of some 2000 spectators gathered across from the prison to cheer and celebrate. Many liberal commentators were appalled. Some contended that it was a spectacle on a par with Bundy's own callous disrespect for human life. One headline read: "Exhibition witnessed outside prison was more revolting than execution." What nonsense! As C. S. Lewis observed in his commentary on the Psalms: "If the Jews cursed more bitterly than the Pagans this was, I think, at least in part because they took right and wrong more seriously." It is long past time for us all to being taking right and wrong more seriously....

## Seeds of Anarchy

As we have seen, most discussions of the death penalty tend to focus on whether it should exist for murder or be abolished altogether. The issue should be reframed so that the question instead becomes whether or not it should be imposed for certain terrible crimes in addition to murder (such as habitual law-breaking, clearly proven cases of rape, and monstrous child abuse).

In 1953 the renowned British jurist Lord Denning asserted: "Punishment is the way in which society expresses its denunciation of wrongdoing; and in order to maintain respect for law, it is essential that the punishment for grave crimes shall adequately reflect the revulsion felt by a great majority of citizens for them." Nineteen years later, U.S. Supreme Court Justice Potter Stewart noted (while nevertheless concurring in the Court's 1972 opinion that temporarily banned capital punishment) that the "instinct for retribution is part of the nature of man and channeling that instinct in the administration of criminal justice serves an important purpose in promoting the stability of a society governed by law. When people begin to believe that organized society is unwilling or unable to impose upon criminal offenders the punishment they 'deserve,' then there are sown the seeds of anarchy—of self-help, vigilante justice, and lynch law."

To protect the innocent and transfer the fear and burden of crime to the criminal element where it belongs, we must demand that capital punishment be imposed when justified and expanded to cover terrible crimes in addition to murder.

# NO ↩

Eric M. Freedman

# The Case Against the Death Penalty

On Sept. 1, 1995, New York rejoined the ranks of states imposing capital punishment. Although the first death sentence has yet to be imposed, an overwhelming factual record from around the country makes the consequence of this action easily predictable: New Yorkers will get less crime control than they had before.

Anyone whose public policy goals are to provide a criminal justice system that delivers swift, accurate, and evenhanded results—and to reduce the number of crimes that actually threaten most people in their daily lives—should be a death penalty opponent. The reason is simple: The death penalty not only is useless in itself, but counterproductive to achieving those goals. It wastes enormous resources—fiscal and moral—on a tiny handful of cases, to the detriment of measures that might have a significant impact in improving public safety.

Those who believe the death penalty somehow is an emotionally satisfying response to horrific crimes should ask themselves whether they wish to adhere to that initial reaction in light of the well-documented facts:

*Fact: The death penalty does not reduce crime.*

Capital punishment proponents sometimes assert that it simply is logical to think that the death penalty is a deterrent. Whether or not the idea is logical, it is not true, an example of the reality that many intuitively obvious propositions—*e.g.*, that a heavy ball will fall faster if dropped from the Leaning Tower of Pisa than a light one—are factually false.

People who commit capital murders generally do not engage in probability analysis concerning the likelihood of getting the death penalty if they are caught. They may be severely mentally disturbed people like Ted Bundy, who chose Florida for his final crimes *because* it had a death penalty.

Whether one chooses to obtain data from scholarly studies, the evidence of long-term experience, or accounts of knowledgeable individuals, he or she

From Eric M. Freedman, "The Case Against the Death Penalty," *USA Today Magazine* (March 1997). Copyright © 1997 by The Society for the Advancement of Education. Reprinted by permission.

145

will search in vain for empirical support for the proposition that imposing the death penalty cuts the crime rate. Instead, that person will find:

- The question of the supposed deterrent effect of capital punishment is perhaps the single most studied issue in the social sciences. The results are as unanimous as scholarly studies can be in finding the death penalty not to be a deterrent.
- Eighteen of the 20 states with the highest murder rates have and use the death penalty. Of the nation's 20 big cities with the highest murder rates, 17 are in death penalty jurisdictions. Between 1975 and 1985, almost twice as many law enforcement officers were killed in death penalty states as in non-death penalty states. Over nearly two decades, the neighboring states of Michigan, with no death penalty, and Indiana, which regularly imposes death sentences and carries out executions, have had virtually indistinguishable homicide rates.
- Myron Love, the presiding judge in Harris County, Tex. (which includes Houston), the county responsible for 10% of all executions in the entire country since 1976, admits that "We are not getting what I think we should be wanting and that is to deter crime.... In fact, the result is the opposite. We're having more violence, more crime."

*Fact: The death penalty is extraordinarily expensive.*

Contrary to popular intuition, a system with a death penalty is vastly more expensive than one where the maximum penalty is keeping murderers in prison for life. A 1982 New York study estimated the death penalty cost conservatively at three times that of life imprisonment, the ratio that Texas (with a system that is on the brink of collapse due to underfunding) has experienced. In Florida, each execution runs the state $3,200,000—six times the expense of life imprisonment. California has succeeded in executing just two defendants (one a volunteer) since 1976, but could save about $90,000,000 *per year* by abolishing the death penalty and re-sentencing all of its Death Row inmates to life.

In response, it often is proposed to reduce the costs by eliminating "all those endless appeals in death penalty cases." This is not a new idea. In recent years, numerous efforts have been made on the state and Federal levels to do precisely that. Their failure reflects some simple truths:

- Most of the extra costs of the death penalty are incurred prior to and at trial, not in postconviction proceedings. Trials are far more likely under a death penalty system (since there is so little incentive to plea-bargain). They have two separate phases (unlike other trials) and typically are preceded by special motions and extra jury selection questioning—steps that, if not taken before trial, most likely will result in the eventual reversal of the conviction.

- Much more investigation usually is done in capital cases, particularly by the prosecution. In New York, for instance, the office of the State Attorney General (which generally does not participate in local criminal prosecutions) is creating a new multi-lawyer unit to provide support to county district attorneys in capital cases.
- These expenses are incurred even though the outcome of most such trials is a sentence other than death and even though up to 50% of the death verdicts that are returned are reversed on the constitutionally required first appeal. Thus, the taxpayers foot the bill for all the extra costs of capital pretrial and trial proceedings and then must pay either for incarcerating the prisoner for life or the expenses of a retrial, which itself often leads to a life sentence. In short, even if all post-conviction proceedings following the first appeal were abolished, the death penalty system still would be more expensive than the alternative.

In fact, the concept of making such an extreme change in the justice system enjoys virtually no support in any political quarter. The writ of *habeas corpus* to protect against illegal imprisonment is available to every defendant in any criminal case, whether he or she is charged with being a petty thief or looting an S&L. It justly is considered a cornerstone of the American system of civil liberties. To eliminate all those "endless appeals" either would require weakening the system for everyone or differentially with respect to death penalty cases.

Giving less due process in capital cases is the opposite of what common sense and elementary justice call for and eventually could lead to innocent people being executed. Since the rate of constitutional violations is far greater in capital cases than in others—capital defendants seeking Federal *habeas corpus* relief succeed some 40% of the time, compared to a success rate of less than five percent for non-capital defendants—the idea of providing less searching review in death penalty cases is perverse.

Considering that the vast majority of post-conviction death penalty appeals arise from the inadequacies of appointed trial counsel, the most cost-effective and just way of decreasing the number of years devoted to capital proceedings, other than the best way—not enacting the death penalty—would be to provide adequate funding to the defense at the beginning of the process. Such a system, although more expensive than one without capital punishment, at least would result in some predictability. The innocent would be acquitted speedily; the less culpable would be sentenced promptly to lesser punishments; and the results of the trials of those defendants convicted and sentenced to death ordinarily would be final.

Instead, as matters now stand, there is roughly a 70% chance that a defendant sentenced to death eventually will succeed in getting the outcome set aside. The fault for this situation—which is unacceptable to the defense and prosecution bars alike—lies squarely with the states. It is they that have created the endless appeals by attempting to avoid the ineluctable monetary costs of death penalty systems and to run them on the cheap by refusing to provide adequate funding for defense counsel.

*Fact: The death penalty actually reduces public safety.*

The costs of the death penalty go far beyond the tens of millions of dollars wasted in the pursuit of a chimera. The reality is that, in a time of fixed or declining budgets, those dollars are taken away from a range of programs that would be beneficial. For example:

- New York State, due to financial constraints, can not provide bullet-proof vests for every peace officer—a project that, unlike the death penalty, certainly would save law enforcement lives.
- According to FBI statistics, the rate at which murders are solved has dropped to an all-time low. Yet, empirical studies consistently demonstrate that, as with other crimes, the murder rate decreases as the probability of detection increases. Putting money into investigative resources, rather than wasting it on the death penalty, could have a significant effect on crime.
- Despite the large percentage of ordinary street crimes that are narcotics-related, the states lack the funding to permit drug treatment on demand. The result is that people who are motivated to cure their own addictions are relegated to supporting themselves through crime, while the money that could fund treatment programs is poured down the death penalty drain.

*Fact: The death penalty is arbitrary in operation.*

Any reasonably conscientious supporter of the death penalty surely would agree with the proposition that, before someone is executed by the state, he or she first should receive the benefits of a judicial process that is as fair as humanly possible.

However, the one thing that is clear about the death penalty system that actually exists—as opposed to the idealized one some capital punishment proponents assume to exist—is that it does not provide a level of fairness which comes even close to equaling the gravity of the irreversible sanction being imposed. This failure of the system to function even reasonably well when it should be performing excellently breeds public cynicism as to how satisfactorily the system runs in ordinary, non-capital cases.

That reaction, although destructive, is understandable, because the factors that are significant in determining whether or not a particular defendant receives a death sentence have nothing at all to do with the seriousness of his or her crime. The key variables, rather, are:

- Racial discrimination in death-sentencing, which has been documented repeatedly. For instance, in the five-year period following their re-institution of the death penalty, the sentencing patterns in Georgia and Florida were as follows: when black kills white—Georgia, 20.1% (32 of 159 cases) and Florida, 13.7% (34 of 249); white kills white—Georgia, 5.7% (35 of 614) and Florida, 5.2% (80 of 1,547); white kills black—

Georgia, 2.9% (one of 34) and Florida, 4.3% (three of 69); black kills black—Georgia, 0.8% (11 of 1,310) and Florida, 0.7% (three of 69).

A fair objection may be that these statistics are too stark because they fail to take into account other neutral variables—*e.g.*, the brutality of the crime and the number and age of the victims. Nevertheless, many subsequent studies, whose validity has been confirmed in a major analysis for Congress by the General Accounting Office, have addressed these issues. They uniformly have found that, even when all other factors are held constant, the races of the victim and defendant are critical variables in determining who is sentenced to death.

Thus, black citizens are the victim of double discrimination. From initial charging decisions to plea bargaining to jury sentencing, they are treated more harshly when they are defendants, but their lives are given less value when they are victims. Moreover, all-white or virtually all-white juries still are commonplace in many places.

One common reaction to this evidence is not to deny it, but to attempt to evade the facts by taking refuge in the assertion that any effective system for guarding against racial discrimination would mean the end of the death penalty. Such a statement is a powerful admission that governments are incapable of running racially neutral capital punishment systems. The response of any fair-minded person should be that, if such is the case, governments should not be running capital punishment systems.

- Income discrimination. Most capital defendants can not afford an attorney, so the court must appoint counsel. Every major study of this issue, including those of the Powell Commission appointed by Chief Justice William Rehnquist, the American Bar Association, the Association of the Bar of the City of New York, and innumerable scholarly journals, has found that the quality of defense representation in capital murder trials generally is far lower than in felony cases.

  The field is a highly specialized one, and since the states have failed to pay the amounts necessary to attract competent counsel, there is an overwhelming record of poor people being subjected to convictions and death sentences that equally or more culpable—but more affluent—defendants would not have suffered.

- Mental disability. Jurors are more likely to sentence to death people who seem different from themselves than individuals who seem similar to themselves. That is the reality underlying the stark fact that those with mental disabilities are sentenced to death at a rate far higher than can be justified by any neutral explanation. This reflects prejudice, pure and simple.

*Fact: Capital punishment inevitably will be inflicted on the innocent.*

It is ironic that, just as New York was reinstating the death penalty, it was in the midst of a convulsive scandal involving the widespread fabrication of evidence by the New York State Police that had led to scores of people—

including some innocent ones—being convicted and sentenced to prison terms. Miscarriages of justice unquestionably will occur in any human system, but the death penalty presents two special problems in this regard:

- The arbitrary factors discussed above have an enormous negative impact on accuracy. In combination with the emotional atmosphere generally surrounding capital cases, they lead to a situation where the truth-finding process in capital cases is *less* reliable than in others. Indeed, a 1993 House of Representatives subcommittee report found 48 instances over the previous two decades in which innocent people had been sentenced to death.
- The stark reality is that death is final. A mistake can not be corrected if the defendant has been executed.

How often innocent people have been executed is difficult to quantify; once a defendant has been executed, few resources generally are devoted to the continued investigation of the case. Nonetheless, within the past few years, independent investigations by major news organizations have uncovered three cases, two in Florida and one in Mississippi, where people were put to death for crimes they did not commit. Over time, others doubtless will come to light (while still others will remain undiscovered), but it will be too late.

The fact that the system sometimes works—for those who are lucky enough to obtain somehow the legal and investigative resources or media attention necessary to vindicate their claims of innocence—does not mean that most innocent people on Death Row are equally fortunate. Moreover, many Death Row inmates who have been exonerated would have been executed if the legal system had moved more quickly, as would occur if, as those now in power in Congress have proposed, Federal *habeas corpus* is eviscerated.

The death penalty is not just useless—it is positively harmful and diverts resources from genuine crime control measures. Arbitrarily selecting out for execution not the worst criminals, but a racially determined handful of the poorest, most badly represented, least mentally healthy, and unluckiest defendants—some of whom are innocent—breeds cynicism about the entire criminal justice system.

Thus, the Criminal Justice Section of the New York State Bar Association—which includes prosecutors, judges, and defense attorneys—opposed reinstitution of the death penalty because of "the enormous cost associated with such a measure, and the serious negative impact on the delivery of prosecution and defense services throughout the state that will result." Meanwhile, Chief Justice Dixon of the Louisiana Supreme Court put it starkly: "Capital punishment is destroying the system."

# POSTSCRIPT

## Is Capital Punishment Justified?

In their arguments, Lee and Freedman cite some of the same facts and figures but draw opposite conclusions. Both, for example, note how expensive it is to keep prisoners on death row for so many years while appeals continue. Lee, however, draws from this the conclusion that appeals should be limited, while Freedman uses it to show that it costs taxpayers less to keep a felon in prison for life than to try to kill him.

Note that Lee does not rest his case for capital punishment on deterrence. He calls deterrence a "bonus" but not a primary justification. What really counts, he says, is whether or not the accused has "earned" the death penalty. For a similar argument developed at greater length, see Walter Berns, *For Capital Punishment: Crime and the Morality of the Death Penalty* (Basic Books, 1979). Directly opposed to the contention that capital punishment is moral is the view of the late judge Lois G. Forer: "Killing human beings when carried out by government as a matter of policy is, I believe, no less abhorrent than any other homicide." Forer's case against capital punishment is presented in her book *A Rage to Punish: The Unintended Consequences of Mandatory Sentencing* (W. W. Norton, 1994). For a moving account of how one condemned man was put into the electric chair *twice* (the first time the jolt was not enough to kill him) after losing a Supreme Court appeal based on "double jeopardy" and "cruel and unusual punishment," see chapter 10 of Fred W. Friendly and Martha Elliott, *The Constitution: That Delicate Balance* (Random House, 1984). *Dead Man Walking: An Eyewitness Account of the Death Penalty in the United States* by Helen Prejean (Vintage Books, 1994) is an impassioned account by a Catholic nun of her friendship with two death row inmates and her pleas for the abolition of capital punishment. Prejean makes all the expected arguments against capital punishment, but the book's power lies in her account of executions. (This story has been made into a motion picture of the same name.)

How often are innocent people convicted of crimes punishable by death? How often are these innocent people executed? In *In Spite of Innocence: Erroneous Convictions in Capital Cases* (Northeastern University Press, 1992), Michael L. Radelet, Hugo Adam Bedau, and Constance E. Putnam describe more than 400 incidents in which they contend that wrongful convictions in capital cases occurred as a result of confused eyewitness testimony, perjury, coerced confessions, or police conspiracy.

More recently, in *The Death Penalty in America: Current Controversies* (Oxford University Press, 1998), Hugo Adam Bedau has compiled essays by opposing scholars, recent Supreme Court decisions, and the status of the death penalty worldwide in a comprehensive sourcebook that touches on virtually all death penalty issues and points of view.

# ISSUE 9

## Do We Need Tougher Gun Control Laws?

**YES: Carl T. Bogus**, from "The Strong Case for Gun Control," *The American Prospect* (Summer 1992)

**NO: Daniel D. Polsby**, from "The False Promise of Gun Control," *The Atlantic Monthly* (March 1994)

### ISSUE SUMMARY

**YES:** Writer Carl T. Bogus argues that even local gun control laws will reduce the number of gun-related crimes.

**NO:** Professor of law Daniel D. Polsby contends that not only does gun control not work, it may actually increase the incidence of robbery and other gun-related crimes.

A slow but significant decline in the murder rate and violent crime in the United States generally began in 1992. By 1998 the murder rate had declined to its lowest level in three decades. But the country was in for a shocking series of gun murders by young people directed primarily at other young people in schools.

In 1998 alone, two boys, aged 11 and 13, shot at classmates and teachers from the woods in Arkansas, killing 4 students and 1 teacher and wounding 10 others during a false fire alarm; a 14-year-old boy killed a teacher and wounded 2 students at a dance at a Pennsylvania middle school; an 18-year-old killed his ex-girlfriend's new boyfriend in the parking lot of a Tennessee high school; and 15-year-old Kip Kinkel killed 2 students and wounded 22 others in an Oregon high school cafeteria. A day before the shooting, Kinkel had been arrested and released to his parents after it was discovered that he had a gun at school. His parents were later found dead in their home. The nation's deadliest school shooting took place the following year at a Colorado high school, when two students, aged 17 and 18, killed 12 students and a teacher and wounded 23 before they killed themselves.

These tragic events brought to public attention the shocking fact that in a single year more than 4,000 children are killed by guns in the United States. In May 2000 the Million Mom March brought several hundred thousand mothers and others to the Washington Mall to advocate more gun control. The demonstrators urged licensing, safety checks, and limiting purchases to one handgun per month.

What has been done? What can be done? Can gun control make a difference, or are the causes of gun violence and its reduction to be found elsewhere?

In November 1993, after seven years of wrangling, Congress finally passed the Brady Bill. For several years, James Brady, a press secretary to President Ronald Reagan who was partially paralyzed by a bullet intended for Reagan in 1981, had been heading a campaign to regulate handguns. The National Rifle Association (NRA) and other opponents of gun control had fought hard against any such legislation, and Republican presidents had largely agreed with the NRA position that the best way to curb gun violence is not to ban guns but to stiffen penalties against those who use them illegally. But President Bill Clinton threw his support behind the Brady Bill, and it was enacted by Congress.

The Brady Act, requiring a background check on potential gun purchasers, has resulted in the rejection of 100,000 prospective gun buyers, but criminals can buy weapons on the black market or abroad, obtain them in informal transactions, and steal them.

The year following passage of the Brady Act, Congress confirmed the fears of those who argued that it would be the opening wedge for more gun control. The 1994 crime act included a ban on assault weapons. An assault weapon has a magazine capable of holding many rounds that can be fired each time the trigger is pulled. The 1994 law placed a 10-year ban on the manufacture and sale of 19 types of assault weapons as well as copycat models and certain other guns with features similar to assault weapons.

Is it too late to curb gun possession in the United States? There are at least 200 million guns in private hands in the United States, and approximately one-half of all American households contain at least one gun. This has not changed much over the past 40 years, which means that most people who buy guns already own guns. In some rural areas, it is unusual for a household not to have a gun.

Advocates and opponents differ in their assessments of the consequences of gun control laws. Those supporting gun control point to Great Britain and Japan, which have very tough firearm laws and very low murder rates. Opponents respond that low murder rates in these countries result from their cultures. They point to countries like Switzerland, New Zealand, and Israel, where firearms are prevalent and murder rates are very low. Opponents also echo the National Rifle Association's argument that "guns do not kill people; people do." Supporters of gun control point out that it is harder to kill (especially large numbers of) people without guns.

In the following selections, Carl T. Bogus and Daniel D. Polsby focus on the consequences of gun control and reach opposed conclusions. Bogus presents evidence suggesting that, even with other demographic factors held nearly constant, there is less gun-related crime in areas that have gun control. Polsby argues that gun control, by keeping guns out of the hands of law-abiding citizens, may tempt criminals to a more indiscriminate use of firearms.

Carl T. Bogus  **YES**

# The Strong Case for Gun Control

**W**hile abhorring violence, Americans generally believe that gun control cannot do much to reduce it. A majority of Americans questioned in a 1992 CBS-*New York Times* poll responded that banning handguns would only keep them away from law-abiding citizens rather than reduce the amount of violent crime. Many serious scholars have accepted the argument that the huge number of guns already in circulation would make any gun control laws ineffective. Until recently, it has been difficult to answer these objections. But in the past few years, new research has demonstrated that some gun control laws do work, dramatically reducing murder rates.

Gun violence is a plague of such major proportions that its destructive power is rivaled only by wars and epidemics. During the Vietnam War, more than twice as many Americans were shot to death in the United States as died in combat in Vietnam. Besides the 34,000 Americans killed by guns each year, more than 60,000 are injured—many seriously—and about a quarter of a million Americans are held up at gunpoint.

Measures that demonstrably reduce gun violence would gain wide public support. But that has been exactly the problem: A public that approves of gun control by wide margins also is skeptical about its effectiveness and even its constitutionality. Both of these sources of doubt can now be put to rest.

## A Tale of Two Cities

Perhaps the most dramatic findings about the efficacy of gun control laws come from a study comparing two cities that have followed different policies for regulating handguns: Seattle, Washington and Vancouver, British Columbia.[1] Only 140 miles apart, the two cities are remarkably alike despite being located on opposite sides of an international border. They have populations nearly identical in size and, during the study period (1980-86), had similar socio-economic profiles. Seattle, for example, had a 5.8 percent unemployment rate while Vancouver's was 6.0 percent. The median household income in Seattle was $16,254; in Vancouver, adjusted in U.S. dollars, it was $16,681. In racial and ethnic makeup, the two cities are also similar. Whites represent 79 percent of

From Carl T. Bogus, "The Strong Case for Gun Control," *The American Prospect* (Summer 1992).
Copyright © 1992 by New Prospect, Inc. Reprinted by permission.

*Figure 1*

### Aggravated Assaults per 100,000 People, 1980–1983, by Weapon

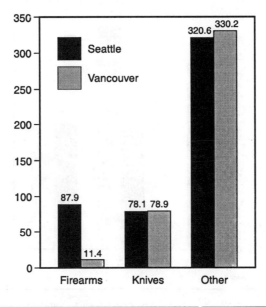

Source: John Henry Sloan, et al., "Handgun Regulations, Crime, Assaults, and Homicide," *The New England Journal of Medicine*, Nov. 10, 1988, pp. 1256–62. Reprinted by permission.

Seattle's inhabitants and 76 percent of Vancouver's. The principal racial differ-ence is that Asians make up a larger share of Vancouver's population (22 percent versus 7 percent). The two cities share not only a common frontier history but a current culture as well. Most of the top ten television shows in one city, for example, also rank among the top ten in the other.

As one might expect from twin cities, burglary rates in Seattle and Van-couver were nearly identical. The aggravated assault rate was, however, slightly higher in Seattle. On examining the data more closely, the Sloan study found "a striking pattern." There were almost identical rates of assaults with knives, clubs and fists, but there was a far greater rate of assault with firearms in Seattle. Indeed, the firearm assault rate in Seattle was nearly eight times higher than in Vancouver [see Figure 1].

The homicide rate was also markedly different in the two cities. During the seven years of the study, there were 204 homicides in Vancouver and 388 in Seattle—an enormous difference for two cities with comparable populations. Further analysis led to a startling finding: the entire difference was due to gun-related homicides. The murder rates with knives—and all other weapons excluding firearms—were virtually identical, but the rate of murders involving

*Figure 2*

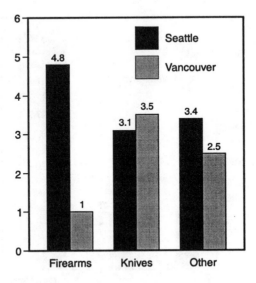

**Murders per 100,000 People, 1980–1986, by Weapon**

Source: John Henry Sloan, et al., "Handgun Regulations, Crime, Assaults, and Homicide," *The New England Journal of Medicine*, Nov. 10, 1988, pp. 1256–62. Reprinted by permission.

guns was five times greater in Seattle [see Figure 2]. That alone accounted for Seattle having nearly twice as many homicides as Vancouver.

People in Seattle may purchase a handgun for any reason after a five-day waiting period; 41 percent of all households have handguns. Vancouver on the other hand, requires a permit for handgun purchases and issues them only to applicants who have a lawful reason to own a handgun and who, after a careful investigation, are found to have no criminal record and to be sane. Self-defense is not a valid reason to own a handgun, and recreational uses of handguns are strictly regulated. The penalty for illegal possession is severe—two years' imprisonment. Handguns are present in only 12 percent of Vancouver's homes.

The Seattle-Vancouver study provides strong evidence for the efficacy of gun control. Sloan and his colleagues concluded that the wider proliferation of handguns in Seattle was the sole cause of the higher rate of murders and assaults. The study answered other important questions as well.

- *Do handguns deter crime?* If handguns deter burglary, the burglary rate in Seattle—where so many more homes have handguns—should have been lower than the burglary rate in Vancouver. But it was not.
- *How often are handguns used for self-defense?* Less than 4 percent of the homicides in both cities resulted from acts of self-defense.

- Perhaps most important: *If handguns are unavailable, will people merely use other weapons instead?* The answer must be "no." Otherwise, the cities would have had similar total murder rates and Vancouver would have had higher rates of homicide with other weapons.

A more recent study measured gun control legislation more directly.[2] In 1976 the District of Columbia enacted a new gun control law. Residents who lawfully owned firearms had sixty days to reregister them. After the sixty-day period, newly acquired handguns became illegal. Residents could continue to register rifles and shotguns, provided they purchased them from licensed dealers and complied with other regulations.

The researchers compared gun-related violence in the nine years prior to the law's enactment with the following nine years. They also compared the experience within the District with that of the immediately surrounding metropolitan area. The law was, of course, only in force within the boundaries of the District itself and not in contiguous areas of Maryland and Virginia that belong to the same metropolitan area, as the Census Bureau defines it.

The results of the study were surprising even to the most ardent gun control advocates. Within the District, gun-related homicides fell by more than 25 percent and gun-related suicides declined by 23 percent. Meanwhile, there was no statistically significant change in either gun-related homicides or suicides in the adjacent areas. Here again the data demonstrated that people did not switch to other weapons: within the District there was no statistically significant change in either homicides or suicides with other weapons.

Perhaps most surprising of all was the suddenness of the change. Any decline in murders and suicides was expected to be gradual, as the number of weapons in the district slowly shrank. Yet homicides and suicides abruptly declined when the law went into effect. The D.C. law, therefore, had a significant and virtually immediate benefit.

The D.C. study demonstrates that gun control can work in the United States. Despite the similarities between Seattle and Vancouver, some critics of the Sloan study have suggested that Canada and the United States are sufficiently different to make extrapolations questionable. The D.C. study shows that even local gun control laws can be effective in the U.S. Previously, the prevailing opinion was that only national legislation could be effective. Critics said that if local laws blocked handgun purchases, buyers would simply import one from a nearby area. Many people probably do just that, and there is little doubt that national legislation would be far more effective.

Washington D.C.'s gun control law has not transformed the city into a utopia. It has remained a violent city and—along with many other large cities—its murder rate rose sharply in the last few years of the study (1986–88), when the use of "crack" cocaine was increasing. Yet the fact remains that for the full nine-year period after the gun control law was enacted, the mean D.C. murder rate was more than 25 percent lower and its mean suicide rate was 23 percent lower than in the preceding nine years. The effect of the law was not only immediate but sustained as well.

## Why Gun Control Works

The gun lobby is fond of saying, "If guns are outlawed, only outlaws will have guns." What's wrong with this picture?

The National Rifle Association (NRA) slogan leads us to envision two groups—solid citizens and hardened criminals—but the real world cannot be neatly divided into good guys and bad guys. Many people are law-abiding citizens until they become inflamed in a domestic dispute, a drunken argument in a bar, even a fender-bender on the highway. Murder is usually an act of rage; it is more often impulsive than premeditated. In fact, 80 percent of all murders occur during altercations and 71 percent involve acquaintances, including lovers, family members, and neighbors. Only 29 percent of those arrested for murder are previously convicted felons.

Rage can pass quickly, but if there is a gun available, even a few seconds may not be soon enough. Of course, enraged lovers and brawlers use other weapons, but it is better to be attacked with anything other than a gun. Guns are, by far, the most lethal weapons. The second deadliest is the knife, but knife attacks result in death only one-fifth as often as those with guns.

For the same reason that it is better to face a knife than a gun in a lover's quarrel, it is better to be robbed at knife point rather than gunpoint. There are good reasons to believe that reducing the number of guns in the general population will reduce them in the hands of muggers and robbers. Prison inmates report that they acquired one-third of their guns by stealing them, typically in home burglaries. There are also people at the margin—not yet career criminals but drifting in that direction—who are more inclined to have guns if they are cheap and readily available. And since handguns are lawful almost everywhere, these people do not even have to cross a psychological Rubicon to get a gun.

⋞⊙⋟

Many of the people at the margin are youngsters. Nearly 70 percent of all serious crimes are committed by boys and young men, ages fourteen to twenty-four. Many of them are not yet career criminals. They are the children of despair, kids from dysfunctional families and impoverished communities who thirst for a feeling of importance. They are angry, immature, and unstable. In the 1950s, they carried switchblades, but since the early 1960s they have increasingly been carrying handguns. Packing a gun makes them feel like men, and it just takes a little alcohol or drugs, a buddy's dare, or a moment of bravado to propel them into their first mugging or holdup of a convenience store. Many juvenile robbers say that they did not intend to commit a robbery when they went out. The nation will be a less dangerous place if these kids go out without guns.

There is a frightening increase in the number of youngsters carrying guns. The National Adolescent Student Health Survey discovered that by 1987, nearly 2 percent of all eighth and tenth graders across the nation said that they carried a gun to school within the past year. A third of those said they took a gun to school with them every day, which translates into more than 100,000 students packing a pistol all the time. In just the first two months of 1992, more than a hundred firearms were confiscated in New York City schools.

And kids are not just carrying guns, they are using them. New York City was shaken earlier this year when, moments before Mayor David Dinkins was to give a speech to the students at Brooklyn's Thomas Jefferson High School, a fifteen-year-old pulled out a Smith & Wesson .38 and killed two other students. Had it not been for the mayor's presence at the school, the shootings might not have been front-page news.

It is somewhat disingenuous to be shocked about youths with handguns. Kids emulate adults. They live in a society that has not attached a sense of gravity to owning handguns. In half of the fifty states, handguns are completely unregulated; anyone may walk into a gun shop and buy a handgun just as easily as a quart of milk at a grocery. Most of the other states have only modest handgun regulations; four states, for example, have forty-eight hour waiting periods. Except in a very few locales, automobiles are regulated far more rigorously than handguns.

There are 35 million handguns in the United States; a quarter of all homes have at least one handgun in them. We can tell a teenage boy that he is really safer if he does not pack a gun. But why should he believe adults who keep handguns in their nightstand drawers, even though they have been told that a gun in the home is six times more likely to be used to shoot a family member than an intruder?

For more than a decade some observers, such as Charles Silberman, have noted a rising tide of savagery. Today, for example, my morning newspaper carries a report about a robbery at a local McDonald's restaurant. A man with a pistol demanded the restaurant's cash, which the manager immediately gave him. The robber then told the manager and two other employees to lie down, and proceeded to shoot two to death while one of the three ran away. Not long ago it would have been extraordinarily rare for a robber—with the money in his hand—to kill his victims gratuitously; now it seems commonplace. We may wonder what impels someone to top off a robbery with a double murder, but whatever the motive, the handgun makes that act possible.

⟶⟐⟵

We are also witnessing a bewildering escalation in suicides. In 1960 there were about 19,000 suicides in the United States; now there are more than 30,000 each year. (This represents a rise in the suicide rate from 10.6 per 100,000 in 1960 to 12.4 per 100,000 in 1988.) Nearly two-thirds of all suicides in the United States are committed with firearms, more than 80 percent of those with handguns. The rising number of suicides is due almost completely to firearm suicides. While the number of suicides with other weapons has remained relatively stable (even slightly declining over the past two decades), the number of firearm suicides has more than doubled since 1960.

Why should that be so? If someone really wants to kill himself, is he not going to find a way to do so regardless of whether a handgun is available? This is something of a trick question. The rabbit in the hat is the phrase "really wants to kill himself" because suicide, like murder, is often an impulsive act, particularly among the 2,000 to 3,000 American teenagers who commit suicide each year. If an individual contemplating suicide can get through the moment of dark despair, he may reconsider. And if a gun is not available, many potential suicides will resort to a less lethal method, survive, and never attempt suicide again. Nothing is as quick and certain as a gun. The desire to die need only last as long as it takes to pull a trigger, and the decision is irrevocable.

In the Seattle-Vancouver study, the researchers found a 40-percent higher suicide rate among the fifteen- to twenty-five-year-olds in Seattle, a difference they discovered was due to a firearm suicide rate that is ten times higher among Seattle adolescents. Other research reveals that a potentially suicidal adolescent is *seventy-five times* as likely to kill himself when there is a gun in the house.[3]

This is the one area, however where the type of gun may not matter. While more than 80 percent of all gun-related suicides are with handguns, research suggests that when handguns are not available, people attempting suicide may just as readily use long guns. But many homes only have a handgun, and reducing the number of homes with handguns will therefore reduce the number of suicides.

## What Kind of Gun Control Works?

No one suggests that gun control legislation will be a panacea. Nevertheless, the strong evidence is that the right kind of gun control legislation can reduce murders, suicides, and accidents substantially in the United States.

First and foremost, gun control means controlling handguns. Handguns account for only about one-third of all firearms in general circulation, but they are used in more than 75 percent of all gun-related homicides and more than 80 percent of all gun-related robberies. No other weapon is used nearly so often to murder: While handguns are used in half of all murders in America, knives are used in 18 percent, shotguns in 6 percent, rifles in 4 percent.

Two basic approaches are available to regulate handguns. One is to allow anyone to have a handgun, except for individuals in certain prohibited categories such as convicted felons, the mentally ill, drunkards, and the like. This approach is fatally flawed. The vast majority of people who end up abusing handguns do not have records that place them in a high-risk category. Whenever someone commits a murder, we can in retrospect always say that the murderer was mentally unstable, but it is not easy to check potential handgun purchasers for signs of instability or smoldering rage. There is no test to give. Many mentally unstable individuals have no record of psychiatric treatment and, even if they do, their records are confidential. Because we want to encourage people who need psychological help to seek treatment, legislation that would open psychiatric records to the government or place them in some national data bank would be counterproductive. Moreover, even someone who clearly falls into a prohibited category, such as a convicted felon, can easily circumvent this system by sending a surrogate to purchase a handgun for him.

✸

The second approach, known as a need-based or a restrictive permitting system, allows only people who fall within certain categories to own handguns. Handgun permits are, of course, issued to law enforcement personnel, but among the general population someone who wants a handgun permit must demonstrate a special need. Simply wanting a handgun for self-defense is not enough, but someone who can provide a sufficiently concrete reason to fear attack would be granted a handgun permit. Sportsmen can obtain special permits, but their handguns must be kept under lock and key at a gun club. It may inconvenience them, but when public safety is balanced against recreation, public safety must win out.

Many states have similar systems for permits to carry a concealed weapon in public, but in the United States only New Jersey and a few cities have true need-base permitting systems for handgun possession. Canada adopted this system nationally in 1978....

Handgun registration should be part of a restrictive permitting system. Owners should be required to register their handguns, and a permanent identification number should be engraved on every handgun. All transfers should be recorded. Everyone who has a driver's license or owns a car understands such a system, and even 78 percent of gun owners in America favor the registration of handguns, according to a 1991 Gallup poll.

✸

With one exception, long guns do not present the same kind of threat to public safety as handguns. The exception, of course, is assault weapons. We remember how Patrick Purdy fired his AK-47 into a schoolyard in Stockton, California. In less than two minutes, he fired 106 rounds at children and teachers, killing five and wounding twenty-nine.

The NRA argues that it is impossible to differentiate an assault weapon from a standard hunting rifle—and to some extent it is right. Both hunting rifles and the assault weapons that are sold to the general public are semi-automatic. With a semi-automatic, firing repeat rounds requires pulling the trigger back for each one; with an automatic weapon, one must only pull the trigger back once and keep it depressed. This, however, is an inconsequential difference. A thirty-round magazine can be emptied in two seconds with a fully automatic weapon and in five seconds with a semi-automatic.

The way to regulate long guns, therefore, is to limit the size of magazines. Civilians should not be permitted to have magazines that hold more than five rounds. This simply means that after firing five rounds one must stop, remove the empty magazine and either reload it or insert another full magazine. No hunter worth his salt blasts away at a deer as if he were storming the beach at Guadalcanal, and therefore this is no real inconvenience for hunters. But as Patrick Purdy demonstrated with his seventy-five-round magazine in Stockton, large-capacity magazines pose an unreasonable danger to public safety and should not be available to civilians.

The gun lobby urges that instead of regulating handguns (or assault weapons), severe and mandatory penalties should be imposed on persons who violate firearm laws. The weight of the evidence, however, suggests that these laws are not as effective. In 1987, for example, Detroit enacted an ordinance that imposed mandatory jail sentences on persons convicted of unlawfully concealing a handgun or carrying a firearm within the city. The strategy was to allow the general population to keep guns in their homes and offices but to reduce the number of people carrying guns on the streets. After evaluating the law, researchers concluded that, at best, "the ordinance had a relatively small preventive effect on the incidence of homicides in Detroit."[4] The researchers were, in fact, dubious that there was any effect. An analysis of the case histories of more than a thousand persons charged under the ordinance revealed that only 3 percent spent time in prison. With overcrowded jails, judges choose instead to incarcerate people convicted of more serious crimes. This is consistent with other studies of mandatory sentencing laws.[5] . . .

Blame for the failure of gun control is generally laid at the feet of the NRA, but the problem is not so much a zealous minority as it is a quiescent majority. There has not been a sufficiently clear understanding of why the majority of Americans want gun control but do not want it enough to make it a priority in the voting booth. Much effort has been wasted describing the magnitude and horror of gun violence in America. The gun lobby has taken one broadside after another—from television network specials and newsweekly cover stories—all to no avail.

In talking about the horror of gun violence, however, the news media are preaching to the converted. Americans are aware of the level of gun violence, and they detest it. But news specials decrying gun violence may unwittingly have the same effect as the entertainment media's glorification of gun violence. They only reinforce a sense of hopelessness. If things could be different, Americans think, they would be. Otherwise, the carnage would not be tolerated. The media portrayals may also have a numbing effect. Research shows that if people are frightened but believe there is no way to escape or to improve conditions, the fear becomes debilitating.

Majority passivity is rooted in the belief that the status quo is immutable. It is this attitude that gun control advocates must try to change, by communicating the evidence that gun control laws do work. Americans know how bad gun violence is; they must now hear the evidence that reducing the violence is possible.

# Notes

1. John Henry Sloan, et al., "Handgun Regulations, Crime, Assaults, and Homicide," *The New England Journal of Medicine,* Nov. 10, 1988, pp. 1256–62.

2. Colin Liftin, et al., "Effects of Restrictive Licensing of Handguns on Homicide and Suicide in the District of Columbia," *The New England Journal of Medicine,* Dec. 5, 1991, pp. 1615–1649.

3. David A. Brent, et al., "The Presence and Accessibility of Firearms in the Homes of Adolescent Suicides," *Journal of the American Medical Association,* Dec. 4, 1991, pp. 2989–93.

4. Patrick W. O'Carroll, "Preventing Homicide: An Evaluation of the Efficacy of a Detroit Gun Ordinance," *American Journal of Public Health,* May 1991, pp. 576–81.

5. Alan Lizotte and Marjorie A. Zatz, "The Use and Abuse of Sentence Enhancement for Firearms Offenses in California," *Law and Contemporary Problems* (1986), pp. 199–221.

Daniel D. Polsby  **NO**

# The False Promise of Gun Control

During the 1960s and 1970s the robbery rate in the United States increased sixfold, and the murder rate doubled; the rate of handgun ownership nearly doubled in that period as well. Handguns and criminal violence grew together apace, and national opinion leaders did not fail to remark on the coincidence.

It has become a bipartisan article of faith that more handguns cause more violence. Such was the unequivocal conclusion of the National Commission on the Causes and Prevention of Violence in 1969, and such is now the editorial opinion of virtually every influential newspaper and magazine, from *The Washington Post* to *The Economist* to the *Chicago Tribune*. Members of the House and Senate who have not dared to confront the gun lobby concede the connection privately. Even if the National Rifle Association [NRA] can produce blizzards of angry calls and letters to the Capitol virtually overnight, House members one by one have been going public, often after some new firearms atrocity at a fast-food restaurant or the like. And last November they passed the Brady bill.

Alas, however well accepted, the conventional wisdom about guns and violence is mistaken. Guns don't increase national rates of crime and violence —but the continued proliferation of gun-control laws almost certainly does. Current rates of crime and violence are a bit below the peaks of the late 1970s, but because of a slight oncoming bulge in the at-risk population of males aged fifteen to thirty-four, the crime rate will soon worsen. The rising generation of criminals will have no more difficulty than their elders did in obtaining the tools of their trade. Growing violence will lead to calls for laws still more severe. Each fresh round of legislation will be followed by renewed frustration.

Gun-control laws don't work. What is worse, they act perversely. While legitimate users of firearms encounter intense regulation, scrutiny, and bureaucratic control, illicit markets easily adapt to whatever difficulties a free society throws in their way. Also, efforts to curtail the supply of firearms inflict collateral damage on freedom and privacy interests that have long been considered central to American public life. Thanks to the seemingly never-ending war on drugs and long experience attempting to suppress prostitution and pornography, we know a great deal about how illicit markets function and how costly to the public attempts to control them can be. It is essential that we make use of this experience in coming to grips with gun control.

From Daniel D. Polsby, "The False Promise of Gun Control," *The Atlantic Monthly* (March 1994). Copyright © 1994 by Daniel D. Polsby. Reprinted by permission.

The thousands of gun-control laws in the United States are of two general types. The older kind sought to regulate how, where, and by whom firearms could be carried. More recent laws have sought to make it more costly to buy, sell, or use firearms (or certain classes of firearms, such as assault rifles, Saturday-night specials, and so on) by imposing fees, special taxes, or surtaxes on them. The Brady bill is of both types: it has a background-check provision, and its five-day waiting period amounts to a "time tax" on acquiring handguns. All such laws can be called scarcity-inducing, because they seek to raise the cost of buying firearms, as figured in terms of money, time, nuisance, or stigmatization.

Despite the mounting number of scarcity-inducing laws, no one is very satisfied with them. Hobbyists want to get rid of them, and gun-control proponents don't think they go nearly far enough. Everyone seems to agree that gun-control laws have some effect on the distribution of firearms. But it has not been the dramatic and measurable effect their proponents desired.

Opponents of gun control have traditionally wrapped their arguments in the Second Amendment to the Constitution. Indeed, most modern scholarship affirms that so far as the drafters of the Bill of Rights were concerned the right to bear arms was to be enjoyed by everyone, not just a militia, and that one of the principal justifications for an armed populace was to secure the tranquillity and good order of the community. But most people are not dedicated antiquitarians, and would not be impressed by the argument "I admit that my behavior is very dangerous to public safety, but the Second Amendment says I have a right to do it anyway." That would be a case for repealing the Second Amendment, not respecting it.

## Fighting the Demand Curve

Everyone knows that possessing a handgun makes it easier to intimidate, wound, or kill someone. But the implication of this point for social policy has not been so well understood. It is easy to count the bodies of those who have been killed or wounded with guns, but not easy to count the people who have avoided harm because they had access to weapons. Think about uniformed police officers, who carry handguns in plain view not in order to kill people but simply to daunt potential attackers. And it works. Criminals generally do not single out police officers for opportunistic attack. Though officers can expect to draw their guns from time to time, few even in big-city departments will actually fire a shot (except in target practice) in the course of a year. This observation points to an important truth: people who are armed make comparatively unattractive victims. A criminal might not know if any one civilian is armed, but if it becomes known that a large number of civilians do carry weapons, criminals will become warier.

Which weapons laws are the right kinds can be decided only after considering two related questions. First, what is the connection between civilian possession of firearms and social violence? Second, how can we expect gun-control laws to alter people's behavior? Most recent scholarship raises serious questions about the "weapons increase violence" hypothesis. The second question is emphasized here, because it is routinely overlooked and often mocked when noticed; yet it is crucial. Rational gun control requires understanding not only the relationship between weapons and violence but also the relationship between laws and people's behavior. Some things are very hard to accomplish with laws. The purpose of a law and its likely effects are not always the same thing. Many statutes are notorious for the way in which their unintended effects have swamped their intended ones.

In order to predict who will comply with gun-control laws, we should remember that guns are economic goods that are traded in markets. Consumers' interest in them varies. For religious, moral, aesthetic, or practical reasons, some people would refuse to buy firearms at any price. Other people willingly pay very high prices for them.

Handguns, so often the subject of gun-control laws, are desirable for one purpose—to allow a person tactically to dominate a hostile transaction with another person. The value of a weapon to a given person is a function of two factors: how much he or she wants to dominate a confrontation if one occurs, and how likely it is that he or she will actually be in a situation calling for a gun.

Dominating a transaction simply means getting what one wants without being hurt. Where people differ is in how likely it is that they will be involved in a situation in which a gun will be valuable. Someone who *intends* to engage in a transaction involving a gun—a criminal, for example—is obviously in the best possible position to predict that likelihood. Criminals should therefore be willing to pay more for a weapon than most other people would. Professors, politicians, and newspaper editors are, as a group, at very low risk of being involved in such transactions, and they thus systematically underrate the value of defensive handguns. (Correlative, perhaps, is their uncritical readiness to accept studies that debunk the utility of firearms for self-defense.) The class of people we wish to deprive of guns, then, is the very class with the most inelastic demand for them—criminals—whereas the people most likely to comply with gun-control laws don't value guns in the first place.

## Do Guns Drive Up Crime Rates?

Which premise is true—that guns increase crime or that the fear of crime causes people to obtain guns? Most of the country's major newspapers apparently take this problem to have been solved by an article published by Arthur Kellermann and several associates in the October 7, 1993, *New England Journal of Medicine.* Kellermann is an emergency-room physician who has published a number of influential papers that he believes discredit the thesis that private ownership of firearms is a useful means of self-protection. (An indication of his wide influence is that within two months the study received almost 100 mentions in publications and broadcast transcripts indexed in the Nexis data base.) For this study Kellermann and his associates identified fifteen behavioral and fifteen environmental variables that applied to a 388-member set of homicide victims, found a "matching" control group of 388 nonhomicide victims, and then ascertained how the two groups differed in gun ownership. In interviews Kellermann made clear his belief that owning a handgun markedly increases a person's risk of being murdered.

But the study does not prove that point at all. Indeed, as Kellermann explicitly conceded in the text of the article, the causal arrow may very well point in the other direction: the threat of being killed may make people more likely to arm themselves. Many people at risk of being killed, especially people involved in the drug trade or other illegal ventures, might well rationally buy a gun as a precaution, and be willing to pay a price driven up by gun-control laws. Crime, after all, is a dangerous business. Peter Reuter and Mark Kleiman, drug-policy researchers, calculated in 1987 that the average crack dealer's risk of being killed was far greater than his risk of being sent to prison. (Their data cannot, however, support the implication that ownership of a firearm causes or exacerbates the risk of being killed.)

Defending the validity of his work, Kellermann has emphasized that the link between lung cancer and smoking was initially established by studies methodologically no different from his. Gary Kleck, a criminology professor at Florida State University, has pointed out the flaw in this comparison. No one ever thought that lung cancer causes smoking, so when the association between the two was established the direction of the causal arrow was not in doubt. Kleck wrote that it is as though Kellermann, trying to discover how diabetics differ from other people, found that they are much more likely to possess insulin than nondiabetics, and concluded that insulin is a risk factor for diabetes.

*The New York Times,* the *Los Angeles Times, The Washington Post, The Boston Globe,* and the *Chicago Tribune* all gave prominent coverage to Kellermann's study as soon as it appeared, but none saw fit to discuss the study's limitations. A few, in order to introduce a hint of balance, mentioned that the NRA, or some member of its staff, disagreed with the study. But readers had no way of knowing that Kellermann himself had registered a disclaimer in his text. "It is possible," he conceded. "that reverse causation accounted for some of the association we observed between gun ownership and homicide." Indeed, the point is stronger than that: "reverse causation" may account for *most* of the association between gun ownership and homicide. Kellermann's data simply do not allow one to draw any conclusion.

If firearms increased violence and crime, then rates of spousal homicide would have skyrocketed, because the stock of privately owned handguns has increased rapidly since the mid-1960s. But according to an authoritative study of spousal homicide in the *American Journal of Public Health,* by James Mercy and Linda Saltzman, rates of spousal homicide in the years 1976 to 1985 fell. If firearms increased violence and crime, the crime rate should have increased throughout the 1980s, while the national stock of privately owned handguns increased by more than a million units in every year of the decade. It did not. Nor should the rates of violence and crime in Switzerland, New Zealand, and Israel be as low as they are, since the number of firearms per civilian household is comparable to that in the United States. Conversely, gun-controlled Mexico and South Africa should be islands of peace instead of having murder rates more than twice as high as those [in the United States]. The determinants of crime and law-abidingness are, of course, complex matters, which are not fully understood and certainly not explicable in terms of a country's laws. But gun-control enthusiasts, who have made capital out of the low murder rate in England, which is largely disarmed, simply ignore the counterexamples that don't fit their theory.

If firearms increased violence and crime, Florida's murder rate should not have been falling since the introduction, seven years ago, of a law that makes it easier for ordinary citizens to get permits to carry concealed handguns. Yet the murder rate has remained the same or fallen every year since the law was enacted, and it is now lower than the national murder rate (which has been rising). As of last November 183,561 permits had been issued, and only seventeen of the permits had been revoked because the holder was involved in a firearms offense. It would be precipitate to claim that the new law has "caused" the murder rate to subside. Yet here is a situation that doesn't fit the hypothesis that weapons increase violence.

If firearms increased violence and crime, programs of induced scarcity would suppress violence and crime. But—another anomaly—they don't. Why not? A theorem, which we could call the futility theorem, explains why gun-control laws must either be ineffectual or in the long term actually provoke more violence and crime. Any theorem depends on both observable fact and assumption. An assumption that can be made with confidence is that the higher the number of victims a criminal assumes to be armed, the higher will be the risk—the price—of assaulting them. By definition, gun-control laws should make weapons scarcer and thus more expensive. By our prior reasoning about demand among various types of consumers, after the laws are enacted criminals should be better armed, compared with noncriminals, than they were before. Of course, plenty of noncriminals will remain armed. But even if many noncriminals will pay as high a price as criminals will to obtain firearms, a larger number will not.

Criminals will thus still take the same gamble they already take in assaulting a victim who might or might not be armed. But they may appreciate that the laws have given them a freer field, and that crime still pays—pays even better, in fact, than before. What will happen to the rate of violence? Only a relatively few gun-mediated transactions—currently, five percent of armed robberies committed with firearms—result in someone's actually being shot (the statistics are not broken down into encounters between armed assailants and unarmed victims, and encounters in which both parties are armed). It seems reasonable to fear that if the number of such transactions were to increase because criminals thought they faced fewer deterrents, there would be a corresponding increase in shootings. Conversely, if gun-mediated transactions declined—if criminals initiated fewer of them because they feared encountering an armed victim or an armed good Samaritan—the number of shootings would go down. The magnitude of these effects is, admittedly, uncertain. Yet it is hard to doubt the general tendency of a change in the law that imposes legal burdens on buying guns. The futility theorem suggests that gun-control laws, if effective at all, would unfavorably affect the rate of violent crime.

The futility theorem provides a lens through which to see much of the debate. It is undeniable that gun-control laws work—to an extent. Consider, for example, California's background-check law, which in the past two years has prevented about 12,000 people with a criminal record or a history of mental illness or drug abuse from buying handguns. In the same period Illinois's background-check law prevented the delivery of firearms to more than 2,000 people. Surely some of these people simply turned to an illegal market, but just as surely not all of them did. The laws of large numbers allow us to say that among the foiled thousands, some potential killers were prevented from getting a gun. We do not know whether the number is large or small, but it is implausible to think it is zero. And, as gun-control proponents are inclined to say, "If only one life is saved..."

The hypothesis that firearms increase violence does predict that if we can slow down the diffusion of guns, there will be less violence; one life, or more, *will* be saved. But the futility theorem asks that we look not simply at the gross number of bad actors prevented from getting guns but at the effect the law has on *all* the people who want to buy a gun. Suppose we succeed in piling tax burdens on the acquisition of firearms. We can safely assume that a number of people who might use guns to kill will be sufficiently discouraged not to buy them. But we cannot assume this about people who feel that they must have guns in order to survive financially and physically. A few lives might indeed be saved. But the overall rate of violent crime might not go down at all. And if guns are owned predominantly by people who have good reason to think they will use them, the rate might even go up.

Are there empirical studies that can serve to help us choose between the futility theorem and the hypothesis that guns increase violence? Unfortunately, no: the best studies of the effects of gun-control laws are quite inconclusive. Our statistical tools are too weak to allow us to identify an effect clearly enough to persuade an open-minded skeptic. But it is precisely when we are dealing with undetectable statistical effects that we have to be certain we are using the best models available of human behavior....

## Administering Prohibition

Assume for the sake of argument that to a reasonable degree of criminological certainty, guns are every bit the public-health hazard they are said to be. It follows, and many journalists and a few public officials have already said, that we ought to treat guns the same way we do smallpox viruses or other critical vectors of morbidity and mortality—namely, isolate them from potential hosts and destroy them as speedily as possible. Clearly, firearms have at least one characteristic that distinguishes them from smallpox viruses: nobody wants to keep smallpox viruses in the nightstand drawer. Amazingly enough, gun-control literature seems never to have explored the problem of getting weapons away from people who very much want to keep them in the nightstand drawer.

Our existing gun-control laws are not uniformly permissive, and, indeed, in certain places are tough even by international standards. Advocacy groups seldom stress the considerable differences among American jurisdictions, and media reports regularly assert that firearms are readily available to anybody anywhere in the country. This is not the case. For example, . . . in Chicago and the District of Columbia, excepting peace officers and the like, only grandfathered registrants may legally possess handguns. Of course, tens or hundreds of thousands of people in both those cities—nobody can be sure how many—do in fact possess them illegally.

Although there is, undoubtedly, illegal handgun ownership in the United Kingdom, especially in Northern Ireland (where considerations of personal security and public safety are decidedly unlike those elsewhere in the British Isles), it is probable that Americans and Britons differ in their disposition to obey gun-control laws: there is reputed to be a marked national disparity in compliance behavior. This difference, if it exists, may have something to do with the comparatively marginal value of firearms to British consumers. Even before it had strict firearms regulation, Britain had very low rates of crimes involving guns; British criminals, unlike their American counterparts, prefer burglary (a crime of stealth) to robbery (a crime of intimidation).

Unless people are prepared to surrender their guns voluntarily, how can the U.S. government confiscate an appreciable fraction of our country's nearly 200 million privately owned firearms? We know that it is possible to set up weapons-free zones in certain locations—commercial airports and many courthouses and, lately, some troubled big-city high schools and housing projects. The sacrifices of privacy and convenience, and the costs of paying guards, have been thought worth the (perceived) gain in security. No doubt it would be possible, though it would probably not be easy, to make weapons-free zones of shopping centers, department stores, movie theaters, ball parks. But it is not obvious how one would cordon off the whole of an open society.

Voluntary programs have been ineffectual. From time to time community-action groups or police departments have sponsored "turn in your gun" days, which are nearly always disappointing. Sometimes the government offers to buy guns at some price. This approach has been endorsed by Senator Chafee and the *Los Angeles Times*. Jonathan Alter, of *Newsweek*, has suggested a variation on this theme: youngsters could exchange their guns for a handshake with Michael Jordan or some other sports hero. If the price offered exceeds that at which a gun can be bought on the street, one can expect to see plans of this kind yield some sort of harvest—as indeed they have. But it is implausible that these schemes will actually result in a less-dangerous population. Government programs to buy up surplus cheese cause more cheese to be produced without affecting the availability of cheese to people who want to buy it. So it is with guns. . . .

The solution to the problem of crime lies in improving the chances of young men. Easier said than done, to be sure. No one has yet proposed a convincing program for checking all the dislocating forces that government assistance can set in motion. One relatively straightforward change would be reform of the educational system. Nothing guarantees prudent behavior like a sense of the future, and with average skills in reading, writing, and math, young people can realistically look forward to constructive employment and the straight life that steady work makes possible.

But firearms are nowhere near the root of the problem of violence. As long as people come in unlike sizes, shapes, ages, and temperaments, as long as they diverge in their taste for risk and their willingness and capacity to prey on other people or to defend themselves from predation, and above all as long as some people have little or nothing to lose by spending their lives in crime, dispositions to violence will persist.

This is what makes the case for the right to bear arms, not the Second Amendment. It is foolish to let anything ride on hopes for effective gun control. As long as crime pays as well as it does, we will have plenty of it, and honest folk must choose between being victims and defending themselves.

# POSTSCRIPT

## Do We Need Tougher Gun Control Laws?

What does the Second Amendment mean? In its entirety it reads, "A well regulated Militia, being necessary to the security of a free State, the right of the people to keep and bear Arms, shall not be infringed." Does this confer an unqualified right to bear arms? Or is it a right conditioned by the clause preceding the statement of right? Does the militia refer to the people generally, or does it specifically relate to the organized ("well regulated") military bodies of state and national guards and the armed forces?

Wayne LaPierre, chief executive officer and spokesman for the National Rifle Association (NRA), has written *Guns, Crime, and Freedom* (Regnery, 1994), which may be the most authoritative defense of the NRA's unqualified opposition to gun control. Gary Wills, in "To Keep and Bear Arms," *The New York Review of Books* (September 21, 1995), argues that the constitutional right to bear arms is limited to its military usage.

As far back as 1976, Barry Bruce-Briggs anticipated some of the arguments made by Polsby. See "The Great American Gun War," *The Public Interest* (Fall 1976). For a similar view, see Don B. Kates, Jr., *Restricting Handguns: The Liberal Skeptics Speak Out* (North River Press, 1979). Neal Bernards, *Gun Control* (Lucent Books, 1991) and David E. Newton, *Gun Control: An Issue for the Nineties* (Enslow, 1992) are both attempts to summarize fairly the chief arguments for and against gun control. To put the issue of guns in a larger historical perspective, readers may wish to examine the impact of the American frontier, with its gunslinging heroes and villains, on modern American culture. Richard Slotkin's *Gunfighter Nation* (Atheneum, 1992) is an illuminating study of this enduring American myth.

In *More Guns, Less Crime: Understanding Crime and Gun-Control Laws* (University of Chicago Press, 1998), John R. Lott argues that weapons in the possession of law-abiding people deter crime. A related defense of gun ownership is examined in the editorial "Gun Availability and Violent Death," *American Journal of Public Health* (June 1997). In a 1993 survey gun owners indicated that in an incident during the previous year, someone "almost certainly would have" died if a gun had not been used for protection. In contrast, 38,000 people died in that year because of injuries due to firearms. The result would appear to be that guns took far fewer lives than they saved. But how exaggerated are the estimates of certain death? How many of the deaths by firearms might have taken place by other means if guns had not been available? The public debate continues.

# ISSUE 10

## Does Affirmative Action Advance the Cause of Racial Equality?

**YES: Clarence Page**, from *Showing My Color* (HarperCollins, 1996)

**NO: Shelby Steele**, from *The Content of Our Character: A New Vision of Race in America* (St. Martin's Press, 1990)

### ISSUE SUMMARY

**YES:** Journalist Clarence Page argues that although affirmative action is not a perfect remedy, it has benefited minorities and, in some cases, increased opportunities for whites as well.

**NO:** Professor of English Shelby Steele argues that affirmative action demoralizes both blacks and whites and that racial preferences do not empower blacks.

**W**e didn't land on Plymouth Rock, my brothers and sisters—Plymouth Rock landed on *us!*" Malcolm X's observation is borne out by the facts of American history. Snatched from their native land, transported thousands of miles —in a nightmare of disease and death—and sold into slavery, blacks were reduced to the legal status of farm animals. Even after emancipation, blacks were segregated from whites—in some states by law, and by social practice almost everywhere. American apartheid continued for another century.

In 1954 the Supreme Court declared state-compelled segregation in schools unconstitutional, and it followed up that decision with others that struck down many forms of official segregation. Still, discrimination survived, and in most southern states blacks were either discouraged or prohibited from exercising their right to vote. Not until the 1960s was compulsory segregation finally and effectively challenged. Between 1964 and 1968 Congress passed the most sweeping civil rights legislation since the end of the Civil War. It banned discrimination in employment, public accommodations (hotels, motels, restaurants, etc.), and housing; it also guaranteed voting rights for blacks and even authorized federal officials to take over the job of voter registration in areas suspected of disenfranchising blacks. Today, several agencies in the federal government exercise sweeping powers to enforce these civil rights measures.

But is that enough? Equality of condition between blacks and whites seems as elusive as ever. The black unemployment rate is double that of whites, and the percentage of black families living in poverty is nearly four times that of whites. Only a small percentage of blacks ever make it into medical school or law school.

Advocates of affirmative action have focused upon these *de facto* differences to bolster their argument that it is no longer enough just to stop discrimination. The damage done by three centuries of racism now has to be remedied, they argue, and effective remediation requires a policy of "affirmative action." At the heart of affirmative action is the use of "numerical goals." Opponents call them "racial quotas." Whatever the name, what they imply is the setting aside of a certain number of jobs or positions for blacks or other historically oppressed groups. Opponents charge that affirmative action penalizes innocent people simply because they are white, that it often results in unqualified appointments, and that it ends up harming instead of helping blacks.

Affirmative action has had an uneven history in U.S. federal courts. In *Regents of the University of California v. Allan Bakke* (1978), which marked the first time the Supreme Court directly dealt with the merits of affirmative action, a 5–4 majority ruled that a white applicant to a medical school had been wrongly excluded due to the school's affirmative action policy; yet the majority also agreed that "race-conscious" policies may be used in admitting candidates —as long as they do not amount to fixed quotas. Since *Bakke,* Supreme Court decisions have gone one way or the other depending on the precise circumstances of the case. In recent years, however, most of the Court's decisions seem to have run against affirmative action programs. For example, the Court has ruled against federal "set-aside" programs, which offer fixed percentages of federal contracts to minority-owned firms, although in the past it has permitted them. A more direct legal challenge to affirmative action was handed down by a federal appeals court in 1996 when it struck down the affirmative action policy of the University of Texas law school on grounds that it discriminated against whites, Asians, and other groups. The university appealed the case, but the Supreme Court declined to review it.

The most radical popular challenge to affirmative action was the ballot initiative endorsed by California voters in 1996. Proposition 209 banned any state program based upon racial or gender "preferences." Among the effects of this ban was a sharp decline in the numbers of non-Asian minorities admitted to the elite campuses of the state's university system, especially Berkeley and UCLA. (Asian admissions to the elite campuses either stayed the same or increased, and non-Asian minority admissions to some of the less-prestigious branches increased.)

In the following selections, Clarence Page contends that affirmative action programs are necessary to undo the damage caused by centuries of slavery and segregation, while Shelby Steele contends that affirmative action has not solved the problem of inequality but has simply resulted in a kind of cosmetic racial "representation."

 **YES**

# Supply-Side Affirmative Action

O ccasionally I have been asked whether I ever benefited from affirmative action in my career. Yes, I respond. You might say that my first jobs in newspapers came as a result of an affirmative action program called "urban riots."

Most newspapers and broadcast news operations in America were not much interested in hiring black reporters or photographers when I graduated from high school in 1965. Nevertheless, I asked the editor of the local daily if he had any summer jobs in his newsroom. I knew I was good. I was an honors graduate and feature editor at the local high school's student newspaper. I had a regional award already glistening on my short resume. Still, I was not picky. I would be delighted to mop floors just to get a job in a real newsroom.

And it was not as if I did not have connections. The editor had known me since I had been one of his newspaper's carriers at age twelve. Still, it was not to be. He told me the budget would not allow any summer jobs for any young folks that year. Then the very next day I found out through a friend that the newspaper did have an opening after all. The editors had hired a white girl a year younger than I, who also happened to be a reporter under my supervision at the student newspaper, to fill it.

Don't get mad, my dad advised me, just get smart. Get your education, he said. "Then someday you can get even!"

My saintly, interminably patient schoolteacher grandmother, dear old Mother Page, also helped ease my tension. "Son," she said, "just prepare yourself, for someday the doors of opportunity will open up. When they do, you must be ready to step inside."

Little did she know that that very summer, riots would erupt in the Watts section of Los Angeles. More than four hundred riots would explode across the nation over the next three years. Suddenly editors and news directors across the country were actively looking to hire at least a few reporters and photographers who could be sent into the "ghetto" without looking too conspicuous.

Many of the black journalists hired in that talent raid, much of it waged on the staffs of black publications and radio stations, would bring Pulitzers and other honors to their new bosses, dispelling the notion that they were mere "tokens" and confirming the depth of talent that had been passed over for so long. Women soon followed. So did Hispanics, some of whom had worked for

From Clarence Page, *Showing My Color* (HarperCollins, 1996). Copyright © 1996 by Clarence Page. Reprinted by permission of HarperCollins Publishers, Inc.

years with Anglo pseudonyms to get past anti-Latino prejudices; Asians; and Native Americans.

Times have changed. Twenty-two years after it became the first newspaper to turn me down for a job, my hometown daily became the first to purchase my newly syndicated column. The advice of my elders ("Just prepare yourself") had come to fruition.

You might say that it took me only twenty years to become an "overnight success."

Yet it is significant that I and other "first blacks" hired in the nation's newsrooms felt pretty lonely through several years of "tokenism" before affirmative hiring—or, if you prefer, "diversity hiring"—policies began to take hold at the dawn of the 1970s. The message to us journalists of color was clear: White managers did not mind hiring a few of us now and then, but they didn't want to make a habit of it, not until policies came down from the top stating in military fashion that "you *will* hire more women and minorities."

So, of all the arguments I have heard various people make against affirmative action, I find the least persuasive to be the charge that it makes its recipients feel bad. Stanford law professor Barbara Babcock had the proper response to that notion when President Jimmy Carter appointed her to head the civil rights division of the Justice Department. When she was asked in a press conference how it felt to think that she had gotten the job because she was a woman, she replied that it felt a lot better than thinking that she had *not* gotten the job because she was a woman.

True enough. Most white males have not felt particularly bad about the special preferences they have received because of their race and gender for thousands of years. Why should we? Believe me, compared to the alternative, preferential treatment feels better.

Nor have I heard many express a nagging doubt about their ability to "hack it" in fair competition with others. Quite the opposite, privileged groups tend to look upon their privilege as an entitlement. Whatever guilt or misgivings they may have are assuaged by the cottage industry that has grown up around bolstering the self-esteem of white people. Books like Charles Murray and Richard J. Herrnstein's *Bell Curve* are intended, at bottom, to answer this deep yearning. Much is made in the book about how whites perform fifteen percentage points higher on average than blacks do on standardized tests and that this may easily explain why whites earn more money than blacks. Little is made of how Asian Americans perform fifteen percentage points higher than whites, yet they have hardly taken over management or ownership of American corporations.

Or, as one of my black professional friends put it, "Since we all know that hardly any of us is really all-black, I want to know how come we only got all the dumb white folks' genes?"

The notion that Babcock should feel bad about her appointment is based on the pernicious presumption that, simply and solely because she is a woman, she must be less qualified than the man who normally would be preferred simply because he was a man.

Charles Sykes, in *A Nation of Victims: The Decay of the American Character* (1993), says that those who insist on affirmative action really are arguing that "minorities" (he speaks little of women) cannot meet existing standards, and that ultimately affirmative action forces all minorities to "deal with the nagging doubt that its policies stigmatize all successful minority individuals."

Another critic of affirmative action, Dinesh D'Souza, resident scholar at the American Enterprise Institute, goes so far as to say in his inflammatory *The End of Racism: Principles for a Multiracial Society* (1995) that most of us middle-class blacks should be stigmatized because we owe our prosperity, such as it is, to affirmative action. He then speculates that middle-class blacks must suffer "intense feelings of guilt" because "they have abandoned their poor brothers and sisters, and realize that their present circumstances became possible solely because of the heart-wrenching sufferings of the underclass."

Yet nothing in affirmative action law calls for the unqualified to be hired regardless of merit. Even "special admissions" minority students are selected from among those who already have met the standards required to do the college's work.

Affirmative action calls only for "merit" standards to be more inclusive. Affirmative action, properly implemented, *widens the pool* of qualified candidates who will be considered. This often benefits qualified white males, too, who would otherwise have been bypassed because of nepotism, favoritism, and other unnecessarily narrow criteria. My favorite example is the University of Indiana Law School's decision in 1969 to broaden its acceptance criteria to open doors to bright, promising applicants who showed high potential but, for the present, had not scored as well as other applicants in a highly competitive field. The goal of the program was to offer a second chance to disadvantaged students like those who could be found in abundance in Gary and other urban centers, but the program was not limited to them. Several white students got in, too. One was a well-heeled De Pauw University graduate named J. Danforth Quayle. He later became vice president of the United States. He apparently had not scored well enough to qualify for the law school under existing criteria, but, like him or not, he did have potential. Some people are late bloomers. . . .

Arguments against affirmative action fall under the following general categories:

**"We don't need it anymore"**  The work of early feminists and the civil rights movement did their job, but now it is time to move on. The nation has outgrown employment and educational discrimination. Nonwhite skin may actually be an advantage in many businesses and schools. The market is ultimately color-blind and would be fair, if only those infernal lawyers and government regulators would get out of the way.

**Comment**  Americans hate intrusions into their marketplace, unless the intrusions benefit them. I would argue that bias is as natural as xenophobia and as common as apple pie. Until opportunities are equalized enough to encourage women and minorities to have more trust in the free marketplace, there will be a glaring demand for extraordinary measures to target what is actually only a quite modest amount of jobs, scholarships, and contracts to minorities.

**"Racism has reversed"**    This is David Duke's claim. Whites, particularly white males, now suffer a distinct disadvantage in the workplace and in college applications. Affirmative action sets racial "quotas" that only reinforce prejudices. Besides, two wrongs do not make a right.

**Comment**    Not anymore, Conservative court decisions in the 1990s actually have shifted the burden of proof in hiring, promotions, publicly funded scholarships, and contract set-aside cases from whites and males to minorities and women. If women and minorities ever had a time of supremacy under the law, it is gone. Conservative court opinions have worked hastily to restore white male primacy.

**"It cheats those who need help most"**    The biggest beneficiaries of affirmative action have been, first, middle-class women and, second, advantaged minorities. It misses the less qualified "underclass."

**Comment**    It is easy to criticize a program that fails to reach goals it never was intended to achieve. The argument that affirmative action benefits those who need help the least falsely presumes affirmative action to be (1) an anti-poverty program and (2) a program that forces employers and colleges to accept the unqualified. It is neither. It is an equal opportunity process that, by that definition, helps most those who are best equipped to take advantage of opportunities once they are opened. I find it ironic that many of the same critics who argue that affirmative action is anti-competitive and bad for business can so quickly spin on a dime to complain that it also is uncharitable.

For example, the biggest black beneficiaries of affirmative action have been working-class blacks who had skills but were shut out of slots for which they were fully qualified in higher-paying blue-collar semiskilled, service, craft, police, and firefighter jobs because of restrictive unions and other discriminatory policies. Before President Nixon signed an executive order in 1972 calling for vigorous affirmative action among federal contractors, few black carpenters, plumbers, and other skilled building tradesmen were allowed to receive union cards. Only when construction boomed high enough to hire all available whites were skilled black tradesmen given union cards, and then only temporary cards, on a last-hired, first-fired basis. Significantly, within months of signing the executive order, Nixon was campaigning for reelection against racial "quotas." His executive order had come not so much out of his best intentions for blacks as out of a keen desire to drive a political wedge between minorities and labor-union whites.

Other examples can be found in the southern textile industry, which, under government pressure in the middle and late 1960s, finally hired blacks into their predominantly female workforce as laborers, operatives, and service and craft workers. "As a result, these black women—many of whom had spent their working lives cleaning other people's homes for a few dollars a day—tripled their wages, an enormous improvement in the quality of their lives," Gertrude Ezorsky, a Brooklyn College philosophy professor, wrote in *Racism & Justice: The Case for Affirmative Action* (1991). "I conclude that affirmative action has not merely helped a 'few fortunate' blacks."

**"Be like the model minorities"**    Behave more like Asians and, for that matter, hardworking immigrant African and West Indian blacks who appear to get along just fine despite racism and without affirmative action. In one notable screed, backlash journalist Jared Taylor's *Paved with Good Intentions: The Failure of Race Relations in America*, asks the question: Why do blacks continue in spite of civil rights reforms and outright preferential treatment to bring so much trouble on themselves and others with family failures, violent crimes, and drug abuse? Black leaders are no help, says Taylor, for they have become "shakedown artists" who encourage excuses, handouts, and self-pity that generate a "denial of individual responsibility." Why, oh why, asks Taylor, don't blacks simply behave more like Asian immigrants in "taking possession of their own lives"?

**Comment**    Opponents of affirmative action invented the "model minority" myth to stereotype Asian-American success in misleading ways that don't benefit Asians or anyone else. According to the myth, Asians succeed better academically and earn higher household income than whites despite racial discrimination and without the benefit of affirmative action. Quite the contrary, goes the myth, affirmative action sets quota ceilings on Asian participation, much like those that once limited enrollment of Jews in the Ivy League. So, therefore, affirmative action actually is harmful, both to minority initiative and to Asian success.

It's an attractive myth, but reality is a bit more complicated. There is a significant difference, for example, between *household* income and *individual* income. Asian household income, like the household income of immigrant blacks from the West Indies, exceeds white household income because more individuals in the house are likely to be working. Asian individual income still lags behind whites at every income level, from the bottom, where low-income Hmongs and many Filipinos, in particular, suffer poverty not unlike that of poor blacks and Hispanics, to the upper levels of corporate management, where a new set of myths continue to stereotype Asians as "not quite American" or "good at rational skills, but not 'people skills.' " Asian-American friends whose families have been here for several generations speak of being asked routinely, "You speak such good English; how long have you been in this country?" More ominous to many Asians are the horror stories like that of Vincent Chin, a Chinese-American who was beaten to death one night in the early 1980s by two disgruntled Detroit auto workers who were angry at competition by Japanese automakers....

**"Give meritocracy a chance"**    Free market zealots like University of Chicago law professor Richard Epstein, who believes all "irrational discrimination" would disappear in an unfettered marketplace, have called for the elimination of anti-discrimination laws, saying the market will punish those who turn aside talented workers or customers with money in their pockets just because of race or ethnicity. D'Souza agrees with Epstein's bold assertion that anti-discrimination laws actually get in the way of women and minorities who would prefer to hire family members. He calls for an end to all anti-discrimination laws except those that apply solely to government.

**Comment**  "Merit" by whose standard? Market forces do count, but so do culture and personal prejudices. Segregation cost white businesses valuable consumer business, yet, even in the North, where it was required only by local custom, not by government, many refused to serve blacks anyway.

Any intrusions into the marketplace trouble free-market conservatives like Epstein and D'Souza, but the larger question we Americans must ask ourselves is this: What kind of country do we want? There is no neutral "color-blind" approach to the law that has for centuries been tilted against women and minorities. It either defends the status quo, which is imbalanced by race and gender, it shifts some benefits to certain groups, or it shifts benefits away from those groups. Do we want rampant irrational completely unfair discrimination reminiscent of the Jim Crow days that dehumanizes large numbers of Americans while we wait for the vagaries of the marketplace to catch up? Or do we want to shape law and social practice to encourage people to mix, get to know each other better, and ultimately reduce tensions?

**"It encourages balkanization"**  Affirmative action opens social wedges that threatens to replace the basic American melting pot creed with a new "balkanization."

**Comment**  Anyone who thinks American society was *less* balkanized in the 1950s and 1960s was not only color-blind but also quite deaf to the complaints of people of color. If there were less racial or gender friction in major newsrooms, campuses, and other workplaces, it is only because there was no race or gender in them except white men.

Racism and sexism have not disappeared, it is widely agreed, they have only become more subtle—"gone underground"—making them less easy to detect, harder to root out. Most of us tend to ignore our own prejudices unless someone points them out. If individuals wish to discriminate in their private social world, that's their business. But discrimination in hiring and promotional practices is everyone's business. With the courts already jammed and the complaint mechanisms of the Equal Employment Opportunity Commission suffering backlogs of two years or worse, especially after Americans with Disabilities Act cases were layered onto its already overtaxed, underfunded enforcement mechanisms, promises of enforcement of individual complaints were simply not enough to make up for cruel realities. Even when the courts do reach guilty verdicts, they often impose racial or gender quotas onto the plaintiffs as part of the penalty and remedies. Such court-ordered mandates are, by the way, the only real "quotas" that are allowed under civil rights law and only as a last resort to remedy particularly egregious cases of historic discrimination, such as the police and fire department hiring and promotion practices in cities like

Chicago, Memphis, and Birmingham. Yet even these quotas have been quite modest, used sparingly, and, beginning in the 1980s, steadily rolled back by the courts, even while the numbers showed modest progress in the face of the enormous problem.

What most people call rigid "quotas" are actually quite flexible goals and timetables, a distinction that has diminished in the public mind in recent years as conservative politicians have, with remarkable success, attacked flexible goals and timetables with as much vigor as they once reserved for attacking rigid quotas.

**"Focus on class not race"**    In attempts to salvage some rudiments of affirmative action in the face of a conservative onslaught, some centrists have argued for programs that reach out to the most needy, regardless of race or gender. If such programs are conducted equitably, a preponderance of minorities will be brought in anyway, without the dubious air of unfairness.

The ghetto "underclass" has not benefited from affirmative action, University of Chicago sociology professor William Julius Wilson writes in *The Truly Disadvantaged* (1987) because this group is "outside the mainstream of the American occupational system." For this group, Wilson advocates macroeconomic policies aimed at promoting economic growth to replace inner-city manufacturing jobs lost since the 1950s and on-the-job training programs.

Each of these arguments has some merit and much myth. Left to our own devices, most of us unfortunately will discriminate, often in ways too subtle for us to notice even when we do it. Either way, such irrational discrimination occurs and is not healthy for a diverse society. . . .

America will not have racial equality until opportunities are equalized, beginning at the preschool level, to build up the supply of qualified applicants for the new jobs emerging in information-age America. The American ideal of equal opportunity still produces rewards, when it is given a real try. It needs to be tried more often. Affirmative action is not a perfect remedy, but it beats the alternative, if the only alternative is to do nothing.

# NO

**Shelby Steele**

# Affirmative Action: The Price of Preference

In theory, affirmative action certainly has all the moral symmetry that fairness requires—the injustice of historical and even contemporary white advantage is offset with black advantage; preference replaces prejudice, inclusion answers exclusion. It is reformist and corrective, even repentant and redemptive. And I would never sneer at these good intentions. Born in the late forties in Chicago, I started my education (a charitable term in this case) in a segregated school and suffered all the indignities that come to blacks in a segregated society. My father, born in the South, only made it to the third grade before the white man's fields took permanent priority over his formal education. And though he educated himself into an advanced reader with an almost professorial authority, he could only drive a truck for a living and never earned more than ninety dollars a week in his entire life. So yes, it is crucial to my sense of citizenship, to my ability to identify with the spirit and the interests of America, to know that this country, however imperfectly, recognizes its past sins and wishes to correct them.

Yet good intentions, because of the opportunity for innocence they offer us, are very seductive and can blind us to the effects they generate when implemented. In our society, affirmative action is, among other things, a testament to white goodwill and to black power, and in the midst of these heavy investments, its effects can be hard to see. But after twenty years of implementation, I think affirmative action has shown itself to be more bad than good and that blacks—whom I will focus on in this essay—now stand to lose more from it than they gain.

In talking with affirmative action administrators and with blacks and whites in general, it is clear that supporters of affirmative action focus on its good intentions while detractors emphasize its negative effects. Proponents talk about "diversity" and "pluralism"; opponents speak of "reverse discrimination," the unfairness of quotas and set-asides. It was virtually impossible to find people outside either camp. The closest I came was a white male manager at a large computer company who said, "I think it amounts to reverse discrimination, but I'll put up with a little of that for a little more diversity." I'll live with a little of the effect to gain a little of the intention, he seemed to be saying. But this only makes him a halfhearted supporter of affirmative action. I think

From Shelby Steele, *The Content of Our Character: A New Vision of Race in America* (St. Martin's Press, 1990). Copyright © 1990 by Shelby Steele. Reprinted by permission of St. Martin's Press, LLC.

many people who don't really like affirmative action support it to one degree or another anyway.

I believe they do this because of what happened to white and black Americans in the crucible of the sixties when whites were confronted with their racial guilt and blacks tasted their first real power. In this stormy time white absolution and black power coalesced into virtual mandates for society. Affirmative action became a meeting ground for these mandates in the law, and in the late sixties and early seventies it underwent a remarkable escalation of its mission from simple anti-discrimination enforcement to social engineering by means of quotas, goals, timetables, set-asides and other forms of preferential treatment.

Legally, this was achieved through a series of executive orders and EEOC [Equal Employment Opportunity Commission] guidelines that allowed racial imbalances in the workplace to stand as proof of racial discrimination. Once it could be assumed that discrimination explained racial imbalances, it became easy to justify group remedies to presumed discrimination, rather than the normal case-by-case redress for proven discrimination. Preferential treatment through quotas, goals, and so on is designed to correct imbalances based on the assumption that they always indicate discrimination. This expansion of what constitutes discrimination allowed affirmative action to escalate into the business of social engineering in the name of anti-discrimination, to push society toward statistically proportionate racial representation, without any obligation of proving actual discrimination.

What accounted for this shift, I believe, was the white mandate to achieve a new racial innocence and the black mandate to gain power. Even though blacks had made great advances during the sixties without quotas, these mandates, which came to a head in the very late sixties, could no longer be satisfied by anything less than racial preferences. I don't think these mandates in themselves were wrong, since whites clearly needed to do better by blacks and blacks needed more real power in society. But, as they came together in affirmative action, their effect was to distort our understanding of racial discrimination in a way that allowed us to offer the remediation of preference on the basis of mere color rather than actual injury. By making black the color of preference, these mandates have reburdened society with the very marriage of color and preference (in reverse) that we set out to eradicate. The old sin is reaffirmed in a new guise.

But the essential problem with this form of affirmative action is the way it leaps over the hard business of developing a formerly oppressed people to the point where they can achieve proportionate representation on their own (given equal opportunity) and goes straight for the proportionate representation. This may satisfy some whites of their innocence and some blacks of their power, but it does very little to truly uplift blacks.

A white female affirmative action officer at an Ivy League university told me what many supporters of affirmative action now say: "We're after diversity. We ideally want a student body where racial and ethnic groups are represented according to their proportion in society." When affirmative action escalated into social engineering, diversity became a golden word. It grants whites an egalitarian fairness (innocence) and blacks an entitlement to proportionate representation (power). *Diversity* is a term that applies democratic principles to races and cultures rather than to citizens, despite the fact that there is nothing to indicate that real diversity is the same thing as proportionate representation. Too often the result of this on campuses (for example) has been a democracy of colors rather than of people, an artificial diversity that gives the appearance of an educational parity between black and white students that has not yet been achieved in reality. Here again, racial preferences allow society to leapfrog over the difficult problem of developing blacks to parity with whites and into a cosmetic diversity that covers the blemish of disparity—a full six years after admission, only about 26 percent of black students graduate from college.

Racial representation is not the same thing as racial development, yet affirmative action fosters a confusion of these very different needs. Representation can be manufactured; development is always hard-earned. However, it is the music of innocence and power that we hear in affirmative action that causes us to cling to it and to its distracting emphasis on representation. The fact is that after twenty years of racial preferences, the gap between white and black median income is greater than it was in the seventies. None of this is to say that blacks don't need policies that ensure our right to equal opportunity, but what we need more is the development that will let us take advantage of society's efforts to include us.

I think that one of the most troubling effects of racial preferences for blacks is a kind of demoralization, or put another way, an enlargement of self-doubt. Under affirmative action the quality that earns us preferential treatment is an implied inferiority. However this inferiority is explained—and it is easily enough explained by the myriad deprivations that grew out of our oppression —it is still inferiority. There are explanations, and then there is the fact. And the fact must be borne by the individual as a condition apart from the explanation, apart even from the fact that others like himself also bear this condition. In integrated situations where blacks must compete with whites who may be better prepared, these explanations may quickly wear thin and expose the individual to racial as well as personal self-doubt.

All of this is compounded by the cultural myth of black inferiority that blacks have always lived with. What this means in practical terms is that when blacks deliver themselves into integrated situations, they encounter a nasty little reflex in whites, a mindless, atavistic reflex that responds to the color black with alarm. Attributions may follow this alarm if the white cares to indulge them, and if they do, they will most likely be negative—one such attribution is intellectual ineptness. I think this reflex and the attributions that may follow it embarrass most whites today, therefore, it is usually quickly repressed. Nevertheless, on an equally atavistic level, the black will be aware of the reflex his color triggers and will feel a stab of horror at seeing himself reflected in this way. He, too, will do a quick repression, but a lifetime of such stabbings is what constitutes his inner realm of racial doubt.

The effects of this may be a subject for another essay. The point here is that the implication of inferiority that racial preferences engender in both the white and black mind expands rather than contracts this doubt. Even when the black sees no implication of inferiority in racial preferences, he knows that whites do, so that—consciously or unconsciously—the result is virtually the same. The effect of preferential treatment—the lowering of normal standards to increase black representation—puts blacks at war with an expanded realm of debilitating doubt, so that the doubt itself becomes an unrecognized preoccupation that undermines their ability to perform, especially in integrated situations. On largely white campuses, blacks are five times more likely to drop out than whites. Preferential treatment, no matter how it is justified in the light of day, subjects blacks to a midnight of self-doubt, and so often transforms their advantage into a revolving door.

Another liability of affirmative action comes from the fact that it indirectly encourages blacks to exploit their own past victimization as a source of power and privilege. Victimization, like implied inferiority, is what justifies preference, so that to receive the benefits of preferential treatment one must, to some extent, become invested in the view of one's self as a victim. In this way, affirmative action nurtures a victim-focused identity in blacks. The obvious irony here is that we become inadvertently invested in the very condition we are trying to overcome. Racial preferences send us the message that there is more power in our past suffering than our present achievements—none of which could bring us a *preference* over others.

When power itself grows out of suffering, then blacks are encouraged to expand the boundaries of what qualifies as racial oppression, a situation that can lead us to paint our victimization in vivid colors, even as we receive the benefits of preference. The same corporations and institutions that give us preference are also seen as our oppressors. At Stanford University minority students —some of whom enjoy as much as $15,000 a year in financial aid—recently took over the president's office demanding, among other things, more financial aid. The power to be found in victimization, like any power, is intoxicating and can lend itself to the creation of a new class of super-victims who can feel the pea of victimization under twenty mattresses. Preferential treatment rewards us for being underdogs rather than for moving beyond that status—a misplacement of incentives that, along with its deepening of our doubt, is more a yoke than a spur.

But, I think, one of the worst prices that blacks pay for preference has to do with an illusion. I saw this illusion at work recently in the mother of a middle-class black student who was going off to his first semester of college. "They owe us this, so don't think for a minute that you don't belong there." This is the logic by which many blacks, and some whites, justify affirmative action—it is something "owed," a form of reparation. But this logic overlooks a much harder and less digestible reality, that it is impossible to repay blacks living today for the historic suffering of the race. If all blacks were given a million dollars tomorrow morning it would not amount to a dime on the dollar of three centuries of oppression, nor would it obviate the residues of that oppression that we still carry today. The concept of historic reparation grows out of man's need to impose a degree of justice on the world that simply does not exist. Suffering can be endured and overcome, it cannot be repaid. Blacks cannot be repaid for the injustice done to the race, but we can be corrupted by society's guilty gestures of repayment.

Affirmative action is such a gesture. It tells us that racial preferences can do for us what we cannot do for ourselves. The corruption here is in the hidden incentive *not* to do what we believe preferences will do. This is an incentive to be reliant on others just as we are struggling for self-reliance. And it keeps alive the illusion that we can find some deliverance in repayment. The hardest thing for any sufferer to accept is that his suffering excuses him from very little and never has enough currency to restore him. To think otherwise is to prolong the suffering.

Several blacks I spoke with said they were still in favor of affirmative action because of the "subtle" discrimination blacks were subject to once on the job. One photojournalist said, "They have ways of ignoring you." A black female television producer said, "You can't file a lawsuit when your boss doesn't invite you to the insider meetings without ruining your career. So we still need affirmative action." Others mentioned the infamous "glass ceiling" through which blacks can see the top positions of authority but never reach them. But I don't think racial preferences are a protection against this subtle discrimination; I think they contribute to it.

In any workplace, racial preferences will always create two-tiered populations composed of preferreds and unpreferreds. This division makes automatic a perception of enhanced competence for the unpreferreds and of questionable competence for the preferreds—the former earned his way, even though others were given preference, while the latter made it by color as much as by competence. Racial preferences implicitly mark whites with an exaggerated superiority just as they mark blacks with an exaggerated inferiority. They not only reinforce America's oldest racial myth but, for blacks, they have the effect of stigmatizing the already stigmatized.

I think that much of the "subtle" discrimination that blacks talk about is often (not always) discrimination against the stigma of questionable competence that affirmative action delivers to blacks. In this sense, preferences scapegoat the very people they seek to help. And it may be that at a certain level employers impose a glass ceiling, but this may not be against the race so much as against the race's reputation for having advanced by color as much as by competence. Affirmative action makes a glass ceiling virtually necessary as a protection against the corruptions of preferential treatment. This ceiling is the point at which corporations shift the emphasis from color to competency and stop playing the affirmative action game. Here preference backfires for blacks and becomes a taint that holds them back. Of course, one could argue that this taint, which is, after all, in the minds of whites, becomes nothing more than an excuse to discriminate against blacks. And certainly the result is the same in either case—blacks don't get past the glass ceiling. But this argument does not get around the fact that racial preferences now taint this color with a new theme of suspicion that makes it even more vulnerable to the impulse in others to discriminate. In this crucial yet gray area of perceived competence, preferences make whites look better than they are and blacks worse, while doing nothing whatever to stop the very real discrimination that blacks may encounter. I don't wish to justify the glass ceiling here, but only to suggest the very subtle ways that affirmative action revives rather than extinguishes the old rationalizations for racial discrimination.

In education, a revolving door; in employment, a glass ceiling.

I believe affirmative action is problematic in our society because it tries to function like a social program. Rather than ask it to ensure equal opportunity we have demanded that it create parity between the races. But preferential treatment does not teach skills, or educate, or instill motivation. It only passes out entitlement by color, a situation that in my profession has created an unrealistically high demand for black professors. The social engineer's assumption is that this high demand will inspire more blacks to earn Ph.D.'s and join the profession. In fact, the number of blacks earning Ph.D.'s has declined in recent years. A Ph.D. must be developed from preschool on. He requires family and community support. He must acquire an entire system of values that enables him to work hard while delaying gratification. There are social programs, I believe, that can (and should) help blacks *develop* in all these areas, but entitlement by color is not a social program; it is a dubious reward for being black....

Preferences are inexpensive and carry the glamour of good intentions—change the numbers and the good deed is done. To be against them is to be unkind. But I think the unkindest cut is to bestow on children like my own an undeserved advantage while neglecting the development of those disadvantaged children on the East Side of my city who will likely never be in a position to benefit from a preference. Give my children fairness; give disadvantaged children a better shot at development—better elementary and secondary schools, job training, safer neighborhoods, better financial assistance for college, and so on. Fewer blacks go to college today than ten years ago; more black males of college age are in prison or under the control of the criminal justice system than in college. This despite racial preferences.

The mandates of black power and white absolution out of which preferences emerged were not wrong in themselves. What was wrong was that both races focused more on the goals of these mandates than on the means of the goals. Blacks can have no real power without taking responsibility for their own educational and economic development. Whites can have no racial innocence without earning it by eradicating discrimination and helping the disadvantaged to develop. Because we ignored the means, the goals have not been reached, and the real work remains to be done.

# POSTSCRIPT

## Does Affirmative Action Advance the Cause of Racial Equality?

$\mathbf{M}$uch of the argument between Steele and Page turns on the question of "color blindness." To what extent should our laws be color-blind? During the 1950s and early 1960s, civil rights leaders were virtually unanimous on this point. Martin Luther King, Jr., in a speech given at a civil rights march on Washington, said, "I have a dream that my four little children will one day live in a nation where they will not be judged by the color of their skin but by the content of their character." This was the consensus view in 1963, but today it may need to be qualified: In order to *bring about* color blindness, it may be necessary to become temporarily color-conscious. But for how long? And is there a danger that this temporary color consciousness may become a permanent policy?

Girardeau A. Spann's *The Law of Affirmative Action: Twenty-Five Years of Supreme Court Decisions on Race and Remedies* (New York University Press, 2000) is a comprehensive chronicle of the Supreme Court's involvement with the affirmative action issue from *DeFunis v. Odegaard* in 1974 through the cases decided in the Court's 1998–1999 term. Clint Bolick, in *The Affirmative Action Fraud: Can We Restore the Civil Rights Vision?* (Cato Institute, 1996), argues that racial and gender preferences deepen racial hostilities and undermine individual freedom without doing minorities much good. This argument is also advanced by Paul Craig Roberts and Lawrence M. Stratton in *The New Color Line: How Quotas and Privilege Destroy Democracy* (Regnery, 1995). In *The Color Bind* (University of California Press, 1998), Linda Chavez recounts the battles over California's Proposition 209, a ballot initiative opposed by the author. Columnist Jim Sleeper's *Liberal Racism* (Viking, 1997) is critical of affirmative action and other race-based programs, as is a book by *ABC News* reporter Bob Zelnick, *Backfire: A Reporter's Look at Affirmative Action* (Regnery, 1996). Barbara Bergmann supports affirmative action in *In Defense of Affirmative Action* (Basic Books, 1996), while Stephan Thernstrom and Abigail Thernstrom, in their comprehensive survey of racial progress in America entitled *America in Black and White: One Nation, Indivisible* (Simon & Schuster, 1997), argue that it is counterproductive.

Affirmative action is one of those issues, like abortion, in which the opposing sides seem utterly intransigent. But there may be a large middle sector of opinion that is simply weary of the whole controversy and may be willing to support any expedient solution worked out by pragmatists in the executive and legislative branches of the government.

# ISSUE 11

# Should Hate Speech Be Punished?

**YES: Charles R. Lawrence III**, from "Crossburning and the Sound of Silence: Antisubordination Theory and the First Amendment," *Villanova Law Review* (vol. 37, no. 4, 1992)

**NO: Jonathan Rauch**, from "In Defense of Prejudice: Why Incendiary Speech Must Be Protected," *Harper's Magazine* (May 1995)

## ISSUE SUMMARY

**YES:** Law professor Charles R. Lawrence III asserts that speech should be impermissible when, going beyond insult, it inflicts injury on its victims.

**NO:** Author Jonathan Rauch maintains that there can be no genuine freedom of expression unless it includes the freedom to offend those who oppose the expressed opinion.

In 1942, on a busy public street in Rochester, New Hampshire, a man named Walter Chaplinsky was passing out literature promoting the Jehovah's Witnesses, which would have been all right except that the literature denounced all other religions as "rackets." As might be expected, Chaplinsky's activities caused a stir. The city marshal warned Chaplinsky that he was on the verge of creating a riot and told him that he ought to leave, whereupon Chaplinsky answered him in these words: "You are a Goddamned racketeer... a damned Fascist, and the whole government of Rochester are Fascists or agents of Fascists." Chaplinsky was arrested for disturbing the peace, and he appealed on the grounds that his First Amendment right to free speech had been violated. The Supreme Court of the United States ruled unanimously against him. In *Chaplinsky v. New Hampshire* (1942) the Court said that his words were "fighting words," not deserving of First Amendment protection because they were "likely to provoke the average person to retaliation."

In 1984 a Texan named Gregory Lee Johnson stood in front of Dallas City Hall, doused an American flag in kerosene, and set it on fire while chanting, "Red, white, and blue, we spit on you." When he was arrested for flag desecration, he appealed to the Supreme Court on grounds of free speech—and won. In *Texas v. Johnson* (1989) the Court ruled that flag burning was a form of "symbolic speech" protected by the First Amendment.

So Chaplinsky used his mouth and was punished for it, and Johnson burned a flag and was not. How do we square these decisions, or should we? If a state can punish a person for calling someone a "Goddamned racketeer," can it also punish someone for shouting racial epithets?

Some municipalities have enacted laws that punish "hate speech" directed at women and minorities. The intention of these codes and laws is to ensure at least a minimum of civility in places where people of very diverse backgrounds must live and work together. But do they infringe upon essential freedoms?

In 1992 the Supreme Court confronted this issue in a case testing the constitutionality of a St. Paul, Minnesota, statute punishing anyone who displays symbols attacking people because of their "race, color, creed, religion, or gender." A group of St. Paul teenagers had burned a cross in the yard of a black family. Prosecutors used this newly enacted law, which raised the essential issues in the case: Did the statute violate freedoms guaranteed by the First Amendment? If so, why? In its decision of *R. A. V. v. St. Paul* (1992), the Court gave a unanimous answer to the first question. All nine justices agreed that the statute was indeed a violation of the First Amendment. But on the second question—*why* was it a violation?—the Court was deeply divided. Four members thought that it was unconstitutional because it was "overbroad," that is, worded in such general language that it would reach beyond the narrow bounds of speech activities that the Court has deemed punishable. But the majority, in an opinion by Justice Antonin Scalia, struck down the statute for a very different reason: because it contained "content discrimination." By punishing speech that attacks people because of their "race, color, creed, religion, or gender," it was prohibiting speech "solely on the basis of the subjects the speech addresses." A statute punishing speech may not single out specific categories like race or creed for protection, for to do so is to involve the state in deciding which sorts of people deserve protection against "hate speech."

In response to increasing incidents of highly derogatory racial, religious, and sexual remarks and writing on college campuses, a number of colleges adopted speech codes that went beyond what the Supreme Court had characterized as "fighting words" in *Chaplinsky*. These restrictions prompted outcries that "political correctness" was stifling the expression of unpopular ideas. Lower federal courts voided antidiscrimination codes at the Universities of Michigan and Wisconsin as overbroad and vague, calling into question similar codes at other public and private institutions.

However, the Supreme Court in *Wisconsin v. Mitchell* (1993) unanimously upheld a hate crimes law. This case was distinguished from hate speech cases in that the speech per se was not punished, but the determination that hatred inspired the commission of a crime could be the basis for increasing the penalty for that crime.

In the following selections, Charles R. Lawrence III argues that speech has the power to inflict injury and curtail the freedom of the victims of hate. Jonathan Rauch defends incendiary speech on the ground that the rights of all are better protected by pluralism than purism.

191

 **YES**

# Crossburning and the Sound of Silence: Antisubordination Theory and the First Amendment

In the early morning hours of June 21, 1990, long after they had put their five children to bed, Russ and Laura Jones were awakened by voices outside their house. Russ got up, went to his bedroom window and peered into the dark. "I saw a glow," he recalled. There, in the middle of his yard, was a burning cross. The Joneses are black. In the spring of 1990 they had moved into their four-bedroom, three-bathroom dream house on 290 Earl Street in St. Paul, Minnesota. They were the only black family on the block. Two weeks after they had settled into their predominantly white neighborhood, the tires on both their cars were slashed. A few weeks later, one of their cars' windows was shattered, and a group of teenagers had walked past their house and shouted "nigger" at their nine-year-old son. And now this burning cross. Russ Jones did not have to guess at the meaning of this symbol of racial hatred. There is not a black person in America who has not been taught the significance of this instrument of persecution and intimidation, who has not had emblazoned on his mind the image of black men's scorched bodies hanging from trees, and who does not know the story of Emmett Till.[1] One can only imagine the terror which Russell Jones must have felt as he watched the flames and thought of the vulnerability of his family and of the hateful, cowardly viciousness of those who would attack him and those he loved under cover of darkness.

This assault on Russ Jones and his family begins the story of *R.A.V. v. City of St. Paul,* the "hate speech" case recently decided by the United States Supreme Court. The Joneses, however, are not the subject of the Court's opinion. The constitutional injury addressed in *R.A.V.* was not this black family's right to live where they pleased, or their right to associate with their neighbors. The Court was not concerned with how this attack might impede the exercise of the Joneses' constitutional right to be full and valued participants in the political community, for it did not view *R.A.V.* as a case about the Joneses' injury. Instead, the Court was concerned primarily with the alleged constitutional injury to those who assaulted the Joneses, that is, the First Amendment rights of the crossburners.

From Charles R. Lawrence III, "Crossburning and the Sound of Silence: Antisubordination Theory and the First Amendment," *Villanova Law Review,* vol. 37, no. 4 (1992), pp. 787–804. Copyright © 1992 by Villanova University. Reprinted by permission. Some notes omitted.

There is much that is deeply troubling about Justice Scalia's majority opinion in *R.A.V.* But it is the utter disregard for the silenced voice of the victims that is most frightening. Nowhere in the opinion is any mention made of the Jones family or of their constitutional rights. Nowhere are we told of the history of the Ku Klux Klan or of its use of the burning cross as a tool for the suppression of speech. Justice Scalia turns the First Amendment on its head, transforming an act intended to silence through terror and intimidation into an invitation to join a public discussion. In so doing, he clothes the crossburner's terroristic act in the legitimacy of protected political speech and invites him to burn again.

"Let there be no mistake about our belief that burning a cross in someone's front yard is reprehensible," writes Justice Scalia at the close of his opinion. I am skeptical about his concern for the victims. These words seem little more than an obligatory genuflection to decency. For even in this attempt to assure the reader of his good intentions, Justice Scalia's words betray his inability to see the Joneses or hear their voices. "Burning a cross in *someone's* front yard is *reprehensible*," he says. It is reprehensible but not injurious, or immoral, or violative of the Joneses' rights. For Justice Scalia, the identity of the "someone" is irrelevant. As is the fact that it is a *cross* that is burned.

When I first read Justice Scalia's opinion it felt as if another cross had just been set ablaze. This cross was burning on the pages of U.S. Reports. It was a cross like the cross that Justice Taney had burned in 1857,[2] and that which Justice Brown had burned in 1896.[3] Its message: "You have no rights which a white man is bound to respect (or protect).[4] If you are injured by this assaultive act, the injury is a figment of your imagination that is not constitutionally cognizable."[5]

For the past couple of years I have been struggling to find a way to talk to my friends in the civil liberties community about the injures which are ignored in the *R.A.V.* case. I have tried to articulate the ways in which hate speech harms its victims and the ways in which it harms us all by undermining core values in our Constitution.

The first of these values is full and equal citizenship expressed in the Fourteenth Amendment's Equal Protection Clause. When hate speech is employed with the purpose and effect of maintaining established systems of caste and subordination, it violates that core value. Hate speech often prevents its victims from exercising legal rights guaranteed by the Constitution and civil rights statutes. The second constitutional value threatened by hate speech is the value of free expression itself. Hate speech frequently silences its victims, who, more often than not, are those who are already heard from least. An understanding of both of these injuries is aided by the methodologies of feminism and critical race theory that give special attention to the structures of subordination and the voices of the subordinated.

My own understanding of the need to inform the First Amendment discourse with the insights of an antisubordination theory began in the context of the debate over the regulation of hate speech on campus. As I lectured at universities throughout the United States, I learned of serious racist and anti-Semitic hate incidents. Students who had been victimized told me of swastikas appearing on Jewish holy days. Stories of cross burnings, racist slurs and vicious verbal assaults made me cringe even as I heard them secondhand. Universities, long the home of institutional and euphemistic racism, were witnessing the worst forms of gutter racism. In 1990, the Chronicle of Higher Education reported that approximately 250 colleges and universities had experienced serious racist incidents since 1986, and the National Institute Against Prejudice and Violence estimated that 25% of all minority students are victimized at least once during an academic year.

I urged my colleagues to hear these students' voices and argued that *Brown v. Board of Education* and its antidiscrimination principle identified an injury of constitutional dimension done to these students that must be recognized and remedied. We do not normally think of *Brown* as being a case about speech. Most narrowly read, it is a case about the rights of black children to equal educational opportunity. But *Brown* teaches us another very important lesson: that the harm of segregation is achieved by the meaning of the message it conveys. The Court's opinion in *Brown* stated that racial segregation is unconstitutional not because the "physical separation of black and white children is bad or because resources were distributed unequally among black and white schools. *Brown* held that segregated schools were unconstitutional primarily because of the message segregation conveys—the message that black children are an untouchable caste, unfit to be educated with white children." Segregation stamps a badge of inferiority upon blacks. This badge communicates a message to others that signals their exclusion from the community of citizens.

The "Whites Only" signs on the lunch counter, swimming pool and drinking fountain convey the same message. The antidiscrimination principle articulated in *Brown* presumptively entitles every individual to be treated by the organized society as a respected, responsible and participating member. This is the principle upon which all our civil rights laws rest. It is the guiding principle of the Equal Protection Clause's requirement of nondiscriminatory government action. In addition, it has been applied in regulating private discrimination.

The words "Women Need Not Apply" in a job announcement, the racially exclusionary clause in a restrictive covenant and the racial epithet scrawled on the locker of the new black employee at a previously all-white job site all convey a political message. But we treat these messages as "discriminatory practices" and outlaw them under federal and state civil rights legislation because they are more than speech. In the context of social inequality, these verbal and symbolic acts form integral links in historically ingrained systems of social discrimination. They work to keep traditionally victimized groups in socially isolated, stigmatized and disadvantaged positions through the promotion of fear, intolerance, degradation and violence. The Equal Protection Clause of the Fourteenth Amendment requires the disestablishment of these practices and systems. Likewise, the First Amendment does *not* prohibit our accomplishment of this compelling constitutional interest simply because those discriminatory practices are achieved through the use of words and symbols.

The primary intent of the cross burner in *R.A.V.* was not to enter into a dialogue with the Joneses, or even with the larger community, as it arguably was in *Brandenburg v. Ohio*. His purpose was to intimidate—to cast fear in the hearts of his victims, to drive them out of the community, to enforce the practice of residential segregation, and to encourage others to join him in the enforcement of that practice. The discriminatory impact of this speech is of even more importance than the speaker's intent. In protecting victims of discrimination, it is the presence of this discriminatory impact, which is a compelling government interest unrelated to the suppression of the speaker's political message, that requires a balancing of interests rather than a presumption against constitutionality. This is especially true when the interests that compete with speech are also interests of constitutional dimension.

One such interest is in enforcing the antidiscrimination principle. Those opposed to the regulation of hate speech often view the interest involved as the maintenance of civility, the protection of sensibilities from offense, or the prohibition of group defamation. But this analysis misconstrues the nature of the injury. "Defamation—injury to group reputation—is not the same as discrimination—injury to group status and treatment." The former "is more ideational and less material" than the latter, "which recognizes the harm of second-class citizenship and inferior social standing with the attendant deprivation of access to resources, voice, and power."

The Title VII paradigm of "hostile environment" discrimination best describes the injury to which victims of racist, sexist and homophobic hate speech are subjected. When plaintiffs in employment discrimination suits have been subjected to racist or sexist verbal harassment in the workplace, courts have recognized that such assaultive speech denies the targeted individual equal access to employment. These verbal assaults most often occur in settings where the relatively recent and token integration of the workplace makes the victim particularly vulnerable and where the privately voiced message of denigration and exclusion echoes the whites-only and males-only practices that were all-too-recently official policy.

*Robinson v. Jacksonville Shipyards, Inc.,* a Title VII case that appears to be headed for review in the Supreme Court, presents a clear example of the tension between the law's commitment to free speech and its commitment to equality. Lois Robinson, a welder, was one of a very small number of female skilled craftworkers employed by Jacksonville Shipyards. She brought suit under Title VII of the Civil Rights Act of 1964, alleging that her employer had created and encouraged a sexually hostile, intimidating work environment. A U.S. District Court ruled in her favor, finding that the presence in the workplace of pictures of women in various stages of undress and in sexually suggestive or submissive poses, as well as remarks made by male employees and supervisors which demeaned women, constituted a violation of Title VII "through the maintenance of a sexually hostile work environment." Much of District Court Judge Howell Melton's opinion is a recounting of the indignities that Ms. Robinson and five other women experienced almost daily while working with 850 men over the course of ten years. In addition to the omnipresent display of sexually explicit drawings, graffiti, calendars, centerfold-style pictures, magazines and cartoons, the trial record contains a number of incidents in which sexually suggestive pictures and comments were directed at Robinson. Male employees admitted that the shipyard was "a boys' club" and "more or less a man's world."

The local chapter of the American Civil Liberties Union (ACLU) appealed the District Court's decision, arguing that "even sexists have a right to free speech." However, anyone who has read the trial record cannot help but wonder about these civil libertarians' lack of concern for Lois Robinson's right to do her work without being subjected to assault.

The trial record makes clear that Lois Robinson's male colleagues had little concern for advancing the cause of erotic speech when they made her the target of pornographic comments and graffiti. They wanted to put the usurper of their previously all-male domain in her place, to remind her of her sexual vulnerability and to send her back home where she belonged. This speech, like the burning cross in *R.A.V.*, does more than communicate an idea. It interferes with the victim's right to work at a job where she is free from degradation because of her gender.

But it is not sufficient to describe the injury occasioned by hate speech only in terms of the countervailing value of equality. There is also an injury to the First Amendment. When Russ Jones looked out his window and saw that burning cross, he heard a message that said, "*Shut up, black man, or risk harm to you and your family.*" It may be that Russ Jones is especially brave, or especially foolhardy, and that he may speak even more loudly in the face of this threat. But it is more likely that he will be silenced, and that *we* will lose the benefit of his voice.

Professor Laurence H. Tribe has identified two values protected by the First Amendment. The first is the intrinsic value of speech, which is the value of individual self expression. Speech is intrinsically valuable as a manifestation of our humanity and our individuality. The second is the instrumental value of speech. The First Amendment protects dissent to maximize public discourse, and to achieve the great flowering of debate and ideas that we need to make our democracy work. Both of these values are implicated in the silencing of Russ Jones by his nocturnal attacker.

For African-Americans, the intrinsic value of speech as self-expression and self-definition has been particularly important. The absence of a "black voice" was central to the ideology of European-American racism, an ideology that denied Africans their humanity and thereby justified their enslavement. African-American slaves were prevented from learning to read and write, and they were prohibited from engaging in forms of self-expression that might instill in them a sense of self-worth and pride. Their silence and submission was then interpreted as evidence of their subhuman status. The use of the burning cross as a method of disempowerment originates, in part, in the perpetrators' understanding of how, in the context of their ideology, their victims are rendered subhuman when they are silenced. When, in the face of threat and intimidation, the oppressors' victims are afraid to give full expression to their individuality, the oppressors achieve their purpose of denying the victims the liberty guaranteed to them by the Constitution.

When the Joneses moved to Earl Street in St. Paul, they were expressing their individuality. When they chose their house and their neighbors, they were saying, "This is who we are. We are a proud black family and we want to live here." This self-expression and self-definition is the intrinsic value of speech.

The instrumental value of speech is likewise threatened by this terrorist attack on the Joneses. Russ and Laura Jones also brought new voices to the political discourse in this St. Paul community. Ideally, they will vote and talk politics with their neighbors. They will bring new experiences and new perspectives to their neighborhood. A burning cross not only silences people like the Joneses, it impoverishes the democratic process and renders our collective conversation less informed.

First Amendment doctrine and theory have no words for the injuries of silence imposed by private actors. There is no language for the damage that is done to the First Amendment when the hateful speech of the crossburner or the sexual harasser silences its victims. In antidiscrimination law, we recognize the necessity of regulating private behavior that threatens the values of equal citizenship. Fair housing laws, public accommodations provisions and employment discrimination laws all regulate the behavior of private actors. We recognize that much of the discrimination in our society occurs without the active participation of the state. We know that we could not hope to realize the constitutional ideal of equal citizenship if we pretended that the government was the only discriminator.

But there is no recognition in First Amendment law of the systematic private suppression of speech. Courts and scholars have worried about the heckler's veto, and, where there is limited access to speech fora, we have given attention to questions of equal time and the right to reply. But for the most part, we act as if the government is the only regulator of speech, the only censor. We treat the marketplace of ideas as if all voices are equal, as if there are no silencing voices or voices that are silenced. In the discourse of the First Amendment, there is no way to talk about how those who are silenced are always less powerful than those who do the silencing. First Amendment law ignores the ways in which patriarchy silences women, and racism silences people of color. When a woman's husband threatens to beat her the next time she contradicts him, a First Amendment injury has occurred. "Gay-bashing" keeps gays and lesbians "in the closet." It silences them. They are denied the humanizing experience of self-expression. We *all* are denied the insight and beauty of their voices.

Professor Mari Matsuda has spoken compellingly of this problem in a telling personal story about the publication of her own thoughtful and controversial *Michigan Law Review* article on hate speech, "Public Response to Racist Speech: Considering the Victim's Story." When she began working on the article, a mentor at Harvard Law School warned her not to use this topic for her tenure piece. "It's a lightning rod," he told her. She followed his advice, publishing the article years later, only after receiving her university tenure and when visiting offers from prestigious schools were in hand.

"What is the sound of a paper unpublished?" writes Professor Matsuda. "What don't we hear when some young scholar chooses tenure over controversial speech? Every fall, students return from summer jobs and tell me of the times they didn't speak out against racist or anti-Semitic comments, in protest over unfairness or ethical dilemmas. They tell of the times they were invited to discriminatory clubs and went along in silence. What is the sound of all those silenced because they need a job? These silences, these things that go unsaid, aren't seen as First Amendment issues. The absences are characterized as private and voluntary, beyond collective cure."

In the rush to protect the "speech" of crossburners, would-be champions of the First Amendment must not forget the voices of their victims. If First Amendment doctrine and theory is to truly serve First Amendment ideals, it must recognize the injury done by the private suppression of speech; it must take into account the historical reality that some members of our community are less powerful than others and that those persons continue to be systematically silenced by those who are more powerful. If we are truly committed to free speech, First Amendment doctrine and theory must be guided by the principle of antisubordination. There can be no free speech where there are still masters and slaves.

## Notes

1. Emmett Till, a 14-year-old boy from Chicago, was killed while visiting relatives in Mississippi in 1955. His alleged "wolf whistle" at a white woman provoked his murderer. CONRAD LYNN, THERE IS A FOUNTAIN: THE AUTOBIOGRAPHY OF A CIVIL RIGHTS LAWYER 155 (1979); *see also* STEPHEN J. WHITFIELD, A DEATH IN THE DELTA: THE STORY OF EMMETT TILL (1988) (recounting story of black teenager murdered for allegedly whistling at white woman).

2. Dred Scott v. Sanford, 60 U.S. (19 How.) 393 (1856).

3. Plessy v. Ferguson, 163 U.S. 537 (1896).

4. Justice Taney, in holding that African Americans were not included and were not intended to be included under the word "citizen" in the Constitution, and could therefore claim none of the rights and privileges which that instrument provides for and secures opined, "[the colored race] had for more than a century before been regarded as being of an inferior order, and altogether unfit to associate with the white race, either in social or political relations; and so far inferior, that they had no rights which the white man was bound to respect." *Dred Scott,* 60 U.S. at 407.

5. In rejecting plaintiff's argument in *Plessy v. Ferguson* that enforced separation of the races constituted a badge of inferiority Judge Brown stated, "[i]f this be so, it is not by reason of anything found in the act, but solely because the colored race chooses to put that construction upon it." *Plessy,* 163 U.S. at 551....

# NO

Jonathan Rauch

## In Defense of Prejudice: Why Incendiary Speech Must Be Protected

The war on prejudice is now, in all likelihood, the most uncontroversial social movement in America. Opposition to "hate speech," formerly identified with the liberal left, has become a bipartisan piety. In the past year, groups and factions that agree on nothing else have agreed that the public expression of any and all prejudices must be forbidden. On the left, protesters and editorialists have insisted that Francis L. Lawrence resign as president of Rutgers University for describing blacks as "a disadvantaged population that doesn't have that genetic, hereditary background to have a higher average." On the other side of the ideological divide, Ralph Reed, the executive director of the Christian Coalition, responded to criticism of the religious right by calling a press conference to denounce a supposed outbreak of "name-calling, scapegoating, and religious bigotry." Craig Rogers, an evangelical Christian student at California State University, recently filed a $2.5 million sexual-harassment suit against a lesbian professor of psychology, claiming that anti-male bias in one of her lectures violated campus rules and left him feeling "raped and trapped."

In universities and on Capitol Hill, in workplaces and newsrooms, authorities are declaring that there is no place for racism, sexism, homophobia, Christian-bashing, and other forms of prejudice in public debate or even in private thought. "Only when racism and other forms of prejudice are expunged," say the crusaders for sweetness and light, "can minorities be safe and society be fair." So sweet, this dream of a world without prejudice. But the very last thing society should do is seek to utterly eradicate racism and other forms of prejudice....

Indeed, "eradicating prejudice" is so vague a proposition as to be meaningless. Distinguishing prejudice reliably and nonpolitically from nonprejudice, or even defining it crisply, is quite hopeless. We all feel we know prejudice when we see it. But do we? At the University of Michigan, a student said in a classroom discussion that he considered homosexuality a disease treatable with therapy. He was summoned to a formal disciplinary hearing for violating the school's policy against speech that "victimizes" people based on

From Jonathan Rauch, "In Defense of Prejudice: Why Incendiary Speech Must Be Protected," *Harper's Magazine* (May 1995). Copyright © 1995 by *Harper's Magazine*. Reprinted by permission. All rights reserved.

"sexual orientation." Now, the evidence is abundant that this particular hypothesis is wrong, and any American homosexual can attest to the harm that the student's hypothesis has inflicted on many real people. But was it a statement of prejudice or of misguided belief? Hate speech or hypothesis? Many Americans who do not regard themselves as bigots or haters believe that homosexuality is a treatable disease. They may be wrong, but are they all bigots? I am unwilling to say so, and if you are willing, beware. The line between a prejudiced belief and a merely controversial one is elusive, and the harder you look the more elusive it becomes. "God hates homosexuals" is a statement of fact, not of bias, to those who believe it; "American criminals are disproportionately black" is a statement of bias, not of fact, to those who disbelieve it. . . .

Pluralism is the principle that protects and makes a place in human company for that loneliest and most vulnerable of all minorities, the minority who is hounded and despised among blacks and whites, gays and straights, who is suspect or criminal among every tribe and in every nation of the world, and yet on whom progress depends: the dissident. I am not saying that dissent is always or even usually enlightened. Most of the time it is foolish and self-serving. No dissident has the right to be taken seriously, and the fact that Aryan Nation racists or Nation of Islam anti-Semites are unorthodox does not entitle them to respect. But what goes around comes around. As a supporter of gay marriage, for example, I reject the majority's view of family, and as a Jew I reject its view of God. I try to be civil, but the fact is that most Americans regard my views on marriage as a reckless assault on the most fundamental of all institutions, and many people are more than a little discomfited by the statement "Jesus Christ was no more divine than anybody else" (which is why so few people ever say it). Trap the racists and anti-Semites, and you lay a trap for me too. Hunt for them with eradication in your mind, and you have brought dissent itself within your sights.

The new crusade against prejudice waves aside such warnings. Like earlier crusades against antisocial ideas, the mission is fueled by good (if cocksure) intentions and a genuine sense of urgency. Some kinds of error are held to be intolerable, like pollutants that even in small traces poison the water for a whole town. Some errors are so pernicious as to damage real people's lives, so wrongheaded that no person of right mind or goodwill could support them. Like their forebears of other stripe—the Church in its campaigns against heretics, the McCarthyites in their campaigns against Communists—the modern anti-racist and anti-sexist and anti-homophobic campaigners are totalists, demanding not that misguided ideas and ugly expressions be corrected or criticized but that they be eradicated. They make war not on errors but on error, and like other totalists they act in the name of public safety—the safety, especially, of minorities.

                          *✿*

The sweeping implications of this challenge to pluralism are not, I think, well enough understood by the public at large. Indeed, the new brand of totalism has yet even to be properly named. "Multiculturalism," for instance, is much too broad. "Political correctness" comes closer but is too trendy and snide. For lack of anything else, I will call the new anti-pluralism "purism," since its major tenet is that society cannot be just until the last traces of invidious prejudice have been scrubbed away. Whatever you call it, the purists' way of seeing things has spread through American intellectual life with remarkable speed, so much so that many people will blink at you uncomprehendingly or even call you a racist (or sexist or homophobe, etc.) if you suggest that expressions of racism should be tolerated or that prejudice has its part to play....

What is especially dismaying is that the purists pursue prejudice in the name of protecting minorities. In order to protect people like me (homosexual), they must pursue people like me (dissident). In order to bolster minority self-esteem, they suppress minority opinion. There are, of course, all kinds of practical and legal problems with the purists' campaign: the incursions against the First Amendment; the inevitable abuses by prosecutors and activists who define as "hateful" or "violent" whatever speech they dislike or can score points off of; the lack of any evidence that repressing prejudice eliminates rather than inflames it. But minorities, of all people, ought to remember that by definition we cannot prevail by numbers, and we generally cannot prevail by force. Against the power of ignorant mass opinion and group prejudice and superstition, we have only our voices. If you doubt that minorities' voices are powerful weapons, think of the lengths to which Southern officials went to silence the Reverend Martin Luther King Jr. (recall that the city commissioner of Montgomery, Alabama, won a $500,000 libel suit, later overturned in *New York Times v. Sullivan* [1964], regarding an advertisement in the *Times* placed by civil-rights leaders who denounced the Montgomery police). Think of how much gay people have improved their lot over twenty-five years simply by refusing to remain silent. Recall the Michigan student who was prosecuted for saying that homosexuality is a treatable disease, and notice that he was black. Under that Michigan speech code, more than twenty blacks were charged with racist speech, while no instance of racist speech by whites was punished. In Florida, the hate-speech law was invoked against a black man who called a policeman a "white cracker"; not so surprisingly, in the first hate-crimes case to reach the Supreme Court, the victim was white and the defendant black.

In the escalating war against "prejudice," the right is already learning to play by the rules that were pioneered by the purist activists of the left. Last year leading Democrats, including the President, criticized the Republican Party for being increasingly in the thrall of the Christian right. Some of the rhetoric was harsh ("fire-breathing Christian radical right"), but it wasn't vicious or even clearly wrong. Never mind: when Democratic Representative Vic Fazio said Republicans were "being forced to the fringes by the aggressive political tactics of the religious right," the chairman of the Republican National Committee, Haley Barbour, said, "Christian-bashing" was the "left's preferred form of religious bigotry." Bigotry! Prejudice! "Christians active in politics are now on the receiving end of an extraordinary campaign of bias and prejudice," said the conservative leader William J. Bennett. One discerns, here, where the new purism leads. Eventually, any criticism of any group will be "prejudice."

Here is the ultimate irony of the new purism: words, which pluralists hope can be substituted for violence, are redefined by purists *as* violence. "The experience of being called 'nigger,' 'spic,' 'Jap,' or 'kike' is like receiving a slap in the face," Charles Lawrence wrote in 1990. "Psychic injury is no less an injury than being struck in the face, and it often is far more severe." This kind of talk is commonplace today. Epithets, insults, often even polite expressions of what's taken to be prejudice are called by purists "assaultive speech," "words that wound," "verbal violence." "To me, racial epithets are not speech," one University of Michigan law professor said. "They are bullets." In her speech accepting the 1993 Nobel Prize for Literature in Stockholm, Sweden, the author Toni Morrison said this: "Oppressive language does more than represent violence; it is violence."

It is not violence. I am thinking back to a moment on the subway in Washington, a little thing. I was riding home late one night and a squad of noisy kids, maybe seventeen or eighteen years old, noisily piled into the car. They yelled across the car and a girl said, "Where do we get off?"

A boy said, "Farragut North."

The girl: "*Faggot* North!"

The boy: "Yeah! Faggot North!"

General hilarity.

First, before the intellect resumes control, there is a moment of fear, an animal moment. Who are they? How many of them? How dangerous? Where is the way out? All of these things are noted preverbally and assessed by the gut. Then the brain begins an assessment: they are sober, this is probably too public a place for them to do it, there are more girls than boys, they were just talking, it is probably nothing.

They didn't notice me and there was no incident. The teenage babble flowed on, leaving me to think. I became interested in my own reaction: the jump of fear out of nowhere like an alert animal, the sense for a brief time that one is naked and alone and should hide or run away. For a time, one ceases to be a human being and becomes instead a faggot.

⚜

The fear engendered by these words is real. The remedy is as clear and as imperfect as ever: protect citizens against violence. This, I grant, is something that American society has never done very well and now does quite poorly. It is no solution to define words as violence or prejudice as oppression, and then by cracking down on words or thoughts pretend that we are doing something about violence and oppression. No doubt it is easier to pass a speech code or hate-crimes law and proclaim the streets safer than actually to make the streets safer, but the one must never be confused with the other. Every cop or prosecutor chasing words is one fewer chasing criminals. In a world rife with real violence and oppression, full of Rwandas and Bosnias and eleven-year-olds spraying bullets at children in Chicago and in turn being executed by gang lords, it is odious of Toni Morrison to say that words are violence.

Indeed, equating "verbal violence" with physical violence is a treacherous, mischievous business. Not long ago a writer was charged with viciously and gratuitously wounding the feelings and dignity of millions of people. He was charged, in effect, with exhibiting flagrant prejudice against Muslims and outrageously slandering their beliefs. "What is freedom of expression?" mused Salman Rushdie a year after the ayatollahs sentenced him to death and put a price on his head. "Without the freedom to offend, it ceases to exist." I can think of nothing sadder than that minority activists, in their haste to make the world better, should be the ones to forget the lesson of Rushdie's plight: for minorities, pluralism, not purism, is the answer. The campaigns to eradicate prejudice—all of them, the speech codes and workplace restrictions and mandatory therapy for accused bigots and all the rest—should stop, now. The whole objective of eradicating prejudice, as opposed to correcting and criticizing it, should be repudiated as a fool's errand. Salman Rushdie is right, Toni Morrison wrong, and minorities belong at his side, not hers.

# POSTSCRIPT

## Should Hate Speech Be Punished?

**M**any forms of hate speech are punished in countries other than the United States, but other democracies do not have the American tradition of freedom of opinion and expression. At the same time, the United States has more races, religions, and nationalities than other countries, giving rise to suspicion, prejudice, and hostility.

On one hand, this diversity has given rise to sharp political disagreement on issues relating to race, religion, women, homosexuals, and others. On the other hand, this diversity has stimulated greater sensitivity to the claims of these groups for equal treatment and social justice. Free speech on controversial issues risks giving offense. At what point, if any, does giving offense curtail the liberty of the offended group? Should such speech be punished?

Nowhere have these questions provoked greater controversy than on college campuses. Do college codes inhibiting or punishing racist, sexist, or other biased speech protect the liberty of the victims of these insults or injuries? Or do they prevent the examination of disapproved beliefs and threaten the suppression of other unpopular ideas?

Steven H. Shiffrin, in *Dissent, Injustice, and the Meanings of America* (Princeton University Press, 1999), argues that Americans should not just tolerate controversial speech, they should encourage it. Timothy C. Shiell, in *Campus Hate Speech on Trial* (University Press of Kansas, 1998), provides background for some of the recent court cases involving hate speech. Edward J. Cleary's *Beyond the Burning Cross: The First Amendment and the Landmark R. A. V. Case* (Random House, 1994) is an account of the attorney who represented the accused youth in *R. A. V. v. St. Paul*. Robert J. Kelly, ed., *Bias Crime: American Law Enforcement and Legal Responses,* rev. ed. (Office of International Criminal Justice, 1993) includes essays on a variety of issues, including religious and gay bias, bias on college campuses, and the Rodney King case, in which four white Los Angeles police officers were filmed beating a black suspect.

Arguing for absolute freedom of expression is Nat Hentoff, *Free Speech for Me—But Not for Thee: How the American Left and Right Relentlessly Censor Each Other* (HarperCollins, 1992). Less absolutist in defending all speech is Cass R. Sunstein, in *Democracy and the Problem of Free Speech* (Free Press, 1993), who attempts to define a distinction between protected and unprotected speech. A case for suppressing speech based on what the authors call "critical race theory" can be found in the essays in Mari J. Matsuda et al., *Words That Wound: Critical Race Theory, Assaultive Speech, and the First Amendment* (Westview Press, 1993).

A somewhat similar argument is developed by Richard Delgado and Jean Stefancic in *Must We Defend Nazis? Hate Speech, Pornography, and the First Amendment* (New York University Press, 1996). The authors insist that free speech must always be weighed against the sometimes-competing values of human dignity and equality. Judith Butler, in *Excitable Speech: A Politics of the Performance* (Routledge, 1997), examines the linguistics of hate and reflects on the implications of speech as a form of conduct. Milton Heumann et al., eds., *Hate Speech on Campus: Cases, Case Studies, and Commentary* (Northeastern University Press, 1997) reprints some classic Supreme Court opinions on free speech as well as excerpts from essays by John Stuart Mill, Herbert Marcuse, and others who have struggled with the question of whether or not freedom should be allowed for "words that wound."

# ISSUE 12

## Does the Religious Right Threaten American Freedoms?

**YES: John B. Judis**, from "Crosses to Bear," *The New Republic* (September 12, 1994)

**NO: Fred Barnes**, from "Who Needs the Religious Right? We All Do," *Crisis* (September 1994)

### ISSUE SUMMARY

**YES:** Reporter John B. Judis argues that politically organized religious conservatives want to impose their views on everyone else.

**NO:** Editor and commentator Fred Barnes argues that religious conservatives are the most stalwart supporters of endangered but vital moral principles in today's America.

Alexis de Tocqueville, a French observer who visited America during the 1830s, wrote that "there is an innumerable multitude of sects in the United States," all of them quite tolerant of each other. What is most important to Americans "is not that all citizens should profess the true religion but that they should profess religion."

America in Tocqueville's time was suffused with religion, which Tocqueville regarded as a good thing because, he contended, religion served as a moral anchor in a freewheeling, libertarian democracy. "Thus, while the law allows the American people to do everything, there are things which religion prevents them from imagining and forbids them to dare."

Tocqueville may have somewhat idealized the degree of religious tolerance in nineteenth-century America. At that time America was overwhelmingly Protestant. Catholicism ("Popery") was not quite respectable, nor was Judaism in many places. But by the middle of the next century, both Catholics and Jews were brought into the broad interreligious consensus that was once confined to Protestant sects. Despite theological differences among the three major faiths, in the 1950s there remained a broad, if somewhat loose, agreement on a variety of moral issues.

Beginning in the 1960s this consensus underwent seismic shifts. Secularism, feminism, and the "sexual revolution" produced strains within all three religions, in some cases dividing them into "liberal" and "conservative" factions. Most of the so-called mainstream Protestant denominations, such as the Episcopalians, Presbyterians, Lutherans, and Methodists, were inclined to adapt their creeds to these new cultural currents, but evangelical and fundamentalist groups emphatically rejected them. Adding to the conflict, groups calling for a "wall of separation" between church and state began a series of legal challenges to all displays of any religious activity in publicly financed institutions.

The genesis of an organized "religious right" began in the 1970s, when many conservative Protestants in the South withdrew their children from public schools and sent them to newly created private religious schools, where children were taught in an atmosphere of traditional moral values. Federal officials, suspecting that the real purpose of these schools was to evade the constitutional mandate of racial desegregation, began challenging their tax-exempt status. Reacting to this challenge, the groups at first mounted a purely defensive campaign to preserve their schools, but as the fight gathered momentum they developed a broader agenda, protesting against abortion, pornography, gay rights, and the teaching of evolution in schools, while seeking to restore the public recognition of religion and traditional values.

Over the past 20 years the religious right has been a force within the Republican Party, helping to mobilize Republican voters and shaping some parts of the Republican agenda. Though its relationship with other groups within the Republican Party is sometimes strained, party leaders have often relied on the religious right in tough political contests. The religious right is a minority, but when energized it can bring to the polls significant numbers of committed voters. At the same time, it should be noted that it has failed to get a Supreme Court majority or consitutional amendments to permit the states to outlaw abortion, to return prayer to public schools, or other public policy changes that it advocates. Nevertheless, most observers agree that the religious right is a force to be reckoned with.

Is the religious right a force for good or evil? Its defenders would say that it performs the very function that Tocqueville said was essential to the preservation of democracy: holding fast to a moral anchor during a time of political turmoil. Its critics, however, can also cite Tocqueville, who was careful to note that the influence of religion on American politics was always indirect. None of the various religions, Tocqueville observed, "lend their support to any particular political system. They are at pains to keep out of affairs and not mix in combinations of parties." By directly participating in the political process, the critics charge, the religious right is attempting to impose its particular brand of morality on the public at large.

These contrasting views are represented in the following selections. John B. Judis argues that the religious right is a danger to democracy because it attempts to use the political process to impose its religious views on others. Fred Barnes argues that religious conservatives serve the Tocquevillian function of preserving the moral principles that prevent democracy from careening into anarchy.

John B. Judis  **YES**

# Crosses to Bear

*Some people have the idea that the [Young Communist Leaguer] is po-
litically minded, that nothing outside of politics means anything. Gosh
no. They have a few simple problems. There is the problem of getting
good men on the baseball team this spring, of opposition from ping-pong
teams, of dating girls, etc. We go to shows, parties, dances and all that.
In short, the YCL and its members are no different from other people
except that we believe in dialectical materialism as the solution to all
problems.*

— Young Communist League pamphlet, circa 1938

In October 1980, when I was covering the South Dakota Senate race
between George McGovern and Republican challenger James Abdnor, I interviewed the Rev. Donald Tottingham, the leader of the state's Moral Majority
chapter and a prime opponent of McGovern's. Tottingham told me how his political activity flowed from his conviction, gleaned from the Bible, that a Satanic
one-world government was imminent. I had similarly extensive, though not
as bizarre, conversations in 1986 with the Rev. Don Lynch, a Muncie, Indiana,
Republican congressional candidate, and in 1992 with W. E. "Bob" McClellan,
a Southern California car dealer and member of the Christian Coalition, who
had been elected to the San Diego City Council the year before. It didn't surprise me that evangelical Christians wanted to talk about the relationship of
their religious beliefs to politics: bringing the "good news" of the gospel to the
unconverted and unconvinced was central to their faith.

But during the last two years, when I've asked leaders of religious right
organizations such as the Christian Coalition about the relationship of religion
to politics, I've gotten hard glances and vague, noncommittal answers. After
staring me down, Steve Sheffler, the field director of the Christian Coalition in
Iowa, responded that the organization's overall goal is "some positive change
in the way the country is going." A prominent national leader of the religious
right would only discuss the relevance of religion to politics if his views were
off the record. Moreover, public spokesmen such as Ralph Reed, the director of
the Christian Coalition, now insist that their organizations are not part of the
"religious right" but of the "pro-family movement."

From John B. Judis, "Crosses to Bear," *The New Republic* (September 12, 1994). Copyright © 1994 by
The New Republic, Inc. Reprinted by permission of *The New Republic*.

Has the movement changed so fundamentally in the last two years that it cannot even be called the religious or Christian right? I don't think so. Rather, what seems to have happened is that the Christian Coalition and smaller organizations of the religious right have come up against the same sort of limits all sectarian movements encounter. They have been forced to recognize that the very principles that bring members into their fold also limit wider public appeal. In response, the religious right's leaders have attempted to change its public face while retaining its private religious attraction.

Such a change has helped the movement gain influence in states such as Texas and Iowa, but in the long run it doesn't resolve the crisis that lies at its heart. Movements that draw a distinction between their private and public discourse inevitably risk schism, on the one hand, and co-optation, on the other. They risk either losing members or losing meaning. Creating a different public face also doesn't resolve the more basic question of what the relationship should be between religion and politics. Ralph Reed's pro-family movement sounds more benign than Tottingham's crusade, but it is probably no less a hazard to America's constitutional principles.

The religious right, defined as a fusion of conservative Christianity and political conservatism, goes back at least to the 1930s and the anti-New Deal crusades of Gerald B. Winrod and Gerald L. K. Smith. The movement's current incarnation, however, dates from the late '70s. It was initially organized by Southern evangelical ministers who wanted to prevent the Internal Revenue Service from removing the tax exemption on the segregated Christian academies they had set up in response to *Brown v. Board of Education.* More broadly, the religious right coalesced in response to Supreme Court decisions limiting school prayer and liberalizing abortion, and to the dramatic changes in American family life and leisure that spurred feminism, gay rights, teenage sexuality and, of course, MTV.

Two kinds of religious organizations emerged from this crucible. The first, epitomized by the Rev. James Dobson's Focus on the Family, defined itself primarily as an educational organization concerned with family issues that were relevant to evangelical Christians, including sex education and abortion. Focus on the Family lobbies the government, but only on these issues, and it does not back candidates. In political terms, it resembles Jewish, Catholic and mainline Protestant pressure groups.

The second kind of organization, more properly termed the "religious right," is typified by the Rev. Jerry Falwell's Moral Majority and the Rev. Pat Robertson's Freedom Council and Christian Coalition. Of these, the coalition is currently the most important, with nearly 1 million registered members, 900 chapters and a $13 million annual budget. All these groups function like political movements and parties—implicitly or explicitly running and endorsing candidates, and even participating as a political faction within the Republican Party. (Many of these organizations are registered as nonprofit with the IRS and must use artful dodges like grading candidates on issues through "Christian scorecards" to get around restrictions on open political endorsements.)

Initially, this new religious right was divided along denominational lines. Anti-Darwinian fundamentalists, who believed the Bible was literally true, gravitated toward Falwell's Moral Majority; Pentecostals and other charismatic Christians, who believed, in addition, that Jesus granted mortals the power to speak in tongues and perform miracles, joined Robertson's Freedom Council. Through the Christian Coalition, Robertson and Reed, to their great credit, have united what Robertson calls "biblical Christians" in a single organization.

Reed tries to portray the coalition as a garden-variety lobby. "We really see ourselves as a kind of faith-based Chamber of Commerce, a kind of League of Women Voters, if you will, for people of faith," he told National Public Radio in June. But if he's looking for an analogy, he's looking in the wrong place. The new religious right doesn't resemble the Chamber of Commerce or other business interests so much as it does the old Socialist and Communist parties. Its members are united by conviction rather than by function or employment; and its goal is not merely to defend certain discrete interests but to win political power on behalf of a broad agenda.

⚜

Like the older leftwing parties, the religious right also draws on a semiorganized base that is many times larger than itself. Many religious activists don't belong to any organized group, but they still take their cues from ministers affiliated with the Christian Coalition; those who belong to smaller Christian organizations, such as the American Family Association, often follow the coalition's lead. At June's Texas Republican convention, for instance, the Christian Coalition was credited with organizing Tom Pauken's victory as state party chairman, even though the coalition probably had an estimated 400 active members among the 6,000 delegates.

The Christian Coalition doesn't have an explicit membership test, but as its name implies, it is for Christians and its organizing functions make clear that it is primarily for those who take the Bible literally. At a founding seminar for the New Jersey Christian Coalition last spring, organizer Clay Mankamyer told the new recruits, "There is no doctrinal statement. Just the principle that we will go by the infallible word of God. Anybody who agrees with that is welcome." The coalition and other organizations of the religious right also take positions that are clearly derived from sectarian biblical political premises. In Iowa and Texas, the Christian Coalition and other groups have gotten the GOP to endorse planks calling for the teaching of "creation science" in the public schools—an invention of fundamentalist Protestants that was meant to replace the theory of evolution. It not only has no scientific backing from biologists, but it has no religious credence outside of a few Protestant sects....

⚜

When the Constitution was written, there were, of course, competing views of the relationship between religion and politics. Some Americans believed the state should actively encourage Protestant religious worship and observance as a means of sustaining a moral and virtuous republic. A few states, such as

Massachusetts and New Hampshire, even maintained religious tests for holding office. But Thomas Jefferson and James Madison, the two leading architects of American democracy, believed that the realm of government should be set apart from that of religion. They maintained that the basic premises of society could be deduced from religion, but could be derived more suitably from natural law and reason. Framing belief in terms of reason allowed public discussion of differing views. By contrast, framing belief and law in religious terms led inevitably to the preference of one religious group over another and to the creation of religious tests for office. More generally, fusing politics and religion could thwart democracy, which depends on reasoned debate. It could also encourage the kind of religious wars that had torn Europe apart.

Jefferson and Madison did not deny that religion played a useful role in inculcating virtue and morality. Jefferson argued that Jesus's "system of morality was the most benevolent and sublime that has been ever taught." Nevertheless, he and Madison thought religious belief would be more likely to flourish if removed from state jurisdiction. And they were right. The United States, as Reinhold Niebuhr once wrote, continues to be "at once the most secular and the most religious of Western nations."

To the consternation of many Americans, the emergence of the religious right has encouraged the trends that Madison and Jefferson feared. At the Texas Republican convention in June [1994], candidates announced their church affiliations. At the Iowa Republican convention the same month, Christian Coalition members made Christian belief a basis for backing a candidate. (Iowa Governor Terry Branstad, the Christian Coalition's Ione Dilley declared, is a politician "who does acknowledge his creator.")

In several states, religious right candidates have been turning school board races into religious contests. [In spring 1994] in a Dallas suburb Christian right candidates, facing two Jewish incumbents, emphasized their church affiliation and religious beliefs at candidate forums. Afterward, Rebecca Morris, one of the defeated incumbents, told an interviewer, "I never know how to deal with the issue 'I'm a Christian and you're not.' " Protestants and Catholics also feel the burden. Said Republican Mary Bennett of the Texas party's elections to choose delegates, "If you didn't say, 'I am a Christian and I attend a certain church,' you were excluded."

In each presidential election since 1980, religious right leaders have argued for supporting the Republicans against the Democrats on religious grounds. In 1992 Operation Rescue founder Randall Terry wrote in his newsletter that "to vote for Bill Clinton is to sin against God." Later, Reed told a conference sponsored by the Center for Ethics and Public Policy that Terry's statement "presented a harsh side of religious belief that is simply inappropriate in a political context." Reed did not say that Terry's views were inappropriate because they imposed a religious test on candidates. They were inappropriate because they were "harsh."

In building its movement, the religious right has run up against another even more formidable wall than that separating church and state. In 1989 the Gallup Poll asked people to rate whom they would like to have as neighbors. Near the bottom, well behind Catholics, Jews, blacks, Koreans, Hispanics, Vietnamese, Russians, and unmarried couples, were "religious fundamentalists." Only members of religious cults were less popular. The poll was about fundamentalists, but the result touches on what bothers many people about the religious right: the suspicion that it is a threat to privacy.

In the last thirty years the Supreme Court has claimed that the right to privacy exists under the "penumbras" of the Bill of Rights. Yet the concept has been a practical part of American life ever since a booming early-twentieth-century economy made it possible for large numbers of citizens to enjoy the kind of education and leisure—including a prolonged period of adolescence—hitherto reserved for the upper classes. This new realm of personal freedom became the basis for new kinds of consumer products, as well as sexual experimentation and novel social arrangements.

The religious right arose, however, partly in response to the trends that emerged from this freedom, and its agenda has consisted of seeking to restrict and regulate personal life. The religious right wants to prohibit abortion; allow employers to hire and fire based on a person's sexual practices; maintain criminal statutes against homosexuality and some kinds of heterosexual practices; and force television networks and stations not to show programs that it deems immoral. Jeff Fisher, the director of the Texas branch of the American Family Association, boasted to me that his group had succeeded in forcing thirteen of seventeen ABC affiliates to take the acclaimed "NYPD Blue" off the air.

While Americans certainly sympathize with some of the religious right's causes—a majority probably opposes taxpayer financing of abortions and insurance coverage of the "domestic partners" of public employees—it's no surprise that they see the movement's overall agenda as an assault on their privacy. They see in the religious right's obsession with homosexuality and soft-core pornography an unruly intolerance that flows from a repressed discomfort with any kind of sexuality. They see in its attempts to dictate television programming a desire to turn every network into Robertson's Family Channel, which intersperses the televangelist's "700 Club" with "Lassie," "Gunsmoke" and "Rin Tin Tin" reruns....

❧

To see the religious right's limits, all you have to do is look at its role in the GOP. The coalition and its allies have taken over the party apparatus in some states, but they have not taken over candidate selection or won the hearts of primary or general election voters. They have yet to elect one of their own to the Senate or governor's office. They have won control of some suburban and rural school boards around the country, and also some state legislative races. That's not much of a takeover, though. And, as in San Diego, these victories often have been followed by reversals.

The movement's greatest political successes have come in Southern and border states that have a high percentage of evangelicals and that, because of their homogeneous religious population, enjoy a much closer relation locally between church and state. Suburban voters in Georgia don't share the same fear of fundamentalism as voters in Portland, Oregon, or Alexandria, Virginia.

In states where Catholics, Jews, mainline Protestants and nonbelievers make up a large percentage of the population, and where there are growing numbers of young middle-class suburbanites, the religious right has proved a divisive force. It has succeeded in taking over Republican Party organizations, but at the expense of participation by moderate voters. The right has cost Republicans dearly in Virginia, Minnesota, Washington, Oregon and California. . . .

Some conservatives, who are uncomfortable with the religious right's quest for a Christian America, still contend that the movement has served a useful purpose by dramatizing the dissolution of the family and the decline of schools. I'd argue the contrary. Because of its reliance on religious explanations, the Christian right has most often slighted these problems. The solutions it has proffered are either harmful or irrelevant.

Take the schools. The religious right candidates I've observed have stood for the reinstitution of school prayer, the elimination or drastic modification of sex education and the introduction of creation science. These are not issues on which the future of our young rests. School prayers are either blatantly discriminatory or meaningless; sex education is, well, complicated; and creation science is bunkum. . . .

Is today's religious right injecting a Christian spirit of compassion and selflessness into American politics? The only group that seems to elicit its compassion is the unborn; it does not display similar compassion, for instance, toward the poor or the victims of AIDS—two obvious groups for which a modern-day Christian might be expected to express concern. Robertson, who in his youth worked among the poor, now has contempt for their suffering. Asked about the welfare system, he quotes Paul's advice on how to deal with disorderly Thessalonians, "If anyone will not work, neither let him eat." And why is the Christian Coalition against community rating of insurance premiums? Reed warns that there will be "massive cross-subsidies from intact, two-parent families with children who lead *healthy* lifestyles to those who do not." Iowa coalition official Steve Sheffler, a former insurance agent, puts it more clearly: families of the healthy will have to pay higher premiums to cover AIDS patients.

It is not a question of what policy government should finally adopt. Perhaps welfare should be eliminated and community rating discouraged. Rather, it is a question of the spirit with which Americans—and Christians—should regard the poor and the terminally ill. The Christian right is, in fact, a perfect example of what happens when the founding principles of church and state are violated. What Jefferson and Madison understood. . . . is that Christianity does not provide a political agenda but rather an underlying social conscience with which to approach politics. Religion plays its most constructive role precisely when church and state are separate.

When the two are fused, however, when organizations acting in the name of Christianity seek political power, then religion becomes subordinate to politics. It becomes infected with the darker egoism of group and nation; it no longer softens and counters our ungenerous impulses but clothes them in holy righteousness.

# NO ↙

**Fred Barnes**

# Who Needs the Religious Right?
# We All Do

T hree things about the Religious Right's influence on the 1992 election and in American politics are of particular interest to me. First, a myth that grew out of the 1992 Republican Convention in Houston. Second, the surprising gains that the Religious Right has made, particularly in the media (National Public Radio presented a fair piece on efforts by the Religious Right to expand into the black and Hispanic communities). And third, the Religious Right's role in keeping alive moral issues and traditional values important to most Americans.

I was in Houston when the myth began. The Religious Right was said to have taken over the convention and to have imposed its own religious views on the Republican Party, with the goal of imposing them on the entire nation. The myth created a media consensus on the convention: that it was intolerant, mean-spirited, exclusive, judgmental, narrow-minded, or worse. When Pat Buchanan gave his speech, I happened to be sitting next to another Washington journalist who is a bellwether of press opinion. At first he loved Buchanan's speech, but two days later his view had changed entirely as had the view of many other press people. Now he felt the convention had turned into a hate-fest because of its domination by the Religious Right. That became the conventional wisdom among reporters in Houston. No, they didn't conspire to reach this conclusion, but as they gathered to trade information and gossip, the consensus emerged that the Religious Right, if not in total control of the convention, at least had a large and pernicious influence there.

The evidence? It was the speeches by Religious Right people, like Pat Buchanan (even though he has little to do with the organized Religious Right). The mainstream press pointed to these speeches more than to the issue of homosexuality and family values. Pat Robertson's speech was cited. So was Marilyn Quayle's, though she didn't dwell on religious issues but talked about feminism and women who don't work.

There were 128 speeches at the convention, only three of which could be considered religious. Just one—Robertson's, which wasn't even given during prime time—could truly be called a Religious Right speech. Yet this was enough for the press to conclude that the Religious Right had dominated the convention.

From Fred Barnes, "Who Needs the Religious Right? We All Do," *Crisis* (September 1994). Copyright © 1994 by Crisis Publishing Company, Inc. Reprinted by permission of The Crisis Publishing Company, Inc., the magazine of The National Association for the Advancement of Colored People.

A week after the convention, a woman television producer—married, with one child—was still furious about Marilyn Quayle's speech, because she felt it attacked women who work. Here's what Mrs. Quayle, who herself has sometimes worked full-time, actually said: "I sometimes think that the liberals are always so angry because they believe the grandiose promises of the liberation movement. They are disappointed because most women do not want to be liberated from their essential natures as women. Most of us love being mothers and wives, which gives us a richness that few men and women get from professional accomplishments alone." This was hardly a broadside against women with full-time jobs. Nonetheless many women and men in the press took it that way.

In any case, the supposed domination of the GOP by the Religious Right didn't contribute heavily to George Bush's defeat in the November election. I think Bush was defeated because he signed the 1990 budget deal. Without that, he would have been re-elected. But in the media the view lingers that the convention was a critical moment that doomed Bush and his re-election chances.

The myth is not confined to the media. Spencer Abraham, executive director of the 1992 House Republican campaign organization, ran for Republican National Chairman after the election and was defeated by Haley Barbour. Abraham talked to each of the 165 members of the Republican National Committee, because they were the electorate choosing the chairman. Amazingly, he found that a majority believed the press view of what happened at the convention, even though they themselves had been there and should have known better. Abraham was regarded as the Religious Right candidate, even though he wasn't.

## Religious Right Gains

My second observation about the Religious Right is the good news that the fog hovering over it is beginning to lift. The hostility toward it has begun to soften. The 1993 races for Virginia governor, lieutenant governor, and attorney general greatly affected press opinion about the Religious Right. Since Virginia is right next door to Washington, D.C., the commercials for the races were on Washington television for national reporters to see. Clearly the Democrats overkilled in their attempts to discredit the Religious Right, trying to make it an issue not only against Michael Farris, a Religious Right favorite who was running for lieutenant governor, but also against George Allen, the Republican gubernatorial candidate. The Democrats cast Allen—who won—as a patsy for Pat Robertson, which he obviously is not.

The backlash in the press, while not sympathetic, was the beginning of a recognition that the Religious Right is a legitimate bloc in the Republican coalition. I don't want to overstate this. But after talking to ten political reporters who followed the Virginia race—Christopher Matthews of the San Francisco *Examiner,*

Gloria Borger of *U.S. News,* Brit Hume of ABC, Eleanor Clift of *Newsweek,* Carl Leubsdorf of the Dallas *Morning News,* Thomas DeFrank of *Newsweek,* syndicated columnist Robert Novak, Morton Kondracke of *Roll Call,* Paul West of the Baltimore *Sun,* and John Mushek of the Boston *Globe*—I found that most agreed the Religious Right is not an evil juggernaut, as they'd previously thought, but rather is a viable element of the Republican Party. They acknowledged that during the campaign the issue of the Religious Right changed from fear of a religious takeover to the unfairness of attacks on people for holding strong religious views. The result is a more positive view of the Religious Right, and that's a gain. The Religious Right has further enhanced its legitimacy with the secular press by tackling non-religious issues, as in the Christian Coalition's decision to air TV ads critical of the Clinton health-care plan.

Moreover, there are other voices now arguing that religious views are a legitimate source of political values and should be included in the public debate. The political left doesn't accept this, insisting that religious people want to impose their views on everyone. But President Clinton dissents from that liberal view, and so does David Wilhelm, the Democratic National Chairman. When Wilhelm spoke to the Christian Coalition, he made a significant concession. He stressed that religious values are fine and legitimate as roots of political views. That's the Religious Right position. It is not the position of most Democrats.

Clinton and Wilhelm declared that people of strong faith should not be ostracized from the public square. Christians, Jews, Muslims, and members of other faiths can properly draw on spiritual teachings to guide their political views. Wilhelm has also noted, "Let us say that while religious motivation is appropriate, it is wrong to use religious authority to coerce support in the public arena."

## The Religious Right's Importance

The third thing I find interesting about the Religious Right is the notion that it is driving people away from the GOP, that most Americans want a party based on serious economic and foreign policy issues, not those horrible social issues. Here the real issue is the Republican Party's strong stand against abortion. If you are part of the élite opinion stream—where it is socially unacceptable to be opposed to abortion—you'll get flak from friends and maybe your spouse for being associated with such a party.

Richard Nixon, in an interview with William Safire, gave his opinion on abortion: "The state should stay out—don't subsidize, and don't prohibit." The view that abortion should be kept out of politics is shared by many other Republican politicians. I think this shows they are ignorant as to the party's real base. They don't understand who grassroots Republicans are.

The Republican Party does not stand a chance of becoming a majority party in America or electing another president without the Religious Right. Vast numbers of Americans are alienated from the Democratic Party, yet are leery of the Republican Party. What attracts them to the GOP is not supply-side economics or hawkishness on foreign policy but serious moral and social concerns. I understand the reluctance of millions of former Democrats to become

Republicans—the thought of being a Republican makes even me wince. But the Religious Right's cluster of issues attracts many of them.

Abortion is an issue that helped George Bush in 1992 and certainly helped George Allen win the governorship of Virginia. Millions of people were also attracted to Republican candidates because they believe in a role for religion in American life. Others became sympathetic to Republicans because they care about, for instance, the injection of gay values into the mainstream of American opinion, or about moral relativism. Whether it's the kind of multiculturalism that shows up in the Rainbow Curriculum in New York or Outcomes-based Education, only the Religious Right keeps all these values issues alive. And the beneficiary is the Republican Party.

There used to be something called the New Right, but it doesn't exist anymore. Its leaders were people like Paul Weyrich (who said in 1985 that the only serious grassroots activity in the Republican Party was religiously based—which is even more true now), Richard Viguerie, and Howard Phillips. But the New Right is now gone, leaving only the Religious Rights.

❧❀❧

If the Religious Right is driven out of the Republican Party, I think values issues —abortion, the role of religion in public life, gay rights, and moral relativism —will all but vanish. It is religious people who keep them on the table. Their departure would cause the Republican Party's base to shrivel dramatically. Republican élites simply do not understand this. I worry when Ralph Reed says that the Christian Coalition is not going to concentrate on opposing abortion because abortion cannot be blocked; instead, they will talk about parental consent and about other important issues like tax cuts. In truth, the Religious Right needs to emphasize the issues that brought its people into politics in the first place—basically moral issues.

The Religious Rights' issues are critical politically not only for the Republican Party but for everybody. They are more important than cutting the capital-gains tax rate or aiding the Bosnian Muslims. They involve the moral upbringing of our children, the character of our citizens and our leaders, the way we regard and treat religious faith and religious believers. If American politicians do not want to grapple with these moral issues, the overarching issues of our era, then what are they in office for?

I do not always agree with the positions of the Religious Right. I am not really concerned, for instance, whether a school-prayer amendment passes. I have also disagreed with their style, although under Ralph Reed it has gotten better. But I give them credit for forcing things onto the national agenda that are critical to the Republican Party and to the rest of us.

In 1989, when Ronald Reagan returned to California on Air Force One, he was asked what his greatest regret was after eight years as president. He said he regretted that he hadn't done more to restrict or end abortion in this country. If an entire party abandons that issue and other moral concerns and ostracizes from the party the people who want to raise those concerns, the regret will ultimately be felt by the entire nation.

# POSTSCRIPT

## Does the Religious Right Threaten American Freedoms?

In spite of their obvious disagreements about the religious right, Judis and Barnes share a few areas of agreement. Judis concedes that some evangelical groups confine themselves to educating the public on their political views, and he seems to have no objection to this. Barnes, while insisting that there is nothing wrong about religious groups playing a direct role in politics, does agree that it is wrong to use religious authority to "coerce" support. But what does "coerce" mean? For example, do threatened boycotts of controversial TV programs constitute "coercion"? Judis, who mentions the case of *NYPD Blue*, apparently thinks so. But many groups, including civil rights and gay rights groups, have also resorted to boycotts of TV programs they do not like. It is sometimes hard to find a bright line between coercion and the legitimate exercise of civil liberties.

Though not a member of any "religious right" organization, William J. Bennett, a former official in the Reagan and Bush administrations, tends to agree with their moral views. See *The De-Valuing of America: The Fight for Our Culture and Our Children* (Summit Books, 1992). On the other hand, David Cantor, of the Anti-Defamation League, has written on what he considers the dangers posed by the religious right. See *The Religious Right: The Assault on Tolerance and Pluralism in America* (Anti-Defamation League, 1994). A kind of middle position is embraced by Stephen L. Carter in *The Culture of Disbelief* (Doubleday, 1994), in which he argues that America can preserve the separation of church and state while embracing a vital religious faith that can actually strengthen it's democracy. Kenneth D. Wald's *Religion and Politics in the United States,* 3rd ed. (Congressional Quarterly Press, 1997) is a balanced treatment of the political impact of religious beliefs, institutions, and practices.

Roman Catholicism is a mainline religion that did not make major adjustments in ethics and theology to accomodate the "cultural revolution" of the 1960s, and in recent years some Catholics have promoted the idea of a political alliance between Catholicism and evangelical Protestantism. The Reverend Richard John Neuhaus, a former Lutheran minister turned Catholic priest, has been prominent among the supporters of it. At the other end, Charles Colson, an evangelical leader and former Nixon aide, is trying to rally support among evangelicals. Neuhaus and Colson were among the signers of a statement of common mission called "Evangelicals and Catholics Together," which was published in the May 1994 issue of *First Things,* a journal edited by Neuhaus, and later as a book, *Evangelicals and Catholics Together: Toward a Common Mission* edited by Neuhaus and Colson (Word, 1995).

# ISSUE 13

# Would "School Choice" Improve the Quality of U.S. Education?

**YES: Gary Rosen**, from "Are School Vouchers Un-American?" *Commentary* (February 2000)

**NO: Judith Pearson**, from *Myths of Educational Choice* (Praeger, 1993)

## ISSUE SUMMARY

**YES:** Editor and author Gary Rosen argues that educational vouchers permitting lower-income parents to afford private schools for their children will raise achievement levels without causing any of the harmful effects that their opponents attribute to them.

**NO:** Social scientist Judith Pearson contends that "school choice" violates the basic principle of equity because it benefits some schools and children at the expense of others.

The United States spends roughly $500 billion annually on public education. Yet studies have shown serious deficiencies in the educational attainments of America's children. In 1998 less than one-third of fourth graders were proficient in reading and less than one-quarter were proficient in writing. In 1996 only one-fifth were at grade level in mathematics. One-third of 17-year-olds cannot identify France on a map of the world, and only about one in ten high school graduates can write proficiently. The problems are particularly severe in the inner cities.

What is wrong in American education, and what can be done about it? To some, the real problem stems from inadequate and inequitable school funding. Teachers' salaries are low compared to those of other professions, and lower still are the salaries of inner-city teachers, whose hardships are further increased by large class sizes, dilapidated buildings, and lack of adequate equipment and support.

Others diagnose the problem differently. From their perspective, the problems have less to do with inadequate funding than with the cultural atmosphere of public schools: stifling bureaucracies, mindless rules, educational fads, anarchical classrooms, and, in the inner cities, schoolyards filled with drugs and fighting. For these critics, the best way to reform education in America is to give parents alternatives to the public schools in their neighborhoods.

A number of alternatives exist. Probably the least controversial is magnet schools, which have been in operation for more than 20 years. Magnet schools have specially trained teachers, modern facilities, and enriched curricula, with the object of bringing students from different races and social classes together for a meaningful educational experience. Another alternative is charter schools, which are schools that are publicly funded yet largely free of direct bureaucratic control by the government. Advocates of charter schools contend that such schools upgrade educational standards by stimulating competition and providing fresh approaches to learning. Opponents charge that they are often mismanaged, tainted by the ideological biases of the groups that run them, and unable to make a significant difference in the students' level of performance.

The most controversial of the "choice" programs is the use of school vouchers—certificates or cash payments by the government for a fixed amount that students can present to a private or public school to cover part or all of the cost of educating the student. The idea for vouchers was first brought up in a 1962 book, *Capitalism and Freedom* by economist Milton Friedman. Friedman was, and is, a libertarian, or one who believes in a very limited role for government. In a perfect world, Friedman asserted, parents would be entirely responsible for their own childrens' education, but since not all can afford those costs, government should finance and regulate education. That does not mean, he insisted, that government has to run the schools. In fact, public administration of schools has led to widespread inefficiency, inequity, and conformity. In place of government administration, Friedman proposed a voucher system. Friedman argued that state governments "could require a minimum level of schooling financed by giving parents vouchers redeemable for a specified maximum sum per child per year if spent on 'approved' educational services."

Friedman's idea received brief attention in the 1960s, then sank into obscurity until the 1980s, when the Reagan administration revived it. In 1986 the administration proposed federal legislation creating a voucher program permitting children to attend private and parochial schools—but, under furious attack from teachers' unions, the administration withdrew the bill and later offered a weaker version financing vouchers only for public schools. Since then, national leaders of both parties have approached "school choice" with considerable caution. In the meantime, voucher programs have cropped up at the state level. Three states—Wisconsin, Ohio, and Florida—have begun voucher programs. All have faced legal challenges by groups claiming that vouchers violate the First Amendment's ban on "the establishment of religion."

The church-state objection is one of the arguments that Gary Rosen, in the following selection, seeks to refute. In Rosen's view, vouchers will not only pass constitutional muster but will raise student achievement levels without harming public education. Opposing that argument, in the second selection, social scientist Judith Pearson contends that school choice violates the basic principles of equity and fairness.

**Gary Rosen**

 **YES**

# Are School Vouchers
# Un-American?

**B**y any measure, public education in America's cities is in deep trouble, and has been for some time. On any given day in Cleveland, almost one of every six students is likely not to show up. In Washington, D.C., a majority of tenth graders never finish high school. And in Los Angeles, school officials recently retreated from a plan to end the practice of "social promotion," realizing that it would have required holding back for a year more than half of the district's woefully unprepared students. Nor do things look any better in the aggregate. As *Education Week* concluded in a special report two years ago, "Most fourth graders who live in U.S. cities can't read and understand a simple children's book, and most eighth graders can't use arithmetic to solve a practical problem."

The response to this dismal situation has taken many shapes in recent years, but none more radical—or more promising—than the idea of school vouchers. Though little more than a thought-experiment as recently as the late 1980's, vouchers are now being used in one form or another in every major American city, providing low-income families with scholarships or subsidies that allow them to send their children to private schools. Of these programs, the great majority are privately financed, currently sponsoring more than 50,000 students nationwide. Considerably more controversial, despite affecting just some 12,000 students, are the three state-funded programs now in operation. In Milwaukee, in Cleveland, and (as of this past fall [1999]) in the state of Florida, qualifying families are using *public* dollars for *private* education, usually at religious schools.

For the teachers' unions, liberal interest groups, and Democratic politicians who are the most determined foes of vouchers, these programs are objectionable not so much for their scope—after all, the number of students involved is but a tiny fraction of the country's school population—as for the precedent they set and the unmistakable message they send. Whether public or private, today's voucher initiatives are an explicit rebuke to the failing inner-city public-school systems whose students are the chief beneficiaries of the new programs. As activists on all sides of the issue recognize, if these pilot programs succeed,

From Gary Rosen, "Are School Vouchers Un-American?" *Commentary* (February 2000). Copyright © 2000 by The American Jewish Committee. Reprinted by permission of *Commentary* and the author.

it is far more likely that school choice for the poor will be transformed from a modest, mostly philanthropic experiment into a full-scale public policy.

⌁◈⌁

And it does, in fact, appear that today's voucher programs are succeeding, at least from the perspective of the families taking part in them. Though isolating the deciding factor in improved test scores is a notoriously difficult business, studies by Harvard's Paul E. Peterson and other social scientists have found that students with vouchers perform at least as well—and often much better— than their peers in public schools.[1] Looking at the question from a different angle, John F. Witte of the University of Wisconsin reports that voucher recipients in Milwaukee have resisted the "normal pattern" of declining achievement among inner-city students, maintaining their test scores relative to national averages even as they enter higher grades. Every study has also found that parents who take advantage of vouchers are vastly more satisfied with the quality of their children's education, a sentiment based on everything from more rigorous homework assignments to better classroom discipline.

Unsurprisingly, given these results, interest in school choice has risen greatly over the last few years among inner-city families. One survey found that 85 percent of the urban poor now favor vouchers; another put support for the idea at 59 percent among blacks and 68 percent among Latinos. As if to prove these figures, when the Children's Scholarship Fund, the largest of the private voucher programs, recently announced its first national lottery for 40,000 scholarships, applications poured in from an astonishing 1.25 million children, all from low-income households. Such desperation, in the view of former Mayor Kurt Schmoke of Baltimore— one of a handful of black Democrats who have dissented from their party's line on education—makes the movement for school choice "part of an emerging new civil-rights battle."

This groundswell of grassroots support has created an increasingly uncomfortable situation for those committed to thwarting school choice. When a federal district judge suspended Cleveland's publicly financed voucher program this past August—setting in motion a series of appeals that is still ongoing—local opinion turned sharply against him, with the *Cleveland Plain Dealer* branding him a "voucher vulture" for his "utter disregard for the needs of children across the city." Within days, the judge felt compelled to reverse his order, allowing the program to carry on, as it has continued to do even in the wake of his ruling in December that it is unconstitutional. So, too, the leading groups in the antivoucher movement have been made to see the political awkwardness in taking a stand that so plainly defies the wishes of low-income families eager to improve the lot of their children.

Many of those making the case against school choice are now willing to concede—grudgingly—that the children who participate in these programs may benefit in some way. But, in their view, this is no compensation for the wider harm that vouchers threaten to do. A lucky few may be helped by the government's willingness to underwrite private education, but society as a whole, they insist, will inevitably suffer from a policy so contrary to our most fundamental civic principles and institutions. Indeed, if the most vociferous critics are to be believed, the idea of school vouchers is not just wrongheaded, it is positively un-American.

**⋅⊶⊙⊷⋅**

The most frequently invoked argument on this score is that allowing public dollars to help support sectarian schools is unconstitutional on its face and strikes at the very heart of our tradition of religious freedom. As the American Civil Liberties Union puts it, "vouchers violate the bedrock principle of separation of church and state," forcing "all taxpayers to support religious beliefs and practices with which they may strongly disagree."

In a more strictly legal vein, voucher opponents point to a series of Supreme Court decisions during the 1970's rejecting various forms of government assistance to religious schools. The first and most important of these decisions, in the landmark case of *Lemon v. Kurtzman* (1971), set out the criteria the Court has used ever since to determine whether a given state action violates the First Amendment by "establishing" religion. Though the Justices themselves have never ruled on the narrow question of whether vouchers may be used for sectarian schools, several lower courts—including the federal district court in Cleveland—have concluded that such programs are unconstitutional under *Lemon* and its judicial progeny. . . .

But the broader concern is that the venerable tradition of the "common school"—ingrained in the national imagination by the experience of generations of successfully assimilated immigrants—will be abandoned in the rush to privatize. Reciting the Pledge of Allegiance in a classroom of diverse peers will give way, it is feared, to the (publicly supported) cultivation of narrow religious and ethnic interests, further damaging our already fragile sense of national identity. As the National Education Association (NEA), the country's largest and most powerful teachers' union, has declared, "At a time when America is fractured by race, religion, and income, we can't afford to replace the one remaining unifying institution in the country with a system of private schools pursuing private agendas at taxpayer expense."

**⋅⊶⊙⊷⋅**

Are the opponents right? Would the spread of school choice, whatever its benefits for a fortunate few, do grave harm to our common culture, and to the republic?

As far as the constitutional question goes, it is useful to start—as these discussions seldom do—with the actual text of the First Amendment, the relevant portion of which reads, "Congress shall make no law respecting an establishment of religion, or prohibiting the free exercise thereof." For most of American history, this language was taken to mean precisely what it says and what its 18th-century authors intended: that the federal government—and the federal government alone—has no authority over religion. The states, by contrast, could do as they wished in these matters, limited only by the protections for religious liberty enshrined in their own constitutions.

All this changed in the 1940's, when the Supreme Court decided through a bit of legal legerdemain that every level of American government was bound by the religion clauses of the First Amendment. Suddenly, the Court found itself having to rule on the constitutionality of a range of church-state relationships over which it previously had had no say, including the question of whether state and local governments could give aid to religious schools, as many of them had been doing for some time.

In the earliest of these cases, the Court showed some willingness to accommodate the practices that had grown up under the old federalism-based arrangement. Thus, the Justices gave their imprimatur to government assistance whose content was plainly secular, like textbooks and reimbursement for transportation. But by the early 1970's, this attitude had changed dramatically. In *Lemon*, the Court ruled that a secular purpose was not enough. In addition, no program aiding sectarian schools could have the "primary effect" of advancing religion or result in an "excessive entanglement" between church and state— a "test," as it turned out in several cases decided shortly thereafter, that effectively banned almost every form of state aid, including such seemingly innocent items as maps, instructional films, and laboratory equipment.

For the past two decades, the Supreme Court has struggled to make sense of these contradictory precedents. Though accepting the basic standard set by *Lemon*, the Justices have tried to apply it in a way that will not automatically find the "establishment" of religion in any program that somehow benefits a sectarian institution. In the most important of these cases—*Mueller v. Allen* (1983), *Witters v. Washington Department of Services for the Blind* (1986), *Zobrest v. Catalina Foothills School District* (1993), and *Agostini v. Felton* (1997)—the Court has upheld several different forms of public aid to students in religious schools. Such assistance is permissible, the Justices have ruled, when it comes about as part of a broader, religiously neutral program and when its benefits accrue to religious schools only indirectly, through the private decisions of individuals.

For school vouchers, the implications could not be clearer. As the highest state courts in both Wisconsin and Ohio have held, the programs currently operating in Milwaukee and Cleveland easily meet the requirements laid down by the Supreme Court: families may opt for a religious *or* a secular school, and the schools themselves receive public funds only as a result of these private choices. Even so strict a church-state separationist as Harvard Law School's Laurence Tribe admits that, "One would have to be awfully clumsy to write voucher legislation that could not pass constitutional scrutiny." ...

⚜

As for the damage that vouchers would supposedly inflict on public schools, the arguments advanced by the teachers' unions and their allies are deeply disingenuous, if not dishonest. From a financial point of view, it is certainly true that public-school budgets are likely to decline as students leave for private institutions, taking some part of their per-pupil funding with them. But it is unclear why this should create any special hardship, since the schools would be losing money only for students whom they are no longer expected to educate. Moreover, because per-pupil support comes from both state and local funds, and vouchers tend to be financed exclusively with the state's share (and often not even all of that), affected public schools already get to keep much of the money earmarked for students who decide to enroll elsewhere—receiving a bonus, in effect, for driving them away. In the 1996–97 school year, this dividend amounted in both Cleveland and Milwaukee to some $3,000 for each departing voucher student.

That the professed concern of the teachers' unions over the financial consequences of vouchers has little to do with the fate of students "left behind" was neatly demonstrated by the journalist Matthew Miller in a recent issue of the *Atlantic Monthly*. Interviewing Bob Chase, the president of the NEA, Miller proposed an experiment in which funding for education would be raised by 20 percent in several cities; every student would receive a voucher for his share of the newly enlarged budget, to be used as he and his parents saw fit. By this means, students who chose to remain in public schools would be guaranteed generous financial support. Chase rejected the idea outright—and did so again even when Miller suggested doubling or even tripling the amount of money. In their approach to vouchers, as to a host of other education reforms proposed in recent years—from giving principals more authority to fire incompetent teachers to expanding the number of independent and (usually) non-unionized "charter" schools—the one great imperative for both the NEA and the AFT has been to preserve the jobs of their members.

No less cynical is the charge that school choice serves only the most capable students, leaving the toughest cases for the public schools. As one study after another has confirmed, the children who use vouchers are hardly distinguishable from their peers, whether in terms of race, income, family background, or academic performance. Nor should this come as a surprise, since these programs do not seek out the most talented students (or, for that matter, allow participating private schools to do so), and are restricted to families that qualify for the federal school-lunch program or meet some other means test. In many cases, in fact, vouchers are used by the *worst*-performing students—for the commonsense reason that their parents are the ones most likely to be unhappy with the public schools. . . .

୶◉ଚ

As for the alarm sounded by critics about the destructive effect vouchers would have on America's democratic ethos, here too there has been much exaggeration, often of a self-serving nature. The fact is that our public schools, whatever their past glories, are not the engines for Americanization that they once were. On the other hand, private schools turn out to do a much better job these days at citizen education, perhaps because their generally more traditional bent has insulated them to some degree from the antipatriotic dictates of multiculturalism.

On the civics portion of the National Assessment of Educational Progress, the results of which were announced this past November, 80 percent of private-school seniors demonstrated basic "civic competency," as compared to just 63 percent of their public-school counterparts—roughly the same margin as prevailed in the scores for fourth and eighth graders as well. Significantly, the test measured both knowledge of government and civic disposition in the broadest sense, including the readiness of students to respect "individual worth and human dignity" and to assume "the personal, political, and economic responsibilities of a citizen."

Private schools also do better at approximating the ideal of the American "melting pot," as studies by Jay P. Greene of the Manhattan Institute have shown. Not only are they more racially integrated than public schools, but they are also home to more interracial friendships and less race-related fighting. As far as voucher programs go, rather than serving as a "subterfuge for segregation," they have usually allowed students to enter more racially mixed schools. This is because private schools in our big cities typically enroll students from different parts of the community, while public schools, even after— or perhaps because of—decades of forced busing, tend to reflect the ethnically homogeneous make-up of their neighborhoods....

⋖◉⋗

This brings us to perhaps the most peculiar feature of the current debate over vouchers: namely, how few liberals have embraced what is so quintessentially liberal a cause. After all, most middle-class Americans already have school choice: they possess the wherewithal either to pick communities where the public schools are good or to pay for private education, and they know how to make the most of public magnet schools and programs for the gifted. Only the less-well-off have to put up with whatever the local school bureaucracy sees fit to provide their children. As John E. Coons, a retired law professor at Berkeley and a long-ignored voucher advocate on the Left, has written, "The rich choose; the poor get conscripted."

But why so many liberals—and, by extension, the Democratic party—are so fiercely resistant to school choice is really no mystery. For decades now, an absolutist and completely ahistorical view of church-state separation has been a defining creed of the American Left. At the same time, and more understandably, liberals remain attached to a public-school system that has served the country well in the past and continues to do so in some ways today, especially in the suburbs. And then there are the teachers' unions, whose three million members stand to lose the most if vouchers succeed, and who are perhaps the most influential constituency in the Democratic party, having sent more delegates to the 1996 Democratic national convention than did the entire state of California.

Still, both politically and morally, the almost frankly reactionary character of the antivoucher position is growing less tenable by the day. While leading Republicans and conservatives speak out for the educational interests of the urban poor, liberal and Democratic standard-bearers continue to stonewall for a status quo that even they must admit is unacceptable—a stance no less embarrassing to the traditions of the Democratic party than to the democratic traditions of the country.

## Note

1. See Peterson's "A Report Card on School Choice," COMMENTARY, October 1997.

# Myths of Educational Choice

## Choice and Revenue

The terms "equal," "equitable," and "fair" bring us to perhaps the thorniest, most muddled issue on the supply side of educational choice—revenue. In fact, school finance is the Gordian knot of education, with or without choice. Education is funded by taxes. Simplicity ends here. Throughout the country, the largest portion of school revenue comes from state and local government. Federal contributions average between 3 percent and 6 percent. The education revenues that come from state and local governments are raised by a combination of state and local taxes. There are probably fifty different combinations of the sales tax, lottery, personal and corporate income tax, interest, dividend, capital gains tax, and, of course, the local property tax. Herein lies the problem.

The particular mix or formula of taxes that most states use to fund education is called the foundation system. Most foundation programs represent a compromise between the right of local districts to support their own schools to the degree they choose through the local property tax levy and the state's responsibility to lessen or modify the impact of extremes in local property wealth subject to taxation. The "foundation" represents the amount of support guaranteed to local districts regardless of property wealth. If a district is so poor that the property tax levy required by the formula does not raise the foundation aid guaranteed, the state makes up the difference. This sounds fair enough, and is certainly an improvement since the days of almost exclusive reliance on the property tax for school revenue.

However, there are several problems. First, the amount guaranteed, the foundation aid or formula allowance, is typically set at a low or minimum level. The setting is done by politicians who try to avoid use of the "T-word." Second, this minimum guaranteed support covers general education revenue, operating funds. It does not cover capital expenditures for buildings, facilities, and equipment. In most states, these expenditures are covered through additional (above the formula) property tax levies. Property-rich districts have the best facilities. Property-poor districts can barely maintain facilities, let alone build and remodel. In a third instance, many states, like Minnesota, have allowed local districts the prerogative of going to the taxpayers for excess levies to raise

From Judith Pearson, *Myths of Educational Choice* (Praeger, 1993). Copyright © 1993 by Judith Pearson. Reprinted by permission of Greenwood Publishing Group, Inc., Westport, CT. References omitted.

additional, discretionary operating funds above the foundation guarantee. This again works to the advantage of property-rich districts. If the property valuation is high, a small levy raises lots of money. In a property-poor district, extremely high levies would be required to raise the same dollars.

As succinctly described by Jonathan Kozol, these disparities resulting from reliance on the property tax are frequently compounded in the large cities and inner city school districts by the disproportionate number of tax-free institutions, such as colleges, hospitals, and museums, which are located within the cities.

> In some cities, according to Jonathan Wilson, former chairman of the Council of Urban Boards of Education, 30 percent or more of the potential tax base is exempt from taxes, compared to as little as 3 percent in the adjacent suburbs. Suburbanites, of course, enjoy the use of these nonprofit, tax-free institutions; and, in the case of private colleges and universities, they are far more likely to enjoy their use than are the residents of the inner cities.

In addition to the traditionally tax-exempt institutions, economic development packages in recent years have added a confusing overlay of property tax-break incentives to lure corporate investment.

Choice programs force increased dependence on the inequitable property tax. Milwaukee public schools lost $2.5 million in state aid as a result of choice. "The school district, therefore, raised its property tax levy by $2.5 million this year to account for the decline in state aid and the increase in required expenditures." In many cases, enrollment choice will initiate hidden but significant tax shifts from the more equitable, progressive state corporate and personal income taxes to the local property taxes—and this will increase inequity....

## Choice and the Constitutions

The Fourteenth Amendment to the U.S. Constitution states:

> No State shall make or enforce any law which shall abridge the privileges or immunities of citizens of the United States; nor shall any State deprive any person of life, liberty, or property, without due process of law, nor deny to any person within its jurisdiction the equal protection of the laws.

Choice will benefit some schools (and some students) at the expense of others. Proponents don't disagree; in fact, that's the purpose. "Choice works, and it works with a vengeance," said Reagan. To even an untrained legal observer, that premise seems to conflict with the Fourteenth Amendment. If an equitable education is not an expressed right in the Constitution, isn't it at least a privilege of all citizens? Shouldn't all citizens in a democracy be equally immune from the deprivations of ignorance? If education is commonly acknowledged as necessary to acquire property, don't all citizens have a property right to an equitable education? If a person is too poor to own property but still pays sales taxes that support education and votes in school elections, doesn't that qualify as citizenship and ownership and constitute a property right deserving of equal protection? Doesn't equal protection mean equal benefit when public money is raised by public officials to provide a public good?

How do all citizens exercise their First Amendment freedoms of speech and press if some citizens can choose a better education than others and if their choices diminish the educational opportunities of others? Isn't the expressed power of the federal government to provide for the general welfare sufficient to imply that some responsibility for the equitable education of all its citizens (upon which its very existence depends) is necessary and proper? Doesn't reading Jefferson and Madison remove any doubt about their original intent?

Perhaps this is nothing but the naive ramblings of an untrained legal mind. After all, the Supreme Court found in the 1973 Rodriguez case that education was not a "fundamental right" under the U.S. Constitution and was not subject to the Equal Protection guarantees. However, the vote was close, 5 to 4. Furthermore, had the case been heard by the Warren Court, the decision might have been different. When choice is factored into the education equation and the inequity balance tips even further, the Supreme Court will undoubtedly have another opportunity to determine whether glaring disparities and absolute deprivation have any equal protection remedy.

In the meantime, education-equity litigation proceeds in over half the states. Almost all state constitutions have specific education clauses that provide for thorough, general, efficient, free, equitable and/or uniform systems of public schools. It does seem ironic that school children are taught to pledge allegiance to the American flag, but it is left to state courts to protect the equality of the classrooms they are taught in. In December 1991, Minnesota District Judge Gary Meyer ruled that parts of the state's school finance system violate the state constitution and result in a "significant imbalance and inequity" between wealthy and poor school districts. He stated that the original goals of the 1971 "Minnesota miracle" which increased the proportion of foundation aid and restricted the use of property taxes had been severely eroded.

Minnesota's education clause reads: "The stability of a republican form of government depending mainly upon the intelligence of the people, it is the duty of the Legislature to establish a general and uniform system of public schools." Judge Meyer also recognized in his decision the emphasis on education in a democratic government and "education's critical importance in supporting the viability of other civil liberties contained in the Bill of Rights." He stated that the mandate of uniformity is not diminished because the legislature has delegated much of its financing authority to local school districts. The rule of uniformity is ultimately the legislature's concern.

If the legislature's responsibility for a general and uniform system of public schools cannot be relegated to local control, how can it be left to individual choice? Any choice system that allows state aid (tuitions, scholarships, vouchers) to follow the students decreases the resources left to educate those who stay behind, many of whom have no effective choice. "General and uniform" become the myths of choice. School districts losing "choice" state revenue are forced into even greater reliance on the inequitable local property tax. The arguments for local control and continued property tax funding, for the right of each school district to address the educational needs of its children in any manner it sees fit, sound as American as the right of parents to choose their children's schools. The rhetoric is American; the consequences are not. That reasoning gave us legal segregation before *Brown vs. Board of Education,* gross inequities before New Jersey (1973), Kentucky (1989), Texas (1989), and so on. Choice will ultimately set off a whole new round of equity litigation.

If the choice systems adopted include public funding for parochial schools, the court challenges will not be limited to equity and equal protection issues. Chubb and Moe advocate such a system: "Our own preference would be to include religious schools as well, as long as their sectarian functions can be kept clearly separate from their educational functions." The initiative filed in California for the November 1992 election would enable parents to send their children to parochial schools at taxpayers' expense, with assurances that those schools would remain free from "onerous regulation." The Pennsylvania Senate has approved a plan that would allow parents to use state stipends to send their children to any public, private, or religious school. In 1991–92, the Bush administration lobbied hard for a multimillion-dollar choice program that included religious schools. Public money for religious education is on deck, and lawyers will benefit from the largest job creation program of the century.

The polls show that a majority of Americans favor school choice. Short-sighted politicians will undoubtedly continue to enact choice legislation, and the courts will be busier than ever. So be it. The courts' role has always been that of a last resort for the

> rights of "politically impotent minorities." By definition, the processes of democracy bode poorly for the security of such rights. Thus, the task of guarding these constitutionally prescribed liberties sensibly falls upon a body that is not politically responsible, that is not beholden to the grace of the excited majoritarianism—the United States Supreme Court. Herein lies the great justification for the power of judicial review, the wisdom of Marbury v. Madison.

The courts have already wrestled for decades over the wall of separation between church and state erected by the establishment clause of the First Amendment. How high is the wall when considering public aid to parochial schools? The current, excessive entanglement standard was first applied by the Supreme Court in *Lemon v. Kurtzman* (1971).

> To be constitutional, a State's school aid law must meet these requirements: (1) the purpose of the aid must be clearly secular, not religious, (2) its primary effect must neither advance nor inhibit religion, and (3) it must avoid an "excessive entanglement of government with religion."

Clearly, the choice programs being proposed will fail to meet these standards. Who will determine how much of the general state aid is spent for secular rather than religious purposes? The government will, and that's got to be excessive entanglement.

Many state constitutions, like Minnesota's, include explicit prohibitions of public aid for religious schools. Article XIII, Section 2, states: "In no case shall any public money or property be appropriated or used for the support of schools wherein the distinctive doctrines, creeds or tenets of any particular Christian or other religious sect are promulgated or taught." In addition, the taxing authority provided in the Minnesota constitution states that taxes can be levied and collected for public purposes only. The Minnesota Bill of Rights is more specific than the federal version and states in Section 16: "Nor shall any man be compelled to attend, erect or support any place of worship, or to maintain any religious or ecclesiastical ministry, against his consent."

There are several concerns, beside the federal and state constitutional issues cited above, about providing public funding for private and parochial schools through a choice system. It is generally accepted that public schools play an important democratizing role in bringing students of different religious, ethnic, and cultural backgrounds together. The draining of resources from the public schools to support private and parochial schools can only erode that primary mission. Choice will further facilitate the separation of children in schools and the reasons for that separation, religious or secular, are most often tied to ethnic, social, racial, or economic differences. It's race and/or class all over again.

Combine private and parochial school choice with deregulatory zeal, and any semblance of fair competition disappears. If public schools are going to be forced to compete with taxpayer-subsidized private schools, do we require compliance with the rules for all players, or do we drop the rules equally for all players? "In most cases, the proponents of private-school choice want it both ways. They want government money on the one hand but freedom from government regulation on the other." If we drop the regulations across the board, do we take the time to examine the reasons for the regulations in the first place? What abuses do we reopen the doors to, and what protections do we eliminate? If regulatory compliance is only required of public schools, then why not scratch Jefferson and simply proceed with a much more deliberate, efficient, and humane dismantling of the public school system?

More likely, choice funding for private and parochial schools will turn out to be a mixed blessing for them in the long run. Government funding means government strings, eventually and inevitably, if not initially.

> If experience elsewhere is any indicator, accountability measures will accompany any substantial flow of money to private schools. The resulting intrusion on the autonomy and independence of the private sector threatens its uniqueness as an alternative to public schools. The publicization of private schools serves neither the schools, their clients, nor American education in general.

While the role of private and parochial schools is not the same as that of public schools in our society, it is no less important. The importance of that role is totally dependent upon the freedom from government involvement or entanglement. Freedom of choice may become a myth for private and parochial schools once they accept government funding, and another thread in the traditional fabric of our democratic society will be torn apart by choice.

The ultimate paradox of choice is that it will inevitably eliminate choices —not for the few, but for the many. There will be fewer schools in rural America and fewer resources and options in the inner city. It's a policy designed to skim the best and write off the rest in the ghettos and a policy that will destroy community and tradition in much of America. As Lewis Finch, former superintendent of the Anoka-Hennepin school district, wrote about Minnesota's open enrollment: "Ultimately, the state will have islands of education excellence surrounded by vast wastelands of deprivation." When schools asked for help, they got choice—"the great placebo."

One business with a vested interest in reading agrees that choice is not the answer. On the September 27, 1991, cover, *Publisher's Weekly* urged President Bush to read Kozol's *Savage Inequalities:*

> It is the story of how, in our public schools, we are creating a country profoundly different from the one our founders envisaged. It is the story of two nations that are separate and unequal in their educational facilities, and tells how this unfair imbalance has been created and maintained by the inequitable distribution of public funds. Clearly, something must be done about American education, but too often those who work to reform it do so through notions of "choice" and "competition," market terms that have no place in a debate on the needs of our poor children. In the end, there is no doubt that we will have to spend money, and a lot of it, to bring genuine equality to our schools.

But President Bush cautioned parents of poor children that money was not a cure for education problems, that "a society that worships money ... is a society in peril." Cold and callous words for parents who only want a fair chance for their kids. Senator Orrin Hatch (R-Utah) said, while pushing Bush's choice program in Congress, "Let's give the low-income parents at least one additional weapon for use for school improvement. Let's give them the ability to walk out." Hatch is right on: Choice is the very least they could give.

Jefferson warned that education would cost. But he also warned that the cost is not more than the "thousandth part" of what will be paid if the people are left in ignorance. We can pay now or pay a lot more later. What if choice sweeps the land and the "failing" public schools are replaced by private "scholarship" schools? What if the new schools turn out to be elitist, separatist, or just plain terrible? What if it becomes necessary to reconstruct rural school districts where there are no schools or communities left, to rebuild urban public schools to bring all poor people into the mainstream of American life?

> At that point it would be incredibly difficult to persuade the middle class to support a substantial new program that would help only people who don't pay taxes. Before taking such an immense risk, we ought to make sure we've tried every possible means of making bad schools better which doesn't involve cutting them loose from the webbing of public life.

Making sure we've tried every possible alternative means more money and emphasis on research. However, the research must be independent and objective, not vulnerable to political pressure or subject to political suppression. This is already a part of the partisan battle over education in Washington with the reauthorization of the Education Department's office of educational research and improvement. "The lightning rod is a proposal to create an independent body to oversee its operations—and prevent the Administration from using the agency to further its political agenda, a longtime concern on Capitol Hill."

We need more information and answers before we launch this massive social experiment. But the information has to be good; the risks are too great, the potential costs too high to settle for anything less.

What if the only cost of choice is not in future repair bills? If Polly Williams takes her children out of the Milwaukee public schools, but her neighborhood erupts as a result of increasing impoverishment and ignorance, what has she gained?

Recall that Jefferson also warned: "Educate and inform the whole mass of the people. Enable them to see that it is their interest to preserve peace and order, and they will preserve them." It is absolutely fundamental to a democratic society that each individual's rights and freedoms are inescapably dependent on everyone else's. As Martin Luther King Jr. wrote from the Birmingham jail, "Injustice anywhere is a threat to justice everywhere."

# POSTSCRIPT

## Would "School Choice" Improve the Quality of U.S. Education?

$R$osen and Pearson agree that America's public school system is badly in need of reform, especially in the inner cities. Their disagreement is on the issue of whether vouchers would help or hurt. Pearson thinks that most inner-city kids would be hurt because the vouchers would help only the elite, leaving the rest to attend public schools that are depleted of resources. Rosen is convinced that school choice would benefit not only the children who leave the schools for better ones but the public schools themselves, since the competition would force teachers and administrators to perform better. These arguments rest upon very different premises about human motivation and the meaning of equality. Is more intense competition the key to better performance from public schools? Or would it just demoralize the schools? Would the benefits of choice reach most families or only those who are highly motivated? If the latter, is that necessarily bad? These are some of the questions to be considered as the issue of school choice is more closely scrutinized.

In *The Manufactured Crisis* (Addison-Wesley, 1995), David C. Berliner and Bruce J. Biddle suggest that most of the evidence of failure cited by critics of public education, from declining SAT scores to rising illiteracy, is bogus and that U.S. public schools are in fact providing an increasingly diverse citizenry with decent opportunities to better themselves. Myron Lieberman, on the other hand, thinks that there is indeed an education crisis, and in *Public Education: An Autopsy* (Harvard University Press, 1993) he attributes the problem to the government's prominent role in education. He proposes replacing the existing system with a three-tier system encompassing public, nonprofit, and for-profit schools, with the latter playing the major role. Peter W. Cookson, Jr., in *School Choice: The Struggle for the Soul of American Education* (Yale University Press, 1994), considers a variety of school choice proposals. While rejecting vouchers, he supports the idea of low-interest loans for poor families who wish to send their children to private or parochial schools. John W. Witte's *The Market Approach to Education: An Analysis of America's First Voucher Program* (Princeton University Press, 2000) examines the strengths and weaknesses of a voucher program in Milwaukee, Wisconsin, and reaches the cautious conclusion that it seems to be working there but would be dangerous to implement universally, at least at the present time. *Learning from School Choice* edited by Paul E. Peterson and Bryan C. Hassel (Brookings Institution, 1998) examines the operation of various school choice programs, including charter schools and vouchers, and generally supports them.

The future of vouchers remains uncertain, in part because of legal challenges to them from the American Civil Liberties Union and other groups that charge that vouchers violate the First Amendment's ban on an "establishment of religion." The Wisconsin plan was upheld by a federal appeals court, and the Supreme Court declined to review the case. The Florida and Ohio voucher plans are still in the lower federal court system. It seems likely that the Supreme Court will eventually have to rule on the constitutionality of this mode of school choice.

# ISSUE 14

# Is Welfare Reform Succeeding?

**YES: Daniel Casse**, from "Why Welfare Reform Is Working," *Commentary* (September 1997)

**NO: Christopher Jencks and Joseph Swingle**, from "Without a Net: Whom the New Welfare Law Helps and Hurts," *The American Prospect* (January 3, 2000)

### ISSUE SUMMARY

**YES:** Policy analyst Daniel Casse argues that the 1996 overhaul of welfare has encouraged long-term welfare clients to find meaningful jobs and to better their lives.

**NO:** Social analysts Christopher Jencks and Joseph Swingle contend that although welfare reforms have helped some people, they have not addressed the "hard core" unemployed, whose lot seems to be getting worse.

No social problem seems more intractable than poverty. Even in America's current upbeat economy, more than 36 million Americans live below the official poverty line (about $15,000 for a family of four). Most are white (though one-third are black), and the largest single age group is children; more than 15 million poor people are under the age of 18, living in families headed by single mothers.

Traditionally, poor families were helped largely through private charities or, at most, by local and state government programs. But in the 1930s the Roosevelt administration established a variety of national antipoverty programs, including public employment projects, old-age pensions, and help for single mothers and their children. This latter aid category has generated much of the controversy over "welfare." The Social Security Act of 1935 contained a provision, later called Aid to Families with Dependent Children (AFDC), that provided grants to needy families who lacked a breadwinner.

AFDC grants were based on the principle of *entitlement*, which meant that there would be a federally defined guarantee of assistance to families with children who met a state's statutory definition of need. It would also guarantee to the state matching grants to help the state pay for assistance to these families.

Little was made of AFDC at the time because divorce was rare and the illegitimacy rate was only about 4 percent. The typical AFDC family in 1935 was not that of a "welfare mother" but a "widow lady" struggling to feed her family after the death of her husband. It was also assumed that the assistance would be of short duration, sufficient to tide things over until the mother remarried, found a job, or moved in with relatives.

Within 30 years, however, the whole context of the program was radically transformed: by the mid-1960s the major category of AFDC recipients consisted of unmarried women and their children, and a substantial portion of them stayed on welfare for many years.

Criticism of AFDC had been building for many years. The main criticism was that it was fostering dependency by handing out money without requiring any work for it. It was the frequent target of Republican politicians, and even many Democrats conceded that the program needed reform. When he first ran for president in 1992, Bill Clinton promised to "end welfare as we know it." He proposed a strict, two-year time limit for people to get off welfare and into productive work. When the Republicans took over Congress in 1995 they decided to put this pledge to the test. During the next year they passed two different versions of welfare reform, both of which Clinton vetoed. But in August 1996 Clinton signed a third version, called the Personal Responsibility Act, which is now part of U.S. public law. The following are among its key provisions:

- It abolishes AFDC, the federally guaranteed program of cash assistance to poor children. Instead, states will get lump sums of federal money to run their own welfare and work-training programs.
- It requires the head of every family to go to work within two years or lose benefits.
- It limits lifetime benefits to five years in most cases.
- It limits the amount of food stamps available to adults who are not raising children.

The signing of this act set off a furious debate on what the effects of the new law would be. Supporters heralded it as a liberation of the poor from the Washington bureaucracy; opponents decried it as a shameful abdication of responsibility that will cause social misery.

In the selections that follow, Daniel Casse argues that the 1996 overhaul of welfare has encouraged long-term welfare clients to find meaningful jobs and to better their lives. Christopher Jencks and Joseph Swingle conclude that although the reforms have helped some people, they have not addressed the "hard core" unemployed, whose situation seems to be getting worse.

**Daniel Casse**

 **YES**

# Why Welfare Reform Is Working

On July 1, [1997], the "end of welfare as we know it," began in earnest. On that day, the federal legislation that President Clinton had signed nearly a year earlier went into effect, terminating a 62-year-old federal entitlement and creating, for the first time, a limit on how long one can receive federal welfare assistance.

In Washington, however, it seems impossible to leave well enough alone. Clinton himself had promised last year to "fix" troublesome portions of the welfare law, and by the end of July, as Congress passed a balanced-budget plan, it became apparent that the law's implementation was still susceptible of political manipulation. In the final days of negotiation over the budget, a passive Republican Congress and a politically alert White House began diluting the potent formula conceived and signed a year earlier and in effect for all of three weeks.

These eleventh-hour changes are not insignificant. But they should not obscure the larger achievement. The welfare-reform legislation that went into effect on July 1 is the most far-reaching policy move of the Clinton presidency —and also, to date, the most successful. Not surprisingly, the President used his July 4 national radio address to crow about it. Since he took office in January 1993, he announced, three million fewer people were on the welfare rolls. Even more impressive was the fact that an astonishing 1.2 million had come off the rolls in the first nine months since the welfare-reform legislation passed Congress and before it formally went into effect. Using rhetoric that was once the preserve of conservative polemicists, the President told the nation on July 4 that "we have begun to put an end to the culture of dependency, and to elevate our values of family, work, and responsibility."

In truth, the legislation itself deserves only part of the credit. Earlier this year, the President's own Council of Economic Advisers concluded that the drop in the number of people on welfare was due in some measure to the healthy economy and also to the wide variety of initiatives that had emerged over the last few years at the state level. We have, indeed, never witnessed such a fertile period of experimentation, with dozens of state legislatures trying new ways to move people off government assistance and onto a path of self-sufficiency. Most of these former recipients have gone successfully into full- or part-time jobs,

From Daniel Casse, "Why Welfare Reform Is Working," *Commentary* (September 1997). Copyright © 1997 by The American Jewish Committee. Reprinted by permission of *Commentary*.

while others, recognizing the new demands the local welfare office will soon place on them, have voluntarily dropped out of the system. With the more comprehensive measures of the federal law now taking effect—and notwithstanding the deleterious changes introduced in the balanced-budget negotiations—we have every reason to expect that these trends will continue.

Not everyone is rejoicing, to be sure. The hand-wringing among some conservatives over the last-minute changes smuggled in by the White House in late July is one thing; but it pales in comparison to the deep distress which the legislation, amended or unamended, has brought to liberal policy circles, not to mention the real rifts which the President's support for welfare reform has caused within his own party. For those who have not wanted to hear that the era of big government is over, the welfare-reform bill has been, indeed, a bitter pill to swallow.

That may explain why, from the beginning, those opposed to the plan repeatedly resorted to a kind of demagoguery that was shameless even by Washington standards. Thus, when the first round of legislation began moving through the Republican-controlled Congress in 1994, Senator Daniel Patrick Moynihan boldly predicted that the result would be "scenes of social trauma such as we haven't known since the cholera epidemics." Not to be outdone, Senator Edward M. Kennedy called an early version of the reform bill "legislative child-abuse."

By the summer of 1996, when it was clear that a bipartisan coalition existed for replacing the federal welfare entitlement with state block grants, time limits, and work requirements, still more alarms were set off. The Urban Institute warned that one million children would fall into poverty, the *New York Times* condemned the bill as "atrocious," and Moynihan pronounced it "an obscene act of social regression." Finally, days after the President signed the legislation, two of his top policy appointees at the Department of Health and Human Services resigned in protest. One of them, Peter Edelman, waited less than six months before publishing an article in the *Atlantic* calling the welfare-reform plan "the worst thing Bill Clinton has done." As Edelman saw it, the new legislation offered a grim future for America's poor:

> [T]here will be suffering.... There will be more malnutrition and more crime, increased infant mortality and increased drug and alcohol abuse. There will be increased family violence and abuse against children and women, and a consequent significant spillover of the problem into the already overloaded child-welfare system and battered-women's shelters.

✦◈✦

... The Personal Responsibility and Work Opportunity Reconciliation Act of 1996 passed both Houses of Congress with considerable bipartisan support. Like all such sweeping pieces of legislation, it makes changes to numerous federal laws and regulations. But the bulk of the legislation is directed at Aid to Families with Dependent Children (AFDC), the Roosevelt-era assistance program that was the target of most of the growing public dissatisfaction with welfare. The new law effectively repeals AFDC and replaces it with a new program known as Temporary Assistance for Needy Families (TANF). In addition, the law introduces four fundamental changes that distinguish it from every attempt at welfare reform that has come before.

First, it ends the federal entitlement to cash assistance. In the past, eligibility for this assistance was means-tested: anyone meeting the income requirements was automatically qualified. Under the new law, each state determines eligibility. Second, the new law gives a block grant to each of the 50 states, permitting it to design a cash-assistance program as it sees fit. Third, the law establishes a five-year lifetime limit on cash assistance and a two-year limit on receiving assistance without working, thus ensuring that welfare cannot become a way of life. Finally, the law requires each state to craft work requirements as part of its welfare program. By the year 2002, states will need to show that at least 50 percent of those receiving welfare are involved in some form of work or training in exchange for benefits.

These changes all come with a catalogue of exemptions, qualifications, and alternative requirements in special cases—a flexibility that guarantees that the actual programs will vary considerably from state to state. The law will not, for example, "throw a million children into poverty." States can exempt 20 percent of their caseload from the time limit, and also convert block-grant money into vouchers for children after their families have reached the limit. Even when the federal limits are triggered, states can continue to spend their own money helping poor families (as they do now). And states may exempt parents of infants from all work requirements, while single parents with children under six will be asked to work only part-time.

Although one would never know it from the critics, left untouched by this reform are a host of poverty-assistance programs. Medicaid, a program still in need of reform, continues to provide health coverage to all poor families under the new welfare law. Public-housing programs remain in effect, as do child-nutrition programs and the Earned Income Tax Credit. The food-stamp program will continue to grow, if at a slower rate. Again contrary to what has been charged, children with serious long-term medical conditions and disabilities will *not* lose their Supplemental Security Income aid; the new law merely narrows the definition of "disability" to exclude some purely behavioral problems.

Most of the bill's critics have also misunderstood the financing behind it. According to the *Washington Post*, the new law "hands the problem to the states and fails to equip them with the resources to solve" it. In fact, the bill represents a giant windfall for state welfare spending. The block grants replacing the old, formula-driven AFDC payments have been fixed at 1994 spending levels—but in the meantime, as the President reminded us in his July 4 radio address, the welfare caseload across the nation has been dropping dramatically. (In Maryland, Oregon, Massachusetts, Oklahoma, and Michigan, the AFDC caseload has shrunk by 20 to 30 percent in the past two years alone.) For many states, then, the new block grants, financed on the basis of the more crowded welfare rolls of two years ago, represent a significant hike in funding—hardly the outcome one would anticipate from a Republican Congress routinely described as mean-spirited, heartless, and insensitive to the needs of the poor.

But most confounding of all to critics of the bill, and most heartening to its supporters, is the fact that welfare reform, in its embryonic stages, has wildly surpassed expectations. In April of [1997], eleven million people were on welfare, the lowest share of the U.S. population since 1970. Nor have any of the widely predicted nightmare scenarios materialized. Even in cities like Milwaukee, where thousands of welfare recipients have dropped off the rolls in the last two years, local shelters and food banks have reported no new surges in demand for their services.

What accounts for these early signs of success? Following the lead of the Council of Economic Advisers, some have suggested that the drop in caseloads is traceable entirely to the current strength of the economy. But this cannot be right. The economy has indeed been strong; yet previous cycles of prosperity have failed to produce anything close to the reductions we see today.

What is different, clearly, is that the *rules* governing welfare dependence have started to change. Indeed, they started to change well before the federal law was passed last year. Impatient with Washington's habitual inaction, both Democratic and Republican governors began introducing time limits, work requirements, and rules designed to promote responsibility in their own state systems. The burgeoning economy has made their work easier, but there is no denying that in states where the rules have changed, the lives and behavior of welfare recipients have also changed, and for the better.

Wisconsin's much-touted reforms are a case in point. In a detailed study published in *Policy Review,* Robert Rector has shown how two new programs in that state, Self-Sufficiency First and Pay for Performance, fundamentally altered the relationship between welfare recipients and government. Implemented in April 1996, the programs required recipients to work in the private sector or perform community service, attend remedial-education classes, or participate in a supervised job search in exchange for AFDC payments or food stamps. Those who did not want to work, take classes, or look for a job were no longer eligible for payments. Seven months after the programs began, the AFDC caseload had dropped 33 percent.

Recent experience in Tennessee, though less widely reported, is no less impressive. As it happens, Tennessee is not subject to the provisions of the new federal law, having won prior approval for an equally comprehensive program of its own. Like the federal law, the Tennessee plan, known as Families First, replaces AFDC with a cash-assistance program that requires recipients to work, go to school, or train while working part-time. Tennessee exempts almost a third of its welfare recipients from the time limits (and from some of the work requirements), and in that respect its plan is even more flexible than the federal law. On the other hand, Tennessee imposes a tighter restriction on the number of consecutive months welfare recipients can receive cash benefits. Finally, everyone eligible for benefits, even if exempt from the work requirements and the time limits, must sign a "personal-responsibility contract" outlining the steps to be taken toward self-sufficiency.

In the first six months of the program, 19,000 Tennesseans left the welfare rolls—a 21-percent drop, unprecedented in the state's history. What makes this reduction more remarkable still is that during these early months no one was being forcibly removed from the rolls by an arbitrary cutoff date. Instead, social-service officials in Tennessee discovered that the mere requirement to show up at a welfare office, sign a statement of personal responsibility, and participate in a work or educational program had a dramatic impact on the lives of people accustomed to receiving a government check without anything being asked of them at all.

Tennessee officials broke down the declining caseload to understand what was taking place. The results are revealing: 5,800 recipients asked that their cases be closed within the first month ("I don't want to be bothered," was a common response). Another 5,500 found work and earned enough money to make them ineligible. Almost a third either refused to sign the personal-responsibility contract, or failed to comply with its terms, or refused to attend classes or begin a job search. The rest moved out of the state. As for those still receiving cash assistance, many appear to be enthusiastically pursuing a route to independence. In the first six months of Families First, 18 percent of this group had found full-time employment; 22 percent were in training or were looking for a job; 19 percent were pursuing adult education; 6 percent had gotten some form of employment mixed with training.

Tennessee's record so far vividly contradicts the most prevalent and long-standing liberal criticism of a decentralized welfare system: that it will spur a "race to the bottom" among the states. Harvard's David Ellwood, who served as an assistant secretary of Health and Human Services and was a point man for the administration's welfare-reform plans before quitting in frustration, has made this criticism most explicitly:

> History is filled with examples of states choosing to ignore poor families or ignoring racial minorities, regions, or types of families. Moreover, if one state's rules differ markedly from those of another, there will be an incentive for migration. It is a lot easier to move poor people from welfare to the state border than from welfare to work. Needs and resources also differ widely across states. The states with the smallest tax base are usually the states with the greatest proportion of poor children and families. Fearful of becoming "welfare magnets," some states may cut benefits and impose more punitive measures than they would otherwise prefer.

On almost every point, the Tennessee example has disproved Ellwood and those who repeat his arguments. Tennessee, a relatively poor Southern state, is also no stranger to racial tensions. With no state income tax, a lean state budget, a recent history of political corruption, and a strong Republican tilt in recent elections, it would hardly seem an ideal candidate for meaningful welfare reform. Yet Tennessee's program *has* promoted work and independence without suddenly snatching away the safety net. Moreover, as part of its reform initiative, the state legislature has actually increased spending on welfare by 22 percent since 1994. Nor is Tennessee unique in this respect. The *New York Times* recently reported that, to the surprise of antipoverty advocates, state legislatures, flush with federal dollars from the welfare-reform bill, have been spending money on day-care services, emergency loans for car repairs, and free subway passes, all designed to make it easier for welfare recipients to find work. . . .

❧

It cannot be stressed enough that the current round of welfare reform is different from all that have preceded it. In the past, reform initiatives simply added a labyrinth of incentives to what remained, at heart, a system of entitlements. Work programs, counseling, job searches, child care, and transportation subsidies are surely limited tools if the recipient knows that at the end of the day, there will be no penalty for failing to respond to the rules and incentives. And the most able welfare recipients *always* knew how to "game" the system.

That is why a legal work requirement and a clear time limit for cash assistance are so crucial. Without the certainty of a fixed cutoff date, workfare programs of the past invariably devolved into another form of open-ended government job training that did little to move the trainee into a real job. The key to the current reform is that it promotes self-sufficiency by *removing* welfare as a long-term alternative.

And that, regrettably, is also where the changes introduced in [the July, 1997] budget agreement are likely to do the most damage. A number of state governors have reacted to these changes by charging that the President has effectively undermined the whole thrust of the legislation. "Even Democratic governors are screaming he's all but killed it," wrote the columnist Paul Gigot in the *Wall Street Journal*.

There is much justice in the governors' complaints. The administration's $3-billion Welfare-to-Work program, for example, was stuffed into the July budget agreement as a payoff to big-city mayors who had been left out of the welfare-reform process. Federal funding for yet another unproven job-preparedness initiative like this one runs counter to the main intent of welfare reform, which is (again) to require work, not training, in exchange for a government check. By permitting such alternatives to thrive, the administration has succeeded in creating yet more loopholes for welfare recipients—the very thing that has repeatedly undone past efforts at reform.

But the administration's attempt to roll back or qualify the progress that has been made has taken on an even more disturbing aspect. Both the President and his Department of Labor have begun to insist that all work performed by welfare recipients, even those in community-service jobs, must be treated as "employment" and therefore subject to the panoply of federal labor regulations. Such an interpretation not only runs contrary to 30 years of sensible precedent, but, by asserting a new and intrusive federal role, it has the very real potential to prevent every new state workfare program from getting off the ground. If the administration has its way, more than two dozen federal requirements would be placed on any workfare position, including the payment of minimum wages (and prevailing wages in construction jobs), payroll taxes for employers, workers'-compensation programs, and so on. It would be hard to conceive a greater obstacle in the path of programs that were intended, after all, to help those most unlikely to find work in the private sector.

As the Republican Congress was notably unenthusiastic about fighting off these rearguard actions against a bill it spent two years struggling to pass, it will now be up to state governments to challenge ongoing efforts to exert federal control over workfare. Still, these legal and technical issues, and others like them, are *all* that remains of the welfare discussion. Which means that the larger debate that began in the early 1980's is finally over....

[W]hat distinguishes the current reform is that it has forced both federal and state governments to take seriously the idea that welfare policy can deter, or encourage, behavior. The fact that Tennessee will increase welfare spending this year tells us nothing in itself. But the fact that Tennessee now holds parents accountable for their children's immunizations and school attendance; that it forces teen parents to stay in school and live at home or with a guardian; and that it provides no additional benefits for single mothers who have additional children while on welfare, means that government is no longer indifferent to the way welfare recipients live and raise their children. All this represents a stark departure from the liberalism that has dominated government policy toward the poor for the last three decades.

Changing the way the poor behave may not make them prosperous, and there will always be critics to insist that until poverty is eradicated, no program can claim success. But by eliminating the certainty that one will be paid whether or not one works or seeks work, we have already taken the most important step on the road toward the end of welfare—and of liberalism—as we have known them.

# NO ⬅

Christopher Jencks and
Joseph Swingle

# Without a Net

The welfare rolls have fallen by almost half since 1994. To assess the impact of this dramatic change, both journalists and social scientists have been talking to families that have left the rolls. But these families are only half the story. Even without welfare reform, nearly half the single mothers on the rolls in 1994 would have left by 1999 simply because their children grew older, they found work, or they got married. But in the absence of welfare reform, most of these mothers would have been replaced by other mothers who had just had their first baby, split up with their husband, or lost their job. Because states have made it far more difficult to get on welfare, most of those who left the rolls were not replaced.

The only way to assess the overall impact of welfare reform is to ask how life has changed for *all* single mothers, including those who no longer even apply for welfare. The most up-to-date information on single mothers comes from the Census Bureau's Current Population Survey (CPS), which collects data every March on about 5,000 unmarried mothers with children under 18. To see how these mothers' lives have changed, we have analyzed the CPS data collected from March 1988 to March 1999, which can help us answer four questions:

- How many single mothers are working?
- How have single mothers' incomes changed since welfare reform began?
- Has declining support from welfare forced more single mothers to double up?
- Are mothers more likely to marry now than they were before reform began?

The answers to these questions are neither as grim as critics of welfare reform feared nor as encouraging as some advocates of reform promised. More single mothers have jobs. Most also have more money, but a small minority is worse off. The proportion of single mothers doubled up with relatives has not changed. Marriage rates, which stopped falling before welfare reform began, have remained flat.

From Christopher Jencks and Joseph Swingle, "Without a Net: Whom the New Welfare Law Helps and Hurts," *The American Prospect* (January 3, 2000). Copyright © 2000 by *The American Prospect*. Reprinted by permission of *The American Prospect* and the authors.

## What the Numbers Tell Us

Welfare reform began in some states in the early 1990s, when Washington began issuing "waivers" allowing states to impose work requirements on certain mothers. But Congress did not abolish Aid to Families with Dependent Children (AFDC) until 1996, and the new system, known as Temporary Assistance for Needy Families (TANF), did not take effect until 1997. The number of households receiving welfare peaked in 1994, two years after the economy began recovering from the recession but three years before TANF took effect [see Figure 1]. By 1996 the rolls had fallen 10 percent, but once TANF took effect, the decline accelerated. Almost everyone agrees that the tightening labor market, the Earned Income Tax Credit (EITC), and welfare reform all played a role in this unprecedented decline.

*Figure 1*

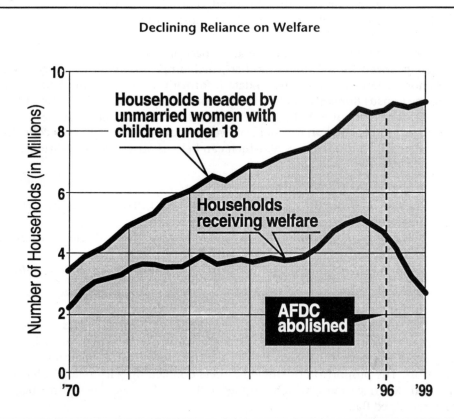

### Declining Reliance on Welfare

*Source:* U.S. Dept. of Health and Human Services and *Current Population Reports.* The 1999 welfare counts are as of March 1999. Earlier counts are annual averages.

The labor market has been tighter in the past few years than at any time since the late 1960s, making it far easier for single mothers to find work in convenient places and at reasonable hours. In addition, the EITC can now raise a single mother's earnings by as much as $2 an hour. The EITC reached this level in 1996, but because many mothers were unaware of the change, its impact on employment has been more gradual. An analysis by David Ellwood concludes that changes in the economy and the EITC together account for about half the decline in the rolls since 1994. The rest is welfare reform.

After TANF became law in 1997, states imposed time limits on welfare receipt. Most also imposed much tougher work requirements. Perhaps most important of all, states concluded that the quickest way to reduce their case load was to open fewer new cases. Many states began"diverting" new applicants into employment programs. Some just hand a mother the "Help Wanted" section and tell her to come back after she has made, say, 30 calls. A lot of mothers never come back. As the word spreads, the number of mothers coming into welfare offices begins to fall.

## More Single Mothers Are Working

Follow-up studies show that most mothers who leave the welfare rolls find jobs, but a large minority do not. Furthermore, some of those who find jobs soon lose them.... Between 1987 and 1996, about 10 percent of all single mothers fell in this category. By 1998 the fraction had climbed to 12 percent [see Figure 2]. This increase is consistent with studies showing that a substantial minority of former recipients are not working.

If a mother has no income for an entire year, she cannot maintain her own household. Such mothers sometimes have to split up their families, but most of them move in with a parent, sibling, or boyfriend. In 1998 such mothers lived in households with incomes averaging about $22,000. Low as this figure is, it is still considerably higher than the household income of the mothers who got welfare. How much of the income was available to support the mother and her children is unclear. Another big worry for these mothers is that they seldom have a legal right to stay in their current households, so if there is a domestic quarrel, they sometimes end up in the streets.

## Incomes Are Rising at the Top but Not at the Bottom

Many surveys have found that even when single mothers work, they often remain poor. Census statistics on poverty do not throw much light on this because they ignore the income mothers get from live-in boyfriends and only provide data on single mothers who head their own household. [Figure 3] shows the total household income of every single mother with children under 18. The income measure includes not only money from jobs, welfare, and the EITC but the estimated value of food stamps, school lunches, subsidized housing, and most other means-tested benefits. The measure does not assign a value to subsidized health insurance because this is worth far more to families with serious health problems than to other people. The income measure also omits the value

*Figure 2*

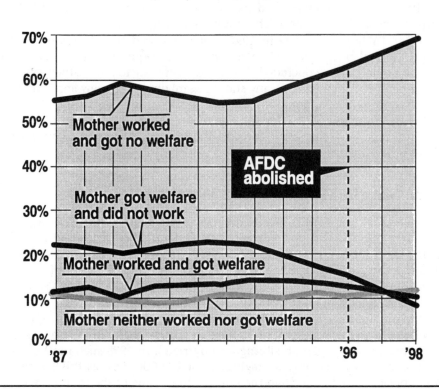

## Working Is Up Among Single Mothers

*Source:* March Current Population Survey. Data in all tables are for single mothers who live with children of their own who are under the age of 18. We count mothers as having worked if they reported working even one week during the year. We count them as having received welfare if anyone in their household received income from public assistance during the year.

of child care subsidies because such data do not exist. We convert income in all years to 1997 dollars.

At the 90th percentile of the distribution for single mothers, household incomes were about $55,000 in 1998, and rising. But mothers at the 50th percentile were just scraping by, with 1998 incomes near $23,000. Mothers at the 10th percentile reported total household incomes of only $9,400. Furthermore, while most single mothers had more income in 1998 than in 1996, those at the 10th percentile reported no gain and those at the 5th percentile actually lost a little ground. Incomes at the 5th percentile averaged only $6,400 in 1997 and 1998, down from $6,900 in 1995 and 1996. But even at the 5th percentile, single mothers were doing better than they had in the late 1980s, when their incomes averaged only $5,600.

At this point the reader should be wondering whether any mother can really make ends meet on less than $10,000 a year, especially when the in-

*Figure 3*

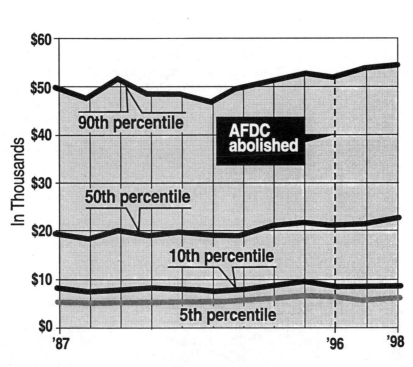

**Single Mothers' Household Incomes**

*Source:* March Current Population Survey. Income is for all household members, after taxes, and includes welfare, the EITC, food stamps, school lunches, and housing subsidies, but not health insurance subsidies.

come measure includes the value of food stamps and housing subsidies. Such skepticism is reasonable. When the Consumer Expenditure Survey asks single mothers how much they spend, those who report incomes below $10,000 mostly spend well over $10,000. A few of these mothers may be living on credit cards, but most are just underreporting their true income. In *Making Ends Meet* (1997), Kathryn Edin and Laura Lein found that almost all unskilled single mothers relied on gifts from family members or boyfriends, or on off-the-books employment to balance their budgets. Mothers are unlikely to report such income to the Census Bureau. But while these mothers are not quite as poor as the CPS implies, Edin and Lein's findings suggest that most of them still experience a lot of material hardship.

[Figure 3] also overstates some mothers' disposable income. The income figures are adjusted to eliminate taxes, but not to eliminate work-related expenses. Now that more single mothers work, they are spending more on child care, transportation, and office clothes. This increase in work-related expenses could mean that some mothers in the lower part of the distribution end up with less money for food, housing, and other necessities. To see how common this is, we need data on single mothers' living conditions. The federal government does collect such data, but not much of the post-1996 data is currently available, so we have to rely on the CPS for clues.

## Doubling Up

When single mothers cannot make ends meet on their own, they usually try to move in with relatives. Thus if welfare reform had left single mothers worse off, we would expect more of them to be doubled up. In fact, the percentage of single mothers living with relatives has not increased [see Figure 4], and neither has the percentage living in a household headed by a nonrelative (usually a boyfriend). The only change in single mothers' living arrangements is that those who head their own households are more likely to report having a nonrelative in their household. Four-fifths of these nonrelatives are boyfriends.

*Figure 4*

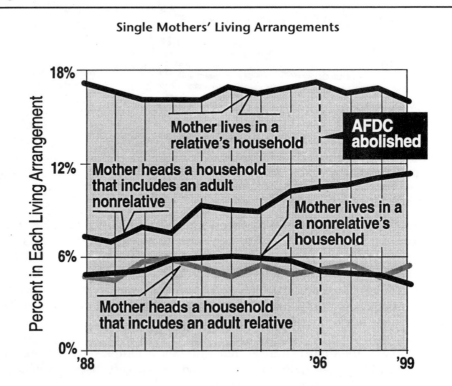

**Single Mothers' Living Arrangements**

*Source:* March Current Population Surveys.

Although more single mothers report live-in boyfriends, it is not clear what this means. Historically, many mothers have had boyfriends whose presence they did not mention to census takers. ("He doesn't *live* here. He's just *staying* here.") As mothers leave welfare, they have less reason to conceal a boyfriend's presence. But single mothers who no longer get welfare and cannot find steady work may also be relying more on problematic men whom they would previously have kept at arm's length. Or couples may just be cohabiting longer before they decide whether to marry.

When mothers are unable to feed their children or keep a roof over their heads, they often send the children to live with relatives. When that is impossible, the kids often end up in foster care, at least for a while. Thus if single mothers were having more trouble making ends meet, we would expect to find more children living apart from both parents. In fact, the number of such children shows no clear trend between 1994 and 1999, fluctuating between 9 and 11 percent among blacks and between 2 and 3 percent among whites.

## Less Health Insurance Coverage

Health insurance coverage has fallen for almost all groups, including single mothers, since the early 1990s. Because almost all poor children are now eligible for Medicaid, while many poor adults are not, we assess changes in coverage by looking at every single mother's household and calculating the percentage of all household members with coverage. From 1987 to 1993, coverage fluctuated between 81 and 82 percent. After 1993 it began to fall. In 1997 and 1998, coverage averaged only 79 percent.

The reason for declining coverage is clear. When a single mother goes on welfare, she is automatically enrolled in Medicaid. In 1993, when the welfare rolls peaked, 40 percent of all single mothers said they had Medicaid. As the rolls fell, Medicaid coverage fell too. By 1998 only 33 percent of single mothers said they had Medicaid coverage. Private coverage increased somewhat as mothers entered the labor force, but not enough to offset the decline in Medicaid.

## Marriage

Although most Americans favored welfare reform primarily because they favored work requirements and time limits, many hoped that eliminating AFDC would also discourage single parenthood, which had spread steadily since the 1960s. [Figure 5] shows that this trend came to a halt in 1994. Single parenthood has not become any *less* common, but the long-term increase has stopped, at least for the moment. [Figure 6] shows changes in the percentage of children born out of wedlock. Here too we see a steady rise from 1970 to 1994. Since 1994 we have been on a plateau.

Both of these figures suggest that the rise of the single-parent family may finally have been arrested. Because this happened well before 1996, welfare reform does not seem a likely explanation. State-by-state analysis reinforces this judgment. Wisconsin began serious welfare reform earlier than almost any other state and has cut its rolls more than any other large state. Yet the proportion of Wisconsin children born to single mothers has not fallen. Indeed, the proportion climbed from 27.1 percent in 1994 to 28.5 percent in 1998—an increase of 1.4 points—at a time when the increase for the nation as a whole was

*Figure 5*

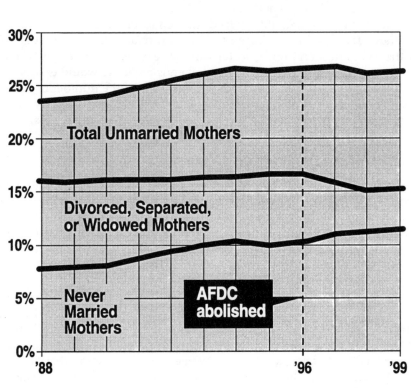

Custodial Parents Who Are Unmarried

*Source:* March Current Population Surveys. Estimates include all households with children under 18 who live with at least one of their parents.

only 0.2 points. David Ellwood has investigated this issue more systematically using data from all 50 states. He has found no evidence that marriage became more popular in states that implemented welfare reform more assiduously.

## What Next?

These are still early days for welfare reform, which did not begin in earnest until 1997. The rolls have been cut in half, but everyone agrees that this was the easy half. Employment among single mothers has increased more than almost anyone expected, but not everyone is finding work, even in today's booming economy. Most surveys of former recipients suggest that their economic situation has not changed much. If we consider all single mothers instead of just former recipients, most are a little better off today than they were in 1996, but the bottom 5 percent seem to be a little worse off. If we could take account of

*Figure 6*

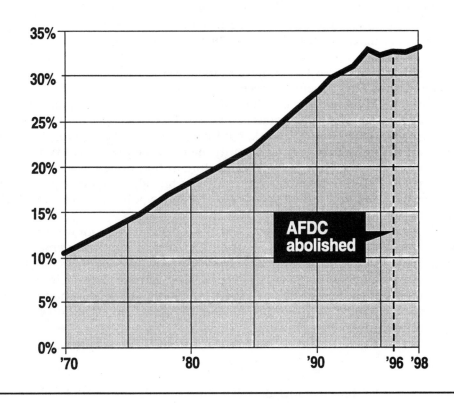

**Children Born Out of Wedlock**

AFDC
abolished

*Source:* National Center for Health Statistics, birth certificate data.

work-related expenses and out-of-pocket health care spending by those who no longer have insurance, we might find that a somewhat larger fraction of single mothers had lost ground.

Strictly economic considerations aside, two facts stand out. First, almost all mothers who are working tell interviewers that they prefer work to welfare. Second, many working mothers report problems finding satisfactory child care. There is a lot of anecdotal evidence that young children are being left alone for long periods. These reports suggest that welfare reform could end up helping parents but hurting their children. Because we have no reliable system for monitoring children's well-being, we will probably never know how welfare reform affected them.

If the welfare rolls were to keep falling at the current rate, TANF would disappear within a few years, but we think that is unlikely. Some current TANF recipients have serious mental or physical problems that make it hard to see how they could get a job, much less keep it. Other current recipients have children with mental or physical problems that demand constant attention at unpredictable times, making employment difficult and child care almost impossible to find. No knowledgeable welfare official believes that every mother currently on the rolls is capable of holding a steady job. But to the best of our knowledge, no state has a well developed plan for dealing with its "hard core" cases.

No one knows how low the rolls can go without a sharp increase in suffering. When Congress abolished AFDC in 1996, it allowed states to exempt a fifth of their case load from time limits. Drawing a line between those who can and cannot work is never easy, as we have learned over the years in battles over eligibility for disability benefits. In theory, any mother whom *no* private employer will hire should presumably be eligible for disability benefits. In practice, that will not always be the case. Some people will be denied benefits because reviewers judge them capable of work, but they will nonetheless fail to find a job. To some, failure to find work will constitute evidence that disability benefits should have been approved. To others, failure to find work will just look like malingering. Whether a state errs more often on the side of excessive generosity or excessive stinginess will ultimately depend on the political climate in which decisions are made.

One big unresolved question is whether popular support for work requirements will lead states to spend more money helping marginally employable single mothers join the labor force. This is happening in a few states, but many states seem to care more about saving money than getting everyone into the labor force. Another unresolved question is how states will handle children who need so much attention from their mother that she cannot hold down a job while responding to their problems.

⋅⋅⋅

There is a disturbing parallel between America's recent effort to eliminate welfare and its earlier effort to deinstitutionalize the mentally ill. When deinstitutionalization began in the late 1950s, we had been locking up and sedating far too many people. Many patients were clearly better off once they left the hospital and began living with relatives or in halfway houses. Many also found that they could hold a job most of the time.

But during the 1970s, after hospitals had discharged the patients who were most likely to succeed in the outside world, two problems arose. First, some civil liberties lawyers became convinced that mental hospitals were just jails by another name, and that involuntary commitment should be subject to the same restrictions as imprisonment. Judges responded by making involuntary commitment increasingly difficult. Second, economic growth slowed during the late 1970s, and real tax revenues stopped rising. As a result, governors began looking for programs to cut. Conservative budget cutters soon formed an unholy alliance with radical civil libertarians, in which both groups sought to empty state mental hospitals. This led to a train wreck.

The housing and psychiatric services that were supposed to help the mentally ill cope after they left the hospital system never materialized, so the mentally ill often ended up homeless. Even patients who sought hospitalization were often turned away, either because the shrinking hospital system had no space or because they did not meet the hospitals' ever-more stringent standards for admission. And patients who threatened or attacked their fellow citizens were often released a few days later, on the grounds they were less disturbed than they had been when they were admitted.

Not many single mothers are mentally ill, but both groups are politically weak. This makes it easy to imagine another alliance between budget cutters and ideologues who think society should insist that every single mother work. Work is increasingly essential for self-respect in America, so given the right kinds of support, most single mothers are probably better off working, at least part time. But almost any good idea can lead to disaster if it is pursued too relentlessly, and the idea that single mothers should work is no exception.

Some single mothers can't manage both employment and parenthood simultaneously. Even those who have the energy and skill to juggle work and parenthood often earn so little that they cannot make ends meet without additional help. If such help is not available, the long-term impact of welfare reform on both single mothers and their children could well turn out to be like the long-term impact of deinstitutionalization on the mentally ill: good for some but terrible for others. This is a worst-case scenario. But it is a possibility we should bear in mind as states keep cutting their welfare rolls.

# POSTSCRIPT

## Is Welfare Reform Succeeding?

**B**oth sides of this welfare debate seem to agree that the 1996 federal overhaul and the changes initiated in the states have resulted in a decline in welfare without the apocalyptic effects predicted by some critics. Where the sides differ is in their expectation of what will happen in the future. Casse is convinced that the decline will continue without an increase in poverty, while Jencks and Swingle worry that the long-term effects of the change will be "good for some but terrible for others."

*Welfare Reform: Race to the Bottom* edited by Sanford F. Schram and Samuel H. Beer (John Hopkins University Press, 2000) consists of essays by writers who are critical of welfare reform, including Frances Fox Piven and the editors themselves. Hans P. Johnson and Sonya M. Tafoya, in *The Basic Skills of Welfare Recipients: Implications for Welfare Reform* (Public Policy Institute of California, 1999), use data from the National Adult Literacy Survey to assess the work skills of adults on welfare and the likelihood that they will be able to get and keep jobs; the authors are not optimistic. In *Catholic Social Teaching and United States Welfare Reform* (Liturgical Press, 1998), Thomas Massaro worries that people who are unable to fend for themselves, especially children, are being pushed aside by the new welfare policy. Private welfare is analyzed and criticized by Chuck Collins and Pam Rogers in *Robin Hood Was Right: A Guide to Giving Your Money for Social Change* (W. W. Norton, 2000). The authors question the results of private charitable spending. "We give to the poor, but poverty prevails.... We donate to shelters, but millions remain homeless." Their solution is to donate to "social change foundations" that work to tackle the root causes of poverty. In *When Work Disappears: The World of the New Urban Poor* (Alfred A. Knopf, 1996), sociologist William Julius Wilson argues that the real issue is not welfare but "the disappearance of work in the ghetto," a problem that he thinks has now reached "catastrophic proportions."

"I hate welfare." The author of those words was not a conservative Republican but Peter Edelman, a former official in the Clinton administration, who resigned in protest after President Clinton signed the Republican welfare reform bill. In a stinging article, "The Worst Thing Bill Clinton Has Done," *The Atlantic Monthly* (March 1997), Edelman predicted "more malnutrition and more crime, increased infant mortality, and increased drug and alcohol abuse" as a result of the new law. Although Edelman professes to "hate" welfare, what bothers him the most about welfare reform are the strict time limits for allowing the poor to stay on welfare (two years in any one stretch and five years total). What happens to those who simply cannot get a job, even after the clock runs out? That still remains the big "what if," and it remains to be seen how it will play out in the next few years.

# ISSUE 15

# Is Socioeconomic Inequality Increasing in America?

**YES: Paul Krugman**, from "The Spiral of Inequality," *Mother Jones* (November/December 1996)

**NO: Christopher C. DeMuth**, from "The New Wealth of Nations," *Commentary* (October 1997)

### ISSUE SUMMARY

**YES:** Economist Paul Krugman maintains that corporate greed, the decline of organized labor, and changes in production have contributed to a sharp increase in social and economic inequality in America.

**NO:** Christopher C. DeMuth, president of the American Enterprise Institute, asserts that Americans have achieved an impressive level of wealth and equality and that a changing economy ensures even more opportunities.

There has always been a wide range in real income in the United States. In the first three decades after the end of World War II, family incomes doubled, income inequality narrowed slightly, and poverty rates declined. Prosperity declined in the mid-1970s, when back-to-back recessions produced falling average incomes, greater inequality, and higher poverty levels. Between the mid-1980s and the late 1990s, sustained economic recovery resulted in a modest average growth in income, but high poverty rates continued.

Defenders of the social system maintain that, over the long run, poverty has declined. Many improvements in social conditions benefit virtually all people and, thus, make us more equal. The increase in longevity (attributable in large measure to advances in medicine, nutrition, and sanitation) affects all social classes. In a significant sense, the U.S. economy is far fairer now than at any time in the past. In the preindustrial era, when land was the primary measure of wealth, those without land had no way to improve their circumstances. In the industrial era, when people of modest means needed physical strength and stamina to engage in difficult and hazardous labor in mines, mills, and factories, those who were too weak, handicapped, or too old stood little chance of gaining or keeping reasonable jobs.

In the postindustrial era into which America has moved, many of the manufactured goods that were once "Made in U.S.A.," ranging from clothing to electronics, are now made by cheaper foreign labor. Despite this loss, America achieved virtually full employment in the 1990s, largely because of the enormous growth of the information and service industries. Intelligence, ambition, and hard work—qualities that cut across social classes—are likely to be the determinants of success.

Far from increasing socioeconomic inequality, in the view of the defenders of the American economic system, the sharp increase in the nation's gross domestic product has resulted in greater prosperity for most Americans. To be sure, the number of superrich has grown, but so has the number of prosperous small business owners, middle-level executives, engineers, computer programmers, lawyers, doctors, entertainers, sports stars, and others who have gained greatly from the longest sustained economic growth in American history. For example, successful young pioneers in the new technology and the entrepreneurs whose capital supported their ventures have prospered, and so have the technicians and other workers whom they hired. Most Americans are better off, according to this view.

By contrast, the detractors deplore what they characterize as a continuing disparity in the distribution of income. There were more people below the poverty line in 1999 (34.5 million) than in 1989 (31.5 million). In 1998 nearly one out of five households was broke (nearly twice as many as in 1962), with nothing to tide them over when confronted with unemployment or a health crisis, not to mention being unable to save for college or retirement. Contrary to the popular cliché, a rising tide does not lift all boats; it does not lift the leaky boats nor those who have no boat.

The contrasting assessment of American society in the following essays could not be sharper. Whereas Paul Krugman examines a variety of factors that sustain and increase inequality, Christopher C. DeMuth outlines a number of social forces that have greatly reduced inequality.

# The Spiral of Inequality

Ever since the election of Ronald Reagan, right-wing radicals have insisted that they started a revolution in America. They are half right. If by a revolution we mean a change in politics, economics, and society that is so large as to transform the character of the nation, then there is indeed a revolution in progress. The radical right did not make this revolution, although it has done its best to help it along. If anything, we might say that the revolution created the new right. But whatever the cause, it has become urgent that we appreciate the depth and significance of this new American revolution—and try to stop it before it becomes irreversible.

The consequences of the revolution are obvious in cities across the nation. Since I know the area well, let me take you on a walk down University Avenue in Palo Alto, California.

Palo Alto is the de facto village green of Silicon Valley, a tree-lined refuge from the valley's freeways and shopping malls. People want to live here despite the cost—rumor has it that a modest three-bedroom house sold recently for $1.6 million—and walking along University you can see why. Attractive, casually dressed people stroll past trendy boutiques and restaurants; you can see a cooking class in progress at the fancy new kitchenware store. It's a cheerful scene, even if you have to detour around the people sleeping in doorways and have to avoid eye contact with the beggars. (The town council plans to crack down on street people, so they probably won't be here next year, anyway.)

If you tire of the shopping district and want to wander further afield, you might continue down University Avenue, past the houses with their well-tended lawns and flower beds—usually there are a couple of pickup trucks full of Hispanic gardeners in sight. But don't wander too far. When University crosses Highway 101, it enters the grim environs of East Palo Alto. Though it has progressed in the past few years, as recently as 1992 East Palo Alto was the murder capital of the nation and had an unemployment rate hovering around 40 percent. Luckily, near the boundary, where there is a cluster of liquor stores and check-cashing outlets, you can find two or three police cruisers keeping an eye on the scene—and, not incidentally, serving as a thin blue line protecting the nice neighborhood behind them.

From Paul Krugman, "The Spiral of Inequality," *Mother Jones* (November/December 1996). Copyright © 1996 by The Foundation for National Progress. Reprinted by permission. Notes omitted.

Nor do you want to head down 101 to the south, to "Dilbert Country" with its ranks of low-rise apartments, the tenements of the modern proletariat —the places from which hordes of lower-level white-collar workers drive to sit in their cubicles by day and to which they return to watch their VCRs by night.

No. Better to head up into the hills. The "estates" brochure at Coldwell Banker real estate describes the mid-Peninsula as "an area of intense equestrian character," and when you ascend to Woodside-Atherton, which the *New York Times* has recently called one of "America's born-again Newports," there are indeed plenty of horses, as well as some pretty imposing houses. If you look hard enough, you might catch a glimpse of one of the new $10 million-plus mansions that are going up in growing numbers.

What few people realize is that this vast gap between the affluent few and the bulk of ordinary Americans is a relatively new fixture on our social landscape. People believe these scenes are nothing new, even that it is utopian to imagine it could be otherwise.

But it has not always been thus—at least not to the same extent. I didn't see Palo Alto in 1970, but longtime residents report that it was a mixed town in which not only executives and speculators but schoolteachers, mailmen, and sheet-metal workers could afford to live. At the time, I lived on Long Island, not far from the old *Great Gatsby* area on the North Shore. Few of the great mansions were still private homes then (who could afford the servants?); they had been converted into junior colleges and nursing homes, or deeded to the state as historic monuments. Like Palo Alto, the towns contained a mix of occupations and education levels—no surprise, given that skilled blue-collar workers often made as much as, or more than, white-collar middle managers.

Now, of course, Gatsby is back. New mansions, grander than the old, are rising by the score; keeping servants, it seems, is no longer a problem. A couple of years ago I had dinner with a group of New York investment bankers. After the business was concluded, the talk turned to their weekend homes in the Hamptons. Naively, I asked whether that wasn't a long drive; after a moment of confused silence, the answer came back: "But the helicopter only takes half an hour."

You can confirm what your eyes see, in Palo Alto or in any American community, with dozens of statistics. The most straightforward are those on income shares supplied by the Bureau of the Census, whose statistics are among the most rigorously apolitical. In 1970, according to the bureau, the bottom 20 percent of U.S. families received only 5.4 percent of the income, while the top 5 percent received 15.6 percent. By 1994, the bottom fifth had only 4.2 percent, while the top 5 percent had increased its share to 20.1 percent. That means that in 1994, the average income among the top 5 percent of families was more than 19 times that of the bottom 20 percent of families. In 1970, it had been only about 11.5 times as much. (Incidentally, while the change in distribution is most visible at the top and bottom, families in the middle have also lost: The income share of the middle 20 percent of families has fallen from 17.6 to 15.7 percent.) These are not abstract numbers. They are the statistical signature of a seismic shift in the character of our society.

The American notion of what constitutes the middle class has always been a bit strange, because both people who are quite poor and those who are objectively way up the scale tend to think of themselves as being in the middle. But if calling America a middle-class nation means anything, it means that we are a society in which most people live more or less the same kind of life.

In 1970 we were that kind of society. Today we are not, and we become less like one with each passing year. As politicians compete over who really stands for middle-class values, what the public should be asking them is, *What* middle class? How can we have common "middle-class" values if whole segments of society live in vastly different economic universes?

If this election was really about what the candidates claim, it would be devoted to two questions: Why has America ceased to be a middle-class nation? And, more important, what can be done to make it a middle-class nation again?

## The Sources of Inequality

Most economists who study wages and income in the United States agree about the radical increase in inequality—only the hired guns of the right still try to claim it is a statistical illusion. But not all agree about why it has happened.

Imports from low-wage countries—a popular villain—are part of the story, but only a fraction of it. The numbers just aren't big enough. We invest billions in low-wage countries—but we invest trillions at home. What we spend on manufactured goods from the Third World represents just 2 percent of our income. Even if we shut out imports from low-wage countries (cutting off the only source of hope for the people who work in those factories), most estimates suggest it would raise the wages of low-skill workers here by only 1 or 2 percent.

Information technology is a more plausible villain. Technological advance doesn't always favor elite workers, but since 1970 there has been clear evidence of a general "skill bias" toward technological change. Companies began to replace low-skill workers with smaller numbers of high-skills ones, and they continue to do so even though low-skill workers have gotten cheaper and high-skill workers more expensive.

These forces, while easily measurable, don't fully explain the disparity between the haves and the have-nots. Globalization and technology may explain why a college degree makes more difference now than it did 20 years ago. But schoolteachers and corporate CEOs typically have about the same amount of formal education. Why, then, have teachers' salaries remained flat while those of CEOs have increased fivefold? The impact of technology and of foreign trade do not answer why it is harder today for most people to make a living but easier for a few to make a killing. Something else is going on.

## Values, Power, and Wages

In 1970 the CEO of a typical Fortune 500 corporation earned about 35 times as much as the average manufacturing employee. It would have been unthinkable to pay him 150 times the average, as is now common, and downright outrageous to do so while announcing mass layoffs and cutting the real earnings of many of the company's workers, especially those who were paid the least to start with. So how did the unthinkable become first thinkable, then doable, and finally—if we believe the CEOs—unavoidable?

The answer is that values changed—not the middle-class values politicians keep talking about, but the kind of values that helped to sustain the middle-class society we have lost.

Twenty-five years ago, prosperous companies could have paid their janitors minimum wage and still could have found people to do the work. They didn't, because it would have been bad for company morale. Then, as now, CEOs were in a position to arrange for very high salaries for themselves, whatever their performance, but corporate boards restrained such excesses, knowing that too great a disparity between the top man and the ordinary worker would cause problems. In short, though America was a society with large disparities between economic classes, it had an egalitarian ethic that limited those disparities. That ethic is gone.

One reason for the change is a sort of herd behavior: When most companies hesitated to pay huge salaries at the top and minimum wage at the bottom, any company that did so would have stood out as an example of greed; when everyone does it, the stigma disappears.

There is also the matter of power. In 1970 a company that appeared too greedy risked real trouble with other powerful forces in society. It would have had problems with its union if it had one, or faced the threat of union organizers if it didn't. And its actions would have created difficulties with the government in a way that is now unthinkable. (Can anyone imagine a current president confronting a major industry over price increases, the way John F. Kennedy did the steel industry?)

Those restraining forces have largely disappeared. The union movement is a shadow of its former self, lucky to hold its ground in a defensive battle now and then. The idea that a company would be punished by the government for paying its CEO too much and its workers too little is laughable today: since the election of Ronald Reagan the CEO would more likely be invited to a White House dinner.

In brief, much of the polarization of American society can be explained in terms of power and politics. But why has the tide run so strongly in favor of the rich that it continues regardless of who is in the White House and who controls the Congress?

# The Decline of Labor

The decline of the labor movement in the United States is both a major cause of growing inequality and an illustration of the larger process under way in our society. Unions now represent less than 12 percent of the private workforce, and their power has declined dramatically. In 1970 some 2.5 million workers participated in some form of labor stoppage; in 1993, fewer than 200,000 did. Because unions are rarely able or willing to strike, being a union member no longer carries much of a payoff in higher wages.

There are a number of reasons for the decline of organized labor: the shift from manufacturing to services and from blue-collar to white-collar work, growing international competition, and deregulation. But these factors can't explain the extent or the suddenness of labor's decline.

The best explanation seems to be that the union movement fell below critical mass. Unions are good for unions: In a nation with a powerful labor movement, workers have a sense of solidarity, one union can support another during a strike, and politicians take union interests seriously. America's union movement just got too small, and it imploded.

We should not idealize the unions. When they played a powerful role in America, they often did so to bad effect. Occasionally they were corrupt, often they extracted higher wages at the consumer's expense, sometimes they opposed new technologies and enforced inefficient practices. But unions helped keep us a middle-class society—not only because they forced greater equality within companies, but because they provided a counterweight to the power of wealthy individuals and corporations. The loss of that counterweight is clearly bad for society.

The point is that a major force that kept America a more or less unified society went into a tailspin. Our whole society is now well into a similar downward spiral, in which growing inequality creates the political and economic conditions that lead to even more inequality.

## The Polarizing Spiral

Textbook political science predicts that in a two-party democracy like the United States, the parties will compete to serve the interests of the median voter—the voter in the middle, richer than half the voters but poorer than the other half. And since ordinary workers are more likely to lose their jobs than strike it rich, the interests of the median voter should include protecting the poor. You might expect, then, the public to demand that government work against the growing divide by taxing the rich more heavily and by increasing benefits for lower-paid workers and the unemployed.

In fact, we have done just the opposite. Tax rates on the wealthy—even with Clinton's modest increase of 1993—are far lower now than in the 1960s. We have allowed public schools and other services that are crucial for middle-income families to deteriorate. Despite the recent increase, the minimum wage has fallen steadily compared with both average wages and the cost of living. And programs for the poor have been savaged: Even before the recent bipartisan gutting of welfare, AFDC payments for a typical family had fallen by a third in real terms since the 1960s.

The reason why government policy has reinforced rather than opposed this growing inequality is obvious: Well-off people have disproportionate political weight. They are more likely to vote—the median voter has a much higher income than the median family—and far more likely to provide the campaign contributions that are so essential in a TV age.

The political center of gravity in this country is therefore not at the median family, with its annual income of $40,000, but way up the scale. With decreasing voter participation and with the decline both of unions and of traditional political machines, the focus of political attention is further up the income ladder than it has been for generations. So never mind what politicians say; political parties are competing to serve the interests of families near the 90th percentile or higher, families that mostly earn $100,000 or more per year.

Because the poles of our society have become so much more unequal, the interests of this political elite diverge increasingly from those of the typical family. A family at the 95th percentile pays a lot more in taxes than a family at the 50th, but it does not receive a correspondingly higher benefit from public services, such as education. The greater the income gap, the greater the disparity in interests. This translates, because of the clout of the elite, into a constant pressure for lower taxes and reduced public services.

Consider the issue of school vouchers. Many conservatives and even a few liberals are in favor of issuing educational vouchers and allowing parents to choose among competing schools. Let's leave aside the question of what this might do to education and ask what its political implications might be.

Initially, we might imagine, the government would prohibit parents from "topping up" vouchers to buy higher-priced education. But once the program was established, conservatives would insist such a restriction is unfair, maybe even unconstitutional, arguing that parents should have the freedom to spend their money as they wish. Thus, a voucher would become a ticket you could supplement freely. Upper-income families would realize that a reduction in the voucher is to their benefit: They will save more in lowered taxes than they will lose in a decreased education subsidy. So they will press to reduce public spending on education, leading to ever-deteriorating quality for those who cannot afford to spend extra. In the end, the quintessential American tradition of public education for all could collapse.

School vouchers hold another potential that, doubtless, makes them attractive to the conservative elite: They offer a way to break the power of the American union movement in its last remaining stronghold, the public sector. Not by accident did Bob Dole, in his acceptance speech at the Republican National Convention, pause in his evocation of Norman Rockwell values to take a swipe at teachers' unions. The leaders of the radical right want privatization of schools, of public sanitation—of anything else they can think of—because they know such privatization undermines what remaining opposition exists to their program.

If public schools and other services are left to deteriorate, so will the skills and prospects of those who depend on them, reinforcing the growing inequality of incomes and creating an even greater disparity between the interests of the elite and those of the majority.

Does this sound like America in the '90s? Of course it does. And it doesn't take much imagination to envision what our society will be like if this process continues for another 15 or 20 years. We know all about it from TV, movies, and best-selling novels. While politicians speak of recapturing the virtues of small-town America (which never really existed), the public—extrapolating from the trends it already sees—imagines a *Blade Runner*-style dystopia, in which a few people live in luxury while the majority grovel in Third World living standards.

# Strategies for the Future

There is no purely economic reason why we cannot reduce inequality in America. If we were willing to spend even a few percent of national income on an enlarged version of the Earned Income Tax Credit, which supplements the earnings of low-wage workers, we could make a dramatic impact on both incomes and job opportunities for the poor and near-poor—bringing a greater number of Americans into the middle class. Nor is the money for such policies lacking: America is by far the least heavily taxed of Western nations and could easily find the resources to pay for a major expansion of programs aimed at limiting inequality.

But of course neither party advanced such proposals during the electoral campaign. The Democrats sounded like Republicans, knowing that in a society with few counterweights to the power of money, any program that even hints at redistribution is political poison. It's no surprise that Bill Clinton's repudiation of his own tax increase took place in front of an audience of wealthy campaign contributors. In this political environment, what politician would talk of taxing the well-off to help the low-wage worker?

And so, while the agenda of the GOP would surely accelerate the polarizing trend, even Democratic programs now amount only to a delaying action. To get back to the kind of society we had, we need to rebuild the institutions and values that made a middle-class nation possible.

The relatively decent society we had a generation ago was largely the creation of a brief, crucial period in American history: the presidency of Franklin Roosevelt, during the New Deal and especially during the war. That created what economic historian Claudia Goldin called the Great Compression—an era in which a powerful government, reinforced by and in turn reinforcing a newly powerful labor movement, drastically narrowed the gap in income levels through taxes, benefits, minimum wages, and collective bargaining. In effect, Roosevelt created a new, middle-class America, which lasted for more than a generation. We have lost that America, and it will take another Roosevelt, and perhaps the moral equivalent of another war, to get it back.

Until then, however, we can try to reverse some of the damage. To do so requires more than just supporting certain causes. It means thinking strategically—asking whether a policy is not only good in itself but how it will affect the political balance in the future. If a policy change promises to raise average income by a tenth of a percentage point, but will widen the wedge between the interests of the elite and those of the rest, it should be opposed. If a law reduces average income a bit but enhances the power of ordinary workers, it should be supported.

In particular, we also need to apply strategic thinking to the union movement. Union leaders and liberal intellectuals often don't like each other very much, and union victories are often of dubious value to the economy. Nonetheless, if you are worried about the cycle of polarization in this country, you should support policies that make unions stronger, and vociferously oppose those that weaken them. There are some stirrings of life in the union movement —a new, younger leadership with its roots in the service sector has replaced the manufacturing-based old guard, and has won a few political victories. They must be supported, almost regardless of the merits of their particular case. Unions are one of the few *political* counterweights to the power of wealth.

Of course, even to talk about such things causes the right to accuse us of fomenting "class warfare." They want us to believe we are all members of a broad, more or less homogeneous, middle class. But the notion of a middle-class nation was always a stretch. Unless we are prepared to fight the trend toward inequality, it will become a grim joke.

 **NO**

# The New Wealth of Nations

The Nations of North America, Western Europe, Australia, and Japan are wealthier today than they have ever been, wealthier than any others on the planet, wealthier by far than any societies in human history. Yet their governments appear to be impoverished—saddled with large accumulated debts and facing annual deficits that will grow explosively over the coming decades. As a result, government spending programs, especially the big social-insurance programs like Social Security and Medicare in the United States, are facing drastic cuts in order to avert looming insolvency (and, in France and some other European nations, in order to meet the Maastricht treaty's criteria of fiscal rectitude). American politics has been dominated for several years now by contentious negotiations over deficit reduction between the Clinton administration and the Republican Congress. This past June, first at the European Community summit in Amsterdam and then at the Group of Eight meeting in Denver, most of the talk was of hardship and constraint and the need for governmental austerity ("Economic Unease Looms Over Talks at Denver Summit," read the *New York Times* headline).

These bloodless problems of governmental accounting are said, moreover, to reflect real social ills: growing economic inequality in the United States; high unemployment in Europe; an aging, burdensome, and medically needy population everywhere; and the globalization of commerce, which is destroying jobs and national autonomy and forcing bitter measures to keep up with the bruising demands of international competitiveness.

How can it be that societies so surpassingly wealthy have governments whose core domestic-welfare programs are on the verge of bankruptcy? The answer is as paradoxical as the question. We have become not only the richest but also the freest and most egalitarian societies that have ever existed, and it is our very wealth, freedom, and equality that are causing the welfare state to unravel.

❧

That we have become very rich is clear enough in the aggregate. That we have become very equal in the enjoyment of our riches is an idea strongly resisted

From Christopher C. DeMuth, "The New Wealth of Nations," *Commentary* (October 1997). Copyright © 1997 by The American Jewish Committee. Reprinted by permission of *Commentary*. Notes omitted.

by many. Certainly there has been a profusion of reports in the media and political speeches about increasing income inequality: the rich, it is said, are getting richer, the poor are getting poorer, and the middle and working classes are under the relentless pressure of disappearing jobs in manufacturing and middle management.

Although these claims have been greatly exaggerated, and some have been disproved by events, it is true that, by some measures, there has been a recent increase in income inequality in the United States. But it is a very small tick in the massive and unprecedented leveling of material circumstances that has been proceeding now for almost three centuries and in this century has accelerated dramatically. In fact, the much-noticed increase in measured-income inequality is in part a result of the increase in real social equality. Here are a few pieces of this important but neglected story.

• First, progress in agriculture, construction, manufacturing, and other key sectors of economic production has made the material necessities of life—food, shelter, and clothing—available to essentially everyone. To be sure, many people, including the seriously handicapped and the mentally incompetent, remain dependent on the public purse for their necessities. And many people continue to live in terrible squalor. But the problem of poverty, defined as material scarcity, has been solved. If poverty today remains a serious problem, it is a problem of individual behavior, social organization, and public policy. This was not so 50 years ago, or ever before.

• Second, progress in public health, in nutrition, and in the biological sciences and medical arts has produced dramatic improvements in longevity, health, and physical well-being. Many of these improvements—resulting, for example, from better public sanitation and water supplies, the conquest of dread diseases, and the abundance of nutritious food—have affected entire populations, producing an equalization of real personal welfare more powerful than any government redistribution of income.

The Nobel prize-winning economist Robert Fogel has focused on our improved mastery of the biological environment—leading over the past 300 years to a doubling of the average human life span and to large gains in physical stature, strength, and energy—as the key to what he calls "the egalitarian revolution of the 20th century." He considers this so profound an advance as to constitute a distinct new level of human evolution. Gains in stature, health, and longevity are continuing today and even accelerating. Their outward effects may be observed, in evolutionary fast-forward, in the booming nations of Asia (where, for example, the physical difference between older and younger South Koreans is strikingly evident on the streets of Seoul).

• Third, the critical *source* of social wealth has shifted over the last few hundred years from land (at the end of the 18th century) to physical capital (at the end of the 19th) to, today, human capital—education and cognitive ability. This development is not an unmixed gain from the standpoint of economic equality. The ability to acquire and deploy human capital is a function of intelligence, and intelligence is not only unequally distributed but also, to a significant degree, heritable. As Charles Murray and the late Richard J. Herrnstein argue in *The Bell Curve,* an economy that rewards sheer brainpower replaces one old source of inequality, socioeconomic advantage, with a new one, cognitive advantage.

⌒◉⌒

But an economy that rewards human capital also tears down far more artificial barriers than it erects. For most people who inhabit the vast middle range of the bell curve, intelligence is much more equally distributed than land or physical capital ever was. Most people, that is, possess ample intelligence to pursue all but a handful of specialized callings. If in the past many were held back by lack of education and closed social institutions, the opportunities to use one's human capital have blossomed with the advent of universal education and the erosion of social barriers.

Furthermore, the material benefits of the knowledge-based economy are by no means limited to those whom Murray and Herrnstein call the cognitive elite. Many of the newest industries, from fast food to finance to communications, have succeeded in part by opening up employment opportunities for those of modest ability and training—occupations much less arduous and physically much less risky than those they have replaced. And these new industries have created enormous, widely shared economic benefits in consumption; I will return to this subject below.

• Fourth, recent decades have seen a dramatic reduction in one of the greatest historical sources of inequality: the social and economic inequality of the sexes. Today, younger cohorts of working men and women with comparable education and job tenure earn essentially the same incomes. The popular view would have it that the entry of women into the workforce has been driven by falling male earnings and the need "to make ends meet" in middle-class families. But the popular view is largely mistaken. Among married women (as the economist Chinhui Juhn has demonstrated), it is wives of men with high incomes who have been responsible for most of the recent growth in employment.

• Fifth, in the wealthy Western democracies, material needs and desires have been so thoroughly fulfilled for so many people that, for the first time in history, we are seeing large-scale voluntary reductions in the amount of time spent at paid employment. This development manifests itself in different forms: longer periods of education and training for the young; earlier retirement despite longer life spans; and, in between, many more hours devoted to leisure, recreation, entertainment, family, community and religious activities, charitable and other nonremunerative pursuits, and so forth. The dramatic growth of the sports, entertainment, and travel industries captures only a small slice of what has happened. In Fogel's estimation, the time devoted to nonwork activities by the average male head of household has grown from 10.5 hours per week in 1880 to 40 hours today, while time per week at work has fallen from 61.6 hours to 33.6 hours. Among women, the reduction in work (including not only outside employment but also household work, food preparation, childbearing and attendant health problems, and child rearing) and the growth in nonwork have been still greater.

There is a tendency to overlook these momentous developments because of the often frenetic pace of modern life. But our busy-ness actually demonstrates the point: time, and not material things, has become the scarce and valued commodity in modern society.

⋖⊙⊱

One implication of these trends is that in very wealthy societies, income has become a less useful gauge of economic welfare and hence of economic equality. When income becomes to some degree discretionary, and when many peoples' incomes change from year to year for reasons unrelated to their life circumstances, *consumption* becomes a better measure of material welfare. And by this measure, welfare appears much more evenly distributed: people of higher income spend progressively smaller shares on consumption, while in the bottom ranges, annual consumption often exceeds income. (In fact, government statistics suggest that in the bottom 20 percent of the income scale, average annual consumption is about twice annual income—probably a reflection of a substantial underreporting of earnings in this group.) According to the economist Daniel Slesnick, the distribution of consumption, unlike the distribution of reported income, has become measurably *more* equal in recent decades.

If we include leisure-time pursuits as a form of consumption, the distribution of material welfare appears flatter still. Many such activities, being informal by definition, are difficult to track, but Dora Costa of MIT has recently studied one measurable aspect—expenditures on recreation—and found that these have become strikingly more equal as people of lower income have increased the amount of time and money they devote to entertainment, reading, sports, and related enjoyments.

Television, videocassettes, CD's, and home computers have brought musical, theatrical, and other entertainments (both high and low) to everyone, and have enormously narrowed the differences in cultural opportunities between wealthy urban centers and everywhere else. Formerly upper-crust sports like golf, tennis, skiing, and boating have become mass pursuits (boosted by increased public spending on parks and other recreational facilities as well as on environmental quality), and health clubs and full-line book stores have become as plentiful as gas stations. As some of the best things in life become free or nearly so, the price of pursuing them becomes, to that extent, the "opportunity cost" of time itself.

The substitution of leisure activities for income-producing work even appears to have become significant enough to be contributing to the recently much-lamented increase in inequality in measured income. In a new AEI study, Robert Haveman finds that most of the increase in earnings inequality among U.S. males since the mid-1970's can be attributed not to changing labor-market opportunities but to voluntary choice—to the free pursuit of nonwork activities at the expense of income-producing work.

Most of us can see this trend in our own families and communities. A major factor in income inequality in a wealthy knowledge economy is age—many people whose earnings put them at the top of the income curve in their late fifties were well down the curve in their twenties, when they were just getting out of school and beginning their working careers. Fogel again: today the average household in the top 10 percent might consist of a professor or accountant married to a nurse or secretary, both in their peak years of earning. As for the stratospheric top 1 percent, it includes not only very rich people like Bill Cosby but also people like Cosby's fictional Huxtable family: an obstetrician married to a corporate lawyer. All these individuals would have appeared well down the income distribution as young singles, and that is where their young counterparts appear today.

That more young people are spending more time in college or graduate school, taking time off for travel and "finding themselves," and pursuing interesting but low- or non-paying jobs or apprenticeships before knuckling down to lifelong careers is a significant factor in "income inequality" measured in the aggregate. But this form of economic inequality is in fact the social equality of the modern age. It is progress, not regress, to be cherished and celebrated, not feared and fretted over.

⋅⟨⟨⊙⟩⟩⋅

Which brings me back to my contention that it is our very wealth and equality that are the undoing of the welfare state. Western government today largely consists of two functions. One is income transfers from the wages of those who are working to those who are not working: mainly social-security payments to older people who have chosen to retire rather than go on working and education subsidies for younger people who have chosen to extend their schooling before beginning work. The other is direct and indirect expenditures on medical care, also financed by levies on the wages of those who are working. It is precisely these aspects of life—nonwork and expenditures on medical care and physical well-being—that are the booming sectors of modern, wealthy, technologically advanced society.

When the Social Security program began in America in the 1930's, retirement was still a novel idea: most men worked until they dropped, and they dropped much earlier than they do today. Even in the face of our approaching demographic crunch, produced by the baby boom followed by the baby bust, we could solve the financial problems of the Social Security program in a flash by returning to the days when people worked longer and died younger. Similarly, a world without elaborate diagnostic techniques, replaceable body parts, and potent pharmaceutical and other means of curing or ameliorating disease—a world where medical care consisted largely of bed rest and hand-holding—would present scant fiscal challenge to government as a provider of health insurance.

Our big government-entitlement programs truly are, as conservatives like to call them, obsolete. They are obsolete not because they were terrible ideas to begin with, though some of them were, but because of the astounding growth in social wealth and equality and because of the technological and economic developments which have propelled that growth. When Social Security was introduced, not only was retirement a tiny part of most people's lives but people of modest means had limited ability to save and invest for the future. Today, anyone can mail off a few hundred dollars to a good mutual fund and hire the best investment management American finance has to offer.

In these circumstances it is preposterous to argue, as President Clinton has done, that privatizing Social Security (replacing the current system of income transfers from workers to retirees with one of individually invested retirement savings) would be good for Warren Buffett but bad for the little guy. Private savings—through pension plans, mutual funds, and personal investments in housing and other durables—are *already* a larger source of retirement income than Social Security transfers. Moreover, although there is much talk nowadays about the riskiness of tying retirement income to the performance of financial markets, the social developments I have described suggest that the greater risk lies in the opposite direction. The current Social Security program ties retirement income to the growth of wage earners' payrolls; that growth is bound to be less than the growth of the economy as a whole, as reflected in the financial markets.

Similarly, Medicare is today a backwater of old-fashioned fee-for-service medicine, hopelessly distorted by a profusion of inefficient and self-defeating price-and-service controls. Over the past dozen years, a revolution has been carried out in the private financing and organization of medical care. The changes have not been unmixed blessings; nor could they be, so long as the tax code encourages people to overinsure for routine medical care. Yet substantial improvements in cost control and quality of service are now evident throughout the health-care sector—except under Medicare. These innovations have not been greeted by riots or strikes at the thousands of private organizations that have introduced them. Nor will there be riots in the streets if, in place of the lame-brained proposals for Medicare "spending cuts" and still more ineffective price controls currently in fashion in Washington, similar market-based innovations are introduced to Medicare.

⚫

In sum, George Bush's famous statement in his inaugural address that "we have more will than wallet" was exactly backward. Our wallets are bulging; the problems we face are increasingly problems not of necessity, but of will. The political class in Washington is still marching to the tune of economic redistribution and, to a degree, "class warfare." But Washington is a lagging indicator of social change. In time, the progress of technology and the growth of private markets and private wealth will generate the political will to transform radically the redistributive welfare state we have inherited from an earlier and more socially balkanized age.

There are signs, indeed, that the Progressive-era and New Deal programs of social insurance, economic regulation, and subsidies and protections for farming, banking, labor organization, and other activities are already crumbling, with salutary effects along every point of the economic spectrum. Anyone who has been a business traveler since the late 1970's, for example, has seen firsthand how deregulation has democratized air travel. Low fares and mass marketing have brought such luxuries as foreign travel, weekend getaways to remote locales, and reunions of far-flung families—just twenty years ago, pursuits of the wealthy—to people of relatively modest means. Coming reforms, including the privatization of Social Security and, most of all, the dismantling of the public-school monopoly in elementary and secondary education, will similarly benefit the less well-off disproportionately, providing them with opportunities enjoyed today primarily by those with high incomes.

I venture a prediction: just as airline deregulation was championed by Edward Kennedy and Jimmy Carter before Ronald Reagan finished the job, so the coming reforms will be a bipartisan enterprise. When the political class catches on (as Prime Minister Tony Blair has already done in England), the Left will compete vigorously and often successfully with the Right for the allegiance of the vast new privileged middle class. This may sound implausible at a moment when the Clinton administration has become an energetic agent of traditional unionism and has secured the enactment of several new redistributive tax provisions and spending programs. But the watershed event of the Clinton years will almost certainly be seen to be not any of these things but rather the defeat of the President's national health-insurance plan in the face of widespread popular opposition.

The lesson of that episode is that Americans no longer wish to have the things they care about socialized. What has traditionally attracted voters to government as a provider of insurance and other services is not that government does the job better or more efficiently or at a lower cost than private markets; it is the prospect of securing those services through taxes paid by others. That is why today's advocates of expanding the welfare state are still trying to convince voters to think of themselves as members of distinct groups that are net beneficiaries of government: students, teachers, women, racial minorities, union members, struggling young families, retirees, and so forth. But as the material circumstances of the majority become more equal, and as the proficiency and social reach of private markets increasingly outstrip what government can provide, the possibilities for effective redistribution diminish. The members of an egalitarian, middle-class electorate cannot improve their lot by subsidizing one another, and they know it.

With the prospects dimming for further, broad-based socialization along the lines of the Clinton health-care plan, the private supply of important social services will continue to exist and, in general, to flourish alongside government programs. Defenders of the welfare state will thus likely be reduced to asserting that private markets and personal choice may be fine for the well-off, but government services are more appropriate for those of modest means. This is the essence of President Clinton's objection to privatizing Social Security and of the arguments against school choice for parents of students in public elementary and high schools. But "capitalism for the rich, socialism for the poor" is a highly unpromising banner for liberals to be marching under in an era in which capitalism has itself become a profound egalitarian force.

⌐◉¬

Where, then, will the battlegrounds be for the political allegiance of the new middle class? Increasingly, that allegiance will turn on policies involving little or no redistributive cachet but rather society-wide benefits in the form of personal amenity, autonomy, and safety: environmental quality and parks, medical and other scientific research, transportation and communications infrastructure, defense against terrorism, and the like. The old welfare-state debates between Left and Right will be transformed into debates over piece-meal incursions into private markets that compete with or replace government services. Should private insurers be required to cover annual mammograms for women in their forties? Should retirement accounts be permitted to invest in tobacco companies? Should parents be permitted to use vouchers to send their children to religious schools? Thus transformed, these debates, too, will tend to turn on considerations of general social advantage rather than on the considerations of social justice and economic desert that animated the growth of the welfare state.

Political allegiance will also turn increasingly on issues that are entirely nonmaterial. I recently bumped into a colleague, a noted political analyst, just after I had read the morning papers, and asked him to confirm my impression that at least half the major political stories of the past few years had something to do with sex. He smiled and replied, "Peace and prosperity."

What my colleague may have had in mind is that grave crises make all other issues secondary: President Roosevelt's private life received less scrutiny than has President Clinton's, and General Eisenhower's private life received less scrutiny than did that of General Ralston (whose nomination to become chairman of the Joint Chiefs of Staff was torpedoed by allegations of an extra-marital affair). There is, however, another, deeper truth in his observation. The stupendous wealth, technological mastery, and autonomy of modern life have freed man not just for worthy, admirable, and self-improving pursuits but also for idleness and unworthy and self-destructive pursuits that are no less a part of his nature.

And so we live in an age of astounding rates of divorce and family break-up, of illegitimacy, of single teenage motherhood, of drug use and crime, of vi-olent and degrading popular entertainments, and of the "culture of narcissism" —and also in an age of vibrant religiosity, of elite universities where madrigal singing and ballroom dancing are all the rage and rampant student careerism is a major faculty concern, and of the Promise Keepers, over a million men of all incomes and races who have packed sports stadiums around the United States to declare their determination to be better husbands, fathers, citizens, and Chris-tians. Ours is an age in which obesity has become a serious public-health prob-lem—and in which dieting, fitness, environmentalism, and self-improvement have become major industries.

It is true, of course, that the heartening developments are in part responses to the disheartening ones. But it is also true that *both* are the results of the economic trends I have described here. In a society as rich and therefore as free as ours has become, the big question, in our personal lives and also in our politics, is: what is our freedom for?

# POSTSCRIPT

## Is Socioeconomic Inequality Increasing in America?

Social Darwinists have long held that a free-enterprise system results in the survival of the fittest. We are not equal in intellect, ambition, energy, or any other critical faculty, and nothing that the government does can make us equal. In their influential and controversial work *The Bell Curve: Intelligence and Class Structure in American Life* (Free Press, 1994), Charles Murray and Richard J. Herrnstein conclude that social factors have only a minor influence on intelligence. Murray returns to this subject in his short book *Income Inequality and IA* (AEI Press, 1998), in which he concludes, "It is time for policy analysts to stop avoiding the reality of human inequality, a reality that neither equalization of opportunity nor a freer market will circumvent."

Michael J. Sandel, in *Democracy's Discontent: America in Search of a Public Philosophy* (Harvard University Press, 1998), calls for a reinterpretation of American values and the role of government in promoting them. Sandel maintains that Americans have abandoned the sense of common interest for politics based on personal choice and that this has led to undesirable trends in court decisions and public policy. The consequences of a widening gulf between the haves and have-nots has been the creation of professional and managerial elites that, according to Christopher Lash, in *The Revolt of the Elites: And the Betrayal of Democracy* (W. W. Norton, 1996), abandon the middle class and betray the idea of democracy for all Americans.

One striking element regarding economic rewards in modern society is the fact that in many markets, a huge disproportion in income exists between the best or near-best and everyone else. Superstars, whether athletes, actors, or CEOs, earn vastly more than those just below them in achievement. This phenomenon is studied in Robert H. Frank and Philip J. Cook, *The Winner-Take-All Society* (Free Press, 1995).

Specific proposals to redistribute income more equally are made by Sheldon Danziger and Peter Gottschalk in *America Unequal* (Harvard University Press, 1995). The reasons why American blacks and whites differ in wealth accumulation are considered by Melvin L. Oliver and Thomas M. Shapiro, in *Black Wealth/White Wealth: A New Perspective on Racial Inequality* (Routledge, 1995). Women and racial minorities are not the only significant groups that believe that they are victims of socioeconomic inequality. *White Trash: Race and Class in America* edited by Matt Wray and Annalee Newitz (Routledge, 1996) is a collection of essays examining the economic, social, and cultural conditions of poor whites.

# ISSUE 16

## Should Abortion Be Restricted?

**YES: Robert H. Bork**, from "Inconvenient Lives," *First Things* (December 1996)

**NO: Mary Gordon**, from "A Moral Choice," *The Atlantic Monthly* (March 1990)

### ISSUE SUMMARY

**YES:** Legal scholar Robert H. Bork concludes that the semantics of "pro-choice" cannot hide the fact that aborting a fetus is killing an unborn child and that most abortions are performed for the woman's convenience.

**NO:** Writer Mary Gordon maintains that having an abortion is a moral choice that women are capable of making for themselves, that aborting a fetus is not killing a person, and that antiabortionists fail to understand female sexuality.

Until 1973 the laws governing abortion were set by the states, most of which barred legal abortion except where pregnancy imperiled the life of the pregnant woman. In that year, the U.S. Supreme Court decided the controversial case *Roe v. Wade*. The *Roe* decision acknowledged both a woman's "fundamental right" to terminate a pregnancy before fetal viability and the state's legitimate interest in protecting both the woman's health and the "potential life" of the fetus. It prohibited states from banning abortion to protect the fetus before the third trimester of a pregnancy, and it ruled that even during that final trimester, a woman could obtain an abortion if she could prove that her life or health would be endangered by carrying to term. (In a companion case to *Roe*, decided on the same day, the Court defined *health* broadly enough to include "all factors—physical, emotional, psychological, familial, and the woman's age —relevant to the well-being of the patient.") These holdings, together with the requirement that state regulation of abortion had to survive "strict scrutiny" and demonstrate a "compelling state interest," resulted in later decisions striking down mandatory 24-hour waiting periods, requirements that abortions be performed in hospitals, and so-called informed consent laws.

The Supreme Court did uphold state laws requiring parental notification and consent for minors (though it provided that minors could seek permission from a judge if they feared notifying their parents). And federal courts have affirmed the right of Congress not to pay for abortions. Proabortion groups, proclaiming the "right to choose," have charged that this and similar action at the state level discriminates against poor women because it does not inhibit the ability of women who are able to pay for abortions to obtain them. Efforts to adopt a constitutional amendment or federal law barring abortion have failed, but antiabortion forces have influenced legislation in many states.

Can legislatures and courts establish the existence of a scientific fact? Opponents of abortion believe that it is a fact that life begins at conception and that the law must therefore uphold and enforce this concept. They argue that the human fetus is a live human being, and they note all the familiar signs of life displayed by the fetus: a beating heart, brain waves, thumb sucking, and so on. Those who defend abortion maintain that human life does not begin before the development of specifically human characteristics and possibly not until the birth of a child. As Justice Harry A. Blackmun put it in 1973, "There has always been strong support for the view that life does not begin until live birth."

Antiabortion forces sought a court case that might lead to the overturning of *Roe v. Wade*. Proabortion forces rallied to oppose new state laws limiting or prohibiting abortion. In *Webster v. Reproductive Health Services* (1989), with four new justices, the Supreme Court pulled back from its proabortion stance. In a 5–4 decision, the Court upheld a Missouri law that banned abortions in public hospitals and abortions that were performed by public employees (except to save a woman's life). The law also required that tests be performed on any fetus more than 20 weeks old to determine its viability—that is, its ability to survive outside the womb.

In the later decision of *Planned Parenthood v. Casey* (1992), however, the Court affirmed what it called the "essence" of the constitutional right to abortion while permitting some state restrictions, such as a 24-hour waiting period and parental notification in the case of minors.

During the Clinton presidency, opponents of abortion focused on what they identified as "partial-birth" abortions; that is, where a fetus is destroyed during the process of birth. President Clinton twice vetoed partial-birth bans that allowed such abortions to save a woman's life but not her health. By early 1998, 22 states adopted such bans, but in 11 of these states challenges to the law's constitutionality were upheld in federal or state courts. In 1998, in the first of these cases to reach the U.S. Supreme Court, the Court let stand without a written opinion (but with three dissenters) a federal court of appeals decision declaring Ohio's law unconstitutional. The Supreme Court did not confront the question of how it would decide a law that narrowly defined the procedure and provided a maternal health exception.

In the following selections, Robert H. Bork argues that even the most embryonic human fetus must inescapably be defined as human life and that most abortions are performed merely to suit the convenience of the pregnant women. Mary Gordon asserts that the fetus removed in most abortions may not be considered a person and that women must retain the right to make decisions regarding their sexual lives.

**Robert H. Bork**　　　　　　　　　　　　　　➡ **YES**

# Inconvenient Lives

Judging from the evidence, Americans do not view human life as sacrosanct. We engage in a variety of activities, from driving automobiles to constructing buildings, that we know will cause deaths. But the deliberate taking of the life of an individual has never been regarded as a matter of moral indifference. We debate the death penalty, for example, endlessly. It seems an anomaly, therefore, that we have so easily accepted practices that are the deliberate taking of identifiable individual lives. We have turned abortion into a constitutional right; one state has made assisted suicide a statutory right and two federal circuit courts, not to be outdone, have made it a constitutional right; campaigns to legalize euthanasia are underway. It is entirely predictable that many of the elderly, ill, and infirm will be killed, and often without their consent. This is where radical individualism has taken us.

When a society revises its attitude toward life and death, we can see the direction of its moral movement. The revision of American thought and practice about life questions began with abortion, and examination of the moral confusion attending that issue helps us understand more general developments in public morality.

The necessity for reflection about abortion does not depend on, but is certainly made dramatic by, the fact that there are approximately a million and a half abortions annually in the United States. To put it another way, since the Supreme Court's 1973 decision in *Roe v. Wade,* there have been perhaps over thirty million abortions in the United States. Three out of ten conceptions today end in the destruction of the fetus. These facts, standing alone, do not decide the issue of morality, but they do mean that this issue is hugely significant.

The issue is also heated, polarizing, and often debated on both sides in angry, moralistic terms. I will refrain from such rhetoric because for most of my life I held a position on the subject very different from the one I now take. For years I adopted, without bothering to think, the attitude common among secular, affluent, university-educated people who took the propriety of abortion for granted, even when it was illegal. The practice's illegality, like that of drinking alcohol during Prohibition, was thought to reflect merely unenlightened prejudice or religious conviction, the two being regarded as much the same.

From Robert H. Bork, "Inconvenient Lives," *First Things* (December 1996). Adapted from *Slouching Towards Gomorrah* by Robert H. Bork (Regan Books, 1996). Copyright © 1996 by Robert H. Bork. Reprinted by permission of HarperCollins Publishers, Inc.

From time to time, someone would say that it was a difficult moral problem, but there was rarely any doubt how the problem should be resolved. I remember a woman at Yale saying, without any disagreement from those around her, that "The fetus isn't nothing, but I am for the mother's right to abort it." I probably nodded. Most of us had a vague and unexamined notion that while the fetus wasn't nothing, it was also not fully human.[1] The slightest reflection would have suggested that non-human or semi-human blobs of tissue do not magically turn into human beings.

Qualms about abortion began to arise when I first read about fetal pain. There is no doubt that, after its nervous system has developed to a degree, the fetus being dismembered or poisoned in the womb feels excruciating pain. For that reason, many people would confine abortion to the early stages of pregnancy but have no objection to it then. There are, on the other hand, people who oppose abortion at any stage and those who regard it as a right at any stage up to the moment of birth. But in thinking about abortion—especially abortion at any stage—it is necessary to address two questions. Is abortion always the killing of a human being? If it is, is that killing done simply for convenience? I think there can be no doubt that the answer to the first questions is, yes; and the answer to the second is, almost always.[2]

⚜

The question of whether abortion is the termination of a human life is a relatively simple one. It has been described as a question requiring no more than a knowledge of high school biology. There may be doubt that high school biology courses are clear on the subject these days, but consider what we know. The male sperm and the female egg each contains twenty-three chromosomes. Upon fertilization, a single cell results containing forty-six chromosomes, which is what all humans have, including, of course, the mother and the father. But the new organism's forty-six chromosomes are in a different combination from those of either parent; the new organism is unique. It is not an organ of the mother's body but a different individual. This cell produces specifically human proteins and enzymes from the beginning. Its chromosomes will heavily influence its destiny until the day of its death, whether that death is at the age of ninety or one month after conception.

The cell will multiply and develop, in accordance with its individual chromosomes, and, when it enters the world, will be recognizably a human baby. From single-cell fertilized egg to baby to teenager to adult to old age to death is a single process of one individual, not a series of different individuals replacing each other. It is impossible to draw a line anywhere after the moment of fertilization and say before this point the creature is not human but after this point it is. It has all the attributes of a human from the beginning, and those attributes were in the forty-six chromosomes with which it began. Francis Crick, the Nobel laureate and biophysicist, is quoted as having estimated that "the amount of information contained in the chromosomes of a single fertilized human egg is equivalent to about a thousand printed volumes of books, each as large as a volume of the Encyclopedia Britannica." Such a creature is not a blob of tissue or, as the *Roe* opinion so felicitously put it, a "potential life." As someone has said, it is a life with potential.

It is impossible to say that the killing of the organism at any moment after it originated is not the killing of a human being. Yet there are those who say just that by redefining what a human being is. Redefining what it means to be a human being will prove dangerous in contexts other than abortion. One of the more primitive arguments put forward is that in the embryonic stage, which lasts about two months after conception, the creature does not look human. One man said to me, "Have you ever seen an embryo? It looks like a guppy." A writer whose work I greatly respect refers to "the patently inhuman fetus of four weeks." A cartoonist made fun of a well-known anti-abortion doctor by showing him pointing to the microscopic dot that is the zygote and saying, "We'll call him Timmy." It is difficult to know what the appearance of Timmy has to do with the humanity of the fetus. I suspect appearance is made an issue because the more recognizably a baby the fetus becomes, the more our emotions reject the idea of destroying it. But those are uninstructed emotions, not emotions based on a recognition of what the fetus is from the beginning.

*❦*

Other common arguments are that the embryo or fetus is not fully sentient, or that it cannot live outside the mother's womb, or that the fetus is not fully a person unless it is valued by its mother. These seem utterly insubstantial arguments. A newborn is not fully sentient, nor is a person in an advanced state of Alzheimer's disease. There are people who would allow the killing of the newborn and the senile, but I doubt that is a view with general acceptance. At least not yet. Equally irrelevant to the discussion is the fact that the fetus cannot survive outside the womb. Neither can a baby survive without the nurture of others, usually the parents. Why dependency, which lasts for years after birth, should justify terminating life is inexplicable. No more apparent is the logic of the statement that a fetus is a person only if the mother values its life. That is a tautology: an abortion is justified if the mother wants an abortion.

In discussing abortion, James Q. Wilson wrote, "The moral debate over abortion centers on the point in the development of the fertilized ovum when it has acquired those characteristics that entitle it to moral respect." He did not, apparently, think the cell resulting from conception was so entitled. Wilson gave an example of moral respect persisting in difficult circumstances: "An elderly man who has been a devoted husband and father but who now lies comatose in a vegetative state barely seems to be alive, . . . yet we experience great moral anguish in deciding whether to withdraw his life support." In response, my wife was moved to observe, "But suppose the doctor told us that in eight months the man would recover, be fully human, and live a normal life as a unique individual. Is it even conceivable that we would remove his life-support system on the ground that his existence, like that of the fetus, is highly inconvenient to us and that he does not look human at the moment? There would be no moral anguish but instead a certainty that such an act would be a grave moral wrong."

It is certainly more likely that we would refuse to countenance an abortion if a sonogram showed a recognizable human being than if only a tiny, guppy-like being appeared. But that is an instinctive reaction and instinctive reactions are not always the best guide to moral choice. Intellect must play a role as well. What if biology convinces us that the guppy-like creature or the microscopic fertilized egg has exactly the same future, the same capacity to live a full human life, as does the fetus at three months or at seven months or the infant at birth? "It is difficult to see," my wife added, "that the decision in the imagined case of the comatose elderly man who in time will recover is different from the abortion decision." In both cases, it is only a matter of time. The difference is that the death of the elderly man would deprive him of a few years of life while the aborted embryo or fetus loses an entire lifetime.

The issue is not, I think, one of appearance, sentience, or anything other than prospective life that is denied the individual by abortion. In introductory ethics courses, there used to be a question put: If you could obtain a hundred million dollars by pressing a button that would kill an elderly Chinese mandarin whom you had never seen, and if nobody would know what you had done, would you press the button? That seems to me the same issue as the abortion decision, except that the unborn child has a great deal longer to live if you don't press that particular button. Most of us, I suspect, would like to think we would not kill the mandarin. The characteristics of appearance, sentience, ability to live without assistance, and being valued by others cannot be the characteristics that entitle you to sufficient moral respect to be allowed to go on living. What characteristic does, then? It must lie in the fact that you are alive with the prospect of years of life ahead. That characteristic the unborn child has.

That seems to me an adequate ground to reject the argument made by Peter Singer last year in the London *Spectator* that supports not only abortion but infanticide. He writes that is doubtful that a fetus becomes conscious until well after the time most abortions are performed and even if it is conscious, that would not put the fetus at a level of awareness comparable to that of "a dog, let alone a chimpanzee. If on the other hand it is self-awareness, rather than mere consciousness, that grounds a right to life, that does not arise in a human being until some time after birth."

Aware that this line leaves out of account the potential of the child for a full human life, Singer responds that "in a world that is already over-populated, and in which the regulation of fertility is universally accepted, the argument that we should bring all potential people into existence is not persuasive." That is disingenuous. If overpopulation were a fact, that would hardly justify killing humans. If overpopulation were taken to be a justification, it would allow the killing of any helpless population, preferably without the infliction of pain.

Most contraceptive methods of regulating fertility do not raise the same moral issue as abortion because they do not permit the joining of the sperm and the egg. Until the sperm and the egg unite, there is no human being. Singer goes on to make the unsubstantiated claim that "just as the human being develops gradually in a physical sense, so too does its moral significance gradually increase." That contention is closely allied to the physical appearance argument and is subject to the same rebuttal. One wonders at measuring moral significance by physique. If a person gradually degenerated physically, would his moral significance gradually decline?

✎❦❧

Many who favor the abortion right understand that humans are being killed. Certainly the doctors who perform and nurses who assist at abortions know that. So do nonprofessionals. Otherwise, abortion would not be smothered in euphemisms. Thus, we hear the language of "choice," "reproductive rights," and "medical procedures." Those are oddly inadequate terms to describe the right to end the life of a human being. It has been remarked that "pro-choice" is an odd term since the individual whose life is at stake has no choice in the matter. These are ways of talking around the point that hide the truth from others and, perhaps, from one's self. President Clinton speaks of keeping abortion "safe, legal, and rare." Why rare, if it is merely a choice, a medical procedure without moral problems?

That there are severe moral problems is becoming clear even to many who favor abortion. That is probably why, as Candace C. Crandall observed last year in the *Women's Quarterly,* "the morale of the pro-choice side of the abortion stalemate has visibly collapsed." The reason: "Proponents of abortion rights overcame Americans' qualms about the procedure with a long series of claims about the benefits of unrestricted abortion on demand. Without exception, those claims have proved false." The proponents claimed that *Roe v. Wade* rescued women from death during unsafe, back-alley abortions, but it was the availability of antibiotics beginning in the 1940s and improved medical techniques that made abortion safe well before *Roe.* It was argued that abortion on demand would guarantee that every child was a wanted child, would keep children from being born into poverty, reduce illegitimacy rates, and help end child abuse. Child poverty rates, illegitimacy rates, and child abuse have all soared. We heard that abortion should be a decision between a woman and her doctor. The idea of a woman and her personal physician deliberating about the choice is a fantasy: women are going to specialized abortion clinics that offer little support or counseling. (Crandall does not address the point, but it is difficult to see that bringing a doctor in for consultation would change the nature of the decision about taking human life.) She does note, however, that many women use abortion for birth control.

Crandall says she sympathizes with abortion-rights advocates. But on her own showing, it is difficult to see why. No anti-abortion advocate could make it clearer that human lives are being destroyed at the rate of 1.5 million a year for convenience.

The author Naomi Wolf, who favors the right to abort, has challenged the feminists whose rhetoric seeks to disguise the truth that a human being is killed by abortion. In a 1995 article in the *New Republic,* she asks for "an abortion-rights movement willing publicly to mourn the evil—necessary evil though it may be—that is abortion." But she asks a question and gives an answer about her support for abortion rights that is troublesome: "But how, one might ask, can I square a recognition of the humanity of the fetus, and the moral gravity of destroying it, with a pro-choice position? The answer can only be found in the context of a paradigm abandoned by the left and misused by the right: the paradigm of sin and redemption."

&⟨❀⟩&

That seems an odd paradigm for this problem. It is one thing to have sinned, atoned, and sought redemption. It seems quite another to justify planning to sin on the ground that you also plan to seek redemption afterward. That justification seems even stranger for repeat abortions, which Wolf says are at least 43 percent of the total. Sin plus redemption falls short as a resolution of her dilemma. If that were an adequate resolution, it would seem to follow, given the humanity of the fetus, that infanticide, the killing of the elderly, indeed any killing for convenience, would be licensed if atonement and redemption were planned in advance.

Nor is it clear why the evil is necessary. It is undeniable that bearing and rearing a child sometimes places a great burden on a woman or a family. That fact does not, however, answer the question whether the burden justifies destroying a human life. In most other contexts, we would say such a burden is not sufficient justification. The fact is, in any event, that the burden need not be borne. Putting the child up for adoption is an alternative. The only drawback is that others will know the woman is pregnant. If that is the reason to choose abortion, then the killing really is for convenience.

But it is clear, in any event, that the vast majority of all abortions are for convenience. In those cases, abortion is used as merely one more technique of birth control. A 1987 survey of the reasons given by women for having abortions made by researchers with the Alan Guttmacher Institute, which is very much pro-abortion, demonstrated this fact. [Table 1] shows the percentage of women who gave the listed reasons.

It is clear that the overwhelming number of abortions were for birth control unrelated to the health of the fetus or the woman. Moreover, of those who were concerned about a possible health problem of the fetus, only 8 percent said that a physician had told them that the fetus had a defect or was abnormal. The rest were worried because they had taken medication, drugs, or alcohol before realizing they were pregnant, but did not apparently obtain a medical confirmation of any problem. Of those aborting because of their own health, 53 percent said a doctor had told them their condition would be made worse by being pregnant. Some of the rest cited physical problems, and 11 percent gave a mental or emotional problem as the reason. Only 1 percent cited rape or incest.

The survey noted that "some 77 percent of women with incomes under 100 percent or between 100 and 149 percent of the poverty level said they were having an abortion because they could not afford to have a child, compared with 69 percent of those with incomes between 150 and 199 percent and 60 percent of those with incomes at or above 200 percent of the poverty level." The can't afford category thus included a great many women who, by most

*Table 1*

| Reason | Total Percentage |
|---|---|
| Woman is concerned about how having a baby could change her life | 76 |
| Woman can't afford baby now | 68 |
| Woman has problems with relationship or wants to avoid single parenthood | 51 |
| Woman is unready for responsibility | 31 |
| Woman doesn't want others to know she has had sex or is pregnant | 31 |
| Woman is not mature enough or is too young to have a child | 30 |
| Woman has all the children she wanted, or has all grown-up children | 26 |
| Husband or partner wants woman to have abortion | 23 |
| Fetus has possible health problem | 13 |
| Woman has health problem | 7 |
| Woman's parents want her to have abortion | 7 |
| Woman was victim of rape or incest | 1 |
| Other | 6 |

reckonings, could afford to have a baby and certainly could have put the baby up for adoption.

This demonstration that abortion is almost always a birth control technique rather than a response to a serious problem with the mother's or the fetus' health must have been a considerable embarrassment to the pro-abortion forces. Perhaps for that reason no survey by them seems to have been reported since. More recent statistics by anti-abortion groups, however, bear out the conclusions to be drawn from the Guttmacher Institute study. The reasons most women give for having an abortion are "social": a baby would affect their education, jobs, lives, or they felt unable to handle it economically, their partners did not want babies, etc.

е☙☙

Perhaps the most instructive episode demonstrating the brutalization of our culture by abortion was the fight over "partial-birth abortions." These abortions are usually performed late in the pregnancy. The baby is delivered feet first until only the head remains within the mother. The aborting physician inserts scissors into the back of the infant's skull and opens the blades to produce a hole. The child's brains are then vacuumed out, the skull collapses, and the rest of the newly made corpse is removed. If the head had been allowed to come out of the mother, killing the baby then would be the criminal act of infanticide.

When it was proposed to outlaw this hideous procedure, which obviously causes extreme pain to the baby, the pro-abortion forces in Congress and elsewhere made false statements to fend off the legislation or to justify an anticipated presidential veto. Planned Parenthood and the National Abortion and Reproductive Rights Action League stated that the general anesthesia given the mother killed the fetus so that there is no such thing as a partial-birth abortion. Physicians promptly rebutted the claim. Local anesthesia, which is most often used in these abortions, has no effect on the baby and general anesthesia not only does not kill the baby, it provides little or no painkilling effect to the baby. The vice president of the Society for Obstetric Anesthesia and Perinatology said the claim was "crazy," noting that "anesthesia does not kill an infant if you don't kill the mother." Two doctors who perform partial-birth abortions stated that the majority of fetuses aborted in this fashion are alive until the end of the procedure.

Other opponents of a ban on partial-birth abortions claimed that it was used only when necessary to protect the mother's life. Unfortunately for that argument, the physician who is the best-known practitioner of these abortions stated in 1993 that 80 percent of them are "purely elective," not necessary to save the mother's life or health. Partial-birth understates the matter. The baby is outside the mother, except for its head, which is kept in the mother only to avoid a charge of infanticide. Full birth is inches away and could easily be accomplished.

No amount of discussion, no citation of evidence, can alter the opinions of radical feminists about abortion. One evening I naively remarked in a talk that those who favor the right to abort would likely change their minds if they could be convinced that a human being was being killed. I was startled at the anger that statement provoked in several women present. One of them informed me in no uncertain terms that the issue had nothing to do with the humanity of the fetus but was entirely about the woman's freedom. It is here that radical egalitarianism reinforces radical individualism in supporting the abortion right. Justice Harry Blackmun, who wrote *Roe* and who never offered the slightest constitutional defense of it, simply remarked that the decision was a landmark on women's march to equality. Equality, in this view, means that if men do not bear children, women should not have to either. Abortion is seen as women's escape from the idea that biology is destiny, to escape from the tyranny of the family role.

❦

Discussions about life and death in one area influence such decisions in others. Despite assurances that the abortion decision did not start us down a slippery and very steep slope, that is clearly where we are, and gathering speed. The systematic killing of unborn children in huge numbers is part of a general disregard for human life that has been growing for some time. Abortion by itself did not cause that disregard, but it certainly deepens and legitimates the nihilism that is spreading in our culture and finds killing for convenience acceptable. We are crossing lines, at first slowly and now with rapidity: killing unborn children for convenience; removing tissue from live fetuses; contemplating creating embryos for destruction in research; considering taking organs from living anencephalic babies; experimenting with assisted suicide; and contemplating euthanasia. Abortion has coarsened us. If it is permissible to kill the unborn human for convenience, it is surely permissible to kill those thought to be soon to die for the same reason. And it is inevitable that many who are not in danger of imminent death will be killed to relieve their families of burdens. Convenience is becoming the theme of our culture. Humans tend to be inconvenient at both ends of their lives.

## Notes

1. I objected to *Roe v. Wade* the moment it was decided, not because of any doubts about abortion, but because the decision was a radical deformation of the Constitution. The Constitution has nothing to say about abortion, leaving it, like most subjects, to the judgment and moral sense of the American people and their elected representatives. *Roe* and the decisions reaffirming it are equal in their audacity and abuse of judicial office to *Dred Scott v. Sandford*. Just as *Dred Scott* forced a southern proslavery position on the nation, *Roe* is nothing more than the Supreme Court's imposition of the morality of our cultural elites.

2. In discussing abortion I will not address instances where most people, however they might ultimately decide the issue, would feel genuine moral anguish, cases, for example, where it is known that the child will be born with severe deformities. My purpose is not to solve all moral issues but simply to address the major ones. Abortions in cases of deformity, etc., are a very small fraction of the total and, because they introduce special factors, do not cast light on the direction of our culture as do abortions of healthy pre-borns performed for convenience.

# NO 🖘

**Mary Gordon**

# A Moral Choice

I am having lunch with six women. What is unusual is that four of them are in their seventies, two of them widowed, the other two living with husbands beside whom they've lived for decades. All of them have had children. Had they been men, they would have published books and hung their paintings on the walls of important galleries. But they are women of a certain generation, and their lives were shaped around their families and personal relations. They are women you go to for help and support. We begin talking about the latest legislative act that makes abortion more difficult for poor women to obtain. An extraordinary thing happens. Each of them talks about the illegal abortions she had during her young womanhood. Not one of them was spared the experience. Any of them could have died on the table of whatever person (not a doctor in any case) she was forced to approach, in secrecy and in terror, to end a pregnancy that she felt would blight her life.

I mention this incident for two reasons: first as a reminder that all kinds of women have always had abortions; second because it is essential that we remember that an abortion is performed on a living woman who has a life in which a terminated pregnancy is only a small part. Morally speaking, the decision to have an abortion doesn't take place in a vacuum. It is connected to other choices that a woman makes in the course of an adult life.

Anti-choice propagandists paint pictures of women who choose to have abortions as types of moral callousness, selfishness, or irresponsibility. The woman choosing to abort is the dressed-for-success yuppie who gets rid of her baby so that she won't miss her Caribbean vacation or her chance for promotion. Or she is the feckless, promiscuous ghetto teenager who couldn't bring herself to just say no to sex. A third, purportedly kinder, gentler picture has recently begun to be drawn. The woman in the abortion clinic is there because she is misinformed about the nature of the world. She is having an abortion because society does not provide for mothers and their children, and she mistakenly thinks that another mouth to feed will be the ruin of her family, not understanding that the temporary truth of family unhappiness doesn't stack up beside the eternal verity that abortion is murder. Or she is the dupe of her husband or boyfriend, who talks her into having an abortion because a child will be a drag on his life-style. None of these pictures created by the anti-choice

From Mary Gordon, "A Moral Choice," *The Atlantic Monthly* (March 1990). Copyright © 1990 by Mary Gordon. Reprinted by permission of Sterling Lord Literistic, Inc.

movement assumes that the decision to have an abortion is made responsibly, in the context of a morally lived life, by a free and responsible moral agent.

## The Ontology of the Fetus

How would a woman who habitually makes choices in moral terms come to the decision to have an abortion? The moral discussion of abortion centers on the issue of whether or not abortion is an act of murder. At first glance it would seem that the answer should follow directly upon two questions: Is the fetus human? and Is it alive? It would be absurd to deny that a fetus is alive or that it is human. What would our other options be—to say that it is inanimate or belongs to another species? But we habitually use the terms "human" and "live" to refer to parts of our body—"human hair," for example, or "live red-blood cells"—and we are clear in our understanding that the nature of these objects does not rank equally with an entire personal existence. It then seems important to consider whether the fetus, this alive human thing, is a *person,* to whom the term "murder" could sensibly be applied. How would anyone come to a decision about something so impalpable as personhood? Philosophers have struggled with the issue of personhood, but in language that is so abstract that it is unhelpful to ordinary people making decisions in the course of their lives. It might be more productive to begin thinking about the status of the fetus by examining the language and customs that surround it. This approach will encourage us to focus on the choosing, acting woman, rather than the act of abortion—as if the act were performed by abstract forces without bodies, histories, attachments.

This focus on the acting woman is useful because a pregnant woman has an identifiable, consistent ontology, and a fetus takes on different ontological identities over time. But common sense, experience, and linguistic usage point clearly to the fact that we habitually consider, for example, a seven-week-old fetus to be different from a seven-month-old one. We can tell this by the way we respond to the involuntary loss of one as against the other. We have different language for the experience of the involuntary expulsion of the fetus from the womb depending upon the point of gestation at which the experience occurs. If it occurs early in the pregnancy, we call it a miscarriage; if late, we call it a stillbirth.

We would have an extreme reaction to the reversal of those terms. If a woman referred to a miscarriage at seven weeks as a stillbirth, we would be alarmed. It would shock our sense of propriety; it would make us uneasy; we would find it disturbing, misplaced—as we do when a bag lady sits down in a restaurant and starts shouting, or an octogenarian arrives at our door in a sailor suit. In short, we would suspect that the speaker was mad. Similarly, if a doctor or a nurse referred to the loss of a seven-month-old fetus as a miscarriage, we would be shocked by that person's insensitivity: could she or he not understand that a fetus that age is not what it was months before?

Our ritual and religious practices underscore the fact that we make distinctions among fetuses. If a woman took the bloody matter—indistinguishable from a heavy period—of an early miscarriage and insisted upon putting it in a tiny coffin and marking its grave, we would have serious concerns about her mental health. By the same token, we would feel squeamish about flushing a seven-month-old fetus down the toilet—something we would quite normally do with an early miscarriage. There are no prayers for the matter of a miscarriage, nor do we feel there should be. Even a Catholic priest would not baptize the issue of an early miscarriage.

The difficulties stem, of course, from the odd situation of a fetus's ontology: a complicated, differentiated, and nuanced response is required when we are dealing with an entity that changes over time. Yet we are in the habit of making distinctions like this. At one point we know that a child is no longer a child but an adult. That this question is vexed and problematic is clear from our difficulty in determining who is a juvenile offender and who is an adult criminal and at what age sexual intercourse ceases to be known as statutory rape. So at what point, if any, do we on the pro-choice side say that the developing fetus is a person, with rights equal to its mother's?

The anti-choice people have one advantage over us; their monolithic position gives them unity on this question. For myself, I am made uneasy by third-trimester abortions, which take place when the fetus could live outside the mother's body, but I also know that these are extremely rare and often performed on very young girls who have had difficulty comprehending the realities of pregnancy. It seems to me that the question of late abortions should be decided case by case, and that fixation on this issue is a deflection from what is most important: keeping early abortions, which are in the majority by far, safe and legal. I am also politically realistic enough to suspect that bills restricting late abortions are not good-faith attempts to make distinctions about the nature of fetal life. They are, rather, the cynical embodiments of the hope among anti-choice partisans that technology will be on their side and that medical science's ability to create situations in which younger fetuses are viable outside their mothers' bodies will increase dramatically in the next few years. Ironically, medical science will probably make the issue of abortion a minor one in the near future. The RU-486 pill, which can induce abortion early on, exists, and whether or not it is legally available (it is not on the market here, because of pressure from anti-choice groups), women will begin to obtain it. If abortion can occur through chemical rather than physical means, in the privacy of one's home, most people not directly involved will lose interest in it. As abortion is transformed from a public into a private issue, it will cease to be perceived as political; it will be called personal instead.

## An Equivocal Good

But because abortion will always deal with what it is to create and sustain life, it will always be a moral issue. And whether we like it or not, our moral thinking about abortion is rooted in the shifting soil of perception. In an age in which much of our perception is manipulated by media that specialize in the sound bite and the photo op, the anti-choice partisans have a twofold advantage over us on the pro-choice side. The pro-choice moral position is more complex, and the experience we defend is physically repellent to contemplate. None of us in the pro-choice movement would suggest that abortion is not a regrettable occurrence. Anti-choice proponents can offer pastel photographs of babies in buntings, their eyes peaceful in the camera's gaze. In answer, we can't offer the material of an early abortion, bloody, amorphous in a paper cup, to prove that what has just been removed from the woman's body is not a child, not in the same category of being as the adorable bundle in an adoptive mother's arms. It is not a pleasure to look at the physical evidence of abortion, and most of us don't get the opportunity to do so.

The theologian Daniel Maguire, uncomfortable with the fact that most theological arguments about the nature of abortion are made by men who have never been anywhere near an actual abortion, decided to visit a clinic and observe abortions being performed. He didn't find the experience easy, but he knew that before he could in good conscience make a moral judgment on abortion, he needed to experience through his senses what an aborted fetus is like: he needed to look at and touch the controversial entity. He held in his hand the bloody fetal stuff; the eight-week-old fetus fit in the palm of his hand, and it certainly bore no resemblance to either of his two children when he had held them moments after their birth. He knew at that point what women who have experienced early abortions and miscarriages know: that some event occurred, possibly even a dramatic one, but it was not the death of a child.

Because issues of pregnancy and birth are both physical and metaphorical, we must constantly step back and forth between ways of perceiving the world. When we speak of gestation, we are often talking in terms of potential, about events and objects to which we attach our hopes, fears, dreams, and ideals. A mother can speak to the fetus in her uterus and name it; she and her mate may decorate a nursery according to their vision of the good life; they may choose for an embryo a college, a profession, a dwelling. But those of us who are trying to think morally about pregnancy and birth must remember that these feelings are our own projections onto what is in reality an inappropriate object. However charmed we may be by an expectant father's buying a little football for something inside his wife's belly, we shouldn't make public policy based on such actions, nor should we force others to live their lives conforming to our fantasies.

As a society, we are making decisions that pit the complicated future of a complex adult against the fate of a mass of cells lacking cortical development. The moral pressure should be on distinguishing the true from the false, the real suffering of living persons from our individual and often idiosyncratic dreams and fears. We must make decisions on abortion based on an understanding of how people really do live. We must be able to say that poverty is worse than not being poor, that having dignified and meaningful work is better than working in conditions of degradation, that raising a child one loves and has desired is better than raising a child in resentment and rage, that it is better for a twelve-year-old not to endure the trauma of having a child when she is herself a child.

When we put these ideas against the ideas of "child" or "baby," we seem to be making a horrifying choice of life-style over life. But in fact we are telling the truth of what it means to bear a child, and what the experience of abortion really is. This is extremely difficult, for the object of the discussion is hidden, changing, potential. We make our decisions on the basis of approximate and inadequate language, often on the basis of fantasies and fears. It will always be crucial to try to separate genuine moral concern from phobia, punitiveness, superstition, anxiety, a desperate search for certainty in an uncertain world.

One of the certainties that is removed if we accept the consequences of the pro-choice position is the belief that the birth of a child is an unequivocal good. In real life we act knowing that the birth of a child is not always a good thing: people are sometimes depressed, angry, rejecting, at the birth of a child. But this is a difficult truth to tell; we don't like to say it, and one of the fears preyed on by anti-choice proponents is that if we cannot look at the birth of a child as an unequivocal good, then there is nothing to look toward. The desire for security of the imagination, for typological fixity, particularly in the area of "the good," is an understandable desire. It must seem to some anti-choice people that we on the pro-choice side are not only murdering innocent children but also murdering hope. Those of us who have experienced the birth of a desired child and felt the joy of that moment can be tempted into believing that it was the physical experience of the birth itself that was the joy. But it is crucial to remember that the birth of a child itself is a neutral occurrence emotionally: the charge it takes on is invested in it by the people experiencing or observing it.

## The Fear of Sexual Autonomy

These uncertainties can lead to another set of fears, not only about abortion but about its implications. Many anti-choice people fear that to support abortion is to cast one's lot with the cold and technological rather than with the warm and natural, to head down the slippery slope toward a brave new world where handicapped children are left on mountains to starve and the old are put out in the snow. But if we look at the history of abortion, we don't see the embodiment of what the anti-choice proponents fear. On the contrary, excepting the grotesque counterexample of the People's Republic of China (which practices forced abortion), there seems to be a real link between repressive anti-abortion stances and repressive governments. Abortion was banned in Fascist Italy and Nazi Germany; it is illegal in South Africa and in Chile. It is paid for by the governments of Denmark, England, and the Netherlands, which have national health and welfare systems that foster the health and well-being of mothers, children, the old, and the handicapped.

Advocates of outlawing abortion often refer to women seeking abortion as self-indulgent and materialistic. In fact these accusations mask a discomfort with female sexuality, sexual pleasure, and sexual autonomy. It is possible for a woman to have a sexual life unriddled by fear only if she can be confident that she need not pay for a failure of technology or judgment (and who among us has never once been swept away in the heat of a sexual moment?) by taking upon herself the crushing burden of unchosen motherhood.

It is no accident, therefore, that the increased appeal of measures to restrict maternal conduct during pregnancy—and a new focus on the physical autonomy of the pregnant woman—have come into public discourse at precisely the time when women are achieving unprecedented levels of economic and political autonomy. What has surprised me is that some of this new anti-autonomy talk comes to us from the left. An example of this new discourse is an article by Christopher Hitchens that appeared in *The Nation* last April, in which the author asserts his discomfort with abortion. Hitchens's tone is impeccably British: arch, light, we're men of the left.

> Anyone who has ever seen a sonogram or has spent even an hour with a textbook on embryology knows that the emotions are not the deciding factor. In order to terminate a pregnancy, you have to still a heartbeat, switch off a developing brain, and whatever the method, break some bones and rupture some organs. As to whether this involves pain on the "Silent Scream" scale, I have no idea. The "right to life" leadership, again, has cheapened everything it touches. ["Silent Scream" refers to Dr. Bernard Nathanson's widely debated antiabortion film *The Silent Scream,* in which an abortion on a 12-week-old fetus is shown from inside the uterus.—Eds.]

"It is a pity," Hitchens goes on to say, "that . . . the majority of feminists and their allies have stuck to the dead ground of 'Me Decade' possessive individualism, an ideology that has more in common than it admits with the prehistoric right, which it claims to oppose but has in fact encouraged." Hitchens proposes, as an alternative, a program of social reform that would make contraception free and support a national adoption service. In his opinion, it would seem, women have abortions for only two reasons: because they are selfish or because they are poor. If the state will take care of the economic problems and the bureaucratic messiness around adoption, it remains only for the possessive individualists to get their act together and walk with their babies into the communal utopia of the future. Hitchens would allow victims of rape or incest to have free abortions, on the grounds that since they didn't choose to have sex, the women should not be forced to have the babies. This would seem to put the issue of volition in a wrong and telling place. To Hitchens's mind, it would appear, if a woman chooses to have sex, she can't choose whether or not to have a baby. The implications of this are clear. If a woman is consciously and volitionally sexual, she should be prepared to take her medicine. And what medicine must the consciously sexual male take? Does Hitchens really believe, or want us to believe, that every male who has unintentionally impregnated a woman will be involved in the lifelong responsibility for the upbringing of the engendered child? Can he honestly say that he has observed this behavior—or, indeed, would want to see it observed—in the world in which he lives?

## Real Choices

It is essential for a moral decision about abortion to be made in an atmosphere of open, critical thinking. We on the pro-choice side must accept that there are indeed anti-choice activists who take their position in good faith. I believe, however, that they are people for whom childbirth is an emotionally overladen topic, people who are susceptible to unclear thinking because of their unrealistic hopes and fears. It is important for us in the pro-choice movement to be open in discussing those areas involving abortion which are nebulous and unclear. But we must not forget that there are some things that we know to be undeniably true. There are some undeniable bad consequences of a woman's being forced to bear a child against her will. First is the trauma of going through a pregnancy and giving birth to a child who is not desired, a trauma more long-lasting than that experienced by some (only some) women who experience an early abortion. The grief of giving up a child at its birth—and at nine months it is a child whom one has felt move inside one's body—is underestimated both by anti-choice partisans and by those for whom access to adoptable children is important. This grief should not be forced on any woman—or, indeed, encouraged by public policy.

We must be realistic about the impact on society of millions of unwanted children in an overpopulated world. Most of the time, human beings have sex not because they want to make babies. Yet throughout history sex has resulted in unwanted pregnancies. And women have always aborted. One thing that is not hidden, mysterious, or debatable is that making abortion illegal will result in the deaths of women, as it has always done. Is our historical memory so short that none of us remember aunts, sisters, friends, or mothers who were killed or rendered sterile by septic abortions? Does no one in the anti-choice movement remember stories or actual experiences of midnight drives to filthy rooms from which aborted women were sent out, bleeding, to their fate? Can anyone genuinely say that it would be a moral good for us as a society to return to those conditions?

Thinking about abortion, then, forces us to take moral positions as adults who understand the complexities of the world and the realities of human suffering, to make decisions based on how people actually live and choose, and not on our fears, prejudices, and anxieties about sex and society, life and death.

# POSTSCRIPT

## Should Abortion Be Restricted?

The real issue dividing Bork and Gordon is whether or not the fetus is fully human, in the sense of being entitled to the treatment that civilized society gives to human beings. Their respective arguments use different methods of proof. Bork reasons from the biological premise that sperm and egg, each with 23 chromosomes, produce a fertilized human organism with the human's full 46 chromosomes; what occurs after that is simply human growth, which no one has the right to interrupt. Gordon reasons from the appearance of the fetus and how people normally react to it. Since even pro-lifers do not conduct funeral services and memorials for the "bloody matter" resulting from an early miscarriage, Gordon reasons, the Supreme Court was therefore right to exclude early fetuses from legal protection. Such reactions, in Bork's view, proceed from "uninstructed emotions, not emotions based on a recognition of what the fetus is from the beginning." Arguably, however, even "uninstructed emotions" have some role in the making of ethical judgments.

Dozens of books have dealt with these questions since the Supreme Court's decision in *Roe v. Wade* in 1973. A comprehensive selection ranging from the proabortion views of Dr. Alan Guttmacher to the antiabortion position of Daniel Callahan can be found in J. Douglas Butler and David F. Walbert, eds., *Abortion, Medicine, and the Law*, 3rd ed. (Facts on File, 1986).

More briefly, most of the legal, ethical, and medical issues are considered in Hyman Rodman, Betty Sarvis, and Joy Walker Bonar, *The Abortion Question* (Columbia University Press, 1987). In *Real Choices* (Multnomah Press, 1994), Frederica Mathewes-Green argues the case against abortion from the standpoint of the harm (physical and psychological) that it inflicts on women. A similar approach is taken by David C. Reardon in *Making Abortion Rare* (Acorn Books, 1996) and in the more recent book he coauthored with Julie Makimaa and Amy Sobie, *Victims and Victors* (Acorn Books, 2000).

Robert M. Baird and Stuart E. Rosenbaum, eds., *The Ethics of Abortion: Pro-Life vs. Pro-Choice*, rev. ed. (Prometheus Books, 1993), contains a wide variety of views, including those of Robert H. Bork, Ronald Dworkin, Anna Quindlen, and Richard Selzer. An unbiased history of abortion as an American political issue can be found in Barbara Hinkson Craig and David M. O'Brien, *Abortion and American Politics* (Chatham House, 1993). In the world arena, Andrzej Kulczycki's *The Abortion Debate in the World Arena* (Routledge, 1999) examines how cultural history, feminist movements, the Catholic Church, and international influences have shaped abortion policies in Kenya, Mexico, and Poland.

If, as Gordon argues, the best way to determine the humanity of the fetus is by its appearance, what of late-term abortions? By the sixth month of pregnancy, the fetus begins to look very much like a baby. Should it then be protected by law? Although she confesses to be "uneasy" about third-trimester abortions (she thinks that they "should be decided case by case"), Gordon suspects that those who advocate bans on late-term abortions are not doing so in good faith. The suspicion between the warring parties to the abortion debate will likely continue, despite efforts by some on both sides to find common ground.

# ISSUE 17

## Should Gay Marriage Be Legalized?

**YES: Andrew Sullivan**, from *Virtually Normal: An Argument About Homosexuality* (Alfred A. Knopf, 1995)

**NO: James Q. Wilson**, from "Against Homosexual Marriage," *Commentary* (March 1996)

### ISSUE SUMMARY

**YES:** Essayist and editor Andrew Sullivan contends that legalizing gay marriage would be a profoundly humanizing step because such marriages, with their honesty, their flexibility, and their equality, could nourish the broader society as well.

**NO:** Social scientist James Q. Wilson asserts that to legalize homosexual marriage would be to enter an untested area that could profoundly damage the already-fragile institutions of marriage and family.

O n May 12, 1979, in Sioux Falls, South Dakota, Randy Rohl and Grady Quinn made history of a sort. They were the first acknowledged homosexual couple ever to receive permission from their high school principal to attend the prom together. The National Gay Task force hailed the event as a milestone in the history of human rights. What the voters of Sioux Falls thought of it cannot be determined (they weren't asked), but if their reactions were similar to those of people who voted on various state and local referenda since that time, they probably were not pleased. In several county and municipal elections, voters were asked to approve resolutions specifically banning discrimination based on "sexual preference," but the voters rejected these resolutions by large majorities. More recently, voters in Colorado approved a resolution denying local jurisdictions the authority to grant homosexuals any rights beyond those granted by the U.S. Constitution. The U.S. Supreme Court struck this down as unconstitutional in 1996, but the passage of the initiative showed that Colorado voters were not ready to include homosexuals among those groups that are entitled to state civil rights protection, such as blacks and women.

Despite these popular rebuffs to "gay rights," the attitude of most Americans toward homosexuals appears to be rather complex and nuanced. A 1995 public opinion poll showed that only 41 percent of the public believed that the homosexual lifestyle should be accepted, a result consistent with those of several earlier polls showing that the majority consider homosexuality "abnormal" and homosexual behavior "immoral." At the same time, however, American voters have defeated resolutions (such as one in California in 1978) that would ban the hiring of homosexuals to teach in public schools, and they have elected public officials who have pledged to uphold "gay rights."

If there is a thread of consistency here, it is this: Americans believe in fair play and equal treatment for people of equal merit; they also, as a rule, believe in minding their own business. Most Americans would agree that what people do in their bedrooms has no place in the public realm. But it is precisely here that the conflict arises, for as many Americans see it, what organized homosexual groups are attempting to do is to bring their private behavior *into* the public realm by making homosexuality a "civil right." Although they are willing to tolerate homosexual behavior in private, most Americans are reluctant to support any measure that appears to give it official recognition.

The raw nerve of this conflict was touched in 1996 when Hawaii's highest state court ruled that the state must present a compelling public reason for prohibiting same-sex marriages. The controversy had national dimensions. Article IV, Section 1, of the Constitution stipulates that "Full Faith and Credit shall be given in each state to the public Acts, Records, and judicial Proceedings of every other State." What that means is that if Hawaii went through with the legalization of same-sex marriage, every state would have to honor it. Gay couples could go to Hawaii to get married, return to their home state, and enjoy all the legal benefits that their state provides for married couples with regard to inheritance, housing, taxation, adoption rights, etc. Reacting to this possibility, Congress adopted the Defense of Marriage Act in 1996, which allowed states to ignore same-sex marriages sanctioned by another state. In 1998 Hawaii voters amended their state constitution to give the legislature authority to ban same-sex marriage, and the following year, the Hawaii Supreme Court, even without the adoption of a new law by the legislature, upheld the old Hawaii statute allowing a marriage license only to a couple composed of a man and a woman.

In 1999 the Vermont Supreme Court held that denying same-sex couples the rights and protections that come with civil marriage violates the state constitution's equality guarantee. In response, in 2000 the Vermont legislature accorded same-sex couples entering into "civil unions" the protections, responsibilities, and benefits of civil marriage. This was the first legislatively sanctioned support for gay marriage. Later in 2000 San Francisco became the first city to compel private businesses to provide all the benefits that they provide to married couples to all other cohabiting couples, regardless of sex. The effect would be to recognize same-sex unions and heterosexual cohabitation as equivalent to legal marriage.

In the following selections, Andrew Sullivan, who is gay, defends the concept of same-sex marriage, which he sees as not only a civil right but as the kind of idea that might add needed flexibility to the institution of marriage. James Q. Wilson expresses concern that legalizing such unions can only weaken the already-fragile framework of marriage.

**Andrew Sullivan**

 **YES**

# Virtually Normal

In everyone there sleeps
A Sense of life lived according to love.
To some it means the difference they could make
By loving others, but across most it sweeps
As all they might have been had they been loved.
That nothing cures.

— Philip Larkin

**I**f there were no alternative to today's conflicted politics of homosexuality, we might be condemned to see the proponents of the four major positions fight noisily while society stumbles from one awkward compromise to another. But there is an alternative: a politics that can reconcile the best arguments of liberals and conservatives, and find a way to marry the two. In accord with liberalism, this politics respects the law, its limits, and its austerity. It places a high premium on liberty, and on a strict limit to the regulation of people's minds and actions. And in sympathy with conservatism, this politics acknowledges that in order to create a world of equality, broader arguments may often be needed to persuade people of the need for change, apart from those of rights and government neutrality. It sees that beneath politics, human beings exist whose private lives may indeed be shaped by a shift in public mores.

This politics begins with the view that for a small minority of people, from a young age, homosexuality is an essentially involuntary condition that can neither be denied nor permanently repressed. It is a function of both nature and nurture, but the forces of nurture are formed so early and are so complex that they amount to an involuntary condition. It is *as if* it were a function of nature. Moreover, so long as homosexual adults as citizens insist on the involuntary nature of their condition, it becomes politically impossible simply to deny or ignore the fact of homosexuality.

This politics adheres to an understanding that there is a limit to what politics can achieve in such a fraught area as homosexuality, and trains its focus not on the behavior of citizens in civil society but on the actions of the public and allegedly neutral state. While it eschews the use of law to legislate culture,

From Andrew Sullivan, *Virtually Normal: An Argument About Homosexuality* (Alfred A. Knopf, 1995). Copyright © 1995 by Andrew Sullivan. Reprinted by permission of Alfred A. Knopf, a division of Random House, Inc.

it strongly believes that law can affect culture indirectly by its insistence on the equality of all citizens. Its goal in the area of homosexuality is simply to ensure that the liberal state live up to its promises for all its citizens. It would seek full public equality for those who, through no fault of their own, happen to be homosexual; and it would not deny homosexuals, as the other four politics do, their existence, integrity, dignity, or distinctness. It would attempt neither to patronize nor to exclude.

This politics affirms a simple and limited principle: that all *public* (as opposed to private) discrimination against homosexuals be ended and that every right and responsibility that heterosexuals enjoy as public citizens be extended to those who grow up and find themselves emotionally different. *And that is all.* No cures or re-educations, no wrenching private litigation, no political imposition of tolerance; merely a political attempt to enshrine formal public equality, whatever happens in the culture and society at large. For these reasons, it is the only politics that actually tackles the *political* problem of homosexuality; the only one that fully respects liberalism's public-private distinction; and, ironically, as we shall see, the only one that cuts the Gordian knot of the shame and despair and isolation that many homosexuals feel. For these reasons, perhaps, it has the least chance of being adopted by homosexuals and heterosexuals alike.

What would it mean in practice? Quite simply, an end to all proactive discrimination by the state against homosexuals. That means an end to sodomy laws that apply only to homosexuals; a recourse to the courts if there is not equal protection of heterosexuals and homosexuals in law enforcement; an equal legal age of consent to sexual activity for heterosexuals and homosexuals, where such regulations apply; inclusion of the facts about homosexuality in the curriculum of every government-funded school, in terms no more and no less clear than those applied to heterosexuality (although almost certainly with far less emphasis, because of homosexuality's relative rareness when compared with heterosexuality); recourse to the courts if any government body or agency can be proven to be engaged in discrimination against homosexual employees; equal opportunity and inclusion in the military; and legal homosexual marriage and divorce....

Its most powerful and important elements are equal access to the military and marriage. The military ban is by far the most egregious example of proactive public discrimination in the Western democracies. By conceding the excellent service that many gay and lesbian soldiers have given to their country, the U.S. military in recent years has elegantly clarified the specificity of the government's unfairness. By focusing on the mere public admission of homosexuality in its 1993 "don't ask, don't tell" compromise, the military isolated the core issue at the heart of the equality of homosexual persons. It argued that homosexuals could serve in the military; that others could know they were homosexuals; that *they* could know they were homosexuals; but that if they ever so much as mentioned this fact, they were to be discharged. The prohibition was not against homosexual acts as such—occasional lapses by heterosexuals were not to be grounds for expulsion. The prohibition was not even against homosexuality. The prohibition was against homosexuals' being honest about their sexuality, because that honesty allegedly lowered the morale of others.

Once the debate has been constructed this way, it will eventually, surely, be won by those advocating the admission of open homosexuals in the military. When this is the sole argument advanced by the military—it became the crux of the debate on Capitol Hill—it has the intellectual solidity of a pack of cards. One group is arbitrarily silenced to protect not the rights but the sensibilities of the others. To be sure, it won the political battle; but it clearly lost the moral and intellectual war, as subsequent court tests demonstrated. It required one of the most respected institutions in American society to impose upon its members a rule of fundamental dishonesty in order for them to perform their duties. It formally introduced hypocrisy as a rule of combat. . . .

If this politics is feasible, both liberal and conservative dead ends become new beginnings. The liberal can campaign for formal public equality—for the abolition of sodomy laws, equal protection in public employment and institutions, the end of the ban on openly gay men and lesbians in the military—and rightly claim that he is merely seeing that all citizens in their public capacity are treated equally. But he can also argue fervently for freedom of expression—for those on both sides of the cultural war—and for freedom of economic contract. And he can concentrate his efforts on the work of transforming civil society, the place where every liberal longs to be.

And the conservative, while opposing "special rights," is able to formulate a vision of what values the society wants to inculcate. He can point to the virtues of a loyal and dedicated soldier, homosexual or heterosexual, and celebrate his patriotism; he can involve another minority group in the collective social good. He can talk about relations between heterosexuals and homosexuals not under the rubric of a minority group seeking preferences from a majority group, but as equal citizens, each prepared and willing to contribute to the common good, so long as they are treated equally by the state.

But the centerpiece of this new politics goes further than this. The critical measure for this politics of public equality–private freedom is something deeper and more emotional, perhaps, than the military.

It is equal access to civil marriage.

As with the military, this is a question of formal public discrimination, since only the state can grant and recognize marriage. If the military ban deals with the heart of what it means to be a citizen, marriage does even more so, since, in peace and war, it affects everyone. Marriage is not simply a private contract; it is a social and public recognition of a private commitment. As such, it is the highest public recognition of personal integrity. Denying it to homosexuals is the most public affront possible to their public equality.

This point may be the hardest for many heterosexuals to accept. Even those tolerant of homosexuals may find this institution so wedded to the notion of heterosexual commitment that to extend it would be to undo its very essence. And there may be religious reasons for resisting this that, within certain traditions, are unanswerable. But I am not here discussing what churches do in their private affairs. I am discussing what the allegedly neutral liberal state should do in public matters. For liberals, the case for homosexual marriage is overwhelming. As a classic public institution, it should be available to any two citizens.

Some might argue that marriage is by definition between a man and a woman; and it is difficult to argue with a definition. But if marriage is articulated beyond this circular fiat, then the argument for its exclusivity to one man and one woman disappears. The center of the public contract is an emotional, financial, and psychological bond between two people; in this respect, heterosexuals and homosexuals are identical. The heterosexuality of marriage is intrinsic only if it is understood to be intrinsically procreative; but that definition has long been abandoned in Western society. No civil marriage license is granted on the condition that the couple bear children; and the marriage is no less legal and no less defensible if it remains childless. In the contemporary West, marriage has become a way in which the state recognizes an emotional commitment by two people to each other for life. And within that definition, there is no public way, if one believes in equal rights under the law, in which it should legally be denied homosexuals. . . .

But perhaps surprisingly . . . one of the strongest arguments for gay marriage is a conservative one. It's perhaps best illustrated by a comparison with the alternative often offered by liberals and liberationists to legal gay marriage, the concept of "domestic partnership." Several cities in the United States have domestic partnership laws, which allow relationships that do not fit into the category of heterosexual marriage to be registered with the city and qualify for benefits that had previously been reserved for heterosexual married couples. In these cities, a variety of interpersonal arrangements qualify for health insurance, bereavement leave, insurance, annuity and pension rights, housing rights (such as rent-control apartments), adoption and inheritance rights. Eventually, the aim is to include federal income tax and veterans' benefits as well. Homosexuals are not the only beneficiaries; heterosexual "live-togethers" also qualify.

The conservative's worries start with the ease of the relationship. To be sure, potential domestic partners have to prove financial interdependence, shared living arrangements, and a commitment to mutual caring. But they don't need to have a sexual relationship or even closely mirror old-style marriage. In principle, an elderly woman and her live-in nurse could qualify, or a pair of frat buddies. Left as it is, the concept of domestic partnership could open a Pandora's box of litigation and subjective judicial decision making about who qualifies. You either are or you're not married; it's not a complex question. Whether you are in a domestic partnership is not so clear.

More important for conservatives, the concept of domestic partnership chips away at the prestige of traditional relationships and undermines the priority we give them. Society, after all, has good reasons to extend legal advantages to heterosexuals who choose the formal sanction of marriage over simply living together. They make a deeper commitment to one another and to society; in exchange, society extends certain benefits to them. Marriage provides an anchor, if an arbitrary and often weak one, in the maelstrom of sex and relationships to which we are all prone. It provides a mechanism for emotional stability and economic security. We rig the law in its favor not because we disparage all forms of relationship other than the nuclear family, but because we recognize that not to promote marriage would be to ask too much of human virtue. . . .

Any heterosexual man who takes a few moments to consider what his life would be like if he were never allowed a formal institution to cement his relationships will see the truth of what I am saying. Imagine life without a recognized family; imagine dating without even the possibility of marriage. Any heterosexual woman who can imagine being told at a young age that her attraction to men was wrong, that her loves and crushes were illicit, that her destiny was single-hood and shame, will also appreciate the point. Gay marriage is not a radical step; it is a profoundly humanizing, traditionalizing step. It is the first step in any resolution of the homosexual question—more important than any other institution, since it is the most central institution to the nature of the problem, which is to say, the emotional and sexual bond between one human being and another. If nothing else were done at all, and gay marriage were legalized, ninety percent of the political work necessary to achieve gay and lesbian equality would have been achieved. It is ultimately the only reform that truly matters.

... It has become a truism that in the field of emotional development, homosexuals have much to learn from the heterosexual culture. The values of commitment, of monogamy, of marriage, of stability are all posited as models for homosexual existence. And, indeed, of course, they are. Without an architectonic institution like that of marriage, it is difficult to create the conditions for nurturing such virtues, but that doesn't belie their importance.

It is also true, however, that homosexual relationships, even in their current, somewhat eclectic form, may contain features that could nourish the broader society as well. Precisely because there is no institutional model, gay relationships are often sustained more powerfully by genuine commitment. The mutual nurturing and sexual expressiveness of many lesbian relationships, the solidity and space of many adult gay male relationships, are qualities sometimes lacking in more rote, heterosexual couplings. Same-sex unions often incorporate the virtues of friendship more effectively than traditional marriages; and at times, among gay male relationships, the openness of the contract makes it more likely to survive than many heterosexual bonds. Some of this is unavailable to the male-female union: there is more likely to be greater understanding of the need for extramarital outlets between two men than between a man and a woman; and again, the lack of children gives gay couples greater freedom. Their failures entail fewer consequences for others. But something of the gay relationship's necessary honesty, its flexibility, and its equality could undoubtedly help strengthen and inform many heterosexual bonds....

As I've just argued, I believe strongly that marriage should be made available to everyone, in a politics of strict public neutrality. But within this model, there is plenty of scope for cultural difference. There is something baleful about the attempt of some gay conservatives to educate homosexuals and lesbians into an uncritical acceptance of a stifling model of heterosexual normality. The truth is, homosexuals are not entirely normal; and to flatten their varied and complicated lives into a single, moralistic model is to miss what is essential and exhilarating about their otherness.

# NO ↵

**James Q. Wilson**

## Against Homosexual Marriage

Our courts, which have mishandled abortion, may be on the verge of mishandling homosexuality. As a consequence of two pending decisions, we may be about to accept homosexual marriage.

In 1993 the supreme court of Hawaii ruled that, under the equal-protection clause of that state's constitution, any law based on distinctions of sex was suspect, and thus subject to strict judicial scrutiny. Accordingly, it reversed the denial of a marriage permit to a same-sex couple, unless the state could first demonstrate a "compelling state interest" that would justify limiting marriages to men and women.... [I]n the meantime, the executive branch of Hawaii appointed a commission to examine the question of same-sex marriages; its report, by a vote of five to two, supports them. The legislature, for its part, holds a different view of the matter, having responded to the court's decision by passing a law unambiguously reaffirming the limitation of marriage to male-female couples.

... [S]ince the United States Constitution has a clause requiring that "full faith and credit shall be given to the public acts, records, and judicial proceedings of every other state," a homosexual couple in a state like Texas, where the population is overwhelmingly opposed to such unions, may soon be able to fly to Hawaii, get married, and then return to live in Texas as lawfully wedded....

Contemporaneous with these events, an important book has appeared under the title *Virtually Normal.* In it, Andrew Sullivan, the editor of the *New Republic,* makes a strong case for a new policy toward homosexuals. He argues that "all *public* (as opposed to private) discrimination against homosexuals be ended.... *And that is all.*" The two key areas where this change is necessary are the military and marriage law. Lifting bans in those areas, while also disallowing antisodomy laws and providing information about homosexuality in publicly supported schools, would put an end to the harm that gays have endured. Beyond these changes, Sullivan writes, American society would need no "cures [of homophobia] or reeducations, no wrenching private litigation, no political imposition of tolerance."

It is hard to imagine how Sullivan's proposals would, in fact, end efforts to change private behavior toward homosexuals, or why the next, inevitable, step would not involve attempts to accomplish just that purpose by using cures

From James Q. Wilson, "Against Homosexual Marriage," *Commentary* (March 1996). Copyright © 1996 by The American Jewish Committee. Reprinted by permission of *Commentary*. Notes omitted.

and reeducations, private litigation, and the political imposition of tolerance. But apart from this, Sullivan—an English Catholic, a homosexual, and someone who has on occasion referred to himself as a conservative—has given us the most sensible and coherent view of a program to put homosexuals and heterosexuals on the same public footing. . . .

✦

Sullivan recounts three main arguments concerning homosexual marriage, two against and one for. He labels them prohibitionist, conservative, and liberal. (A fourth camp, the "liberationist," which advocates abolishing all distinctions between heterosexuals and homosexuals, is also described—and scorched for its "strange confluence of political abdication and psychological violence.") I think it easier to grasp the origins of the three main arguments by referring to the principles on which they are based.

The prohibitionist argument is in fact a biblical one; the heart of it was stated by Dennis Prager in an essay in the *Public Interest* ("Homosexuality, the Bible, and Us," Summer 1993). When the first books of the Bible were written, and for a long time thereafter, heterosexual love is what seemed at risk. In many cultures—not only in Egypt or among the Canaanite tribes surrounding ancient Israel but later in Greece, Rome, and the Arab world, to say nothing of large parts of China, Japan, and elsewhere—homosexual practices were common and widely tolerated or even exalted. The Torah reversed this, making the family the central unit of life, the obligation to marry one of the first responsibilities of man, and the linkage of sex to procreation the highest standard by which to judge sexual relations. Leviticus puts the matter sharply and apparently beyond quibble:

> Thou shalt not live with mankind as with womankind; it is an abomination. . . . If a man also lie with mankind, as he lieth with a woman, both of them have committed an abomination; they shall surely be put to death; their blood shall be upon them.

Sullivan acknowledges the power of Leviticus but deals with it by placing it in a relative context. What is the nature of this "abomination"? Is it like killing your mother or stealing a neighbor's bread, or is it more like refusing to eat shellfish or having sex during menstruation? Sullivan suggests that all of these injunctions were written on the same moral level and hence can be accepted or ignored *as a whole*. He does not fully sustain this view, and in fact a refutation of it can be found in Prager's essay. In Prager's opinion and mine, people at the time of Moses, and for centuries before him, understood that there was a fundamental difference between whom you killed and what you ate, and in all likelihood people then and for centuries earlier linked whom you could marry closer to the principles that defined life than they did to the rules that defined diets.

The New Testament contains an equally vigorous attack on homosexuality by St. Paul. Sullivan partially deflects it by noting Paul's conviction that the earth was about to end and the Second Coming was near; under these conditions, all forms of sex were suspect. But Sullivan cannot deny that Paul singled out homosexuality as deserving of special criticism. He seems to pass over this obstacle without effective retort.

Instead, he takes up a different theme, namely, that on grounds of consistency many heterosexual practices—adultery, sodomy, premarital sex, and divorce, among others—should be outlawed equally with homosexual acts of the same character. The difficulty with this is that it mistakes the distinction alive in most people's minds between marriage as an institution and marriage as a practice. As an institution, it deserves unqualified support; as a practice, we recognize that married people are as imperfect as anyone else. Sullivan's understanding of the prohibitionist argument suffers from his unwillingness to acknowledge this distinction.

><

The second argument against homosexual marriage—Sullivan's conservative category—is based on natural law as originally set forth by Aristotle and Thomas Aquinas and more recently restated by Hadley Arkes, John Finnis, Robert George, Harry V. Jaffa, and others. How is it phrased varies a bit, but in general its advocates support a position like the following: man cannot live without the care and support of other people; natural law is the distillation of what thoughtful people have learned about the conditions of that care. The first thing they have learned is the supreme importance of marriage, for without it the newborn infant is unlikely to survive or, if he survives, to prosper. The necessary conditions of a decent family life are the acknowledgement by its members that a man will not sleep with his daughter or a woman with her son and that neither will openly choose sex outside marriage.

Now, some of these conditions are violated, but there is a penalty in each case that is supported by the moral convictions of almost all who witness the violation. On simple utilitarian grounds it may be hard to object to incest or adultery; if both parties to such an act welcome it and if it is secret, what differences does it make? But very few people, and then only ones among the overeducated, seem to care much about mounting a utilitarian assault on the family. To this assault, natural-law theorists respond much as would the average citizen—never mind "utility," what counts is what is right. In particular, homosexual uses of the reproductive organs violate the condition that sex serve solely as the basis of heterosexual marriage.

To Sullivan, what is defective about the natural-law thesis is that it assumes different purposes in heterosexual and homosexual love: moral consummation in the first case and pure utility or pleasure alone in the second. But in fact, Sullivan suggests, homosexual love can be as consummatory as heterosexual. He notes that as the Roman Catholic Church has deepened its understanding of the involuntary—that is, in some sense genetic—basis of homosexuality, it has attempted to keep homosexuals in the church as objects of affection and nurture, while banning homosexual acts as perverse.

But this, though better than nothing, will not work, Sullivan writes. To show why, he adduces an analogy to a sterile person. Such a person is permitted to serve in the military or enter an unproductive marriage; why not homosexuals? If homosexuals marry without procreation, they are no different (he suggests) from a sterile man or woman who marries without hope of procreation. Yet people, I think, want the form observed even when the practice varies; a sterile marriage, whether from choice or necessity, remains a marriage of a man and a woman. To this Sullivan offers essentially an aesthetic response. Just as albinos remind us of the brilliance of color and genius teaches us about moderation, homosexuals are a "natural foil" to the heterosexual union, "a variation that does not eclipse the theme." Moreover, the threat posed by the foil to the theme is slight as compared to the threats posed by adultery, divorce, and prostitution. To be consistent, Sullivan once again reminds us, society would have to ban adulterers from the military as it now bans confessed homosexuals.

But again this misses the point. It would make more sense to ask why an alternative to marriage should be invented and praised when we are having enough trouble maintaining the institution at all. Suppose that gay or lesbian marriage were authorized; rather than producing a "natural foil" that would "not eclipse the theme," I suspect such a move would call even more seriously into question the role of marriage at a time when the threats to it, ranging from single-parent families to common divorces, have hit record highs. Kenneth Minogue recently wrote of Sullivans's book that support for homosexual marriage would strike most people as "mere parody," one that could further weaken an already strained institution.

To me, the chief limitation of Sullivan's view is that it presupposes that marriage would have the same, domesticating, effect on homosexual members as it has on heterosexuals, while leaving the latter largely unaffected. Those are very large assumptions that no modern society has ever tested.

Nor does it seem plausible to me that a modern society resists homosexual marriages entirely out of irrational prejudice. Marriage is a union, sacred to most, that unites a man and woman together for life. It is a sacrament of the Catholic Church and central to every other faith. Is it out of misinformation that every modern society has embraced this view and rejected the alternative? Societies differ greatly in their attitude toward the income people may have, the relations among their various races, and the distribution of political power. But they differ scarcely at all over the distinctions between heterosexual and homosexual couples. The former are overwhelmingly preferred over the latter. The reason, I believe, is that these distinctions involve the nature of marriage and thus the very meaning—even more, the very possibility—of society. . . .

⁂

Let us assume for the moment that a chance to live openly and legally with another homosexual is desirable. To believe that, we must set aside biblical injunctions, a difficult matter in a profoundly religious nation. But suppose we manage the diversion, perhaps on the grounds that if most Americans skip church, they can as readily avoid other errors of (possibly) equal magnitude.

Then we must ask on what terms the union shall be arranged. There are two alternatives—marriage or domestic partnership.

Sullivan acknowledges the choice, but disparages the domestic-partnership laws that have evolved in some foreign countries and in some American localities. His reasons, essentially conservative ones, are that domestic partnerships are too easily formed and too easily broken. Only real marriages matter. But—aside from the fact that marriage is in serious decline, and that only slightly more than half of all marriages performed in the United States this year will be between never-before-married heterosexuals—what is distinctive about marriage is that it is an institution created to sustain child-rearing. Whatever losses it has suffered in *this* respect, its function remains what it has always been.

The role of raising children is entrusted in principle to married heterosexual couples because after much experimentation—several thousand years, more or less—we have found nothing else that works as well. Neither a gay nor a lesbian couple can of its own resources produce a child; another party must be involved. What do we call this third party? A friend? A sperm or egg bank? An anonymous donor? There is no settled language for even describing, much less approving of, such persons.

Suppose we allowed homosexual couples to raise children who were created out of a prior heterosexual union or adopted from someone else's heterosexual contact. What would we think of this? There is very little research on the matter. Charlotte Patterson's famous essay, "Children of Gay and Lesbian Parents" (*Journal of Child and Development,* 1992), begins by conceding that the existing studies focus on children born into a heterosexual union that ended in divorce or that was transformed when the mother or father "came out" as a homosexual. Hardly any research has been done on children acquired at the outset by a homosexual couple. We therefore have no way of knowing how they would behave. And even if we had such studies, they might tell us rather little unless they were conducted over a very long period of time.

But it is one thing to be born into an apparently heterosexual family and then many years later to learn that one of your parents is homosexual. It is quite another to be acquired as an infant from an adoption agency or a parent-for-hire and learn from the first years of life that you are, because of your family's position, radically different from almost all other children you will meet. No one can now say how grievous this would be. We know that young children tease one another unmercifully; adding this dimension does not seem to be a step in the right direction.

Of course, homosexual "families," with or without children, might be rather few in number. Just how few, it is hard to say. Perhaps Sullivan himself would marry, but, given the great tendency of homosexual males to be promiscuous, many more like him would not, or if they did, would not marry with as much seriousness.

That is problematic in itself. At one point, Sullivan suggests that most homosexuals would enter a marriage "with as much (if not more) commitment as heterosexuals." Toward the end of this book, however, he seems to withdraw from so optimistic a view. He admits that the label "virtually" in the title of his book is deliberately ambiguous, because homosexuals as a group are *not* "normal." At another point, he writes that the "openness of the contract" between two homosexual males means that such a union will in fact be more durable than a heterosexual marriage because the contract contains an *"understanding of the need for extramarital outlets"* (emphasis added). But no such "understanding" exists in heterosexual marriage; to suggest that it might in homosexual ones is tantamount to saying that we are now referring to two different kinds of arrangements. To justify this difference, perhaps, Sullivan adds that the very "lack of children" will give "gay couples greater freedom." Freedom for what? Freedom, I think, to do more of those things that heterosexual couples do less of because they might hurt the children.

❧

The courts in Hawaii and in the nation's capital must struggle with all these issues under the added encumbrance of a contemporary outlook that makes law the search for rights, and responsibility the recognition of rights. Indeed, thinking of laws about marriage as documents that confer or withhold rights is itself an error of fundamental importance—one that the highest court in Hawaii has already committed. "Marriage," it wrote, "is a state-conferred legal-partnership status, the existence of which gives rise to a multiplicity of rights and benefits...." A state-conferred legal partnership? To lawyers, perhaps; to mankind, I think not....

Our challenge is to find a way of formulating a policy with respect to homosexual unions that is not the result of a reflexive act of judicial rights-conferring, but is instead a considered expression of the moral convictions of a people.

# POSTSCRIPT

## Should Gay Marriage Be Legalized?

**S**ince Hawaii backed down from the likelihood that it would become the first state to permit same-sex marriage, the federal Defense of Marriage Act did not have to be invoked by states that did not want to fulfill the Constitution's requirement that every state give "Full Faith and Credit" to the laws of every other state. But Vermont's recent action providing legal sanction for same-sex "civil unions" serves as a reminder that the questions raised in these selections have not been finally answered.

Sullivan's defense of gay marriage has been developed at great length by William N. Eskridge in *The Case for Same-Sex Marriage: From Sexual Liberty to Civilized Commitment* (Free Press, 1996). The legal aspects of same-sex marriage are examined by Mark Strasser in *The Challenge of Same-Sex Marriages: Federalist Principles and Constitutional Protections* (Praeger, 1999). Essays arguing opposing positions can be found in Andrew Sullivan et al., eds., *Same Sex Marriage, Pro and Con: A Reader* (Vintage Books, 1997). A variety of viewpoints will be found in the essays in Robert M. Baird and Stuart E. Rosenbaum, eds., *Same-Sex Marriage: The Moral and Legal Debate* (Prometheus Books, 1997).

Although much public discussion has focused on this issue, those who defend same-sex marriage believe that it must be seen in a larger social context. They argue that this is just one area in which male and female homosexuals are denied equal rights. Shortly after President Bill Clinton took office, he confronted the issue of homosexuals in the armed forces. It was, at least for the time, resolved with a government policy of "don't ask" for superior officers and "don't tell" for homosexual soldiers. The ambiguities inherent in the practice of such a policy has resulted in varying interpretations by military commands and challenges in various courts. It has not resulted in a reduction of the forced withdrawal of homosexuals from the armed forces.

Most law-abiding Americans recoiled from the details of the 1999 murder of Matthew Shepard, a 21-year-old homosexual student at the University of Wyoming who was pistol-whipped before being tied spread-eagle to a fence and left to die in freezing temperatures. Supporters of same-sex marriage argue that the Defense of Marriage Act contributed to a climate of irrational homophobia that was also created by "don't ask, don't tell" policies in the military, an ad campaign that maintains that homosexuality can be "cured," and opposition to civil rights statutes for homosexuals. Critics of same-sex marriage are outraged that their opposition to changing the ancient and spiritual definition of marriage can be linked to an increase in gay-bashing violence, which they abhor.

# ISSUE 18

## Are Americans Taxed Too Much?

**YES: Amity Shlaes**, from *The Greedy Hand: How Taxes Drive Americans Crazy and What to Do About It* (Random House, 1999)

**NO: Citizens for Tax Justice**, from *Are Americans Overtaxed?* (May 24, 2000)

### ISSUE SUMMARY

**YES:** *Wall Street Journal* editorial writer Amity Shlaes maintains that the federal income tax is too high, too complex, and too biased against high-income earners.

**NO:** Citizens for Tax Justice, a nonprofit research and advocacy association dedicated to fair taxation, concludes that taxes are relatively low, fair in distributing the tax burden, and necessary to pay for essential programs.

$B$enjamin Franklin is credited with having first said, "In this world nothing is certain but death and taxes." That does not mean that we have to look forward to either one. When the colonists confronted the collection of taxes by Great Britain, they proclaimed "No taxation without representation" and moved toward revolution and the creation of the United States.

In 1912 the Sixteenth Amendment to the Constitution was adopted, enabling the federal government to levy taxes directly on income. The following year Congress adopted a graduated income tax, ranging from a 1 percent tax on individuals and businesses earning over $4,000 (most Americans did not earn that much) up to 6 percent on incomes over $500,000. Since then, tax rates have gone up and down, but some measure of progressivity—higher rates for higher incomes—has been retained. However, every change in the tax code has produced new deductions, concessions, and loopholes that benefit some groups to the disadvantage of others, lengthen and complicate the law, and stimulate a major tax-filing occupation for accountants and tax lawyers.

No one likes taxes, but upon reflection most Americans are likely to agree with Supreme Court Justice Oliver Wendell Holmes, Jr., that "taxes are what we pay for civilized society." No other way has been devised to pay for such essential services as public education, police and fire protection, roads and public transport, and the military defense of the nation. So the question is not whether or not we should be taxed but how and how much.

By the standards of other nations, American taxes are low. In fact, every other industrial nation has higher rates of taxation, except Japan, whose tax rate is about the same as that of the United States. Nevertheless, Americans appear to respond more favorably than citizens of other countries to proposals to lower taxes. When presidential candidate George Bush in 1988 said, "Read my lips: No new taxes," he enhanced his prospects for election. But when then–president Bush ran for reelection in 1992, his broken promise contributed to his defeat.

It is a rare candidate for high office who will suggest the desirability of raising taxes. At the same time, no serious candidate for the presidency is likely to propose the abandonment of Social Security, Medicare, or other costly programs that have become fixed and probably irrevocable parts of national public policy. When Republican presidential candidate George W. Bush in 2000 proposed nearly $500 billion in tax cuts over the next five years, Democratic presidential candidate Al Gore responded by charging that a tax cut of that magnitude would threaten the survival of Social Security.

Despite the public's general dislike of taxes, difficult and divisive questions need to be resolved. What kinds of taxes should be imposed? While the federal personal income tax is the most important source of government revenue, the federal government and the states employ other types of taxes, including sales, use, property, inheritance, and tariff taxes. Unlike the progressive income tax, there is not much difference between the sales tax people with different incomes pay at the supermarket checkout counter or the gasoline tax that they pay at the gas pump.

But should the income tax be progressive? As the following selections demonstrate, views differ. Given the reduction of the maximum income tax rates in recent decades, there are those who deplore the fact that the system is not as progressive as it had been. On the other hand, in recent years there has been a movement to adopt a flat tax—that is, a single rate of taxation on all income. The appeal of a flat tax is its simplicity, elimination of special interest tax deductions, and, its supporters argue, the ability of high-income earners to invest more and ultimately pay higher taxes. Opponents of a flat tax object to the abandonment of a progressive rate of taxation and the widening of the gap between high- and low-income earners.

How people should be taxed is closely linked to how much people should be taxed. Those who believe that "that government governs best that governs least" would cut government and taxes. Those who would have the American government undertake new roles and responsibilities would disagree. In the following selections, Amity Shlaes maintains that the American tax system is ill-advised with respect to a withholding tax that takes earnings before wage-earners receive them, a tax code that is too complex, a tax rate that is too high, and a tax burden that reduces the productivity and ultimate tax payments of the rich. Citizens for Tax Justice supports the present system because tax revenues cannot be reduced, tax revenues are modest, and tax rates are progressive, although not as progressive as they could be.

# The Greedy Hand

The father of the modern American state was a pipe-puffing executive at R. H. Macy & Co. named Beardsley Ruml. Ruml, the department store's treasurer, also served as chairman of the board of directors of the Federal Reserve Bank of New York and advisor to President Franklin Roosevelt during World War II. In those years Washington was busy marshaling the forces of the American economy to halt Japan and Germany. In 1942, not long after Pearl Harbor, lawmakers raised income taxes radically, with rates that aimed to capture twice as much revenue as in the previous year. They also imposed the income tax on tens of millions of Americans who had never been acquainted with the levy before. The change was so dramatic that the chroniclers of that period have coined a phrase to describe it. They say that the "class tax" became a "mass tax."

The new rates were law. But Americans were ill-prepared to face a new and giant tax bill. A Gallup poll from the period showed that only some 5 million of the 34 million people who were subject to the tax for the first time were saving to make their payment. In those days, March 15, not April 15, was the nation's annual tax deadline.

The Treasury nervously launched a huge public relations campaign to remind Americans of their new duties. A Treasury Department poster exhorted citizens: "You are one of 50,000,000 Americans who must fill out an income tax form by March 15. DO IT NOW!" For wartime theatergoers, Disney had prepared an animated short film featuring citizen Donald Duck laboring over his tax return beside a bottle of aspirin. Donald claimed exemptions and dependent credits for Huey, Dewey, and Louie.

As March 15, 1943 neared, though, it became clear that many citizens still were not filing returns. Henry Morgenthau, the Treasury secretary, confronted colleagues about the nightmarish prospect of mass tax evasion: "Suppose we have to go out and try to arrest five million people?"

## The Macy's Model

Enter Ruml, man of ideas. At Macy's, he had observed that customers didn't like big bills. They preferred making payments bit by bit, in the installment plan, even if they had to pay for the pleasure with interest. So Ruml devised a plan,

From Amity Shlaes, *The Greedy Hand: How Taxes Drive Americans Crazy and What to Do About It* (Random House, 1999). Copyright © 1998 by Amity Shlaes. Reprinted by permission of Random House, Inc.

which he unfolded to his colleagues at the Federal Reserve and to anyone in Washington who would listen. The government would get business to do its work, collecting taxes for it. Employers would retain a percentage of taxes from workers every week—say, 20 percent—and forward it directly to Washington's war chest. This would hide the size of the new taxes from the worker. No longer would the worker ever have to look his tax bill square in the eye. Workers need never even see the money they were forgoing. Withholding as we know it today was born.

This was more than change, it was transformation. Government would put its hand into the taxpayer's pocket and grab its share of tax—without asking.

Ruml hadn't invented withholding. His genius was to make its introduction palatable by adding a powerful sweetener: the federal government would offer a tax amnesty for the previous year, allowing confused and indebted citizens to start on new footing. It was the most ambitious bait-and-switch plan in America's history.

Ruml advertised his project as a humane effort to smooth life in the disruption of the war. He noted it was a way to help taxpayers out of the habit of carrying income tax debt, debt that he characterized as "a pernicious fungus permeating the structure of things." The move was also patriotic. At Macy's, executives had found that a "young man in the comptroller's office who was making $75 or $100 [a week was] called into the navy at a salary of $2,600 and we had to get together and take care of his income tax for him." The young man, Ruml saw, would face a tax bill for a higher income at a time when he was earning less money in the service of his country. This Ruml deemed "an impossible situation."

Ruml had several reasons for wagering that his project would work. One was that Americans, smarting from the Japanese assault, were now willing to sacrifice more than at any other point in memory. The second was that the federal government would be able to administer withholding—six successful years of Social Security showed that the government, for the first time ever, was able to handle such a mass program of revenue collection. The third was packaging. He called his program not "collection at source" or "withholding," two technical terms for what he was doing. Instead he chose a zippier name: "pay as you go." And most important of all, there was the lure of the tax amnesty.

The policy thinkers of the day embraced the Ruml arrangement. This was an era in which John Maynard Keynes dominated the world of economics. The Keynesians placed enormous faith in government. The only thing they liked about the war was that it demonstrated to the world all the miracles that Big Government could work. The Ruml plan would give them the wherewithal to have their projects even, they sensed, after the war ended. Keynesianism also said high taxes were crucial to controlling inflation. The Keynesians saw withholding as the right tool for getting those necessary high taxes.

Conservatives played their part in the drama. Among withholding's backers was the man who was later to become the world's leading free-market economist, Milton Friedman. Decades after the war, Friedman called for the abolition of the withholding system. In his memoirs he wrote that "we concentrated single-mindedly on promoting the war effort. We gave next to no consideration to any longer-run consequences. It never occurred to me at the time that I was helping to develop machinery that would make possible a government that I would come to criticize severely as too large, too intrusive, too destructive of freedom. Yet, that was precisely what I was doing." With an almost audible sigh, Friedman added: "There is an important lesson here. It is far easier to introduce a government program than to get rid of it."

Such questions, though, had no place in the mind of a nation under attack. At the moment what seemed most important was that voters accepted the Ruml plan. Randolph Paul, a Treasury Department official and Ruml critic, wrote resignedly that "his plan had political appeal. Though he conceived the plan as getting people out of debt to the government, the public thought that Ruml had found a very white rabbit"—a magic trick—"which would somehow lighten their tax load."

❦

... Adam Smith described the "invisible hand," the hand of free commerce that brings magic order and harmony to our lives. Thomas Paine wrote of another hand, all too visible and intrusive: "the greedy hand of government, thrusting itself into every corner and crevice of industry." Today the invisible hand is a very busy one. Markets are wider and freer than ever, and we profit from that by living better than before. But the "greedy hand of government" is also at work. Indeed, in relative terms, the greedy hand has grown faster than the invisible hand. In the late 1990s, economists noted with astonishment that federal taxes made up one-fifth of the economy, a rate higher than at any time in American history outside of war. We can not assign the blame for changes of such magnitude to Beardsley Ruml, who was, after all, not much more than a New Deal package man. The real force here is not even withholding, whatever its power. Behind Ruml's withholding lurks Paine's greedy hand.

... Today, more than half of the budget goes to social transfers mandated by expensive programs whose value many Americans question. Working citizens sense that someone is getting something, but that someone is often not they.

The avid tax haters who pop up occasionally in the news are the expression of this national unease. Their froth-mouthed manifestos strike us as extreme—how many of us truly want to "kill the IRS"?—but they reflect something that all Americans feel to some degree. Even the most moderate of us often feel a tick of sympathy when we hear the shouts of the tax haters. We think of our forefathers who felt compelled to rebel against the Crown for "imposing Taxes on us without our consent." We know we live in a democracy, and so must have chosen this arrangement. Yet nowadays we too find ourselves feeling that taxes are imposed on us "without our consent."

Washington doesn't necessarily recognize the totality of this tax frustration. The purview of the House Ways and Means Committee is limited to federal taxes, and so the committee writes tax law as if the federal income tax were the only tax in the country. The commissions that monitor Social Security concern themselves only with the solvency of Social Security, and so ignore the consequences of raising payroll taxes, or taxing pensions, at a time when income taxes are already high. Old programs with outdated aims stay in place. Newer ones, added piecemeal, often conflict with the old.

"Rube Goldberg machine," "unstoppable contraption"—none of the stock phrases adequately captures the complication that is our tax structure. As William E. Simon, a former Treasury secretary, once said, "The nation should have a tax system which looks like someone designed it on purpose." . . .

✧

Americans today are more prosperous than we have ever been. As a nation, we have come very far, so far that even our past is beginning to look different. In the 1960s, 1970s, and even the 1980s, we took Big Government America, the America of the postwar period, to be the only America, an America that permanently supplanted something antiquated. This conviction strengthened when we considered the enormous troubles that plagued us in those decades. Who else but government could end the underclass, right the wrongs of Vietnam, combat inflation?

We can see now that in those years we had a foreshortened view of history. From the heights of our new achievement, we recognize that the Great Society, for all its ideals, was something of an aberration. It is clear now that the self-doubt and gray misgivings of the Vietnam period were, in their way, just a momentary interruption. The inflation of the 1970s was an acute and terrible problem but a short-lived one. Our famous deficit agony—which so many commentators and foreigners alleged would bring us down—has, at least for the moment, receded. Today we are in many ways more like the America of Andrew Jackson or even Thomas Jefferson than we are like the America of Jimmy Carter.

This change was the result of enormous and serious work. We developed microchips and computers that secured our global economic dominance. We started the welfare state and then, when we saw it wasn't working, successfully ended it. We grew a stock market that will provide pensions for the baby boom and beyond. Serious challenges loom ahead. Unpredictable rogue states threaten our national security; the economy will not always live up to its 1990s boom. But we understand now that the key to sustaining our prosperity is recognizing that we are our own best providers. Thinkers from left, center, and right agree: we don't need a nanny state.

This American confidence is not new. It is simply a homecoming to older ideals, ideals that we held through most of our history. Self-reliance is the ultimate American tradition. Even through a good part of the Depression "no handouts" was Americans' self-imposed rule. We are coming to a new appreciation of what Tocqueville admiringly called "self-interest, rightly understood."

Yet we are still saddled with our tax structure, the unwieldy artifact of an irrelevant era.

Unburdening ourselves is not easy, but it is something we have in our power to do. Our impasse, in fact, contains the outline of its own solution, if only we allow ourselves to look at it clearly. What, exactly, does our long struggle with Paine's greedy hand tell us?

*Taxes have to be visible.*    Beardsley Ruml's trap worked because it made taxes invisible. No one today willingly gives a third or a half of his income into a strange hand; we only pay our taxes now because the trap locked shut long ago. We never see our tax bill in its entirety except during the madness of filing season.

When we rewrite our arrangement with government, we need to write into it a tax structure that is clear and comprehensible, whose outlines we can see and consider whenever we choose.

*Taxes have to be simple.*    The tax code is a monster of complexity, but it doesn't have to be. When rules are added to rules, the change may benefit certain classes, but they hurt the rest of us. The best thing is to settle on one system, even if someone shouts that it's not "fair" to everyone.

*Taxes are for revenue.*    For fifty years we have used taxes to steer behavior. Indeed, politicians often used the argument that they were promoting social good through the tax code as window dressing for their real aim: getting at the revenue. None of us likes the result. We are responsible for our own fate; let government take what we choose to give it and then retreat.

*Taxes have to be lower.*    We have managed to achieve prosperity notwithstanding high taxes. But that prosperity would have been greater without those taxes. The microchip, in its way, has allowed us to postpone our date with tax reform.

But epochal transformations like the computer revolution, or the Industrial Revolution for that matter, cannot be counted on to come every decade. Taxes will slow our economy if we don't bring them down to rates that allow us to sustain desirable growth.

*We don't have to load extra taxes on the rich.*    We've learned that a tax system that punishes the rich also punishes the rest of us. Those who have money should pay taxes like everyone else. In fact the rich already carry more of the tax burden than any other income group. Yet history—the history of the 1980s in particular—has shown an amazing thing—that lower rates on the rich produce more revenue from them.

Progressivity has had its day. Let us move on to a tax system that is more worthy of us, one that makes sense for the country.

*It's time to privatize Social Security.*    Many of the core tax problems we face today are in reality Social Security problems. Markets have taught us that they can do a better job than government in providing public pensions. We should privatize a portion of Social Security—at least three of the percentage points that individuals carry.

The only thing to guard against is a privatization that is not a true privatization. When government enters the stock market on behalf of citizens, as many advocates of Social Security privatization would like, that is not privatization. That is expanding the public sector at the cost of the private sector. An office in government that invests on behalf of citizens, as many are proposing, is an office open to enormous moral hazard. To understand this you need only to consider what would happen if the chairman of the Securities and Exchange Commission directly controlled a few hundred million shares of blue-chip stocks.

Individuals need to control their own accounts, just as they control the rest of their money. Government guarantees of returns are also guarantees of disaster. One need only look to our recent history with savings and loans to see that. Raising the ceiling on federal insurance of S & L accounts led to that disaster by giving S & L directors license without accountability. The cost ran into the hundreds of billions, but it was far lower than the cost a government guarantee on privatized Social Security would be.

*Local is good.* The enduring lesson of our schools crisis is that centralizing school finance to the state and federal level has not given us the equity or the academic performance we hoped for. These results have ramifications far beyond schools. The federal government cannot solve everything. Many problems —from school to health care to welfare—are better handled lower down. A wise tax reform is a tax reform that leaves much of the nation's work to the people and the officials they know. Trying to write a federal tax law that addresses all our national problems is a recipe for a repeat of the current trouble.

*We must lock in change.* In the 1980s, through tremendous political and social exertion, the nation joined together to lower tax rates and prune out many of the code's absurdities. Within a few years, Washington had destroyed its own child. This time we must fix our change so the fiddlers can't get at it....

Most Americans are not fire-breathing radicals or Ruby Ridge survivalists. They don't want to "kill the IRS." They just want a common-sense change in the system. And that is what they are telling lawmakers. When Steve LaTourette, a Republican congressman from Ohio, surveyed his constituents, he found that just about half wanted the IRS abolished. But a full three quarters wanted to see the tax code itself abolished. They saw that the code, not the bureaucrats, was the problem.

The second part of the program is to make the change truly permanent through a constitutional amendment. Our nation's last experience of trying to pass a significant-seeming constitutional amendment—the Equal Rights Amendment—was a bitter one. It soured Washington on amendments in general. Hesitation over amendments goes a long way toward explaining the current Republican foundering.

A constitutional amendment that calls for limiting federal taxes, including Social Security, to 25 percent of our income, or even a lower share, would be an important first step out of the logjam. For one thing, states would have to ratify the change, and that would allow us to have a much needed national discussion about taxes. Citizens would have to consider what lawmakers were proposing. This would give voters a chance to get around the lobbies and politicians who have kept the tax debate to themselves. It would get us all back into the discussion.

The third step is to realize that as a people we want to pay taxes. Roosevelt called taxes "the dues we pay for organized society." We still feel that way.

But people want a tax system that doesn't intrude on our private lives while it collects those dues; and we want those dues to be spent in a reasonable, limited way. We want a tax code that, to quote former Treasury secretary William Simon again, looks as if somebody designed it on purpose. Not a giant machine that collects our money merely to feed the monster.

# NO ⤶

Citizens for Tax Justice

# Are Americans Overtaxed?

Are Americans overtaxed? Compared to what? one might ask. Taxes, of course, are a function of public services. If we want the latter, we have to put up with the former. And for the most part, these days the public seems to think the trade-off is worth it.

Federal taxes pay for retirement security for the aged, disability insurance, support for the widowed and orphaned, military might, law enforcement, roads, environmental protection, national parks and a host of other programs, services, protections and obligations that the private sector is ill-equipped to provide. While most Americans inevitably disagree with particular things their tax dollars support and some tax money is clearly misspent, the public programs that most of our tax dollars fund are widely supported.

This shouldn't be surprising. We live in a representative democracy and make our decisions on taxation and spending at the ballot box. Large programs can survive only if the majority supports them. Some small programs can exist with only minority support, but only if a wide range of such programs exist so that a majority gets something they want.

Although most federal programs are popular, federal taxes generally are not. It's not irrational that most people would prefer to get something for nothing. But in the real world government cannot provide the services the public wants without the revenue to pay for them. We tried cutting taxes without reducing outlays in the 1980s, and ended up adding $3 trillion to the national debt. We're paying the price for that now with fully 20 percent of the non-Social Security federal budget going to pay interest.

At least for now, however, the days of enormous budget deficits appear to be behind us. For the first time since 1969, the federal government is operating with a budget surplus. This feat hasn't been accomplished painlessly. Federal taxes as a share of gross domestic product are at a post-war high and government spending as a share of the economy is at its lowest point since 1973.

From Citizens for Tax Justice, *Are Americans Overtaxed?* (May 24, 2000). Copyright © 2000 by Citizens for Tax Justice. Reprinted by permission.

Despite having to pay for the excesses of the past, the federal government is a good deal for Americans. For better or worse, our taxes and our government services are much lower than in other industrialized nations. More important, because the federal tax system is progressive, government is a fair deal for most Americans.

*Figure 1*

### Federal Spending and Revenues As Shares of GDP

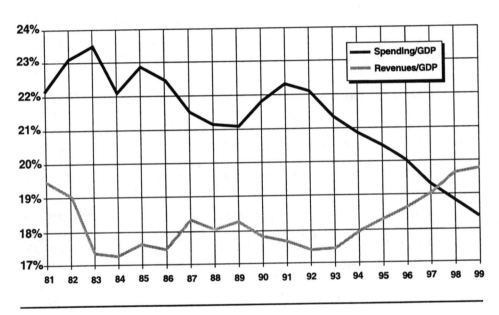

*Sources:* Congressional Budget Office; CTJ.

## America's Taxes Compared to the Rest of the World

In a recent survey of 29 industrialized countries in Europe, North America and Asia, the United States ranked 25th in total national and local taxes as a share of Gross Domestic Product.[1] Taxes in the 29 countries ranged from a high of 52.2 percent of GDP in Denmark to a low of 16.3 percent in Mexico. Total United States taxes (including federal, state and local) were 28.5 percent of GDP—well below the European Union average of 42.4 percent and the 29-country average of 37.7 percent.

Of course, Americans get less in public services because they pay less in taxes. Health insurance and higher education stand out as services that are commonly provided by governments in other countries to a much greater degree than in the United States.

# Who Pays Federal Taxes?

Tax rankings as a share of GDP do not necessarily tell us how much typical citizens pay in taxes. For example, middle-income people living in a country with relatively low overall taxes might rightfully feel overtaxed if that country's taxes fell disproportionately on people in the middle of the income scale.

Fortunately, federal taxes in the United States are progressive. Well-off people pay a greater share of their income in taxes than do low- and middle-income taxpayers. This makes the trade-off between taxes and public services a fair one for most Americans.

To understand who pays federal taxes, we need first to look at the three main kinds of federal taxes we pay. The largest share of federal tax revenues, 49 percent, comes from personal income taxes. Social Security and Medicare payroll taxes raise 33 percent and the corporate income tax contributes 10 percent. An assortment of other taxes, mostly excise taxes, customs duties and estate taxes, fills in the remaining eight percent of federal tax revenues.

# The Federal Personal Income Tax

The federal personal income tax is the key to our progressive federal tax system. Several features of the federal personal income tax make it progressive.

*The standard deduction and personal exemptions are worth more to middle- and low-income families than to the well-off.*   (For married couples this year, the standard deduction is $7,350 and the personal exemption is $2,800 per taxpayer and dependent.) For example, a family of four's $11,200 in personal exemptions exempt almost a quarter of the income of a family making $45,000, but exempt only 10 percent of the income of a four-person family earning $112,000. (For those with very high incomes, personal exemptions are phased-out entirely, and are worth nothing.)

*Progressive tax rates increase as income rises.*   For tax year 2000, marginal income tax rates range from 15 percent on the first portion of income subject to tax up to 39.6 percent on those with the highest incomes. Because the rate brackets apply to income after deductions and exemptions are taken, married couples, for example, typically don't start paying the 28 percent tax rate on any of their income until they make more than about $68,000.

The "marginal" tax rates shown in [Table 2] apply only to the portion of income in each bracket. Thus, even though a married couple with total income of, say, $75,000 may be "in" the 28 percent bracket, the couple pays a 15 percent tax rate on its first $43,850 of taxable income, and pays the 28 percent rate only on the remainder—in this example typically about $6,000. The marginal tax rate approach takes much of the bite out of the higher tax rates even for the minority of taxpayers affected by them.

*Table 1*

### Federal Taxes in 1999 by Income Group, As Shares of Cash Income

| Income Group | Average Income | Taxes We Pay on the Cash Income We See | | | Taxes That Lower Our Pretax Income Before We See It | | | Taxes on Spending (Excise Taxes) | Taxes on Wealth (Estate & Gift) | ALL FEDERAL TAXES |
|---|---|---|---|---|---|---|---|---|---|---|
| | | Personal Income Taxes | Worker Payroll Taxes | Total on Reported Earnings | Employer Payroll Taxes | Corporate Income Taxes | Total That Reduce Earnings | | | |
| Lowest 20% | $8,600 | -3.8% | 4.3% | 0.5% | 3.8% | 0.9% | 4.7% | 3.7% | 0.0% | 8.8% |
| Second 20% | 18,800 | 1.3% | 5.4% | 6.7% | 4.9% | 1.2% | 6.1% | 2.3% | 0.0% | 15.2% |
| Middle 20% | 31,100 | 6.0% | 5.7% | 11.8% | 5.2% | 1.5% | 6.7% | 1.5% | 0.0% | 19.9% |
| Fourth 20% | 50,700 | 9.4% | 6.2% | 15.6% | 5.7% | 1.5% | 7.2% | 1.0% | 0.0% | 23.8% |
| Next 15% | 86,800 | 12.9% | 6.0% | 18.9% | 5.5% | 1.7% | 7.2% | 0.8% | 0.0% | 26.9% |
| Next 4% | 183,000 | 17.4% | 4.3% | 21.7% | 3.4% | 3.4% | 6.9% | 0.3% | 0.3% | 29.1% |
| Top 1% | 915,000 | 24.6% | 1.3% | 25.9% | 1.0% | 7.8% | 8.8% | 0.2% | 2.2% | 37.1% |
| ALL | $50,800 | 12.7% | 4.9% | 17.6% | 4.3% | 2.9% | 7.2% | 1.0% | 0.4% | 26.2% |

*Note:* Taxes on reported earnings include federal personal income taxes and Social Security & Medicare payroll taxes (workers and self-employed). Taxes that reduce pretax income include employer payroll taxes and corporate income taxes. Excise taxes include taxes on gasoline, cigarettes, etc. Estate & gift taxes apply to very large transfers of wealth. Tax rates in the top groups are substantially overstated due to the exclusion of unrealized capital gains, inside build-up on pensions, etc. from income.

*Table 2*

---

### Federal Person Income Tax Rates on Married Couples in 2000

| Taxable Income (after all exemptions and deductions) | Marginal Tax Rate |
|:---:|:---:|
| First $43,850 | 15% |
| From $43,850 to $105,950 | 28% |
| From $105,950 to $161,450 | 31% |
| From $161,450 to $288,350 | 36% |
| Above $288,350 | 39.6% |

---

*Tax credits are targeted to lower- and middle-income families with children.* After the tax rates are applied to taxable income, many taxpayers can use credits to reduce their tax liability. The single largest credit is the earned-income tax credit (EITC), which is available to lower-income families with earned income. Families with children receive higher EITC credits than the childless. Eligibility in 2000 for the EITC is phased-out for families with children between $12,690 and $31,150 of income. The maximum benefit is $2,353 for families with one child and $3,888 for families with two or more children. The EITC is refundable, so families can receive payments above and beyond their federal income tax liability. The second biggest tax credit, also for families with children, equals $500 per child, and is generally available to families making between $25,000 and $100,000.

Because of these progressive features of the income tax, taxpayers in the middle 20 percent pay only 6 percent of their income in personal income taxes. Due to the EITC, the poorest 20 percent actually have a *negative* tax rate of −3.8 percent. On the other hand, taxpayers in the wealthiest one percent of the income scale—those with an average income of $915,000—pay 24.6 percent of their income in federal personal income tax.

Notwithstanding the progressivity of the income tax, every year around April 15th anti-tax groups like to tell Americans that they "work for the government" for a significant portion of the year before they get any benefit from their earnings. That's a very odd concept, since what we pay in taxes comes back to us in government programs that most of us support and all of us benefit from.

But even by the "tax-freedom day" standard, the income tax looks pretty good for most taxpayers. For the lowest-income 20 percent, "income-tax freedom day" is all year long, since there is no federal income tax on the lowest earners. For the second 20 percent, the typical "income-tax freedom day" came on January 3rd in 1999. And for the median-income taxpayer, "income-tax freedom day" came on January 21st.

*Table 3*

**Dates Federal Income Taxes Were Fully Paid in 1999**

| Income Group | Date |
| --- | --- |
| Lowest 20% | No tax |
| Second 20% | Jan 4 |
| Middle 20% | Jan 21 |
| Fourth 20% | Feb 3 |
| Next 15% | Feb 16 |
| Next 4% | Mar 4 |
| Top 1% | Mar 30 |

Although the personal income tax is progressive, it has some very significant loopholes for the well-off. For example, capital gains—income from the sale of stocks and other investments—are taxed at much lower rates than income from wages and other sources. This tax break overwhelmingly benefits those with very high incomes, who have most of the capital gains. Getting rid of tax loopholes such as this and using the resulting revenues to help middle- and low-income families would make the income tax both more progressive and much simpler. But even without such reforms, the overall progressivity of the income tax makes it a very good deal for most Americans.

## Social Security and Medicare Taxes

The second largest source of federal revenues is payroll taxes which are used to pay for Social Security and Medicare. For individuals, the Social Security tax is 6.2 percent of wages up to $76,200 in 2000 (this "cap" is adjusted upwards each year for wage growth). Employers also pay 6.2 percent on wages, for a total Social Security payroll tax of 12.4 percent on wages up to the cap. Self-employed people, who have no employer, pay the full 12.4 percent rate on their earnings.

The Medicare tax is not capped. It adds another 1.45 percent to both the employee and employer sides of the tax, and 2.9 percent to the self-employment tax. Thus, up to the wage cap, payroll taxes total 15.3 percent of earnings, and above the cap, they are 2.9 percent.

Unlike the income tax, payroll taxes apply to the first dollar a person earns, exempt investment income, and are mostly capped. As a result, payroll taxes take only 2.3 percent of the total income of the wealthiest one percent of Americans (who get most of their income from non-wage sources). That's much lower than the 10.9 percent effective payroll tax rate that the middle 20 percent pays, and the 8.1 percent of income paid in payroll taxes by the poorest 20 percent.[2]

Many people find the regressive nature of payroll taxes troubling. Indeed, one reason the earned-income tax credit was adopted was to help offset the payroll taxes of lower-income working people. The structure of the payroll tax is consistent, however, with Social Security's role as a retirement insurance program. Better-off workers receive somewhat greater retirement benefits under the program, but those added benefits are not in proportion to the higher taxes they pay in. Conversely, lower-income workers receive benefits that are high relative to the taxes they pay in to the system.

For most Americans, the payroll tax represents the largest single federal tax they pay (counting the portion paid by businesses as ultimately paid by workers). In fact, almost three-quarters of all taxpayers pay more in payroll taxes than in federal income taxes. But Social Security and Medicare are the direct federal government programs from which most Americans benefit the most.

## Corporate Income Tax

The corporate income tax has been a declining source of revenue for many decades. It was cut drastically in the early seventies and again in the early eighties. Although corporate income tax revenues revived a bit after reforms in the mid-eighties and early nineties, the corporate income tax's effectiveness has been greatly reduced. Multinational corporations have become increasingly aggressive at avoiding paying taxes, and the corporate alternative minimum tax, which had served for a while to ensure that large, profitable corporations pay at least some federal income tax has been gutted in recent years.

Assigning the corporate income tax to the owners of corporations, this tax lowers the cash income of the wealthiest one percent of Americans by 7.8 percent. For the middle 20 percent, the rate is 1.5 percent, and for the poorest 20 percent, only 0.9 percent.

## Other Taxes

Finally, there are several smaller kinds of taxes collected by the federal government. The estate tax, which applies only to the most valuable two percent of estates, is an extremely progressive tax.

Conversely, excise taxes, such as those applied per gallon of gas or per pack of cigarettes, are regressive. Although better-off taxpayers may consume as much or more of the taxed items, middle- and low-income taxpayers pay much more in excise taxes as a share of their incomes. Americans in the top one percent of the income scale pay only 0.2 percent of their income in excise taxes. Those in the middle fifth pay 1.5 percent of their earnings in excise taxes, while excise taxes take 3.7 percent of the income of the poorest taxpayers.

*Figure 2*

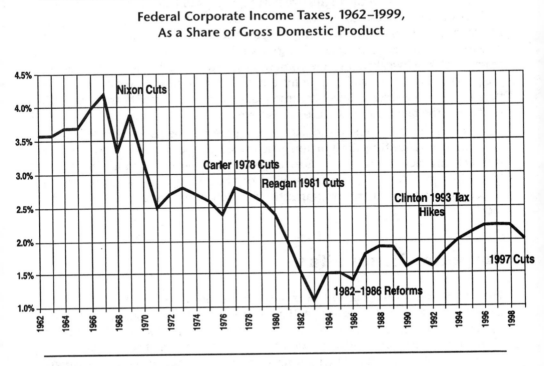

**Federal Corporate Income Taxes, 1962–1999,
As a Share of Gross Domestic Product**

*Source:* Congressional Budget Office

## Adding It All Up

Federal taxes aren't as progressive as they used to be, or as they could be. And state and local taxes aren't progressive at all. But when all the federal taxes are added up, our federal tax system remains progressive—mostly because of the personal income tax. That's only fair, since the people who have the most money have obviously gotten the greatest benefits from our society, and ought to pay more to help support it. Just as important, the well-off have a much greater ability to pay taxes compared to the less fortunate.

Making the well-off pay their fair share through progressive taxes also makes government services considerably less expensive for the rest of us. It's no wonder then, that anti-government ideologues hate progressive taxes. It's precisely because federal taxes are progressive that most of us are not overtaxed compared to what we get from government.

## Notes

1. This survey was of taxes as a share of GDP for 1996. Although the U.S. federal tax burden has increased slightly since 1996, preliminary data shows that well more than half of the surveyed countries also experienced increases in taxes as a share

of GDP, and the few which experienced a relative decline in their tax burdens were not significant enough to affect the ranking of the United States.

2. The reason the payroll tax burden is smaller in the bottom income group than the middle-income group is that a smaller portion of income in this group comes from earned income. There are many retired elderly people in this group as well as families receiving government assistance.

# POSTSCRIPT

## Are Americans Taxed Too Much?

There is an obvious conflict between wanting to keep (and perhaps extend) most of the services and benefits that government provides and simultaneously wanting to lower taxes. There is no free lunch in the federal school lunch program, or the space program, or the National Institutes of Health, or old-age survivors' insurance (Social Security), or a thousand other federal activities. At the same time, Americans are increasingly skeptical about the uses to which their tax money is put. They do not understand how taxes are imposed, and they suspect that somebody else is getting a tax cut at their expense. How else can the increasing size and complexity of the tax code be explained?

The context in which tax policy is debated has changed in recent years. Instead of an annual deficit, the federal government anticipates a surplus in the near future. Should taxes be cut? If so, how and for whom? Should the federal government use this revenue to finance new programs (for example, child care) or expand old programs (for example, pay prescription costs for Medicare patients)? Or should the surplus be used to cut the national debt and thus reduce the interest payments that Congress must appropriate every year?

A critical approach to many so-called reforms of tax policy is taken by Joel Slemroad and Jon Bakija in *Taxing Ourselves: A Citizen's Guide to the Great Debate Over Tax Reform* (MIT Press, 1998). The authors examine the difficulties inherent in various tax reform proposals and conclude that a national sales tax would be difficult to enforce; a broad-based, value-added tax would be highly regressive; a flat tax would also be regressive; and a consumption tax would be more complicated than the present income tax.

The most significant changes in tax policy have occurred in times of crises: the formation of the new nation, the Civil War, World War I, the Great Depression, and World War II. This does not augur well for meaningful tax reform in relatively stable times. The evolution of tax policy is clearly related in W. Elliot Brownlee, *Federal Taxation in America: A Short History* (Cambridge University Press, 1996).

A broad and thoughtful perspective on the relationship of taxation to public policy can be found in *The Government We Deserve: Responsive Democracy and Changing Expectations* by C. Eugene Steuerle, Edward M. Gramlich, Hugh Heclo, and Demetra Smith Nightingale (Urban Institute Press, 1998). In it the authors argue that without restoring citizen-owned government, confidence in public policy and its tax burdens will continue to decline.

## U.S. State Department

View this site for understanding into the workings of a major U.S. executive-branch department. Links explain exactly what the department does, what services it provides, and what it says about U.S. interests around the world, as well as provide other information.

http://www.state.gov

## Marketplace of Political Ideas/University of Houston Libraries

Here is a valuable collection of links to campaign, conservative/liberal perspectives, and political-party sites. There are general political sites, Democratic sites, Republican sites, third-party sites, and much more.

http://info.lib.uh.edu/politics/markind.htm

## NationalJournal.com

This is a major site for information on American government and politics. There are reportage and discussion of campaigns, a congressional calendar, a news archive, and more for politicos and policy makers. Membership is required, however, to access much of the information.

http://nationaljournal.com

## Voice of the Shuttle: Politics and Government Page

This site, created and maintained by Alan Liu of the University of California, Santa Barbara, offers numerous links to political resources on the Internet. In addition to general political resources, categories include general international politics, political theory and philosophy, and political commentary.

http://vos.ucsb.edu/shuttle/politics.html

## American Diplomacy

*American Diplomacy* is an online journal of commentary, analysis, and research on U.S. foreign policy and its results around the world.

http://www.unc.edu/depts/diplomat/

## Foreign Affairs

This page of the well-respected foreign policy journal *Foreign Affairs* is a valuable research tool. It allows users to search the journal's archives and provides indexed access to the field's leading publications, documents, online resources, and so on. Link to dozens of other related Web sites from here too.

http://www.foreignaffairs.org

# PART 4

# America and the World

*W**hat is the role of the United States in world affairs? From what premise—realism or idealism—should American foreign policy proceed? What place in the world does America now occupy, and in what direction is it heading? American government does not operate in isolation from the world community, and the issues in this section are crucial ones indeed.*

- Does China Tend to Threaten World Peace and Stability?

- Should the United States Put More Restrictions on Immigration?

- Is Democracy Desirable for All Nations?

# ISSUE 19

# Does China Tend to Threaten World Peace and Stability?

**YES: Lucian W. Pye**, from "After the Collapse of Communism: The Challenge of Chinese Nationalism and Pragmatism," in Eberhard Sandschneider, ed., *The Study of Modern China* (St. Martin's Press, 1999)

**NO: David M. Lampton**, from "China," *Foreign Policy* (Spring 1998)

## ISSUE SUMMARY

**YES:** Political science professor Lucian W. Pye warns that China is not to be trusted in its economic and political dealings with the United States and other nations.

**NO:** Chinese studies professor David M. Lampton maintains that popular assumptions about China's military, political, and economic objectives are wrong and should be corrected.

In May 2000 the U.S. House of Representatives voted to extend Permanent Normal Trade Relations (PNTR) with China. It was the dramatic climax of a long conflict between opposing groups. President Bill Clinton sponsored PNTR, and he drew on strong support from former presidents Gerald Ford, Jimmy Carter, and George Bush; the leading business interests in the United States; and others who believed that free trade would lead to greater personal freedom in China. Opposed to PNTR were most organized labor, human rights, environmental, and veterans organizations, as well as churches that were critical of China's suppression of religious liberty. Among Clinton's strongest political allies were the Republican leaders of Congress, who had sought his removal from office only a year earlier. His opponents included the Democratic leadership of the House of Representatives.

In a long and emotionally charged debate, the supporters of Permanent Normal Trade Relations argued that closer relations would lead to democratic reforms, that more trade with China would lead to the opening up of a closed society, and that American business owners, workers, and farmers would profit from trade with the one-fifth of the world's population that China represents. If China is treated as a normal country, advocates said, it will in time become one. At the same time, profits for Chinese entrepreneurs and wages for Chinese workers will increase, and the Chinese who prosper from free trade are bound to be less dependent on, and therefore more independent of, the repressive state.

The opponents of PNTR rejected all of these arguments. They cataloged a long list of ways in which China violates truly free trade and suppresses freedom in its continuing imprisonment of political enemies, the use of child and prison labor, the punishment of religious worship by Christians and Buddhists, the flooding of American markets by cheap Chinese goods with no comparable U.S. sales in China, threats to Taiwan (which has sought independence), the conquest of Tibet and the suppression of its culture, and the buildup of Chinese military power. Granting PNTR rewards China when it has made no efforts to change its policies in these areas.

It remained to be seen which view of China and its relationship with America and the world would prevail. What was certain was that China was entering a new stage of its long history. Ancient China was the most advanced and powerful nation in the world. By the nineteenth century, it was victimized and forced to pay tribute to invading European powers. In the twentieth century it was long governed by a dictatorship that had been America's ally in World War II, but a communist revolution put in power the ruling class that governs China today.

By the century's end, China had adopted a kind of pragmatic, state-controlled capitalism that was reaching out to do business with the rest of the world. But it remained a ruthless communist dictatorship, as the world was reminded when Chinese tanks and machine guns crushed student prodemocracy demonstrations in Beijing's Tiananmen Square. After the U.S. State Department criticized China's human rights record, the United States imposed strong sanctions on China in response to China's sale of nuclear-capable technology to Pakistan.

Running for president in 1992, Bill Clinton criticized President George Bush for "coddling criminals" who ran the Chinese government. As president, Clinton came around to a more conciliatory policy and supported most-favored-nation status for China in 1994, opening U.S. markets to Chinese goods. In each of the following years Congress conducted a review of China's human rights and arms proliferation policies in order to determine whether or not to extend favorable trade status, and each year that status was renewed despite the absence of positive change. President Clinton made the move to make America's trade relations with China permanent. But the debate on how America and the world should deal with China is certain to continue.

In the following selections, Lucian W. Pye is harshly critical of China's political motives and behavior and concludes that it must change in fundamental ways in order to improve relations with America. Believing that our understanding of China has been distorted by popular misconceptions of what China wants and does, David M. Lampton takes up each of the indictments of China and seeks to rebut them.

Lucian W. Pye

 **YES**

# After the Collapse of Communism

$\mathbf{B}$ilateral relations between the United States and China are among the most complex and difficult in world politics. It is a relationship stacked with irritants and attractions, clashes but also convergences of interests. Success in managing the relationship is indeed a matter of considerable importance because it is a truism that relations between the one remaining superpower and the largest country in the world will be central for maintaining peace and stability in the Asia-Pacific region. At present, however, Washington and Beijing increasingly confront each other in a state of frustration and barely suppressed aggression, but the craving for better relations is so strong that a single meeting of high officials is enough to raise a chorus of congratulations.

Washington has been torn over what to do about China's pirating of intellectual property rights, its continued flagrant disregard of human rights, its sabre-rattling in the Taiwan Straits, its covert nuclear and missile aid to Pakistan and Iran, and even the smuggling of automatic weapons into America itself. Solutions proposed, such as trade sanctions, would probably hurt American interests more than Chinese, and thus seem foolish, like 'picking up a boulder to drop it on one's own toes'—as the Chinese saying goes. To make matters worse, different agencies of the U.S. government have focused on different issues, and thus there has been little coordination or sense of priorities. Instead of any authoritative guidance for U.S. policy, it is usually the mass media which determine what issues will command attention at any moment. All this means that in Americans' ambivalent love-hate feelings about China, the tilt is ever more towards the latter, to the point that some 65% now have negative views of China.

China, for its part, has been convinced off and on that the United States is a superpower in decline, and thus jealously driven to wanting to 'contain' China, a superpower on the rise. Both reformers and hardliners have been united in the conviction that they must appear firm and bold if they are to make a smooth transition into the post-Deng era. Leading international relations specialists in Beijing were struck with the fact that at the time of the Nixon opening, Washington thought that there was a 'China card' to be played against the Soviet Union. They, of course, knew that China was at the time helpless, indeed truly impotent, because of the chaos of the Cultural Revolution. They

From Lucian W. Pye, "After the Collapse of Communism: The Challenge of Chinese Nationalism and Pragmatism," in Eberhard Sandschneider, ed., *The Study of Modern China* (St. Martin's Press, 1999). Copyright © 1999 by Eberhard Sandschneider. Reprinted by permission of St. Martin's Press, LLC.

could only conclude that the United States must in fact be in serious trouble if it needed China to help balance the Soviet Union. In the years that followed, Chinese analysts have read and believed the literature produced in the United States by the American declinists who argued that America's day was over and that having overreached itself militarily, it was on the downgrade, similar to what happened to Rome and Britain. The Gulf War helped correct this picture of a failed America to some degree, but then the Chinese were quick to pick up on the idea that China is destined in a few years to have the world's largest economy, and thus become truly a world power. Consequently Beijing has become headily self-confident and even boastful—generally ignoring the fact that it has a host of daunting domestic problems. In a spirit of blended glee and indignation, the Chinese rebut every American charge, and point instead to American sins, such as 'dumping its garbage' in China.

In contrast, Washington has remained markedly ambivalent, vacillating between engaging and ignoring China. Its actions have not matched its words, and its words have not reflected careful thought or strong conviction. Statements about China have been made to satisfy various domestic constituencies and have not been backed by actions towards China. Teams of American officials who visit Beijing seem to alternate between beating the drum for greater trade or threatening trade sanctions. In the end though, the one guiding principle seems to be the dream of making money in China's supposedly lucrative market.

The fact that relations with China are troubled should not be surprising, for the relationship has rarely been as close as ritual diplomatic toasts about 'old friendships' would suggest. Except for the brief period of near alliance to fend off the common enemy of Soviet expansionism, there have been just too many fundamental obstacles to make the political relationship as warm as right-thinking people would want it to be. This is particularly disturbing to those Americans who in their private and non-political relations are strongly attracted to the charms they find in Chinese culture and to the outstanding qualities of the wonderful Chinese people. The problems in Sino-American relations are clearly the most acute in the political and diplomatic realms. Even in economics they are not so severe as to prevent American companies from elbowing each other to get advantages [in] trade and investment in China.

It is tempting to suggest that the troubles can be explained by the manifest differences in political culture, history, ideology, and levels of development. Yet, whereas at one time those differences were far greater and therefore misunderstandings more natural, now, despite the economic successes of Deng Xiaoping's reforms which have led to a significant degree of convergence, there have also been greater tensions and frustrations.

One might have hoped that their remarkable accomplishments in economic growth and the manifest improvements in living conditions would have made the Chinese more self-confident and at ease with the outside world, less touchy about slights to their sovereignty or perceived meddling in their internal affairs. However, Chinese successes seem to have only generated greater distrust and frustration. Taking seriously the forecast that in the foreseeable future they will have the world's largest economy, the Chinese feel that they deserve recognition and respect as a superpower-in-waiting. It is not enough that they are already a permanent member of the United Nations Security Council and one of the five nuclear powers, for somehow all their accomplishments of the last two decades have not produced as great a change in their international status as they had expected. Therefore they suspect that there has been a conscious effort to thwart their rise in prestige, and they are sure that the United States must be the black hand behind such a devious plot.

... [T]he central theme of modern Chinese history has been precisely the country's unsuccessful quest for a set of national values and principles which might satisfy the need for a modern national identity. In fact, what led Mao's generation of leaders to go down the dead-end road of Marxism-Leninism was their belief that in that ideology they would find satisfaction for this fundamental need. As a result of that commitment, the Chinese people have been exposed to nearly half a century of unrelenting propaganda attacks against all the ideas, values and symbols associated with China's great historic civilization. Confucianism and Taoism have been steadily denounced as abominable 'feudal remnants' which must be totally purged from the collective memory of the Chinese people. All that was once seen as great in Chinese history has been decried as a part of a curse which had held the Chinese people back in their now all-important race to modernity.

A nationalism without ideals can only generate mindless anti-foreign sentiments....

With Chinese nationalism consisting of little more than ethnicity and xenophobia, the Chinese people tend to vacillate between indiscriminately adoring, indeed almost fawning over, what is foreign, and sudden outbursts of anti-foreign passions. In the main cities there is a frantic striving to be a part of the modern world and to absorb all that foreign popular cultures have to offer. Yet, at the same time, one of the hottest selling books in 1996 was *China Can Say No*, an angry tirade by five journalists who proclaim that the United States is engaged in all manner of devious plots against China, and who in their rage over American complaints about intellectual property rights came up with the bizarre demand that America should be paying 'royalties' for using China's 'great inventions' of paper and gunpowder.[1] ...

The record of Chinese governments, from the warlords right through to the disastrous years of Mao's reign with its Great Leap, which produced the worst famine in all of human history, and the subhuman brutalities of the Cultural Revolution, is unquestionably one of the worst in all history. Therefore it is not surprising that the Chinese must try to blame others in order to put their own failings out of mind. Moreover the current leadership has to block the search for more solid foundations for a modern sense of Chinese nationalism because it cannot afford to allow the Chinese public to reflect on the regime's history of failures. Above all, there cannot be any thought of a 'reversal of the verdict' on Tiananmen, and thus any discussion of a democratic option for China is forbidden....

The same rules of pragmatism which guide their behaviour in their domestic politics will also operate in foreign affairs. This is because the unstructured near-anarchy of post-Cold War international politics resembles to a remarkable degree the world of Chinese Communist factional politics. The Chinese leaders all learned well the Leninist doctrine that the highest right is to support 'truth' with falsehood, and they still cling to that code even as their faith in the ultimate truth of Marxism has come into question. Above all, the Chinese leaders' compelling need to cling to power and to rule without the benefits of a strong set of legitimizing myths, or a believable ideology, will give a strongly opportunistic cast to their behaviour....

This is not the place for a full review of the rules of Chinese pragmatism, but a few of its outstanding features which are most likely to complicate relations between Beijing and Washington need to be noted....

*It pays to be firm, even threatening.* The first cardinal rule of Chinese pragmatism is: never hesitate to seek the advantage that can come from causing worry and fear in others. Real authority knows the value of intimidation. The traditional wording of imperial decrees ended with, 'Now read this, and with fear and trembling, obey'. True obedience demands fear. In all hierarchical relationships it is essential to make subordinates worry about being criticized and punished. The vocabulary of punishment should be used freely to remind people that they are in danger if they displease their superiors. One also proves that one is superior by freely using threatening language. Moreover, it can be expected that in bilateral relations the Chinese will routinely dictate the aggressively declare what the other party should and should not do.

Although the Confucian ideal of leadership stressed benevolence, the Chinese leaders today are more inclined to the Leninist principle of treating opponents as enemies. Moreover, they believe that a reputation for intimidation establishes the idea that one is fearless, indeed possibly even reckless, which they believe will make others cautious in any future dealings....

*Openly play favourites.* Just as the Chinese father feels no need to treat all his children equally but freely plays favorites, so Chinese officials will openly acknowledge who at any time is the favourite among their subordinates. In international relations the Chinese willingness to reveal which states are rising in their favour and which are losing favour is matched only by their practice of making finely calibrated judgments as to which state's power is on the rise and which is in decline. There has been of course, a long tradition in Chinese state-craft of 'playing off one barbarian against another'....

*To make an enemy is also to make new friends.* In the highly fluid political environment that Chinese leaders operate in, there can be much easy talk about 'old friends', but in the actual play of politics the line between friend and enemy is easily crossed. More particularly, leaders do not hesitate in piling demands on friends for they see little risk in turning a friend into an enemy because they believe that with every new enemy there will usually come one or more new friends. In the factional struggles of elite politics there can be quick realignments as a once friendly relationship is broken and everyone involved has to readjust their ties and seek new allies. The Chinese have found that the same rule applies in foreign relations. Conflict with the United States in the 1950s strengthened ties with the Soviet Union; the break with Moscow was quickly followed by the opening to Washington; tensions with Japan help strengthen relations with ASEAN [Association of Southeast Asian Nations]; trade and human rights problems with Washington open the way to better relations with Moscow and Europe, to say nothing of the rest of Asia. Problems with any particular foreign company will only motivate other competing companies to seek favour with China. If there are problems with Jeep there are always the eager Japanese car-makers; difficulties with General Electric can easily lead to better relations with Westinghouse; indeed candidates for joint ventures seem limitless as entrepreneurs from a host of countries seek greedily to profit from China's economic growth. The Chinese also expect that by merely proclaiming a new friendship they can make an old friend jealous and thereby anxious to improve relations with them. Thus, faced with problems with Washington the Chinese have played up symbols of friendship with Moscow.

In both domestic and foreign policy the rule applies that authority should never fear to challenge a friend or ally for not being truly 'faithful' or fully 'reliable'. Suggesting doubt will make the 'friend' work harder to prove the charge false; and if not, there is still psychic satisfaction to be derived from knowing that one's judgment about reliability was right in the first place. Hence, never fear pushing your 'friends' to do more. A good example of this tactic was the way the Chinese treated James McGregor, head of the American Chamber of Commerce in Beijing and the China representative of Dow Jones & Co., who earlier, as a reporter had established a record of faithfully explaining Chinese positions. While in Washington lobbying hard on China's behalf for the continuation of MFN ["Most Favored Nation" status], the Chinese authorities chose that moment to announce tough regulations to exercise control over foreign news services which were particularly damaging to Dow Jones. For Americans the timing of the Chinese action seemed stupid, indeed self-destructive, but according to the Chinese way of thinking the timing was perfect because if Mr. McGregor had slackened in his enthusiasm for selling China on Capitol Hill it would have shown that he was only motivated by material self-interest. So, the Chinese reasoned he would have to carry on his lobbying and try to rationalize what had happened; and they were correct, for this is exactly what happened.

According to this same timing principle, the right moment to arrest a dissident is just before or after a 'friendly' visit by a high US official seeking better relations with China. Just as Secretary of State Warren Christopher was arriving in Beijing to discuss among other things China's human rights record, the Chinese arrested a leading dissident. The Secretary, following the American rule that all trips abroad have to yield 'progress', put the best face he could on his trip, but that was his last visit to China. Within a few years the American press, surreptitiously encouraged by Chinese feeds, began castigating Christopher for visiting Beijing only once while making 24 trips to Damascus to meet with the certifiable tyrant Hafez al-Assad. Score: one up for the Chinese, and a faulted American Secretary of State.

In a similar timing ploy, Beijing arrested Yao Zhenxiang a few days after the U.N. Commission on Human Rights had voted not to criticize China's human rights record. For those who had voted in China's favour to complain would only make them look foolish for having initially supported China. The effect was to consolidate the champions of 'Asian values' and to isolate further the United States and European governments who were said to be trying to 'impose their values on others'. . . .

*Symbols are important, but words are cheap and logical consistency is a hobgoblin of the small mind.*   In Chinese politics it is often quite enough just to manipulate symbols without necessarily changing substantive reality. . . .

Not infrequently, Chinese officials will promise something with the full expectation that the other party should be satisfied with just the symbolic act of the promise, and not expect the promise to be actually kept. . . .

Also, in contrast to American politicians, who will go to extraordinary lengths to uphold the pretence of consistency and to insist that they have always held to the same opinions, Chinese leaders are quite comfortable with changing their positions. They place little value on consistency because they assume that when circumstances change all intelligent people should adjust their positions. These views also mean that it is possible to have dramatic changes and even total reversals of policies in Chinese politics with little stress or consternation. Political right and wrong can suddenly be turned on their heads and nobody seems surprised. It was the Western world and not the Chinese public that was astonished when Chinese politics changed overnight from the ideological politics of the Mao Zedong era to the pragmatic reforms of Deng Xiaoping. Passionate believers in Communism could in less than a year's time become avid capitalists with no more psychic stress than comes with changing from winter to summer clothes. . . .

*Secrecy is invaluable, but discount what is said in private.*   Secrecy envelops the entire workings of the Chinese political process, and it is taken for granted that true power always operates behind the scenes and not in public. Aside from a few ritualistic and essentially theatrical appearances, important leaders strive to be invisible. . . .

Above all, the task of framing a successful China-policy requires an American leadership capable of articulating a compelling vision of what America wants in its relations with both China and Asia in general. Then there needs to be continuous high level engagement with China so as to bring China even more into the international system and thereby encourage Beijing to abandon its more troublesome propensities and to adhere more to standard international practices. Engagement, however, means that Washington must recognize the games and ploys that the Chinese are employing and not be either manipulated or unduly irritated by them. It requires that Washington have a clear and consistent view as to exactly what it wants the relationship to be.

If relations are to become smoother and more stable, China, however, will also have to change, but in a much more fundamental way. The imperative need is for the Chinese as a people to finally succeed in their long quest to find a modern national identity so that they can face the world armed with an appropriate version of nationalism and not be consumed just with xenophobic passions. However, until China is politically opened up enough for the Chinese people as a whole to freely participate in a collective process of articulating a more coherent sense of national identity, other countries will have to deal with a prickly Chinese government and a people who can easily swing between xenophilia and xenophobia. As long as the attempt to define a new nationalism is monopolized by China's autocratic leaders, the result will either be a continuation of Leninist stagnation or some version of national socialism or fascism.

## Note

1. The Chinese seem impervious to embarrassment about using quirky arguments in support of their national interest. Most recently they have believed that they could advance their claims to disputed islands in the South China Seas by insisting that the wreckage of a Song dynasty ship with its cargo of shattered pottery justifies China's rights of ownership.

# NO

David M. Lampton

# China

China is a giant screen upon which outsiders project their hopes and fears. Expectations of economic gain coexist with worries about financial crisis; shrill alarms about Chinese power with dire forecasts of collapse; visions of democratic change with caricatures of current reality. It is time to step back and look at where China is today, where it might be going, and what consequences that direction will hold for the rest of the world.

## China Is a Rogue State With Hegemonic Ambitions

*Not true.* Strident voices in the West assert that the People's Republic of China (PRC) sees little to be gained from being a good international citizen. This view has three defects: 1) The record of the last two decades does not support it; 2) it is not in Beijing's interest to be perceived and treated as a rogue state; and 3) if other nations begin to regard it in that light, they will help bring about the very Chinese behavior they seek to avert.

Consider China's actions as a permanent member of the UN Security Council. Surely, "the next 'rogue' superpower"—to quote one recent characterization of China in the U.S. press—would not have hesitated to throw its weight around over the years. Yet, since 1972, while China has abstained on some Security Council resolutions, it has cast only two vetoes in open session. Although deeply apprehensive of resolutions condoning sanctions or interventions, the PRC has not sought to stop UN missions in the former Yugoslavia, Haiti, Somalia, or Iraq during the Gulf War and thereafter. As Foreign Minister Qian Qichen said in late 1997 about Beijing's position on sanctions against Iraq: "Despite the fact that we have not supported these [UN] resolutions, they must be respected."

This generally constructive stance extends to the growing number of international organizations that China has joined since former leader Deng Xiaoping's opening to the outside world almost two decades ago. In 1977, China belonged to 21 international governmental organizations and 71 international nongovernmental organizations. By 1994, the respective numbers were

From David M. Lampton, "China," *Foreign Policy* (Spring 1998). Copyright © 1998 by The Carnegie Endowment for International Peace. Reprinted by permission of *Foreign Policy*.

50 and 955. In institutions such as the Asian Development Bank, the International Monetary Fund (IMF), and the World Bank, China has been a model citizen. Beijing has also acted responsibly in Asia's recent economic crisis, contributing U.S.$1 billion to the IMF stabilization package for Thailand, clearly conveying its intention to defend the Hong Kong dollar, and (so far) resisting the temptation to devalue its own currency.

Closer to home, the record is mixed. But Beijing's missile exercises in the Taiwan Strait in 1995–96 and its occupation of several reefs in the Spratly Islands must be set next to its concerted and successful efforts during the last decade to improve relations with every country in the neighborhood. In Cambodia, China played an essential role in the settlement leading to UN-sponsored elections. Looking north and west, the PRC has resolved disputes with Kazakstan, Kyrgyzstan, Russia, and Tadjikistan through negotiated agreement. To the south, Beijing has improved relations with Hanoi and New Delhi and joined the Association of South East Asian Nations' regional forum on security.

Beijing's adherence to various international institutions, treaties, and regimes has been best where it has been engaged in writing the rules it is asked to observe and where the international community has made available tangible resources to assist implementation. Indeed, for all the controversy surrounding China's behavior in the field of nonproliferation, it has generally complied with the international nonproliferation regimes to which it has been a full party, including the Treaty on the Non-Proliferation of Nuclear Weapons, the Comprehensive Test Ban Treaty, and the Chemical Weapons Convention. China's relations with Pakistan and Iran have been worrisome. Nonetheless, Beijing addressed these issues during President Jiang Zemin's October 1997 state visit to the United States and reassured the Clinton administration in writing about China's future nuclear cooperation with Iran.

Beijing's compliance has been less praiseworthy in areas where it has not been a member of the rule-writing club, where compliance would conflict with its perceived strategic interests, or where it lacks the necessary resources and enforcement mechanisms. In the case of some missile-related and nuclear technology transfers to Pakistan—long a Chinese strategic ally—Beijing has sought to use its compliance with agreements, or lack thereof, as leverage to obtain stricter adherence in Washington to the Joint Communiqué on Weapons Sales to Taiwan of 1982. Then again, the transfer of ring magnets to Pakistan probably owes less to government directives than to Beijing's inability to exercise effective supervision and control over industries and companies—a problem that bedevils the United States, Great Britain, and other countries with a strong stake in nonproliferation.

# China Is Undertaking a Huge Military Buildup

*Wrong.* There is little uncertainty about China's modest military capabilities, much speculation about what those capabilities may be 20 years hence, and considerable debate about current and future Chinese intentions.

China's defense budget presents a daunting challenge for analysts, not least because much military spending occurs outside the regular defense budget. Those who wish to point to a Chinese threat often use figures from China's defense budget that show a dramatic rise in official spending from 1988 to 1996. However, a 1997 RAND study of China's official defense budget, which adjusts these figures for inflation, suggests that the increase in official defense spending is much less significant.

The Institute for International Strategic Studies and the Stockholm International Peace Research Institute assert that total spending by the People's Liberation Army (PLA) is four to five times the amount officially reported (which Chinese military officers hotly dispute). If true, this would put actual 1996 PLA spending at U.S.$35.5 to 44.4 billion. The Heritage Foundation puts the upper range estimate at U.S.$40 billion. Japan, in 1996, with the American nuclear umbrella and the U.S.–Japan Security Treaty, spent about U.S.$45 billion. China has a long coastline, land borders with 14 states, many of which have presented, and might again present, security problems, and no protective alliance; the PLA also has domestic control responsibilities (as we saw tragically in 1989). And not only do many of China's neighbors have more modern weapons, but as a report recently issued by the Pacific Council on International Policy and RAND noted, "China's military expenditures as a percentage of total defense expenditures by all Asian countries have been decreasing steadily since the mid-1970s."

What about China's development and purchase of advanced technologies? A 1996 report by the U.S. Department of Defense covering 17 families of technologies with military applications shows that, with a few important exceptions (nuclear and chemical technologies among them), China lagged well behind first- and second-tier countries such as France, Israel, Japan, Russia, the United Kingdom, and the United States. True, current estimates of Chinese purchases of advanced technology from Russia during 1990–96 ranged from U.S.$1 to 2 billion annually. By way of comparison, however, the U.S. military spent U.S.$11.99 billion with one American prime defense contractor, Lockheed Martin, in FY 1996 alone.

While it would be foolish to dismiss China's increasing ability to project force beyond its borders and to affect U.S. and other interests, it would be even more foolish to allow exaggerated perceptions of Chinese strength to shape U.S. policy—a development that would stoke nationalist resentment in Beijing and likely fuel support for the very buildup that some U.S. commentators regularly decry.

# A Peaceful Resolution of Taiwan's Status Is Only a Matter of Time

*Maybe not.* The conventional wisdom is that the Taiwan Strait missile crisis from mid-1995 to March 1996 had a sobering effect on Beijing, Taipei, and Washington. In Beijing, there had been those who thought that Washington

*Figure 1*

### China's Defense Budget in Billions of Renminbi (RMB), Official Figures, and Official Figures Adjusted for Inflation

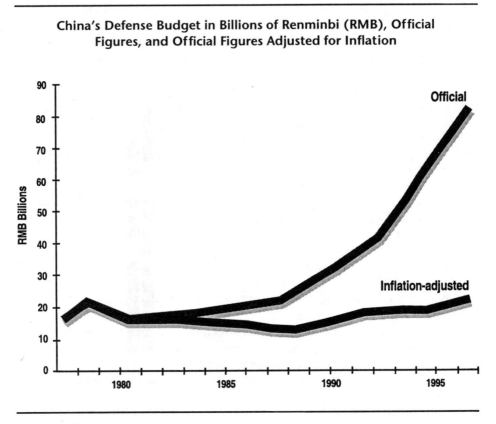

Source: James Mulvenon, the Rand Corporation.

lacked the will to uphold its commitment to a "peaceful resolution" of the Taiwan issue and to stability in East Asia. The March 1996 dispatch of two aircraft carrier groups was a credible assertion of American interest. In Taipei, President Lee Teng-hui and others seemed to have concluded that Beijing could not, or would not, do much about Taiwan's search for a more dignified international role. Beijing's missiles and the resultant dislocations of markets and capital flight were an abrupt comeuppance. And after the PRC missile exercises (particularly those in the spring of 1996), many in the U.S. Congress professed a new appreciation for Beijing's sensitivity to the Taiwan issue. In short, there is now a happy assumption that everyone has become more cautious. One can hope so, but there are other forces at work.

First, something fundamental drives Taipei's search for a greater role in the international community—a changing sense of identity among its population. In recent years, there has been a progressive decline in the percentage of people on Taiwan who consider themselves "Chinese" and a corresponding rise in the percentage identifying themselves as "Taiwanese." Taiwan's ever

*Figure 2*

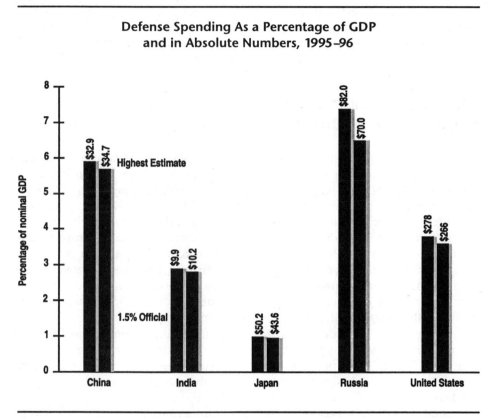

**Defense Spending As a Percentage of GDP
and in Absolute Numbers, 1995–96**

*Note:* The figures above each column report defense expenditures, according to NATO definitions and are converted to billions of U.S. dollars.

*Source: The Military Balance: 1997/98* (London: International Institute for Strategic Studies, 1997).

more competitive political system has given voice to this new, distinct identity. In the Taiwan presidential election of the year 2000, a president may well be elected from the Democratic Progressive Party (DPP), which historically has stood for the island's independence.

Beijing has said it will employ force to prevent independence or outside intervention. How Beijing would actually react to the DPP's assumption of power, how the DPP would lead Taiwan, and how the Taiwanese will respond in an indefinite future are all imponderables. And yet, the answers to these questions will influence whether peace and stability can be maintained in the Taiwan Strait in the years ahead.

There is another part to the equation: How long will Beijing remain "patient?" As Beijing's attention shifts from the return of Hong Kong and Macao (in 1999), it will focus increasingly on "reunification with Taiwan." Not only do PRO leaders worry about trends on Taiwan, they believe that, were the island to achieve de jure independence, their own right to role would be forfeited. Moreover, they fear that areas from Mongolia to Xinjiang to Tibet would use Taiwan's moves to justify their own efforts to break away. Beijing sees everything at stake in the Taiwan issue and is unsure that time works in its favor, despite the ties that about U.S.$35 billion in investment by Taiwan on the mainland create.

In short, continued stability depends on restraint by Beijing, Taipei, and Washington, none of which has an unblemished record of self-control.

# China Will Be the Next Asian Economic Domino to Fall

*Not necessarily.* The financial crash in Northeast and Southeast Asia since mid-1997 is already taking a toll on the PRC. China now faces the prospects of declining regional demand for its exports and stiffening competition from regional economies in other export markets. Its still robust 1997 GDP growth of 8.8 percent was below earlier government forecasts, there are signs that growth will slow further (perhaps to 6 percent), and some Chinese and foreign analysts believe that the PRC may devalue its currency to maintain its export competitiveness. Beijing asserts that it will vigorously resist such a move. Yet, if unemployment rises, growth slows, and domestic exporters apply political pressure, policy could change. Declining asset values in East and Southeast Asia will probably also reduce capital flow to China from the region.

Many of the considerations that have undermined confidence in other Asian financial systems apply to China: a lack of transparency; financial cronyism; banks with huge portfolios of nonperforming loans; poor regulatory systems; property bubbles; heavy borrowing abroad; and new, volatile equity markets.

And yet, China's economy has important differences that may provide a breathing spell. In a forthcoming book, economist Nicholas Lardy lays them out clearly: 1) China's currency is not freely convertible, thereby reducing speculative pressures; 2) Beijing reports hard currency reserves of about U.S.$140 billion, not including the separate resources of Hong Kong; 3) a large proportion of foreign investment in China has come in the form of direct investment in factories and other assets, not hot money put into more volatile stock markets; 4) although Chinese entities have large foreign debts, most are long-term, unlike elsewhere in Asia; and 5) although foreign direct investment has been important for growth over the last 15 years, the high domestic savings rate has been the principal fuel—growth can continue if savings can be more productively utilized.

The key to avoiding a meltdown will be whether Beijing moves to accelerate reform of the banking and state enterprise sectors—an apparent commitment of the current leadership. But deciding and doing are two different things: Will Beijing recapitalize its banks and operate them on sound financial principles? Simply training the personnel to accomplish this is a gargantuan task. And will China tackle the problem of state enterprises (at least 40 percent of which lose money), whose bad debts to the banks are a principal cause of the financial system's current woes? The restructuring of state enterprises and the bankruptcy

*Figure 3*

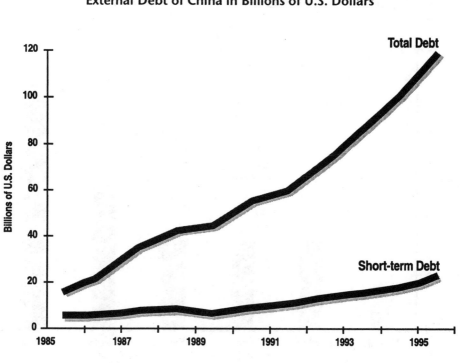

**External Debt of China in Billions of U.S. Dollars**

Source: *China 2020: Development Challenges in the New Century* (Washington, DC: World Bank, 1997).

of many others could put millions more workers onto the streets, just as growth slows. Can China meet these challenges and avoid serious political dislocation? Nobody can be sure.

## China's Large, Fast-Growing Exports Come Principally at the Expense of Jobs in the West

*Wrong.* Chinese exports to the United States and Europe have grown rapidly and often dominate in labor-intensive sectors such as toys, footwear, apparel, and textiles. But PRC exports in these areas generally surged after domestic jobs in these industries had already migrated to Indonesia, South Korea, and Taiwan, and elsewhere in East Asia and Latin America. In garment manufacturing, for example, World Bank data suggests that, especially for the European Union, employment had already fallen sharply before Chinese exports achieved even the relatively low penetration rate of 2 percent. And economist Marcus Noland

*Figure 4*

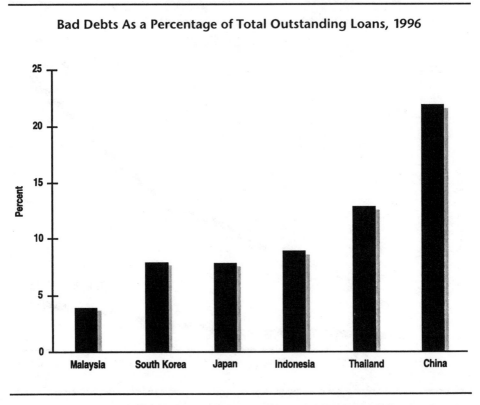

**Bad Debts As a Percentage of Total Outstanding Loans, 1996**

*Source:* Nicholas Lardy, the Brookings Institution. Calculations were made in billions of U.S. dollars.

calculated that from 1988 to 1994, almost 90 percent of the increase in the Chinese share of U.S. consumption had merely displaced imports from other countries. The real fear of Chinese export competition ought to be found in low-cost producing economies, not Main Street, U.S.A. or Europe.

## China Has Been a Bust for U.S. Firms

*Not really.* According to U.S. Commerce Department figures for 1990–96, China was the fastest-growing major U.S. export market. During that period, American exports grew at a compound rate of more than 19 percent, if one includes U.S. exports initially exported to Hong Kong but then reexported to China. The PRC is now America's ninth largest export market. By way of comparison, U.S. exports to Japan grew at 6 percent, and those to Brazil by 15 percent, annually. American-invested joint ventures and wholly owned U.S. subsidiaries in China also increasingly sell goods there; although some of the profit is repatriated to the United States, much is reinvested in China, where it can generate future returns.

However, it is also true that the United States has a mounting trade deficit with China—U.S. government estimates peg it at about U.S.$50 billion for 1997 —a figure that many economists believe overstates the problem. The reality of these rising exports to China and the simultaneously mounting trade deficit suggest that Washington—quite appropriately—is proceeding to secure more market access.

Those who assert that the Chinese market has been a bust have a deeper, more erroneous point. Their implicit assumption is that the United States and other industrialized economies do not have a lot riding on economic relations with China. Wrong. Everyone has a great deal at stake in whether or not China can sustain (and how it sustains) growth as other economies deflate.

# China Is the World's Biggest Intellectual Thief

*Wrong, for now.*   Stealing copyrighted music, software, and movies—the "piracy" of intellectual property rights (IPR)—is a serious and legitimate concern. One 1996 study estimated that "of the 523 million new business software applications used globally during 1996, 225 million units—nearly one in every two— were pirated." China does its share of wrongdoing in this regard. But the sorry fact is that developed nations and Americans themselves inflict the biggest dollar losses on U.S. industry, though the highest piracy rates (the percentage of protected items in use that have been illegally appropriated) are to be found in low-income economies with weak to nonexistent legal structures.

Looking at dollar losses through software piracy in 1996 (and the industry's methodology is subject to criticism for inflating losses), Eastern Europe, Japan, Western Europe, and the United States itself all inflicted greater losses on U.S. industry than China (with 22 percent of the world's population). However, if one looks at the "piracy rate" in 1996, China was surpassed only by Vietnam and Indonesia. Russia and the rest of the Commonwealth of Independent States were close behind.

In short, owners of intellectual property confront a global circumstance in which losses to developed countries (with high rates of personal computer ownership) exceed losses to poorer countries (with fewer PCs, weaker legal and regulatory structures, and more extensive official corruption).

The music recording industry faces similar problems. The Recording Industry Association of America reported in 1996 that lost revenue through CD piracy in Japan came to U.S.$500 million annually—"more than the U.S.$300 million the American record industry says it is losing annually from the far more well-known piracy in China."

China is trying to build an IPR enforcement regime. In addition to constructing a (yet imperfect) framework of domestic law in the late 1980s and 1990s, Beijing signed two agreements with Washington (in 1992 and 1995) and from May 1996 to March 1997 closed 37 factories illegally copying CDs—58 CD and CD-ROM production lines by January 1998. As China develops its own innovators and artists with commercially salable products, demands for stricter IPR protection will grow.

# China Is a Totalitarian State

*Simplistic.* To reject this characterization is not to assert that the PRC is a democracy—it is not. But words should have meaning. Totalitarian refers to a state that has the intention and capability to control nearly all aspects of human behavior, thought, and communication. Totalitarian described the ambitions and, to a considerable extent, the system during much of Mao Zedong's reign, when a trip to Albania was considered broadening and children were expected to inform on parents.

Ironically, many of China's domestic problems and irresponsible behavior abroad—from piracy to proliferation—stem from a lack of central control. Most significantly, between 30 and 200 million people slosh around China in search of temporary employment, encamping in and around cities and creating a potentially volatile pool of poor and discontented citizens.

In fact, for all its imperfections and injustices, China today is freer than it has been at any time in the last five decades. About 40,000 Chinese students are now enrolled in tertiary U.S. educational institutions; during the Soviet Union's entire 70-year history, it never sent that many students to the United States. In 1965, there were 12 television and 93 radio stations in China; today, PLA receiving dishes are sold illegally to citizens who pull in satellite TV. The Internet is growing by leaps and bounds. Newspapers and magazines have become not just more numerous but far more diverse and autonomous. In 1978, the state controlled more than 90 percent of GNP; in 1996, that number was about 45 percent and falling. The state now employs only 18 percent of the work force, compared with more than 90 percent in 1978 (including peasants in communes at that time). In September 1997, at the Fifteenth Party Congress, the concept of "public" ownership was morphed from Marx's concept into "public" in the sense of "initial public offering" of stock. While under Mao the concept of the individual suing the state for damages was inconceivable, it now happens increasingly often.

# China Is Wrecking Hong Kong

*No.* The broadcast networks that spent large sums covering the July 1, 1997, handover to the PRC left disappointed, not at the absence of disaster but at the absence of a "story." The days since then have been notable for both what Beijing has and has not done.

Beijing has not militarized the city, as some feared. There are fewer army troops there under Chinese rule than there were generally in Hong Kong under British governors—reinforcements are, of course, only a few miles away in China proper. Beijing has not stopped political demonstrations, which have continued on an almost daily basis since the night of June 30–July 1, 1997, when Martin Lee, the leader of democratic forces in Hong Kong, spoke to a crowd from the balcony of the Legislative Council. Although it is hard to measure press self-censorship—and there is some, as evidenced by the reluctance of Hong Kong Chinese to show three controversial movies dealing with sensitive subjects—Hong Kong still has one of the most freewheeling journalism communities in Asia. In terms of governance, it appears that the new chief executive, C.H. Tung, has great latitude in leading Hong Kong.

U.S. naval ships have been permitted to continue to make port calls—as of January 1998, 34 naval vessels, including two aircraft carrier battle groups and two nuclear submarines. When equity and property markets throughout the region, including Hong Kong, precipitously declined in the latter half of 1997 and early 1998, Beijing let markets work (even though many PRC interests lost heavily). Chinese leaders also quietly let it be known that China's large hard-currency reserves could be brought to the defense of the Hong Kong–U.S. dollar peg.

Less reassuring has been Beijing's determination, expressed well before the takeover, to reverse British governor Christopher Patten's October 1992 speedup in the agreed-upon process of broadening the popular franchise. Instead, immediately after the handover, a provisional legislative council was installed to sit during the interim period before new elections. The elections that Tung has announced for May 1998 will be widely criticized for narrowing functional constituencies and employing proportional representation in ways that can be expected to weaken the power of Martin Lee's Democratic Party.

On balance, however, Beijing has played a responsible role. This pattern of PRC behavior probably will persist, depending on the fate of China's own reforms, regional economic stability, and whether Hong Kong's own people stay out of the business of promoting political change in the PRC.

# China Is an Effective, Major Player in the Washington Lobbying Game

*Wrong.* No misconception is further from reality. Until May 1995, when Lee Teng-hui was given a visa to visit Cornell University as a result of congressional pressure (by a House vote of 396-0), Beijing paid little heed to Capitol Hill. PRC leaders rested secure in the mistaken belief that when U.S. presidents wish to prevail over Congress, they do.

This inattention to Congress is reflected in a number of ways. Beijing has one law firm under retention in Washington—Taipei is reported to have 14. The PRC has (off and on) one public relations firm in the United States—Taipei has many. Even if one adds to the PRC's legal lobbying expenditures the alleged U.S.$100,000 in illegal campaign contributions that the FBI says may have occurred (although the Thompson committee failed to demonstrate this), China does not rank even among the top 10 nations (or territories) in terms of lobbying efforts. Even Haiti (no. 7) and Angola (no. 9) outspend Beijing!

The PRC recently augmented efforts to bring members of the U.S. Congress to China. Beijing knows that there has been high congressional turnover since 1992, that most members have not traveled much, and that seeing China's dynamism leaves few views unchanged. But the PRC efforts lag well behind Taipei's. In 1996, members of Congress took 58 all-expense paid trips to China—still a distant second to the 139 trips they took to Taiwan. When the numbers for 1997 are in, Beijing probably will be seen to have narrowed the gap considerably.

# POSTSCRIPT

## Does China Tend to Threaten World Peace and Stability?

Can China reconcile communism and capitalism? How will it be changed by the movement toward the production of more goods for export and the investment of foreign capital? Will the dictatorship be moved to release its control over the lives of its people? Will China's increasing involvement in the marketplace of goods make the Chinese government and people more receptive to the marketplace of ideas?

All these questions imply that, for better or worse, China will likely play an increasingly important role in world affairs. Yet there is the possibility that hopes and fears of China's rise to international influence are premature. Industrialization in China has increased the misery of millions of poor people. Unemployment is high, and the gap between the new rich and the poor has been increasing. Many natural resources are lacking, and the cities are overcrowded and polluted. Despite these obstacles, most students of China believe that China must be seriously reckoned with as a nation, economy, and ideology because of its emergence into the modern economy, its desire to play a role in world affairs, its aggressiveness in dealing with neighbors, and the raw determination of its people.

David Zweig, who teaches at the Hong Kong University of Science and Technology, contends that advocates of economic liberalization mistakenly believe that this must inevitably lead to political democratization. In "Undemocratic Capitalism: China and the Limits of Economism," *The National Interest* (Summer 1999), Zweig favors cautious American engagement while the United States observes whether or not China moves in another direction.

China today may not be a first-rate military power, but Aaron L. Friedberg, in "Arming China Against Ourselves," *Commentary* (July–August 1999), argues that China continues to increase its armed forces and has shown great interest in American thermonuclear devices (and may have employed spies to acquire their designs). Given China's threats to Taiwan, says Friedberg, the risk of military action involving the United States cannot be discounted, if the United States is true to its pledge to protect Taiwan's independence.

A standard short history of American-Chinese relations can be found in the fourth edition of Warren I. Cohen, *America's Response to China: A History of Sino-American Relations* (Columbia University Press, 2000). A closer exploration of the modern period is to be found in James H. Mann, *About Face: A History of America's Curious Relationship With China, from Nixon to Clinton* (Alfred A. Knopf, 1999).

# ISSUE 20

## Should the United States Put More Restrictions on Immigration?

**YES: Daniel James**, from "Close the Borders to All Newcomers," *Insight* (November 22, 1993)

**NO: Stephen Moore**, from "Give Us Your Best, Your Brightest," *Insight* (November 22, 1993)

### ISSUE SUMMARY

**YES:** Daniel James, an adviser to Carrying Capacity Network in Washington, D.C., wants a moratorium on immigration, which, he contends, is taking away jobs from American workers, threatening the environment, and breaking up American culture.

**NO:** Economist Stephen Moore insists that immigrants have created more jobs than they have taken away and have greatly enriched the economy and culture.

In 1949 a delegation of Native Americans went to Washington to tell lawmakers about the plight of America's original occupants. After meeting with Vice President Alben Barkley, the delegation got up to leave. But one old Sioux chief stayed a moment longer to deliver a parting word to the vice president. "Young fellow," he said, "let me give you a little advice. Be careful with your immigration laws. We were careless with ours."

As America prospered and offered the hope of opportunity and freedom, increasing numbers of immigrants came to the United States. In the last two decades of the nineteenth century, Congress barred further immigration by convicts, paupers, idiots, and Chinese. That, however, did not stem the tide.

In the half-century between 1870 and 1920, more than 26 million people came to live in the United States. The National Origins Act was adopted in 1924 to restrict the number of new immigrants, ban east Asian immigration (directed at Japan), and establish a European quota based on the population of the United States in 1890, when there had been far fewer new arrivals from eastern and southern Europe. The total number of legal immigrants was later cut again, but still they came.

In 1965 the national origins formula was abandoned, but strict limits on the number of immigrants were retained. The end of quotas spurred a dramatic increase of immigrants from Central and South America and Asia. Between 1965 and 1995, nearly one-half of all immigrants came from Mexico, the Caribbean, and the rest of Latin America, and nearly one-third arrived from Asia. Because they fear deportation, illegal arrivals accept very low wages and poor living conditions.

The number of illegal arrivals from Latin America prompted passage of the Immigration Reform and Control Act of 1987, requiring that employers confirm the legal status of their employees. At the same time, undocumented workers who had entered the United States before 1982 were granted amnesty. However, the flood of illegal immigrants has not been stemmed.

Why do so many people want to come to the United States? They come to flee tyranny and terrorism, to escape the ravages of war, and to join relatives already here. Above all, they come because America offers economic opportunity, in stark contrast to the poverty they endure in their native countries.

Do immigrants endanger or improve the American standard of living? Critics fear that the new immigrants, willing to work longer hours at lower pay, will take jobs away from American workers. Supporters of immigration believe that the new immigrants fill jobs that most Americans do not want and that they stimulate economic growth. Do poor, often uneducated immigrants contribute to urban crowding and the decline of cities? Do they introduce new diseases or reintroduce old ones that have been conquered here?

Do immigrants undermine or enrich American culture? The changing face of the United States has been dramatic in the last quarter-century. California, the most populous state, no longer has a single racial majority. Hispanics defined as whites and blacks who identify themselves as being of Hispanic origin make up the fastest-growing major category. Currently, whites make up 73.6 percent of the population; blacks make up 12 percent; Hispanics, 10.2 percent; and Asians, 3.3 percent. If we project present population trends forward, we can see that still greater change will take place among these populations: By the year 2050 whites will make up 52.8 percent of the population; blacks 13.6 percent; Hispanics, 24.5 percent; and Asians, 8.2 percent. (American Indians are not included here, because they are likely to continue to be less than 1 percent of the population.)

What, if anything, is to be done? California's voters adopted Proposition 187 to cut off all state assistance to illegal immigrants, but its implementation has been blocked in the courts. Congress has acted to deny welfare to illegal immigrants and public education to their children. Some have argued that children born in the United States to illegal immigrants should be denied citizenship. Others have argued that a great wall should be built between the United States and Mexico to discourage illegal entry.

Some of these issues are touched upon in the debate that follows, although the authors place greatest emphasis on economic considerations. Daniel James worries that recent immigration adds immeasurably to America's economic problems. Stephen Moore insists that "immigrants don't just take jobs, they create jobs."

**Daniel James**

 **YES**

# Close the Borders to All Newcomers

**S**trip the rhetoric from the evolving immigration debate and the bottom line becomes crystal clear: We may desire more and more immigrants, but can we afford so many of them? In his recently published memoirs, *Around the Cragged Hill,* George F. Kennan, perhaps [America's] most eminent statesman, goes to the heart of the matter:

> "We are already, for better or for worse, very much a polyglot country; and nothing of that is now to be changed. What I have in mind here are sheer numbers. There *is* such a thing as overcrowding. It has its psychic effects as well as its physical ones. There *are* limits to what the environment can stand."

The sheer numbers are indeed mind-boggling:

- 10.5 million immigrants, including those arriving illegally, entered the U.S. in the 1980s. That topped the previous record of 8.8 million who came here from 1901 to 1910.
- 15 to 18 million more newcomers, both legal and illegal, are projected to reach America in the 1990s, assuming our present immigration policy remains unchanged. Already, the number arriving in this decade is greater than for the same period in the previous decade. And there were nearly 1.2 million immigrants in 1992, 20 percent more than in 1991.
- 30 million immigrants—perhaps as many as 36 million—are expected to arrive in the first two decades of the next century, according to demographic projections and extrapolation of 1991–92 Census Bureau data.

The last two projections indicate that between 45 million and 54 million people—almost equal to the population of Great Britain—will be entering the U.S. in little more than a generation.

Add the 20 million immigrants who arrived from 1965 to 1990, and the grand total who will have entered the U.S. in just over a half-century (1965–2020) will be 65 million to 74 million.

From Daniel James, "Close the Borders to All Newcomers," *Insight* (November 22, 1993). Copyright © 1993 by *Insight.* Reprinted by permission. All rights reserved.

There is no precedent for these numbers anywhere in the world. They constitute the biggest wave of immigration ever to a single country. Called the "fourth wave" of immigration to the U.S., it is really a tidal wave.

Yet the numbers are conservative. Unforeseeable trends in countries that generate immigrants could swell the tidal wave even higher than projected. It is likely, for example, that the demise of Cuba's communist dictatorship would send a flood of refugees to Miami comparable to the 125,000 *Marielitos* who inundated it in 1980.

Mexico is an even bigger concern. In the 1980s, it sent the U.S. nearly 4 million immigrants, more than the total for all of Asia. Two great "push" factors will drive ever more of them northward: high population growth—Mexico's present 90 million inhabitants will become 110 million by 2000—and unemployment/underemployment levels of 40 to 50 percent.

The North American Free Trade Agreement [NAFTA] ... may generate a temporary upsurge in illegal border crossings. It would draw more Mexicans to the relatively affluent north and make entering the U.S. affordable. Meanwhile, an expected rise in imports of cheaper U.S. corn would bankrupt Mexico's peasant class, the *campesinos,* and drive them to seek work stateside. Only years from now would NAFTA create enough jobs to keep Mexicans at home.

The cost to U.S. taxpayers of accepting endless numbers of immigrants is intolerable. We learn from a new study, "The Costs of Immigration," by economist Donald Huddle, that the net 1992 public assistance cost of the 19.3 million immigrants who have settled here since 1970 was $42.5 billion, after subtracting $20.2 billion they paid in taxes.

Huddle examined costs in 22 categories of federal, state and local assistance available to immigrants, including a package of 10 county welfare and health services. The largest net costs for immigrants in 1992 were $16 billion for education (primary, secondary and bilingual), $10.6 billion for health and welfare services and $8.5 billion for Medicaid.

Criminal justice and corrections costs for immigrants were found by Huddle to total more than $2 billion in 1992. The social price was greater: A disproportionately large number of illegals were in prison for committing felonies. In California, they made up 11 percent of all inmates.

Huddle also found that immigrants in 1992 displaced—probably forever—2.07 million American workers. This should answer the oft-debated question: Do immigrants take jobs away from Americans?

It is true that American workers frequently turn down tasks that immigrants willingly perform, such as picking fruit and vegetables under inhumane conditions or making garments in urban sweatshops. But that hardly explains the virtual elimination of blacks from jobs in entire industries. In Los Angeles, unionized blacks have been displaced by nonunion Hispanics in janitorial services, and in Washington, D.C., by Latino immigrants in hotels and restaurants.

The puzzling question is: Why does the U.S. continue to import competition for American workers at a time of high unemployment? The Labor Department reports that 8.5 million Americans, about 6.7 percent of our work force, are unemployed. Our two principal minorities suffer most from jobless-ness—12.6 percent of blacks and 9.7 percent of Latinos—and they are the most vulnerable to displacement.

Immigration costs will rise further in this decade, Huddle forecasts. He projects that from 1993 to 2002, 11.1 million legal and illegal immigrants will be added to the 19.3 million post-1970 immigrants already here, for a total of 30.4 million. Their net cost to taxpayers during the next decade would come to $668.5 billion, which is larger than the $496 billion of the national deficit that President Clinton and Congress have pledged to erase over five years.

Indeed, the savings from reducing immigration could be applied to cut-ting the deficit considerably, with less pain to the taxpayer than paring public services and raising taxes, as the administration proposes. Alternatively, Huddle suggests, such savings could be used to finance investment tax credits to create and maintain 4.1 million private sector jobs, or 1.4 million public works and service jobs, throughout the decade.

Impossible to quantify, but perhaps more devastating in the long run, is the cost of excessive immigration to the environment. As more and more peo-ple are added to our population—already excessive at 260 million—the greater the environmental degradation will be. The immigrants will contribute to in-creasing energy use, toxic waste, smog and urban crowding, all of which affect our mental and emotional health as well as the ecosystem.

Our population is increasing by 3 million a year, a rate faster than that of any other advanced country. California provides an example of what can happen to a nearly ideal environment when it is overwhelmed by too many people. Since 1980, its population has zoomed from 23.7 million to more than 31 million, an increase of almost one-third. As a consequence, Los Angeles and its once pristine bay are all but hopelessly polluted, and San Diego and Orange counties are fast becoming sad miniatures of Los Angeles.

Equally alarming is the impetus that uncontrolled immigration provides to separatism and its obverse, multiculturalism. Those living in areas where there are many other immigrants, such as Los Angeles and Texas's Rio Grande Valley, see no need to learn English and so live in virtual isolation from the general population. As long as these barrios are constantly replenished with newcomers from Mexico—virtually a stone's throw away—their inhabitants will feel less and less need or desire to assimilate. This process encourages a kind of natural separatism that could lead to political separatism.

Richard Estrada, a journalist and scholar, sees an ominous parallel with Quebec: "If Francophone Quebec can bring the Canadian confederation to the brink of disintegration even though France lies an ocean away, should there not at least arise a certain reflectiveness about our Southwest, which lies contiguous to an overpopulated Third World nation?"

A growing number of Americans of all classes and ethnic groups share these concerns about immigration and favor reducing it. For at least two decades, a majority of Americans have expressed in various polls their desire to stop or reduce immigration. In January 1992, a Gallup Poll found that 64 percent of registered voters would vote for a presidential candidate who fa-vored tougher laws on immigration. In December, the Latino National Political

Survey discovered that Hispanics overwhelmingly believed there is too much immigration.

❧

Even politicians who previously shunned immigration as a taboo subject are jumping onto the immigration reform bandwagon. From President Clinton, a Democrat, to California's Gov. Pete Wilson, a Republican, most are clamoring to curb illegal immigration. We can hope that they soon will understand that the main problem, as the public generally has perceived, is legal immigration.

Serious though illegal immigration is, *legal* immigration poses a much graver problem. We receive more than three times as many legal immigrants, including refugees, as illegal ones. Their numbers are projected to grow exponentially, because under the 1990 Immigration Act they are permitted to bring in an endless procession of family members. In 1992, for example, family-related immigrants totaled 594,000, or 49 percent of the 1.2 million immigrants who entered the U.S. that year.

Legal immigrants account for almost three-quarters of the total costs calculated by the Huddle study. Thus, of the $668.5 billion projected net cost to taxpayers for all immigrants from 1993 to 2002, legal immigrants would account for $482 billion. Illegal aliens would cost $186.4 billion.

The most effective way to curb illegal immigration is to declare a moratorium on *all* immigration. Why? If the U.S. clamps down on illegals but permits legal immigration to continue uncontrolled, that tells the world we are not serious about solving either problem, for it is easier to reduce or halt the legal flow than to hunt down those who arrive undercover. To do so would require a mere stroke of the pen and wouldn't cost taxpayers extra—Congress could just reform the Immigration Act of 1990, which is directly responsible for the 40 percent increase to immigration. That would send the unequivocal message to anyone who plans to enter the U.S. that we cannot afford to receive them—at least for the time being.

The message would ring loud and clear to would-be illegal immigrants that we mean business. It must be backed up, however, by a whole range of law enforcement measures that are now on the books but are ignored or not used effectively. In addition, to smoke out illegals and also eliminate the racket in fraudulent documents, Congress should approve a universal ID, much like the health security card that President Clinton displayed when he presented his health plan.

The ID cards would identify those who are legally in the U.S. and entitled to work and receive benefits. Local and state authorities should be directed to share information on illegals with the Immigration and Naturalization Service to aid in apprehending them; at present, authorities deny such information to the INS, in effect protecting illegals.

Instead of sending the National Guard to patrol the border as advocated by some lawmakers. it would be more effective to give the Border Patrol sufficient personnel to do its job. At least 2,000 new agents should be added to the current force of about 4,000, as well as equipment such as better night sensors and new vehicles. The Customs Service will also require additional personnel, particularly if NAFTA is put into effect and vehicular traffic from Mexico increases as expected.

A vital component of any program to curb immigration must be the cooperation of the Mexican government. The White House should take advantage of our cordial relations with Mexico and our growing economic clout to request that our southern neighbor cease its traditional (though unwritten) policy of regarding the U.S. as a safety valve.

A U.S. moratorium on immigration would yield highly positive gains by allowing the 20 million immigrants now within our borders time to assimilate into the mainstream. It would remove the pressure of new millions crowding into inner-city barrios and encourage existing inhabitants to break out of them. This would mitigate the danger of separatism, counter multiculturalist trends, defuse interethnic tensions and reduce crime and violence.

If this prescription sounds like a pipe dream, let us recall that restrictive legislation in 1924 cut immigration to a trickle, allowing enough time for the masses of immigrants the U.S. had then to overcome the obstacles to assimilation. That literally saved America. For when the Japanese struck at Pearl Harbor in 1941 and the U.S. was confronted by their military might plus that of Germany, which already had conquered Europe and had just invaded the Soviet Union, our nation stood united against them. Sadly, one doubts whether today's America, torn by an identity crisis spawned by divisive forces, would be capable of meeting a similar threat.

The United States is headed for a crisis of incalculable magnitude if mass immigration continues unchecked. The argument of those who favor an open border is that immigrants have always contributed to our society, and so they have. But we no longer can afford the world's "huddled masses" when our own are so often homeless and jobless. If we permit immigration to continue uncontrolled, it will explode in a full-blown crisis that will extend beyond the vociferous separatism/multiculturalism debate to engulf us in a violent civil conflict.

America is under siege. It is threatened from without by international terrorism and from within by centrifugal forces that already have revealed their capacity for destruction in bloody riots from Los Angeles to Miami, from Washington to Manhattan.

# NO ↩

**Stephen Moore**

# Give Us Your Best, Your Brightest

For many Americans, the word "immigration" immediately conjures up an image of poor Mexicans scrambling across the border near San Diego to find minimum-wage work and perhaps collect government benefits. Recent public opinion polls confirm that the attitude of the American public toward immigration is highly unfavorable. Central Americans are perceived as welfare abusers who stubbornly refuse to learn English, Haitians are seen as AIDS carriers, Russian Jews are considered to be mafiosi, and Asians are seen as international terrorists. The media reinforce these stereotypes by battering the public with negative depictions of immigrants.

The conception of immigrants as tired, poor, huddled masses seems permanently sketched into the mind of the public, just as the words are sketched irrevocably at the feet of the Statue of Liberty. But the Emma Lazarus poem simply does not describe the hundreds of thousands of people who are building new lives here in the 1990s. It would be more appropriate if the words at the base of the statue read: "Give us your best, your brightest, your most energetic and talented." Why? Because in large part those are the people who come to the United States each year.

Before we start slamming shut the golden door, it might be worthwhile to find out who the newcomers are and how they truly affect our lives.

Anyone who believes that immigrants are a drain on the U.S. economy has never visited the Silicon Valley in California. Here and in other corridors of high-tech entrepreneurship, immigrants are literally the lifeblood of many of the nation's most prosperous industries. In virtually every field in which the United States asserted global leadership in the 1980s—industries such as computer design and softwear, pharmaceuticals, bioengineering, electronics, superconductivity, robotics and aerospace engineering—one finds immigrants. In many ways these high-growth industries are the modern version of the American melting pot in action.

Consider Intel Corp. With profits of $1.1 billion in 1992, it is one of the most prolific and fast-expanding companies in the United States, employing tens of thousands of American workers. It is constantly developing exciting, cutting-edge technologies that will define the computer industry in the 21st century.

From Stephen Moore, "Give Us Your Best, Your Brightest," *Insight* (November 22, 1993). Copyright © 1993 by *Insight*. Reprinted by permission. All rights reserved.

And it is doing all of this largely with the talents of America's newest immigrants. Three members of Intel's top management, including Chief Executive Officer Andrew S. Grove, from Hungary, are immigrants. Some of its most successful and revolutionary computer technologies were pioneered by immigrants, such as the 8080 microprocessor (an expanded-power computer chip), invented by a Japanese, and polysilicon FET gates (the basic unit of memory storage on modern computer chips), invented by an Italian. Dick Ward, manager of employee information systems at Intel, says: "Our whole business is predicated on inventing the next generation of computer technologies. The engine that drives that quest is brainpower. And here at Intel, much of that brainpower comes from immigrants."

Or consider Du Pont-Merck Pharmaceutical Co., an $800 million-a-year health care products company based in Wilmington, Del., which reports that immigrants are responsible for many of its most promising new product innovations. For example, losartan, an antihypertensive drug, was developed by a team of scientists that included two Chinese and a Lithuanian. Joseph Mollica, Chief Executive Officer of Du Pont-Merck, says that bringing together such diverse talent "lets you look at problems and opportunities from a slightly different point of view."

Intel and Du Pont-Merck are not alone in relying on immigrants. Robert Kelley Jr., president of SO/CAL/TEN, an association of nearly 200 high-tech California companies, insists: "Without the influx of Asians in the 1980s, we would not have had the entrepreneurial explosion we've seen in California." David N. K. Wang, vice president for worldwide business operations at Applied Materials Inc., a computer-technology company in California, adds that because of immigration, "Silicon Valley is one of the most international business centers in the world."

Take away the immigrants, and you take away the talent base that makes such centers operate. Indeed, it is frightening to think what would happen to America's global competitiveness if the immigrants stopped coming. Even scarier is the more realistic prospect that U.S. policymakers will enact laws to prevent them from coming.

New research has begun to quantify the contributions of immigrants to American industry. The highly respected National Research Council reported in 1988 that "a large fraction of the technological output of the United States [is] dependent upon foreign talent and that such dependency is growing." Noting that well over half of all scientists graduating with doctorate degrees from American universities and one in three engineers working in the United States are immigrants, the report states emphatically: "It is clear . . . that these foreign-born engineers enrich our culture and make substantial contributions to the U.S. economic well-being and competitiveness."

The United States' competitive edge over the Japanese, Germans, Koreans and much of Europe is linked closely to its continued ability to attract and retain highly talented workers from other countries. A 1990 study by the national Science Foundation says, "Very significant, positive aspects arise from the presence of foreign-born engineers in our society."

For example, superconductivity, a technology that is expected to spawn hundreds of vital new commercial applications in the next century, was discovered by a physicist at the University of Houston, Paul C. W. Chu. He was born in China and came to the U.S. in 1972. His brilliance and inventiveness have made him a top contender for a Nobel Prize.

Of course, if Chu does win a Nobel, he will join a long list of winners who were immigrants in America. In the 20th century, between 20 percent and 50 percent of the Nobel Prize winners, depending on the discipline involved, have been immigrants to the United States. Today there are more Russian Nobel Prize winners living in the U.S. than there are living in Russia.

Public opinion polls consistently reveal that a major worry is that immigrants take jobs from American workers. The fear is understandable but misplaced. Immigrants don't just take jobs, they create jobs. One way is by starting new businesses. Today, America's immigrants, even those who come with relatively low skill levels, are highly entrepreneurial.

Take Koreans, for example. According to sociologists Alendro Portes and Ruben Rumbaut, "In Los Angeles, the propensity for self-employment is three times greater for Koreans than among the population as a whole. Grocery stores, restaurants, gas stations, liquor stores and real estate offices are typical Korean businesses." Cubans also are prodigious creators of new businesses. The number of Cuban-owned businesses in Miami has expanded from 919 in 1967 to 8,000 in 1976 to 28,000 in 1990. On Jefferson Boulevard in Dallas, more than 800 businesses operate, three-quarters of them owned by first- and second-generation Hispanic immigrants. Just 10 years ago, before the influx of Mexicans and other Central Americans, the neighborhood was in decay, with many vacant storefronts displaying "for sale" signs in the windows. Today it is a thriving ethnic neighborhood.

To be sure, few immigrant-owned businesses mature into an Intel. In fact, many fail completely. Like most new businesses in America, most immigrant establishments are small and only marginally profitable. The average immigrant business employs two to four workers and records roughly $200,000 in annual sales. However, such small businesses, as President Clinton often correctly emphasizes, are a significant source of jobs.

It should not be too surprising that immigrants are far more likely than average U.S. citizens to take business risks. After all, uprooting oneself, traveling to a foreign culture and making it requires more than the usual amount of courage, ambition, resourcefulness and even bravado. Indeed, this is part of the self-selection process that makes immigrants so particularly desirable. Immigrants are not just people—they are a very special group of people. By coming, they impart productive energies on the rest of us.

This is not just romanticism. It is well-grounded in fact. Countless studies have documented that immigrants to the United States tend to be more skilled, more highly educated and wealthier than the average citizen of their native countries.

Thomas Sowell, an economist and senior fellow at the Hoover Institution in Stanford, Calif., reports in his seminal study on immigration, "Ethnic America," that black immigrants from the West Indies have far higher skill levels than their countrymen at home. He also finds that the income levels of West Indies immigrants are higher than those of West Indies natives, American blacks and native-born white Americans.

Surprisingly, even illegal immigrants are not the poverty-stricken and least skilled from their native countries. Surveys of undocumented immigrants from Mexico to the United States show that only about 5 percent were unemployed in Mexico, whereas the average unemployment rate there was about three times that level, and that a relatively high percentage of them worked in white-collar jobs in Mexico. In addition, surveys have found that illiteracy among undocumented Mexicans in the U.S. is about 10 percent, whereas illiteracy in Mexico is about 22 percent.

Perhaps the greatest asset of immigrants is their children, who tend to be remarkably successful in the U.S. Recently, the city of Boston reported that an incredible 13 of the 17 valedictorians in its public high schools were foreign-born—from China, Vietnam, Portugal, El Salvador, France, Italy, Jamaica and the former Czechoslovakia. Many could not speak a word of English when they arrived. Public high schools in Washington, Chicago and Los Angeles also report remarkably disproportionate numbers of immigrant children at the top of the class. Similarly, Westinghouse reports that over the past 12 years, about one-third of its prestigious National Science Talent Search winners have been Asians. Out of this group might emerge America's next Albert Einstein, who himself was an immigrant.

So one hidden cost of restricting immigration is the loss of immigrants' talented and motivated children.

In the past century, America has admitted roughly 50 million immigrants. This has been one of the largest migrations in the history of the world. Despite this infusion of people—no, because of it—the United States became by the middle of the 20th century the wealthiest nation in the world. Real wages in America have grown more than eightfold over this period. The U.S. economy employed less than 40 million people in 1900; today it employs nearly 120 million people. The U.S. job machine had not the slightest problem expanding and absorbing the 8 million legal immigrants who came to this country in the 1980s. Eighteen million jobs were created.

But what about those frightening headlines? "Immigration Bankrupting Nation." "Immigrants Displacing U.S. Workers." "Foreigners Lured to U.S. by Welfare."

Here are the facts. The 1990s census reveals that roughly 6 percent of native-born Americans are on public assistance, versus 7 percent of the foreign-born, with less than 5 percent of illegal immigrants collecting welfare. Not much reason for alarm. Because immigrants tend to come to the United States when they are young and working, over their lifetimes they each pay about $20,000 more in taxes than they use in services, according to economist Julian Simon of the University of Maryland. With 1 million immigrants per year, the nation gains about $20 billion more than cost. Rather than fiscal burdens, immigrants are huge bargains.

Nor do immigrants harm the U.S. labor market. A comprehensive 1989 study by the U.S. Department of Labor concluded: "Neither U.S. workers nor most minority workers appear to be adversely affected by immigration—especially during periods of economic expansion." In the 1980s, the top 10 immigrant-receiving states—including California, Florida, Massachusetts and Texas—recorded rates of unemployment 2 percentage points below the U.S. average, according to the Alexis de Tocqueville Institution in Arlington, Va. So where's the job displacement?

We are now witnessing in America what might be described as the return of the nativists. They are selling fear and bigotry. But if any of their allegations against immigrants are accurate, then America could not have emerged as the economic superpower it is today.

In fact, most Americans do accept that immigration in the past has contributed greatly to the nation's economic growth. But they are not so sanguine in their assessment of present and future immigrants. It is strangely inconsistent that Americans believe that so long-standing and crucial a benefit is now a source of cultural and economic demise.

Shortly before his death, Winston Churchill wrote, "The empires of the future are the empires of the mind." America is confronted with one of the most awesome opportunities in world history to build those empires by attracting highly skilled, highly educated and entrepreneurial people from all over the globe. The Andrew Groves and the Paul Chus of the world do not want to go to Japan, Israel, Germany, France or Canada. Almost universally they want to come to the United States. We can be selective. By expanding immigration but orienting our admission policies toward gaining the best and the brightest, America would enjoy a significant comparative advantage over its geopolitical rivals.

By pursuing a liberal and strategic policy on immigration, America can ensure that the 21st century, like the 20th, will be the American century.

# POSTSCRIPT

## Should the United States Put More Restrictions on Immigration?

There is no accurate census of illegal immigrants, but the best estimate is that 5 million persons have entered the United States illegally within the past 10 years. What are the consequences for American society? The issue of immigration encompasses both legal and illegal immigrants. Immigration policy should begin by examining who comes and the consequences for the nation. Who are they, and what impact do they have? What do they cost, and what do they contribute?

Until the early years of the new republic, immigrants were predominantly white, English-speaking, Protestant Europeans and African slaves who were forcibly brought to the New World. This soon changed, and for a half-century —until the adoption of laws restricting immigration in the 1920s—Catholics and Jews, southern and eastern Europeans, most of them non-English speakers, came to the United States. Since World War II, Asian and Hispanic immigrants have come in ever-increasing numbers. George Henderson and Thompson Olasiji's *Migrants, Immigrants, and Slaves: Racial and Ethnic Groups in America* (University Press of America, 1995) is a useful introduction to the patterns of immigration into the United States.

Georgie Anne Geyer's *Americans No More* (Atlantic Monthly Press, 1996) is a lament on the decline of civic life in America as a result of both legal and illegal immigration. Geyer does not deplore illegal immigration but the recent tendency of legal immigrants to resist assimilation. Peter Brimelow, in *Alien Nation: Common Sense About America's Immigration Disaster* (Random House, 1995), catalogs what he perceives to be the consequences of what he calls America's "immigration disaster." Brimelow argues that no multicultural society has lasted.

In opposition to Brimelow's view, Sanford J. Ungar, in *Fresh Blood: The New American Immigrants* (Simon & Schuster, 1995), argues, "To be American means being part of an ever more heterogeneous people and participating in the constant redefinition of a complex, evolving cultural fabric." Somewhere in between multiculturalists like Ungar and assimilationists like Brimelow and Geyer is Peter D. Salins. In *Assimilation, American Style* (Basic Books, 1997), Salins argues that the naturalization process is the best means for absorbing the flood of immigrants who arrive in America each year.

Often forgotten in these debates are the experiences of the immigrants themselves. Newer immigrants to America have recounted some of these experiences in recent books by and about them. In *Becoming American: Personal Essays by First Generation Immigrant Women* (Hyperion, 2000), Ghanaian-American writer Meri Nana-Ama Danquah brings together the personal recollections and reflections by immigrant women from Europe, Latin America, Africa, Asia, and the Caribbean. In *American by Choice: The Remarkable Fulfillment of an Immigrant's Dreams* (Thomas Nelson, 1998), Sam Moore describes his rise in America from a poor Lebanese immigrant to president and CEO of Thomas Nelson Publishers, a major religious publishing house. A more troubling account of the immigrant experience is that of Mary C. Waters, in *Black Identities: West Indian Immigrant Dreams and American Realities* (Harvard University Press, 2000). Waters finds that when West Indian immigrants first arrive, their skills, knowledge of English, and general optimism carry them forward, but later on, a variety of influences, from racial discrimination to low wages and poor working conditions, tend to erode their self-confidence.

Americans confront a choice. On the one hand, there are the ethical and political consequences of restricting immigration into a country whose attraction to poor or persecuted people is as great as its borders are vast. On the other hand, there are the problems of absorbing new, generally non-English-speaking populations into an economy that may have to provide increasing public support and a society whose traditions and values may clash with those of the newcomers.

# ISSUE 21

# Is Democracy Desirable for All Nations?

**YES: Robert Kagan**, from "Democracies and Double Standards," *Commentary* (August 1997)

**NO: Robert D. Kaplan**, from "Was Democracy Just a Moment?" *The Atlantic Monthly* (December 1997)

### ISSUE SUMMARY

**YES:** Author and editor Robert Kagan argues that democracy has taken root in many nations that never had it before, in large measure due to American intervention, with desirable consequences for American security and prosperity.

**NO:** Foreign correspondent Robert D. Kaplan contends that recent experience demonstrates that not all nations have the conditions in which democracy can thrive, that some nations prosper without it, and that democracy may be less important in the future.

T he most thoughtful advocates of democracy do not claim that it provides a cure for all that ails us. Rather, they argue, it is simply the best way—far and away the best, say its most ardent advocates—of organizing societies to deal with public issues. Winston Churchill acknowledged that he was not the first to express the sentiment in his famous observation, "No one pretends that democracy is perfect or all-wise. Indeed, it has been said that democracy is the worst form of government except all those other forms that have been tried from time to time."

Writing about the United States more than 150 years ago, Alexis de Tocqueville expressed his belief that the spread of democracy was irresistible, but he also concluded that the American example of the 1830s might not be the best for either America's future or the rest of the world. Tocqueville warned that democracy must "adapt its government to time and place, and to modify it according to men and conditions." With the belief of hindsight and an awareness of the ways in which democracy has developed, we may ask, Can those adaptations and modifications be sufficient to meet the needs of all nations and cultures? Is it possible that democracy is neither inevitable nor desirable at some times, under some circumstances, and in some places?

The evidence of the past quarter century is encouraging to those who believe in the triumph of democracy. President Bill Clinton has asserted that, for the first time in human history, more people live in democracies than any other form of government. Throughout Latin America and in parts of Asia, Africa, and Eastern Europe in which democracy was previously unknown, personal freedoms, free elections, and a free press have become familiar. By contrast, Freedom House, a private organization devoted to the spread of democracy, estimated in 1996 that only one-fifth of the world's population lived in free societies, two-fifths in partly free nations, and another two-fifths in countries that were not free.

What are the necessary conditions for democracy? The most basic requirement is economic: the existence of a minimally adequate standard of living that provides enough food and other basic necessities. No population would choose a ballot over bread or other basic dietary staples. Implicit is the existence of employment that is adequate to ensure that individuals will continue to be able to meet these needs.

The fundamental political requirement for democracy is literacy, which goes beyond the ability to read and write to an awareness of one's responsibilities and rights in a democratic society. Political pundit Walter Lippmann observed, "No amount of charters, direct primaries, or short ballots will make a democracy out of an illiterate people." In this respect, democracy sets a high standard that many nations may not be able to meet.

More debatable is the claim of a social requirement: the sense of a shared destiny that cuts across racial, ethnic, and religious differences to create a common bond that ensures stability and a willingness to abide by the results of the last election, no matter how opposed the losers may be. The idea is that although the best public policy may not be made by counting heads, it is far better than breaking them, as appeals court judge Learned Hand once said.

Should America seek to export democracy? "The world must be made safe for democracy," was President Woodrow Wilson's plea when he urged Congress to involve the United States in World War I. Since then America has often sought the expansion of democracy, but it has also given military and economic assistance to governments that were undisguisedly antidemocratic. America's foreign policy often hinges on a choice between morality (what's good?) and practicality (what's good for America?). Those who urge American commitment to the spread of democracy argue that the idealistic and pragmatic approaches now coincide because the security of the United States is endangered by the presence of authoritarian regimes.

In the first of the following selections, Churchill's argument for democracy is echoed by Robert Kagan, who concludes, "Democracy is not the solution to the world's problems. But it is a better solution than the alternatives." He adds, relevant to America's relations with the rest of the world, "And it is the only solution the United States can ever support with a modicum of enthusiasm or consistency." In the second selection, Robert D. Kaplan suggests that democracy may be rendered irrelevant as a result of the globalization of economic enterprise, culture, electronic communications that transcend all boundaries, and material prosperity that leaves less time and thought for public concerns.

**Robert Kagan**

 **YES**

# Democracies and Double Standards

For citizens of the world's most powerful democracy, it ought to be a source of satisfaction, and even of pride, that peoples all over the planet have struggled to adopt our model of government—and, in recent years, have succeeded in doing so at an astonishingly high rate. In the wave of democratization that swept the world between the late 1970's and early 1990's, more than 30 nations of widely diverse cultures and locales became democratic. Many of these transformations would once have been unimaginable: democracy in Taiwan? in Nicaragua? in Romania? in South Africa? Although some have since faltered and slipped back toward dictatorship, in most democracy has sunk its roots deeply and appears to be settling in for a long stay.

The United States played a central part—indeed, an indispensable part—in spurring and supporting this global transition. To be sure, in Latin America and Asia, growing economies and indigenous political forces made dictatorship more precarious. Within the Soviet empire, stagnation and decay hollowed out Communist tyranny from within. But in the absence of American exhortation, pressure, and in some cases direct intervention, these broad historical trends could easily have been cut short by guerrilla victories, military coups, or violent repression. Instead, they were seized upon by local leader after local leader, from Corazon Aquino and José Napoleon Duarte to Lech Walesa and Boris Yeltsin, each of whom was favored with American support at the crucial turning point.

Can anyone doubt that the spread of democracy these past twenty years has been a good thing, both for the United States and for the world? To contemplate today's situation is to appreciate anew the wisdom of American policymakers in the late 70's and throughout most of the 1980's who placed a special value on promoting democratic governance abroad as part of America's grand strategy. Indeed, given the remarkable success of this policy, one would have every reason to expect that it continues to command a great deal of support in the foreign-policy establishment and among American public officials.

But one would be wrong.

⋘◉⋙

Over the past four or five years, a new pessimism, a new indifference, and even a new distaste for the promotion of democracy abroad have rippled through

From Robert Kagan, "Democracies and Double Standards," *Commentary* (August 1997). Copyright © 1997 by The American Jewish Committee. Reprinted by permission of *Commentary*. Some notes omitted.

intellectual circles and out into the political arena. The assault comes from many different directions: from both the Right and the Left, from isolationists and internationalists, from the avatars of realism and the apostles of free-trade liberalism. But for all its diversity, the trend is unmistakable. The policies that helped shape the present, democratic era are losing legitimacy.

As one rather remarkable illustration, consider two "data points." In 1991, the distinguished Harvard political scientist Samuel P. Huntington published a book, *The Third Wave: Democratization in the Late Twentieth Century,* which exhaustively chronicled and unapologetically celebrated the advance of democracy around the world from the late 1970's onward. Although Huntington recognized some significant obstacles to the further extension of this trend—not least, the limits on political pluralism and individual rights that might be imposed by certain cultures, especially the Islamic and the Confucian—he reminded his readers that similar arguments had once been made about the inhibiting effects of Catholicism, and had been proved wrong in Spain, Portugal, Poland, and Latin America. Cultures need not be "permanent obstacles to development in one direction or another," he wrote. "Cultures evolve."

Thanks to broad, impersonal forces like economic growth, "time," Huntington concluded in 1991, was "on democracy's side." Still, though economic development and modernization helped make democracy possible, only "political leadership makes it real." Democracy would continue to spread only "to the extent that those who exercise power in the world and in individual countries want it to spread." Urging the United States to take a leading role in the process, Huntington departed from the analytic mode of the social scientist to propose, at several points in his book, "Guidelines for Democratizers."

Now for our second data point. It could not have been very long before the Huntington who wrote ringingly in 1991 that "I believe... democracy is good in itself and... has positive consequences for individual freedom, domestic stability, international peace, and the United States of America" began revising his optimism downward. By 1994, he had published an article in *Foreign Affairs,* "The Clash of Civilizations," in which he outlined the view—later developed in a book of the same title—that culture, or civilization, pretty much determined politics after all. As he would put it in another article in *Foreign Affairs* two years later, such hallmarks of democracy as the separation of spiritual and temporal authority, pluralism, the rule of law, representative government, and respect for individual rights and liberties were a product of European civilization, and "the belief that non-Western peoples should adopt Western values, institutions, and culture is, if taken seriously, immoral in its implications." The message now was that the United States and the West should stay out of the affairs of other civilizations and tend to their own—which happened, by the way, to be in a perilous state of decline.

❧

Huntington's may be the starkest but is far from the only example of the swift journey traveled by many foreign-policy thinkers from optimism to skepticism, and from participation, however qualified, in the euphoria occasioned by the spread of democracy and the downfall of Soviet Communism to denunciation of that euphoria. One can discern the origins of the new dourness in the virtually uniform response among intellectuals to Francis Fukuyama's 1989 article, "The End of History." In that now-famous work, Fukuyama suggested that the collapse of Communism augured nothing less than "the end point of mankind's ideological evolution and the universalization of Western liberal democracy as the final form of human government." Although Fukuyama conspicuously did *not* say this spelled an end to all human troubles, he was taken as saying it, and the reaction was fierce. It was not enough to prove that Fukuyama had exaggerated the good news; it was necessary to declare that he was entirely wrong, and that the news was in fact bad.

The harbingers of bad news have multiplied in the intervening years. We have been told that the world, far from being in somewhat greater harmony as a result of the spread of democratic government, is really *Out of Control* (the title of a 1993 book by Zbigniew Brzezinski) or in a state of *Pandaemonium* (the title of a book by Daniel Patrick Moynihan in the same year). The Yale historian Paul Kennedy, undeterred by history's refutation of his 1988 work, *The Rise and Fall of the Great Powers* (in which he had warned of the impending bankruptcy of the United States under the weight of "imperial overstretch"), produced, in *Preparing for the Twenty-first Century* (1993), a new catalogue of global horrors: population explosions, disease, growing disparities of wealth, environmental catastrophe, the breakdown of nation-states. In "The Coming Anarchy," an influential article in the *Atlantic Monthly* later fleshed out in the portentously titled book, *The Ends of the Earth*, Robert D. Kaplan gave "personal meaning" to Kennedy's tale of miseries by providing a worldwide tour of the future now awaiting us: "Poverty, the collapse of cities, porous borders, cultural and racial strife, growing economic disparities, [and] weakening nation-states."

Although Huntington himself has not fully endorsed the new "chaos paradigm," the picture he has painted in the last few years suggests the futility of any efforts at amelioration. In a world in which, as he wrote last year, "the word 'genocide' has been heard far more often . . . than it was in any half-decade during the cold war," talk of supporting the further spread of democracy seems not only silly but misguided. In a *New York Times* op-ed piece, Robert Kaplan has suggested that we "shift our emphasis in the third world from holding elections to promoting family planning, environmental renewal, road building, and other stabilizing projects." What many third-world countries now need, in Kaplan's view, is not democracy, which tends rather to weaken than to strengthen society, but a dictatorship that can lead them through the stages of economic development necessary before democratic government becomes thinkable.

Kaplan is not alone in proposing that democracy may not only be too difficult for some people to achieve but actually bad for them. Two political scientists from Columbia University, Edward D. Mansfield and Jack Snyder, have discovered a hitherto unknown "historical pattern" linking "democratization, belligerent nationalism, and war." Reinterpreting the origins of the Crimean war, World War I, and such modern conflicts as the wars between Serbia and Croatia and between Armenia and Azerbaijan; and citing the fact that "the electorate of Russia's partial democracy cast nearly a quarter of its votes [in 1993] for the party of radical nationalist Vladimir Zhirinovsky," Mansfield and Snyder have concluded, with mathematical precision, that

> states that make the biggest leap, from total autocracy to extensive mass democracy—like contemporary Russia—are about twice as likely to fight wars in the decade after democratization as are states that remain autocracies.

Indeed, the splitting-up of the Soviet behemoth into fifteen new states has provided ample fodder for the new debunkers of democracy. In seven of those states democracy is intact though precarious, while in the remaining eight it is either increasingly flawed or absent. But these eight make up fully half of a worldwide list compiled by Thomas Carothers of the Carnegie Endowment as proof positive of a "retrenchment" that "is stripping away the illusions that have surrounded the pro-democratic enterprise of recent years." Similarly with the break-up of Yugoslavia, where, according to Mansfield and Snyder, the "inexorable pressure for democratization" is what allowed the old elites to create "a new basis for legitimacy through nationalist propaganda and military action." After all, Fareed Zakaria, the managing editor of *Foreign Affairs,* pointed out in early 1996, it was through the quintessentially democratic procedure of elections that a "xenophobic dictator," Slobodan Milosevic, could consolidate his power in Serbia.

To the list of bad things produced by democracy has been added, finally, the deeply problematic outcome of elections in the Islamic world. In Algeria in 1992, such elections seemed certain to yield a victory by Muslim radicals, and were therefore canceled by the military. In Turkey, elections in 1995 produced a victory for the Welfare party, whose leader, Necmettin Erbakan, upon taking power in 1996, set about encouraging Islamic fundamentalism at home and courting the radical governments of Iran, Iraq, and Libya abroad; he was forced from his perch this year by the secular Turkish military. In both cases, it took a violation of democratic process to put a halt to what the democratic process had alarmingly yielded, and in both cases many observers and government officials heaved a sigh of relief: surely, they reasoned, it is better to have in place an orderly authoritarian government we can work with than a radical one we cannot.

~·❦·~

Irronically, that is the kind of reasoning that Jeane J. Kirkpatrick pursued many years ago in these pages in "Dictatorships and Double Standards,"[1] the seminal and wide-ranging article which led to her appointment as U.S. ambassador to the United Nations and influential adviser on foreign policy to the newly elected Ronald Reagan.

Kirkpatrick came at the issue from within the context of that historical moment. Specifically, her article was aimed at the blunderings of the Carter administration in foreign affairs over the preceding three years, and the "double standard" referred to in her title was this: the administration, and its liberal supporters, had reacted with punitive outrage to violations of human rights perpetrated by right-wing regimes allied to the United States, while taking a relatively accommodating view of the far more systematic abuses of Communist tyrannies that were actively threatening American interests around the world. Worse, by hectoring our allies and pressuring them to democratize overnight, the Carter administration, she argued, had transformed two such allies, Iran and Nicaragua, into hostile, radical dictatorships.

But much of Kirkpatrick's essay also transcended the particular issues of the day and was meant to enunciate durable political truths, however hard she thought they might be for some Americans to swallow. One of these was that dictatorships, like the poor, would always be with us. At a time when the number of democracies outside Western Europe, the United States, and Canada could be counted on one hand, Kirkpatrick declared, quite accurately, that "most governments in the world are, as they always have been, autocracies of one kind or another." And yet, she went on, "no idea holds greater sway in the mind of educated Americans than the belief that it is possible to democratize governments, anytime, anywhere, under any circumstances."

This idea, in Kirkpatrick's judgment, was simply false. In "Dictatorships and Double Standards" she took sharp issue with the notion of modernization's inevitability (an idea associated with the work of Samuel P. Huntington), and went out of her way to slam Zbigniew Brzezinski, the main foreign-policy intellectual in the Carter administration, for his insistence on viewing the world not from the "perspective of American interests or intentions" but from that of "the modernizing nation and the 'end' of history." Although Kirkpatrick did not deny that U.S. policy could "encourage [the] process of liberalization and democratization" in some autocratic regimes, she came close to doing so. The attempt should certainly not be made, she wrote, "at a time when the incumbent government is fighting for its life against violent adversaries." Moreover, the proposed reforms would have to be "aimed at producing gradual change rather than perfect democracy overnight." And "gradual" did not mean a few years. "Decades, if not centuries" might be "required for people to acquire the necessary disciplines and habits."

⌘

Eighteen years and more than 30 new democracies later, Kirkpatrick's intellectual followers include, amazingly enough, some of the main targets of her criticisms in 1979—and on both the Left and the Right. On the Left, especially in the giddily optimistic crowd of free-trade liberals, some of the same people who wanted the United States to topple Somoza and the Shah in 1979, and who denounced "constructive engagement" with South Africa in the 1980's, today argue with equal passion for "constructive engagement" with China. A hefty portion of the Right similarly defends a tolerant attitude toward China, as well as other dictatorial regimes, on the solid Kirkpatrickian grounds that we cannot and must not expect "perfect democracy overnight."

To be sure, the new debunkers of democratization have had to digest the inconvenient fact that democracy can, indeed, spring up "anytime, anywhere, under any circumstances." But this does not appear to have fazed them.

Whether the subject is Indonesia, a classic authoritarian government, or, more incongruously, China, which still retains many of the defining characteristics of a totalitarian society, the current wisdom holds that tyrannies should be given time to evolve naturally, which is to say, as Kirkpatrick explained, "slowly."

In one sense, of course, the return of the Kirkpatrick thesis is only part of a broader resurgence of an older and more established tradition in foreign policy: namely, "realism." In the 1950's and 1960's, the leading prophets of this influential school of thought, Hans J. Morgenthau and George E. Kennan, constantly warned against "crusades" on behalf of democracy, which they thought would lead either to nuclear holocaust or to the immoral dominance of one power—the United States—over every other.[2] Kennan, for one, did not much care for democracy, believing that, in Latin America and other less developed parts of the world, it made for weak and untrustworthy allies in the fight against Communism. And as for democracy in the United States, he once compared it to a dinosaur with a "brain the size of [a] pin."

Today, modern realists from Huntington to Owen Harries, the editor of the *National Interest,* complain about the "arrogance" of American efforts to impose our values on others, while some echo Kennan's view that democracies may be too weak to withstand the onslaught of radicals (in today's circumstances, these are usually not Communists but religious fundamentalists). Still others, like Henry Kissinger, admire the "Asian values" which allegedly form the basis of political society in Singapore, Indonesia, and China: in particular, the emphasis on "order" and "community" over individual rights and freedoms. And the aversion to promoting democracy abroad is also heavily influenced, just as it was in the past, by a deep pessimism about the health of democracy here at home.

This is especially, but not exclusively, true among conservatives. If, in the 1950's, the realists' hostility to ideological crusades was closely related to their disgust at what they perceived to be the wild and irresponsible behavior on display during the McCarthy era, today many conservatives are worried about the balkanization of American culture, about the impact of immigration and multiculturalism on our national identity, about threats to the American family, about an overweening government bureaucracy on the one hand and rampant individual license on the other. "The central issue for the West," Huntington warns in *The Clash of Civilizations,* "is whether, quite apart from any external challenges, it is capable of stopping and reversing the internal processes of decay."

✤

It is hard to say just how much this pessimism about democracy at home has influenced the reorientation of attitudes toward foreign policy, but one suspects it is quite a bit. What is clear, in any case, is that this reorientation has spread far beyond the think tanks and the universities and has profoundly affected the world of policy-makers.

A year ago, a panel of experts, former senior officials, and members of Congress produced a report on American interests in the post–cold-war era. . . .

The panel listed those interests under the categories of color-coded poker chips. Blue-chip interests were "vital," that is, "strictly necessary to safeguard and enhance the well-being of Americans in a free and secure nation." Red-chip interests, deemed "extremely important," represented conditions that "if compromised would severely prejudice but not strictly imperil the ability of the U.S. government to preserve American well-being. There were five of the former sorts of interest, eleven of the latter.

Then came the white chips, among which, at last, democracy made its appearance: the panel deemed it "just important" that the United States promote this interest, but only in "strategically important states" and only "as much as feasible without destabilization." A broader approach, "enlarging democracy elsewhere or for its own sake," was listed at the very bottom, as a translucent chip—something "intrinsically desirable" but having no major effect on the ability of the U.S. government to safeguard the freedom, security, and well-being of Americans.

A decade ago, these conclusions, by these people, would surely have provoked considerable discussion. They would have been taken, and rightly, as a strong repudiation of the policy followed by the Reagan administration, which had made a very high priority out of promoting democracy in such places as El Salvador, Chile, the Philippines, and South Korea, as well as in Eastern Europe and within the Soviet Union. Today, however, the report's hierarchy of interests aroused not the smallest hint of controversy. Nor was it meant to: rather, it was a conventional representation of conventional thinking.

⁐◉⁐

It is true that the Clinton administration, at least until recently, has tilted against this prevailing wind. Indeed, the President and his top advisers have declared the "enlargement" of the democratic sphere to be something of a red-chip or even a blue-chip goal, and in some areas their rhetoric has been complemented by action. Thus, the administration has devoted considerable energy to supporting democratic forces in Russia, often in the face of indifference and skepticism in Congress and the foreign-policy establishment. It has used the process of NATO enlargement as a means of both preserving and encouraging democratic reforms in former Warsaw Pact countries. It played an important role in the continuing transition to democracy in South Africa. In Latin America, it helped support a crucial, second free election in Nicaragua, blocked a military coup in Paraguay and another in Guatemala, and, in a very bold move for which it was harshly condemned by Republicans, even used force to restore a democratically-elected president in Haiti.

More recently, though, the administration's commitment has faltered. Instead of treating the "enlargement" of the democratic world as a high American priority, it has increasingly settled into the establishment view that democracy is only a white or translucent chip and hence subject to barter in return for other benefits, especially of the economic or commercial variety. As Thomas Carothers correctly notes, the administration has "shied away" from pushing hard for democratic reform in Nigeria (which has oil); it has kept largely silent about the move toward authoritarian rule in Kazakhstan (which also has oil); it has been unwilling to take a hard line against the increasingly authoritarian president of Armenia, Levon Ter-Petrosian (there is a domestic constituency for continuing aid to Armenia); and it has been sporadic, at best, in its support for democratic reforms in Croatia and Serbia. In Asia, though willing to apply sanctions against tiny and inconsequential Burma for suppressing the democratic movement of Aung San Suu Kyi, Clinton has placed the avidity of American business for "emerging markets" in China and Indonesia ahead of concerns about those regimes' tyrannical practices.

In short, what we are seeing in the administration's moves, as in the experts' report, is the emergence of a new consensus, created more by default than by design and based on today's version of a double (or, rather, multiple) standard. Democracy is to be supported in Western Europe and parts of Central and Eastern Europe, but not necessarily in Southeastern Europe. It is to be celebrated in those Asian nations, like Taiwan, Japan, and South Korea, which have already chosen the democratic path; but in those that have not, we are to respect the dictators' right to impose "Asian values" on their people. (In Hong Kong, this may require some particularly uncomfortable contortions, but the pain will pass.) In Latin America, democracy is to be supported almost everywhere, except (if you are a conservative) Haiti or (if a liberal) Cuba. Democracy is altogether too dangerous to support in the Islamic world, except, partially, in Turkey, which is a member of NATO. In the states that once made up the former Soviet Union, the issue is largely one of culture: the peoples of the Baltic states, Russia, and Ukraine are to be held to a much higher standard than the peoples of the Caucasus and Central Asia. As for the African nations, if they hold elections, we will be happy; if they cancel them, or start slaughtering each other, we can rest content in the knowledge that they were not ready for elections in the first place.

━◦◉◦━

Two decades ago, it may have made sense to be pessimistic about the prospects for democracy. As Jeane Kirkpatrick noted at the time, autocracy in one form or another was the norm, democracy the rare and fragile exception. Much less understandable is today's dour and cynical view, which is so at odds with the global experience of the intervening two decades.

*Are* some of the world's new democracies unstable or faltering? Of course they are. But the largest chunk of these troubled nations lies in a part of the world—the former Soviet Union—that possesses a number of unique qualities. The main problem is not that such newly independent states as Tajikistan, Uzbekistan, Turkmenistan, Belarus, and Kazakhstan have no history of democracy; there is plenty of evidence from elsewhere in the world that this need not be an insuperable obstacle to democratization. The far greater problem is that they have no history of independent nationhood. Their institutions, such as they are, are the provincial remnants of the Soviet system. As Alexander J. Motyl notes in this year's Freedom House survey, most of the non-Russian Soviet republics began their lives lacking almost everything—"elites, civil society, rule of law, and the market"—necessary to support almost *any* form of government. It is certainly disappointing that democracy in about half of these countries is in trouble, but the miracle is that it continues to survive in so many. And in any case it is an analytical error to lay disproportionate stress on these failures in any objective global assessment....

That the African picture is a mixed one is powerfully proved by the horrors of Rwanda and Burundi, the brutal tyranny of Nigeria, and the turmoil of the Democratic Republic of Congo (formerly Zaire). But given Africa's history, and given the long-term failure of the United States and other democracies to address themselves to its political problems, the wonder once again is that the continent's record is as mixed as it is.

If it is one kind of mistake to overstate the bad news by measuring today's much-improved reality against some imagined utopia, a much bigger mistake is to shape our policy around the failures. The notion, for instance, that we would do better to focus on economic development, on establishing the alleged "prerequisites" of democracy rather than democracy itself, simply ignores the lessons of the recent past. As the political analyst Adrian Karatnycky has noted, the states of the former Soviet empire that "have made the greatest progress in creating market economies" have, for the most part, also been those "that have made the greatest progress in consolidating their democratic transitions." Conversely, the failure to achieve economic reform has been most notable in states showing the least progress toward political reform. These findings, Karatnycky argues,

> contradict the argument that economic reform can successfully be implemented by authoritarian rulers who [allegedly] can take decisive and unpopular steps because they are not inhibited by public opinion, ... rival political parties and movements, or free trade unions.

What about the idea that democracy leads to instability, bloody ethnic conflict, and war? Surely no one can seriously believe it would have been better to preserve the Soviet or Titoist tyrannies intact after 1989—let alone that this would have been possible. The collapse of these regimes did, indeed, unleash ethnic conflicts and innumerable border disputes. But was democratization to blame? Absent the firm intervention of outside powers, would the break-up of Yugoslavia have been more peaceful if the successor governments had been more uniformly tyrannical? If this century has taught us anything, it is that dictators are perfectly capable of whipping up ethnic and/or nationalist hysteria, and of initiating genocide, for their own purposes.

Finally, the claim by Edward Mansfield and Jack Snyder that states in transition to democracy are twice as likely to engage in war cannot withstand scrutiny. Even leaving aside their interpretation of earlier historical events, it is simply wrong to conclude that today's Russia is more warlike because nearly a quarter of the Russian electorate voted in 1993 for a radical nationalist, or because Boris Yeltsin used murderous force against the breakaway republic of Chechnya. The fact is that Zhirinovsky reached his political zenith in 1993, and his support has dwindled ever since. Russia's new democratic system, meanwhile, has compelled the Kremlin to give up its disastrous effort to crush the Chechen revolt. (In the czarist era, Russia fought wars of this nature for decades.) And democratic Russia has likewise peacefully negotiated a settlement with democratic Ukraine for control of Sevastopol and the Black Sea fleet; somehow, one doubts that Stalin, or even Gorbachev, would have been so accommodating. If, in sum, today's Russia offers evidence of anything, it is the generally pacifying effect of democracy on a leadership not traditionally known for its pacific policies.

⊷

Democracy is not the solution to the world's problems. But it is a better solution than the alternatives. And it is the only solution the United States can ever support with a modicum of enthusiasm or consistency.

This, certainly, was the hard-learned lesson of the Reagan era. Contrary to what everyone expected at the time, the Reagan administration did not ultimately conduct its foreign policies according to the Kirkpatrick thesis, though for a time it tried to do so by instituting closer ties, or at least less hostile relations, with certain dictatorial regimes in Latin America and elsewhere. (Reagan himself had fond feelings for the Philippine dictator, Ferdinand Marcos.) But the practice proved unsustainable, and for a simple reason.

Reagan, who was no realist in the Kissingerian mode, elevated the global struggle with Communism to a high priority; rather than accept a condition of permanent coexistence, he took steps to try to undo Communism whenever and wherever the opportunity beckoned. A couple of years into his first term, however, administration officials began to realize that such a battle against the world's most formidable tyranny could not be won by a policy that was officially sanguine about lesser and friendlier tyrannies. It could not be won, that is, under a double standard. And so, instead of accepting the permanence and legitimacy of friendly dictatorships, the administration set about pressing them to reform, often not under conditions of relative calm and safety but when, precisely, they were engaged in "fighting for [their] life against violent adversaries," and not over decades or centuries but quickly.

In El Salvador, in the Philippines, in Chile, and elsewhere, the Reagan team found a way to accomplish this without suffering the fate of the Carter administration in Iran and Nicaragua. In the countries where the "Reagan doctrine" was applied, democratic reformers did indeed gain strength and guerrillas and terrorist groups were indeed weakened. This record looks all the more impressive in the light of today's sober warnings that we should support democracy abroad only when the risks to our security, or to our oil, or to our export markets, are negligible.

One area in which the Reagan-era experience holds obvious implications today is the Islamic world. Clearly it is in our interest to prevent radical fundamentalist regimes from taking power there. In fact, the battle against the radicals in Iran, in Sudan, and in Afghanistan should be waged more tenaciously than it has been. Simultaneously, however, we could and should be holding authoritarian regimes in the Middle East to higher standards of democracy, and encouraging democratic voices within those societies, even if it means risking some instability in some places. At the height of the cold war, the strategic risks in Central America and in Asia were at least as great as they are today in the Middle East—and the gamble, once taken, paid off.

The real question before us today is the same question Samuel P. Huntington posed, in Lincolnesque fashion, seven years ago: "How long can an increasingly interdependent world survive part-democratic and part-authoritarian?" Huntington's point was not that the world would ever *become* completely one or the other, but that a modern, closely interconnected world must move generally either in one direction—i.e., toward greater liberty—or in another—toward greater tyranny. Although the United States may not have the final say over the outcome, as the leading power our say can well be determinative. If we act wrongly, we may lose something even more valuable than our relative security.

✦

For the day we adopt a neutral attitude toward the fate of democracy in the world is the day we deny our own essence, an essence rooted in a commitment to certain principles which we believe to be universal. Anyone worried about our national identity, and about the challenge posed to it by the balkanization of our culture, must know that we can hardly expect to unite our own country if we decide that those principles apply only in a few, rare circumstances and to a limited number of fortunate peoples. Nor can we expect to achieve renewal at home if we conduct ourselves abroad in a mood of despair and cynicism about the very things we hold most dear.

It is often argued that vitality abroad depends first on vitality at home. But the reverse is also true: the active defense of our principles abroad has encouraged us to support them even more vigorously at home. The fight against Nazism and Communism in the 1940's and 50's helped build a national consensus behind the civil-rights movement. In the Reagan era, confidence about America's beneficial role in the world was closely linked with confidence about the democratic project at home. This is a point on which the Samuel P. Huntington of 1991 needed no instruction. "Other nations," he wrote,

> may fundamentally change their political systems and continue their existence as nations. The United States does not have that option. Hence Americans have a special interest in the development of a global environment congenial to democracy.

There is no stasis in international affairs. Some day, the world may well turn back toward autocracy. The United States, the world's leading democratic power, could lose a major war to some rising, nondemocratic power. Or some calamity, whether man-made or not, may devastate the civilization we have created. But precisely because nothing lasts forever, and in the full knowledge that democracy is not inevitable but requires constant effort by those who mean to sustain it, the task facing us is to preserve and extend the democratic era as far into the future as possible. As it happens, and precisely because of the success of earlier policies, the present moment is one of relative safety, and therefore one that offers special opportunities. It would be a timeless human tragedy if, out of boredom, laziness, carelessness, or unfounded gloom, we failed to seize them.

## Notes

1. November 1979.
2. I have written on the realists at greater length in "American Power—A Guide for the Perplexed," COMMENTARY, April 1996.
3. "1997 Freedom Around the World," *Freedom Review,* January 1997.

**Robert D. Kaplan**

 **NO**

# Was Democracy Just a Moment?

In the fourth century A.D. Christianity's conquest of Europe and the Mediterranean world gave rise to the belief that a peaceful era in world politics was at hand, now that a consensus had formed around an ideology that stressed the sanctity of the individual. But Christianity was, of course, not static. It kept evolving, into rites, sects, and "heresies" that were in turn influenced by the geography and cultures of the places where it took root. Meanwhile, the church founded by Saint Peter became a ritualistic and hierarchical organization guilty of long periods of violence and bigotry. This is to say nothing of the evils perpetrated by the Orthodox churches in the East. Christianity made the world not more peaceful or, in practice, more moral but only more complex. Democracy, which is now overtaking the world as Christianity once did, may do the same.

The collapse of communism from internal stresses says nothing about the long-term viability of Western democracy. Marxism's natural death in Eastern Europe is no guarantee that subtler tyrannies do not await us, here and abroad. History has demonstrated that there is no final triumph of reason, whether it goes by the name of Christianity, the Enlightenment, or, now, democracy. To think that democracy as we know it will triumph—or is even here to stay —is itself a form of determinism, driven by our own ethnocentricity. Indeed, those who quote Alexis de Tocqueville in support of democracy's inevitability should pay heed to his observation that Americans, because of their (comparative) equality, exaggerate "the scope of human perfectibility." Despotism, Tocqueville went on, "is more particularly to be feared in democratic ages," because it thrives on the obsession with self and one's own security which equality fosters.

I submit that the democracy we are encouraging in many poor parts of the world is an integral part of a transformation toward new forms of authoritarianism; that democracy in the United States is at greater risk than ever before, and from obscure sources; and that many future regimes, ours especially, could resemble the oligarchies of ancient Athens and Sparta more than they do the current government in Washington. History teaches that it is exactly at such prosperous times as these that we need to maintain a sense of the tragic, however unnecessary it may seem.

From Robert D. Kaplan, "Was Democracy Just a Moment?" *The Atlantic Monthly* (December 1997). Copyright © 1997 by Robert D. Kaplan. Reprinted by permission.

... Those who think that America can establish democracy the world over should heed the words of the late American theologian and political philosopher Reinhold Niebuhr:

> The same strength which has extended our power beyond a continent has also ... brought us into a vast web of history in which other wills, running in oblique or contrasting directions to our own, inevitably hinder or contradict what we most fervently desire. We cannot simply have our way, not even when we believe our way to have the "happiness of mankind" as its promise.

The lesson to draw is not that dictatorship is good and democracy bad but that democracy emerges successfully only as a capstone to other social and economic achievements. In his "Author's introduction" to *Democracy in America,* Tocqueville showed how democracy evolved in the West not through the kind of moral fiat we are trying to impose throughout the world but as an organic outgrowth of development. European society had reached a level of complexity and sophistication at which the aristocracy, so as not to overburden itself, had to confer a measure of equality upon other citizens and allocate some responsibility to them: a structured division of the population into peacefully competing interest groups was necessary if both tyranny and anarchy were to be averted.

The very fact that we retreat to moral arguments—and often moral arguments only—to justify democracy indicates that for many parts of the world the historical and social arguments supporting democracy are just not there....

The demise of the Soviet Union was no reason for us to pressure Rwanda and other countries to form political parties—though that is what our post–Cold War foreign policy has been largely about, even in parts of the world that the Cold War barely touched. The Eastern European countries liberated in 1989 already had, in varying degrees, the historical and social preconditions for both democracy and advanced industrial life: bourgeois traditions, exposure to the Western Enlightenment, high literacy rates, low birth rates, and so on. The post–Cold War effort to bring democracy to those countries has been reasonable. What is less reasonable is to put a gun to the head of the peoples of the developing world and say, in effect, "Behave as if you had experienced the Western Enlightenment to the degree that Poland and the Czech Republic did. Behave as if 95 percent of your population were literate. Behave as if you had no bloody ethnic or regional disputes."

States have never been formed by elections. Geography, settlement patterns, the rise of literate bourgeoisie, and, tragically, ethnic cleansing have formed states. Greece, for instance, is a stable democracy partly because earlier in the century it carried out a relatively benign form of ethnic cleansing—in the form of refugee transfers—which created a monoethnic society. Nonetheless, it took several decades of economic development for Greece finally to put its coups behind it. Democracy often weakens states by necessitating ineffectual compromises and fragile coalition governments in societies where bureaucratic institutions never functioned well to begin with. Because democracy neither forms states nor strengthens them initially, multiparty systems are best suited to nations that already have efficient bureaucracies and a middle class that pays income tax, and where primary issues such as borders and power-sharing have already been resolved, leaving politicians free to bicker about the budget and other secondary matters.

Social stability results from the establishment of a middle class. Not democracies but authoritarian systems, including monarchies, create middle classes—which, having achieved a certain size and self-confidence, revolt against the very dictators who generated their prosperity. This is the pattern today in the Pacific Rim and the southern cone of South America, but not in other parts of Latin America, southern Asia, or sub-Saharan Africa....

Foreign correspondents in sub-Saharan Africa who equate democracy with progress miss this point, ignoring both history and centuries of political philosophy. They seem to think that the choice is between dictators and democrats. But for many places the only choice is between bad dictators and slightly better ones. To force elections on such places may give us some instant gratification. But after a few months or years a bunch of soldiers with grenades will get bored and greedy, and will easily topple their fledgling democracy. As likely as not, the democratic government will be composed of corrupt, bickering, ineffectual politicians whose weak rule never had an institutional base to start with: modern bureaucracies generally require high literacy rates over several generations. Even India, the great exception that proves the rule, has had a mixed record of success as a democracy, with Bihar and other poverty-wracked places remaining in semi-anarchy. Ross Munro, a noted Asia expert, has documented how Chinese autocracy has better prepared China's population for the economic rigors of the post-industrial age than Indian democracy has prepared India's.

Of course, our post–Cold War mission to spread democracy is partly a pose. In Egypt and Saudi Arabia, America's most important allies in the energy-rich Muslim world, our worst nightmare would be free and fair elections, as it would be elsewhere in the Middle East. The end of the Cold War has changed our attitude toward those authoritarian regimes that are not crucial to our interests—but not toward those that are. We praise democracy, and meanwhile we are grateful for an autocrat like King Hussein, and for the fact that the Turkish and Pakistani militaries have always been the real powers behind the "democracies" in their countries. Obviously, democracy in the abstract encompasses undeniably good things such as civil society and a respect for human rights. But as a matter of public policy it has unfortunately come to focus on elections....

The current reality in Singapore and South Africa, for instance, shreds our democratic certainties. Lee Kuan Yew's offensive neo-authoritarianism, in which the state has evolved into a corporation that is paternalistic, meritocratic, and decidedly undemocratic, has forged prosperity from abject poverty. A survey of business executives and economists by the World Economic Forum ranked Singapore No. 1 among the fifty-three most advanced countries appearing on an index of global competitiveness. What is good for business executives is often good for the average citizen: per capita wealth in Singapore is nearly equal to that in Canada, the nation that ranks No. 1 in the world on the United Nations' Human Development Index. When Lee took over Singapore, more than thirty years ago, it was a mosquito-ridden bog filled with slum quarters that frequently lacked both plumbing and electricity. Doesn't liberation from filth and privation count as a human right? Jeffrey Sachs, a professor of international trade at Harvard, writes that "good government" means relative safety from corruption, from breach of contract, from property expropriation, and from bureaucratic inefficiency. Singapore's reputation in these regards is unsurpassed. If Singapore's 2.8 million citizens ever demand democracy, they will just prove the assertion that prosperous middle classes arise under authoritarian regimes before gaining the confidence to dislodge their benefactors. Singapore's success is frightening, yet it must be acknowledged.

Democratic South Africa, meanwhile, has become one of the most violent places on earth that are not war zones, according to the security firm Kroll Associates. The murder rate is six times that in the United States, five times that in Russia. There are ten private-security guards for every policeman. The currency has substantially declined, educated people continue to flee, and international drug cartels have made the country a new transshipment center. Real unemployment is about 33 percent, and is probably much higher among youths. Jobs cannot be created without the cooperation of foreign investors, but assuaging their fear could require the kind of union-busting and police actions that democracy will not permit. The South African military was the power behind the regime in the last decade of apartheid. And it is the military that may yet help to rule South Africa in the future. Like Pakistan but more so, South Africa is destined for a hybrid regime if it is to succeed. The abundant coverage of South Africa's impressive attempts at coming to terms with the crimes of apartheid serves to obscure the country's growing problems. There is a sense of fear in such celebratory, backward-looking coverage, as if writing too much about difficulties in that racially symbolic country would expose the limits of the liberal humanist enterprise worldwide. . . .

## "World Government"

Authoritarian or hybrid regimes, no matter how illiberal, will still be treated as legitimate if they can provide security for their subjects and spark economic growth. And they will easily find acceptance in a world driven increasingly by financial markets that know no borders.

For years idealists have dreamed of a "world government." Well, a world government has been emerging—quietly and organically, the way vast developments in history take place. I do not refer to the United Nations, the power of which, almost by definition, affects only the poorest countries. After its peacekeeping failures in Bosnia and Somalia—and its $2 billion failure to make Cambodia democratic—the UN is on its way to becoming a supranational relief agency. Rather, I refer to the increasingly dense ganglia of international corporations and markets that are becoming the unseen arbiters of power in many countries. . . .

Of the world's hundred largest economies, fifty-one are not countries but corporations. While the 200 largest corporations employ less than three fourths of one percent of the world's work force, they account for 28 percent of world economic activity. The 500 largest corporations account for 70 percent of world trade. Corporations are like the feudal domains that evolved into nation-states;

they are nothing less than the vanguard of a new Darwinian organization of politics. Because they are in the forefront of real globalization while the overwhelming majority of the world's inhabitants are still rooted in local terrain, corporations will be free for a few decades to leave behind the social and environmental wreckage they create—abruptly closing a factory here in order to open an unsafe facility with a cheaper work force there. Ultimately, as technological innovations continue to accelerate and the world's middle classes come closer together, corporations may well become more responsible to the cohering global community and less amoral in the course of their evolution toward new political and cultural forms. . . .

The level of social development required by democracy as it is known in the West has existed in only a minority of places—and even there only during certain periods of history. We are entering a troubling transition, and the irony is that while we preach our version of democracy abroad, it slips away from us at home.

# The Shrinking Domain of "Politics"

I put special emphasis on corporations because of the true nature of politics: who does and who doesn't have power. To categorize accurately the political system of a given society, one must define the significant elements of power within it. Supreme Court Justice Louis Brandeis knew this instinctively, which is why he railed against corporate monopolies. Of course, the influence that corporations wield over government and the economy is so vast and obvious that the point needs no elaboration. But there are other, more covert forms of emerging corporate power.

The number of residential communities with defended perimeters that have been built by corporations went from 1,000 in the early 1960s to more than 80,000 by the mid-1980s, with continued dramatic increases in the 1990s. ("Gated communities" are not an American invention. They are an import from Latin America, where deep social divisions in places like Rio de Janeiro and Mexico City make them necessary for the middle class.) Then there are malls, with their own rules and security forces, as opposed to public streets; private health clubs as opposed to public playgrounds; incorporated suburbs with strict zoning; and other mundane aspects of daily existence in which—perhaps without realizing it, because the changes have been so gradual—we opt out of the public sphere and the "social contract" for the sake of a protected setting. Dennis Judd, an urban-affairs expert at the University of Missouri at St. Louis, told me recently, "It's nonsense to think that Americans are individualists. Deep down we are a nation of herd animals: micelike conformists who will lay at our doorstep many of our rights if someone tells us that we won't have to worry about crime and our property values are secure. We have always put up with restrictions inside a corporation which we would never put up with in the public sphere. But what many do not realize is that life within some sort of corporation is what the future will increasingly be about." . . .

Corporations, which are anchored neither to nations nor to communities, have created strip malls, edge cities, and Disneyesque tourist bubbles. Developments are not necessarily bad: they provide low prices, convenience, efficient work forces, and, in the case of tourist bubbles, safety. We need big corporations. Our society has reached a level of social and technological complexity at which goods and services must be produced for a price and to a standard that smaller businesses cannot manage. We should also recognize, though, that the architectural reconfiguration of our cities and towns has been an undemocratic event—with decisions in effect handed down from above by an assembly of corporate experts.

"The government of man will be replaced by the administration of things," the Enlightenment French philosopher Henri de Saint-Simon prophesied. We should worry that experts will channel our very instincts and thereby control them to some extent. For example, while the government fights drug abuse, often with pathetic results, pharmaceutical corporations have worked *through* the government and political parties to receive sanction for drugs such as stimulants and anti-depressants, whose consciousness-altering effects, it could be argued, are as great as those of outlawed drugs.

The more appliances that middle-class existence requires, the more influence their producers have over the texture of our lives. Of course, the computer in some ways enhances the power of the individual, but it also depletes our individuality. A degree of space and isolation is required for a healthy sense of self, which may be threatened by the constant stream of other people's opinions on computer networks.

Democratic governance, at the federal, state, and local levels, goes on. But its ability to affect our lives is limited. The growing piles of our material possessions make personal life more complex and leave less time for communal matters. And as communities become liberated from geography, as well as more specialized culturally and electronically, they will increasingly fall outside the realm of traditional governance. Democracy loses meaning if both rulers and ruled cease to be part of a community tied to a specific territory. In this historical transition phase, lasting perhaps a century or more, in which globalization has begun but is not complete and loyalties are highly confused, civil society will be harder to maintain. How and when we vote during the next hundred years may be a minor detail for historians. . . .

## Umpire Regimes

This rise of corporate power occurs more readily as the masses become more indifferent and the elite less accountable. Material possessions not only focus people toward private and away from communal life but also encourage docility. The more possessions one has, the more compromises one will make to protect them. The ancient Greeks said that the slave is someone who is intent on filling his belly, which can also mean someone who is intent on safeguarding his possessions. Aristophanes and Euripides, the late-eighteenth-century Scottish philosopher Adam Ferguson, and Tocqueville in the nineteenth century all warned that material prosperity would breed servility and withdrawal, turning people into, in Tocqueville's words, "industrious sheep."

... The mood of the Colosseum goes together with the age of the corporation, which offers entertainment in place of values. The Nobel laureate Czeslaw Milosz provides the definitive view on why Americans degrade themselves with mass culture: "Today man believes that there is *nothing* in him, so he accepts *anything,* even if he knows it to be bad, in order to find himself at one with others, in order not to be alone." Of course, it is because people find so little in themselves that they fill their world with celebrities. The masses avoid important national and international news because much of it is tragic, even as they show an unlimited appetite for the details of Princess Diana's death. This willingness to give up self and responsibility is the sine qua non for tyranny....

A continental regime must continue to function, because America's edge in information warfare requires it, both to maintain and to lead a far-flung empire of sorts, as the Athenians did during the Peloponnesian War. But trouble awaits us, if only because the "triumph" of democracy in the developing world will cause great upheavals before many places settle into more practical—and, it is to be hoped, benign—hybrid regimes. In the Middle East, for instance, countries like Syria, Iraq, and the Gulf sheikhdoms—with artificial borders, rising populations, and rising numbers of working-age youths—will not instantly become stable democracies once their absolute dictators and medieval ruling families pass from the scene. As in the early centuries of Christianity, there will be a mess.

Given the surging power of corporations, the gladiator culture of the masses, and the ability of the well-off to be partly disengaged from their own countries, what will democracy under an umpire regime be like?

## The Return of Oligarchy?

... [T]he differences between oligarchy and democracy and between ancient democracy and our own could be far subtler than we think. Modern democracy exists within a thin band of social and economic conditions, which include flexible hierarchies that allow people to move up and down the ladder. Instead of clear-cut separations between classes there are many gray shades, with most people bunched in the middle. Democracy is a fraud in many poor countries outside this narrow band: Africans want a better life and instead have been given the right to vote. As new and intimidating forms of economic and social stratification appear in a world based increasingly on the ability to handle and analyze large quantities of information, a new politics might emerge for us, too—less like the kind envisioned by progressive reformers and more like the pragmatic hybrid regimes that are bringing prosperity to developing countries.

... If democracy, the crowning political achievement of the West, is gradually being transfigured, in part because of technology, then the West will suffer the same fate as earlier civilizations.

# POSTSCRIPT

## Is Democracy Desirable for All Nations?

The questions raised by Kagan and Kaplan are as complex as they are important. At least one prominent American political scientist, Samuel P. Huntington, has shifted his position from a positive view of the likelihood of democratic domination in the future in *The Third Wave: Democratization in the Late Twentieth Century* (University of Oklahoma Press, 1991) to a more negative outlook in *The Clash of Civilizations and the Remaking of the World Order* (Simon & Schuster, 1996). Another analysis that argues that democracy has not established the claim of its ultimate triumph is found in Albert Somit and Steven A. Peterson, *Darwinism, Dominance, and Democracy* (Praeger, 1997).

Evidence regarding the successes and failures in the transition from autocracy to democracy can be found in recent studies. Barry M. Hager, in *Limiting Risks and Sharing Losses in the Globalized Capital Market* (Johns Hopkins University Press, 1998), examines Mexico's 1994–1995 financial crisis and the 1997 Asian crisis affecting Thailand, Indonesia, Korea, and Japan, and considers how the world's response to crises is related to other aspects of international relations, including support for democracy. Walter O. Oyugi et al., eds., *Democratic Theory and Practice in Africa* (Heinemann, 1998), offers a wide-ranging examination of new African democracies.

It is likely that the rise of global corporations and the worldwide communications made possible by the Internet will diminish the importance of national boundaries and, to a considerable extent, homogenize national and ethnic cultures. Will such changes adversely affect the movement toward democracy? A pessimistic answer is offered by Donald N. Wood in *Post-Intellectualism and the Decline of Democracy: The Failure of Reason and Responsibility in the Twentieth Century* (Praeger, 1997).

President John F. Kennedy's ringing proclamation in 1961 that the United States was ready to "pay any price, bear any burden, meet any hardship, support any friend, oppose any foe, to assure the survival and the success of liberty" suggested that America has a unique role in spreading democracy. Consider the following facts, which are much more evident now than when Kennedy spoke four decades ago: English has become the language that links educated people throughout the world. The United States is the sole military superpower. American movies and music threaten to overwhelm the popular culture of other nations. And, despite the challenge of Japan, America is the world's only information superpower. Perhaps the decline of cultural distinctions and the evolution of a global culture of shared interests is a measure of enhanced communications and understanding. Insofar as this is occurring, it provides for the United States not only an enormous commercial opportunity but also the opportunity to promote liberties identified with democracy.

# Contributors to This Volume

## EDITORS

**GEORGE McKENNA** is a professor of political science and chair of the Department of Political Science at City College, City University of New York, where he has been teaching since 1963. He received a B.A. from the University of Chicago in 1959, an M.A. from the University of Massachusetts in 1962, and a Ph.D. from Fordham University in 1967. He has written numerous articles in the fields of American government and political theory, and his publications include *American Populism* (Putnam, 1974) and *American Politics: Ideals and Realities* (McGraw-Hill, 1976). He is the author of the textbook *The Drama of Democracy: American Government and Politics,* 3rd ed. (Dushkin/McGraw-Hill, 1998).

**STANLEY FEINGOLD,** recently retired, held the Carl and Lily Pforzheimer Foundation Distinguished Chair for Business and Public Policy at Westchester Community College of the State University of New York. He received his bachelor's degree from the City College of New York, where he taught courses in American politics and political theory for 30 years, after completing his graduate education at Columbia University. He spent four years as Visiting Professor of Politics at the University of Leeds in Great Britain, and he has also taught American politics at Columbia University in New York and the University of California at Los Angeles. He is a frequent contributor to the *National Law Journal* and *Congress Monthly,* among other publications.

## STAFF

Theodore Knight   List Manager
David Brackley   Senior Developmental Editor
Juliana Gribbins   Developmental Editor
Rose Gleich   Administrative Assistant
Brenda S. Filley   Director of Production/Design
Juliana Arbo   Typesetting Supervisor
Diane Barker   Proofreader
Richard Tietjen   Publishing Systems Manager
Larry Killian   Copier Coordinator

# AUTHORS

**FRED BARNES** is executive editor of *The Weekly Standard* and a former senior editor and White House correspondent for *The New Republic.* He is cohost, with Mort Kondracke, of *The Beltway Boys* on the Fox News Channel. And from 1988 to 1998, he was a regular panelist on *The McLaughlin Group.*

**WILLIAM J. BENNETT** is a Distinguished Fellow of the Heritage Foundation and codirector of Empower America. He served as chairman of the National Endowment for the Humanities and secretary of education under President Ronald Reagan and as President George Bush's "drug czar." He has authored or edited a number of books, including *Children's Book of Faith* (Doubleday, 2000) and *The Index of Leading Cultural Indicators: American Society at the End of the Twentieth Century,* rev. and exp. ed. (WaterBrook Press, 1999).

**CARL T. BOGUS** is an associate professor at Roger Williams University School of Law in Bristol, Rhode Island. He is also a contributor to *The American Prospect.*

**ROBERT H. BORK** is the John M. Olin Scholar in Legal Studies at the American Enterprise Institute in Washington, D.C., a privately funded public policy research organization. He is also a former U.S. Court of Appeals judge for the District of Columbia Circuit.

**STEPHEN G. BREYER** is an associate justice of the U.S. Supreme Court. He received his A.B. from Stanford University in 1959, his B.A. from Oxford University in 1961, and his LL.B. from Harvard University in 1964. A former U.S. Circuit Court of Appeals judge, he was nominated to the Supreme Court by President Bill Clinton in 1994.

**DANIEL CASSE** is senior director of the White House Writers Group, a public policy communications firm.

**CITIZENS FOR TAX JUSTICE** is a nonpartisan, nonprofit research and advocacy organization dedicated to fair taxation at the federal, state, and local levels.

**ARCHIBALD COX** is the Carl M. Loeb University Professor Emeritus of Law in the School of Law at Harvard University. He is the author of *The Warren Court* (Harvard University Press, 1968), *Freedom of Expression* (Harvard University Press, 1981), and *The Court and the Constitution* (Houghton Mifflin, 1988). He was a Watergate special prosecutor in 1973.

**THOMAS E. CRONIN,** a professor of political science, is president of Whitman College in Walla Walla, Washington. He earned his Ph.D. in political science from Stanford University and has taught at a number of colleges and universities, including the Universities of North Carolina and California, Brandeis, Stanford, and Princeton. He has also held the McHugh Professorship of American Institutions and Leadership at Colorado College in Colorado Springs. His many publications include *Direct Democracy: The Politics of Initiative, Referendum, and Recall* (Replica Books, 2000) and *The Paradoxes of the American Presidency,* coauthored with Michael A. Genovese (Oxford University Press, 1998).

**CHRISTOPHER C. DeMUTH** is president of the American Enterprise Institute for Public Policy Research.

**RONALD DWORKIN** is a professor of law at New York University in New York City and the University Professor of Jurisprudence at Oxford University in Oxford, England.

**ERIC M. FREEDMAN** is a professor of law in the School of Law at Hofstra University. He chairs the Committee on Civil Rights of the Association of the Bar of the City of New York and is a member of the association's Special Committee on Representation in Capital Cases. He earned his M.A. at Victoria University of Wellington in New Zealand and his J.D. at Yale University. He is coauthor, with Monroe H. Freedman, of *Group Defamation and Freedom of Speech: The Relationship Between Language and Violence* (Greenwood, 1995).

**MICHAEL A. GENOVESE** is a professor of political science at Loyola Marymount University in Los Angeles, California. He is the author of *A Splendid Misery: The Ebb and Flow of Presidential Power* (Oxford University Press, 2000) and *The Watergate Crisis* (Greenwood, 1999).

**MARY ANN GLENDON** is the Learned Hand Professor of Law in the School of Law at Harvard University. She is the author of *A Nation Under Lawyers: How the Crisis in the Legal Profession Is Transforming American Society* (Farrar, Straus & Giroux, 1994).

**MARY GORDON** is a novelist and short-story writer. She is the author of *Penal Discipline: Female Prisoners* (Gordon Press, 1992), *The Rest of Life: Three Novellas* (Viking Penguin, 1993), and *The Other Side* (Wheeler, 1994).

**DANIEL JAMES** is an adviser to Carrying Capacity Network in Washington, D.C., an organization that focuses on issues pertaining to the carrying capacity of the Earth, including immigration, population, and the environment. He is the author of *Illegal Immigration—An Unfolding Crisis* (University Press of America, 1991).

**CHRISTOPHER JENCKS** is the Malcolm Wiener Professor of Social Policy in the John F. Kennedy School of Government at Harvard University. Among his publications are *The Black-White Test Score Gap,* coedited by Meredith Phillips (Brookings Institution Press, 1998) and *The Homeless* (Harvard University Press, 1995).

**JOHN B. JUDIS** is a fellow of the Woodrow Wilson International Center for Scholars in Washington, D.C., and a senior editor at *The New Republic.* He is also a regular contributor to *The American Prospect* and the author of *The Paradox of American Democracy: Elites, Special Interests and the Betrayal of the Public Trust* (Pantheon Books, 2000).

**ROBERT KAGAN** is the Alexander Hamilton Fellow at American University and a contributing editor at *The Weekly Standard.* He is also the author of *A Twilight Struggle: American Power and Nicaragua 1977–1990* (Free Press, 1996).

**ROBERT D. KAPLAN** is a contributing editor at *The Atlantic Monthly* and the author of several books, including *To the Ends of the Earth: A Journey at the Dawn of the Twenty-First Century* (Vintage Books, 1997).

**ANTHONY KING** is a professor of political science at the University of Essex and the author of *Running Scared: Why America's Politicians Campaign Too Much and Govern Too Little* (Martin Kessler Books, 1997).

**IRVING KRISTOL** is publisher of *The National Interest* and a fellow of the American Enterprise Institute, a privately funded public policy research organization located in Washington, D.C.

**PAUL KRUGMAN** is a professor of economics at the Massachusetts Institute of Technology. He is the author of many books, including *Pop Internationalism* (MIT Press, 1996) and *The Accidental Theorist: And Other Dispatches from the Dismal Science* (W. W. Norton, 1998).

**DAVID M. LAMPTON** is the George and Sadie Hyman Professor of China Studies and director of China studies in the School of Advanced International Studies at Johns Hopkins University in Washington, D.C. He is a former president of the National Committee on U.S.-China Relations and a former director of the China Policy Studies Program at the American Enterprise Institute. His many publications include *Same Bed, Different Dreams: Managing U.S.-China Relations, 1989–2000* (University of California Press, 2001). He received his Ph.D. in political science from Stanford University.

**CHARLES R. LAWRENCE III** is a professor in the School of Law at Georgetown University in Washington, D.C. He is coauthor, with Mari J. Matsuda, of *We Won't Go Back: Making the Case for Affirmative Action* (Houghton Mifflin, 1997) and *Affirmative Action* (Houghton Mifflin, 1997).

**DANIEL LAZARE** is a freelance writer based in New York City, who has written for *The Village Voice, Dissent,* and *In These Times.*

**ROBERT W. LEE** is a contributing editor at *The New American* and the author of *The United Nations Conspiracy* (Western Islands, 1981).

**ROBERT W. McCHESNEY** is a research professor in the Institute of Communications Research and the Graduate School of Library and Information Science at the University of Illinois at Urbana-Champaign. He is the author of *Rich Media, Poor Democracy: Communication Politics in Dubious Times* (University of Illinois Press, 1999) and coauthor, with John Nichols, of *It's the Media, Stupid!* (Seven Stories Press, 2000). He earned his Ph.D. in communications at the University of Washington in 1989.

**STEPHEN MOORE** is director of fiscal policy study at the Cato Institute in Washington, D.C., a public policy research foundation. He is the author of *Power and Corruption: The Rotten Core of Government and Big Business* (Frog, 1999) and *Social Welfare Alive!* 2d ed. (Stanley Thornes, 1998).

**CLARENCE PAGE** is a Pulitzer Prize–winning journalist for the *Chicago Tribune.* He is coauthor, with Leanita McClain, of *What Killed Leanita McClain? Essays on Living in Both Black and White Worlds* (Noble Press, 1995).

**JUDITH PEARSON** has over 20 years of experience as a public school educator in Minnesota, the first state to experiment with choice in education.

**DANIEL D. POLSBY** is the Kirkland and Ellis Professor of Law at Northwestern University in Evanston, Illinois. He has also held academic positions at Cornell University, the University of Michigan, and the University of Southern California. He has published numerous articles on a number of subjects related to law, including employment law, voting rights, broadcast regulation, and weapons policy.

**SAMUEL L. POPKIN** is a professor of political science at the University of California, San Diego. He has been an active participant in and an academic analyst of presidential elections for over 20 years, and he served as a consultant to the Clinton campaign in 1992, for which he worked on polling and strategy.

**LUCIAN W. PYE** is the Ford Professor of Political Science Emeritus in the Center for International Studies at the Massachusetts Institute of Technology in Cambridge, Massachusetts. He was also the president of the American Political Science Association in 1998–1999. His research focus has been in the field of comparative politics with special emphasis upon Asian political cultures and development, and he is the author of *The Spirit of Chinese Politics*, 2d ed. (Harvard University Press, 1992).

**STEVEN RATTNER** is an investment banker and managing director of Lazard Frères & Co. LLC., where he specializes in media mergers and acquisitions. He has also worked as a managing director at Morgan Stanley and as a reporter for the *New York Times.*

**JONATHAN RAUCH** is a writer for *The Economist* in London and the author of *Kindly Inquisitors: The New Attacks on Free Thought* (University of Chicago Press, 1993).

**WILLIAM H. REHNQUIST** became the 16th chief justice of the U.S. Supreme Court in 1986. He engaged in a general practice of law with primary emphasis on civil litigation for 16 years before being appointed assistant attorney general, Office of Legal Counsel, by President Richard Nixon in 1969. He was nominated by Nixon to the Supreme Court in 1972.

**GARY ROSEN** is the associate editor of *Commentary* and the author of *American Compact: James Madison and the Problem of Founding* (University Press of Kansas, 1999).

**AMITY SHLAES** is an editorialist on tax policy at the *Wall Street Journal.* Her writing has also been published in *Commentary* and *The New Yorker,* and she is the author of *Germany: The Empire Within* (Farrar, Straus & Giroux, 1991).

**BRADLEY A. SMITH,** a professor in the Capital University Law School in Columbus, Ohio, was confirmed by the U.S. Senate as a member of the nonpartisan, six-member Federal Elections Commission in May 2000. He has also practiced law with the law firm Vorys, Sater, Seymour & Pease; worked as a consultant in the field of health care; and served as U.S. vice consul in Ecuador. He earned his J.D. from Harvard Law School.

**SHELBY STEELE** is a research fellow at the Hoover Institution who specializes in the study of race relations, multiculturalism, and affirmative action. He received the National Book Critic's Circle Award in 1990 in the general nonfiction category for his book *The Content of Our Character: A New Vision of Race in America* (St. Martin's Press). He has written extensively for the *New York Times* and the *Wall Street Journal,* and he is also a contributing editor at *Harper's* magazine. His most recent book is *A Dream Deferred: The Second Betrayal of Black Freedom in America* (HarperCollins, 1999).

**ANDREW SULLIVAN** is a former editor of *The New Republic.* He received a B.A. in modern history and modern language from Oxford University in 1984 and an M.A. in public administration and a Ph.D. in political science from Harvard University in 1986 and 1990, respectively. His articles have been published in the *New York Times,* the *Wall Street Journal, Esquire, The Public Interest,* and the *Times* of London. He is also the author of *The Distant Intimacy* (Random House, 1999).

**JOSEPH SWINGLE** is on the faculty of the Quantitative Reasoning Program at Wellesley College in Wellesley, Massachusetts.

**JAMES Q. WILSON,** a criminologist and sociologist, is the James Collins Professor of Management and Public Policy at the University of California at Los Angeles, where he has been teaching since 1985. He has studied and advised on issues in crime and law enforcement for nearly 25 years, serving on a number of national commissions concerned with public policy, and he has authored, coauthored, or edited numerous books on crime, government, and politics, including *Bureaucracy: What Government Agencies Do and Why They Do It* (Basic Books, 1989), *American Government* (Houghton Mifflin, 1996), and *The Moral Sense* (Simon & Schuster, 1997).

# Index

W9-BTA-478

Praise for Peter Slevin's

# MICHELLE OBAMA

One of *Booklist*'s Top Ten Biographies of 2015

"Thoughtful. . . . Ripe with revelations about [Michelle Obama's] deeply complicated relationship with her own position as an Ivy League–educated black woman. . . . Provides richly rendered context for Mr. Obama's 2008 campaign, when Mrs. Obama suddenly became a litmus test." —*The New York Times Book Review*

"[A] meticulously reported, close-up look. . . . A detailed portrait of an ambitious, civic-minded woman with a track record for getting things done." —*The Florida Times-Union*

"Makes a convincing case that Mrs. Obama's popularity today has more to do with events that took place on the south side of Chicago decades ago than with the work of an image maker in the East Wing of the White House." —*The Wall Street Journal*

"Impressively reported and researched. . . . Fast-paced." —*Chicago* magazine

"Richly detailed prose. . . . There are tons of little-known nuggets revealed in the book, offering readers a closer look at the Mrs. Obama they never knew." —NBC.com

"[An] intimate view of her life. . . . The most comprehensive portrait to date of the nation's first African-American first lady." —*Atlanta Blackstar*

"The most ambitious and authoritative book about [First Lady Michelle Obama] yet. Richly reported, beautifully written, thoughtful in its judgments and revelatory in its details . . . a work that does justice to Michelle Obama in a fresh way."
—John Heilemann, coauthor of
*Game Change* and *Double Down*

"The life of Michelle Obama is a uniquely American story, and Peter Slevin tells it beautifully in this deft, revealing work. . . . Slevin also paints a rich picture of Chicago's South Side during the past century and the family and forces that helped shape this exceptional woman."
—David Axelrod, former Senior Advisor to the President, director of the Institute of Politics at the University of Chicago

"Slevin is dogged in his reporting, nuanced in his storytelling, and thoughtful in his analysis. He tells us not only who this historic first lady is, but also how she came to be. In the process, he reveals much about our times and our culture."
—Robin Givhan, Pulitzer Prize–winning critic
for *The Washington Post*

"Compelling. . . . [An] exhaustive and thoughtful portrait. . . . Will delight the most ardent Michelle Watchers."
—Patrik Henry Bass, *The Book Reader* (NY1)

"An amazing, eye-opening biography that begins on Chicago's South Side and ends in the White House. . . . A rich, powerful portrait at once revealing of Mrs. Obama and of ourselves as Americans." —Dexter Filkins, author of *The Forever War*

Peter Slevin

# MICHELLE OBAMA

Peter Slevin spent a decade on the national staff of *The Washington Post* before joining Northwestern University's Medill School of Journalism, where he is an associate professor. He has written extensively about Barack and Michelle Obama, as well as political campaigns and policy debates from one end of the country to the other. Slevin graduated from Princeton and Oxford. He lives with his family in Evanston, Illinois.

# MICHELLE OBAMA

## A LIFE

## Peter Slevin

VINTAGE BOOKS
A Division of Penguin Random House LLC
New York

FIRST VINTAGE BOOKS EDITION, JANUARY 2016

Copyright © 2015 by Peter Slevin

All rights reserved. Published in the United States by Vintage Books,
a division of Penguin Random House LLC, New York, and distributed
in Canada by Random House of Canada, a division of Penguin Random
House Canada Ltd., Toronto. Originally published in hardcover in
the United States by Alfred A. Knopf, a division of Penguin
Random House LLC, New York, in 2015.

Vintage and colophon are registered trademarks of
Penguin Random House LLC.

Grateful acknowledgment is made to Gotham Books for permission to
reprint excerpts from *A Game of Character: A Family Journey from Chicago's
Southside to the Ivy League and Beyond* by Craig Robinson and Mim Eichler
Rivas, copyright © 2010 by Craig Robinson. Used by permission of Gotham
Books, an imprint of Penguin Publishing Group, a division of
Penguin Random House LLC.

The Library of Congress has cataloged the Knopf edition as follows:
Slevin, Peter.
Michelle Obama : a life / by Peter Slevin.—First edition.
pages cm
1. Obama, Michelle, 1964–
2. Presidents' spouses—United States—Biography.
3. African American women lawyers—Biography.
4. African American lawyers—Biography.   I. Title.
E909.O24 S58 2015   973.932092—DC23
[B] 2014041100

Vintage Books Trade Paperback ISBN: 978-0-307-94931-8
eBook ISBN: 978-0-307-95883-9

Book design by Cassandra J. Pappas

www.vintagebooks.com

Printed in the United States of America
10   9   8   7   6   5

*For Kate*

# Contents

# MICHELLE OBAMA

# Introduction

In June 2010, when Michelle Obama cast her eyes across the class of graduating high school seniors from one of Washington's most troubled black neighborhoods, she saw not only their lives, but her own. The setting was Constitution Hall, where the Daughters of the American Revolution had prevented opera singer Marian Anderson from performing in 1939 because she was black. So much had changed in seven decades, and yet much had not. Michelle spoke to the graduates about the troubles facing African American children in Anacostia, and she spoke about racism. She pointed out that the neighborhood within sight of the U.S. Capitol once was segregated and that black people had been prohibited from owning property in parts of the community. "And even after those barriers were torn down," she said, "others emerged. Poverty. Violence. Inequality."

Michelle drew a straight line from her struggles with hardship and self-doubt in working-class Chicago to the fractured world the Anacostia students inhabited thirty years later. She told them about being written off, about feeling rejected, about the resilience it takes for a black kid in a public school to become one of the first in her family to go to college. "Kids teasing me when I studied hard. Teachers telling me not to reach too high because my test scores weren't good enough. Folks making it clear with what they said or didn't say that success wasn't meant for a little girl like me from the South Side of Chicago." As she spoke of her parents—their sacrifices and the way they pushed her "to reach for a life they never knew"—her voice broke and tears came to her eyes. As the students applauded in support, Michelle went on, "And if Barack were here, he'd say the same thing was true for him. He'd tell you it was hard at times growing up without a father. He'd tell you that his family didn't have a lot of money. He'd tell you he made plenty of mistakes and wasn't always the best student."

She knew that many of the Anacostia students faced disruptions and distractions that sometimes made it hard to show up, much less succeed. It might be family turmoil or money troubles or needy relatives or children of their own. Or maybe the lack of a mentor, a quiet place to study, a lucky break. "Maybe you feel like no one has your back, like you've been let down by people so many times that you've stopped believing in yourself. Maybe you feel like your destiny was written the day you were born and you ought to just rein in your hopes and scale back your dreams. But if any of you are thinking that way, I'm here to tell you: *Stop it.*"

There were no cheap lines in Michelle's speech that day, seventeen months after she arrived in the White House as the unlikeliest first lady in modern history. In a voice entirely her own, she reached deep into a lifetime of thinking about race, politics, and power to deliver a message about inequity and perseverance, challenge and uplift. These were the themes and experiences that animated her and set her apart. No one who looked like Michelle Obama had ever occupied the White House. No one who acted quite like her, either. She ran obstacle courses, she danced the Dougie, she hula-hooped on the White House lawn. She opened the executive mansion to fresh faces and voices and took her show on the road. She did sitcoms and talk shows and participated in cyber showcases and social media almost as soon as they were invented. Cameras and microphones tracked her every move. Maddening though the attention could be, she tried to make it useful. Amid a characteristic media fuss about a new hairstyle, she said of first ladies, "We take our bangs and we stand in front of important things that the world needs to see. And eventually, people stop looking at the bangs and they start looking at what we're standing in front of."

Michelle's projects and messages reflected a hard-won determination to help the working class and the disadvantaged, to unstack the deck. She was more urban and more mindful of inequality than any first lady since Eleanor Roosevelt. She was also more steadily, if subtly, political. Not political in ways measured by elections or ephemeral Beltway chatter, although she made clear her convictions from many a campaign stage. Rather, political as defined by spoken beliefs about how the world should work and purposeful projects calculated to bend the curve. Her efforts unfolded in realms that had barely existed for African Americans a generation earlier, a fact that informed and complicated her work. "We live in a nation where I am not supposed to be here," she once said.

Michelle's prospects as first lady delighted her supporters and helped get Barack elected, but her story and its underpinnings remained unfamiliar to many white Americans in a country where black Americans often felt relegated to a parallel universe. "As we've all said in the black community, we don't see all of who we are in the media. We see snippets of our community and distortions of our community," Michelle said. "So the world has this perspective that somehow Barack and Michelle Obama are different, that we're unique. And we're not. You just haven't seen us before." She belonged to a generation that came of age after the civil rights movement. It was fashionable in some circles for people to declare that they no longer saw race, but translation would be required. As her friend Verna Williams put it, "So many people have no idea about what black people are like. They feel they know us when they really don't." Lambasted early as "Mrs. Grievance" and "Barack's Bitter Half," Michelle knew the burden of making herself understood. One of her favorite descriptions of her Washington life came from a California college student who described the role of first lady as "the balance between politics and sanity."

During her years in the spotlight, Michelle became a point of reference and contention. She built and nurtured her popularity and emerged as one of the most recognizable women in the world. "You do not want to underestimate her, ever," said Trooper Sanders, a White House aide. Indeed, Michelle seemed to stride through life, full of confidence and direction. Comfortable in her own skin, friends always said. Authentic. But when asked what she would say to her younger self, as an interviewer flashed her high school yearbook photo onto a giant screen, Michelle paused to consider. "I think that girl was always afraid. I was thinking 'Maybe I'm not smart enough. Maybe I'm not bright enough. Maybe there are kids that are working harder than me.' I was always worrying about disappointing someone or failing."

At Constitution Hall, addressing 158 Anacostia seniors dressed in cobalt blue gowns, Michelle shared her history and her self-doubt. She offered advice and encouragement but skipped the saccharine. "You can't just sit around," she instructed. "Don't expect anybody to come and hand you anything. It doesn't work that way." She asked them to think about the obstacles faced by Frederick Douglass, their neighborhood's most illustrious former resident, born into slavery and self-educated in an era when it was illegal to teach slaves to read or write. His mother died when he was a boy and he never knew his father. But he made it, "persevering through thick and thin," and spent decades fighting for equality. She also asked them to consider the current occupants of the White House. "We see ourselves in each and every one of you. We are living proof for you, that with the right support, it doesn't matter what circumstances you were born into or how much money you have or what color your skin is. If you are committed to doing what it takes, anything is possible. It's up to you."

# ONE

# Chicago's Promise

I n the DuSable High School swim team photograph, Fraser C. Robin-son III stands in dark swimming trunks in the back row, third from the left. He is bare-chested, lean and fit. His arms are strong and his gaze is sure. The year was 1953 and the seventeen-year-old senior was close to having all the formal education he would get. In five years, he would be an army private on his way to Germany. In five more, he would be married and a father, a Democratic precinct worker soon to be on the payroll of the city of Chicago. The work he would do for much of his life, tending high-pressure boilers at a water-filtration plant, was tedious labor done in eight-hour shifts and it paid just enough for him to get by. At home, where he invested his considerable smarts and energy in his family, the swimming days of his youth would give way, far too soon, to years of physical decline. Multiple sclerosis left his brain increasingly unable to control his body. He walked with a limp, then a cane, then crutches; finally he used an electric scooter. Before work, his children watched him struggle to fasten the buttons on his blue work shirts. After work, he would sometimes call them to help carry shop-ping bags up the stairs to their apartment. Known on the job as Robbie, to his family as Diddley, he worked long after he could have taken dis-ability. "The gutsiest guy I have ever known," said water plant colleague Dan Maxime.

In 2008, sixteen years after Fraser Robinson died, Michelle told voters that her father remained her north star. "I am constantly trying to make sure that I am making him proud," she said. "What would my father think of the choices that I've made, how I've lived my life, what careers I chose, what man I married? That's the voice in my head that keeps me whole and keeps me grounded and keeps me the girl from the South Side of Chicago, no matter how many cameras are in the room, how many autographs people want, how big we get." That voice in her head emerged from Fraser's own South Side upbringing and the narrow but steady path he followed. The oldest of five surviving siblings born to a deeply religious mother and an ambitious father who arrived from South Carolina in the Great Migration, he secured a foothold in the working class. He was the least professionally accomplished of the children, but he occupied a central position in the family—"the glue," a cousin said—and he propelled his own two children yet further. Fraser was the one to whom the others turned with their problems, the one who kept track of the family lore, the one who worked hardest to knit together a large clan with its share of triumphs, failures, and frustrations. In the final lines of her speech to the 2008 Democratic National Convention, Michelle called on voters to elect her husband Barack as president "in honor of my father's memory and my daughters' future." She would also say that year, on the cusp of occupying a White House perch that she would devote to opening doors for others, "I remember his compassion. I remember the words, his advice, the way he lived life, and I am trying each and every day to apply that to how I raise my kids. I want his legacy to live through them. Hopefully it will affect the kind of first lady I will become because it's his compassion and his view of the world that really inspires who I am, who I want my girls to be, and what I hope for the country."

Fraser's story, and hers, begins in the Chicago of the 1930s, when any child of the first wave of the great black migration learned what was expected of him. Fraser would come to know possibility and the rewards of discipline and perseverance, lessons he would bequeath to Michelle and her older brother, Craig. He would encounter, too, the profound obstacles that faced African Americans in Chicago in the middle of the twentieth century, despite living hundreds of miles up the well-traveled Illinois Central tracks from the South of slavery and Jim Crow.

RICHARD WRIGHT, author of the memoir *Black Boy*, pulled into Chicago on a bitterly cold day in 1927, seeking a job more than anything. Not yet twenty, he was hungry and weighed less than 125 pounds, the minimum weight for a postal worker. He was uncertain about what lay ahead, but he was sure there was nothing for him in Memphis, where he had earned $8 a week, with little chance of advancement, as an errand boy in an optical company. "I could calculate my chances for life in the South as a Negro fairly clearly now," he wrote, remembering the decision to head north. Wright's white co-workers in Memphis belittled his choice, and as he rumbled into town aboard a northbound train, the Chicago that he spied through the window hardly seemed encouraging. That first glimpse "depressed and dismayed me, mocked all my fantasies," he wrote. Once he stepped off the train, however, he witnessed scenes that brightened his mood. Before he left the station, he saw that a black man could buy a newspaper "without having to wait until a white man was served." He saw black people and white people striding along purposefully, strikingly unmindful of one another. "No racial fear," he thought. Yet for a young black man born near Natchez, Mississippi, even the encouraging scenes triggered anxiety: "I knew that this machine-city was governed by strange laws and I wondered if I would ever learn them."

The blessings of Chicago, as Wright and later waves of migrants would find, were mixed. The sense of freedom was undeniable. Indeed, for many, it was overwhelming. Many of the rules were different, and in a better way. Streetcars had no seating code. Work paid better. Decent public schools beckoned, even if overcrowding forced many black schools to operate on double shifts. Chicago offered a rich menu of music, culture, and religion, not to mention gambling, liquor, and pursuits of a less savory kind. On the one hand, so many people crowded into African American districts marked by invisible boundaries that it sometimes seemed there was no room to move. On the other, the concentrated South Side community generated energy and drive and, for some, a common purpose. Sociologists St. Clair Drake and Horace R. Cayton described "a city within a city," and likened the intersection of 47th Street and South Parkway to a busy town square. In their study, *Black Metropolis*, published in 1945, they sketched a "continuous eddy of faces." Within view on a typical morning were black doctors, dentists, police officers, shopkeepers, and clerks, along with newsstands selling black-owned newspapers that included the *Defender,* the *Bee,* the *News-Ledger,* and the *Metropolitan News.* In one direction was a library named for Dr. George Cleveland Hall, chief of staff at Provident Hospital. In another was the Regal Theater, scene of performances by Cab Calloway and Louis Armstrong, Lena Horne and Duke Ellington, Lionel Hampton and Nat King Cole. Starting in 1939, the Regal was managed by a black man, a significant achievement for the time. As New York's Harlem Renaissance ebbed away, in its place stood Chicago. One writer would christen the South Side "the capital of black America."

Four years after Wright arrived, Fraser C. Robinson Jr. alighted on the South Side. He had traveled north and west from a small town in coastal South Carolina called Georgetown—in honor of King George II, not George Washington. It was known locally for rice farming, timber mills, and the plantation economy. Robinson was born in 1912 to a one-armed father as imperious as he was successful, a lumber company worker and businessman who owned his own home on an integrated block. Just one generation earlier, and for generations before that, the family had lived in slavery, when countless Robinsons and their kin were owned by white people. After the Civil War came and went and Abraham Lincoln signed the Emancipation Proclamation, they stayed put. They continued to speak Gullah, a distinctive English-based creole language descended from languages brought from West Africa.

African American voters held a majority in Georgetown as late as 1900, when the town's white leaders decided enough was enough. The tipping point came in September, when hundreds of black residents massed outside the county jail to protect a black barber named John Brownfield from a lynching. A white sheriff's deputy had tried to arrest Brownfield for failing to pay a poll tax. There was a scuffle. The deputy caught a bullet from his own gun and died a few hours later. Brownfield went to jail on suspicion of murder. As word spread that white men were organizing a lynching party, as many as a thousand black residents gathered outside the jail and chanted "Save John!" The demonstrations grew, and Georgetown's white mayor persuaded the state's governor to send soldiers to restore order.

In court, Brownfield was convicted and sentenced to death for capital murder, while he and eight others were found guilty of crimes connected to the protests. White community leaders formed a White Supremacy Club and used literacy tests and poll taxes to cull black citizens from voter rolls. By 1902, only 110 of the city's 523 voters were black. The same was true in other southern states. In Louisiana, about 130,000 black people were registered to vote in 1896; in 1904, the total was 1,342. In Alabama, 2 percent of eligible black men were registered "and they risked serious reprisals if they attempted to exercise their right to vote." With the white minority firmly in control, the portents looked uniformly bad. "The whites in power," wrote Rachel Swarns in *American Tapestry*, a study of Michelle Obama's ancestry, "made it clear that there was no future for ambitious black men in Georgetown."

Finishing Howard High School at the end of the 1920s, Fraser Robinson Jr. considered himself "a young man destined for better things." Others saw him the same way. A skilled debater and strong student, he envisioned college and perhaps a career in the emerging field of electronics. But he felt certain that such a future did not await him in Georgetown, where he found himself working in a timber mill as the Depression took hold. "He wanted a different kind of life. He had high hopes," recalled his daughter, Francesca. When a friend left for Chicago, Fraser followed.

FROM THE START, things went poorly for the man who would one day be Michelle's exacting paternal grandfather. Jobs in Chicago were scarce and Fraser always seemed to be a temporary hire. He set up pins in a bowling alley. He washed dishes. He worked in a laundry and undertook the workaday chores of a handyman. It soon became clear that college was out of the question, as was a career in electronics. To get steady work as an electrician required membership in a union that barred African Americans. He eventually found a regular income with the Depression-era Works Progress Administration, but the money did not stretch far. As he made his way, he gave up the African Methodist Episcopal church of his youth in favor of a South Side Pentecostal church called Full Gospel Mission. There, he began courting a focused and prayerful teenager in the choir, LaVaughn Johnson. She was the daughter of Phoebe Johnson and her husband, a sometime Baptist preacher who had done duty as a Pullman porter and owner of a shoe repair shop. After a quiet stretch in Evanston, Illinois, in the 1920s, the Johnsons moved around as he sought stable work. Financial pressure brought trouble, and their marriage came undone. James moved out, leaving Phoebe on the South Side with their seven children, the oldest twenty-seven, the youngest five. LaVaughn stayed in school, but soon began spending her off hours working alongside her mother in the homes of white families. She did laundry and took care of children in Hyde Park, where her granddaughter Michelle would live seventy years later in relative splendor.

Fraser and LaVaughn married in October 1934. He was twenty-two years old, three years removed from South Carolina. She was nineteen, barely eight months out of high school. In August 1935, they had a son and named him Fraser C. Robinson III. The city, in the teeth of the Great Depression, was overflowing with unskilled black laborers who had streamed into town in search of something like a future. The pace of migration was startling. In 1910, one in fifty Chicago residents was black; in 1940, it was one in twelve. During those thirty years, the city's African American population grew 530 percent, to 277,731 residents. The population would continue to climb during the boom years of World War II and beyond as passenger trains delivered thousands of new residents each month to the imposing Illinois Central terminal, within sight of the downtown skyscrapers. Chicago was called the city of big shoulders, not the city of open arms, and the vast majority of African Americans found themselves squeezed into a slice of the South Side called the Black Belt. Some called it North Mississippi. To others, it was Darkie Town.

Segregation in housing was the rule. For years, white community leaders used restrictive covenants and race-minded civic organizations—known without irony as "improvement associations"—to keep blacks out. Mob violence and intimidation played a part. The Federal Housing Administration, founded in 1934, refused to insure mortgages in neighborhoods that were home to more than a small number of black people. The policy, known as redlining, meant that banks would not loan money to most African Americans, which kept property largely out of reach. In 1940, when Michelle's father was five years old, three-fourths of Chicago's black population lived in neighborhoods that were more than 90 percent black. Fully 350 of the city's 935 census tracts had not a single black resident. Housing in the Black Belt tended to be inhospitable and, as more African Americans arrived from the South, increasingly cramped. To accommodate the newcomers and line their own pockets, landlords carved buildings into smaller and smaller units, often without plumbing, even as they charged rents far higher than white people paid elsewhere in the city.

Overcrowding and poor sanitation contributed to rates of illness and death that were higher among black Chicagoans than among white ones. Tuberculosis in 1940 was five times more prevalent among black residents. Three black infants died before their first birthday for every two white infants who did. By 1945, more than half of the Black Belt was considered "blighted" by city planners and real estate assessors. Equality was at best a mirage, at worst a hoax. Which is not to say that Chicago did not hold out hope for a better future. But the equation was a complicated one. The deck was stacked, and it would remain that way well into Michelle's lifetime. As Barack Obama would say of his in-laws and their lives in the 1960s, "They faced what other African American families faced at the time—both hidden and overt forms of racism that limited their effort to get ahead."

IN THE MID-1930S, when Michelle's father was born, money was tight in the Robinson household. LaVaughn again took up housecleaning. She gave birth to Nomenee in July 1937 and later to a third son, John, who died as a baby. Under the strains that grew as the decade passed, the relationship between husband and wife that had started strongly ended abruptly. By the end of the 1930s, the elder Fraser was through with the marriage. Soon after, he was through with Chicago, at least for the time being. He enlisted in the army in March 1941, giving his height as five feet, eight inches, and his weight as 153 pounds. A form noted his marital status as "separated, without dependants [sic]."

LaVaughn's day-to-day challenges grew harder. Living on East 57th Street near State Street, she turned to public assistance before finding her way into a federal job, working in the publications office at the U.S. Department of Agriculture. Her sons visited her there. With Fraser leading the way, the boys climbed aboard a northbound streetcar and stepped off downtown. They rode upstairs in an elevator cage and visited their mother in the room where she operated a mimeograph machine. To help with the boys during the early years, LaVaughn looked to friends and relatives. She relied especially on two older women from Georgetown, who sometimes spoke Gullah as the children listened. She also remained close to her church, taking young Fraser and Nomenee with her to Full Gospel Mission on Sundays. The storefront church had rigid rules and lively music. "If a church doesn't jump, so to speak, I don't feel that there's any holy spirit there," said Nomenee, who called it a wonderful experience. He remembered the boost he got from a pastor who called him "my little preacher" and told him he had a gift for words. As for his mother, in his telling she was "religiously sheltered" while growing up and, as an adult, always proper and "very, very prayerful." Finding a way to blend faith with a measure of professional ambition, LaVaughn would go on to manage a Moody Bible Institute store in Chicago, the first African American woman to do so. In 1958, her twenty-two-year-old son Fraser gave her a Bible for Mother's Day. Fifty-five years later, with Michelle holding that Bible in the Blue Room, Barack Obama would take the oath of office for his second term in the White House.

Although money was always scarce, LaVaughn strongly encouraged Fraser and Nomenee in musical and artistic pursuits. "Everything educational, they got it," her sister Mary Lang said. They learned to swim and ice-skate and to always do their schoolwork. Money mattered, but

Nomenee recalled a time when his mother's caution about his safety trumped her concern about the family's finances. For Christmas one year, he received a set of molds in the shapes of Mickey Mouse, Donald Duck, Pluto, and other Disney characters. "I just loved that little toy because you had some plaster and you'd take that off and let it sit and harden. You'd shellac them and paint them. So, one day, I just decided to keep making them. I had forty sitting on the table or something. I came up with this idea that I'm going to sell them." He put them in an old shoebox and asked his mother to buy him a receipt book. "I never told her what I was doing. I said I'm going to try to go into business. She was just laughing."

While his mother was at work, Nomenee began walking through the neighborhood, knocking on apartment doors. "I said, 'Miss, would you like to buy one of these? Thirty-five cents, three for a dollar.' You know, she'll say, 'Honey, come here, look at this! Look at this little boy!' So, one week, I collected thirteen-something dollars, a lot of money. I put it on the table in front of Mom." Shocked, she asked where the money had come from. Nomenee said he had gone into business selling Disney figures and reminded her that she was the one who had bought the receipt book. LaVaughn was not amused. "Don't you dare go out there again knocking on people's doors," she told her son. "Somebody's going to snatch you." That ended the sales enterprise.

World War II took Fraser Jr. to Europe and, by his children's accounts, made him stronger. He worked with radios and climbed in rank in a segregated unit, years before President Harry Truman ordered the military's integration in 1948. "I think he finally had the opportunity to use his skills and gifts in the army. He had a sense of autonomy in some respects," said Francesca, his only daughter, born in Chicago long after the war. Fraser would return to the South Side, but for years he kept a certain distance from the family. "He'll come by once a year or so and take us to the circus. That was our encounter with him," said Nomenee, who recalled visits to a railroad fair in downtown Chicago and occasional trips to the movies. His father lived just a few blocks away, but it might as well have been across the state. His mother knew the location; the children did not.

After Fraser's army stint and several years back on the South Side, he returned to the family, which in time would grow to include three more children. They were Andrew, Carlton, and Francesca, named for a friendly Italian woman who delivered milk and eggs to Fraser and other black American soldiers bivouacked near her farm. It had been more than a decade since his departure, but he rejoined the household as a prideful man, confident and often stern, a disciplinarian possessed of firm ideas about right and wrong. It was no accident that he became a master sergeant during his army years. He could be hard on the boys, recalled Nomenee, who said he challenged his father's authority more than his brother did. Once, in Nomenee's early teens, his father started to whip him for a misdeed, now forgotten. Young Fraser stepped in. "He happened to hear me screaming. He came in and said, 'That's enough, Dad. That's enough.' He held his hands and Dad couldn't move, couldn't pull away. We never had any whippings after that." When he was raising his own children years later, Fraser III would not spank them. He left that chore to his wife.

When Fraser III and Nomenee grew older, they were expected to work in addition to fulfilling their school responsibilities. "We had to contribute. It's not like we were making that much money, but it's just that that was Dad's system," said Nomenee, who recalled that one boy might be responsible for the phone bill, another for the light bill or groceries. One of Fraser's first jobs was as a dairy helper, hefting glass bottles of Wanzer Dairy milk—motto: *"Wanzer on milk is like sterling on silver"*—to customers' doorsteps and returning with the empties. He worked on the horse-drawn cart of a vegetable deliveryman, also for a hat-maker and a cleaning company. Being a swimmer on his high school team, the Sea Horses, Fraser sometimes found work as a lifeguard. When he could, Fraser passed along his old jobs to Nomenee, two years younger. "We had to be hustlers, in the positive sense of hustling," Nomenee said. "We had to figure out ways."

LAVAUGHN WAS DETERMINED to open a door to a wider world for her children. In the mid-1940s, when he was about eleven years old, Fraser caught a bus on Saturday mornings to the Art Institute of Chicago, a grand beaux-arts edifice on Michigan Avenue. There, he discovered painting and sculpture. With classmates at what was then called the Junior School, he worked in an array of disciplines. One of his teachers was Nelli Bar Wieghardt, a German-Jewish sculptor and refugee from wartime Europe. "Her style was very open, looking to discover what strengths the student had and encouraging them," said Richard Hunt, another black student of hers, born the same year as Fraser. "More embracing than strict," Hunt said, and less wedded to academic conventions than to approaches more abstract and flowing. Hunt remembered lunch discussions about race relations in the United States. Wieghardt was startled by what she found after "escaping and coming to the land of the free and then discovering what it was in terms of black-white relations." For Hunt, who traveled to the Junior School on Saturdays from the bustling working-class streets of Englewood, one discipline led to another as he studied drawing and painting, watercolors and oils, still life and figures. Looking back after becoming a professional sculptor, he remembered an eclectic and engaging array of Art Institute instructors. Classrooms and studios were tucked into basement spaces, but, just upstairs, students had the run of a flourishing museum. "The teachers might suggest, 'Why don't you go up and look at Rodin?'"

Fraser's passion for art was understated, but enduring. It set him apart at DuSable High School, where his interests ran from painting and sculpture to swimming and boxing. A full-page photograph in the 1953 *Red and Black*, the school yearbook, shows him dressed in a sport coat, sculpting a bust. "You'd hardly know he was around," said classmate Reuben Crawford. "He was going about the business of being the business, as we used to say. He was very quiet and into his art." If he could have afforded it, Michelle said later, her father would have made art his profession. "He was quite an artist," Nomenee agreed, acknowledging a certain envy that started at an early age. He saw Fraser, who led parades and took trips as a young drum major, as smoothly talented and sociable, a steady soul who made friends easily. He had fashion sense and style. "He was very self-confident," his brother said. "He was secure with himself."

.   .   .

FRASER CELEBRATED his seventeenth birthday in 1952, shortly before starting his final year at DuSable. The previous year, Nelson Algren had published his essay *Chicago: City on the Make*, mocking the bilious self-promotion of city leaders and their notion of Chicago as a place where color did not matter. He argued that race relations were grounded in a "protean awareness of white superiority everywhere, in everything." Algren, a white novelist later known for his novel about heroin addiction, *The Man with the Golden Arm*, told of rents pegged higher for black residents, and restaurants and bars that were unofficially, but certainly, off-limits. "Make your own little list," he wrote. "Of the streets you mustn't live on, the hotels where you can't register, the offices you can't work in and the unions you can never join."

Among DuSable students, many of them children of the Great Migration, blackness was widely discussed and understood. It was not only a fact of life, it was the X factor in their futures. Encounters with racism, studied in school and experienced outside, would shape their thinking and their decisions, not least about what lessons to teach the next generation. The high school itself was named for Jean-Baptiste Point du Sable, a black fur trader regarded as the first permanent settler of Chicago. Born in 1745 in what is now Haiti, his story was important to the high school's identity from the time it was christened in 1936. "We were taught the history of Jean-Baptiste Point du Sable," said Charlie Brown, a 1954 DuSable graduate who reported that African American history lessons stretched throughout the school year. Students regularly discussed "all the hardships the black people went through."

One of the most freewheeling and influential teachers during Fraser Robinson's years at DuSable was the main art teacher, Margaret Burroughs, who laced her lessons with African American history and current events. A young girl when she moved to Chicago from Louisiana with her family in the early 1920s, she joined the NAACP Youth Council as a teenager and studied at the Art Institute on her way to helping create a South Side art center and the DuSable Museum of African American History. Beseeching her students to take pride in their history, she instructed them to press onward when "faced with abhorrence of everything that is black." Burroughs's attitudes and activism were evident, not just to her students, but to higher-ups at the Chicago Board of Education who summoned her downtown in 1952 to explain herself. At first, she thought she might be getting a promotion. Instead, they questioned her views of communists and their sympathizers, including Earl Browder and one of her heroes, Paul Robeson. Burroughs said she was never given a reason, but she suspected it was her advocacy of black history, which, she said, "was considered subversive at the time."

The central message at DuSable was perseverance in the face of inequality, the idea that it was important to know the past but not be bound by it. Painted above the stage in DuSable High's ornate auditorium were the words "Peace if possible, but justice at any rate." The phrase came from Wendell Phillips, a white abolitionist in the nineteenth century and president of the American Anti-Slavery Society. "An agitator by profession," a prominent historian called him. Nearly sixty years after graduation, Charlie Brown could recite the DuSable epigram from memory. To him, the eight words registered as a demand for fairness, for it was undeniable that African Americans faced long odds. "When you lived in Chicago back then," he said, "you understood how white society described a black person, or a Negro. One drop of blood, you were a Negro." Brown was the star of the DuSable basketball team, a six-foot-two forward on the 1953 and 1954 squads that won the city title and became the first all-black teams to compete downstate in the Illinois state tournament. When DuSable played a white team, the coach warned his players to be at least 20 points ahead entering the fourth quarter, especially if it was an away game. "We didn't look for any favorable calls from the refs," Brown said. "In those days, racism was not hidden at all."

LONG BEFORE the civil rights movement became national news, African American adults on the South Side of Chicago often conveyed a message that acknowledged the obstacles without surrendering to them. Young people learned that they needed to work hard to prove themselves; they needed to be twice as good as whites to get just as far. They had less room for error than their white peers. Unfair? Yes, but that was the deal. No cavalry would ride to their rescue. "If one word came out of my father's mouth more than any other word, it was discipline, self-control," said Bernard Shaw, who grew up on the South Side and became an on-air reporter for CNN. "My mother used to say, 'It's not what you do, it's how you do it.' My father used to say, 'It's not what you say, it's how you say it.'" Yet these were not the standard admonitions that parents of any ethnicity might deliver about character and good manners. Rather, the Shaws were instructing their son on how to succeed in a society dominated by white people. "Racism pervaded city life," he said. "It certainly trickled down to the high school level." To succeed, as Fraser's classmate Reuben Crawford had said, you had to be about the business of being the business.

Children of the Great Migration learned that their job was to reach a higher rung than the one their parents occupied. "You *had* to do better. So much was expected of you," said Crawford, whose father supported his family by working two jobs, one of them as a window washer for the Chicago Board of Education. "You knew to respect your elders and do what you had to do. No nonsense, that was the key." Crawford played the clarinet, made the honor roll, and held an after-school job, working as a busboy at Gus' Good Food on North Dearborn. He learned a trade, dye-setting. The values ran deep. Going to church every Sunday was not required, but the moral imperative was strong: "Just do what you're supposed to do when you're interacting with people. Treat all people alike. Don't misuse them. That's God's will."

The message was very much the same at Fraser and LaVaughn Robinson's dinner table, said Capers Funnye, a nephew, who recalled "an absolute conviction for what's right. You don't embarrass your family. You don't embarrass yourself." He ascribed a "tenacity" to the elder Fraser, recalling his message to the younger generation, especially to black boys: "You don't have time to be a slacker. If that's what you want to be, you're wasting your life. You're in competition. And as a person who's a Negro, you have to work twice as hard. You have to always be willing to step forward to prove your worth. You have to adjust to the situation. Move forward." In a world of equal opportunity, Fraser might have become a college professor, believed Funnye, who attended Howard University, converted to Judaism, and became a South Side rabbi. Indeed, some people who knew Fraser in South Carolina in the early years called him "professor." He "encouraged striving, he encouraged pushing," Funnye said. If someone in the family were wasting talents and opportunities, he would demand, "What are you doing? We don't have time for this." Although the system might be rigged, the message was to carry on, steadfast and undaunted.

MICHELLE'S FATHER, FRASER III, TURNED TWENTY in 1955, the summer of Emmett Till. On August 28, two white men in a Mississippi Delta town kidnapped the visiting fourteen-year-old from his great-uncle's house, lynched him, and dropped his body, weighted with a hundred-pound cotton gin fan, into the Tallahatchie River. His alleged crime was whistling at a white woman who tended a shop in rural Money, Mississippi. After Till's mutilated body reached Chicago on an Illinois Central train, his mother, Mamie Till Bradley, decreed that the casket should remain open so that "all the world" would bear witness. For anyone living in the city—and certainly on the South Side, where mourners paid their respects at the A. A. Rayner & Sons Funeral Home—there was no avoiding the shocking news. The papers were filled with it. A photographer from *Jet* magazine took photographs, one with Bradley looking on. "Few photographs . . . can lay claim to equally universal impact upon black observers," wrote historian Adam Green, who traced the ripples. Langston Hughes and Gwendolyn Brooks wrote poems about the case. James Baldwin made it the foundation of his play *Blues for Mister Charlie*. Eldridge Cleaver and Anne Moody said the killing influenced their political paths. Muhammad Ali told an interviewer, "I couldn't get Emmett Till out of my mind."

In Chicago, thousands upon thousands of people filed past the casket during five days of shock and mourning that ended with a large funeral service at the Roberts Temple Church of God in Christ. Before the month was out, a rally at the city's Metropolitan Church had attracted another ten thousand. Three months later, Rosa Parks refused to give up her seat on a city bus in Montgomery, Alabama. One thought running through her head as she sat there, she said many years later, was Till's death.

BY THE TIME of Till's murder, Fraser Robinson Jr. was earning his living in a post office job offered to war veterans, a valuable pathway to the middle class in an era when prejudice often limited private-sector opportunity. It was not electrical engineering, his long ago dream, but it was steady and it allowed him to salt away some savings. He was a frugal man who believed that when you put money in the bank, you never take it out. Settling back in together as a family, he and LaVaughn took a step rare for African Americans at the time and bought an apartment. It was located in the Parkway Gardens Homes, rising on fifteen acres at the old White City Amusement Park grounds in Woodlawn, just east of the rail yards. Parkway Gardens, described as "the largest mutually-owned apartment project to be owned and operated by Negroes in America," got its start in 1945. It was an initiative of the Dining Car Workers Union, whose leaders aimed to ease living conditions for the black laborers who crowded into scarce and substandard dwellings during the World War II manufacturing boom. In the immediate postwar years, 20 percent of the nation's steel was made in Chicago, and jobs were more plentiful than housing. Beyond delivering 694 apartments in 35 buildings, the shared ownership model of Parkway Gardens was designed to make decent housing more affordable and keep slumlords at bay. After an initial payment—$2,500 for families who had signed up by 1949—co-op owners paid a monthly amount at something less than market rates. The project, built with several million dollars in Federal Housing Administration support, made it easier to own property at a time when African Americans rarely had access to credit on the same terms as white people. The complex opened in the early 1950s and was completed in 1955. In 2011, Parkway Gardens was added to the National Register of Historic Places.

The ceremony to lay the Parkway Gardens cornerstone in September 1950 attracted political notables from across the city including, as keynote speaker, civil rights leader Mary McLeod Bethune who considered the ownership model "the opening of a new frontier to progress." Michelle Obama would live in Parkway Gardens, across the hall from her grandparents, for the first eighteen months of her life. In future years, she would visit often from her childhood home in nearby South Shore.

FRASER AND LAVAUGHN ROBINSON'S MOVE into an apartment of their own in the 1950s signified advancement, a solid step on a road that would carry each of their five children through high school, in some cases through college and graduate school, and into the middle class. They reached Parkway Gardens in a decade that would advance the slow-growing consensus that racial discrimination was wrong, symbolized most publicly by the Supreme Court's 1954 ruling in *Brown v. Board of Education*. Yet court victories masked as much as they promised. It was two steps forward, a step or two back. At times, success itself was thwarted. Carl Hansberry was a banker, real estate investor, and unsuccessful Republican candidate for Congress. In 1937, he secretly bought a house in a white part of Woodlawn, not far from the University of Chicago. He wanted not only to provide for his family, but to challenge housing restrictions, called restrictive covenants, a form of legalized segregation designed to prohibit black residents from living in certain places. "Literally howling mobs surrounded our house," his daughter Lorraine wrote, calling the block "hellishly hostile." Although a neighbor sued and Illinois courts ordered the Hansberry family to leave, the U.S. Supreme Court ruled otherwise in November 1940, invoking a procedural issue, not the constitutional question. By then, the Hansberrys had given up on the new house at 6140 Rhodes Avenue and returned to a home in the heart of the Black Belt, where they hosted many figures in the black cultural elite, including W. E. B. Du Bois, Paul Robeson, Duke Ellington, Langston Hughes, and Joe Louis.

Eighteen years after the ruling, a group of actors gathered in New York to rehearse a play written by Lorraine Hansberry, who said the drama was largely autobiographical. "Mama," she wrote to her mother, "it is a play that tells the truth about people, Negroes and life, and I think it will help a lot of people to understand how we are just as complicated as they are . . . people who are the very essence of human dignity." The play was *A Raisin in the Sun,* and it became the first drama by a black author to reach Broadway. Hansberry set the story in a black neighborhood on the South Side, the very one where she grew up and the Robinsons now lived. The central character is Lena Younger, a black domestic worker who receives an insurance windfall of $10,000, a princely sum. To help her family escape their shabby apartment, she uses some of the money to buy a house in a white neighborhood. Appalled, the white community sends an emissary to buy her out. Lena struggles with what to do and announces that her family will reject the payoff. They will not surrender to self-doubt or to the connivings of their foes. "We ain't never been that poor," she explains. "We ain't never been that . . . dead inside." Even as she moves up and out, however, she is aware that not everyone in their old neighborhood, or even their own family, will make it. For many black families like them, the dilemma of obligation—to oneself, to family, to others—would become a feature of life, a perpetually renewing riddle. After seeing a revival of *A Raisin in the Sun* in 2014, Michelle would declare the play "one of America's greatest stories," and call it one of her favorites.

FRASER III SPENT his final stretch of high school living at Parkway Gardens and making his way to DuSable for class. After graduation in 1953, he enrolled at the University of Illinois at Navy Pier, a temporary campus built to accommodate the post–World War II college boom. He ran out of money, dropped out, and soon was helping to support his brother Nomenee, who would graduate from the Illinois Institute of Technology with a degree in architecture. Fraser joined the army in May 1958 at age twenty-two, prompting younger brother Andrew, not yet eight years old, to cry in worry that Fraser was going off to war. But these were the quiet years between the end of the Korean War and the start of hostilities in Vietnam. His first stop was Fort Leonard Wood, 130 miles southwest of St. Louis. Eight days later, he was on his way to

Fort Riley, Kansas. Six months after that, he headed to southern Germany.

At Fort Riley, soldiers converged from all over the country for eight weeks of basic training and eight weeks of advanced combat preparation. Once they reached their barracks near Munich, they joined the 24th Infantry Division, soon to be commanded by Major General Edwin Walker. A complicated figure, Walker had directed the federal troops that defended the integration of Little Rock's Central High School in 1957, but he was bounced from the army in 1961 for distributing right-wing political messages to soldiers under his command in Germany. In 1962, he was arrested for demonstrating against James Meredith's enrollment at the University of Mississippi. Walker demanded a spirit of discipline and dedication built on the presumption that a cold war in the era of superpower competition could quickly become hot. Drill time and physical training seemed endless, the rules unbending. "You fell out for formation every day. Every Saturday morning you had barracks inspection and God help you if everything wasn't perfect," recalled Joe Hegedus, who served in a mortar battery in Fraser's regiment. Before he left active duty, Fraser would win an expert marksmanship qualification with a rifle and a sharpshooter's qualification with a machine gun. He was awarded a good conduct medal and left active duty on May 23, 1960, as a private first class. He would complete his service with four years on the roster of the Illinois National Guard.

FRASER TURNED TWENTY-FIVE the summer after he returned home to the South Side. He looked for work and spent time with a young woman named Marian Shields. Chicago was teeming, and in flux. As African Americans continued to migrate northward, the city was home to 500,000 more black residents in 1960 than it was in 1940. It was now nearly thirty years since his father's generation had arrived from the old Confederacy and for all of Fraser Jr.'s frustrations, the family seemed to be gaining traction. In the next decade, it would be the turn of Fraser III and Marian to see what they could make for their children of Chicago's gruff promise.

# TWO

# South Side

Fraser Robinson and Marian Shields met through mutual friends when he was nineteen and she was seventeen, a senior at Englewood High. They broke up before he went into the army and got back together when he returned. They were vibrant, energetic, and athletic. Their interests were eclectic, their feet were on the ground, and they laughed a lot. Less than six months after Fraser returned from Germany, they were married in Woodlawn on October 27, 1960. The presiding African Methodist Episcopal minister was the Reverend Carl A. Fuqua, who doubled as executive secretary of the Chicago NAACP. On January 17, 1964, Marian gave birth to Michelle, who joined their oldest son, Craig, not quite two. The Robinsons' ambitions ran more to family happiness and their children's advancement than to professional success, particularly after Fraser was hit with multiple sclerosis. In the family's shorthand, Marian was the disciplinarian, while Fraser was the motivator and "philosopher in chief." Emerging from complicated families in a city that recognized them first and foremost as black, they saw it as their mission to provide strength, wisdom, and a measure of insulation to Michelle and Craig. Attitudes were changing, if slowly, and opportunities were growing. But the lessons echoed the ones their own parents had taught: Play the hand you were dealt and do it without complaint. "If it can be done, you can do it," Marian once said, describing the family motto. "It's a matter of choice."

Neither Fraser nor Marian finished college, a disappointment that fueled the push they gave to their children. Fraser served on reserve status with the Illinois National Guard and, like his father, worked at the post office. Three days before Michelle's birth, he started the city water plant job that he would keep until his death. Marian spent an unsatisfying two years studying to be a teacher, a profession favored by her parents but unattractive to her. She worked at Spiegel, the retail company, and then stayed home with the children until Michelle was in high school. "I come from a very articulate, well-read, highly productive, strong moral background. We weren't rich but we had the same aspirations as middle- and upper-middle-class African American families . . . ," Michelle explained in 2005. "People tend to either demonize or mythologize black communities that aren't wealthy. But my experience is that my community was very strong, the parents had strong values—the same as other people have throughout this country."

MARIAN SHIELDS ROBINSON WAS BORN in Chicago on July 30, 1937. Her parents arrived in the city as grade-school children, each already knowing much about sadness and loss. Rebecca Jumper and Purnell Shields came from the South, one from North Carolina, one from Alabama. Born early enough in the new century that people were alive who had lived in slavery, they joined the growing tide that became the Great Migration, attracted to what writer Isabel Wilkerson, borrowing from Richard Wright, called "the warmth of other suns." They traveled to the big city with adults who were determined to escape the race-based constraints of the South and grasp the economic opportunities that Chicago appeared to offer. Marian's parents arrived roughly a decade before Fraser C. Robinson Jr. and lived through the 1920s there. Married by age twenty, they would raise seven children on the South Side. But their path was hardly smooth, professionally or personally. By the end of their lives, they would be living apart.

Rebecca Jumper, Michelle's maternal grandmother, was born in 1909 in North Carolina, the seventh child in the family and the first to be born away from the Virginia farm where her father, James Jumper, had been an illiterate sharecropper. The family had followed relatives across the state line to Leaksville, where businesses sprouted to mill the cotton, process the tobacco, and hew the trees grown nearby. James worked as a laborer and his wife, Eliza Tinsley Jumper, the daughter of former slaves, took in laundry, scrubbing other people's clothes on a washboard. As adults, they both learned to read and Eliza could write "a little." Before Rebecca was ten years old, however, her parents died, perhaps in an influenza outbreak that killed thousands of people in North Carolina, the majority of them black. The family split apart. Rebecca joined her mother's younger sister, Carrie Tinsley Coleman, and her husband, John, who had moved north in 1907. After starting in Baltimore, they were on their way to Chicago to try their luck. They settled on the bustling South Side as a cobbled-together family of three. As an adult, Rebecca found work as a seamstress. "The women in my family were dressmakers," said Marian, who would also learn to sew. John went to work in a meatpacking plant, not five years after Upton Sinclair wrote his dark history of the industry, *The Jungle*. He then found work as a plasterer.

Purnell Shields, too, knew loss at a young age. He was born in Birmingham, Alabama, in 1910, the newest member of a family that had climbed several rungs since slavery. The city was deeply segregated and would remain so for decades, yet his grandfather had succeeded as a businessman and acquired property. His father, Robert Lee Shields, worked as a Pullman porter—desirable work that delivered a solid income, a measure of prestige, and a window onto a wider world. Purnell was not yet ten when his father died suddenly, leaving his mother, Annie Shields, to pay the bills while caring for her two children. Her work life until then had consisted of working at home as a seamstress, and she struggled with the new responsibilities. She soon remarried. Her new husband was a tailor. With Purnell and his sister, the family moved from Alabama to Chicago in the early 1920s.

Purnell, working in a syrup factory by the time he was nineteen, would spend much of his adult life as a carpenter and handyman whose passions ran to music, especially jazz. When he was a young man, Chicago was a music mecca. "When I finally came to Chicago on May 9,

1930," said Floyd Campbell, a renowned drummer of the era, "there was plenty of work for musicians. I used to say that there were at least 110 full-time musicians working on salaries of up to $75 a week within a one-block radius of 47th Street and South Parkway. There were two bands at the Regal Theater and three large orchestras working at the Savoy Ballroom. . . . Chicago was a musician's town." The greats, the sidemen, and the dreamers flowed through town in the years to come. Louis Armstrong and Earl Hines. Bessie Smith and King Oliver. Duke Ellington and Cab Calloway. Count Basie and Benny Goodman. Ella Fitzgerald and Gene Krupa. They all played at the Lincoln Gardens Cafe or the enormous Savoy Ballroom, capacity four thousand, or in the galaxy of other South Side clubs.

It was clear to everyone who spent time with Purnell Shields that jazz animated him. "He played it 24 hours a day on the highest volume he could put it on," recalled Michelle, who credited him with presenting her with her first album, *Talking Book,* released by Stevie Wonder in 1972. She reported that he had speakers in every room, including the bathroom, and quoted her mother as saying of her upbringing, "You learn to sleep through jazz." Craig said the grandfather they called Southside was "by calling a chef, drummer and jazz aficionado, an impresario and all around magnet who made everyone in the family gravitate to his side." He experienced frustration, as well, particularly about the racism he encountered throughout his life. He was denied better jobs and pay because, as an African American, he could not join a labor union. "I had a father who could be very angry about race," Marian once said. "My father was a very angry man."

IN NO DECADE since the Civil War and Reconstruction had race been more consistently central to the national conversation than it was in the 1960s, when Fraser and Marian were beginning to raise their children. The Kerner Commission, delivering its 1968 report on racial unrest in America's cities, made its elemental conclusion plain on the very first page: "Our nation is moving toward two societies, one black, one white—separate and unequal." The commission, established by

President Lyndon B. Johnson during the angry summer of 1967, and chaired by Illinois governor Otto Kerner Jr., was hardly stacked with iconoclasts or seers. Rather, months of testimony and analysis yielded the inescapable conclusion that America's cities were bitterly broken and black people were getting the short end of the stick. "Segregation and poverty have created in the racial ghetto a destructive environment totally unknown to most white Americans," wrote the eleven members of what was officially named the National Advisory Commission on Civil Disorders. "What white Americans have never fully understood— but what the Negro can never forget—is that white society is deeply implicated in the ghetto. White institutions created it, white institutions maintain it, and white society condones it." In establishing the commission, President Johnson declared that the nation should attack, as a matter of "conscience," the urban conditions that bred despair and violence: "All of us know what those conditions are: Ignorance, discrimination, slums, poverty, disease, not enough jobs."

What the commission found in cities across the country was commonplace in Chicago, where progress toward equal opportunity had been grudging in the aftermath of the 1948 Supreme Court decision in *Shelley v. Kraemer,* which ended racially restrictive housing covenants, and the 1954 ruling in *Brown v. Board of Education.* Protests had been launched and civic battles fought, notably over segregated schools, but avenues to advancement through education, work, and politics remained stubbornly narrow. When the Reverend Martin Luther King Jr. decided to carry his nonviolent southern protest movement to the urban north in 1966, he chose Chicago. To draw attention to slum housing and discrimination, he made a show of moving his family into a dilapidated West Side apartment with a broken boiler and stairwells that stank of urine.

That same year, a team of university researchers concluded that poverty and lack of opportunity in Chicago's African American neighborhoods owed much to discriminatory policies in housing and employment. Redlining and usurious contract-buying practices were common. Although the income of an average black family in 1966 was just two-thirds of the income of an average white family, average rents were identical. Noting that rents and home prices in African American neighborhoods were artificially high. Academics called it a "color tax" and demonstrated the ways that housing discrimination rippled through other aspects of the lives of black citizens: "This difference has its source in the prejudice that deprives the Negro of the free choice of his residence. Regardless of his living standards or of his preferences, the Negro is confined to certain areas of the city. Residential segregation by extension tends toward segregation of residentially oriented facilities such as schools, parks, libraries, beaches and public transportation lines." Schools became increasingly overcrowded with black children, but the Chicago public school leadership refused to redraw boundaries to allow black students to fill unused classroom space in largely white schools.

As for employment, the gap was stark. Black people were generally unwelcome in jobs in the Loop, the city's downtown business center. A 1966 report on major Chicago businesses by the U.S. Equal Employment Opportunity Commission found that white workers were ten times more likely than black workers to have professional or managerial jobs and five times more likely to have sales jobs. Black employees were three times more likely than whites to be laborers or service workers. In raw numbers, the survey found that African Americans held 4.5 percent of the 33,769 white-collar jobs in the insurance industry and 12 percent of the 78,385 retail jobs. In the health care field, black people were found to have 7.9 percent of the 23,783 white-collar jobs.

All ten of Chicago's poorest communities were in the so-called "Negro Belt" on the city's South and West Sides. Seven of the ten communities were found to be at least 90 percent nonwhite. Meanwhile, only one in sixty-five African Americans lived in neighborhoods that were at least 90 percent white. The most downtrodden neighborhood in the city was Altgeld, on the city's far southern edge, where Barack Obama would work as a community organizer in the 1980s.

WOODLAWN, WHERE MICHELLE LIVED for the first eighteen months of her life across the hall from Fraser and LaVaughn Robinson in

Parkway Gardens, was also going downhill. The community's population was expanding and becoming increasingly African American, with Woodlawn moving from 40 percent nonwhite in 1950 to 98 percent nonwhite in 1966. It was also becoming poorer by every measure, its housing stock deteriorating, juvenile delinquency rising, and jobs moving away. "Statistically, Woodlawn had become just another slum," wrote one author. In 1965, when Craig was three years old and Michelle was one and a half, the Robinsons moved about three miles away to a house on a quiet street in South Shore, a middle-class neighborhood in transition from all white to all black. At the time, some called the move going "way out south." They packed up their things, from Fraser's artwork to the children's toys, and settled into the upstairs apartment of a red-brick bungalow purchased that year by Marian's aunt, Robbie Shields Terry, a strong-willed schoolteacher active in the Woodlawn AME church choir, and her husband, William Terry, a Pullman porter. With no children of their own, they liked the idea of having the young Robinson family close by. The apartment was small, but the house had a yard in front and back with plenty of room to turn cartwheels.

At about the time Marian and Fraser were moving to 7436 South Euclid Avenue, Gloria and Leonard Jewell bought a home two blocks south. "Because it was an integrated neighborhood," Gloria Jewell told a *Chicago Tribune* reporter in 1967. "We wanted to bring up our two children, ages 5 and 4, in a world that would be far more pleasant than it had been to us." She said, "People here are dedicated and have high standards." Gloria worked as a Head Start coordinator after earning a teaching certificate. Leonard was a commercial artist who had studied and taught at the Art Institute of Chicago but was routinely denied jobs because he was African American. One of the first black families in the 7600 block of South Euclid, the Jewells stayed and built a life even as a steady stream of white people moved out. "I had the best childhood ever. It was awesome," said Leonard Jewell Jr., known as Biff to his friends, including Craig Robinson. "I had so much fun. There were tons of kids, we played tons of games. It was all outside, simple stuff. Riding your bike, playing softball, playing football. There was always something going on. Climbing my garage, swinging from the trees into my backyard. It was a blast."

Two blocks away it would not be long before Craig and Michelle could ride their bikes on the sidewalk and around the block to the back alley. Across East 75th Street was a large city park with a grass field and playground equipment. Its name, Rosenblum Park, signified an earlier wave of South Shore residents, now moving out. When they were old enough, Craig and Michelle could walk safely to class at Bryn Mawr Elementary, where Marian, one of the very few stay-at-home mothers in the neighborhood, volunteered her time. "There were good schools, that's why people moved, and it was the reason *we* moved," Marian said. "It was fine with me that it was changing. Some people felt the schools were too geared to whites. People were very conscious and wanted black artists in the schools. My point was just to go to school and learn what you have to learn." To the children, it seemed pretty great. Craig called it "the Shangri-La of upbringings."

IN 1966, when Martin Luther King arrived in North Lawndale, a grittier precinct on Chicago's West Side, he found a latticework of racial politics so intricate that it made him long for the television-ready segregationists in Selma and Birmingham. Not that the hatred in Chicago was any milder, he would soon conclude, for the structural inequality that hindered and harmed black people had deep roots. King began leading interracial vigils and protest marches in support of open housing. He met with gang members, civic activists, and city officials. Pickets stood outside real estate offices and banks, instructing passersby about discrimination that kept more people from doing what the Robinsons did. In the city's central business district demonstrators carried signs that read "We are here because the Savings and Loan Associations refuse to loan money to Negroes who wish to buy beyond the ghetto."

On July 10, six months into what became known as the Chicago Freedom Movement, King headlined a rally on a ninety-eight-degree day at Soldier Field, where tens of thousands of people listened to performances by B.B. King, Mahalia Jackson, Peter, Paul, and Mary, and sixteen-year-old Stevie Wonder. Several thousand then marched three miles to City Hall, where King emulated Martin Luther and taped a parchment with fourteen demands to an outside door. Five days later, a neighborhood argument over opening fire hydrants for black children in the brutal summer heat had ricocheted into riots that left two dead, hundreds under arrest, six police officers wounded by gunfire, $2 million in property damage, and four thousand National Guardsmen patrolling the streets.

The troubles continued. Three weeks later, King led a march of 550 white and black Freedom Movement supporters through Marquette Park, a white southwest Chicago neighborhood. Despite the deployment of two hundred police officers in riot helmets to protect the demonstrators, the protest turned ugly. The marchers, including Andrew Young and Jesse Jackson, were met with rocks, bricks, and cherry bombs; forty-two people were hospitalized. White youths slashed tires and set fire to marchers' cars, which were identified by their "End Slums" stickers. King addressed 1,700 supporters a few days later by saying the protests and the picket lines would continue: "I *still* have faith in the future. My brothers and sisters, I *still* can sing 'We Shall Overcome.'" The next afternoon, when King returned to Marquette Park, an angry crowd of more than four thousand white people was waiting. One sign read "King Would Look Good with a Knife in His Back." A King supporter who had helped plan the march route heard a singsong chant to the tune of the Oscar Mayer Weiner jingle:

> *I wish I were an Alabama trooper.*
> *This is what I would truly love to be.*
> *Because if I were an Alabama trooper,*
> *Then I could kill the niggers legally.*

A rock hurled by someone in the crowd hit King behind his right ear and knocked him to the ground. Someone else threw a knife; it missed him and stuck in the shoulder of a white heckler. The three-mile march continued, as did the attack, with windows shattering, bones breaking, and men setting protesters' cars afire. Six Chicago policemen, seen by the crowd as collaborators, were cornered and beaten until reinforcements fired gunshots into the air and rescued them. "I have never in my life seen such hate," King told reporters later. "I've been in many demonstrations all across the South, but I can say that I have never seen—even in Mississippi and Alabama—mobs as hostile and hate-filled as I've seen in Chicago. I think the people from Mississippi ought to come to Chicago to learn how to hate."

The protests, the bad publicity, and the potential for more conflict pushed Mayor Richard J. Daley and the business community to promise modest action. But when King left town, the status quo remained undisturbed. "We should have known better," King's Southern Christian Leadership Conference ally Ralph Abernathy said later, "than to believe that we could come to Chicago and right its wrongs with the same tactics we had used in Montgomery, Birmingham and Selma." What the Chicago project did, however, was demonstrate to a national audience that racism in the mid-1960s was not confined to the byways of the old Confederacy. The violence and vitriol in the heartland, wrote author Taylor Branch, "cracked a beguiling, cultivated conceit that bigotry was the province of backward Southerners, treatable by enlightened but firm instruction." In the aftermath of the bloody Chicago campaign, the editors of the *Saturday Evening Post* wrote, "We are all, let us face it, Mississippians."


THE TUMULT EXPOSED a mean side of Chicago, a city dominated by Daley, a quintessential political boss who was elected to six terms between April 1955 and December 1976. More than any mayor in twentieth-century America, Daley perfected the power of patronage to bend the city to his vision and his will. He earned the loyalty of many, co-opted others, and bulldozed the rest. This was particularly true in the growing black community, which experienced Daley's tactical largesse as a limited blessing. "Daley had a special weak spot. He never accepted African American Chicagoans on an equal basis," said Leon Despres, an independent white South Side alderman who often found himself on the lonely end of 49–1 city council votes. "He used their committeemen and officeholders to get votes. He allotted them their mathematical share of patronage. He reserved the highest offices for whites. He resisted a genuine opening of the police and fire departments. He arranged the construction of the Dan Ryan Expressway to serve, he hoped, as a barrier to expansion of black residence. He resisted genuine fair housing legislation as long as he could."

By the early 1960s, there were six African American aldermen on the city council. They were known derisively as the Silent Six for their supple responses to Daley's demands. The mayor granted his loyalists considerable license to dispense jobs to constituents, so long as election day turnout was high and aldermen voted the right way when called upon. At its height, the Chicago machine controlled as many as forty thousand patronage jobs, by one estimate, ranging from gardeners, garbagemen, and drivers to city inspectors and department heads. For some, patronage meant respectable work at a decent salary, a path to the middle class. For others, it was a gateway to greased palms; cash flowed from numbers rackets, business schemes, and kickback operations that were limited only by the boundaries of human imagination. For still others, it was a ladder to public office. Very few people stepped into one of the fifty city council seats during the Daley years without a nod from the man who ruled City Hall.

Everything was a transaction and everyone understood the rules. "It was impossible to do business in Chicago at that time without dealing with Mayor Daley," said John Johnson, the African American chairman of the downtown media company that published *Jet* and *Ebony*. "You couldn't cut a deal with underlings; you had to see him personally. Which meant that you were personally obligated to him." Harold Washington, who became the city's first black mayor in 1983, got his start with the machine. So did Eugene Sawyer, who took office when Washington died. William Barnett, a precinct captain who later became one of the Silent Six, said matter-of-factly, "We gave out jobs. A man had to carry his precinct to keep his." A former Black Panther named Bobby Rush would say in 1975 that Barnett's perspective had been "blunted by the taste of polish from Mayor Daley's boots," but defenders argued that the bargain made by the Silent Six was not entirely venal, particularly when work possibilities for African Americans were so limited. "You went along with things in order to make sure that we were able to help people," Sawyer told the *Chicago Tribune* after he himself became mayor. "They were people who wanted somehow to break that shackle, but they had so many people that would get hurt, so many people who would lose jobs and positions." Far down the food chain, precinct workers owed the jobs that sustained their families to the labor they did for the machine. "There are no virgins in Chicago politics," Sawyer said. "We all started in the Daley machine."

Sawyer's political mentor was Robert Miller, one of the Silent Six. A funeral director by profession, Miller ran the 6th Ward on the South Side, dispensing favors, getting out the Democratic vote, and toeing the party line. Miller not only understood patronage as the way politics was played, but defended the tradeoffs as the price of progress for his black constituents. Just as Sawyer owed his job on the city payroll to Miller, who put him to work at the city water plant in June 1959, so did Nomenee Robinson, Michelle's uncle, who talked his way through the 6th Ward patronage system into a water plant job one year later. As Robinson recalled the moment, he was attending the Illinois Institute of Technology, helped to a scholarship by Robert Chorley, director of the Woodlawn Boys Club. When Chorley asked what he intended to do for the summer, Robinson replied, "Mr. Chorley, I need a good job." The year before, Robinson had worked as a city janitor and he was looking to move up. Chorley wrote a letter of introduction and sent him to Miller, who dispatched him to City Hall. There, he met Matthew Danaher, Daley's patronage chief, who had started as the mayor's driver and risen to become the 11th Ward alderman before his indictment on federal bribery charges. Danaher, in turn, sent Robinson to see the public works commissioner, James Wilson, who thumbed through a thick employment ledger.

"Okay, we have this laborer job," Wilson said. "How's that fit you?" Robinson took a chance and said that, well, he had held a better job before. Wilson turned back to the ledger and saw a different slot. "Chlorine attendant," he said. "It's like an engineer's job at the old water tower. Are you up to that?" Robinson asked how much it paid. When Wilson said it paid $543.50 a month, Robinson was floored. It was a sum equal to the median family income for a Chicago family of four. He accepted on the spot. Miller, of course, asked something of

Robinson in return, assigning him to be an assistant precinct captain. As Robinson recalled, "He put it very nicely: 'If this conflicts with your studies, you let me know.'" Miller tied the request in a bow, but both parties understood that declining was not an option.

Fraser Robinson followed his younger brother into a low-level job with the machine, serving as a Democratic precinct captain and reporting to the city water department. He was twenty-eight years old when he started work as a water plant "station laborer," or janitor, for a salary of $479 a month. One of his colleagues in later years was Dan Maxime, a white man from the North Side who had started working for the Democratic machine in 1957. When Maxime got his first patronage job, serving as a Cook County zoning inspector, he said it was "the beginning of the good old days of politics. With the graft, even for the cop on the street. When you got stopped, he asked for your license and you had either a five- or a ten-dollar bill you handed him with your license. We were all part of the system. Every election was war and the Republicans were the enemy. You did everything you needed to win that war. That included stealing votes." But Fraser Robinson was not one to falsify registrations or steal votes, Maxime said. "He wasn't the type. He was strait-laced. Just the salt of the earth."

For Fraser, the role of precinct captain suited his outgoing personality. It was also "a ladder, a stepping stone to a job," said his brother Andrew. The water plant job, while tedious, afforded him a steady living with reasonable hours. In five years, he had been promoted to foreman at $659.50 a month, and seven months later, in May 1969, he began tending boilers for $858 a month. He would keep that job until his death. Marian recalled that Fraser "felt local politics was the most important" and saw his precinct work as a way to do good works. "He loved trying to help people. The city was set up so that precinct captains were the go-between with the city," she said. "If they needed an answer, he was the liaison. He was always going to the precinct. He would head there in the evening. He loved to talk." She called him "a visiting kind of person."

. . .

THE HOUSE AT 7436 South Euclid Avenue where the Robinsons lived was neither the nicest nor the poorest on a quiet street stretching three blocks north to a commercial strip on East 71st Street that would later be called Emmett Till Way. It had two entrances on the south side, with one door leading to a staircase that rose to their second-floor apartment. With help from Marian's father, Purnell, the Robinsons turned two rooms and a kitchen into a home for a family of four. The parents took the bedroom while Purnell installed paneling that divided a narrow living room into a shared bedroom and play space—later, a homework space—for Michelle and Craig. The kitchen, down a hallway from the children's room, did double duty as the dining room, and the family shared a single bathroom. "If I had to describe it to a real estate agent, it would be 1BR, 1BA," Craig said. "If you said it was 1,100 square feet, I'd call you a liar."

"Everything that I think about and do," Michelle said later, "is shaped around the life that I lived in that little apartment in the bungalow that my father worked so hard to provide for us." The family made a point of sitting down to dinner together every evening, apart from the nights when Fraser pulled the late shift at the water plant, a twenty-minute drive up Lake Shore Drive to downtown Chicago. Aunt Robbie gave piano lessons to the children, who played outdoors together in good weather. When Craig rode the bicycle he got for Christmas, Michelle followed on her new tricycle. "It was almost as if we were twins, rather than siblings close in age," Craig recalled. There are stories of practical jokes played in the dark and scenes that made the children fall out laughing. Also, all sorts of contests, from hunts through dictionaries and encyclopedias to a jumping game staged by Fraser, who sometimes put a quarter atop a door jamb for young Craig to leap and reach. Michelle had an Easy Bake Oven and a passel of Barbie dolls, including the impossibly contoured blonde Malibu Barbie—the first doll she owned—and a black Barbie imitation. "I liked everything Barbie. I was a big Barbie doll kid and every Christmas, I got a new Barbie. One year, I got the Barbie townhouse and the camper." Only later, after she started to read the work of Maya Angelou, particularly her poem "Phenomenal Woman," did she reflect on the cultural messages contained in the curves of the tiny-waisted plastic figurines. Barbie seemed to be "the standard for perfection," she said later. "That was what the world told me to aspire to."

AT THE ROBINSON HOUSE, Fraser made time when he returned from work to play sports with the kids—baseball, basketball, soccer, football. He gave Craig a pair of boxing gloves and taught him how to use them. Craig remembers boxing with Michelle, who told the International Olympic Committee in Copenhagen that her father "taught me how to throw a ball and a mean right hook better than any boy in my neighborhood." She described herself as "kind of a tomboy" and recalled sports as "a gift I shared with my dad." The children were limited to one hour of television a day. *The Brady Bunch* was a particular favorite of Michelle's, and she developed an encyclopedic knowledge of the show. For the parents, nights out of the house on their own were a rarity. The family typically devoted Saturday nights to games: Chinese checkers, Monopoly, a bluffing game called Hands Down, and, later, epic Scrabble battles. From an early age, Michelle hated to lose.

When the weather was warm, in a house without air conditioning, the children staged camping trips on the back porch, later converted to a bedroom for Craig. During football season, they backed the Bears, with Fraser parking himself in front of the television on Sunday afternoons. They rooted for the White Sox, the nearby South Side baseball team. But they invested more passion in the Cubs, the team that played in the North Side's iconic Wrigley Field. The star was the effervescent Ernie Banks, ace fielder, slugger, and two-time National League most valuable player who had once earned $7 a day in the Negro Leagues. Fans called him Mr. Cub. He and two black teammates, Billy Williams and Ferguson Jenkins, reached the Baseball Hall of Fame despite years on desultory squads that never saw the first inning of a World Series. Craig once said he considered baseball his main sport as a young boy. He liked to imagine himself as the next Ernie Banks.

When Michelle launched her healthy eating campaign during her husband's first term in the White House, she recalled how active she had been as a girl in South Shore. The streets were safe and Bryn Mawr Elementary still had recess. Before school, she played freeze tag and other games in the schoolyard until the bell rang, "and after school we'd head home to our neighborhood and play outside for hours. There were always plenty of kids around, and we'd play softball or a game called Piggy with a batter, a pitcher, a catcher, and a 16-inch softball rather than the standard 12-inch ones." When a fielder caught a batted ball on the fly or on one bounce, the fielder got to bat. "Later, we played chase, which was basically just boys chasing girls and then girls chasing boys. And all the girls in the neighborhood knew how to jump Double Dutch. We would also ride on our bikes and ride around for hours."

MARIAN DEVOTED considerable time to the education of her children, starting when they were young. Craig recalled his mother's diligence in teaching him to read at age four, before he started school. She was ready with flash cards and, as soon as he showed an interest, spent hours with him, describing the letters and sounds and how they connected. He was far ahead of his classmates when he arrived at Bryn Mawr. When she tried the same strategy with her daughter, the little girl refused. "I guess she figured she could figure out how to read on her own, but she was too young to say that," Marian recalled. On her way to becoming grandmother in residence at the White House, Marian would report that Michelle's younger daughter, Sasha, then age seven, reminded her of Michelle at the same age. "Just like Sasha. She always had her own opinions about things and she didn't hesitate to say so, because we allowed it." LaVaughn Robinson, Michelle's paternal grandmother, told a co-worker that Michelle was "hard-headed" and needed a spanking from time to time, but that she and Craig were good kids. A friend, meanwhile, recalled hearing Michelle tell a story about a Bryn Mawr teacher who complained to Marian about the girl's attitude. "Her mom told the teacher, 'Yeah, she's got a temper, but we decided to keep her anyway.'"

The Robinsons' standards for achievement were very high, but they emphasized effort and attitude over grades. They instructed the children that hard work would be rewarded. And it was. Michelle skipped second grade, and Craig, who remembered being bored in second grade, skipped third. It was known as "doing a double." When they finished eighth grade at Bryn Mawr two years apart, Craig was the valedictorian of his class and Michelle was the salutatorian of hers. In making clear the importance of education—not just attending school, but excelling—Marian and Fraser used their own experience as an example, explaining to Michelle and Craig how much they regretted not finishing college. "We told the kids how dumb it was," Marian said.

The lessons at home expanded on what the children learned in school and filled gaps in a Chicago Public Schools curriculum that could not keep up with the politically charged times. The Civil Rights Act and the Voting Rights Act had both become law, yet the children would see on Sunday drives through the city and summer trips to the South that segregation and bigotry endured. Martin Luther King was assassinated in April 1968, when Michelle was four years old, sparking riots in black neighborhoods on the West Side and across the country. When Bryn Mawr lesson plans began to include black history and Craig began asking questions, Marian bought a set of encyclopedias "written from the black perspective," as Craig put it. "Now I could understand not only what the tragedy of Dr. King's killing meant, but also what he represented in terms of the dream of equality that belonged to all races," Craig recalled. "I also learned why 'turn the other cheek' wasn't always easy to do and a little more about other civil rights leaders in [the] 1960s like Malcolm X." It was no coincidence that Malcolm was Craig's middle name. In 1962, he said, his mother "read an article about his work and, as she was looking for a middle name for a boy if she should have one, decided Malcolm had a nice ring to it." Or, as he put it another time, "Now, you've got to remember, my dad grew up in the Black Panther era—my middle name is Malcolm!"

In the tumult of the 1960s, Malcolm X personified an array of images of black people in America, some of them contradictory. He was the petty criminal born as Malcolm Little and known as Big Red who spent time behind bars. He was the ascetic who preached against drugs, deceit, and moral decay. Lanky and stylish, operating from behind silver and black glasses that lent him a studious air, he befuddled white questioners with calm rejoinders about the fundamental rights that any decent society owed its citizens. Yet he also raised his fist in a black power salute. He advocated separatism and militancy, and asked what progress nonviolent protest had ever delivered to African Americans. He dismissed the 1963 March on Washington, which culminated in King's "I Have a Dream" speech, as the "farce on Washington."

Through all of Malcolm's intellectual and spiritual wanderings, even many African Americans who were skeptical or disdainful of his fulminations drew strength from his personal narrative and his celebration of blackness. Jackie Robinson, the first black baseball player in the major leagues, offered up his opinion in *The Defender* in March 1964. The piece appeared in the weeks after Cassius Clay defeated Sonny Liston for the heavyweight boxing title and converted to Islam, becoming Muhammad Ali. Robinson said the new champ, who called himself "the greatest," was loud and sometimes crude, but his message of black self-worth was right. "I am not advocating that Negroes think they are greater than anyone else," Robinson said. "But I want them to know that they are just as great as other human beings." He said critics missed the point in worrying that Ali and Malcolm X would entice Negroes to become Black Muslims. The black people who marched for civil rights "want more democracy, not less," Robinson said. "They want to be integrated into the mainstream of American life, not invited to live in some small cubicle of this land in splendid isolation. If Negroes ever turn to the Black Muslim movement, in any numbers, it will not be because of Cassius or even Malcolm X. It will be because white America has refused to recognize the responsible leadership of the Negro people and to grant us the same rights that any other citizen enjoys in this land."

"Before Malcolm X," wrote cultural critic Ta-Nehisi Coates, "the very handle we now embrace—*black*—was an insult. We were *coloreds* or *Negroes*, and to call someone *black* was to invite a fistfight. But Malcolm remade the menace inherent in that name into something mystical—*Black Power; Black Is Beautiful; It's a black thing, you wouldn't understand. . . .* For all of Malcolm's invective, his most seductive notion was that of collective self-creation: the idea that black people could, through force of will, remake themselves." In *Dreams from My Father,* his memoir about his search for identity, young Barack Obama wrote of Malcolm X that his "repeated acts of self-creation spoke to me. The blunt poetry of his words, his unadorned insistence on respect, promised a new and uncompromising order, martial in its discipline, forged through sheer force of will. All the other stuff, the talk of blue-eyed devils and apocalypse, was incidental to that program." As president, Obama said he found Malcolm's theology, analysis, and policy advice to be "full of holes." And yet, he told writer David Remnick, Malcolm gave voice to the growing conviction in the African American community that black people must believe in themselves and assert their worth. "If you think about it, of a time in the early 1960s, when a black Ph.D. might be a Pullman porter and have to spend much of his day obsequious and kowtowing to people, that affirmation that 'I am a man, I am worth something,' I think that was important. And I think Malcolm X probably captured that better than anybody."

WHEN MICHELLE AND CRAIG WERE in elementary school, Marian made herself a familiar presence among the teachers and students. Fraser also spent time in their classrooms, and other relatives pitched in. Aunt Robbie ran an operetta workshop for children in the school district, once casting Craig as Hansel in *Hansel and Gretel* when he was in second grade. He had a singing part, as did Michelle, who wore a tutu and played the good fairy. Singing a solo was "humiliating," she said, but the performance was a win. "I liked it because of the costume."

Robbie was a formidable presence. Always had been. Years before, she had lived with Marian's large family at 6449 South Eberhart Avenue, helping with the children in ways that, as Marian recalled, "my mother would not or could not." She became youth choir director at the politically progressive Woodlawn AME church and, in 1943, registered for a church and choral music workshop at Northwestern University. Late on a summer night, when she arrived at Willard Hall to claim her room, a clerk informed her that Negroes were not permitted to spend the night on campus. Although it was nearly midnight, the clerk sent her to a rooming house for "coloreds" elsewhere in Evanston. Robbie reported the news to Woodlawn's pastor, the Reverend Archibald J. Carey Jr., who mustered a *Chicago Defender* reporter and an officer of the Chicago Civil Liberties Committee to investigate. "We know that Negroes prefer to live with members of their own race," a school official told the delegation. Five months later, backed by the Woodlawn church, Robbie sued Northwestern in state court, alleging discrimination. The lawsuit charged that the university had treated her as "inferior to other normal young American women and unfit to live and associate with them."

Robbie, who became the Woodlawn choir director, retained her high standards, a trait that ran in the family. "She was friendly, but that music had to be perfect," remembered Betty Reid, who sang at Woodlawn and rehearsed from time to time at the South Euclid house. "Let me tell you, in the middle of your performance, if you were off-key, she would stop. 'We are going to start at *this* place. If you aren't interested in singing, you should just sit this out.' We would feel so embarrassed, but she wanted to make sure you never made that error again. She was a hard taskmaster, but the choirs and the performers were right on target." Reid became a friend, sometimes giving Robbie a ride home from church. Later, Reid would leave Woodlawn and minister to her own congregation. She presided over Fraser's memorial service in 1991.

Michelle said both sides of the family had a "strong connection to faith and religion," although she and Craig were infrequent worshippers as children. They sometimes attended Woodlawn, which was preferred by the Shields family, and sometimes the Baptist church favored by the Robinsons. She remembered enduring the endless Chicago winters with the help of romps in a church basement much larger than the cellar at 7436 South Euclid. As an adult, she said she wanted her own daughters to have "a basic foundation, understanding and respect for [a] higher being . . . because it's what I grew up with." In religious matters as with many other things, Fraser and Marian left it to the children to choose their own way. Their approach, according to Craig, was to expose them to church and encourage them "to explore and find our own basis for faith by thinking for ourselves." After his father's funeral years later, Craig noted that Betty Reid's remarks were not "about how Fraser had gone on to a better place, which would have been counter to his belief that life is what it is, here on earth."

THROUGH THE YEARS, Craig and Michelle frequently described their childhood as an idyll rooted in family solidarity that flowed from their parents' evident affection for each other and their determination to get the parenting equation right. "That love for one another," Craig wrote, "was simply a fact of our lives, the foundation of the strong family unit they chose to build, and the reason they always seemed to be happy to me—even when circumstances might have dictated otherwise." Fraser and Marian made clear their rigorous expectations for achievement and citizenship, while deploying a sense of humor that, among other things, kept the children from getting too big for their britches. Craig recalled their parents as "relentless." Michelle, who remembered "a mother who pushed me," cleaned the bathroom every Saturday, scrubbing the sink and toilet and mopping the floor. She and her brother took turns doing the dishes. The parents "didn't overdo the praise," yet something in the mix kept the children from being overly concerned with the negative opinions of others. "It was very disciplined and there was a lot of accountability," Craig said. "But there was a whole lot of respect, a whole lot of love, and the biggest thing I think my parents gave us was self-esteem." They also modeled a sense of responsibility, to oneself and others, that would be echoed in countless choices Michelle made as an adult.

The freedom granted to Michelle and Craig to make their own decisions was not unlimited. It existed within a framework that emphasized hard work, honesty, and self-discipline. There were obligations and occasional punishment. But the goal was freethinking. "Don't be a follower," Marian told her children. "You follow people for one reason and they'll lead you for another." She advised them to use their heads, yet not to be afraid to make mistakes—in each case always learning from what goes wrong. "If it sounds like they are using good judgment," she said, "then you don't settle on the rules, because you want them early on to start making decisions on their own. I think that gives kids a lot of confidence."

The highs and lows of Marian's own childhood taught her some enduring lessons, ones that she would pass along. She attended segregated schools. In her extended family, she saw struggle and sacrifice alike. "That's where we got our understanding that it was going to be hard, but you just had to do whatever it takes," she said. "We all went to church. I was a Brownie. I was a Girl Scout. We all took piano lessons. We had drama classes. They took you to the museum, the Art Institute. They did all these things, but I don't know how." She saw to it that Craig and Michelle went to the symphony, the opera, and the city's fine museums. Recalling times in her childhood when she "resented it when I couldn't say what I felt," she also aimed to raise her children to stand up, speak up, and always ask why. "More important, even, than learning to read and write was to teach them to think. We told them, 'Make sure you respect your teachers, but don't hesitate to question them. Don't even allow us to just say anything to you.'"

It was understood in the Robinson household that no matter what obstacles Michelle or Craig faced because of their race or their working-class roots, life's possibilities were unbounded. Fulfillment of those possibilities was up to them. No excuses. Not that the strategy emerged fully formed when the kids were born. Marian said she raised her children "by ear, day by day." She explained, "You know, we always tried to look at things like we might not be right. I learned a lot from my kids simply because I didn't pretend to act like I knew everything, and my husband was good at that, too. Kids can be smart if you let them; they can think on their own."

From the Robinsons' vantage point on the South Side in the 1960s and 1970s, prejudice and opportunity existed side by side. Amid the undeniable perils, Marian and Fraser recognized that their children would inhabit a world of greater possibility than the one that had greeted their own coming of age a generation earlier. They calculated that a black child stepping into the tumult of modern urban America would find a certain independence of mind to be not just an asset, but a necessity.

# THREE

# Destiny Not Yet Written

Fraser and Marian Robinson mastered the art of the Sunday drive, a form of entertainment that matched their budget and not incidentally furthered their educational goals for their children. In the early 1970s, gas was affordable and the city beckoned in all of its complexity. When they had time, the family would pile into the Buick Electra 225—Fraser called it the "deuce and a quarter"—and meander through Chicago neighborhoods as the children asked questions and Fraser told stories. With Fraser at the wheel and the children in the back seat, Marian would sit with her back against the passenger door to watch her family as the conversation unfolded. Michelle's exploration of the wider world began on those drives and would continue on neighborhood bicycle rides, treks across town to high school, summer trips across state lines, and, one day, airplane flights to the East Coast to attend university. Fraser was a devoted reader of books and newspapers, as was Marian, and he was the keeper of the family lore. As he drove, he connected the scenes spooling beyond the windows with stories and wisdom he kept stashed in his head, drawing on his own experiences and his long, solitary hours tending the equipment that kept the city's tap water flowing. Craig Robinson, who loved hearing stories about the family, remembered the Sunday drives as important moments in the children's consideration of life beyond the relative comfort and neighborliness of South Shore.

In 1974, when Craig was twelve and Michelle was ten, one expedition led the Robinsons to a neighborhood lined with mansions. Craig asked why so many of the homes had an extra little house in the back. "My parents explained that those were carriage houses where black folks who took care of the family stayed," he recalled. "Thus began a conversation about racism and classism, integration and segregation, along with the history of slavery and Jim Crow." In South Shore by this time, there were few white residents and the children encountered few white people on their daily rounds. If they experienced animosity in those early years, it was likely from African American kids who heard their good grammar, saw their classroom diligence, and accused them of "trying to sound white." On that particular Sunday drive, the children wanted to know why some kids, black and white, were judgmental and mean. Marian remarked that meanness often stemmed from insecurity. Fraser said it was important to understand the nature of ignorance instead of dismissing it without reflection. The antidote to meanness was self-knowledge. No one can make you feel bad, they said, if your values are solid and you feel good about yourself. "When you grow up as a black kid in a white world, so many times people are telling you—sometimes not maliciously, sometimes maliciously—you're not good enough," Craig said later. "I remember [my father] saying you don't want to do things because you're worried about people thinking they're right; you want to do the right things. You grow up not worrying about what people think about you."

The national debate about racism was intense in the early 1970s, thanks, on the positive side, to the civil rights movement and, on the negative, to Republican president Richard Nixon's adoption of a race-baiting "Southern strategy." Opportunities for African Americans were unquestionably growing. Legalized discrimination was ebbing, aided by federal law, and the "firsts" were piling up, even if the few exceptions continued to prove the rule. Yet obstacles aplenty remained. In Chicago, the world of young African Americans was different in degree, but not in kind, from the city their parents had known in their youth. The lessons they heard—grounded in education, personal responsibility, and self-esteem—emerged from the experience of the generations that preceded them, including the ones that had flowed north during the Great Migration. For Michelle and Craig, that meant wisdom imparted by Fraser and Marian, but also by their four grandparents and a sprawling extended family on the South Side. Fraser was one of five children, Marian one of seven. It required considerable concentration simply to name all the cousins.

Purnell Shields, Michelle's maternal grandfather, was the jazz lover called Southside. He was lively, a good cook, and a master of barbecue whose home became "the headquarters for every special occasion," Michelle said. Beyond birthdays, holidays, and his annual Fourth of July extravaganza, she recalled visiting frequently, "packed into his little house, eating those ribs for dinner, talking and laughing, listening to jazz, playing cards late into the night. And then, when we could barely keep our eyes open, Southside would jump up and ask, 'Anybody want cheeseburgers and milkshakes?' He didn't want us to leave." One of Purnell's most memorable messages, said his daughter Grace Hale, came the day she arrived home in tears and told her father that other children did not like her. "They might not like you, but you need to make sure they respect you. Always work to get respect outside, but get your love at home," he replied, adding, "Don't ever come to me again with something so unimportant." Michelle's maternal grandmother, Rebecca Shields, was a model of a different sort. She raised her children, then returned to school in her fifties to become a licensed practical nurse, learning to speak French along the way. "Very smart, but very quiet," Hale recalled. "Sometimes you didn't even know she was in the room."

Michelle owed her middle name to her paternal grandmother, LaVaughn Robinson, who was formidable in her own way, becoming the first African American woman to manage a Moody Bible Institute store. When customers were scarce, she chose sections of scripture and prayed with her fellow workers. "She had very strong values," said store clerk Jacquelyn Thomas, who reported to her. "She would tell us how we should dress, how we should carry ourselves as Christian young women." Thomas considered her "a beautiful lady," and yet felt troubled by the way LaVaughn treated her. "I used to think she was picking on me. The other girl, she didn't make her do the things she made me do. I would go home and pray on it." But the teaching and prodding made sense after LaVaughn announced that she was moving, reluctantly, to South Carolina following Fraser's retirement. It turned out that she wanted Thomas to succeed her and had been preparing her for the role.

Yet no one carved a stronger profile in the family than LaVaughn's husband, Fraser C. Robinson Jr., who delivered acerbic lessons in nonsense avoidance to his grandchildren whenever they visited. If he had been born white, Michelle once said, he would have been a bank president. Despite his teenage aspirations in South Carolina in the 1920s, he retired fifty years later from the Chicago workforce as a post office employee, his dreams unfulfilled. Michelle saw "a discontent about him." Even Craig, who tended to look on the bright side, described him as "scowling" and "very stern." He said the crusty grandfather they called Dandy was "not always enjoyable to be around." Fraser was, however, punctilious in all things. "As precise as a drill sergeant when it came to the use of the English language," Craig said. He liked to use unfamiliar words. If the children did not recognize them, he would send them to the dictionary. "On one visit," Craig recalled, "I went to greet him and as soon as I said hello, Grandpa barked, 'Well, that was perfunctory!' . . . Sure enough, before I could respond, he asked, 'Do you know what *perfunctory* means?' 'No, I don't know.' 'Then go look it up!' . . . But then he smiled, which was not only shocking, since it was so rare, but also made me wonder if it made him happy to use a word we didn't know." Years later, when Craig coached basketball at Oregon State University, his players found a dictionary permanently positioned in the locker room.

Fraser Jr. was fiercely disciplined and famously tight with a nickel, recalled his nephew, Capers Funnye, born in 1952. To borrow money from him was to invite a lecture about responsibility. "His whole demeanor was that men have to be responsible." Fraser's own record, of course, was mixed. He had left LaVaughn and his two young boys on their own for many years, although when he returned to the family, he stayed for good. "He was wrestling with something that you and I would never be able to understand," reported his second son, Nomenee, who said he made it through college and graduate school without his father's help, drawing on scholarships, summer jobs, and other sources of money, including loans from his brother Fraser. His father did not show up for Fraser's graduation from DuSable High, Nomenee's graduation from Hyde Park High, where he was a top student, or his college commencement. Younger brother Andrew said his father "didn't exactly spew love or anything. Everything was his way or no way or the highway." This was true no matter how grand the success. "When I was at my ballgames and winning awards at the Museum of Science and Industry for my drawings, he wouldn't come or say anything. When I was quarterback in the city championship, he didn't come. We had to do it on our own."

Nomenee went to India with the Peace Corps, where a 1962 photograph in *The New York Times* showed him meeting Jacqueline Kennedy. He later worked for the federal Office of Economic Opportunity and, in 1971, graduated from Harvard Business School. To his surprise, his father broke with precedent and traveled to Cambridge for the commencement ceremony. After his father's death in 1996, Nomenee discovered among his father's papers a folder marked EENEMON—his name spelled backward. In the folder was a thick stack of newspaper stories that mentioned his son, whose achievements had drawn local attention. The family found something else that stunned them: the frugal soul who refused to pay for his sons' college education had died a prosperous man, leaving a six-figure sum to LaVaughn.

FRASER JR. ALSO DRUMMED into the grandchildren a larger message fundamental to their upbringing, one that Fraser III and Marian and countless other African American parents perfected in the 1960s. The message was rooted in a paradox that required elders to hold two seemingly contradictory ideas in mind simultaneously. One was the fact that the playing field was tilted away from their children because of their race and class. The other was the conviction that a combination of love, support, perseverance, and upright living could win out.

Michelle sketched the juxtaposition in a speech to a largely black audience in South Carolina during the first presidential campaign. On the one hand, she spoke of the "veil of impossibility that keeps us down and keeps our children down—keeps us waiting and hoping for a turn that may never come. It's the bitter legacy of racism and discrimination and oppression in this country." On the other, she said her grandfather Fraser "filled my brother and me with big dreams about the lives we could lead. He taught me that my destiny had not been written before I was born—that my destiny was in my hands."

Whatever their frustrations and demons, Michelle's grandfathers did not appear to be fixated on the injustices of the past. Nor were her parents. Whether because the history was too painful or too much of a distraction or a little of both, the elders did not want their children to feel beaten down by knowledge of the barriers that had halted their own progress. Even Purnell, whom Marian perceived as angry about racism, "did not let it carry over," she said. "We couldn't be racially divisive. That wasn't allowed. We could not be prejudiced." This was typical for the times. Sterling Stuckey, who graduated from DuSable High School in 1950, had an uncle with an Ivy League degree, from Cornell. Yet the best work his uncle could find in those days was managing a business that sold ice. "An ice house!" Stuckey marveled. "But never did he say something discouraging to the young people in the family. He said, 'Things will be different for you.'"

"Parents were trying not to burden their children, but to give them hope and keep them moving forward," said Rachel Swarns, who traced Michelle's family back to slavery, finding white ancestors and slaves on both sides of the family tree, along with generations of travail. The unspoken message from Fraser and LaVaughn was pragmatic. "We want you to get what you can. We want you to look forward. We don't want you to look back," remembered daughter Francesca Gray, who graduated from Simmons College. Limiting excavations of the past, the adults created a buffer, a security zone that made it possible for many African American children to grow up in a nurturing, optimistic world even as prejudice persisted up the street or around the corner or a bus ride away. Michelle noticed and later paid homage, praising "the mothers and the fathers who taught their children to stand with dignity during a time when it was hard to get our kids to dream big."

THE LESSON WAS FAMILIAR to Deval Patrick, who grew up in an impoverished family on the South Side. "We didn't think of it as segregation," he said, "just the neighborhood." He saw elders who had every reason to surrender to cynicism, yet they told him he could shape his future. Seven years older than Michelle, he endured penury worse than anything faced by the Robinsons, particularly after his father, a baritone saxophonist, split for New York to play with the Sun Ra Arkestra. The day his father stormed away from the family in a rage, four-year-old Deval ran after him. "Go home! Go home!" his father shouted. A block from their apartment, he turned and slapped Deval, knocking him to the ground. "From that position, I watched him walk away," said Patrick, whose childhood was punctuated by his mother's stint on welfare, gang threats on his way to DuSable, and summer days wishing his family could afford orange juice. His bright and able grandfather, Reynolds Wintersmith, worked for more than fifty years as a South Shore Bank janitor, sweeping floors and cleaning toilets four blocks from the Robinsons' house on South Euclid Avenue.

"I was surrounded by adults who had every reason to curb my dreams," Patrick said. "My grandparents had grown up with Jim Crow. My mother knew all too well the humiliation of poverty and betrayal." Yet he and his older sister reached adulthood with "just no sense at all that there were limits on us," confident that they could chart their own course. "The true gift of my childhood," he called it. With an unexpected boost from a white South Side teacher who relayed news of a scholarship possibility, Patrick escaped to boarding school at Milton Academy, then earned two degrees from Harvard before being elected the first African American governor of Massachusetts. "They did not want me trapped by bitterness, but liberated to believe that the wider world could be a special place," Patrick said. It was only much later that he realized how far his family had gone to protect him. His grandmother's decision to pack food for the family's monthly visits to Kentucky was not about saving time or money on the road. Rather, it was an attempt to avoid the indignity of stopping at roadside restaurants that refused to serve black customers.

CRAIG ROBINSON DID NOT REALIZE how little money the family had, or how small their apartment was, until he reached Princeton in 1979. At that point, he concluded that the Robinsons were "poor." His father had received regular raises at the water plant, and the family kept its expenses down through general frugality and the chance to share the house on South Euclid. When they took a vacation, it was by car. When they went out, it was usually to dinner at a relative's house. When they went to a drive-in movie, Marian popped the popcorn at home. Desserts were reserved for Sunday dinner and Fraser cut Craig's hair, saving the expense of a barber. "Lunch on school days was often a sandwich made from leftovers. Going to the circus once a year was a big deal. Getting pizza on Friday was a treat," Michelle said, noting that pizza was often reserved as a reward for good grades. The purpose of a rare visit to State Street or Michigan Avenue was usually not to shop, but to peer into the windows of bustling stores decorated for Christmas. "If the TV broke and we didn't have any money to have it fixed, we could go out and buy another one on a charge card," Marian explained, "as long as we paid the bills on time."

One day when Craig was in elementary school and feeling inquisitive about the family finances, he caught up with his father at the kitchen table and asked, "Are we rich?" He told Fraser that it looked as though they were rich, since Marian did not work outside the home and Fraser had a steady city job. When Fraser received his next paycheck, instead of putting it in the bank, he cashed it and brought home a wad of cash, probably about $1,000. When he spread out the bills on the foot of the bed, it was more money in one place than Craig had ever seen. "Wow, we are rich!" he exclaimed. Then Fraser pulled out the family's bills, for electricity, gas, telephone, rent, and the monthly car payment. He had a stack of envelopes and he placed the matching amount of money in each. He set aside money for groceries and each of the ordinary costs of a typical month. When he was finished, a lone $20 bill remained. Craig said gamely that $20 still seemed like a lot. "You get to keep $20 every time you get paid?" Fraser reminded Craig of the trips to the drive-in and the occasional takeout meal. There was nothing left.

IN CONTRAST TO his own father, Fraser C. Robinson III channeled great energy into the children he called "Cat" and "Miche" and took very public pride in their doings and accomplishments. He would even make time for them in the mornings after an overnight shift, which ran from 10 p.m. to 6 a.m., sometimes fixing their breakfast before he headed to bed. He attended Craig's games and Michelle's dance recitals. He spent hours with Craig on neighborhood courts, and shot baskets with him at Dukes Happy Holiday Resort, a rustic getaway in central Michigan where the Robinsons sometimes rented a cabin, and helped him find a principled coach who would teach him well. He took Craig with him to the barbershop, so that his son could hear the talk of the day—advising him, however, not to repeat the bawdy jokes to his mother. He dispensed aphorisms. One favorite was "A smart man learns from his own mistakes; a wise man learns from the mistakes of others." There was something about Fraser that made his children want to live up to his high standards. "If you disappointed my dad, everybody was, like, crying," reported Craig, who said he did not drink his first beer until a college recruiting trip. "I never had any friends who could talk me into doing something that my parents would be disappointed in. Never. Because it was the ultimate insult to me as a son to disappoint my mom and dad."

Friends and relatives universally described Fraser as gregarious and generous, honorable and trusted. "Unofficial counselor to family, friends and strangers all around Chicago," as Craig once put it. "Fraser was the type of person, whatever he did, he put his all into it. Whatever he did, he did it all the way," said Grace Hale, Marian's sister. "The way he thought about his job. The way he went out there every day, determined to make it. The way he insisted that his children would get an education. He always assumed he would make a way for them to get their education. He wanted the best for them and he gave it to them—and he never got to see it." When Marian's uncle William Terry's health failed, Fraser would check on him before leaving for work and again when he arrived home. He would shave Terry's whiskers, cut his hair, bathe him, and take him to the toilet. To others in the family, he listened well and was not shy about offering advice. "That's where I went to talk about my issues in life, wife, children. We would get a bottle of Old Fitz and ginger ale and some beer nuts and sit down and really talk. He taught me a lot," said Nomenee, who described being dismissed at times by other relatives as a vagabond or, worse, a schemer. "Not that I always made the best decisions, but whatever decisions I made and I wanted to recover from, he wanted the best for me. I always felt that way. He could put things in perspective."

A major source of Fraser's perspective was his debilitating multiple sclerosis. The illness held him back on many fronts, not least in pursuing his passion for painting and sculpture. "Before he got really sick and had to work and raise us, he probably, if he had his choice, would have been an artist," Michelle said. Multiple sclerosis is unpredictable in whom it afflicts and how seriously. It also is notoriously difficult to diagnose, but by 1965, the year he turned thirty and the family moved to South Shore, it seemed likely that he had the disease. Long before the children knew why he was ill, they saw that he was becoming weaker, walking with a limp and struggling against tremors to button his work uniform. "I never knew my father as a man who could run," Michelle once told an audience. He walked first with a cane, then with one crutch, the kind with a cuff that wraps around the arm. Then with two and then with a walker. By the time the children were in college, he used a wheelchair and a motorized scooter.

"Even as a kid, I knew there were plenty of days when he was in pain. And I knew there were plenty of mornings when it was a struggle for him to simply get out of bed," Michelle told delegates to the 2012 Democratic National Convention. "But every morning I watched my father wake up with a smile, grab his walker, prop himself against the sink, and slowly shave and button his uniform. And when he returned home after a long day's work, my brother and I would stand at the top of the stairs of our apartment, patiently waiting to greet him, watching as he reached down to lift one leg and then the other to slowly climb his way into our arms." He took pride in not going to the doctor, Michelle said, and he almost never missed a day of work. By all accounts, he did not complain about yet another bad break in a life afflicted with more than his fair share. Michelle, who often talked about the example her father set, did not volunteer details about how her father's illness had influenced her, but there were signs in her preference for organization and discipline. "When you have a parent with a disability," she said, "control and structure become critical habits, just to get through the day."

Dan Maxime started work at the water plant in 1970 and remembered Fraser walking with a limp even then. As the years went by, he watched his health decline. "Here's a guy who could have gone on medical disability," Maxime said. "Every day, he worked. He was the gutsiest guy I have ever known in my life. He was honest, conscientious, hardworking. Here he had this disability and he never complained about it. A mild-mannered guy. I only heard him cuss once." It happened one payday, when a co-worker stopped by the plant to pick up his paycheck, then called in sick two hours later when he was due to start his shift. Maxime recalled attending one of Craig's basketball games, impressed that Craig had addressed him as Mr. Maxime. "We had a lot of laughs. We talked a lot of sports. . . . Every time there was some kind of accomplishment by Craig or Michelle, he would always tell me. 'Guess what? Craig made his first dunk today.'"

Nor was he timid about sharing his pride and good feelings with the children themselves. Fraser "thought he had the greatest kids that God ever gave anyone," Marian told an interviewer. None of it was lost on Craig or Michelle. "To have a family, which we did, who constantly reminded you how smart you were, how good you were, how pleasant it was to be around you, how successful you could be, it's hard to combat. Our parents gave us a little head start by making us feel confident," Craig said. "It sounds so corny, but that's how we grew up."

BEFORE MICHELLE was old enough to ride by herself on the trains that rumbled along 71st Street, her bicycle provided an escape. A favorite destination, and the apogee of one of her first solo rides, was Rainbow Beach, a large patch of public sand on the shores of Lake Michigan, an easy pedal from home. Michelle sometimes gathered friends, riding their own bikes, to join her. At a city-run summer camp there, ten-year-old Michelle missed out on the best camper award because of her salty tongue. "I was going through my cursing stage," she said. "I didn't real-ize until my camp counselor at the end came up and said, 'You know, you would have been best camper in your age group, but you curse so much.'" The news floored her. "And I thought I was being cool."

The fact that Rainbow Beach could occupy a spot on Michelle's itin-erary in the mid-1970s was a sign of changing times. Barely a dozen years earlier, the stretch of sand and water from 75th Street to 79th Street was contested territory, as more African Americans moved beyond the borders of the traditional Black Belt. White lifeguards and beachgoers made it clear that black people were not welcome, prompting protests. In July 1961, an interracial group of demonstrators, including members of the NAACP Youth Council, staged a "freedom wade-in." Opponents threw rocks, injuring demonstrators. Although the conflict was history to the South Shore kids of Michelle's generation, Craig had an encoun-ter in the 1970s that reinforced a sense that the city was making only halting progress. One warm day, he was riding his new bicycle, bought at Goldblatt's department store, along the lake at Rainbow Beach. A black Chicago police officer ordered him off the bike and accused him of stealing it. Craig protested, to no avail, and the officer drove the boy and the bicycle home. Standing in the front yard, Marian lectured the officer for a good half hour about jumping to conclusions about black children as Craig watched from an upstairs window. She insisted that the officer return the next day and apologize. He did.

Leonard Jewell Jr., Craig's friend from the 7600 block of South Euclid, considered bike rides an important part of his South Shore childhood. He recalled the feeling of freedom when he pedaled east toward the lake, away from his block. Yet he, too, had one ride that troubled him for years. It happened when he rode with elementary school friends to South Shore Country Club, home to a nine-hole golf course and pri-vate beach. The country club, originally open only to white Protestants, refused to allow Jews or African Americans to join. A white gatekeeper

stopped the bike-riding group. "He said, 'You guys can't come in here.'"
Jewell felt sure they were turned away because of their skin color, and he
said the hurt was "horrible." But just as Rainbow Beach had yielded to
changing times, so would the club. As whites moved away, membership
dwindled and the place was put up for sale. One group of bidders was
headed by Muhammad Ali, who lived nearby. In the end, the Chicago
Park District purchased the property. In 1992, Michelle and Barack held
their wedding reception there.

AS MICHELLE PROPELLED herself through school, she developed a
ferocious work ethic. "Michelle works harder than anyone I know,"
Craig once said. "I'd come home from basketball practice and she'd
be working. I'd sit down on the couch and watch TV. She'd keep working. When I turned off the TV, she'd still be working." Although they
were two grades apart at Bryn Mawr, they both attended an accelerated learning program at Kennedy-King College, where Michelle took
classes in biology and French. Jewell, who joined them there, recalled
an engaging day each week away from the neighborhood. While he,
too, skipped a grade, he recalled that Michelle and Craig worked harder
than he did, a trait that he traced to the ethos that infused the Robinson household. Fraser and Marian, he said, were "strong, strong,
strong, like steel." They honored values that seemed beyond his reach.
"Mrs. Robinson, I loved her a lot. I would not want to piss her off, ever.
Mr. Robinson, I was really scared of. I was so much of a chameleon
back then, I remember my grandmother telling me, 'You have to have
more of a backbone, you have to have character.' And I'm like, 'What is
character?'"

Jewell tumbled through a series of identity crises before becoming
a successful Chicago veterinarian. "I set my own schedule when I was
in eighth grade. And when I got into high school, I was making my
own activities, I was calling the shots. I remember sitting at the kitchen
table with Mr. Robinson and he could just look right through me. He
was kind of stoic and quiet and tough. I felt like such a phony." Jewell
could not help but notice the contrast in the way the two families lived.

"We had so much. My house was like fucking elegance, and they were crammed in this little, tiny, itsy-bitsy space. It was a box. One little cubicle was Michelle's place and one little cubicle was Craig's. They had a small living area and this itsy-bitsy kitchen and one little tiny bathroom. They were the most disciplined people I have ever known."

Michelle hated to be bad at anything. She "really does hate to lose, and that's why she's been so successful," Craig once said. One of her first pursuits was piano, guided by Aunt Robbie. Craig played, too, on the upright that was parked along a wall in the upstairs apartment, but not nearly as well or as diligently. "She would practice the piano for so long, you'd have to tell her to stop," her mother said. By the time Michelle was a teenager, she played Broadway show tunes, jazz, and pop songs. To soothe Craig's nerves before a basketball game, she would play the *Peanuts* cartoon theme song. At the games themselves, Michelle and Marian were regulars. They loved easy wins, but could not bear suspense. If the game was close and the clock was ticking down, they would turn away or leave the gym.

The children did not have the only competitive streaks in the family. In 1996, shortly before she turned sixty, Marian competed in the sprints at the Illinois Senior Olympics, running 50 meters in 9.39 seconds and 100 meters in 20.19 seconds. She finished third in her age group in both events. The following year, she turned sixty and ran faster—8.75 in the 50 and 18.34 in the 100—and won both races in the 60-to-64 category. She finished second in both events in 1998. After a fall and an injury, she stopped competing. "If I can't do it fast, I'm not doing it," Marian said at age seventy. "You don't run just to be running. You run to win."

Michelle herself, although competitive and skilled at sports in a sports-minded house, generally avoided joining teams, although she put in some time with the track squad. "Tall women *can* do other things. I wasn't going to be typecast that way," she said. She would grow to five feet, eleven inches, yet basketball was Craig's sport and she was already known as Craig Robinson's little sister in many other things. She started with ballet as a girl and continued to dance at Whitney M. Young High School, where a 1981 yearbook photograph shows her in a leotard onstage, springing off her left foot, her right leg raised high, toe extended, arms stretched out for balance, her body fully under control. As an adult, Michelle hung on her wall a photograph of Judith Jamison doing her iconic solo dance performance, "Cry," which choreographer Alvin Ailey dedicated in 1971 to "all black women everywhere—especially our mothers." Jamison wrote that her character in the dance "represented those women before her who came from the hardships of slavery, through the pain of losing loved ones, through overcoming extraordinary depressions and tribulations. Coming out of a world of pain and trouble, she has found her way—and triumphed."

MICHELLE'S HIGH SCHOOL WAS NAMED for a black man born into segregation in Kentucky. Whitney Young took control of the National Urban League in 1961 and maneuvered the organization into a position of influence. Yet at a time of growing racial ferment, Young drew criticism among some African Americans for courting the support of Lyndon Johnson and white business leaders. Pushing for what would become known as affirmative action, he saw himself as a bridge and considered constructive compromise a virtue. "I think to myself, should I get off this train and stand on 125th Street cussing out Whitey to show I am tough? Or should I go downtown and talk to an executive of General Motors about 2,000 jobs for unemployed Negroes." Michelle learned his story and praised him. In 2013, at a White House film screening of *The Powerbroker: Whitney Young's Fight for Civil Rights,* a documentary about his life, she told schoolchildren that Young "drew on his decency. He drew upon his intelligence and his amazing sense of humor to face down all kinds of discrimination and challenges and all kinds of threats."

The high school named for him was something of an experiment when it opened in 1975, a magnet school designed to mix talented students of different races and ethnicities. It would "force you outside your bubble," said Ava Greenwell, a black graduate from the South Side. The Chicago Urban League called the school "probably the finest ever built in Chicago. It has facilities, equipment and a curriculum plan which give it unique power to attract students." The league had been pushing the concept for years, while recognizing the quandary the new public school created: Each year, several hundred students would win a coveted spot, but thousands of Chicago teenagers would be left behind in second-rate schools. "We are delighted with the recent progress of the magnet school idea," league director James W. Compton said. "But we do not want this idea to be advanced at the cost of neglecting the interests of areas and people who need help first."

By 1974, as the city's African American population grew, 51.7 percent of high school students were black, along with 57.8 percent of elementary school students. Only 28.3 percent of elementary school students were white. At Whitney Young, enrollment goals by race and ethnicity were explicit. By design the school would draw students from all over the city. Plans called for a student body that was 40 percent black, 40 percent white, and 10 percent Spanish-speaking, with 5 percent "other," and 5 percent in the patronage-friendly category of "principal's option." Overall, when geography was factored in, the principal's option accounted for 10 percent of all students. Academically, at least 80 percent of entering students would be "average or above" on citywide test scores. Principal Bernarr E. Dawson, in describing the waiting list, said the information accompanying the applicant's name would include residence, race, sex, "achievement grouping," and comments from the applicant, teachers, and counselors. He said he would choose "in such a way that students' characteristics are best matched with the educational program of Whitney Young."

Opened two years before Michelle arrived, the school brought together teenagers from the South, West, and North Sides. The fortunate ones who made their way to a rundown area just west of downtown Chicago soon discovered that Whitney Young was an island—some thought an oasis—populated by students who would not otherwise have met. They studied, attended classes, and hung out together on campus. But when they scattered to their homes in far-flung neighborhoods, they often would not see each other again until the morning bell. Jeffrey Wilson was in the group of students that entered in 1975. He played center and defensive tackle on the football team and sang in the choir. It felt odd to be away from his West Side neighborhood, where he had friends from the earliest years of elementary school. Instead of walking to a nearby school, he rode an L train and walked the last two blocks.

"Whitney Young was built in the middle of a slum. It was barren," Wilson recalled. "There were different mills and factories, brick buildings, around. And most of them were empty. There was a skid row just two blocks away on Madison, where transient and homeless people walked through the neighborhood all the time. We'd be at football practice and they'd be standing on the sideline. Sometimes they'd talk to us in the middle of practice." Wilson said the school's purpose and spirit were clear. "It was a grand experiment in integration at a time when Chicago was considered the most segregated city in the country. I think we just dealt with it matter-of-factly. I had white friends. I had black friends. I had white male friends, white female friends." At the same time, as an African American student, he learned that there were neighborhoods where a black teenager should not go. "It wasn't all that unusual for a black kid to go off to a certain neighborhood and get his brains beaten in. That affected all of us," said Wilson, who appreciated the ways that life inside the school was different from life outside. "At the end of the day, back in those days, your white friends went where they went and your black friends went where they went. The only time they would mingle would be at school or an event connected to school, or if you were dating someone in another neighborhood." Wilson laughed about the classroom material delivered by Chicago daily life. "Particularly for the social studies teachers, it was like Christmas. They got to bring the message directly to where we lived. It wasn't abstract."

Wilson remembers feeling tugged between different worlds, not just between white and black, but within different black communities. His upbringing was thoroughly working class in a family so large—he had seven siblings—that they could never go anywhere in the same car. His father came from Mississippi and worked as a mixer at Entenmann's bakery. His mother came from Alabama and spent twenty-eight years working on a conveyor belt at Sara Lee. Starting at 4 a.m. more than an hour's drive away, she fit dough into pans before they rolled into the oven. His parents delivered a clear and timeless message: Life is hard.

You can make it. Keep pushing. Education, education, education. Yet when Wilson enrolled at Whitney Young, some kids in the neighborhood mocked him. They said he must be so special, so smart, so stuck up. One of Wilson's defenses was to talk black, even at Whitney Young. In the hall one day, he said to a friend, "I'm fixin' to go to the gym," but in his telling, the words were guttural and slurred, something like "Ahmfinninuhgotagym." A French teacher overheard and said, "Young man, why did you say that?" Wilson repeated the phrase. The teacher motioned him into her classroom, closed the door, and commanded, "Don't ever say that again." She made him say the sentence correctly several times and sent him back into the hall. "Not two minutes later, someone else asked me where I was going and I said it the same way, 'Ahmfinninuhgotagym.'" The teacher was still watching. "I saw her fixing me with this icy stare and I never did it again." He loved being at Whitney Young. "We enjoyed being in school that much, we would stay and watch the basketball team, the volleyball team, the swim team just practice."

MICHELLE WAS THIRTEEN when she started riding public transportation from the South Side to Whitney Young, then in its third year of operation. She caught a bus not far from her house and traveled a route that led to Lake Shore Drive, then about eight miles north along Lake Michigan into a thicket of skyscrapers downtown. From there, she caught another bus or a train and walked the final stretch. The trip took at least an hour in each direction. In the depths of Chicago's winters, she would travel both ways in the dark. Sometimes, to get a seat on the crowded northbound bus, she would catch a different bus south and board the downtown bus a few stops earlier. The maneuver could take thirty minutes, but it guaranteed her a chance to sit and study. Her frequent traveling companion and closest friend was Santita Jackson, daughter of the Reverend Jesse Jackson, the civil rights leader and future presidential candidate. The girls visited one another's homes as teenagers and remained close as young adults. Santita would sing at Michelle's wedding.

For the Robinsons, the distance was daunting, but the decision to apply to the new magnet school was straightforward. South Shore High School had been plagued by construction defects, vandalism, and a lack of supplies since its opening. Envisioned as a "model in function and design" when proposed in the mid-1960s, it had opened two years late, millions of dollars over budget and still unfinished. Craig bypassed the school to attend the all-male Mount Carmel High School, where he played varsity basketball and described himself as "the outsider, the racial minority and the brainy athlete I had always been." In attending Whitney Young, Michelle knew she was taking a valuable step beyond the limitations of her neighborhood high school, yet just like James W. Compton, the Chicago Urban League director, and Lena Younger in *A Raisin in the Sun,* she also knew that hundreds of her peers would not have the same option. It was the kind of thing she noticed from a young age. When she and Craig shared a bedroom, they often compared notes before they fell asleep. He said, "My sister always talked about who was getting picked on at school or who was having a tough time at home."

Once at Whitney Young, Michelle built on the work she had done in the gifted program at Kennedy-King and the record that had made her salutatorian of her eighth-grade class. She sang in a choir that traveled around the city. She helped organize social activities and ran for office, becoming treasurer of her senior class after a close race that required her to give a speech that jangled her nerves. She served on the publicity committee for school fundraisers, took Advanced Placement classes, and made the National Honor Society, whose president was Santita Jackson. College was the goal, she said. "I signed up for every activity that I could fill up my applications with, and I focused my life around the singular goal of getting into the next school of my dreams . . . It seemed like every paper was life or death, every point on an exam was worth fighting for." She earned extra money by teaching piano, babysitting, and training the occasional dog. Her senior year, she worked in a bookbinder's shop and witnessed at close range the lives of adult co-workers who were low on options and relegated to doing the same repetitive job for the rest of their working days.

A trait not lost in the transition to high school was Michelle's confidence in challenging authority. A typing teacher at Whitney Young told the students that their grades would be calculated according to their typing speed. By the end of the course, Michelle typed enough words per minute to earn an A, according to the teacher's chart, but the teacher said she simply did not give As. "She badgered and badgered that teacher," Marian said. "I finally called her and told her, 'Michelle is not going to let this go.'" Another time, a substitute teacher did not know her name. "Michelle said, 'What is my name?'" her mother related. "She sat on his desk until he knew her name. I told her, 'Michelle, don't sit on a teacher's desk.'" Michelle's diligence paid off. In addition to her job in the bindery, she spent several summers as a typist at the Association of Medical Assistants, where her aunt Grace Hale worked.

Michelle's ambitions grew at Whitney Young as her gaze expanded. As a young girl, she wanted most to be a mother, "because that's who I saw. I saw my mom caring for me. Those were the games that I played. I didn't play doctor, I didn't play lawyer." New professional imaginings developed toward the end of her high school years. For a time, she thought she would become a pediatrician, but she felt she was not strong enough in math and science and, anyway, did not much like those subjects. Test taking was a weakness, although in her mother's eyes, smarts were not the problem. "I'm sure it was psychological, because she was hardworking and she had a brother who could pass a test just by carrying a book under his arm," Marian said. "When you are around someone like that, even if you are okay, you want to be as good or better."

The disparity in work ethic and test results was also something Craig thought about. "She saw I never studied. I could always take tests and do well," he said. "She always studied. She was always up late, until 11 or 12 o'clock, doing homework." She burned the candle at the other end, too. Frustrated that the house felt crowded and noisy, she sometimes rose at 4:30 or 5 a.m. to do homework when she could hear herself think. Marian recalled those late nights, telling Michael Powell of *The New York Times*, "She'd study late but she had a discipline about her. I would ask, 'Aren't you through yet?' And she'd just keep going. She's always been pretty good in school, and if she works for the grade, you'd better give it to her. She was very independent, very strong-willed."

MICHELLE GRADUATED thirty-second in her class, solid if not stellar. As she headed to college, she received a small scholarship from a South Side foundation created by Ora C. Higgins, who had helped integrate Spiegel, the Chicago retailer. The company was ahead of its time in 1945, when M. J. Spiegel hired Higgins, a Chicago Urban League fieldworker, as a "personnel counselor" and tasked her with hiring hundreds of African Americans for the company's catalog business and its twenty-six Chicago department stores. She recruited and hired workers in dozens of capacities, from secretaries and typists to stencil cutters, commercial artists, accountants, and packers. Word got around fast, particularly at a time when decent jobs for African Americans were scarce. "They said, 'Go to Spiegel. There's a black lady there who can get you hired,'" recalled Reuben Crawford, Fraser Robinson's high school classmate, who worked on a Spiegel loading dock. Another beneficiary was Marian, who worked as a Spiegel secretary as a young woman. Seeing Higgins's success, other department stores hired her, making her a noted Chicago figure. She earned two degrees from Northwestern University, and in the 1960s, traveled to Washington, where she spoke at the Labor Department and had her picture taken with President Johnson.

Higgins was Michelle's great-great-aunt. She was a regular at Shields family gatherings, as was her daughter, Murrell Duster, a college administrator who was married to Benjamin C. Duster III, a civil rights lawyer and grandson of Ida B. Wells. "They talked about everything," Murrell Duster said of the family gatherings. "My mother always talked about human rights. We were very aware as children of what was going on in Chicago and other places." When Higgins turned 100 in 2010, Michelle sent a letter of congratulations from the White House, saying what an inspiration she had been.

AS MICHELLE WAS FINISHING high school, Craig was taking his final exams at the end of his sophomore year at Princeton. He had starred at

Mount Carmel and played well at a summer basketball camp in Wisconsin that was scouted by a Princeton assistant coach. When the Ivy League program flew him east for a recruiting trip, the school's head coach, Pete Carril, picked him up at the Newark, New Jersey, airport wearing a trademark gray sweatshirt and messily smoking a cheap White Owl cigar. Craig, who remembered equating Princeton and Yale with "Princestone" and "Shale" in *The Flintstones* cartoons, appreciated the attention. He was all the more impressed when Carril flew out to Chicago and made his way to South Euclid Avenue, where he climbed the steep stairs and met the Robinsons. One day, the mail brought a fat acceptance letter. Craig said, "People reacted as if I were Neil Armstrong just come back from the moon."

Marian recalls being clear with Craig that Princeton was the right choice: "It's like I say, 'You're tall and black. Nobody's going to notice the smartness.' So you had to go." Yet there was the matter of money. Craig felt torn. Other colleges were offering him full scholarships, while Princeton's financial aid package would require Fraser and Marian to come up with perhaps $3,000 toward the yearly cost. "It might as well have been $2 million to me," Craig said years later. As his mother stood at the sink doing the dinner dishes one night, Craig sat at the kitchen table and told his father that he craved the chance to go to an Ivy League school, but he was thinking of accepting an offer from the University of Washington. Good school, good coach, good basketball program—and it was a free ride. His father did not react with histrionics or tell his son what to do. Rather, after a deep sigh, he nodded and stroked his chin and said in a measured voice, "Well son, you know I'd be awfully disappointed if I thought you were making a decision this important on the basis of what we could afford." Craig said nothing after the conversation with his father. He simply agreed to think about it overnight, but he felt elated, "like the weight of the world was being lifted off my shoulders." His father's offer, as his health worsened and Michelle remained at home, testified to a "generosity greater than I have ever witnessed in any other human being." Craig, who later learned that his parents financed much of their share of his Princeton education with credit cards, would recall that conversation as one of the most important of his life.

Michelle's view, when it came time to apply to college, was that if Craig could get into Princeton, she could, too. By her reckoning, she was just as smart and certainly worked harder. Her counselors at Whitney Young, however, did not see it that way. They said her grades and scores were too low and her sights were too high. Their assessment knocked her off stride, leaving her feeling uncertain. "It made me mad, too," she said more than thirty years later. The moment would stay with her, becoming an essential component of her campaign stump speech and her message to young audiences. She folded her story into the narrative of Barack Obama's run for president. His election, she said, would send a message to "thousands of kids like me who were told, 'No.' 'Don't.' 'Wait.' 'You're not ready.' 'You're not good enough.' See, I am not supposed to be here. As a black girl from the South Side of Chicago, I wasn't supposed to go to Princeton because they said my test scores were too low." Michelle applied to Princeton and Harvard, as well as the University of Illinois and the University of Wisconsin. Her Princeton essay was "long, long," recalled Marian, who said Michelle "talked her way in." Like her brother, she was accepted and soon was on her way. She was stepping up and out, making the biggest leap of her young life.

# FOUR

# Orange and Blackness

Princeton in September 1981 was a world away from the South Side. It was a world away from most of the world, in fact. From the leaded glass and gargoyles to the sleek and sculpted columns of I. M. Pei, the campus telegraphed privilege, a trait the university leadership did not hesitate to advertise. Every freshman knew that Nassau Hall was home to the Continental Congress in 1783 and that Princetonians had populated America's top tier since the beginnings of the republic. *Dei sub numinae viget* read the Latin saying etched on Princeton's orange and black shield. Translated, the phrase meant "under God she flourishes," but wags rendered it as "God went to Princeton." Princeton's leaders touted the institution as a pinnacle of undergraduate education and had the applicant pool to prove it. Of 11,602 aspirants to the class of 1985, only 17.4 percent were admitted, a very low acceptance rate at the time. Among them were more high school valedictorians, class officers, team captains, and newspaper editors than anyone could count.

President William Bowen addressed them on September 13, 1981, the last time they would gather as a class before commencement week nearly four years later. Standing among towering stone pillars and stained glass in the grandly opulent Princeton chapel, he urged them toward a path of self-discovery and purpose. He invited them to aim high and advocated learning for its own sake, "not merely as a means to some more prosaic end." It would be a shame, he said, to choose narrow goals too easily achieved, ones that in retrospect "turn out to be trivial." He challenged them to pursue "lives lived generously, in service to others," and asserted that "the most worthwhile goals are often elusive and almost always just beyond reach."

For a text, Bowen read aloud a translation of Constantine P. Cavafy's poem "Ithaka," an ode to the joys of a great, lifelong journey. Ithaka was the home of Odysseus and the talismanic destination of his adventures after the fall of Troy. Bowen made an explicit reference to the racial divide that plagued Princeton and the country at large. "I sometimes feel," he told the freshmen, "that in developing friendships, especially those that require us to reach across such complex boundaries as race and religion, we are too self-protecting. . . . You can spare yourselves discomfort by keeping your distance, by remaining safely aloof, by maintaining what are largely superficial friendships. But if you do, you will deprive yourselves, and others, of one of the greatest opportunities for learning and for personal growth."


MICHELLE ROBINSON REACHED campus three weeks early to attend an orientation for minority students and other freshmen who might want extra time to adjust. Five months shy of her eighteenth birthday, she was daunted at first, a trepidation shared by many of her classmates. "When I first got in," she remembered, "I thought there's no way I can compete with these kids. I mean, I got in, but I'm not supposed to be here." During the first days on campus, she felt overwhelmed. Her sense of being at a loss was symbolized by the bedsheets she brought from home, too small for the standard university-issue mattress. She stretched the bottom sheet as far as she could from the head of the bed, then draped her covers over the part that the sheet did not reach. She slept with her feet resting on the bare mattress. Then there were the clothes, the furniture, and the cars. "I remember being shocked by college students who drove BMWs," she said. "I didn't even know parents who drove BMWs."

Michelle sometimes felt her head was barely above water. Her first semester, she took a class in Greek mythology and found herself "struggling just to keep up." On the midterm, she got a C. "The very first C I'd ever gotten and I was devastated." She pressed ahead, talking repeatedly with the professor and pouring heart and soul into her final paper. She soon discovered a secret of elite American universities: The tricky part is getting in the door; flunking out is hard to do. She gravitated to the sociology department and the Third World Center, created in 1971 as an oasis for the growing community of students of color. The center featured discussions about race, black culture, and the African diaspora, and served as a social hub. For Michelle, who found a work-study job there and was elected to the governing board, it became a refuge. Following the pattern set at Whitney Young, she chose not to join a sports team, nor did she try to prove her mettle in campus politics. She made close friends and stayed grounded during her first foray into an upper-crust realm where African Americans and, especially, African American women, were a distinct minority.

It helped, when Michelle arrived, that she had a significant anchor in Craig, who was entering his junior year as a sociology major and basketball star who spun records at Third World Center parties. His early jitters foretold her own. When he stepped off a bus on Nassau Street on a muggy August afternoon in 1979, he felt as though he was entering "a world that existed practically in its own time and space continuum." It seemed that every second classmate had come up with a medical breakthrough or published a novel. By the time he received his midterm grades, he was standing at a pay phone, trying to keep from crying. He had agreed to an adviser's recommendation that he enroll in the engineering program, but his record showed one C, two Ds, and an F. A worrier by nature, especially anxious about disappointing his parents, Craig told his father that he was not sure he would make it. "Maybe I'm over my head," he said. "Maybe I shouldn't be here. Maybe coming here I reached too far."

Fraser interrupted and told him to pull himself together. You won't be finishing first in your class, he said, but you won't be finishing last, either. With a Princeton degree in your pocket, Fraser said, "Y people will care what your grade was in freshman calculu recalled his father saying that the Ivy League school had ch not because he was "just like everybody," but "because of v me distinctive and because of the contribution that I could make to the school." Reassured, Craig stuck it out, although he did switch out of engineering. He later said that he loved history and African American studies, but gained the most from philosophy and religion classes—and the on-court tutelage of coach Pete Carril, who would be named to the basketball hall of fame.

AS A FRESHMAN, Michelle was "enormously concerned as all young people are, especially black women, with identity problems," said sociology professor Marvin Bressler, who befriended Michelle and Craig and supervised the beginnings of her senior thesis. "There existed in universities at that time various competing strains of what an ideal minority should be. She had to make up her mind to what extent she regarded herself as black, as a woman, as simply a person." The matter of making up her mind was not an exercise performed in a vacuum. For all of its remarkable academic offerings, Princeton was by tradition and reputation the most southern of the elite northern universities. Michelle would write that the school was "infamous for being racially the most conservative of the Ivy League colleges." The color barrier remained virtually unbroken for two hundred years after the university's founding in 1746. The dawn of the civil rights movement prompted the admissions office to declare in 1963, "Princeton is actively seeking qualified Negro applicants," yet it was years before any entering class included more than 20 African American students. The class of 1985 included just 94 black students, or 8.2 percent of the entering cohort of 1,141 students. The class was also unbalanced along gender lines, with 721 men and 420 women, a dozen years after Princeton admitted women for the first time. Tuition, room, and board cost roughly $10,000 her first year.

Not for the last time, Michelle felt herself walking in two worlds, one black and the other white. She was living what W. E. B. Du Bois in 1897 called "two-ness." For Du Bois, who not incidentally had been a black man at Harvard, it was the idea that an African American was in a perpetual struggle to reconcile his blackness with his Americanness,
‘ be both a Negro and an American without being cursed and spit

upon . . . , without having the doors of Opportunity closed roughly in his face." Being a Negro at the end of the nineteenth century, Du Bois suggested, was to face a looming question from white people: "How does it feel to be a problem?" He observed that a black man often felt at sea, striving to develop an independent identity yet enduring "double-consciousness, this sense of always looking at oneself through the eyes of others, of measuring one's soul by the tape of a world that looks on in amused contempt and pity."

Hilary Beard, a friend of Michelle's who arrived on campus one year earlier, had been stunned by what she found. "I grew up around a lot of white people. What was new to me was to be around white people who had had so little exposure to people of color. Nothing prepares you to have somebody you don't know, and shares a room with you, ask you something like if your skin color rubs off. I didn't just get asked that once. I got asked that all the time. I was suddenly confronted with negative assumptions about me and people who looked like me that I had never encountered before. It was shocking. I was unprepared. It was a lot, to be dropped in the middle of this environment and be confronted with that as part of your transition."

Minority students, more than most of their white peers, faced profound choices tied to race and ethnicity. For Michelle, questions about race, class, and values would inform her academic pursuits and her senior thesis, which explored issues of identity and purpose among black Princeton graduates. She wrote in the introduction, "My experiences at Princeton have made me far more aware of my 'Blackness' than ever before. I have found that at Princeton, no matter how liberal and open-minded some of my White professors and classmates try to be toward me, I sometimes feel like a visitor on campus; as if I really didn't belong. Regardless of the circumstances under which I interact with Whites at Princeton, it often seems as if, to them, I will always be Black first and a student second."

THE FIRST SIGN THAT Michelle would encounter racism at Princeton happened before classes even started. One of her freshman year roommates was a white teenager named Catherine Donnelly. She had been raised in New Orleans by her schoolteacher mother, Alice Brown, who labored, much as the Robinsons had, to position her daughter for a first-rate education. Catherine was settling into her fourth-floor room in Pyne Hall on her first day when Craig Robinson dropped by. He was searching for Michelle, who was not there. Catherine headed up campus and told her mother the news: One of her roommates was black.

Brown was horrified. She first called her own mother, who recommended pulling Catherine out of school and driving right back to New Orleans. That seemed extreme, so Brown charged into the student housing office and demanded a room change. "I told them we weren't used to living with black people, Catherine is from the south," Brown said. Hoping to strengthen her hand, she returned to her room at the tony Nassau Inn, where she and a friend called everyone they knew with Princeton connections and beseeched them to intervene. Nothing worked. The housing office said no beds were available.

Second semester, when a room came open, Donnelly moved out. At that point, she was simply glad to escape a cramped room. She had come to admire and enjoy Michelle, although they traveled in entirely different circles. She called her "one of the funniest people I've ever known." Donnelly had forgotten about Michelle Robinson a quarter century later when she noticed a lovely black woman with long fingers and a familiar face, the one whose husband was running for president. She did an Internet search to test her hunch and was chagrined to learn that she was right. Looking back to her freshman year, she regretted not standing up to her mother. By then, she had another reason to shake her head at her family's prejudice. Donnelly, a high school homecoming queen and basketball captain, had come out as a lesbian while at Princeton. When she did, she felt judged, and she learned a few things about being an outsider.

TO BE BLACK at Princeton was to be anything but unthinking. Racial politics compelled African American students to make decisions about how to live their blackness—where to sit in the dining hall, where to live on campus, where to socialize, what friends to make and what causes to claim. The pressures came not just from white teachers and classmates, but from African Americans. Walking in a black world was not without its own dilemmas. Indeed, it was possible to sketch not just two worlds confronting a black student at Princeton, but three or more, each tugging in a different direction. "There were those black students who wanted to be part of the storied Princeton they had heard about," said Ruth Simmons, one of a relative handful of black faculty members during Michelle's time at Princeton. "There were those who 'hung' black and those who did that to an extreme degree and did tend to resent people who were too impressed with the white society of Princeton." Simmons, who would later become president of Smith College and Brown University, felt the pressure herself. "You had to prove yourself to everybody."

Robin Givhan knew this well. She graduated from Princeton in 1986, one year after Michelle, and went on to win a Pulitzer Prize for criticism at *The Washington Post*. A black woman from Detroit, she visited the Third World Center from time to time—"it was a little like checking in with family"—but decided not to become a regular. "I didn't want this Third World place to be the focus of my social life, because if I had wanted that, I would have gone to Howard." She never forgot a speech at the center early in her Princeton career by a student from, she thinks, the Organization for Black Unity (OBU), a group that Michelle joined. "I had no idea who this guy was. He basically was giving this spiel about what it meant to be black at Princeton and what it entailed and what you should think. I felt what he was saying was, 'You are not black.' I remember coming back to my dorm and being just so upset about it, a little tearful."

By contrast, Sharon Holland felt a pull toward the Third World Center, which counted more than two hundred members. "I wanted to create a different social life for myself," said Holland, a doctor's daughter raised in Washington, D.C. Like Michelle, she took a job there, answering telephones, taking messages, typing memos, running errands. "An amazing time to be at the center. Lots of outreach, lots of attempts at multi-ethnic community building." She recalled her Princeton years as a mix of highs and lows as she struggled to chart a path that was not constrained by white privilege or what she called black "codes of responsibility," unwritten rules about how a black person should act toward other black people. Those were "some of the best of times," said Holland, who would become an American studies professor at the University of North Carolina, "but they were also really difficult times."

Some afternoons, as Michelle drifted into the Third World Center after class, she entertained Jonathan Brasuell, the young son of the center's director. His favorite tune was the theme song from *Peanuts*, the same song she had played to calm her brother's nerves before basketball games back in Chicago. Hilary Beard remembers Michelle playing the piano as Jonathan, not yet ten, sat beside her on the bench. "She took time to talk with him," Beard said, "not at him." Michelle worked with center director Czerny Brasuell to start an after-school program for the children of Princeton staff, principally young children of color whose parents wanted "a program that would be more sensitive to the needs of their children." Simmons was one of them. She enrolled her daughter and became a Third World Center regular. Recruiting black professors to Princeton was difficult "because of the isolation that African American families felt," Simmons said. "We spent so much time there as a family and faculty and staff because it was the one place we could go where we could feel part of that community. Just as we felt very comfortable there, others felt very uncomfortable with the activities of the Third World Center because it was, in a way, an activity that resegregated the campus."

As a place for discussions about social justice at home and abroad, the center welcomed speakers with political views to the left of much of the Princeton student body and more international in scope. Craig Robinson called it a "sanctuary." "You learned about politics, you learned about culture, you learned about people from different backgrounds. . . . I remember using those debates as practice for my in-class debates, and how I felt so fortunate to have that kind of support that made me feel good about going into class and competing." On weekends, the TWC, as it was often called, was central to Michelle's social life. "She was generally where the party was," said Ken Bruce, two years ahead of Michelle at Princeton, adding that "black parties mostly revolved around the music and dancing, and less around drinking or anything like that." Michelle ate meals at Stevenson Hall, and she lived on campus for four years, as did almost all of her classmates. She was active in the Organization for Black Unity and helped bring speakers to campus, recalled classmate and OBU officer Lauren Robinson, later Lauren Ugorji, who became Princeton's vice president for communications. She said Michelle also played a role in the Black Thoughts Table, an informal forum where African Americans and other interested students could talk about social and political questions. "As a black student at Princeton at that time," Ugorji said, "whether you wanted to deal with race issues or not, you had to."

While at Princeton, Michelle walked the runway in an occasional fashion show. At a February 1985 benefit that helped raise $15,000 for Ethiopian famine relief, she modeled a sleeveless red velvet gown and a voluminous white floor-length dress. She was pictured in a photograph on the front page of the school newspaper, *The Daily Princetonian*. To raise money for a local after-school program, she wore a yellow peasant skirt intended to suggest the Caribbean countryside. The student designer, Karen Jackson Ruffin, said she asked Michelle to model the skirt "because she is so tall and carries herself so well. Michelle is very mellow and she said, 'Sure.'"

Sometimes, Michelle and Beard would team up to do Third World Center errands. "If I drove, I would speed," Beard said. "Michelle would drive the speed limit. We were twenty years old, we were supposed to speed and do dumb, reckless things. Michelle would always do the right thing." The same qualities struck Beard that would strike Michelle's friends through the years. She was independent without being arrogant or aloof; she was "always rooted in her values." When people sought her advice, and many did, she listened carefully and did not simply react, "unlike the rest of us who were twenty and thought we knew so much. When you're twenty and you go to Princeton, you think you're smart and life is about you." As Beard recalled it, "Her thoughts were never the popular opinion or the Princeton opinion or the black opinion."

Beard also said Michelle was a "fighter" who had "feistiness in her spirit." That came out in amusing ways, as when Michelle was annoyed with her French teacher. "Michelle's always been very vocal about anything. If it's not right, she's going to say so," Marian Robinson said. "When she was at Princeton, her brother called me and said, 'Mom, Michelle's here telling people they're not teaching French right.' She thought the style was not conversational enough. I told him, 'Just pretend you don't know her.'" Her convictions emerged in sharper ways, as well. After Crystal Nix became the first black editor of *The Daily Princetonian*, Michelle disapproved of a story about an African American politician. She told Nix in a calm voice, "You need to make sure that a story like that doesn't run again." In her senior year, Michelle felt punched in the stomach when a professor assessed her work by telling her, "You're not the hottest thing I've seen coming out of the gate," despite the fact that she had aced his class. Her response was revealing: "I decided that I was going to do everything in my power to make that man regret those words. . . . I knew that it was my responsibility to show my professor how wrong he was about me." She became his research assistant and poured herself into the effort. He noticed and offered to write an extra letter of recommendation. She concluded that she had "shown not just my professor, but myself, what I was capable of achieving."

Brasuell took Michelle on her first trip to New York and made her feel welcome in her Princeton apartment, which Michelle described as "a place of peace and calm." But her most memorable experience was folding Craig and Michelle into a rental car for a surprise Mother's Day expedition to the Carolinas, an overnight drive from central New Jersey. The Robinsons dropped Czerny and young Jonathan in North Carolina and continued to Georgetown, South Carolina, to see their grandparents, Fraser and LaVaughn. After the visit, they picked up their traveling partners on the way back north. Time was short. "It was sort of like, 'Are we crazy?' But it was worth it," said Brasuell, who invited Michelle to be a bridesmaid at her wedding. "There was an evenness about her, a self-assurance about her, a consistent center of gravity about the way she moved in the world." Marvin Bressler, the professor who supervised the junior year independent work that led to Michelle's sociology thesis, remembered her for a combination of discipline—"she has a certain puritanical streak"—and sense of humor, which he called "impish." He described her as thoughtful, prone to reflection, and committed to what he considered social responsibility. "One of the things that is always said about her is that she was grounded," said Bressler, who traced the trait to her parents, who sometimes visited. The Robinsons, he said, seemed to step from the pages of *The Saturday Evening Post* like characters in a Norman Rockwell painting. "That family more nearly embodied that conception than any I've ever seen," Bressler said. He recalled Craig, the Ivy League's best basketball player, a two-time player of the year, holding court in the lobby of Jadwin Gymnasium after games, "his mother standing next to him, tugging at his sleeve and saying, 'How's your senior thesis, Craig?' He knew it was funny. Their father, he was disabled, was barely able to conceal his pride. He knew as a male you weren't supposed to go around being sentimental about your children, but he was. That kind of thing sustained her."

ON A STRETCH of Prospect Street known as the province of the university's private eating clubs, the Third World Center was the odd building out. For generations, sophomores took part in "bicker," the clubs' fraternity-like interview and assessment process that determined who would receive invitations, or bids, and which bids the most coveted students would accept. Next door to the center was the all-male Tiger Inn, famous on campus for its boisterous parties. Across the street, behind a low red-brick wall and a swinging gate, was Cottage Club, whose alumni included Secretary of State John Foster Dulles, basketball star and U.S. senator Bill Bradley, and writer F. Scott Fitzgerald, author of *The Great Gatsby*. As an undergraduate, Fitzgerald began writing a Princeton-based novel in the upstairs library at Cottage and later published it as *This Side of Paradise*. Princeton's president, John Grier Hibben, said after reading the book, "I cannot bear to think that our young men are merely living four years in a country club and spending their lives wholly in a spirit of calculation and snobbishness."

Seventy years later, many of the clubs of Michelle's era had dropped their selective status, and most admitted women, several relenting under the pressure of a civil liberties lawsuit. For all of the progress, the clubs along Prospect Street remained overwhelmingly white, while the service workers tended to be African Americans or immigrants. Black students in Michelle's generation learned to walk with care down Prospect on party nights. "Even walking across Prospect Street when a lot of people had had a lot to drink was a very challenging experience. People would say things, they would shout things, they wouldn't give you space on the sidewalk. It was almost like they felt a sense of ownership and they felt we were supplementary guests," said Ken Bruce, a Princeton junior when Michelle arrived. "I don't think they looked at us as equivalent stakeholders at the time, and I think it was hard for us to look at ourselves as equivalent stakeholders." Bruce, an African American engineering student who played football, ran track, and went on to become a New York investment manager, sometimes found himself the only black face in class. "Across the board," he said, "students and professors saw us as black first."

ONE COMPLICATING FACTOR—some would say *the* complicating factor—for African American students in the Ivy League in the 1980s was affirmative action. A policy that delivered opportunity could also be an unwelcome cloud, especially in relations with white students and faculty. The effort, begun in the mid-1960s, was straightforward enough: Identify talented black students who previously would have gone unnoticed and invite them into the club, even if their record appeared weaker than those of white students. One result was to create a reflexive doubt in the minds of skeptics about the worthiness and smarts of black students. The policy was also deeply unpopular among the public at large. At Princeton, where the admission of a black student often meant the rejection of a white student, perhaps the son or daughter of an alumnus, the tension was unmistakable. The dangling question, which trailed African American students like a shadow, was whether they belonged. "There were the beginnings of a lot of resentment about affirmative action. People asked you over dinner what your SAT scores were," Sharon Holland recalled of the early 1980s. Lauren Ugorji remembered the slights clearly: "The question that bothered me most was, 'Why are you here?'"

The public purposes of affirmative action, a policy described more precisely in Britain as "positive discrimination," were clear enough. When it came to college, the objective was to give an increasing number of black children opportunities that were comparable to ones enjoyed for generations by white children. In the wake of the civil rights movement and assessments by the likes of the Kerner Commission, credible research suggested that black students were paying the costs of racial subjugation endured by them, their parents, and their parents' parents, all the way back to slavery times. Compared with a white child, a black child born in the United States in the 1960s was likely to have less money, fewer models of achievement, and a poorer education. All of which, it was assumed, translated to lower scores on standardized tests and rejection letters from selective universities. When combined with the likelihood that African American families had less financial wherewithal to pay the high costs of competitive schools, it became clear to some progressive thinkers that equality of opportunity would not come naturally, at least not any time soon. In 1965, President Lyndon Johnson argued the case in a speech at Howard University. The Civil Rights Act of 1964, he said, was an important step, but an insufficient one. "You do not take a person who, for years, has been hobbled by chains and liberate him, bring him up to the starting line in a race and then say, 'You are free to compete with all the others'—and still justly believe you have been completely fair." One year later, Harvard Law School began admitting black law students with standardized test scores markedly lower than those of their white classmates, and other schools followed suit.

In 1978, three years before Michelle reached Princeton, the battle over the fairness of affirmative action policies reached the Supreme Court in the case of *Regents of the University of California v. Bakke.* The instigator was Alan Bakke, a white medical school applicant who said he was rejected by the University of California–Davis in favor of minority students with inferior credentials. He sued, citing Title VI of the Civil Rights Act, which stated that no program receiving federal money can discriminate "on grounds of race, color, or national origin." The high court was divided. Four justices agreed with Bakke, while four justices said racial preferences were justified to overcome the residual effects of past discrimination. Justice Lewis Powell cast the deciding vote, concluding that Bakke should not have to pay for wrongs committed by others. But Powell also cited the educational benefits of various kinds of diversity and ruled that universities could consider race when deciding who should be admitted, just as they might consider grades, test scores, orchestral achievements, or speed in the 100-yard dash. The decision left it to admissions officers to determine how to weigh an applicant's many traits. Standardized tests, increasingly shown to be culturally biased against disadvantaged minority students, would be just one factor. This benefited high-achieving black and Hispanic students while persuading critics that white students were now the losers in a rigged game.

"WE CREATED A COMMUNITY within a community," Michelle once said, discussing the challenges of being a minority student at Princeton. She also used space on her senior yearbook page to talk about what sustained her: "There is nothing in this world more valuable than friendships. Without them you have nothing." She grew particularly close to two women. One was Angela Kennedy, the third of three African American siblings to attend Princeton, each of whom would develop a richly meaningful career. The other was Suzanne Alele, born in Nigeria and raised partly in Jamaica before finishing high school in suburban Maryland. The three women were inseparable. They lived in dormitory rooms, using the workaday desks, dressers, and single beds provided by the university. No sofa, no television. "We couldn't afford any furniture, so we just had pillows on the floor, and a stereo," reported Kennedy, who said they listened to a lot of Stevie Wonder and "giggled and laughed hysterically." During spring break one year, they went on a ski trip with a Jewish student group. "We were three black women on a trip with all of these white Jewish kids. We stuck out like sore thumbs, but we had a great time."

Angela Sadie Edith Kennedy grew up in the nation's capital, where her father was a postal clerk and her mother commuted to work as a teacher at the upscale and very white Chevy Chase Elementary School, known in the neighborhood as Rosemary. Henry Harold Kennedy Sr., born in 1917 in Covington, Louisiana, "never forgave American society for its racist treatment of him and those whom he most loved," recalled Angela's brother, Randall Kennedy, a Harvard Law School professor whose research and teaching focused on race and society. He described his father as "an intelligent, thoughtful, loving man who, tragically, had good reason to doubt his government's allegiance to blacks and, thus, to himself." He attended segregated schools, saw doors closed to him because of his race, and watched as African Americans were "terrorized and humiliated by whites without any hint of disapproval from public authorities." His children saw their strong-willed father being humiliated and never forgot it. As Randall Kennedy told the story, his father was pulled over several times by white police officers as he drove the family to South Carolina, "simply because he was a black man driving a nice car. I am not making an inference here. This is what the police openly said." As the children watched, the officers would instruct Kennedy to behave himself, since he was not "up north" any longer. Their lectures would end with the words "Okay, boy?" There would be a pause as the policeman waited for Kennedy's response. "My dad reacted in a way calculated to provide the maximum safety to himself and his family: 'Yassuh,' he would say with an extra dollop of deference."

And yet, just as Michelle would recall of her elders, the Kennedy parents made clear that there would be no hand-wringing or excuses. Nor, by the way, would there be any talk of taking to the streets and getting arrested at civil rights protests. "We were expected to get a great education and be excellent at whatever we did. Racism? So what? Overcome it by being better," said Henry H. Kennedy Jr., Angela's oldest brother, who came of age during the civil rights years. All three Kennedy children chose legal careers after graduating from Princeton. Henry attended Harvard Law School and became, at thirty-one, the youngest judge appointed to D.C. Superior Court, later becoming a U.S. district judge. Randall went to Oxford on a Rhodes Scholarship and then to Yale Law School before clerking for Supreme Court justice Thurgood Marshall. Angela wrote a senior thesis titled "Attitudes Toward Femininity and Masculinity of Princeton University Women" and graduated from Howard Law School. She dedicated her professional life to defending indigent clients at the D.C. Public Defender Service, remaining close to Michelle during the White House years. Asked how the three children managed to prosper, Randall Kennedy described an approach that echoed life on South Euclid. He said of his parents, "They created a family that told the kids that they were deeply loved, no matter what. They also told the family, the kids, to be ambitious and to go out into the world and do what you want to do. They were not people who stood over us every minute. . . . They did have a rule that said to the kids, especially once we turned 11 or 12: 'You have to be interested in something. You have to have a particular passion. Frankly, we don't care what that passion is, but you have to have a passion.' "

SUZANNE ALERO ALELE HAD LIVED in the United States for only two years when she reached Princeton in late summer 1981. Born four days after Michelle and half a world away, she spent her early childhood in Lagos, the Nigerian capital, where her parents were doctors with medical degrees from prominent universities in the United Kingdom. Her mother was an obstetrician-gynecologist, her father a specialist in nuclear medicine who graduated from the University of London. They spoke Itsekiri and English at home. Alele spent the first half of high school in Jamaica and the second half in Bethesda, Maryland, where she attended a large suburban high school. She high-jumped and ran the hurdles, took advanced classes in biology and physics, and made the county honor roll. She was also an accomplished pianist, winning a certificate of merit at a London music school and performing in a folk music group during her time in Jamaica.

What fascinated Alele academically, she said in her Princeton application, were biology and biochemistry. "What are the important items in the food that I eat? Why am I 5'10" tall and why do I look like my mother?" She learned several computer languages and, as a teenager, envisioned a career in applied mathematics. Teachers commented on her "originality" and clear understanding of difficult subjects. "Integrity and a real sense of responsibility and purpose," wrote Sharon Hell-ing, her Advanced Placement biology teacher. "Compassionate beyond her years," wrote guidance counselor Dorothy J. Ford.

At Princeton, Alele took science classes, ran track, and became manager of the lightweight football team. She staffed the help desk at the computer center and joined the International Center. Her academic record was mixed—she found herself on disciplinary probation—but she graduated with a degree in biology after writing her senior thesis on the molecular basis of abnormal red blood cells in sickle-cell anemia, a hereditary disease that primarily afflicts people of African descent. Friends admired her for her ability to resist the pressure to conform. "Suzanne was the spirit that we all should have, the voice inside you that tells you to listen to your own heart," Czerny Brasuell said. Michelle, more cautious and conventional by nature, said her friend "always made decisions that would make her happy and create a level of fulfillment. She was less concerned with pleasing other people, and thank God."

While Alele counted herself a member of the Third World Center, she decided to bicker at selective eating clubs. She was invited to join Cap and Gown, a club with a decidedly upper-crust feel across the alley from Cottage Club. There, she knew Terri Sewell, who had been mentored by Michelle through a Third World Center program designed to support new black students on campus. Sewell arrived at Princeton from Alabama. She had graduated as valedictorian of her class at Selma High School, where her father taught math and her mother, the first black woman on the Selma City Council, worked as a librarian. She attended Brown Chapel AME Church, the starting point of Martin Luther King Jr.'s fateful Selma-to-Montgomery march. "She never accepted the status quo," Sewell's mother once said, "from grade school on up." At Princeton, she became a varsity cheerleader and junior class president and wrote an award-winning senior thesis, "Black Women in Politics: Our Time Has Come." After graduation, she moved on to Oxford and Harvard Law School. In 2010, she became the first black woman elected to Congress from Alabama.

·  ·  ·

MICHELLE SPENT the summers after her freshman and sophomore years in Chicago, living on Euclid Avenue and commuting to the downtown office of the executive director of the American Association of Medical Assistants. She spent much time as a typist, later lamenting that meaningful internships and summer jobs with community groups "seemed to be a luxury that a working-class kid couldn't afford." Such positions paid little, if anything, and students on financial aid could not justify giving up a paycheck for the adventure or the experience. "I felt guilty to even ask parents who were already working hard to let me take a summer or a semester off to do something like that," Michelle said during the White House years in praising a law designed to triple the size of AmeriCorps, a national service program underwritten by the federal government. "So, oftentimes I never asked. I studied. I worked. I worked and I studied. . . . I had to work all the time because I had to have enough money for books for the year and I had to help out with tuition."

In 1984, the summer before her senior year, Michelle and Angela signed up as counselors at a camp in the Catskills for underprivileged girls from New York City. They reported to Camp Anita Bliss Coler— Camp ABC, for short—sixty-five miles north of Manhattan, where 216 girls between the ages of nine and twelve arrived for one of four two-week summer sessions, sleeping in wooden cabins without doors, electricity, or running water, taking long hikes, and listening to nature, often for the first time. Activities at the rustic facility, one of four *New York Times* Fresh Air Fund camps, ranged from swimming and dance to sewing and pottery. Many of the games organized by counselors were noncompetitive, designed to build trust and self-esteem. Each day, the girls sang grace before lunch. "Being in the woods builds up their confidence," camp director Beverly Entarfer said in 1985. "Especially the girls [who] have been told that they can't do this and they can't do that. Well, they go walking through the forest at night without a flashlight, build a fire or go without hot water for a while, and they find out they can do a lot."

Urban church groups and community service organizations chose the campers. In 1984, the summer Michelle was there, some campers came from the Rheedlen Foundation, whose educational director was

Geoffrey Canada, the future head of the Harlem Children's Zone. Canada believed that many impoverished children could get ahead if they had support and caught a break. These were fundamentally good kids, he said, who lacked the experiences and opportunities considered elemental in a middle-class upbringing elsewhere. "Average kids with a chance," he called them. His thinking would mirror Michelle's own. As first lady, she called Canada "one of my heroes."

At first, Canada was skeptical that the Fresh Air Fund adventures would make a difference. He pointed out that many children in his program, economically disadvantaged and living in broken or violent households, were two years behind their peers in reading and math. Their summers were, at best, unstructured and all of the kids had "a problem with adult authority." In the end, however, he concluded that the summer projects worked. The children got out of town, they tasted something new, they learned about themselves. "I liked the hayride, and getting away from my enemies in the city," an eleven-year-old girl said of Camp ABC in the summer of 1984. Another camper in the same era said, "The first time I came here, I liked the nights here, the way you could sit by the lake, talk to people with the moon shining." Counselors who converged on the camp from the United States and Europe also tended to grow. Helen Macmillan, a young Scottish woman who worked at Camp ABC the year Michelle was there, said, "You learn a lot about yourself here—what you can't tolerate, what your boundaries are, and what makes you mad."

WHEN MICHELLE RETURNED to Princeton for her senior year, the politics-plagued Los Angeles Olympics were over and Ronald Reagan was coasting toward a lopsided reelection victory during a stretch that would see five of six presidential elections won by Republicans. Her largest task before graduation was her senior thesis, which would combine her sociology studies with her interest in African American affairs. She spent many hours designing and refining a study of the racial attitudes and habits of black Princeton alumni, trying to assess the likelihood that successful African Americans would work to help less fortunate black people. Her sixty-four-page paper revealed much about the questions that interested her as she tried to square her upbringing on the South Side of Chicago with the elite world she now inhabited.

In a survey sent to four hundred black alumni, she asked their reaction to nine statements about "lower class Black Americans and the life they lead." Among the choices were "I feel guilty that I may be betraying them in some way" and "I feel ashamed of them; they reflect badly on the rest of us." Other options included "I feel lucky that I was given opportunities that they were not given" and "I feel they must help themselves." The final choice: "There is no way they can be helped; their situation is hopeless." For each statement, she asked the respondents to mark boxes ranging from "very true" to "false." The six-page survey also asked the graduates about their upbringing, their heroes, their connection to God, their relationships of various kinds with white people and black people, and how they perceived those relationships before, during, and after their time at Princeton.

The thesis was built on twin truths that applied beyond Princeton as African American class differences grew. The first was that some black people were making their way to ever higher rungs on the ladder. The second was that vast numbers of black people were being left behind. Michelle and her friends had opportunities their parents could hardly have imagined, a fact they recognized every time they sat down to Christmas dinner with their extended families. The broad racial solidarity of the civil rights movement was giving way to economic stratification. It was an "illusion" of the Civil Rights Act, wrote University of Chicago sociologist William Julius Wilson in 1978, "that when the needs of the black middle class were met, so were the needs of the entire black community." As it happened, it was Wilson's drives through the nicest parts of South Shore, Michelle's increasingly middle-class Chicago neighborhood, that crystallized his recognition of the growing divide. But where did the obligations lie? Michelle had been taught from childhood that every rising African American must reach back with a helping hand. It was a familiar understanding—"From those to whom much is given, much is expected"—and she considered it part of her cultural DNA. Now she was asking whether success far above the norm had changed the equation.

Michelle's literature review sketched a continuum of opinion about black identity and the wide array of essentially political choices available to African Americans in U.S. society. At one end of the spectrum, she borrowed a 1967 definition of black power from Charles V. Hamilton and former Freedom Rider and Student Nonviolent Coordinating Committee leader Stokely Carmichael. "Before a group can enter the open society, it must close ranks," they wrote in *Black Power: The Politics of Liberation in America.* "By this, we mean that group solidarity is necessary before a group can operate effectively from a bargaining position of strength in a pluralistic society." From Andrew Billingsley's *Black Families in White America,* she described the idea that African Americans must take responsibility for black communities and "define themselves by new 'Black' standards different from the old White standards." And from the other end of the spectrum, distant from Hamilton and Carmichael, she cited the conciliatory position of her thesis adviser, Walter L. Wallace, who taught a class called "Race and Ethnicity in American Society." In his *Black Elected Officials,* he argued that blacks and whites must work together toward "representative integration." Michelle wrote that such integration, according to Wallace and his co-author, James E. Conyers, meant the inclusion of black politicians and public servants in "various aspects of politics." She explained, "They discuss problems which face these Black officials who must persuade the White community that they are above issues of race and that they are representing all people and not just Black people." Michelle's description strikingly foreshadowed a challenge that she and her husband would face twenty-two years later as they aimed for the White House.

To say that during her Princeton years she could not envision an African American president is like saying that the sun rises and sets every day. Even the acceptance of black people as equals seemed unlikely. The "White cultural and social structure will only allow me to remain on the periphery of society, never becoming a full participant," she wrote in her thesis. Indeed, Michelle believed that there existed a separate "Black culture" and "White culture." Among the reasons she perceived black culture to be different were "its music, its language, the struggles, and a 'consciousness' shared by its people." Those elements "may be attributed to the injustices and oppressions suffered by this race of people which are not comparable to the experience of any other race of people through this country's history." She expected her research to show that the more thoroughly a Princeton student or graduate became immersed in white culture, the less connected that person would feel to the plight of lower-class black people—the "black underclass," as Wilson described it, "in a hopeless state of economic stagnation, falling further and further behind the rest of society." But, to Michelle's surprise, the eighty-nine surveys returned by black alumni did not confirm her hypothesis. Black graduates could, and did, care about the fate of African Americans who had been less successful.

To Michelle, the most interesting finding suggested that African American students identified more with other black people while they were at Princeton than they had before or after. Indeed, after graduation the sense of identification "decreased dramatically." She called it her major conclusion. The survey did not address the reasons, but Michelle offered two. Calculating the ages of the respondents, she reasoned that most had been on campus in the 1970s and might have sought solidarity in keeping with the teachings of the black power movement. Her other theory was rooted in the isolation that she and others felt. Noting that the university had just five tenured African American professors, a small African American studies program, and only the Third World Center "designed specifically for the intellectual and social interests of Blacks," she suggested that black students turned to each other for support "because it is likely that other Blacks are more sensitive to respondents' problems."

As for her own views of Princeton and life beyond, she wrote that her sense of alienation made her more determined to muster her skills "to benefit the Black community." And yet in a season when recruiters for blue-chip banks and companies descended on Princeton, she felt her professional aspirations shifting and the temptation of a large paycheck growing. "It is conceivable," she wrote, "that my four years of exposure to a predominately White, Ivy League university has instilled within me certain conservative values. For example, as I enter my final year at Princeton, I find myself striving for many of the same goals as my White classmates—acceptance to a prestigious graduate or professional school or a high paying position in a successful corporation." Howard Taylor, a sociology professor who helped advise Michelle while she was working on her thesis, said she "was not an assimilationist, but she wasn't a wild-eyed militant, either. She was able to straddle that issue with great insight."

The questions Michelle was asking represented familiar territory for black students at the time, said fellow graduate Ken Bruce. "How her experience at Princeton would affect her place in society, that's pretty much what all of us were thinking. You get this great education and what do we do with that, both in the majority environment and in our minority environment?" Few questions seemed to have easy answers, and one conundrum led to another, even about where to live. "Do you become the wealthiest person in a black neighborhood," Bruce asked, "or the only black person in a white neighborhood?"

MICHELLE EARNED sociology department honors. Her thesis also won an honorable mention and a $50 prize from the African American studies program. The questions she raised would stay with her. "One of the points I was making, which is a reality for black folks in majority white environments, is it is a very isolating experience, period. The question is how do people deal with that isolation. Does it make you cling more to your own community or does it make you try to assimilate more? Different people handle that in different ways," Michelle said in 2007. Tacking to the value of diversity, she continued, "It is incumbent on us, whether we are in city government or sitting around the corporate boardroom or in policy or education, to have critical masses of diverse voices at the table. I challenged my colleagues in the nonprofit world to look around and say, 'What does the leadership look like? Does it look like you? What are you doing to branch out and to make sure there aren't just one or two black folks, women, or Hispanics around the table?' In all sectors, we still struggle with that. At many of the top universities, we still struggle with that. That's one of the core points that comes out of my thesis and I don't think that's changed significantly since I wrote it. We've made marginal change. The question for

Princeton is what does the ratio of underrepresented minority students look like today? What about faculty? What about top administrators? Those are the questions we have to continue to ask as a country."

ALTHOUGH MICHELLE WORRIED that her time at Princeton would diminish her desire to serve, there never seemed much chance that she would forget her South Side roots. For one thing, her parents had drilled the message of community deep into her consciousness. "We teased them about how some people went away to college and never came back to their community," Marian said of Michelle and Craig. For another, Michelle nurtured a connection to family not five blocks from the lush Princeton campus. From time to time, she crossed Nassau Street and the town-gown divide to visit a woman who lived in a small apartment at 10 Lytle Street, just downhill from the gates of the university. Born in 1914, barely two generations removed from slavery, the woman was raised in rural South Carolina and made her way to Princeton to find work. When Michelle knew her, she was cooking and cleaning for a prosperous white family. Although her name was Ernestine Jones, Michelle knew her as Aunt Sis, for she was a younger sister of her paternal grandfather, Fraser C. Robinson Jr. How sweet it was, considering the southern world that Jones had known and the Princeton she had first encountered, that two of her brother's grandchildren would graduate from one of the finest schools in the land.

Four years at Princeton left Michelle freshly conflicted about her own ambitions. "My goals after Princeton are not as clear as before," she wrote in her thesis. The picture-book university, with its neo-Gothic quadrangles of carved stone and its clutches of self-assured white people, was an elite realm that delivered an elite education. It was a combination that cut both ways, reminding her all too often that she was a black student from the Chicago working class, while also telling her that Michelle LaVaughn Robinson could play in the big leagues. After another summer back home, she moved on to Harvard Law School, where the opportunities and the conundrums presented themselves anew.

# FIVE

# Progress in Everything
# and Nothing

Harvard Law School, when Michelle arrived in 1985, was a lofty perch, every bit as privileged as Princeton, but certainly more competitive once classes began. Some critics derided the school as a factory, in part because it was the largest law school in the country, in part because it turned out so many corporate lawyers. At graduation, diligence would be rewarded with admission to the upper echelons of American society. It was no accident that nearly half of the Supreme Court justices appointed after 1955 bore a Harvard pedigree or that Michelle pressed ahead with her application after being waitlisted, despite being accepted everywhere else she applied. The place had an undeniable mystique, polished and perpetuated by the 1973 film *The Paper Chase,* whose iconic Professor Kingsfield explains theatrically to his cowed students, "You come in here with a skull full of mush and you leave thinking like a lawyer." Chicago writer Scott Turow turned anxiety into memoir in *One L,* published in 1977. He said Harvard beckoned "those of us compulsively pursuing some vague idea of distinction." A former federal prosecutor who wrote a string of crime thrillers, he drew a stark portrait of the first-year pressures. "It is Monday morning, and when I walk into the central building, I can feel my stomach clench," he wrote. "For the next five days I will assume that I am somewhat less intelligent than anyone around me. At most moments I'll suspect that the privilege I enjoy was conferred as some kind of peculiar hoax. I will be certain that no matter what I do, I will not do it well enough." Years later, Turow said being at Harvard meant "feeling like you were playing an unwinnable game of king of the hill."

For many black students, the hill seemed yet steeper. Robert Wilkins would go on to become president of Harvard's Black Law Students Association and a judge on the high-profile U.S. Court of Appeals for the D.C. Circuit. But as he finished his undergraduate chemical engineering degree at a small school in Terre Haute, Indiana, Harvard seemed a mirage. "I almost didn't apply," he said. "And if I applied, I probably couldn't afford it. And if I could afford it, I probably wouldn't like it. *The Paper Chase* was all I knew." Wilkins described himself as a "small-town kid who didn't really know that much about the world." But he did apply, and he got in. In spring 1986, the Black Law Students Association (BLSA) invited him to its annual gathering of students past, present, and future. He remembers being broke and unable to afford the trip until a visiting fraternity brother said he could drive him as far as Philadelphia, where he could catch a train to Cambridge. Wilkins felt welcomed that weekend. The students he met, including Michelle—"You can't really forget her because she's a tall, striking woman"—impressed him not only as smart and substantive, but caring.

The discovery of community and common cause was unexpected, considering the school's cutthroat reputation. Yet the attitude, a kind of constructive embrace, would shape many of the black students who enrolled at Harvard in the mid-1980s, particularly those who became active in campus efforts to diversify the faculty and curriculum. "The black community at Harvard was really sustaining to me," said Verna Williams, a close friend of Michelle's who grew up in Washington, D.C., and preceded Wilkins as BLSA president. Williams moved uncertainly into one of the world's great crossroads of the elite, doubting that she would measure up, yet she discovered people with similar experiences "who were really, really smart and really cool—the most amazing people I had ever met." Harvard struck her as a better fit than Yale, particularly because of her interests in race and social justice. True, she found the whiteness and maleness of the Harvard faculty "stunning." But she felt encouraged by the recent recruitment of black professors, and the black students, numbering 170 among the 1,796 students on campus in 1985, struck her as "more active and more dynamic" than their counterparts in New Haven. "We had a critical mass of black folks," she said. "Why would you go to Yale?"

It was certainly a contrast from twenty years earlier, when barely one percent of U.S. law students were black, and one-third of those attended predominantly African American schools. Being at Harvard with smart, committed black people, Williams said, was "a lifesaver for me. It contributed to the formation of my identity as a black professional, as a black woman. Feeling like I have this opportunity, I have this incredible opportunity, and it's not just about me. It wasn't just about me when I got here, and it can't be just about me when I get out of here." Williams remembered bull sessions in the cluttered basement offices of the Black Law Students Association, where friends including Michelle discussed conundrums of obligation and purpose. " 'What are you going to do for black folks when we get out of here?' We did think a lot about that, about what it means to be a lawyer, what it means to be a black lawyer." Such questions became central to Michelle's thinking at Harvard and beyond, connecting the lessons of the South Side with her experiences at Princeton and her looming career decisions.

THE 575 1L STUDENTS of the Harvard Law School class of 1988 split into sections to move through their introductory year of torts, contracts, and constitutional law. The required classes tended to be less than scintillating, with plenty of rote learning in the mix. It was law school, after all, and it was all-consuming. Michelle had been known for her discipline at Princeton, so self-controlled that she imposed a personal ban on all-nighters. At Harvard, too, she stayed focused and, according to friend Jocelyn Frye, avoided being "caught up in all that goes with being at an elite law school. She was a regular person. We had fun." To help pay the bills, she held a campus job and added to her Princeton debt by taking out loans. One year, she worked as a research assistant for Randall Kennedy, the law professor brother of Angela, her college roommate. With her friends, she sat in front of a big television set in the BLSA office on Thursday nights to watch *L.A. Law* and *The Cosby Show,* the most popular show on television, featuring the Huxtables, an upper-middle-class black family headed by Cliff, a gregarious obstetrician, and Clair, a smart and plainspoken lawyer. Their oldest daughter, Sondra, went to Princeton and planned to be a lawyer, but veered in another direction, deciding to open a wilderness store, instead. When she announced that she had changed her mind, her mother erupted. "Change it back!" she demanded. "After all that money we spent sending you to Princeton? Sondra, you owe us $79,648.22 and I want my money now!" The line got a big laugh, but Clair was also making a deeper point about contributing to society, according to Phylicia Rashad, the actress who played her. "Parents know their children," Rashad said, "and Clair wasn't telling her daughter to become a lawyer just to be a lawyer—but don't cop out."

As the Harvard students bumped along with varying degrees of competence and sanity, Williams noticed that her classmate seemed unusually serious and self-possessed, but not in a preening, call-on-me way. "She was not the person in class who was constantly raising her hand, showing she's smarter than everyone," Williams said. "But you know she's got it going on. She's got the quiet air of confidence—and it's confidence, not arrogance." Jocelyn Frye saw her in similar terms, describing Michelle as "down-to-earth, reasonable, practical, solution-oriented." She explained, "The thing about law school is that you get caught up in the theory so much. She has always been a person who's thinking about the bottom line—here's what makes sense, here are the practical results we can and should be trying to achieve."

Toward the end of every Harvard student's first year came the moot court competition, the first exercise where the students could stand up in a courtroom setting and act the part of the lawyers they would soon become. When it came time to choose partners, Williams made a beeline for Michelle. Her calculation was simple: "She's really cool and really smart, I'd better ask her before someone else does." It was a criminal case. The details escaped her memory, but Williams recalled that as they set to work, there was an easy way and a harder way to proceed. They chose the harder way: an evidentiary hearing to prevent the prosecution from entering a weapon into evidence. Williams was struck again by Michelle's cool forcefulness. "Damn, she is good," she thought to herself, watching as Michelle pushed the envelope and drew objections from opposing counsel. "She is saying something that she knows is objectionable, and she's just going to do it. The kind of question, 'How long have you been beating your wife?' Look at her, she knows she's not supposed to be doing that. She's so confident."

They lost the motion to suppress the evidence, but their friendship blossomed. Williams was the more overtly vocal and political, while Michelle generally preferred roles out of the spotlight—helping indigent clients of the school's legal aid bureau, adding heft to BLSA's annual conference, and doing some editing for a student-run law journal that aspired to be a vehicle and a voice for African American legal minds. "Michelle always, everything she wrote, the things that she was involved in, the things that she thought about, were in effect reflections on race and gender," said Charles Ogletree, a high-profile Harvard professor who mentored her. "And how she had to keep the doors open for women and men going forward."

IN THE SPRING of 1986, Michelle's first year in Cambridge, she volunteered as an editor for the *Harvard BlackLetter Journal,* which had been created a few years earlier on the largely white campus to address questions of race and rights from a black perspective. This was the journal's third issue and the editors presented a discussion of "The Civil Rights Chronicles," an allegorical essay by African American law professor Derrick Bell published in the November 1985 issue of the *Harvard Law Review.* The article ran as The Foreward, the review's annual disquisition on the previous Supreme Court term. In selecting Bell to write the piece, student editors Elena Kagan, Carol Steiker, and William B. Forbush III signalled the prominence of discussions about race and the law. "All the talk and the debates were shifting to race," said Kagan, a 1986 graduate who became dean of the law school and later a Supreme Court justice appointed by Barack.

The *BlackLetter Journal* had gotten its start in the late 1970s as a blend of essays, poetry, news, and interviews. "A voice for black expression," later editors would say. In 1984, students relaunched the journal as a race-conscious alternative to the lofty law review, which had never had a black president until Barack was elected to the position in 1990. The goal was to produce "scholarly presentations of legal issues of interest to blacks. . . . without some of the stylistic constraints of other law reviews." The editors were hungry to squeeze into the conversation, but the journal was underfunded, understaffed, and decidedly outside the mainstream. Entirely different, in other words, from the hypercompetitive law review, which was as much a part of Harvard's self-image as the elegant law library, with its 1.4 million volumes and the inscription over the main entrance that read *Non sub homine sed sub deo et lege,* or "Not under man, but under God and law."

For African Americans, the law review had long proved difficult to navigate, even from the inside. Kenneth Mack, a Harvard student in the late 1980s and later a faculty member, called his time on the law review "the most race-conscious experience of my life." He said prejudices crossed political and ideological lines. "Many of the white editors were, consciously or unconsciously, distrustful of the intellectual capacities of African-American editors or authors. Simply being taken seriously as an intellectual was often an uphill battle." Bradford Berenson, politically conservative and white, said, "I've worked at the Supreme Court. I've worked at the White House. I've been in Washington now for almost 20 years. And the bitterest politics I've ever seen, in terms of it getting personal and nasty, was on the *Harvard Law Review.*"

In the Spring 1986 issue of the *BlackLetter Journal,* nine of the twelve articles directly responded to Bell's "Chronicles." Two others dealt with affirmative action, including one by Harvard professor Elizabeth Bartholet entitled "The Radical Nature of the Reagan Administration's Assault on Affirmative Action." The staff dedicated the issue to Bell's fictional protagonist and muse, Geneva Crenshaw, a confident black lawyer in the 1960s whose "pride in her color and her race," Bell wrote, "flourished at a time when middle class 'Negroes' (as we then insisted on being called) were ambivalent about both." Crenshaw saw herself continuing the work of nineteenth-century black abolitionists Sojourner Truth and Harriet Tubman, crediting them with an inner vision that allowed them to "defy and transcend the limits that the world tried to impose on their lives." In Bell's telling, Crenshaw, recently hired as a law professor at Howard University, is driving to a voter registration meeting during the Mississippi Freedom Summer of 1964 when a white driver runs her off the road. She survives in a catatonic state, emerging twenty years later to survey American race relations and conclude, "We have made progress in everything, yet nothing has changed." She says, "It is incredible that our people's faith could have brought them so much they sought in the law and left them with so little they need in life."

Despite a string of victories for African Americans in courthouses and statehouses across the land, Crenshaw is perplexed that the United States has made so little progress on racial fairness. "What is impossible is making the public understand that blacks continue to endure subordinate status, despite the legal advances of the last two decades," Crenshaw laments. "Blacks demand nothing more than their rightful share of opportunities long available to whites. But whites believe that blacks are demanding privileges they have not earned to remedy injustices they have not suffered."

Charismatic and soft-spoken, Bell was an engaging provocateur whose high-profile protests against Harvard's disappointing minority-hiring practices put him at the center of the school's racial politics. Prone to wage his fights through sit-ins and threats to resign, he challenged the persistence of racial bias, questioning not just Ivy League demographics, but the very role of laws and lawyers in building a more equitable society. He believed that racism was pervasive in the American establishment and could not be sliced out with a scalpel or a lawsuit. As a principal proponent of critical race theory, he argued that racism was more than simply a random array of bigots who said and did bigoted things. Rather, he posited racism as an attitude and an affliction embedded in laws, legal institutions, and relationships—"a legal system which disempowers people of color." He considered it the product of a history of black subjugation so distant in the minds of most white people that attempts to shift the balance were dismissed as a form of racism in reverse. Bans on overt discrimination allowed some talented

African Americans—"the spotlighted few," he labeled them; W. E. B. Du Bois called them "the talented tenth"—to rise and prosper. Yet, even as they rose, the vast majority of black people remained hostage to stubbornly enduring patterns of inequality.

Bell cited the work of William Julius Wilson, the prominent Chicago sociologist who wrote in *The Declining Significance of Race* that "the patterns of racial oppression in the past created the huge black underclass, as the accumulation of disadvantages were passed on from generation to generation." In Bell's view resistance was essential. He believed significant progress, if it ever came, would emerge from the ground up, assisted by a recognition by white people that black advancement served their own interests. "History gets made through confrontation. Nothing gets done without pushing," Bell said during one of his many standoffs with the Harvard administration. Harvard professor Robert Clark cracked in 1987, "This is a university, not a lunch counter in the Deep South." Bell's retort: "I feel that Harvard is long overdue for change, just like the South was."

When it came to the Harvard curriculum, Bell's thinking led him to develop a set of positions about faculty diversity that went well beyond the assertion that women and African Americans deserved to join the faculty as a matter of equitable hiring practice. In an argument that Michelle would advance in a 1988 essay for incoming students, Bell said that women and faculty of color enhance university teaching because of who they are, how they teach, and what experiences they carry into classrooms and corridors. "Even liberal white scholars have to imagine oppression, and have to imagine they are not oppressors," Bell said upon publication of *We Are Not Saved,* his book based on the "Chronicles." "Black people have stories and experiences that provide the basis not only for their lives but for their scholarship."

As a former NAACP attorney who did not attend a prestigious law school or clerk for a federal judge, Bell did not forget that he owed his own job to students who pressed Harvard to hire a tenured black professor during the civil rights ferment of the late 1960s. "You'll be the first, but not the last," Harvard president Derek Bok told him when offering him a spot on the faculty. That proved true, but barely. In 1967,

Harvard Law School had fifty-three tenured faculty, all of them white men. Twenty years later, when Michelle was there, the school had sixty-one tenured faculty, including five white women, but still only two black men and not a single woman of color. In other words, 96 percent of the faculty at one of the country's most elite and ostensibly progressive law schools was white.

THE CAMPUS AIR may have been rarefied, but developments at Harvard reflected the dawning national realization that so much and yet so little had changed in matters of race and opportunity. More than thirty years after *Brown v. Board of Education,* African Americans were winning elections and stepping into academic and corporate positions in greater numbers. But the decade in race relations was largely defined by the presidency of Ronald Reagan, who launched his 1980 campaign with an endorsement of states' rights in Neshoba County, Mississippi, where three civil rights workers were murdered in 1964. He peppered his public speeches with exaggerated or apocryphal stories about Cadillac-driving welfare queens and "young bucks" who bought T-bone steaks with food stamps. Reagan opposed affirmative action programs, a product of the Civil Rights Act of 1964, as a fount of unfair advantage. He curtailed the enforcement work of the Justice Department's civil rights division and tried to defund the Legal Services Corporation. To run the Equal Employment Opportunity Commission, he appointed Clarence Thomas, a future Supreme Court justice and unabashed foe of affirmative action.

The political debate between Reagan and his antagonists carried over to the law school. In 1987, as the country celebrated the two-hundredth anniversary of the Constitution, Harvard and the National Conference of Black Lawyers hosted a scholarly conference, "The Constitution and Race: A Critical Perspective." The gathering provided "time for re-evaluation in the midst of the pomp and circumstance." Bell was the keynote speaker, and black Harvard professors Charles Ogletree and David Wilkins led workshops. For all of the glorification of "original intent" by conservatives—this was the year of Reagan's highly contentious nomination of Robert Bork to the Supreme Court, an event that drew campus protests—many Harvard students and faculty thought "original sin" was more like it. After all, the men who built the framework of American democracy wrote a contradiction into the nation's founding documents when they promised liberty but permitted slavery. They did not endorse voting rights for women, black people, or men without property. Indeed, many of the founders owned slaves.

On campus, students and instructors not only discussed the causes and costs of three centuries of racial inequality, but asked what could change and how. Was it appropriate to promote diversity as a tool of learning? Was affirmative action a legitimate approach? "We were trying to search for the meaning of all that. We were writing about that and talking about it," Robert Wilkins said. In the fiery debate over affirmative action, critics not infrequently questioned the abilities of African American students, who were outnumbered nine to one. "The absence of minorities feeds the perception that blacks are not qualified to be here . . . as students, as professors, and as future lawyers," Verna Williams said at the time. "The idea that we're here as a twist of fate is totally false, when in fact to be here we've had to sustain a great deal of stress, along with the abuse that we experience on a daily basis as African Americans." Williams's comments appeared in a profile written for a special report of the Black Law Students Association's *Memo,* a newsletter designed to share the wisdom of the class of 1988 with newer students. That year seemed "as good a time as there has ever been to recognize, celebrate and preserve the achievements of black students at Harvard Law School," according to an editor's note. Black students in the class led more Harvard organizations than ever before. Among them were the *Women's Law Journal,* the *Harvard Journal on Legislation,* and the *Civil Rights and Civil Liberties Law Review,* as well as the Legal Aid Bureau, Students for Public Interest Law, and even the Harvard Law School Republicans. The longest essay in the fifty-page newsletter was written by Michelle, who devoted more than three thousand words to an appeal for greater faculty diversity.

In the essay, "Minority and Women Law Professors: A Comparison of Teaching Styles," she spoke up for a more human understanding of law and the work of lawyers and argued that women and people of color connected with students in fresh and valuable ways. She suggested, referring to *The Paper Chase*, that space should be cleared for instructors who did not conform to the Professor Kingsfield model of imperious superiority. However cinematic, the image of law school cultivated in *The Paper Chase* and Scott Turow's *One L* constrained student expectations and influenced faculty teaching styles—and not in a good way, she argued. "In the name of tradition, these images serve to mold perceptions of what one should look for in a 'genuine' law school experience. . . . Unfortunately, this sense of security and comfort that students find with traditional notions of the law school experiences engenders an inherent distrust of anything that does not resemble or conform to those notions." Michelle predicted that old-school teaching models, if left unchallenged, would be replicated in the hiring process. Instructors who tested boundaries would find themselves on the outs with a majority of students and undervalued in hiring and promotion. "The faculty's decisions to distrust and ignore non-traditional qualities in choosing and tenuring law professors merely reinforces racist and sexist stereotypes," she said.

Michelle chose three instructors—two black men and one white woman—to study and interview. She concluded that all three had received a chilly reception from white male colleagues and faced hostility from some students. A number of students, "solely on the basis of race and sex . . . feel justified in rudely challenging their authority and doubting [their] credibility," she wrote. But when given the chance, minority and women faculty were able "to introduce innovative methods of teaching and to invoke their perspectives on different issues. Now, unlike before, students are being made to see how issues of class, race and sex are relevant to questions of law. Not only do students find that these issues are relevant, they are finding them interesting."

Different as they were from the traditional faculty, the professors she chose were also quite different from one another. Charles Ogletree grew up in Merced, California, his father a truck driver, his mother a housekeeper, one from Alabama, the other from Arkansas. A counselor recognized his talent, and he thrived at Stanford University "despite academic and cultural disadvantages stemming from inadequate basic educational training," Michelle wrote. Ogletree, known to friends as Tree, had doubts about the merits of law school, but he enrolled at Harvard after concluding that legal training would make him a more effective advocate. He served as president of the National Black Law Students Association and the organization's Harvard chapter.

On a different path, David Wilkins was the son of a black graduate of Harvard Law School. He attended the University of Chicago Laboratory Schools, won honors as a Harvard undergraduate, and made the *Harvard Law Review* before clerking for Justice Thurgood Marshall. The third professor, Martha Minow, was raised in a world of some privilege as the daughter of former Federal Communications Commission chairman Newton Minow. She earned a master's degree in education at Harvard, graduated at the top of her Yale Law School class, clerked for Marshall, and developed specialties in human rights and the status of women and racial and religious minorities. When Michelle wrote the essay, Minow was the only one of the three with tenure. Ogletree and Wilkins would later be awarded tenure and Minow would be named law school dean.

"IN PROFESSOR OGLETREE's criminal law class," Michelle wrote, students "could close their eyes and imagine what it would be like to see him in action in a courtroom. Like a successful trial, this professor approaches each class with a game plan and he merely uses the Socratic Method to extract from students the information necessary to make that plan work. He manages to do this, however, without interrogating students with confusing questions designed to catch them off-guard. Inflections in his voice are always calm, soothing and patient, but yet he is able to get to the point very quickly and with the precision of an artist." Ogletree used role-playing, assigning students to play prosecutor and defense attorney. He served as moderator, "interjecting or intervening when necessary." Discussing an issue that would remain relevant for decades, he told Michelle that context counted. "When we talk about whether or not a stop and frisk is permissible, it makes a difference to see how a stop and frisk can be abused against certain groups and, therefore, students will not be as willing to say that such a procedure is acceptable." Years later, Ogletree said he pushed Harvard students "to understand that they're here for a reason, and it's not just to work at law firms and be successful in and of itself."

David Wilkins, in Michelle's account, adopted a more traditional approach, in part because he felt a need to demonstrate his own authority. He told her, "You don't think that I'm going to walk into a class of Harvard Law students being young, looking even younger, black and a first-time teacher and say, 'Hey guys, call me Dave!'" Michelle said Wilkins encouraged class participation without using intimidation or motivation-by-fear. "I make it a point not to cut off or treat any comment as stupid," he said. "Also, I run my class in a way that makes discussion important and I absolutely forbid any hissing or booing." He told Michelle that he wanted to create an atmosphere where minorities and women felt comfortable speaking out. He also made sure that students were exposed to uncommon or unfamiliar reasoning. "Part of the reason why I'm here, as opposed to a white professor," Wilkins said, "is to bring issues of race, class and other issues into the classroom and make them part of the debate. I want to show students how a lot of what goes on in cases is fueled by issues of race and class."

Michelle likened being a student in Minow's family law class to being a member of the studio audience during a taping of *The Phil Donahue Show.* Like Donahue, the prototype of the empathetic daytime talk show host, Minow paced the classroom, "probing deeply," using smiles and humor as she worked to make everyone feel welcome. She told Michelle that sharp analysis remained essential, but that "safety and a sense of reinforcement is more likely to produce motivation and learning than fear." A by-product of her openness was the stream of students who sought her advice. "Students come to me because I look like someone who listens and cares," Minow told her. "And partly because they know that I won't turn them away. It's important for students to feel they have a place to go."

In her essay, Michelle called for new approaches to the recruitment and assessment of law school faculty. She emphasized hands-on teaching and the human side of education, rather than intellectual heft for its own sake. Let others count angels on the head of a pin; she cared about outcomes. Her interests and, indeed, her orientation to the world were close to the ground. An emerging professional skeptic, she wanted to know how the law connected to real lives, not least to African American ones. Thus, she highlighted Ogletree's "primary objective" as bringing "reality into the classroom." She cited Wilkins's efforts to demonstrate the roots of conflict and noted that Minow did whatever she could "to shake students out of the complacency of being in a classroom and to force them to think long and hard." Describing Michelle's own approach, Wilkins said later that she thought hard and spoke up. She listened to others, he said, and yet was "strong on what her opinions were. She was always the person who was asking the question, 'What does this have to do with providing real access and real justice for real people? Is this fair? Is this right?' She was always very clear on those questions."

THE DISCUSSION MOVED from theory to practice when Michelle volunteered at Harvard's Legal Aid Bureau, a student-run clinic for low-income clients. She worked in a small house on the edge of campus and rode a shuttle to a down-at-the-heels Boston neighborhood. The volunteers met with clients and the attorneys for the opposing party, whether a landlord, a spouse, the gas company, or perhaps a state or federal agency. They drafted pleadings and occasionally argued the issues in court. In return for hands-on experience, students were expected to devote at least twenty hours a week to their cases. For some, the bureau defined their identity. Notable bureau alumni included Supreme Court justice William J. Brennan Jr. and Massachusetts governor Deval Patrick. Yet only a small subset of each Harvard class volunteered, about sixty students a year.

At the clinic's seventy-fifth anniversary celebration in 1988, public interest lawyer Alan Morrison suggested that all graduates should spend a year with a legal services organization after collecting their diplomas. "You can't begin to approach the problems of the poor unless you have experienced them directly," he said. "Working for poor people shows you the difference between the lives of the people who have to fight the system and those who simply enjoy it." Ronald Torbert, an African American student who led the bureau during Michelle's third year, wished more African American students were among the volunteers. "A large number of our clients are blacks and minorities. Lots of folks just don't have the background experience to understand," Torbert said.

Michelle worked with clients on at least six cases between September 1986 and June 1988, when she graduated. Three are listed in bureau records as family cases, a category that encompassed domestic disputes, divorce, and custody fights. Two were housing cases, which a bureau administrator said were probably evictions. One was a matter whose details are not reflected in the files. A 1988 bureau summary referred to a case in which her client's opponent had no attorney. It said Michelle "experienced the tactical difficulty of negotiating against a *pro se* party in the tense emotional environment of visitation and custody issues." In each of her cases, Michelle was the lawyer of record and would have been responsible for developing her strategy, consulting if necessary with one of the bureau supervisors. Ogletree, who ran a trial advocacy workshop, described Michelle as "tenacious." He said Michelle's work flowed from a sense of purpose grounded in her South Side upbringing and "a commitment to her father, who did not go to college, that she would pursue her talents to help her community."

Supervisor Ilene Seidman recalled a visit by Michelle to a satellite court in a white, upper-crust Boston suburb. "People looked at her as though she was an exotic bird. You didn't see women on the bench or in the courtroom in the same way you do now, and certainly not out of the city. Definitely very few women of color." Michelle had labored over a careful memorandum for the judge, Seidman said, while the opposing counsel, a white courthouse regular, had come unprepared. "So she's sitting very upright and serious with her beautiful memo and the other lawyer is flailing around. The judge started really admonishing the other lawyer, 'She did this beautiful memo; you didn't do anything.'" Things went well. On the forty-five-minute ride back to Cambridge in

Seidman's minivan, they replayed the events with delight. "She had just been in a situation that might have made some people justifiably angry, because she had been treated like an alien," Seidman said. But the two women shook their heads and laughed. Michelle was "keenly aware of everything going on around her and had a very mature way of assessing what she would respond to and how."

THE LEGAL AID BUREAU STINT was the only time in Michelle's career when she practiced street-level law, although it was far from the last time she would pay attention to working-class Americans in need. It was a persistent dilemma, what to do with the education and opportunity presented by Princeton and Harvard. She conceded that she had been neither selfless nor particularly purposeful when she set out for Cambridge. "Law school was one of those 'Okay, what do I do next? Don't want to work,'" she said in 1996. "It was less a thoughtful experience than 'Hey, this is a good way to develop a good income. Being a lawyer is prestigious and socially acceptable.'" She worked at corporate law firms in Chicago after each of her first two years at Harvard and entertained lucrative offers to start her career the same way. By the same token, the conversation about responsibility and purpose coursed through her law school years. "There was a real sense among the black students at Harvard of the old adage 'From those to whom much is given, much is expected,'" said Robert Wilkins, the former Black Law Students Association president. Even as they themselves were struggling with where to land, Michelle and several friends saw a vehicle in the group's spring alumni conference, a once-substantive forum that by the mid-1980s had become little more than a social event. They decided to add a measure of meaning about the law, lawyering, and black responsibility. Areva Bell Martin, who co-chaired the 1987 gathering, said one theme "permeated" it: "You guys, this is not just about you going to a cushy firm on Wall Street and doing the fat cat part . . . You will be doing your community and your family a disservice if you leave here and buy your penthouse apartment and never do anything else. There's more to your life than your own personal gain."

The temptations of corporate law firms could be hard to resist, as Michelle was learning. Big-city firms flew Harvard students into town, put them up in fine hotels, and wined and dined them "like you wouldn't believe. We were treated like celebrities," said Martin, who remembered taking more than a half-dozen trips early in her Harvard career. Many students succumbed to the allure, not least some who graduated with substantial student loan debt, including Martin, whose upbringing in a St. Louis housing project was harder than most. She described the BLSA conference as an attempt to present an alternative narrative, for use immediately or later: "Yes, you're privileged. Yes, these firms are courting you. Yes, you'll be offered these huge salaries. But there's more to it and don't get caught up in it."

The BLSA conference, as Martin and the other organizers saw it, needed to convey a sense of purpose, even as it developed into a more effective recruiting and networking event for law firms and students. The organizers set out to lure not just alumni and African Americans in private practice, but also black lawyers who had chosen public interest law, elective office, and other forms of public service. The keynote speaker in 1987 was L. Douglas Wilder, lieutenant governor of Virginia. In 1988, Michelle's third year, it was Bruce M. Wright, a retired New York Supreme Court justice. Known for spotlighting racial disparities in the criminal justice system, Wright titled his 1996 memoir *Black Justice in a White World*. In 1935, Wright had been admitted to Princeton, but when he showed up on campus, administrators saw the color of his skin and refused to allow him to enroll. He sat on his trunk on the sidewalk for several hours as his father drove from New York to pick him up. Asked later why he did not protest, he replied, "I was timid then. And there was a campus police officer standing there." Wright did receive a response in 1939 when he finally asked Princeton why he had been turned away. Radcliffe Heermance, director of admissions, replied that Princeton had a nondiscrimination policy, but that southern students in particular would not approve. "My personal experience," Heermance wrote in a letter that Wright was carrying when the university publicly embraced him in 2001, "would enforce my advice to any colored student that he would be happier in an environment of others of his race."

Jocelyn Frye was one of the spring conference organizers that year, joining Michelle and fellow student Karen Hardwick. Raised in Washington, D.C., the daughter of federal workers, Frye would become Michelle's policy director in the White House. She attended the National Cathedral School and the University of Michigan before alighting at Harvard in 1985. She was glad to find a critical mass of motivated and accomplished black students who shared a number of experiences and goals. "There's no other black student at Harvard who's going to think 'What the heck are you doing at Harvard?'" Frye said. "It was nice to be around people like that and not to feel you were being fitted in boxes that people created for you."

Her feelings of good fortune about being at Harvard aside, Frye came to believe that the law school administration should do more on issues of diversity. "There weren't enough of us. There weren't enough faculty of color. I think Harvard is like any other institution that is a predominantly white institution: They are not good about doing a meaningful assessment of their strengths and weaknesses. They think they're better than they are." She went on, "We had—and we should have—higher expectations for schools that are considered the best or among the best in the country. If you want to brag about Harvard being the preeminent law school, you ought to be able to brag about Harvard being the preeminent law school with faculty and students of color." In May 1988 many of the most active members of BLSA would take a very public step to adjust the balance.

BLSA LEADERS HAD BEEN MEETING in small groups to discuss protest options since April 1988, when law school dean James Vorenberg announced that he was stepping down. The new dean would be Professor Robert Clark, who had been dismissive of Derrick Bell's protests. The students, concluding that the moment before Vorenberg's departure was an opportunity to petition for faculty diversity, decided on an overnight sit-in in Vorenberg's office, where they would present a dozen demands. Seeking maximum publicity, they drafted a mock complaint resembling a lawsuit and assembled a list of likely media outlets. The target was May 10, two days before a full faculty meeting. One objective was to be invited to the meeting to argue their case.

When Robert Wilkins presented the plan to BLSA members, the response was far from the unanimous support he had expected. It was exam season and some students said they could not afford to take time away from their books. Others worried that an arrest would hurt their professional chances. Wilkins reminded his audience that a generation of protesters in the South had risked beatings and jail for their convictions and, anyway, nothing so severe was going to happen in the hushed halls of Harvard Law. Whether or not they joined the sit-in, he and others argued, BLSA members should not weaken the impact of the demonstration by voting against it. The leadership counted enough votes to go forward.

Geneva Crenshaw would have been proud. The vote was a victory, however modest, for Derrick Bell's cherished activism and the narrowing of the distance between theory and practice. Verna Williams described a determination to make BLSA "something more, not a social club," and she gave Bell some of the credit. "He said nothing's going to happen unless you speak up. He was always reminding us of that." If three years at Harvard had confirmed anything to the most politically active students, it was the elemental lesson from Frederick Douglass that power concedes nothing without a demand.

THE TWENTY-FOUR-HOUR SIT-IN began on schedule on Tuesday, May 10. Roughly fifty students participated, the majority of them African American. The BLSA leadership called it a "study vigil." Television news footage showed students seated quietly in Vorenberg's suite preparing for exams. Wilkins presented the demands to the dean, among them that the law school hire a black female professor that year and add at least twenty women or members of minority groups in tenured or tenure-track jobs over the next four years. The list called on the administration to do more to prepare black and minority students to teach law and to "diversify the curriculum to reflect the experience of people of color and women," a page from Bell's playbook and Michelle's

BLSA essay. For good measure, the students also demanded that Bell be named the next dean and Ogletree be offered tenure. A student press release said the protest had become necessary when Vorenberg and the faculty appointments committee showed "a refusal to take any concrete steps or make any tangible commitment." The statement went on to say that minority hiring was important to address "the breadth of legal issues that face America's lawyers. Many of these issues are now omitted by the predominately White male faculty."

In response, Vorenberg made no promises on hiring, but pledged to support a broadening of the curriculum and efforts to give students a stronger voice. Wilkins was permitted to speak to the faculty at its meeting, the day after the sit-in ended. He recalled a decidedly mixed reaction from the assembled professors. Some applauded, some folded arms, some showed stern faces. At least one faculty member did not look up from his newspaper.

GRADUATION DAY DAWNED GRAY, but the rain-soaked outdoor ceremony in Harvard Yard carried the familiar pomp of commencement exercises everywhere, this one all the sweeter because it was Harvard. The recipients of honorary degrees at the university's 337th commencement included soprano Jessye Norman, economist John Kenneth Galbraith, and Nobel Peace Prize winner Óscar Arias from Costa Rica, who admonished the graduates to acknowledge their rare and privileged position and embrace the accompanying responsibilities. "The majority of young people in this world are neither here nor in other university graduations," he said. "That majority, if they are lucky, got up early today to plow fields or to start up machines in factories. Young people like yourselves are dying in futile wars or barely subsisting with no hope. The privilege of knowledge bears a social responsibility." Harvard president Derek Bok, too, spoke of civic duty that day. He lamented the low salaries paid to teachers and public servants and contrasted those roles with the career choices of the graduates of Harvard Law. He pointed out that just 2 percent of the graduates of one of the most prestigious law schools in the country entered government jobs right after graduation. An even smaller number, he said, chose public interest or legal aid work. The vast majority joined corporate law firms.

After the ceremony, David Wilkins saw from a distance the Robinson family sheltering under an arch. Michelle was there, elegant and tall, her brother Craig still taller, and Marian Robinson standing with them. Fraser, who would die less than three years later, sat alongside in a wheelchair. Wilkins introduced himself to the Chicago visitors. "Harvard Law School is a hard place," he told them. "It's a hard place for anybody, but it's a particularly hard place for black students and more for black women students. Michelle not only did well in this place, but she did something quite unique: She tried to change it. I don't know what your daughter's going to do, but I promise you, whatever she decides to do, she's going to be somebody special."

Michelle was leaving Harvard more confident and skilled, if not necessarily more certain about her direction, than when she arrived nearly three years before. For all of the impassioned discussion about purpose, she chose corporate law, returning to the name-brand Chicago firm where she had worked the previous summer, stepping onto the cushy corporate track that she had mused about at Princeton. The new job would cover some bills and provide some legal experience. And then she would see. In the Harvard yearbook, her parents bought space for a message, reminding her with proud bemusement that she might have fancy degrees from Harvard and Princeton, but she was still a South Side girl, still a Robinson: "We knew you would do this fifteen years ago when we could never make you shut up."

# SIX

# Finding the Right Thing

W hen Michelle packed her boxes in Cambridge and moved back
to Chicago after seven years in the Ivy League, she traded one
privileged institution for another, embarking on the corporate path that she had begun to foresee in her college years. She started
work in the summer of 1988 as a first-year associate at Sidley & Austin,
one of the city's most prominent firms—very white, very male, very
pleased with its blue-chip client list. By education and affiliation, she
was now a certified member of the elite, and from her first day on the
job, she was earning more money than her parents combined. And
yet she was no closer to resolving her essential dilemma, the one that
had informed so many conversations at Princeton and Harvard: What
is possible for a black person, especially a black woman, in America?
What is desirable? What is right when judged by whom?

It was more than Michelle's fine education that made her new career
possible, although the pair of diplomas inked in Latin offered impressive evidence of her potential. The fact was, Chicago was changing. The
city she found when she returned to the bungalow on South Euclid was
not the Chicago of Richard Wright or her grandfathers or her parents. It
was not the city where a talented young black woman's options ranged
about as far as the nearest classroom or secretarial pool. Nor was it the
Chicago of Richard J. Daley, who had wielded power atop a largely white
power structure from 1955 until his death in 1976. A generation after

Martin Luther King's northern campaign fizzled, black economic and political clout was growing. African Americans accounted for nearly 40 percent of the city's population, sprawling across dozens of square miles. There were more than one million black people within the city limits, compared with 240,000 in 1930, when Michelle's grandparents were coming of age. With the population and the changing times came greater opportunity and perhaps the biggest shift of all: The mayor of Chicago during much of Michelle's time away had been Harold Washington, a black man.

Chicago's election, in 1983, of its first African American mayor came later than most. Five years after New Orleans and Oakland. Ten years after Detroit, Atlanta, and Los Angeles. Sixteen years after Cleveland and Gary. Frustration with the white establishment had been growing, fueled by the unequal treatment of black neighborhoods and residents. Anger had spiked in 1968, as it had in many cities, with the assassination of Martin Luther King Jr., and again in 1969 when Chicago police raided an apartment and killed Fred Hampton and Mark Clark, leaders of the Black Panthers. In 1972, police mistreated two black dentists, Herbert Odom and Daniel Claiborne, fueling the conviction that the rock-no-boats strategy of the Silent Six black aldermen had run its course. "I have been asked why it took me so long to take a stand," Representative Ralph Metcalfe, an Olympic gold medalist who had been one of the six, said that year as he broke with Daley and the Democratic machine. "My answer is this: It's never too late to become black. And I suggest some of you try becoming black also."

After Daley's death in December 1976, Harold Washington lost the race to succeed him. In 1983, however, he rode into office with the backing of an energized coalition. The election, for all the progress it represented, also revealed the city's enduring racial fissures. Washington received just 11 percent of the white vote in the primary. Many white Democrats chose race over party and voted Republican in the general election. But the bitterness of the campaign and the lateness of the date made the achievement all the sweeter for Washington's supporters, particularly residents of the heavily black communities on the South Side and West Side. It was like the moment in *The Wizard of Oz* when the

Wicked Witch of the West melts away. Washington had paid his own dues to Daley and the Democratic machine, rising within it, yet his election promised progress and patronage alike.

"His picture was everywhere," wrote a young community organizer who arrived in Chicago in July 1985, two years into Washington's tenure. "On the walls of shoe repair shops and beauty parlors; still glued to lampposts from the last campaign; even in the windows of the Korean dry cleaners and Arab grocery stores, displayed prominently, like some protective totem." A black barber in Hyde Park asked the organizer if he had been in Chicago during the election. No, the newcomer said, he had not. The barber explained, "Had to be here before Harold to understand what he means to the city. Before Harold, seemed like we'd always be second-class citizens." Another man spoke up and said it was "plantation politics." The barber agreed. "That's just what it was, too. A plantation. Black people in the worst jobs. The worst housing. Police brutality rampant. But when the so-called black committeemen came around election time, we'd all line up and vote the straight Democratic ticket. Sell our soul for a Christmas turkey. White folks spitting in our faces and we'd reward 'em with the vote."

The new organizer who went to the barber shop and recalled the conversation was Barack Obama, who spent three years doing grass-roots political work on the South Side. He headed off to Harvard Law School in 1988, just as Michelle was settling into her job at the law firm. They would not meet until the following year.

A FEW MONTHS AFTER Washington won a second term, Alan Greene sat down to dinner in Cambridge with twenty-three-year-old Michelle Robinson. It was the fall of 1987 and she was in her final year at Harvard, starting to choose among job offers from prominent Chicago law firms. One of those firms was Chadwell Kaiser, whose specialty was complex business litigation, particularly the profitable work of defending corporations against anti-trust complaints. She had spent the summer after her first year of law school at Chadwell, where the partners had been impressed. It was unusual for the firm to hire a first-year law student, but Michelle was "so obviously a quality candidate," Greene said. The lawyers were struck by her aptitude for the law, her self-confidence, and her accomplishments at Princeton and Harvard. Greene described her as "hard-charging" and "sophisticated," not somebody "you would just stick in a library to do research." And there was something else. Michelle was a talented black woman entering a hypercompetitive field that for decades had been very white and mostly male. The firm needed her. Not because it was the moral thing to do—an argument that was appealing but insufficient—but because its business model demanded it.

"Our firm, like everybody else in the mid-eighties, was realizing that the world of law firms was too insular," Greene said. The firm's interest in Michelle, he said, "started with the idea that here is somebody who seems to get along fine." If all went well and she proved to be as talented as she appeared, she could become a magnet for black clients and minority lawyers, as well as for other clients who valued a diverse team. The firm had once been entirely Protestant, male, and white, only later hiring Catholics, Jews, and women. "So, she would be the next breakthrough in the firm. That's a lot of pressure and it didn't seem to faze her, which was one of the things in her favor."

Despite Greene's entreaties, Michelle chose to start her career at Sidley & Austin, a larger, more dynamic, and marginally more diverse firm—the clients of one black Sidley attorney included Muhammad Ali and boxing promoter Don King. It was not a hasty decision; hasty was not her style. She aimed to build her credentials and start to repay student loans that totaled tens of thousands of dollars. She had a good idea of the air she would breathe, having been a summer associate at Sidley the previous year. The firm was founded in 1866, five years before the Chicago Fire tore through the heart of the city. It was a classic white shoe operation that had expanded and changed through mergers and collaborations. One of the firm's best-known partners in the modern era was Newton Minow, a Democrat, who, as director of the Federal Communications Commission, famously decried television as a "vast wasteland." Yet the firm's politics were broadly Republican, and there was no disguising the fact that the firm's business was distinctly corporate. There would be no trips to distant courthouses to work with indigent clients, no sit-ins for change. When she rode the elevator to her office on the forty-seventh floor of a downtown skyscraper, she was halfway to the clouds. And yet, as the novelty wore off, she would recognize ruefully that she could stand in her gleaming window and still not quite see the South Side neighborhood of her youth.

MICHELLE'S ASSIGNMENTS as a young associate at Sidley ranged from the AT&T account to a series of marketing matters for Coors beer and Barney, the purple dinosaur on public television. One colleague said the work could be thankless and, frankly, dull—for example, reading storyboards to determine whether a beer advertisement conformed to television industry rules and standards. "I knew Michelle was frustrated," said John Levi, a senior partner who remained a friend. "Things in that group were unsettled at that time." Colleagues recall her efforts as thorough and her voice as independent. "She was very at ease with herself. Confident in her attitude. I don't think she suffered fools easily," said Mary Hutchings Reed, one of the firm's few senior women attorneys, who supervised Michelle in Sidley's intellectual property group. Other young lawyers had stronger records when they were hired, but Michelle's personality and high standards stood out, another senior colleague recalled. "A lot of people come with great résumés, but without a lot of common sense and without the kind of personal strength that she had," said Nate Eimer, who joined the firm in 1973. "She was very poised, she was extremely articulate, she was very smart, she obviously was not intimidated by anything or anybody," Eimer said. "She was the perfect associate, the perfect lawyer for Sidley. She would have done extraordinarily well had she stayed there."

Early on, in a conversation with Levi, Michelle volunteered to play a role in the firm's recruiting efforts. She had not been at Sidley for a year, but Levi invited her to sift applications from Harvard students, and help recruit the best of them. He reasoned that she knew the school, possessed a winning personality, and would speak positively about the firm. The fact that she was African American was a bonus. In the next step of Sidley's hiring and orientation process, her race played a role. "There was always a bit of an effort to introduce black people who were coming through to black people who were here, just to let them know they wouldn't be the sole black person here," said Steven Carlson, a white Princeton graduate who had been Michelle's first contact at Sidley. That year, the firm invited a black first-year law student from Harvard to join Sidley's class of summer associates in 1989, just as Chadwell Kaiser had done with Michelle. He was a star and the firm wanted him to have a good summer. Would Michelle, the higher-ups wanted to know, be his adviser?

ON HIS FIRST DAY, Barack was late. Michelle took note. Despite what she described as "all this buzz about this hotshot," she expected to be unimpressed. For one thing, after examining the photograph he had sent for the Sidley directory, she concluded that he was not much of a looker. It was the ears, she later said. For another, she knew how little it sometimes took for well-meaning white people to be wowed by a black person. Everyone was making a big fuss, she thought to herself, because Barack was "probably just a black man who can talk straight."

"But he walked into the office and we hit it off right away because he is very charming and he was handsome—I thought he was handsome. And I think we were attracted to each other because we didn't take the whole scene as seriously as a lot of people do. He liked my dry sense of humor and my sarcasm. I thought he was a really good, interesting guy, and I was fascinated with his background because it was so different than mine." How different? "Well, Barack grew up in a multiracial environment," she explained in 1996. "His mother is white, his father is Kenyan, he lived in Hawaii." He had spent several years as a child in Indonesia with his anthropologist mother and he had seen some of the world. His worldliness gave him a dimension that she did not encounter on the South Side or among the well-heeled lawyers at Sidley, where "you tend to find people that sort of fit one mold."

Not that she intended to date him. That would be going too far. Besides, as she told her mother while feeling luckless at love, she had sworn off romance that summer, declaring, "I'm going to focus on me." Michelle had dated an array of young men all the way back to high school, when she went to the Whitney Young prom with David Upchurch. She had posed for a photo that night in a silken evening gown with a V neck and a thigh-high slit, a pattern she chose and modified, insisting on the slit. Her mother did the sewing. At Harvard, one beau was law student Stanley Stocker-Edwards, the adopted son of singer Patti LaBelle. Nothing lasted. She said later, "My family swore I would never find a man that would put up with me."

WHEN BARACK ARRIVED at Sidley, it was the second time he had lit out for Chicago. His background was, indeed, exotic, and he had made many ports of call in his search for purpose and identity. His parents met in the autumn of 1960 at the University of Hawaii, where his mother, Stanley Ann Dunham, born in Kansas, had just enrolled as a seventeen-year-old freshman. Barack Hussein Obama Sr. was six years older, married, with one child in Kenya and another on the way. Within a few weeks of the start of classes, Ann was pregnant. She left school after the first semester and the couple quietly married in a county courthouse in Wailuku. At the time, laws prohibiting interracial marriage were on the books in twenty-one states. Barack Hussein Obama II was born in Honolulu on August 4, 1961, at Kapiolani Maternity and Gynecological Hospital. In Arabic, Barack means "blessed by God," while Hussein means "good" or "handsome." Within months, his parents had split up and young Barack would see his father only once more, when he was ten years old. For four years in his childhood, he lived with his mother and her Indonesian husband, Lolo Soetero, in Jakarta. His younger sister was born there. Dissatisfied with the Indonesian elementary schools, his mother often awakened him at 4 a.m. and tutored him, sometimes for as long as three hours. When Barack complained, her refrain was always the same: "This is no picnic for me either, buster."

By the time Barack was ten, Ann had decided he should be schooled in the United States. While she stayed in Indonesia to continue her research, he moved to Honolulu, where he lived in a small apartment with his middle-class midwestern grandparents, Stanley and Madelyn Dunham. They, too, had married young, eloping before her eighteenth birthday, on the night of her high school prom. During World War II, Stanley served in the Third Armored Division while Madelyn, known to the family as Toot, worked in a B-29 bomber factory. After Ann was born, their peripatetic existence took them to California, Oklahoma, Texas, Washington State, and, eventually, Hawaii, where Stanley found work in a furniture store and Madelyn worked as a bank secretary. Stanley was a bluff man, a dreamer and a drinker considerably less industrious than his wife. Basically a good man but "too old and too troubled to provide me with much direction," Barack said. They "stayed married through thick and thin," said Charles Payne, Madelyn's younger brother, who retired in 1995 as assistant director of the University of Chicago library. "They were both strong-willed persons and Stanley believed that he was the master of the household in all things. Madelyn made the money that paid the rent. In fact, Madelyn was the one, year after year, who got up and went to work and earned some money. Stanley could never do that consistently." In Payne's view, it was the women in Barack's life—his mother and his grandmother—who set the terms and the tone: "They were both very strong and tended toward the domineering." Musing about their impact on the future president, he said, "Well, he ended up pretty strong himself." Barack, in fact, once told Michelle, "You know, I got my toughness from Toot."

When Barack—then known as Barry—returned to Honolulu from Jakarta, his family enrolled him in the elite, private Punahou Academy. In *Dreams from My Father: A Story of Race and Inheritance,* the memoir he published at age thirty-three, Barack described a directionless adolescence. "Indifferent" was how he recalled himself. He played basketball, studied only as much as necessary, and smoked so much pot that he and his friends called themselves the Choom Gang. "I rebelled," he once said, "angry in the way that many young men in general, and young black men in particular, are angry, thinking that responsibility and hard work were old-fashioned conventions that didn't apply to me." By senior year, he had doubts about going to college. His mother asked him one day whether he was being a little casual about his future. He mused that he might stay in Hawaii, take a few classes, maybe get a part-time job. "She cut me off before I could finish," he said. "I could get into any school in the country, she said, if I just put in the effort. 'Remember what that's like? Effort? Damn it, Bar, you can't just sit around like some good-time Charlie, waiting for luck to see you through.'"

Barack roused himself. He made his way to Occidental College in Southern California. "A few miles from Pasadena," he wrote, "tree-lined and Spanish-tiled. The students were friendly, the teachers encouraging." In Hawaii, he had spent time with Frank Marshall Davis, a dashiki-wearing black nationalist poet and former Chicago newspaperman. Before Barack set out for the mainland, Davis warned him that the price of admission to college was "leaving your race at the door, leaving your people behind," a bluntly phrased version of the dilemma that absorbed Michelle at Princeton and Harvard. Davis said the experience would give the young man "an advanced degree in compromise." Indeed, when he arrived at Occidental—a first-rate school, but no one's idea of the Ivy League—Barack found that most of the concerns of black students "seemed indistinguishable from those of the white kids around us. Surviving classes. Finding a well-paying gig after graduation. Trying to get laid. I had stumbled upon one of the well-kept secrets about black people: that most of us weren't interested in revolt; that most of us were tired of thinking about race all the time; that if we preferred to keep to ourselves, it was mainly because that was the easiest way to stop thinking about it."

His own internal conversation about race and identity, however, was deep and unremitting, a product of his biracial heritage and an upbringing unconventional in white and black terms alike. Hawaii, Indonesia, the absent Kenyan father. Even the Dunhams. "We always just thought of Barack as just being Barack. Not black or white. Another family member who was just like us, only not quite," Charles Payne said. Barack said his grandmother more than once "uttered racial or ethnic stereotypes that made me cringe" and "once confessed her fear of black men who passed her by on the street." He came to envy, perhaps idealize, traits he saw in black students from working-class urban neighborhoods, young people who came from Watts or Compton or, as it happened, Chicago. In *Dreams from My Father,* which relied on composites of characters from his life, he assigned the role of alter ego to a black woman from the South Side.

He called her Regina, Latin for "queen," and identified her as an Occidental student, "a big, dark woman who wore stockings and dresses that looked homemade." She was studious—she spent a lot of time in the library—and she helped organize black student events. She had an evenness about her, an honesty and authenticity that "made me feel like I didn't have to lie." Her father was absent, her mother was struggling to pay the bills in a Chicago apartment cold in winter and so hot in summer that people sometimes slept outdoors to keep cool. Regina, he wrote, spent many "evenings in the kitchen with uncles and cousins and grandparents, the stew of voices bubbling up in laughter. Her voice evoked a vision of black life in all its possibility, a vision that filled me with longing—a longing for place, and a fixed and definite history."

When Barack told Regina that he envied her memories, she started to laugh. Confused, he asked why. "Oh Barack," she said, "isn't life something? And here I was all this time wishing I'd grown up in Hawaii." Barack published *Dreams* six years after meeting Michelle. They were married by then and he had been steeped in her South Side life, even living with her for a time in the house on Euclid. In his second book, *The Audacity of Hope,* he would use similar language to describe the real-life Michelle and her family.

ONE THING THAT STRUCK Michelle that first summer in Chicago was the way Barack seemed to move so easily among many different worlds. She also saw a sense of purpose not tied to wealth or corporate success. The Sidley brass took a keen interest, hoping to lure him back to the firm for good. He went to one cloth-napkin lunch after another. A member of Sidley's executive committee took him to a board meeting, while Newt Minow urged him to enhance his credentials by becoming a federal law clerk. The estimable attorneys saw what the Harvard professors saw. "Barack Obama, One L!" wrote constitutional scholar

Laurence Tribe on his desk calendar on March 29, 1989, commemorating an encounter with the first-year student. "I was impressed by his maturity and his sense of purpose, his fluency. Barack wasn't just a wonk of some kind. He cared about how people ticked."

The man was undeniably smart and smooth and it did not take long before Michelle found him intriguing "in every way you can imagine. He was funny. He was self-deprecating. He didn't take himself too seriously. He could laugh at himself. I mean, we clicked right away." But she hesitated to date him. She thought it might be inappropriate, given the responsibility conferred by Sidley in assigning her to be his mentor. And quite possibly tacky, should two of the firm's relatively few black professionals find themselves in a romantic relationship. "When I first met him, I fell in deep *like*," Michelle explained. "Right off the bat, I said, 'This guy can be my friend. We're going to be friends.' And it was later on, when he pressed for a little more than friendship, that's what I pushed away from. Because I thought, you know, we're working together." She even tried to set him up with her friends. Over the course of several weeks, with no small amount of verbal jousting, Barack wore her down, challenging her professed reasons one by one. Along the way, she learned something more about him: "He is very persistent."

"So," she recalled, "I said, okay, we'll go on this one date, but we won't call it a date. I'll spend the day with you." The day arrived sunny and warm. Michelle was living in South Shore. Barack had an apartment in nearby Hyde Park, not far from the University of Chicago. They started at the Art Institute, where Michelle's father had studied forty years earlier. They ate lunch in the museum's leafy stone courtyard to the sounds of a jazz combo and then took a long walk to see the new Spike Lee movie, *Do the Right Thing*. Afterward, they had a drink on the ninety-sixth floor of the John Hancock building, as the city and the lake stretched into the distance. "I was sold," she said.

Barack saw many things to like in Michelle, including her beauty: "I thought she looked real good." He admired her "strong sense of herself and who she is and where she comes from." But he also spotted a trait that was not part of her public persona. "In her eyes," he said later, when Michelle was in her early thirties, "you can see a trace of vulnerability, or at least I do, that most people don't know, because when she's walking through the world, she is this tall, beautiful, confident woman and extremely capable. But there is a part of her that is vulnerable and young and sometimes frightened and I think seeing both of those things is what attracted me to her." Michelle's vulnerability flowed from a sense that life was "terrifyingly random," Barack wrote in *The Audacity of Hope*. He said he spotted "the slightest hint of uncertainty, as if, deep inside, she knew how fragile things really were, and that if she ever let go, even for a moment, all her plans might quickly unravel."

One afternoon after a Sidley picnic, they went for ice cream in Hyde Park. As they sat on a curb outside Baskin-Robbins, they shot the breeze. Barack told Michelle how he had once scooped ice cream at a Baskin-Robbins in Hawaii. He said he would like to meet her family. He asked if he could kiss her.

"WE SPENT THE REST of the summer together," trading stories and getting to know one another, Barack wrote in *The Audacity of Hope*. To impress him, she borrowed her mother's seafood gumbo recipe, persuading him that she was a more versatile cook than she actually was. She was saving money by living with her parents in the Euclid house, which Fraser and Marian had bought from Aunt Robbie for $10 in April 1980. Later, when he was president and Michelle told acquaintances the story of their courtship and what attracted her to him, Barack chirped merrily, "Black man with a job! Black man with a job!"

Barack said it was not until he met Michelle's family that he "began to understand her." In the Robinson household in those early days, he saw what he described as joy. He said visiting the bungalow on Euclid was like "dropping in on the set of *Leave It to Beaver*." Beyond Fraser, Marian, and Craig, who graduated from business school and became a Chicago investment banker, "there were uncles and aunts and cousins everywhere, stopping by to sit around the kitchen table and eat until they burst and tell wild stories and listen to Grandpa's old jazz collection and laugh deep into the night." It was language that echoed his descriptions in *Dreams* of Regina's extended family and its effect on him. The contrast could hardly have been greater between his untethered life and the world of the Robinson and Shields clans, so numerous and so firmly anchored in Chicago. He felt embraced and it surprised him. "For someone like me, who had barely known his father, who had spent much of his life traveling from place to place, his bloodlines scattered to the four winds, the home that Fraser and Marian Robinson had built for themselves and their children stirred a longing for stability and a sense of place that I had not realized was there."

MICHELLE WAS STRUCK by Barack's community organizing work and the way he still talked about making a difference. He seemed to care little about the legal profession's traditional ladders of success, and even less about money. He reported to Sidley in serviceable clothes— "cruddy" was Michelle's word. His only pair of shoes was a half size too small and he drove a car so rusty that she could sit in the passenger seat and see the road through a hole in the door. "He loved that car. It would shake ferociously when it would start up. I thought, 'This brother is not interested in ever making a dime.'" He had graduated from Columbia University in 1983 after becoming more serious about his studies and transferring from Occidental. He worked in New York City for Business International, a publishing operation that produced newsletters and research reports, and he considered working in Harold Washington's administration. But when he wrote to the mayor's office, he received no reply. If he had cared more about money, he would not have answered a newspaper ad and spent three years before law school in Chicago, working for the Developing Communities Project, where the starting pay was $12,000 a year, plus $1,000 to buy a rattletrap.

The project descended from the work of Saul Alinsky, a Chicago organizer best known for his cagey opposition to Daley and his authorship of a book that was part manual, part manifesto, called *Rules for Radicals*. Still in New York, Barack aced the interview, took the job, and set off for Chicago. His mission was to mobilize the largely apolitical residents of Altgeld Gardens and Roseland to demand a fairer shake from the government—more attention, better services, a stronger chance of pulling their neighborhoods together. Fellow organizer Mike Kruglik said Barack possessed "a basic belief in the humanity of the folks on the South Side and their right to a decent life" and was "emotionally committed to African Americans getting ahead." Political critics who disapproved of Alinsky's philosophy, real or imagined, later accused Barack of being an acolyte. In fact, athough his supervisor, Gregory Galluzzo, liked to describe himself as Alinsky's St. Paul, Barack borrowed some bits and discarded others, crafting his own strategies as he went.

Looking back, Barack said the work gave him "the best education I ever had." In those deathly poor neighborhoods where he worked with African American ministers, he found persistent racial inequality that defied the progress that had erased the worst of segregation. He interviewed black Chicagoans, heirs to the Great Migration, whose family history mirrored Michelle's, with grandparents barred from labor unions and parents kept out of good schools and jobs because of their skin color. Some had succeeded, while many others had stalled out, perhaps permanently. It was the paradox of the talented tenth all over again. He was troubled by "this dual sense, of individual advancement and collective decline." The need was clear enough, but what to do? Feeling his way, Barack saw limits to what he could accomplish as a local organizer and set out for Harvard, thinking maybe he could do more as a lawyer or a politician.

Back in Chicago that summer after his first year of law school, he invited Michelle to join him as he met South Side residents he had known as an organizer. It was there, in a church basement, watching Barack talk with African Americans living from paycheck to paycheck, that she fell in love. His theme that day was the world as it is and the world as it should be. "He said that all too often we accept the distance between the two and we settle for the world as it is, even when it doesn't reflect our values and aspirations," Michelle said in a campaign speech. "But he reminded us that we also know what the world should look like. He said we know what fairness and justice and opportunity look like, and he urged us to believe in ourselves, to find the strength within ourselves to strive for the world as it should be." Barack's talk that day, in a year that would see peaceful revolutions across Central Europe and an unarmed man defying a column of tanks in China's Tiananmen Square, stayed with Michelle long after they were married. It would take two years and two jarring emotional blows before she quit Sidley, but what she saw in Barack strengthened her view that there was more to life than billable hours.

In Barack, Michelle felt she had found a man whose values meshed with her own, someone with whom she could share a purposeful life. "There are a lot of women who have the boxes—did he go to the right school, what is his income? It was none of that," Michelle told British high school girls in 2011.

It was how he felt about his mother. The love that he felt for his mother. His relationship to women. His work ethic. We worked together in a firm. He did his work, and he was good, and he was smart, and I liked that. And he was low-key. He wasn't impressed with himself, and he was funny. And we joked a lot. And he loved his little sister. And he was a community organizer—I really respected that. Here we are in a big law firm, right? And everybody was pushing to make money. He was one of the smartest students at Harvard Law School, one of the smartest associates in our firm. He had the chance to clerk for the Supreme Court and I thought, "Well, you're definitely going to do that, right?" Only a few people even have the chance to do that. He was, like, "Not really. I think I can do more work working with folks in churches." I was like, whoa, that's different. And he meant it. It wasn't a line. He wasn't trying to impress me. It was those kinds of values that made me think, "you don't meet people like that often." And when you couple that with talent, and he's cute. You know, I always thought he would be useful."

"WE GAVE IT a month, tops," Craig Robinson said after Michelle introduced Barack to the family. Not because there was anything wrong with him. He was quick, engaging, handsome, and six-foot-two, which mattered to Michelle, who stood nearly six feet tall. "But we knew he was going to do something wrong, and then it was going to be too bad for him. She held everybody to the same standard as my father, which was very high." Craig usually found no reason to dislike Michelle's boyfriends, but "you sort of felt sorry for them because you knew it was just a matter of time before they were getting fired." He called her "one tough girl" and made clear that she could be demanding. "She's very accomplished, so she needs someone as accomplished as her, and she also needs someone who can stand up to her. So, we in the family, we were just hoping she could hang onto this guy, because it was readily apparent he could stand up to her."

Marian, no pushover, was favorably impressed with Barack. "She found that he never talked about himself. He was always focused on who was around him," Michelle said. "He was somebody that shared the values of our family. He believed in honesty, treated people with respect and kindness, no matter who they were." Marian had white cousins and aunts who had married into the family, and one of her brothers married a white woman. But she was wary of Barack's biracial heritage. "A little bit," she said. "That didn't concern me as much as had he been completely white. And I guess that I worry about races mixing because of the difficulty, not so much for prejudice or anything. It's just very hard."

Barack's odds remained unclear. Fraser always said that you could tell a lot about a man by the way he played basketball. So one day Michelle asked Craig to include Barack in a pickup basketball game and report back. "When she asked me, I thought, 'Oh, no, she's going to make me be the bad guy,'" Craig said. But Barack was neither selfish with the ball nor shy about taking an open shot. He got extra points for not being overly deferential to his girlfriend's big brother during that first session, where they played for hours on a public court near Lake Michigan. "Confident without being cocky, selfless without being wimpy, and willing to sublimate his ego for the team. I gave her a good report."

After the summer in Chicago, Barack returned to Harvard for his second year of law school while Michelle continued her work at Sidley. He pursued a job in a different Chicago firm, but his plans to spend a leisurely summer in the Windy City were interrupted by his ground-breaking February 1990 election to the presidency of the *Harvard Law Review.* Never in its 104-year history had a black person led the esteemed journal, and his election drew media attention. He told *The New York Times* that he expected to spend two or three years at a law firm, then return to community work or enter Chicago politics. "The fact that I've been elected shows a lot of progress. It's encouraging," Barack, then twenty-eight, told the reporter. "But it's important that stories like mine aren't used to say that everything is okay for blacks. You have to remember that for every one of me, there are hundreds or thousands of black students with at least equal talent who don't get a chance."

FOUR MONTHS LATER, Suzanne Alele died.

Michelle's effervescent Princeton friend, the one she admired for making decisions based on fulfillment, not expectations, lost a fight with cancer on June 23, 1990. She was only twenty-six, barely five years out of college. Her devastated friends had pulled together during her illness, supporting her in Washington, D.C., where she had become a computer specialist at the Federal Reserve after earning an MBA. Angela Kennedy, who helped organize a memorial fund, said of Michelle, "If Suzanne or I picked up the phone and needed or wanted anything, she was here in a heartbeat. Suzanne's death was the first time I really got to see the depth of her love for her friends, how loyal she is." Alele's passing had a profound effect on Michelle, putting into focus frustrations she was feeling at Sidley and reminding her, against the backdrop of Barack's more purposeful inclinations, that the choice was hers to make. If she herself died young, she wondered, was being a corporate lawyer "how I would want to be remembered in life. Was I waking up every morning feeling excited about work and the work I was doing? The answer to the question was no."

She soon suffered an even deeper blow. Her father, after many years of living with multiple sclerosis, had been growing weaker. He started having breathing problems, but delayed telling anyone. One late winter night, Marian awakened to find him struggling for air. He passed out.

She called an ambulance. Doctors at the University of Chicago found a host of problems, including a large growth in his airway and bleeding ulcers. Surgeons operated, but unable to get enough oxygen to his brain, he slipped into a coma. The family gathered and Barack flew in from Boston to be with Michelle. On March 6, 1991, at age fifty-five, still employed at the water plant, Fraser died. He was buried a few days later at Lincoln Cemetery on the South Side. In their grief, Michelle and Craig argued over the wording of a remembrance. "Would you just stop it?" Marian demanded. "Do you know why you're arguing? You're arguing because you miss your father." The three of them burst into tears.

At the gravesite, Michelle rested her head on Barack's shoulder. "As the casket was lowered," Barack wrote later, "I promised Fraser Robinson that I would take care of his girl. I realized that in some unspoken, still tentative way, she and I were already becoming a family."

MICHELLE KNEW THAT she needed to find more meaning in her professional life. Exactly how, she had no clear idea, but she knew she had to leave Sidley. Among other factors, she was increasingly uncomfortable with the money she was making. She asked herself, figuratively, "Can I go to the family reunion in my Benz and be comfortable, while my cousins are struggling to keep a roof over their heads?" More than the matter of dollars and cents, she saw that making a difference in the city where her cousins, neighbors, and friends lived was important to her. "Just like that, I'd lost two of the people I loved most in the world," she told North Carolina A&T students in 2012. "So there I was, not much older than all of you, and I felt like my whole world was caving in. And I began to do a little bit of soul searching. I began to ask myself some hard questions. Questions like, 'If I die tomorrow, what did I really do with my life? What kind of a mark would I leave? How would I be remembered?' And none of my answers satisfied me."

# SEVEN

# Assets and Deficits

The file that landed on Valerie Jarrett's desk in Chicago City Hall was relayed by a colleague who had just interviewed a startlingly impressive young woman dissatisfied with her job at Sidley & Austin. The colleague was Susan Sher, a senior attorney for Mayor Richard M. Daley, elected two years earlier to his father's old job. Sher quickly realized that she could not tempt Michelle Robinson with a position in the legal department. "I don't want to be a lawyer," Michelle told her. "I want to do public service, but I think lawyers look at things from too narrow a perspective." Not wanting to let her get away, Sher alerted Jarrett, who was on the lookout for talented recruits, especially African Americans. Jarrett was so impressed after meeting Michelle that she offered her a job in the mayor's office on the spot. On the receiving end, Michelle was gratified and intrigued, but wary. She had an unusual request: Would Jarrett be willing to meet with her boyfriend, Barack Obama, and talk things over?

"He wanted to kick my tires," Jarrett recalled. The three of them—Jarrett the oldest at thirty-four, Barack turning thirty, and Michelle twenty-seven—met for dinner at a restaurant in the West Loop. Jarrett, who would become a friend, mentor, and one of the most powerful players in the Obama White House, recalled that Barack did much of the talking. He spoke little about himself. "I remember him, in a very nonthreatening way, tickling out what I was all about. He did it not in an intimidating way, but in a way that made me want to talk." He wanted to know where she was born. Iran, she told him. "He wanted to know how I'd gone from being born in Iran to Mayor Daley's office." That was a longer story.

Born in November 1956, Valerie Bowman had grown up in a highly educated family with ambitions to match. "Valerie, put yourself in the path of lightning," her grandmother used to tell her. For an African American family in the middle of the twentieth century, the educational lineage was exceedingly rare. "Everybody in my mother's generation went to college," said Jarrett's mother, Barbara Taylor Bowman, who was born in Chicago in 1928. "And the generation before that went to college. My grandfather, his brothers, all of their kids and, of course, us. We all went to college." One great-grandmother attended seminary at Oberlin before the Civil War. One grandfather was the first black graduate of the Massachusetts Institute of Technology and a deputy to Booker T. Washington at the Tuskegee Institute. Her father was the first black chairman of the Chicago Housing Authority, and she herself graduated from Sarah Lawrence College in 1950. Two weeks later, she married James Bowman, a dentist's son born in 1923 in Washington, D.C. He and his siblings all attended college, with Jim earning two degrees from Howard University. Yet, for all of their drive and success, the Bowmans experienced prejudice firsthand. Barbara recalled that, as one of about thirty black students at an integrated South Side elementary school, no white child would hold her hand as they walked into the building after recess.

In the Bowman family, the messages about racial identity were as clear as the ones about the importance of education. "My grandmother always kept telling us that they cannot make you uncomfortable; only you can make yourself uncomfortable," Barbara recalled. She said her grandmother could have passed as white, "but she took pride in being black and I also took pride in being black. . . . My great-grandmother, she took her stick and she would say, 'You know, you are a Negro. You should always be proud of that.'"

Valerie spent much of the first six years of her life outside the United States because her father was fed up with racial inequality in Chicago, where he had embarked on a medical career. With two internships behind him, he became the first African American resident at St. Luke's Hospital. Showing up for work in 1947, he was told that black employees were expected to use the back entrance. He defied the dictum and walked through the front door. The next day, he arrived to find other black employees waiting out front to walk through the door with him. He spent three years as chairman of pathology at Provident Hospital and three more as an army pathologist in Colorado, but when Provident executives invited him to return in 1955, they offered him less than half the salary white doctors were making. That was the breaking point. He said, "My wife and I decided that we were not going back to anything that smacked of segregation."

"We said, 'Let's look for someplace to go, and we may or may not ever come back,'" Jim Bowman recalled. He accepted a job as pathologist at Nemazee Hospital in Shiraz, an ancient crossroads in southern Iran, not far from the Persian Gulf. When they finally did head back to Chicago, following a stint in London, it was largely for Valerie's sake. "Because she didn't know who she was, and we wanted her to know who she was. In those days, we were called Negroes, but when we would say to our daughter, 'You are Negro,' she would say, 'Well, what does that mean?' We tried to explain it to her, but she said, 'Everywhere I look, I see lots of people with dark skin, but they are not called Negroes. Why aren't they called Negroes?'"

As educators who prospered in Chicago after their return, the Bowmans passed their wisdom along to their students, as well as to their daughter. Barbara Bowman helped create the Erikson Institute, a graduate program in early childhood education. Born seven years before Michelle's father, she told students that her generation took a certain satisfaction in confronting racism. "Because it was so hard, we thought about ourselves as being made stronger by the struggle." Jim Bowman told his black medical students at the University of Chicago that feeling sorry for themselves would get them nowhere. "In order to compete, you have to be better than the rest," he said. "You can't be just as good. You have to be better. And once you realize that and stop feeling sorry for yourself, then and only then will you succeed."

Like Michelle, Valerie became a lawyer at a blue-chip firm before reporting to City Hall, but she arrived by a different path. She attended the private University of Chicago Laboratory Schools and graduated from prep school in Massachusetts before attending Stanford and the University of Michigan. Well into adulthood, by her own account, she was "painfully shy." In the Chicago legal community in the 1980s, she felt much the same lack of fulfillment that Michelle would experience a few years later. She worked in plush surroundings on the seventy-ninth floor of the Sears Tower, then the world's tallest building. "I had a great office overlooking the sailboats on Lake Michigan, but I was miserable. A friend advised me to think about city government. I was hesitant. I was on my path and, miserable as I might be, it was my path. But Harold Washington had become the first black mayor of Chicago, and I made the move."

GIVEN HER OWN INITIAL DOUBTS, Jarrett was not surprised by the questions posed by Michelle and Barack over dinner. Michelle had long been suspicious of politics and the practitioners of its more unsavory arts. She knew from growing up as the daughter of a Democratic precinct captain the many ways that City Hall could seem remote, at best, from the lives of average citizens. Abner J. Mikva, an independent Democrat first elected to Congress in 1968, put it more bluntly. Until Washington's 1983 election, he said, "there was no reason to be happy with Chicago politics if you were black." Washington's tenure was messy and short. He died at his desk in November 1987 and was followed briefly in office by Eugene Sawyer, appointed by the city council. Now occupying the fifth-floor office was the unproven scion of Richard J. Daley, who had ruled City Hall for twenty-one years without paying more attention than absolutely necessary to his African American constituents.

Barack was a student of Chicago politics, and Jarrett recalled that he had "a certain trepidation" about Michelle working in the highly politicized office of the mayor, where she would not have a network to nourish and protect her. "She was a political novice," Jarrett said. "Was Mayor Daley going to be committed to the kinds of ideas Michelle cared about? Was he going to do only what he wanted to do or was he open to ideas? I think I convinced her that, together, we could do some unique things for the city." As they moved on to other subjects, Jarrett sensed that during the rest of the evening the younger couple was silently assessing whether they should trust her judgment. The experience told Jarrett that "before they were married, they were best friends. They had each other's back."

There was, of course, the matter of money. Although Michelle had concluded that finances would not be the deciding factor in her professional choices, the quest for fulfillment was going to cost her. Leaving Sidley for City Hall meant cutting her salary roughly in half, to $60,000 a year, when she still had significant student loan debt. "It just seemed incredible at the time that she'd leave," Angela Kennedy, her Princeton friend, said. The elder Robinsons had always counseled Michelle and Craig that if they took a job for the money alone, "ultimately you're not going to make enough money to put up with the mess." But even her father, aware before his death of her restlessness, had been concerned about a move. He asked Michelle, "Don't you want to pay your student loans?"

From the time she was young, Michelle had watched her pennies even as she made calculated indulgences. One was a Coach handbag she bought with her babysitting money. Marian gasped when Michelle informed her of the cost, telling her daughter that she would never spend such a crazy amount on a purse. Right, Michelle answered, but you'll go through ten handbags in the time I have this one. In fact, without the debt from her years at Princeton and Harvard, Michelle said she might have gone straight from Sidley to a nonprofit or a grassroots organization, a move she would make less than two years after reporting to City Hall. "City government, in addition to being interesting, was less of a setback to me, and I could manage that," she said. "My stint in city government was amazing. I was very young, but got a lot of responsibility."

AS MICHELLE WAS SETTLING into a job in the Daley administration, Barack was choosing an unconventional path of his own, one substantially less lucrative than the ones open to him as president of the *Harvard Law Review*. He spurned coveted judicial clerkships and six-figure law firm positions even though he could have had his pick. Instead, he cobbled together an eclectic array of jobs and pursuits, to the frustration of his mother and grandmother, who had both known financial hardship. His mother, Ann, in fact, had once been on food stamps. They believed Barack should fill his own pockets before he tried to save the world. Madelyn Dunham, his grandmother, "despaired" about his early choices, said her brother, Charles Payne. "We all thought Barack was going to make a lot of money. Because he was so good, so well spoken and, even with his dark skin, so white. Barack could fit in anywhere and he did. And with a Harvard law degree." He recalled his sister lamenting that she did not know what Barack was doing with his life. "Sometimes she was supporting six or seven people and her great hope was that Barack would make an awful lot of money and there wouldn't be these money problems."

Mikva, then a judge on the U.S. Court of Appeals for the D.C. Circuit, tried and failed to recruit Barack for a clerkship following his law review election. Barack informed Mikva that he intended to return to Chicago and go into politics. His political ambitions at that moment remained unchanneled, but they were not entirely unknown. He was twenty-six years old and on his way to Harvard when he had a drink in Chicago with Bruce Orenstein, an organizer for the United Neighborhood Organization. The two men had worked on a proposal, supported by Harold Washington, to fund South Side neighborhood improvements with fees from local landfills. After they ordered beers, Barack asked Orenstein what he wanted to be doing in ten years. Orenstein said he hoped to be making film documentaries and batted the question back to Barack. In ten years, Barack said, he wanted to be mayor of Chicago.

Back in Chicago after graduation, Barack lived with Michelle on the top floor of the Euclid Avenue house, upstairs from Marian Robinson, as he studied for the Illinois bar exam. As he considered his future, he set out not only to identify opportunities, but to preserve options, including political ones. He wanted no baggage that might later limit his choices or his chances. "Barack thinks about everything. He doesn't do things serendipitously," said attorney Judson Miner, who shared long lunches with Barack that summer of 1991, often at a local Thai restaurant. "He has got one life and he has got to figure out, 'How do I use it effectively? How do I position myself?'" Fresh from the intellectual ferment at Harvard, Barack was discussing with Miner the pros and cons of using the courts as a tool for social change.

Miner, two decades older, had served two years as Harold Washington's corporation counsel, or principal city attorney, and led a small progressive law firm housed in a red-brick townhouse just north of downtown. The firm, then known as Davis, Miner, Barnhill & Galland, made its name in civil rights law while advising nonprofit organizations and doing some general litigation. When he read of Barack's election as *Harvard Law Review* president, Miner had called the law review office. The person who answered essentially told him to take a number. He left a message. Barack telephoned Miner at home that night and surprised him by knowing of his work in the Washington administration. As their conversations unfolded, Miner encouraged him to come to work at the firm, promising that he could choose assignments "that would let him sleep soundly at night." At the same time, it was clear to both men that the activist, anti-establishment nature of the work might carry other costs, two years into what would become the twenty-two-year reign of Mayor Richard M. Daley. Barack "knew full well that the mayor of Chicago was not enamored of us," Miner said, recalling that some people warned Barack against joining the firm. Being labeled an independent Democrat could be a liability, but Barack was sufficiently savvy about Chicago's fractured politics to know that the approach could have the twin benefits of suiting his personality and winning more votes than it would cost him.

Barack signed on at Miner's firm, which represented most of the city's African American aldermen and worked with the Mexican-American Legal Defense and Education Fund. Barack took the side of minority residents in Chicago who challenged Citibank's mortgage practices. He worked on behalf of black voters and aldermen in a St. Louis voting rights case and helped develop a novel legal theory to defend an Illinois redistricting map that had been challenged on grounds of reverse discrimination. For several years, he devoted time to *Barnett v. Daley,* which sought greater representation for African American voters in Chicago. An appellate court said the case tested "the outer limits of minority rights in redistricting situations." Barack also did legal work for the Reverend Arthur M. Brazier's Apostolic Church of God in Woodlawn, as well as a community health network for low-income residents and two nonprofit organizations intent on developing affordable housing. Miner said Barack's efforts were "enormously thoughtful."

As Miner had pledged, the work did feel worthwhile to Barack, and if he did not always sleep soundly, it was more likely due to his tendency to overcommit. While he was working out details with the law firm, he was under contract to write a book that started as a reflection on American race relations and ended as a memoir. He accepted the challenge of registering tens of thousands of new voters and agreed to teach constitutional law at the University of Chicago. And there was his relationship with Michelle, who was not content to be just one item on an endless list. He loved her; it wasn't that. He wanted to be a good partner; it wasn't that, either. He simply wanted to do a lot of things, he wanted to do them well and, it often seemed, simultaneously, a tall order even for Barack Obama.

AS VALERIE JARRETT HAD OBSERVED, he and Michelle were very much a couple, but there was the question of marriage. Not one to wait in silence, Michelle made clear in 1991 that she was ready. "If this isn't leading to marriage, then, you know, don't waste my time," she told him. He usually replied by saying they had a great relationship, why did they need a piece of paper to confirm it? He did not get far with that argument, as anyone who knew Michelle could have told him. "He would sometimes say, 'If two people love each other, what is marriage?'" she recalled. "And I would say, 'Marriage is everything.'" Meanwhile, without telling her, he quietly spoke with her family about his intentions. One night, at a fine dinner for two, ostensibly to celebrate his efforts on the Illinois bar exam, Michelle again raised the question of marriage and began haranguing him for his refusal to commit. Dessert came. On Michelle's plate was a box containing an engagement ring. She was floored, and thrilled. Barack laughed, "That kind of shuts you up, doesn't it?"

THEY WERE MARRIED on October 3, 1992, at Trinity United Church of Christ, the Reverend Jeremiah A. Wright Jr. officiating. It was Barack who first joined the church—motto: "Unashamedly Black and Unapologetically Christian"—near the end of his community organizing days. Trinity offered a sense of community and mission. Anything but staid, it was especially popular with African American professionals, who were variously provoked, entertained, or inspired by Wright's theatrical sermons. One of Barack's signature lines, and the title of his second book, *The Audacity of Hope,* came from Wright—as did trouble for his presidential campaign.

Standing in for their father, Craig walked his sister down the aisle. For the reception, the party moved to the South Shore Cultural Center, formerly the no-Negroes-allowed South Shore Country Club, now owned by the Chicago Park District. In a ballroom facing Lake Michigan, maid of honor Santita Jackson sang Stevie Wonder's "You and I (We Can Conquer the World)," a song Michelle cherished from *Talking Book,* the first record album she owned. It was also the first record album Barack bought with his own money. The bride wore a dramatic white gown. Barack dressed in white tie. The families dined, danced, and got to know each other. Barack's mother, Ann, was there from Indonesia; she was soon to start a job at Women's World Banking, a New York nonprofit that used microfinance to help low-income women establish businesses. Madelyn Dunham, Barack's grandmother Toot, made the trip from Hawaii. "Everybody was delighted with Michelle," said her brother, Charles Payne. "I think people thought Barack was damn lucky to get her."

Family and friends of the bride and groom recognized the strength in each that would help the other. Barack struck Craig as a partner who would appreciate Michelle and earn her respect. Michelle's personality reminded Payne of the inner toughness of Barack's mother and grandmother. For Kelly Jo MacArthur, a colleague of Michelle's at Sidley, the analogy was hydrogen and oxygen: "We understood that together they were going to be so much more than they would have been individually." Harvard law professor David Wilkins recalled the moment he heard that Michelle and Barack were getting married: "I remember thinking to myself, 'That's perfect.' He has somebody who will complement him perfectly, both by being unbelievably supportive and by being unbelievably tough and honest. I said that's what Barack Obama needs. He's going to get every temptation in the world and she is going to ground him."

AT CITY HALL, still in her late twenties, Michelle was one of several staff members with the title of administrative assistant, a moniker that only sounded like a fancy title for secretary. When Jarrett became the commissioner of Planning and Economic Development, Michelle joined her. There, in pursuit of jobs, services, and advancement in neglected neighborhoods, she had money to spend and scissors sometimes just sharp enough to cut red tape. Michelle's job was "operational," as a friend put it. She was a troubleshooter whose interests and assignments ranged widely. She worked on business development, but also on issues connected to infant mortality, mobile immunization, and after-school programs. Her portfolio included black neighborhoods unused to attention from the mayor's office. One question was whom to help. Another was how. An elemental question, said colleague Cindy Moelis, was "whether city government could have a positive impact."

Michelle proved to be flexible and practical, capable of steering her way through a problem, colleagues said. Co-worker Sally Duros recalled Michelle as a "straight shooter" who moved with confidence despite her inexperience. "She was not the type of person who would do you wrong," Duros said, referring to infighting in the bureaucratic vortex of a city powered by politics. "She had a strong value system, a strong sense of what she wanted to do, and so she wasn't going to put up with people who were giving her crap, which is a pretty tough stance to take in City Hall." Duros worked with Michelle on a project designed to improve the distribution of Community Development Block Grants, a program that used federal dollars to attract economic activity to hardscrabble communities. The program was administered downtown, which proved inefficient and ineffective. A better approach, Michelle believed, was to pipe the money directly into the neighborhoods and help recipients avoid the wasteful effects of patronage and graft. "I remember a sense of frustration about the pace of decision making in government and the complexity of the number of characters and actors involved," said David Mosena, Mayor Daley's chief of staff when Michelle was hired. He remained a mentor. "She was 'Let's get this done. Don't tell me stupid stories, don't lie to me, don't BS.' She's got a great laugh and a great smile, but I don't recall her telling a lot of jokes and yukking around the water fountain. She wanted to see things get accomplished."

The city job got Michelle into working-class communities far from the antiseptic corridors of the downtown office towers, and it gave her a taste of the possibilities of government. But it also delivered an education in the obstacles and the infighting that so often inhibited worthy projects. She felt dissatisfied, as she had at Sidley. "It still wasn't enough, because city government is like a corporation in many ways," she said later. Not eighteen months into the job, she was ready to move on. "She wanted to be on her own, wanted direct control, wanted to see the results of her actions," Mosena said. The answer would be an organization called Public Allies.

WHILE MICHELLE WAS WORKING at City Hall, Barack took time to run Project Vote, a drive that added more than 100,000 African American voters to the rolls ahead of the 1992 election. He raised money, hired ten people, recruited seven hundred volunteer registrars, and saturated black radio with the slogan "It's a Power Thing." His goal was to energize Chicago's African American community in ways not seen since Harold Washington's campaigns and help make Carol Moseley Braun the second black U.S. senator elected since Reconstruction. He was calculating where he could make the biggest difference, said his boss, Sandy Newman, who was struck by the way he expanded the scope of the job. Barack raised more money than any of Project Vote's state directors ever had. "It wasn't part of the job description, but it was part of what he did," Newman said. "He did a great job of enlisting a broad spectrum of organizations and people, including many who did not get along well with one another."

For his financial team, Barack turned to John Rogers, a black Princeton graduate, friend of Craig Robinson, and chairman of Ariel Capital, a mutual fund he started. Rogers was joined by John Schmidt, a well-connected white lawyer who had been Richard M. Daley's chief of staff and a candidate for Illinois governor. For grassroots help, he not only developed an array of supporters, but he approached them in ways that made them feel valued. It was no accident that the techniques reflected his community organizing experience. "He went around to each of us individually, sat us down, and said, 'Here's what I'd like to do. It's daunting.' He'd say things like, 'Do you think we should do this? What role would you like to play?' One-on-one is what we call it in organizing. It's such a sign of respect," said Madeline Talbott, chief organizer for Illinois ACORN. "Everybody else just puts out an email and says 'Y'all come.' Barack doesn't do that. He talked to people individually and it's just so different." West Side alderman Sam Burrell called it the most efficient campaign he had seen in twenty years in politics.

There was no doubt that his own political future was on Barack's mind. Asked at the end of 1992 about running for office, he answered, "Who knows? But probably not immediately." He then smiled and said to his interviewer, "Was that a sufficiently politic 'maybe'? My sincere answer is I'll run for office if I feel I can accomplish more that way than agitating from the outside. I don't know if that's true right now." He was just thirty-one years old, but his work at Project Vote earned him attention and contacts. The following year, *Crain's* magazine named him to its list of "40 Under 40" rising stars. The magazine noted his passion for social justice, his commitment to the wonky concept of "building institutions," and his decision to teach classes on racism and the law at the University of Chicago. "If you have the chance to go to Harvard Law School, it's no accomplishment to be a partner in a law firm," Barack said. "It's an accomplishment to make a difference."

Despite its praise, the magazine also demonstrated that he might not have the ideal name for the political future he was beginning to imagine for himself. The brief story spelled his name incorrectly three different ways, identifying him as "Borock Oboma" in the first paragraph and "Barock" in the third.

THE IDEA THAT BECAME Public Allies, the organization Michelle would join after leaving City Hall, emerged from the minds of two young women looking to attract members of their generation to public service. Vanessa Kirsch and Katrina Browne polished the concept in November 1991 at a Wingspread conference in Wisconsin, where one invitee was Barack Obama. On the roster of participants, he listed his address as the Robinson bungalow and his profession as "writer." At first, the new organization took a very Washington name, the National Center for Careers in Public Life. But as several participants drove away from the conference in a van, they discussed how young people so often were seen as public enemies. Public Allies was born. They received an early grant from Elspeth Revere at the John D. and Catherine T. MacArthur Foundation and, soon, federal backing for a program that would provide training and public service apprenticeships. After the first class of "Allies" graduated in Washington, D.C., in 1993, Kirsch and Browne looked to start a chapter in Chicago. In search of an executive director, they turned to Barack, who had become a board member. He pointed them toward Michelle and stepped down from the board as the search proceeded.

The job called for creating a mentoring and internship program. The director would build a curriculum, recruit a board, raise money, choose a diverse array of Allies—thirty per year at first, then forty—and find positions for them. Four days a week for ten months, Allies served as apprentices. Some went to City Hall, where Michelle retained her contacts, while others worked with education programs, youth development agencies, economic development projects, and environmental organizations. One lawyer did legal work in a Hispanic neighborhood. Time on Fridays and some evenings was reserved for leadership training sessions and team projects. Jacky Grimshaw, a former Harold

Washington aide, was one of the board members who interviewed Michelle. Grimshaw's first impression: "Boy, she's tall!" Michelle spoke confidently about how to structure and administer the program and how to connect with young people from a wide array of backgrounds. "She was quick to smile. She was very personable. She had that warm personality, which is what we were looking for," Grimshaw said. "We were talking about young persons who needed guidance and we needed a young person to be their leader. She was a perfect fit." Grimshaw also felt sure that anyone admitted to the Chicago program would see that Michelle was direct. There would be no trifling.

As Michelle developed the leadership training and community organizing components of Public Allies, she drew on the ideas of John McKnight and Jody Kretzmann, Northwestern University faculty members who had spotted a flaw in the way outsiders typically perceived the neighborhoods they were trying to help. As they saw it, do-gooders too often failed to appreciate the abilities of people they were trying to help and too rarely drew on them for solutions. Calling their model ABCD, for Asset-Based Community Development, they said solutions needed to be crafted from the inside out and the ground up. Projects should build on neighborhood efforts in order to avoid becoming beholden to outsiders, their theories and their money. A key goal was self-reliance. Only if the project were practical and made sense to the residents would it be sustainable. And only if it were sustainable would it make the neighborhood stronger.

Michelle introduced these concepts to Allies she recruited from across Chicago, adopting a training manual published by McKnight and Kretzmann. Each Ally received a copy during "Core Week," when the concepts were introduced and the coaching and team building began. The manual proposed ways of asking questions and listening, an approach considered preferable to marching into a neighborhood to prescribe and command. It emphasized outreach to residents who had ideas and energy but did not carry the label of "community leader." Successful workers would recognize a suffering neighborhood as a glass half empty, but work with it as a glass half full. They would see assets, in other words, not just deficits.

Kretzmann met for coffee with Michelle as she developed her curriculum. He saw how the theories resonated with her understanding of Chicago's black neighborhoods. Once the Allies were on board, Michelle recognized how much she enjoyed the mentoring and teaching side of the job, recalling the role that elders had played in her own life and the importance of reaching back, just as she had discussed in her Princeton thesis and all those conversations at Harvard. It all fit. "My mom and dad would always say that if just a few people would come back and live in the community, it would make all the difference in the world," Michelle said. "We talked about it a lot."

At each step in her life, Michelle stretched herself in fresh ways, moving from South Shore to Whitney Young to Princeton to Harvard to Sidley to City Hall. The same was true at Public Allies. Most important, she was in charge. The organization was not prestigious, the job was not lucrative, and there was no guarantee of success, but it was hers. "The first thing that was mine and I was responsible for every aspect of it," Michelle said. "It sounded risky and just out there." She described her three-year stint as executive director as the first time in her working life that her talents and her passions converged. In 1995, not two years after starting, she oversaw a budget of $1,121,214, with about half coming from the U.S. government through what had become the AmeriCorps program. Summing up her experience after reaching the White House, she said, "I was never happier in my life than when I was working to build Public Allies."

MICHELLE ATTRACTED young Allies from DePaul University and the University of Chicago and a few from Harvard Law—but also from housing projects such as Cabrini-Green and tough neighborhoods like Little Village and North Lawndale, where the Reverend Martin Luther King Jr. had tried nearly thirty years earlier to expose the wrongs of poverty and discrimination. Some Allies came equipped with only a high school equivalency degree. A few had criminal pasts. Many had trouble at home and little experience with high standards. "She didn't care if you were one of the cool kids. She cared if you were one of the kids who really wanted it," said Jobi Petersen Cates, a member of Michelle's first Public Allies class. "She would pick the one on the edge of her seat. It had nothing to do with intellect or breeding, but that they were itching to get going. That quality of enthusiasm and earnestness was more important than just about anything else." In bringing a wide range of people together, one of Michelle's essential goals was to teach them to walk in unfamiliar worlds, a challenge for sheltered and unsheltered young people alike. "There's nothing funnier," she once said, "than to watch a kid who believes they know it all actually come across some real, tough problems in communities that test every fiber of what they believe." On the flip side, she said, nothing was finer than to see a kid without a high school diploma sit with college graduates and realize that his "ideas are just as good, sometimes even better." Bethann Hester, a white woman who started as an Ally and then joined the staff, recalled that "the most powerful thing she ever taught me was to be constantly aware of my privilege. . . . Michelle reminded me that it's too easy to go and sit with your own. She can invite you in a kind of aggressive way to be all you can be."

If Michelle had only been seeking diversity of palette, she could have chosen well-mannered candidates of varying complexions from comfortable middle-class households. That would have been the path taken by a person "who wants to just look like they're doing well," said Cates, a white Northwestern graduate. But that was not Michelle's approach. "She would always take risks on kids from lower-income neighborhoods—and in Chicago, that correlates with race—just to make sure that they got a chance. She was willing to drive them hard and take extra time, in addition to being executive director, to push these guys. These aren't easy guys to work with." Cates continued, "The people who had privilege coming into the program, she didn't encourage us any less, she didn't push us any less hard. But I got the sense that part of her mission in life was to push all these incredible people not to be left behind, not to let their lives go. She was hard on them, but also didn't kick them out."

Krsna Golden was just eighteen when Michelle recruited him for her first class of Public Allies after meeting him at a leadership awards ceremony. By his own account, he had been in trouble—dabbling in petty crime, running with tough guys, being expelled from school—before straightening up. He was smart, equipped with a big vocabulary and a probing mind, and he was a talker. Michelle complimented him on his ability to parse problems, but she wanted him to come up with solutions. "She has a knack for building as she destroys. If she's addressing one of your weaknesses, she makes it a priority to fill in the gaps with strengths and how, if you apply yourself, you can change," Golden said. "She doesn't let people off the hook . . . but there's a charisma in there that makes you feel like, even if you're in a hard place with her, you're okay. You're still safe, you're still like one of her cubs." Under Michelle's tutelage, Golden won an award that took him to Washington and she helped him travel to Germany on a cultural exchange. He was uncommonly bright, she assured him, but he was in danger of wasting his talents. "She told me, 'Go back to school, go back to school, go back to school.'" *Stanford*, she said, *Stanford*. Two decades later, still smart, still verbal, still thoughtful while cutting hair on the South Side, Golden sometimes wished he had listened and made it past barber college.

Public Allies sought to teach young recruits how to build relationships and achieve results. This happened during their internships, but also at training sessions in the group's downtown offices. It was in the weekly group sessions, Michelle said, "where the magic happened." Sometimes, however, the magic was slow in coming. One night during her third year, a discussion grew so heated that an angry Ally punched a hole in an office door. When Michelle arrived at work the next morning, she did not expel him. Rather, she explained to him that his anger was self-defeating because it removed his ideas from the discussion. "You can't be punching doors here. You lose credibility when you do that. You know what I mean?" she said, according to Leif Elsmo, a long-time colleague. Another day, Michelle sat down with an Ally who was charming but often showed up late, equipped with an elaborate excuse. The young man said he had woken up that morning and taken a drink of booze from the refrigerator. His troubled mother had then asked him to stay home and help her. "I hear that," Michelle replied, "but that can't be how you're defining your choice for the morning. . . . Here are some ways you need to deal with that. This is about you."

It was a tense moment with a kid who was "pretty far gone," said Julie Sullivan, a staff member in the room that day. She said Michelle delivered a message that was equal parts firm and empathetic. "And not in a ridiculous 'Pull yourself up by your bootstraps' way," Sullivan said. "It was realistic and understanding of what people are going through." Michelle did not, however, have polite words for black Allies who tried to use race or upbringing as a crutch, particularly if their pitch included bad-mouthing white people for a lack of understanding. In a page she could have taken from the Shields and Robinson family handbooks, she made clear that young black men had no room for error. A mediocre white kid might be able to skate by on charisma or connections, his competence assumed or his failings forgiven. Less so his black counterpart. Cates, who later worked in City Hall, remembered supervising an African American Ally who did not do his work and resisted earnest efforts to keep him on track. She reported the trouble to Michelle, who "didn't indulge that situation for five seconds. She didn't use kid gloves."

Sullivan was impressed with Michelle's ability to be "understood anywhere" as she crossed back and forth among Chicago's disparate realms. She recalled drives in Michelle's Saab. "We'd go from some burned-out shithole on the West Side, where she's talking to really scary people, and then we'd go downtown to a meeting" with Daley's chief of staff. "She was unafraid to put issues on the table and talk about them clearly. She always had a really, really uncanny combination of unruffled calm and extreme clarity about what needed to happen next, whether it was in the small picture or the big picture. You couldn't not respect her, even if you were mad at her."

When issues of race and class surfaced in Public Allies staff discussions and training sessions, as they always did, Michelle had little tolerance for dogma or meandering debate. Getting from Point A to Point B was her focus, an approach that would become a hallmark of her professional and political life. Paul Schmitz, who ran the Milwaukee office of Public Allies at the time, said Michelle was the person who would say during a discussion, "That's nice, but we've got to get things done."

·   ·   ·

ONE OF MICHELLE'S TASKS was to find places for the Allies to work. To do so, she drew on a web of relationships that grew with her membership in the 1993 class of Leadership Greater Chicago, an extracurricular networking and education program for promising young leaders in business, government, and other city realms. Valerie Jarrett and John Rogers preceded her in the program. Among those who followed were Barack's close friends Marty Nesbitt and Eric Whitaker; Craig's first wife, Janis Robinson; and future U.S. education secretary Arne Duncan. Michelle persuaded an array of colleagues and friends to talk with Allies, with one eye toward the Allies' edification and another toward their future employment. One of the speakers she imported was Barack, steeped in the ways of community organizing and something of a student of John McKnight's in the 1980s. For all of Barack's talent, some Allies and staff members later laughed ruefully that they had barely noticed him, so dazzled were they by Michelle. To them, he was just Michelle's husband, a likable guy doing some teaching and lawyering somewhere in town.

What Barack brought to the Public Allies training sessions, however, was his knowledge of grassroots organizing and his experience of trying to pry results from City Hall. He often talked about power dynamics. "It was very focused on thinking about how you build constituencies within communities," said Kelly James, who attended the training as an Ally in 1997, after Michelle left the organization, and later took Barack's classes at the University of Chicago Law School. Teaching in Socratic style, he challenged his charges to examine their own thinking and move beyond conventional battle lines, many of them established during the civil rights era. He counseled them to find places where interests intersected and opponents could agree. And, as Michelle always counseled, to focus laser-like on results. Disadvantaged communities cannot be seen as "mere recipients or beneficiaries," Barack said in 1995. "The thrust of our organizing must be on how to make them productive, how to make them employable, how to build our human capital, how to create businesses, institutions, banks, safe public spaces—the whole agenda of creating productive communities. That is where our future lies. The right wing talks about this, but they keep appealing to that old individualistic bootstrap myth: Get a job, get rich and get out."

In a heartbeat, the Ivy-educated couple could have gotten out. They chose to stay, but both began looking for a bigger set of tools. In the end, both chose to work from the inside. For Barack, the answer was politics. In 1995, he decided to run for the Illinois state senate, concluding that a political perch offered leverage that community organizing could not deliver. For Michelle, it was bridge building at the University of Chicago, a privileged and remote institution that tended to see the surrounding South Side black community as an unkempt and threatening backyard. She viewed her role as breaking down barriers between the university and the community. Beyond the sense of purpose, the job paid better, with fewer obligations than Public Allies, where she had served as chief cook and bottlewasher for three nonstop years. And, too, she and Barack wanted children.

The Public Allies job "just wasn't big enough," said board member Sunny Fischer, who hosted a goodbye party at her home, where Michelle grew "a little teary." Barack and Michelle had been guests there before, enthusiastic and witty partners in political conversation with the Fischers and an eclectic array of friends whom they also saw elsewhere in Chicago, including former Weather Underground leaders William Ayers and Bernardine Dohrn. The two had become academics and Hyde Park Little League baseball regulars after years on the lam. Fischer remembered Michelle at the farewell party as "the warmest I've ever seen her." She was thirty-two years old and she felt she had accomplished much, designing the Chicago operation and building it from the ground up. Michelle had loved creating an organization, particularly this one, but Fischer never thought she would stay forever. "I always got the sense," Fischer said, "that there was a restlessness in her, that there was something else she could be doing that had more impact, that could move social change a little faster."

# EIGHT

# A Little Tension with That

For decades, the relationship of the overwhelmingly white University of Chicago to the surrounding African American community had been unsavory bordering on hostile. It seemed an unlikely place for Michelle to land. "I grew up five minutes from the university and never once went on campus. All the buildings have their backs to the community," she said. "The university didn't think kids like me existed, and I certainly didn't want anything to do with that place." Yet here she was in September 1996 reporting to work on the inside as director of a student community service program—"as fate would have it," she mused, recognizing the irony. She set out to bridge gaps of privilege and race, often finding herself walking in parallel worlds, serving as a kind of translator. The job had its bureaucratic side, but it provided freedom to devise projects that might make a difference. "What I found was that working within the institution gave me the opportunity to express my concerns about how little role the university plays in the life of its neighbors," Michelle said. "I wanted desperately to be involved in helping to break down the barriers that existed between the campus and the community."

The university's neo-Gothic spires had long stood like watchtowers along the green Midway Plaisance, where the first Ferris wheel carved steam-powered circles in the air during the 1893 World's Columbian Exposition. The Midway bequeathed its name to carnivals around the country, and the university, bankrolled in the 1890s by John D. Rockefeller, became a magnet for smart and sober scholarship. The intellectual ferment was recognized with dozens of Nobel Prizes and one of the country's most famous scientific discoveries. In a squash court beneath Stagg Field on December 2, 1942, Manhattan Project researchers produced the first self-sustaining atomic reaction, a precursor of nuclear weapons. It was said only half in jest that modern-day undergraduates would look up from their readings of Hegel and Dostoevsky and declare that the Hyde Park campus was the place "where fun goes to die."

After World War II, the university found itself doubtful about its future in Hyde Park, roughly seven miles south of downtown Chicago. In some ways, Hyde Park was a rare oasis in a segregated city, a place where middle-class black families could aspire to live alongside similarly situated white people. But as the population pressure from the Great Migration grew and barriers fell, administrators feared an influx of low-income African American residents that would repel white faculty and students. The university endorsed restrictive covenants and channeled money to white neighborhood organizations that fought to keep black people out. As Chicago courts stopped enforcing the covenants and the Supreme Court outlawed them in 1948, the university's white leadership gave thought to abandoning the leafy cloisters. "The gutters were full of half-pint whiskey bottles and crime was on the increase," declared one 1950 report, describing a two-block stretch of 55th Street that included 53 bars. By one estimate, 20,000 white people moved out of Hyde Park and neighboring Kenwood in the next six years, while 23,000 nonwhites moved in. Between 1940 and 1956, the nonwhite population went from 4 percent to 36 percent.

University leaders, in the end, chose to stay, but they took radical steps to create a buffer zone. Their method was urban renewal. "Social engineering on a vast and unprecedented scale," wrote University of Chicago historian and dean John W. Boyer. Drawing heavily on federal funding, the administration oversaw plans that displaced hundreds of small businesses and thousands of residents. The largest of the projects led to the demolition of buildings where 4,371 families lived. In all, 2,534 of those families were black, most living on low incomes. "Of those who did not return to Hyde Park, the percentage of blacks was substantially greater than whites," Boyer reported. By 1970, the university and an array of government agencies had spent $100 million on the effort. In place of the old dwellings, the university erected housing unaffordable to most of the black families who had lived there. The goal was to generate real estate prices high enough to "regulate both the number and 'quality' of blacks remaining," wrote historian Arnold R. Hirsch. The project prompted critics to scoff that "urban renewal" really meant "Negro removal." One of the university's most attention-getting opponents was Saul Alinsky, the community organizer whose mobilizing methods influenced Barack.

As the years passed, the University of Chicago endured, but only slowly adapted. On the summer day in 1976 when Boyer, a white man, was awarded his Ph.D., his working-class mother revealed her surprise that he had chosen to study at the university. She had been told by her mother that "people like us don't go there." Boyer explained, "It's not that the university wasn't racist. Of course it was. But it also sent signals to working-class whites—the sense of drawing up the drawbridge, of creating a moat." In racial terms, the leadership and the student body looked nothing like Chicago, much less the South Side. One of the country's most elite universities resided smack in the middle of the largest concentration of African Americans in the country, yet it often seemed to residents that the institution treated its neighbors as a species to be catalogued or, worse, ignored. As late as 1994, soon before Michelle started her job, Barbara Bowman recoiled when someone spoke of the university's "illustrious history" at a campus meeting. The erudite Bowman, an expert in early childhood development and the mother of Valerie Jarrett, could not resist setting the record straight. "You know," she said to the man, "I appreciate what you are saying, but you have to remember that as a black woman I was excluded from the leadership of that 'wonderful' community you are talking about. And so it is very hard for me now to think that it really was all that wonderful back then. In fact, it makes me very angry when you say that it was all that wonderful without recognizing that it excluded *any* black people from positions of leadership."

. . .

THIS TERRITORY WAS NOT unfamiliar to Michelle. She knew something about upper-crust universities from her time at Princeton and Harvard. She also had a snapshot of life on the Hyde Park campus from her mother, who worked as a secretary in the university's legal office in the 1970s, when Michelle was in high school. From the start in September 1996, it was clear to her thirty-two-year-old self that she had work to do. "I know the community does not trust and understand the university, and the university does not trust and understand the community," Michelle said. "Until you can bridge those gaps and hear out both sides and understand why they are afraid, you can't really have a conversation." Her job, director of the University Community Service Center, was a new one that owed its creation to a faculty-student committee that found the university wanting on volunteerism. She aimed to have an impact on nearby neighborhoods, as well as on University of Chicago students. To succeed, she needed to design programs and sell them to her superiors, including Boyer. She also had to find agencies and organizations where students would be welcomed and put to good use.

Michelle built a small staff and set out to increase student awareness of the city's geography, arranging bus tours beyond the Hyde Park campus. She developed a summer internship program infused with lessons from Public Allies and the Asset-Based Community Development approach. Called Summer Links, the project provided ten-week internships that included half-day training sessions on such themes as race relations, welfare reform, affordable health care, and homelessness. Separately, she developed a series of monthly conversations on urban issues, including one timed to coincide with the hundredth anniversary of the U.S. juvenile justice system. The panel included a former juvenile offender, a priest, and a teacher who had worked in a Cook County youth detention center. Barack was on the panel, as was William Ayers, the former Weather Underground leader and federal fugitive, who had recently published a book on juvenile justice. "Students and faculty explore these issues in the classroom, but it is an internal conversation,"

Michelle said. "We know that issues like juvenile justice impact the city of Chicago, this nation and—directly or indirectly—this campus. This panel gives students a chance to hear about the juvenile justice system not only on a theoretical level, but from the people who have experienced it."

Her interest in reaching out to African American residents beyond the campus, however, was largely incidental to the university's focus on its own students. Boyer was looking for ways to attract and satisfy students at a time when the university was struggling. Improvements in the surrounding communities and the residents' attitudes toward the university were welcome, but secondary. When Boyer became dean of the college in 1992, the University of Chicago was accepting nearly 75 percent of applicants. In his first year, 15 percent of the freshman class flunked out or dropped out, a statistic that would have gotten him fired at Harvard or Yale, "like, within two minutes." Soon after university president Hugo Sonnenschein announced plans to increase student enrollment by one thousand, Boyer was glad to see Michelle walk through the door. He reasoned that her concentration on community service would give the college "a broader and more diverse profile, in the sense that our students came here not just to read Shakespeare and take calculus and debate the meaning of life well into the night." Michelle was "convinced that the university was too inward-looking," he said. He called their efforts "a convergence of what she wanted to do and what I was interested in doing."

In Michelle, Boyer saw someone as pragmatic as he was, and as oriented toward results. Smart and tough, he said, persistent without being abrasive, "quite strategic in getting the resources she needed to accomplish her goals." Given the university's racial history, he was pleased to find that she seemed more interested in plotting the future than rehashing the past. He would not have been sympathetic to the argument that the university owed something to black South Side residents because of its history of bigotry, what he called a "reparations mentality." She recognized that the community service program needed to benefit the students and "not just make us into some kind of NGO that would go out and do good in the neighborhood. I wasn't interested in investing money in things that did not have some payoff for the education of our students. My job is dean of the college. I'm not here to save the world, even though I hope the world could be saved."

Michelle expanded the scope of her office during her five years on the job. Many African American students, seeking a campus haven, considered the community service center a gathering spot, said Melissa Harris-Perry, who taught a course on black women's social activism and relied on Michelle and her colleagues to find internships for her students. "They really saw her as an ally and a voice for their interests," she said. Until Michelle arrived, Samuel Speers, associate dean of the university chapel, had served as the primary adviser to the community service center. He recalled her as savvy about navigating the university hierarchy and the politics of the surrounding neighborhoods. "She would wade right in. She's not afraid of conflict, but she also doesn't seek it. You had the sense she had the ear of the university president and the ear of the wider community." Race was never far from the discussion. "You cannot do community-based work in Hyde Park and not engage questions of race," Speers said.

Michelle did not win all of her battles. She argued unsuccessfully that students should get course credit for their volunteer work, a position that Arthur Sussman, who had hired her, considered "toxic" among university faculty. "It was possible that other elite schools were doing it," he said, "but that was not going to be the Chicago way." Overall, Michelle sought to expand the service program while ensuring that neighborhood organizations gained from the collaboration. That lesson stuck with Leif Elsmo, who followed Michelle to the university from Public Allies and worked with her for nearly fourteen years. She taught him to be "sensitive about the promises we made to communities," he said. "We had to fulfill what we said we were going to do, because communities have been failed so many times."

IN 1995, as Michelle was about to welcome her third class of Public Allies and start the job search that would take her to the university, Barack was still doing several things part-time. He enjoyed decent success, but was hardly a player. He taught law at the University of Chicago. He handled public interest cases at Davis, Miner, Barnhill & Galland. He conducted community organizing training sessions, and he served on boards of directors, including the Woods Fund, the Joyce Foundation, and The Chicago Annenberg Challenge. When he published *Dreams from My Father* that year and did a reading at 57th Street Books in Hyde Park, he was the amiable guy from the neighborhood, not a literary star. A grand total of nine people showed up for a reading at Eso Won Books, the leading African American bookstore in Los Angeles. Many years later, the reissued *Dreams* would make Barack and Michelle rich, with several million copies in circulation, but the first printing did not sell enough copies to earn back its $30,000 advance. For all of the buzz about his talents, it was safe to say that Barack's great promise remained unfulfilled. No one felt it more than he did.

Alice Palmer, in 1995, was the state senator from the Illinois 13th Senate District, a swath of South Side turf that included the Obamas' Hyde Park apartment and stretched south and west into tougher working-class neighborhoods. Progressive and well connected, she tended her political garden and faced no foreseeable electoral threat. She spotted a chance to move up the ladder when Representative Mel Reynolds, a black former Rhodes Scholar, became the latest in a string of Chicago politicians to be indicted, in his case for having sex with a sixteen-year-old campaign volunteer and obstructing justice. His conviction and forced exit meant a special election. When Palmer entered the congressional race, Barack declared himself a candidate for her state senate seat, but not before exacting a promise that if she lost, she would not jump back into the senate contest. He also lent his name to her congressional candidacy, an awkward proposition. Her principal opponent was Jesse Jackson Jr., son of a certain other Jesse Jackson, the Operation PUSH leader and two-time presidential candidate, and brother of Michelle's friend Santita Jackson, who had sung at the Obamas' wedding just three years earlier.

Palmer lost the Democratic primary to Jackson, placing third with just 10 percent of the vote. She reiterated that she would not try to keep her senate seat, but her reluctance soon disappeared. With the backing of South Side stalwarts including the elder Jackson and Emil Jones Jr., the Democratic leader of the state senate, she declared that she would run for her old job, after all. "Michael Jordan can come back and so have I," she asserted. A number of her loyalists leaned on Barack to drop out. He refused. The way he saw it, a deal was a deal. After Palmer's team cut corners in collecting signatures to qualify for the ballot, Barack challenged the validity of her petitions and those of the three other Democratic candidates. The board of elections disqualified all four. He was in. The November election against a pair of minor candidates would be just a formality.

Michelle had doubts about the wisdom of a political career. Indeed, she had no truck with politicians or their ways, but she worked hard for Barack's election. "Michelle was determined to run a top-notch campaign, no cheesiness," said Barack's campaign manager, Carol Anne Harwell. "She brought elegance and class to the campaign. She was the taskmaster and she was very organized, even if she didn't know a lot about politics then. When we started collecting petitions, we would set a goal for, say, two hundred signatures that day. There would be a blizzard and we would come back with only a hundred and fifty. Michelle would be furious and we'd have to go out and get the rest." Asked why she went along with Barack's plans despite her misgivings about the profession, she answered, "Because I believe in him."

"How can you impact the greatest number of people? We always debated this," Michelle said, "because my view was, well, you can also impact a lot of people if you're the principal of a high school or a great teacher or a great dad. I wasn't a proponent of politics as a way you can make change." Her mistrust of politics was deeply rooted and would linger long into Barack's political career. "We as a family were extremely cynical about politics and politicians," her brother Craig said. That view was all but inescapable on the South Side in the second half of the twentieth century, a period scarred by schoolhouse inequity, economic neglect, and political corruption that no single politician could fix. Abner Mikva, former Democratic congressman and federal judge, traced Michelle's dissatisfaction to race. "Michelle had a black life in black Chicago," he said. "You can't have any brains and not be influenced in a big way, and pretty negatively."

Beyond her doubts that meaningful change could be produced in the well of the Illinois senate, Michelle worried that Barack would be eaten alive. "I don't trust the people in there," she told interviewer Mariana Cook in May 1996, two months after the primary. "I think he's too much of a good guy for the kind of brutality, the skepticism." Michelle also saw Barack's political aspirations as a threat to the life she wanted for herself—a life fundamentally comfortable, controlled, and private. "When you are involved in politics, your life is an open book and people can come in who don't necessarily have good intent," she said. "I'm pretty private and like to surround myself with people that I trust and love." She wanted to make a difference, sure, but she also wanted a full partner. She saw children in her future, as well as travel and quality time with friends and family. These happened to be among the things Barack had said he wanted when they married, but his entry into politics threatened to create a much different reality. He would be even less available. Gone, in fact. It was one thing for him to surprise her by saying he wanted to go to Bali for a month to work on *Dreams* soon after their California honeymoon. It would be quite another for him to drive three hours to Springfield most Mondays for who knew how many years. And that was if he did not make the jump to Congress or the Senate in far-off Washington. In 1996, Michelle rated the chances as "strong" that Barack would make politics his career. "There is a little tension with that," she acknowledged, but she was trying to keep an open mind. "In many ways, we are here for the ride, just sort of seeing what opportunities open themselves up."

FOR SOMEONE WHO HAD imagined himself running Chicago one day, and maybe the country, the life of a small-time pol in Springfield, Illinois, would seem to hold all the allure of a ten-cent prize at a boardwalk arcade. Yet, his first election behind him, Barack tore into his new work, determined to learn the riddles of power even as he discovered that being a junior member of the minority party gave him virtually no influence. Entrenched senators rolled their eyes at his transparent ambition and his floor speeches, which tended to be lofty and overlong. Some of the fiercest jabs came from black colleagues who mocked his biracial ancestry, his Harvard education, and his home turf in the bourgeois precincts of Hyde Park. To them, he seemed all too eager to accept half a loaf. "He was not any kind of mystery to me," declared Rickey Hendon, a senator from Chicago's suffering West Side. "My friends with all those degrees like to compromise and live in nice rich neighborhoods. They don't see things as they really are. You're not as willing to compromise if you see the poverty all the time." It was a riff that played in different ways depending on the audience. Barack, after all, did tend to see the middle ground as the most likely path to progress, not to mention the functioning of the republic. He was pragmatic. In statewide and national campaigns, that would be seen as a net positive. But in large segments of the black community in the years ahead, the criticism would be rendered in shorthand: Was he black enough?

For all of his pleasure in the power of words, Barack took little satisfaction in scoring rhetorical points if he lost on substance. Sound bites, he said in a 1996 interview, were "dishonest." They masked complexity and disguised "the very real conflicts between groups that are going to have to be resolved through compromise." He had considered the possibilities and limitations of politics for many years before he entered the arena, and he had received no shortage of warnings. Back in Hawaii, former Chicago newsman Frank Marshall Davis advised him that black students emerge from college with an "advanced degree in compromise." A decade later, when Barack gave up community organizing, John McKnight agreed to write a law school recommendation letter, but not before he tacked on a lecture about the price Barack would pay. The cost of surrendering his grassroots role, McKnight predicted, would be the loss of his intellectual integrity. "What you have been doing every day is creating polarities, conflict, and confrontation in order to get to the table. You are a person taking a position that you believe in and that feels a certain way," McKnight told him. "I can tell you that if you get into the heart of politics, the important thing you will be doing is compromise. You will be an architect of compromise."

The discussion had deep roots in African American political history. Modern variants of black political style and substance stretched from the calculations of the Chicago aldermen known as the Silent Six through Whitney Young, the Reverend Martin Luther King Jr. and the Black Panthers, to the post–civil rights era maneuverings of the Congressional Black Caucus and a raft of big-city mayors. Barack and Michelle shared a conviction that racial grievance, however righteous, was not a winning strategy. Results were what mattered most. "We have no shortage of moral fervor," Barack told Hank De Zutter of the *Chicago Reader* in 1995. "The biggest failure of the civil rights movement was in failing to translate this energy, this moral fervor, into creating lasting institutions and organizational structures."

Policymakers could find common ground, Barack argued, if only they could dispense with their partisanship and their invective long enough to discover it. "What if a politician," he told De Zutter as he began his state senate run, "were to see his job as that of an organizer, as part teacher and part advocate, one who does not sell voters short but who educates them about the real choices before them? As an elected public official, for instance, I could bring church and community leaders together easier than I could as a community organizer or lawyer. We would come together to form concrete economic development strategies, take advantage of existing laws and structures, and create bridges and bonds within all sectors of the community."

Barack knew he was making a choice and he could guess how various constituencies might react. He had been leading training sessions and doing some lawyering for the Association of Community Organizations for Reform Now, the grassroots anti-poverty group better known as ACORN. As he entered politics, he alerted ACORN organizer Madeline Talbott that he would have to move toward the political center to be effective. "I may not be as liberal as ACORN members want me to be," he told her. "I may believe some things and do some things that ACORN members believe are too middle of the road." Talbott, inclined to cut him some slack, took his remarks as evidence that he wanted to make a difference and was realistic about what it would take. "He felt the need to give me fair warning, which was unusual. People just thought Barack was so talented even then," she said. Friends sometimes nudged him and said he would be president some day. "He would pooh-

pooh it always and say, 'Don't be ridiculous. I'm just trying to pay off some bills. Leave me alone.'"

THE FRESHMAN SENATOR FOUND his way, partly as a result of the good offices of Emil Jones, a gruff and savvy arm-twister and former city sewer inspector. Although the senior senate Democrat had backed Palmer, he watched with grudging respect as Barack refused to quit the race. In Springfield, Jones saw potential in his eagerness, his work ethic, and his smarts. The freshman struck him as "very aggressive," if a touch naive. "He thought you could press a button and it would be done." Over time, Barack developed a style that was methodical, inclusive, and ever pragmatic. "He wasn't a maverick," said Cynthia Canary, a lobbyist on good-government issues. "There were other legislators I would turn to if I just wanted to make a lot of noise."

Typically spending three nights a week in Springfield, Barack dropped by the ubiquitous cocktail hours that capped the statehouse workday and made friends and occasional allies over golf and poker, leaning across ideological lines to befriend Republicans and some of the more conservative Democrats. Even there, his innate caution came through. One regular at a poker game of legislators and lobbyists described Barack as competitive, yet supremely careful and hard to read. "One night, we were playing and things weren't going very well for me," recalled Larry Walsh, a white state senator. "I had a real good hand and Barack beat me out with another one. I slammed down my cards and said, 'Doggone it, Barack, if you were a little more liberal in your card playing and a little more conservative in your politics, you and I would get along a lot better.'"

Barack, pushed forward by Jones, registered bipartisan successes, negotiating the first ethics reform in Illinois in twenty-five years and brokering a bill that established mandatory taping of interrogations and confessions in death penalty cases. When he was not working, he often had long telephone conversations with Michelle. He remembered storytelling and laughter, "sharing the humor and frustrations of our days apart." Michelle remained unpersuaded. Politics as practiced in Springfield struck her as petty, oily, and, frankly, beneath him. "Barack," she would tell him, "this business is not noble."

MICHELLE GAVE BIRTH to Malia Ann Obama, their first daughter, on July 4, 1998, about eighteen months after Barack started commuting to Springfield. Malia took her middle name from Barack's mother, who had died of cancer in November 1995 at the age of fifty-two. Home after the legislative session ended, Barack described the period after Malia's birth as "three magical months." They sang songs to the little girl and snapped a passel of pictures. But when the legislature resumed work, Barack returned to his weekly commute, two hundred miles each way. The burden of having an often absent husband grated on Michelle, who now had an infant at home and a demanding job at the University of Chicago. Michelle switched to a schedule with fewer hours and lower pay. She welcomed the flexibility, but the workload seemed much the same. "It's like, oh, so you take half a salary and you do the same amount of work," she said. "They don't take anything off your plate." Although the legislature was considered a part-time job, and Barack was usually in Chicago from Thursday to Monday with summers off, he often had evening meetings to attend, legal work to finish, or law school papers to grade. "The strains in our relationship began to show," he said.

Money was becoming an increasing worry for Michelle, despite a joint income that would reach $240,000 in 2000. They were not hurting, but the dollars were going out nearly as fast as they were coming in, paying for a full-time nanny, a mortgage, and student debt. "We didn't pick cheap ones," she once said of their college and law school choices. They paid more each month toward their student loans than they did toward the 2,200-square-foot Hyde Park condominium that they purchased in 1993 for $277,500. Their down payment was about $111,000, with a small assist from Barack's grandmother. And now there was private school and college to think about. Barack continued to care little about money, sometimes forgetting to seek reimbursement for his senate expenses until reminded by an aide. He had no expensive hobbies or tastes and draped his thin frame in a wardrobe of standard-issue suits, business shirts, black sport shirts, and khakis, waiting until his clothes were threadbare to buy anything new. He played golf, but typically on public courses, including the links at the former South Shore Country Club. After he was elected to state office, he sold a black Saab 900S for $2,500 to one of Michelle's former Public Allies, partly to put himself behind the wheel of a more politically palatable American-made car.

IF YOU WANT to be president, it does not take long to realize the stairway to the stars is not in Springfield, even if the Illinois legislature was Abraham Lincoln's first elective office. Barack considered himself burdened by "chronic restlessness," and barely two years into his state senate tenure, he was feeling antsy. The Chicago mayor's office was out. Richard M. Daley won his fourth term in February 1999. His grip on power seemed firm after he swamped U.S. Representative Bobby Rush, whose reputation dated to his past leadership of the Chicago chapter of the Black Panther Party. But Rush's defeat gave Barack an idea. On the eve of a new century, he saw Rush as a 1960s throwback who was not half the congressman his constituents deserved. Against the advice of friends, mentors, and Michelle, he announced that he would challenge Rush, a fellow Democrat. Only after Barack had entered the race in September 1999 did he do any polling. When he did, he quickly learned that Rush, whatever his troubles against Daley when he ran citywide, enjoyed 90 percent name recognition and a 70 percent approval rating in his district. Only one in nine voters had ever heard the name of his challenger, Barack Obama.

In a district that was 69 percent African American and where the median household income was $24,140, Barack promised "new leadership." But he never found his voice, or at least a voice that would connect with working-class black voters who saw no good reason to turn Rush out of office. For all of his brainpower, Barack was wordy on the stump. He struck many preachers, politicians, and business leaders as being too full of himself and in too much of a hurry. Rush and a well-worn challenger named Donne Trotter, a fellow state senator, delighted in attacking Barack for his Hawaiian roots and his bohemian tastes. In this audience, it was not a plus to teach constitutional law at the University of Chicago or to claim the title of community organizer after growing up on a Pacific island. Barack "went to Harvard and became an educated fool. . . . We're not impressed with these folks with these eastern elite degrees," Rush said that year, striking the not-black-enough chord. "Barack is a person who read about the civil rights protests and thinks he knows all about it." Lu Palmer, a black radio host, alluded to Barack's time at Harvard and said, "If you so impress white folks at these elite institutions, and if they name you head of these elite institutions, the *Harvard Law Review*, that makes one suspect." Trotter dispensed with code and asserted that "Barack is viewed in part to be the white man in blackface in our community."

Barack protested that the appeal to street cred stereotypes sold the African American community short and sent a lousy message to black kids that "if you're well educated, somehow you're not keeping it real." Michelle felt the same way, later explaining her frustration with African Americans who "use intellect and race as a way to drive a wedge between certain people in their own community." The attack reminded her of her girlhood: "You talk a certain type of English and then you have to cover that up on your way to school so you don't get your butt kicked. You know, we grew up with that." But even if Barack could find a winning message, which was doubtful, he never had much chance to engage. On October 19, a month after Barack entered the race, Rush's twenty-nine-year-old son Huey—named for Black Panther Party founder Huey P. Newton—was shot during a robbery outside his South Side home. He died a few days later.

Rush was heartsick and Barack had no choice but to curtail his campaigning. A few weeks later, Rush's elderly father died. It was January before the campaign resumed in earnest. By then, Barack had left himself open to criticism that verged on ridicule. He was in the habit of flying to Hawaii for the Christmas holidays with Michelle to enjoy the tropical weather and see his aging grandmother, Madelyn Dunham. Amid campaign demands and a legislative debate about gun regulations, his staff urged him to forgo the trip. But he tried to squeeze the vacation into five days between Christmas and New Year's, vowing to see Toot and "reacquaint myself" with Michelle and eighteen-month-old Malia. On the home front things were going no better than the electoral contest. "Tired and stressed," he said, "we had little time for conversation, much less romance."

While they were gone, Republican governor George Ryan called the Illinois legislature into special session to vote on a gun control bill that had his support and the backing of the Democratic caucus. On the day Barack and Michelle were scheduled to fly back to Chicago, Malia had a high fever. The family stayed put. Barack missed the vote, and the gun bill failed by five votes. Rush and Trotter were quick with criticism, and the *Chicago Tribune* called out Barack and several other politicians by name in a searing editorial that began "What a bunch of gutless sheep."

Barack returned home to the headlines two days later, "a wailing baby in tow, Michelle not speaking to me." Although his absence had not decided the gun bill's fate, he now had to fight the impression that he had been sipping drinks on a Hawaiian beach while the legislature fought to make Chicago's streets safer—at the very time Rush was a public face of the pain of gun violence. Barack, aware that he would lose, woke up every morning with a sense of dread, "realizing that I would have to spend the day smiling and shaking hands and pretending that everything was going according to plan." To compound his misery, President Bill Clinton jetted to Chicago to campaign for Rush and make a commercial reminding listeners of Huey Rush's death. By the time Barack arrived at his election night party, the media had already called the race. He lost by thirty points.

THE THUMPING SENT Barack into a funk, what Springfield aide Dan Shomon called his "morose period." Barack hated the fact that he had been so certain and so wrong. It did not help that he had spent more than he took in, even lending $9,500 to his campaign. The race, he said, left the household "more or less broke." He not only had to ask donors for cash to retire $60,000 in campaign debt, he had to face the people who said "I told you so." Or who bit their tongues and said nothing, which in some ways was worse, for it was easy to imagine their silent pity or disdain. You might attribute defeat to circumstances beyond your control, Barack said, but "it's impossible not to feel at some level as if you have been personally repudiated by the entire community, that you don't quite have what it takes, and that everywhere you go the word 'loser' is flashing through people's minds." The defeat bruised his formidable confidence. He began to wonder whether it was all over, this experiment with politics. Maybe he did not have the skills to match his ambition. Maybe Michelle was right when she urged him to find something a little more respectable, a little more lucrative, and a lot more family friendly.

The clouds were slow to part. Hoping it would be "a bit of useful therapy," several friends urged him to go to the August 2000 Democratic National Convention in Los Angeles, where Democrats would send Vice President Al Gore into battle against Texas governor George W. Bush. Although he had set aside that summer for catching up on his legal work and spending time with Michelle and Malia, he decided to go. When he landed at the Los Angeles airport, he made his way to the Hertz counter and handed over his American Express card. "I'm sorry, Mr. Obama, but your card's been rejected," the clerk said. "That can't be right," he replied. "Can you try again?" He had reached his credit limit. On the telephone, he worked out something with American Express, but the week improved little from there. He was not a delegate, and the chairman of the 189-member Illinois delegation said he could not spare a floor pass. To see the show, Barack occasionally accompanied friends into convention center skyboxes, "where it was clear I didn't belong." After watching most of the first two nights of political speeches on television monitors, he decided he was wasting his time. Long before Gore's nomination and acceptance speech, he caught a flight home.

DURING THEIR COURTSHIP and the early years of their marriage, Michelle and Barack had set out to braid their independent lives into a unified whole, finding synergy in the work they did and the ambitions they shared. One of the marriage's strengths, Barack said in 1996, four years after their wedding, was their ability to "imagine the other person's hopes or pains or struggles." Michelle said Barack helped her "kind of loosen up and feel comfortable with taking risks and not doing things the traditional way." Barack, meanwhile, understood Michelle's pull toward "stability and family, certainty." In their different approaches, however, they recognized the potential for friction. "How we approach that tension is going to be really important," Barack said.

One source of strength was the way they pulled together amid early difficulties in starting a family. Julie Sullivan, Michelle's Public Allies colleague, described this period as particularly hard on Michelle and recalled that Barack was "really wonderful," even with his mother dying at the same time. "I've seen that relationship go through some life stresses," Sullivan said, "and they've always just had a really nice way about each other." But as parents, Barack said, they "argued repeatedly" about how to balance their obligations to work and family. At times, Michelle felt she was all but singlehandedly raising Malia and running the household while leading the student community service office. This did not feel like an equal partnership. This was not the life she had expected to lead. She told him more than once, "You only think about yourself. I never thought I'd have to raise a family alone."

On June 10, 2001, Michelle gave birth to daughter Natasha. By that point, on the eve of Barack's fortieth birthday, the downward slide was clear. "My wife's anger toward me seemed barely contained," he said. He had vowed not to be the shirker his father had been. Indeed, his role model was Michelle's father, Fraser Robinson, said his friend Valerie Jarrett. And yet it was as a husband and father that he was most disappointed in himself. Michelle's displeasure forced him to confront the ways he was falling short. His old-school assumptions about gender roles contributed mightily, although he did not see it at first. "As far as I was concerned, she had nothing to complain about," he said. He believed Michelle was being unfair. "After all, it wasn't as if I went carousing with the boys. I made few demands of Michelle—I didn't expect her to darn my socks or have dinner waiting for me when I got home. Whenever I could, I pitched in with the kids. All I asked for in return was a little tenderness. Instead, I found myself subjected to endless negotiations about every detail of managing the house, long lists of the things that I needed to do or had forgotten to do, and a generally sour attitude. I reminded Michelle that compared to most families, we were incredibly lucky. I reminded her as well that for all my flaws, I loved her and the girls more than anything else. My love should be enough, I thought."

When Natasha, known to one and all as Sasha, was just three months old, Barack and Michelle got the scare of their lives. One night, they heard her crying. It was not unusual for her to wake up, but "there was something about the way she was crying," Barack said later. They called the pediatrician, who met them at his office in the morning. Examining Sasha, he correctly suspected meningitis, a potentially fatal inflammation of the membranes surrounding the brain and spinal cord, and immediately sent them to the emergency room. "We were terrified," Michelle said. Sasha, still tiny, underwent a spinal tap. As nurses administered antibiotics, her parents stayed close for three days, "not knowing whether or not she was going to emerge okay," Barack said. "I can't breathe," he told Jarrett when she visited. His world "narrowed to a single point. I was not interested in anything or anybody outside the four walls of that hospital room—not my work, not my schedule, not my future." The antibiotics worked. Sasha recovered. So, too, did their marriage, if more slowly.

IT WAS AT ABOUT this time that Barack most seriously considered an exit from politics. The legislative process felt incremental, the fundraising deadening, the banquets always too long. "The bad food and stale air and clipped phone conversations with a wife who had stuck by me so far but was pretty fed up with raising our children alone." Michelle was openly questioning his priorities, and he wondered if it was time to move on to "more sensible pursuits, like an athlete or an actor who had fallen short of the dream." The door was open at the University of Chicago, where he was teaching popular constitutional law courses. Students loved him, and he enjoyed the mental gymnastics of challenging their exuberant thinking. A tenure-track appointment would connect him more closely to the intellectual life of the Hyde Park campus and deliver lifetime job security. Instead of the long commute to Springfield, he could walk to work. Yet it was an insular world and he was hardly inspired by the legal writing expected of the professoriat. They didn't call it the ivory tower for nothing. Another door led to corporate law, where he could pull down big money in a hurry. Sidley & Austin and any number of other firms would hire him in a flash and gladly pay him a salary deep into six figures. But a decade after he first rejected that path, he saw nothing to suggest that he would find it any less soul-deadening. The same was true of a host of opportunities in business and finance that could have been his for the asking.

Philanthropy, however, caught his eye. The Joyce Foundation, which distributed about $55 million a year to projects connected to such challenges as schools, urban violence, campaign reform, and the environment, was looking for a new president. The job would pay well, it would be close to home, the hours would be manageable, and the work could have an impact. Barack was already on the foundation board, so he knew the players and the mission. He prepared seriously for his interview with board members, working on a strategy with Dan Shomon, his senate aide.

But when he went into the meeting, he was shaking. Shomon said Barack was more fearful that he would get the job than that he would be turned down. Yes, he had been frustrated at times with Springfield and he had felt "completely mortified and humiliated" by the loss to Rush. He was anxious to please Michelle, make time for his daughters, and add some order to his life. But winning the job would mean quitting the legislature. His political career might be over. Board members sensed his uncertainty. One told him, "For God's sake, Barack, this is a great job. But you don't want it." Indeed, he realized, he did not.

Michelle, for all of her frustration, felt his anguish. "It's hard to look at somebody with the talents and gifts of Barack and say, 'Go do something smaller than what you could do,'" she said. Also watching the drama unfold was Maya Soetero-Ng, Barack's half sister, named for poet Maya Angelou the year after the publication of *I Know Why the Caged Bird Sings*. Barack agonized, honestly unsure whether to give politics another chance, Soetero-Ng recalled. "And at the same time," she said, "I think he felt a stirring within and the sense that he was destined for something bigger."

# NINE

# Just Don't Screw It Up

The University of Chicago brass gathered under a tent with local notables in November 2001 to break ground for a $135 million state-of-the-art children's hospital. Michelle was there in her new role as director of community outreach for the university medical center. Barack dropped by, a local state senator. Through the crisp morning air came the voice of a man on a bullhorn. His name was Omar Shareef, and he was leading a band of protesters who said the university was not giving enough business to African American construction workers. Michelle had only been on the job for a few weeks, but she calculated that this was a community affairs matter. She walked up to Shareef and invited him to talk things over.

Michelle had been on maternity leave after Sasha's birth, giving little thought to her career, when the new job opportunity came up. Susan Sher and Valerie Jarrett, who had opened doors for her at City Hall a decade earlier, proposed her for the role. Sher was the medical center's general counsel and Jarrett sat on the board of trustees. Michelle felt torn about working while the girls were young, but her reluctance freed her to seek a substantial salary and, especially, a flexible schedule. The day of the interview, with no babysitter, Michelle bundled up Sasha, who was still nursing, and took her along. "This is my life," she told hospital president Michael Riordan. Charmed and impressed, he met her terms. She could hardly say no. Not only did the job suit her practical side, it carried the explicit goal of helping South Side communities, a mission largely absent from the University Community Service Center post that she had occupied for the previous five years. It would be her most ambitious job yet. It would also be the last time that her work and her identity would be so independent of Barack.

Michelle saw the largely undefined hospital perch as a way to build on her earlier work and help connect the university with the surrounding neighborhoods. She told colleagues when she was hired that the university hospital, with its staff of 9,500, needed to send people into the community. Borrowing from her Asset-Based Community Development experience, she scheduled staff volunteer days in grittier parts of the city and took trustees and senior staff on field trips. Stepping from a bus at a chosen intersection, the passengers would see in one direction a street of broken-down and boarded-up houses, suggesting decay. Then she would have them turn to see a block of renovated homes with sparkling windows and fresh paint. At her instigation, the hospital supported a Christmas pageant at the Reverend Arthur Brazier's Apostolic Church of God and participated in Bud Billiken Day and the country's oldest African American parade, started in 1929 by *Chicago Defender* publisher Robert S. Abbott. Michelle's father and her uncle Nomenee had belonged to the Billiken club as young children. She also took part in the medical school's summer pipeline program, designed to draw under-the-radar minority students toward science and medicine. Urging them to study hard and recognize where education could take them, her message echoed her work at Public Allies and presaged her efforts as first lady. The heart of her pitch, said a colleague, was an admonition not to be a victim of circumstance.

Explaining her goals for the medical center, Michelle wrote in 2005 that the University of Chicago needed to adjust its priorities. "It's not enough to be at the forefront of medicine if we're not respected in the community," she said, maintaining that the university talked "too much about the negative and we don't embrace all the great assets of the community that surrounds us." Yet she had words of advice for neighboring black residents, too. "The community also has to be open to the new direction and new leadership that is here. And sometimes we have a tough time stepping away from the past." She included herself in both camps: the *we* of the university and the *we* of the black community. Describing herself as "a regular little black girl from the South Side," she said, "Somebody like me, who has feet in both worlds, can help to bridge the gap and create solutions."

WHEN MICHELLE DISCUSSED minority hiring with Omar Shareef, the man with the bullhorn, she brought colleagues from the university. Shareef brought fellow activists. One of his partners, the Reverend Gregory Daniels, was decidedly unimpressed. He complained afterward that the protesters were being fobbed off on underlings "who have jobs to protect or do not have the best interest of blacks at heart." He cited Michelle specifically and demanded that she be removed, claiming that she was working with the university leadership to split the African American community. He called it the "Willie Lynch method," a reference to an apocryphal 1712 story about a Virginia slave master who advocated divide-and-conquer tactics to keep black people in line. Michelle persisted, however, and within a month of the protest, the medical center reached a deal with Shareef's African-American Contractors Association. In return for his promise to end the protests, the university pledged to deliver business to qualified minority-run companies.

Minority contracting was a concern of Michelle's during a stint as head of the Chicago Transit Authority's citizens advisory board— Jarrett was CTA chairman at the time—and it would become a significant part of her portfolio during the seven years she spent at the medical center. She saw the strategy as a way to support businesses run by African Americans, Hispanics, and women, and to pump money directly into surrounding communities. To strengthen the contracting program, she hired the Chicago Urban League's diversity monitor, Joan Archie, a CTA consultant. The hospital made progress and won awards. From the 2002 to 2008 budget years, 42.9 percent of the medical center's spending on new construction went to firms run by minorities or women, a total of $48.8 million, according to university figures. In Michelle's final year on the job, the medical center channeled another

$16.2 million to such firms for goods and services, or 5.7 percent of the overall budget.

Kenneth P. Kates, the hospital's chief operating officer, recalled a meeting where the white owner of a large firm thought he could nod agreeably and ignore the minority hiring requirements. Michelle, however, was "tenacious," he said, and the owner got no more business until he met the hospital's demands. Kates called her a quick thinker who brooked no nonsense yet managed to be collegial. "She would not shy away from taking a position. No matter what it was, you always knew where she stood," Kates said. "She was very good at laying out why she thought she was right. Some people come across as holier than thou. That was not her at all. She never took herself too seriously." After Michelle got to work, he said, the hospital's attention to the black community became "staggeringly different."

Michelle also pushed for greater access to the exclusive University of Chicago Laboratory Schools, which Malia and Sasha attended from an early age. She was among a group of board members convinced that "Lab," a private school coveted by parents across the city, had wrongly reduced its commitment to diversity by race and class and needed to do more. Opponents countered that allocating more slots for diversity would hurt the university's recruiting efforts by limiting spaces for the children of faculty and staff. "Let's just look at the facts," she would say, according to John Rogers, a friend and fellow board member who would later become chairman. "She has this enormous passion to make sure the Lab School remains this diverse, welcoming place for people of color and people of different socioeconomic backgrounds. It took a lot of courage and conviction to push the agenda. Not only to push the diversity, which can be uncomfortable in a public setting, but also the admissions policy."

SMILING AND SHAKING HANDS, Barack worked a Chicago ballroom in the summer of 2003. The event was a fundraiser for Bill Clinton's charitable foundation, but Barack saw it as a chance to talk up his latest quixotic quest: a run for the U.S. Senate. Few people had heard of

Barack at that point, surely not enough to make a cerebral Hawaiian-born man named Barack Obama just the third African American elected to the Senate since Reconstruction. "I saw Barack working the crowd," recalled Geoffrey Stone, a constitutional law scholar and University of Chicago provost. "He was going from person to person, taking their elbows and shaking their hands and looking them in the eye. I was watching this for a while and I thought, 'Ach, what a waste.'"

What chance did he have, this unproven black pol, one of fifty-nine Illinois state senators, a sometime lawyer and law professor who so recently had lost a congressional race by thirty percentage points? It was highly unlikely that he would make it through the primary against a large field of Democrats who were prominent, wealthy, or both. Even if he did, it seemed probable that he would face a moderate Republican incumbent with deep pockets who wielded the advantages of office. Stone found himself standing next to Barack at the shrimp bowl. "Why are you wasting your time on this?" Stone asked him. "Watching you work the crowd like this, it's sort of pathetic. Why don't you make a decision, commit yourself. I think you really could have a career as an academic. I think we'd give you an appointment." In other words, Stone was thinking, *Make something of yourself.*

"He took my elbow," Stone recalled, "and looked me in the eye and said, 'Geof, I really appreciate that. I hear you. I know what you're saying. But I really feel I have a responsibility and a sense of opportunity and I just have to give it a try.' I remember thinking as he turned back to go into the crowd, *What a putz.*"

Much had changed since Barack's jarring defeat in the 2000 congressional race and his flirtation with the Joyce Foundation. He had climbed out of his funk. He had won a third term in Springfield and was driving around the state, learning about places that bore no resemblance to the South Side. Among them were the long reaches of Illinois that lay closer to Memphis and Little Rock than to Chicago. If he were going to build a winning coalition and win statewide office, he would need voters in places like these. He was nothing if not self-critical, and he intently studied his mistakes in the Bobby Rush debacle. He worked on his delivery, which had sometimes come across as wonkish or disdainful. He redoubled his legislative efforts and made the rounds of the pols, preachers, and money people in Chicago who had scoffed at his candidacy. If he decided not to give up on politics, maybe losing to Rush would turn out to be a lucky break, like flunking a midterm with six weeks left until the final. "A wake-up call," said Bill Daley, the mayor's politically minded younger brother. "He didn't seem to get bitter. He didn't turn on people. He engaged people more and worked it. And then he decided to throw the bomb, and rightly so."

Before he could enter the U.S. Senate contest, Barack not only had to convince himself, he had to persuade Michelle. It was late 2002 when Valerie Jarrett hosted a meal among friends to discuss the prospect. She included Marty Nesbitt, a businessman and one of Barack's closest friends, and John Rogers, a childhood friend of Jarrett's and a backer of Barack's as far back as the 1992 Project Vote campaign. Michelle was there, too, of course. She held the most important vote and seemed to be leaving little doubt about how she would cast it. "Walking into that lunch we were resolved we were going to talk him out of this," Jarrett said. "No one thought it was a good idea, Michelle being the most clear that it was a bad idea." Looking back, Michelle recalled her reservations: "It was, gosh, this is going to be painful and hard for me, for us. Let's not go through this again."

Yet Barack was equally resolved. He told the group that he had spotted a golden opening this time and explained why he thought he could top a field that would eventually number seven Democrats and eight Republicans. He laid out his reasoning and acknowledged the risk, especially the blow to his reputation and his prospects if he became a two-time loser. He promised Michelle that it was up or out. "I'm willing to gamble. I know if I lose, I'm probably done," he said. "I have the most to lose and I have confidence that I can win—and I can't do it without you guys."

The friends were sold. "He's really hard to say no to," said Jarrett, who agreed on the spot to be his finance chair. Nesbitt and Rogers, meanwhile, pledged to work their connections to raise money. Early in his deliberations, Barack had totaled up the money he thought he could raise. When he added the column of numbers, the figure barely reached $500,000, roughly what he had raised in losing to Rush in a district with fewer than one-twentieth of the state's population. Barack once mused that Michelle gave a green light to his candidacy "more out of pity than conviction."

For Michelle, getting to yes meant overcoming yet again her doubts about politics and her dislike of political life. She had to trust Barack not to repeat his miscalculations in running for Congress. She was also considering their finances. An improbable victory would mean setting up a second household in Washington when she was already feeling pressed. "I don't like to talk about it, because people forget his credit card was maxed out," she told writer David Mendell. "My thing is, this is ridiculous. 'Even if you do win, how are you going to afford this wonderful next step in your life?' And he said, 'Well, then I'm going to write a book, a good book.' And I'm thinking, 'Snake eyes there, buddy. Just write a good book, yeah, that's right. Yep, yep, yep. And you'll climb the beanstalk and come back down with the golden egg, Jack.'"

The couple took out a second mortgage just to get through the campaign season. On the eve of the Democratic primary in March 2004, the *Chicago Sun-Times* placed Barack's net worth between $115,000 and $250,000. When Michelle joked that losing might not be the worst outcome, friends knew she was not entirely kidding. Michelle said wryly about her role as political wife, "It's hard, and that's why Barack is such a grateful man."


MICHELLE, IN FACT, had been doing a lot of thinking about her life amid the gloom of Barack's losing run for Congress and the dark period that followed. The frustrations crystallized anew after Sasha was born, a period when Barack was traveling the state. She was torn. She felt the familiar tension of wanting to be a good mother and not spread herself too thin. At the same time, she had a sense of purpose, two Ivy League degrees, and plenty of unfulfilled professional drive. She had excelled at work in ways that Barack had not. She had built the Chicago office of Public Allies from scratch, and she had designed and run many components of the University of Chicago's community service program. At the hospital, she inherited a staff of two and would build a twenty-three-member team. It sometimes bothered her that Barack's career always took priority over hers. Like many professional women of her age and station, Michelle was struggling with balance and a partner who was less involved—and less evolved—than she had expected.

Michelle was sometimes in tears "because she couldn't figure out how to juggle everything that she was doing," Barack recalled. Competing visions of herself were at war, he said, "the desire to be the woman her mother had been, solid, dependable, making a home and always there for her kids; and the desire to excel in her profession, to make her mark on the world and realize all of those plans she'd had on the very first day that we met." She was certain that she was performing neither of her main roles well. Yet for all of her frustrations, Michelle was not prepared to leave the workforce and become part of what *The New York Times* dubbed the opt-out generation—educated, accomplished women who quit white-collar jobs to raise their children. Beyond her attraction to professional pursuits, including the chance to preserve her independence and her earning capacity, she doubted she had the temperament to tend children full-time. "Work is rewarding. I love losing myself in a set of problems that have nothing to do with my husband and children. Once you've tasted that, it's hard to walk away," she said. "The days I stay home with my kids without going out, I start to get ill. My head starts to ache."

Michelle realized she was spending an awful lot of energy tugging on Barack to be different: to put his socks in the hamper, hang up his coat, put the butter away, stop smoking, be home with the family. All the while, she was working at the university, running the household, embracing her extended family, and acting as chief organizer of the lives of two small girls. It was exhausting. Through the fog of fatigue, it dawned on her that she was staking too much on Barack changing in ways that seemed increasingly unlikely. He did have a guilty conscience about his absences, he told friends, suggesting that she could probably coax or cajole a few minor adjustments. But she decided the better course was to address what she could hope to control. That meant, first of all, her own frame of mind. "Figuring out how to carve out what kind of life I want for myself beyond who Barack is and what he wants," Michelle said. "I cannot be crazy, because then I'm a crazy mother and I'm an angry wife."

One epiphany came as she stewed over the fact that she was always the one who dragged herself out of bed to feed Sasha. The couple operated on different circadian rhythms, with Michelle usually asleep by 10 p.m., if not earlier, and Barack savoring the quiet apartment into the wee hours, writing, reading, or watching sports. "I am sitting there with a new baby, angry, tired and out of shape," she said. "The baby is up for that 4 o'clock feeding and my husband is lying there, sleeping." It dawned on her that if she escaped to the gym, Barack would have to get up to feed Sasha. So, she started slipping out of the house before dawn to drive to a gym in Chicago's West Loop. By the time she arrived home, Barack would have Sasha and Malia up and fed.

Michelle made peace with the situation, and with Barack. If he was not home because he was out raising money or commuting to a distant job, "it didn't mean he wasn't a good father or didn't care. I saw it could be my mom or a great babysitter who helped. Once I was okay with that, my marriage got better." She said looking back, "The big thing I figured out was that I was pushing to make Barack be something I wanted him to be for me. I believed that if only he were around more often, everything would be better. So I was depending on him to make me happy. Except it didn't have anything to do with him. I needed support. I didn't necessarily need it from Barack."

Her mother's advice helped. "Don't sweat the small stuff. Get up. Get over it. He's a good man. Don't be mad at him," Marian Robinson told her daughter. Reflecting on her daughter's journey, Marian offered a theory about what it took for Michelle to come to terms with her marriage. In Marian's view, Michelle needed to accept the fact that her husband was different from the father she revered. "I just think that's a normal thing that people go through," she said. "The sooner you realize that's the case, the more successful you are."

Barack did some reckoning of his own and saw how unthinking he had been. Although he had lived much of his life in the households of strong women—his mother, his grandmother, and now Michelle—he tended to float above the details, never quite focusing on how certain things got done or where the burden fell. He realized that Michelle was right. The burden most often fell on her, "no matter how much I told myself that Michelle and I were equal partners, and that her dreams and ambitions were as important as my own." His role at home? "Sure, I helped, but it was always on my terms, on my schedule. Meanwhile, she was the one who had to put her career on hold." Whether it was scheduling activities for Malia and Sasha or staying home when the girls got sick or the babysitter cancelled, the task usually fell to Michelle, whatever the implications for her professional life. To some men of his generation, raised in the 1960s and 1970s by women who worked, such observations amounted to commonplaces. Barack, however, was a little slower on the uptake. At the end of what Michelle called "an important period of growth in our marriage," he attributed their endurance to "Michelle's strength, her willingness to manage these tensions and make sacrifices on behalf of myself and the girls." He said he had learned his lesson.

NOT THAT HE WOULD be around much during the Senate campaign. As the race intensified, Barack became less and less available. There was cash to raise, by the million. There were rings to kiss and umpteen hands to shake. Nearly every Sunday, it seemed, he headed to a black church on the South Side or West Side, laboring to build credibility among working-class African Americans who had largely rejected him in the campaign against Bobby Rush. He sounded a lot less Ivy League one day after the Internet bubble had burst, when he talked about U.S. economic troubles during an appearance at Pleasant Ridge Missionary Baptist Church: "We ain't seen no recovery on the West Side. We don't see no recovery in East St. Louis. . . . If there ain't no jobs, there ain't no recovery." The campaign was difficult, and it often seemed that the arrow pointed down. Barack called press conferences that nobody attended. He sat through church services and union meetings where no one acknowledged his presence. He sometimes drove alone downstate, a trip lasting hours, to find just two or three voters waiting for him.

Yet he found himself happy. Really happy. "Freed from worry by low expectations, my credibility bolstered by several helpful endorsements, I threw myself into the race with an energy and joy that I'd thought I'd lost. . . . I felt like working harder than I'd ever worked in my life." Adjustments to the work-life balance, it seemed, would wait.

At first, Barack's six Democratic opponents seemed to pose an array of threats. Dan Hynes was the scion of a prominent Chicago political family close to the Daleys. Blair Hull was a wealthy newcomer who would spend $29 million of his own money on the race. Gery Chico was a former Chicago School Board president who had served as Mayor Richard M. Daley's chief of staff. Joyce Washington was an African American health care executive who threatened to split the crucial black vote. With Hull and Hynes considered the frontrunners, Michelle offered a pithy comment about Illinois politics and the meaning of Barack's candidacy a few days before the Democratic primary. She urged her audience to send a message to the political establishment and to African American children alike. Introducing Barack at the Community Fellowship Missionary Baptist Church, she said, "I am tired of just giving the political process over to the privileged. To the wealthy. To people with the right daddy."

Month by month, the campaign gathered steam, fueled by Barack's legislative success in Springfield, his elbow grease, and, perhaps most of all, his ability to win favor among progressive Democrats, most of them white. Some of the very qualities that doomed his congressional candidacy in a predominantly African American district were now working in his favor. In a stroke of good fortune, it also turned out that his opponents were less formidable than they appeared, with Hynes a lackluster campaigner and Hull undone by divorce records that alleged he had cursed, punched, and menaced his former wife.

In the final weeks, Barack broke through. His campaign husbanded its cash for a burst of television advertising when voters were most likely to be making up their minds. The message, a harbinger of campaigns to come, centered on branding Barack as ethical and upbeat, a skilled legislator who worked across party lines in Springfield and would labor to change the tone in Washington. A new advertising slogan would become his signature: "Yes, we can." At first, Barack did not like the line. It sounded corny. But strategist David Axelrod thought it had a certain simple assertiveness, and Michelle believed it would work with African American voters disenchanted, as she was, with Illinois politics. "She understood before he did that it had some power," said Forrest Claypool, a Chicago politician and consultant who worked in Axelrod's firm. The television ads began running and Barack "took off like a rocket."

On March 16, 2004, Barack swamped the rest of the Democratic field. Surprisingly, given the large field, he piled up 53 percent of the vote and avoided a runoff. He also regained his swagger.

THEN CAME THE BIGGEST BREAK of a very big year: John Kerry, his party's prospective presidential nominee, invited Barack to deliver the keynote speech at the Democratic National Convention in Boston. "We believe he represents the future of the party," Kerry spokeswoman Stephanie Cutter said simply. Barack would get twenty minutes in the brightest of political spotlights just four years after he failed to land a floor pass to the festivities. For a politician who had never won an office higher than state senator—who had *lost* his only race for Congress—the odds of landing the assignment were incalculable. But there he was, putting Kerry's name into nomination against President George W. Bush and pulling his own name, which writer Scott Turow once said "rhymes uncomfortably with Osama," out of obscurity. On July 27, 2004, as he prepared to speak, he had butterflies. Michelle gave him a hug, looked him straight in the eye, and said, "Just don't screw it up, buddy." And they laughed.

Screw it up he didn't. The soaring speech by the unknown politician caught the delegates by surprise, producing paroxysms in Boston's Fleet Center and Democratic households across television land. "This guy's going places!" one newscaster crowed. David Mendell, in the hall for the *Chicago Tribune,* recalled the scene: "Michelle sees this happening and she has tears streaming down her cheeks. I'm sitting in the crowd and a woman next to me is crying, bawling her eyes out. She just keeps screaming, 'This is history! This is history!'"

"Tonight is a particular honor for me because, let's face it, my presence on this stage is pretty unlikely," Barack began. He traced his family history to a village in Kenya and a small town in Kansas. Piecing together bits of his Senate stump speech and the values that drove him into public service, he spoke of the social contract and a politics greater than the partisanship and petty sniping that defined the era.

*If there's a child on the South Side of Chicago who can't read, that matters to me, even if it's not my child. If there's a senior citizen somewhere who can't pay for their prescription and having to choose between medicine and the rent, that makes my life poorer, even if it's not my grandparent. If there's an Arab-American family being rounded up without benefit of an attorney or due process, that threatens my civil liberties. It is that fundamental belief—I am my brother's keeper, I am my sister's keeper—that makes this country work. It's what allows us to pursue our individual dreams, yet still come together as a single American family.*

Barack went on to tell the crowd that "there's not a liberal America and a conservative America, there's the United States of America. There's not a black America and white America and Latino America and Asian America. There's the United States of America." He insisted that he was not speaking of "blind optimism." Rather, he was issuing a call to service grounded in the historical argument that progress comes when people fight for it. He wove a sense of optimism for the country into the narrative of his life, borrowing a line passed among black churches, and invoked by his pastor at Trinity United Church of Christ, the Reverend Jeremiah A. Wright Jr. It was the "audacity of hope."

*It's the hope of slaves sitting around a fire singing freedom songs; the hope of immigrants setting out for distant shores . . . the hope of a skinny kid with a funny name who believes that America has a place for him, too. Hope in the face of difficulty, hope in the face of uncertainty, the audacity of hope: In the end, that is God's greatest gift to us, the bedrock of this nation, a belief in things not seen, a belief that there are better days ahead.*

The cheers rang on and on. The next day, the circus began. Barack was in demand, for interviews, television appearances, campaign stops, autographs. He was becoming a pop icon. Debra Messing, star of one of the most popular sitcoms on television, *Will & Grace,* soon had a memorable dream on the show: she was showering with the candidate and he was "Ba-racking my world." His Senate gamble—one more shot, up or out—could hardly be paying off bigger. He was famous, and he and Michelle would soon be rich, with the reissue of *Dreams from My Father* and his signature on a $1.9 million contract to write two more books. The looming question was no longer whether he would reach the Senate, which seemed a foregone conclusion. It was whether he would seek the presidency.

IF BARACK WAS a helium balloon, Michelle was the one holding the string. In public, she developed a wry patter designed to affirm his humanity and just maybe keep his ego in check. "Absolutely the messiest person in the household," she said when Oprah Winfrey interviewed them. She called his home office "the hole." When he interjected, she replied, "You had dirty clothes on top of the basket this morning. And I'm just like, 'There's a basket with a lid. Lift it up. Put it in.'" Besides, she would say later, the country needed leaders "who have their feet on the ground." Michelle also tried to put a ceiling on voters' expectations, for their benefit and her husband's. "Barack is not our savior. I want to tell it to the whole country and I will if I get the opportunity," she informed a crowd at Illinois State University. "There are many of us who want to lay all of our wishes, fears and hopes at the feet of this young man, but life doesn't work that way and certainly politics doesn't work that way." It was an observation that would prove prescient.

Michelle played her part on the campaign trail, speaking up for Barack, standing in for him, raising money. She and the girls accompanied him when he went to the summer home of Penny Pritzker to seek the support of the prominent Chicago Democrat, businesswoman, and Hyatt heiress. Very occasionally, the Obamas campaigned as a foursome, an experiment in family togetherness that proved challenging.

Michelle was no more convinced than before that politics was a worth-while pursuit, at one point that year calling it "a waste of time." But he was in it to win it, as the saying goes, and so was she. On the stump, she vouched for his motives by contrasting her own disdain for the profession with Barack's abiding faith. "I didn't believe that politics was structured in a way that could solve real problems for people, so you can imagine how I felt when Barack approached me to run for state senate," she told the audience at Illinois State. "I said, 'I married you because you're cute and you're smart, but this is the dumbest thing you could have ever asked me to do.' Fortunately for all of us, Barack wasn't as cynical as I was."

In a campaign where Barack's race mattered to voters in myriad ways, Michelle also offered a sturdy defense of his commitment to urban African Americans. The shorthand question confronting the Hawaiian-born, Harvard-educated candidate—*Is he black enough?*—replayed the caricature and the criticism advanced by Barack's opponents in the congressional campaign. Michelle would have none of it. Leaning heavily into her own history, she told a Chicago interviewer, "I'm as black as it gets. I was born on the South Side. I come from an obviously black family. We weren't rich. I put my blackness up against anybody's blackness in this state, okay, and Barack is a black man. And he's done more in terms of meeting his commitments and sticking his neck out for this community than many people who criticize him. And I can say that because I'm *black*."

IN HYDE PARK, Michelle continued to carry the weight of what used to be called homemaking, taking care of the girls' welfare while also pressing forward with her work at the University of Chicago. She started her fourth year at the medical center—her ninth at the university—and continued to build a loyal, tightly knit team. Looking back, she said she loved her work, but it was never easy. "Balancing a full-time job and the round-the-clock needs of my family. Juggling the recital and the conference calls. Making the endless to-do lists that I never got through and often lost. Feeling like I was falling short at work and at home." To make the gears turn at work, she set a standard of efficiency that would become familiar to aides through the years. When, for example, her hospital outreach team proposed a community meeting on a Saturday, cutting into family time, Michelle wanted evidence that the purpose was clear, the scheduling was essential, and the meeting would run on time. "It was never willy-nilly or just to meet," said Leif Elsmo, her longtime deputy. Her colleague Kenneth Kates also recalled the family imperative. Time was valuable and time away from the girls was precious. "The girls came first," he said. "Period."

To make the logistics work, Michelle employed babysitters and paid a housekeeper to corral the flotsam of their busy lives. She also made efforts to look out for herself in other ways. An inveterate list maker, she put herself on her own to-do list, as one aide put it. She also took stock of society's gendered roles. "What I notice about men, all men, is that their order is me, my family, God is in there somewhere. But me is first," Michelle said. "And for women, me is fourth, and that's not healthy." She cared about food and, increasingly, about fashion. She took an occasional trip to a spa. She had hair and manicure appointments with Michael Flowers, better known as Rahni, owner of Van Cleef Hair Salon in downtown Chicago. She first visited the salon with her mother as a teenager, and later took Malia and Sasha. Located in a refurbished church on West Huron Street, the salon was welcoming and busy. Having your hair done at Van Cleef's was a sign of status for black women in Chicago. "A stellar, classy place. If you can, you do, if you know what I mean," said Haroon Rashid, a Van Cleef stylist who founded an organization to support the DuSable Museum of African American History.

Marian Robinson remained a consistent and welcome presence for the Obama family, living less than fifteen minutes away in the Euclid bungalow and working downtown as a secretary. She cut back her hours to help look after the girls on weekday afternoons. Sometimes Michelle took Malia and Sasha to meetings, as did Barack. Dan Hynes recalled seeing Barack at a Saturday morning candidate forum without Michelle. Sasha was two years old, Malia was five. He was "trying to herd these two little kids and they're knocking things over and taking

pamphlets and throwing them. And here he is trying to be this dignified Senate candidate." It was an established household rule, however,
that the girls were not to be trotted out on the campaign trail as props,
although they appeared at ritual election night celebrations. A day or
two after Rod Blagojevich won his second term as Illinois governor in
2002, historian James Grossman bumped into Barack in the produce
section at the Co-Op, a Hyde Park grocery store. Grossman mentioned
that the camera-ready Blagojevich, a sometime Elvis impersonator
who would later land in federal prison on a corruption conviction, had
stood onstage and prompted his small daughter to wave to the crowd.
"If I did that even once," Grossman recalled Barack saying, "I would be
divorced."

It went without saying that Barack's triumphs did not give unalloyed
satisfaction to Michelle. She saw his rise pulling him yet further from
the home life she preferred. Even for Barack, who seemed to delight
in his cascading successes, the victories could be bittersweet. The day
after he scaled the heights in Boston with his convention speech, he
said, "Malia is six years old and, you know, I can't believe it, but a third
of her childhood is over already." When someone asked how much of
her childhood he had missed because of politics, he said, "Too much."

IN YET ANOTHER lucky Barack bounce, Jack Ryan, his Republican
opponent, quit the Senate race because of revelations that he had tried
to pressure his actress wife—Jeri Ryan, who appeared in *Star Trek*:
*Voyager*—into having public sex with him in nightclubs. That left
Barack without an opponent until the Illinois GOP recruited Alan
Keyes, a sharply conservative black Harvard graduate with no ties to
Illinois. It was a preposterous choice. By the end, Barack was so far
ahead that he had time to cement his star status and earn some political
IOUs by campaigning across the country for other Democrats.

"I don't take all the hype too seriously," Barack said on one of those
trips, acknowledging that he had gotten "some unbelievable breaks." As
a jet chartered by his campaign waited on a nearby tarmac, he insisted
that it was not going to his head. "The attention has come very rapidly

and late. I'm a forty-three-year-old who has worked in obscurity for twenty years on the issues I'm working on now. I'm married with two kids. I've been on the receiving end of bad press. I know what it's like to struggle to pay the bills, know what it's like to lose." He described himself as someone who tried not to get too high when things were going well or too low when the bottom seemed to fall out. "I'm a big believer in not jinxing myself by thinking I've got it made," he added when the plane was airborne. "I get more nervous when things are going well."

Things went well. In fact, they could hardly have gone better. On November 2, 2004, Barack became the country's only black senator and just the third elected since the 1880s. When the votes were counted, Barack had won 70 percent of the vote to Keyes's 27 percent, the largest Senate victory margin in Illinois history. Amid the clamor of his swearing-in ceremony at the U.S. Senate in January 2005, Michelle rolled her eyes in bemusement at the turn their lives had taken. "Maybe one day," she laughed, "he will do something to warrant all this attention."


THE BIGGEST QUESTION the Obamas faced after the Senate victory was where Michelle and the girls would live. It would be difficult for her to move away from Chicago, where she was firmly rooted in her professional life, her family, and her social circle. She looked at houses in the Maryland suburbs, but somehow she could not see herself being happy there. And even though living near the nation's capital would mean more family time with Barack when the Senate was in session, he would often need to make the reverse commute to Illinois, leaving them behind in a city where her network was small. They decided to stay in Hyde Park and find a bigger house—a much bigger one, now that they were flush. Money was pouring in, from the sale of *Dreams,* as well as from Michelle's most recent promotion and raise, which more than doubled her earnings to $273,000 a year. She also joined the board of TreeHouse Foods, which paid her $51,000 in her first full year as a director. In July 2005, the Obamas spent $1.65 million on a red-brick neo-Georgian house with four fireplaces at 5046 South Greenwood Avenue. The home, Michelle said, would be her refuge.

The house purchase, as it happened, was fraught, for Barack had made the mistake of consulting real estate investor Antoin Rezko, a prominent Democratic campaign contributor and future convicted felon who made a habit of befriending up-and-coming Illinois politicians. The house and an adjacent corner lot were for sale by the same owner, but the price of the two together was more than Barack and Michelle wanted to pay. When the Obamas closed on the house in July 2005, Rezko's wife bought the lot on the same day. Seven months later, the Obamas purchased a piece of the empty lot and folded it into their property. Rezko would later go to federal prison for conspiring with Blagojevich to profit illegally from state business, a clandestine scheme under way at the time of the Greenwood Avenue transaction. There was no evidence that the Obamas did anything illegal. They had occasionally dined with the Rezkos. Tony Rezko contributed to Barack's campaigns. Barack called him a friend. But he said he missed the warning signals, including news coverage about shady deals and a political buzz that seemed to foretell Rezko's fall. Barack said of the real estate transaction in 2006, "There's no doubt that this was a mistake. 'Boneheaded' would be accurate. There's no doubt I should have seen some red flags in terms of me purchasing a piece of property from him." *New York Times* columnist Maureen Dowd asked in print why Obama's "tough, smart and connected" wife, the skeptical and careful one with the Harvard law degree and the eye on the bottom line, did not see trouble coming.

The Rezko incident did no permanent harm to the Obama brand, but it revealed the deep waters into which Michelle would soon plunge. Everything she did would be examined for motive, for plan, for her ability to execute without mishap. She was navigating the political netherworld without a map. Her promotion to vice president of community and external affairs at the University of Chicago raised eyebrows, coming as it did shortly after Barack's election to the Senate. Hospital executives denied to reporters that her elevation had anything to do with his political success. They said the institution was afraid of losing her and that her pay package was in line with the salaries of other vice presidents. This was the first of many times the Obamas would be questioned about their finances and their connections, much to Michelle's frustration. "It's just like, dang, is that what you think? Is that who you think we are? Of all the stuff that we have done over our lifetimes and how Barack has carried himself as a politician, I mean, it's like, is there any basis for that assumption?" she asked in a December 2007 interview with *Chicago Tribune* reporter John McCormick. She was also sensitive to sotto voce suggestions that she was getting ahead professionally because of his success. "The problem is that in this modern day life, where you've got a wife who works—and I've got a job—there is going to be some appearance of something. I can't even think, could I be a babysitter? I really do think about this. What could I do where I would get credit for it completely?"

BY STAYING IN CHICAGO, Michelle found a way to do well and do good without giving up her profession, even if Barack's absences made her life more difficult. Equipped with her new title, she launched the Urban Health Initiative, the most ambitious project of her career. As Valerie Jarrett put it, "We are going to change the way we deliver health care and change life on the South Side of Chicago." It started with a cost-benefit analysis. The university, which estimated that it treated one in ten South Side residents, found that disadvantaged and often uninsured residents were using the emergency room as a primary care clinic. This was not only expensive and time-consuming for patients, who might wait hours to see a doctor for a routine complaint. It was also expensive for the hospital, which calculated that it cost about $1,100 each time a patient walked through the door. Every patient who was running short of insulin or suffering an asthma attack was taking the attention of medical staff trained and equipped to do more complex work. A family doctor or clinic could perform the same service for $100, but one in every four patients who reported to the emergency department had no doctor.

What the hospital saw as a more rational way to allocate resources and expertise, Michelle saw also as an opening to improve options for poorly served residents. The inequity in access to health care was a subject she knew through personal and professional experience. There was her father's long struggle with multiple sclerosis and the haggling that Barack's mother had done with insurance companies as she was dying of cancer. There were relatives with debilitating health problems, limited insurance, and unsteady access to quality care. And, on the flip side, there was the relief she experienced, when Sasha contracted meningitis and Malia suffered an asthma attack, of dialing a doctor, going to a first-rate hospital, and being able to pay.

The scale of Chicago's health care deficit was startling. Among the 1.1 million inhabitants of the sprawling South Side of one of the nation's largest cities, there was no logic to health care, and certainly no system that anyone might recognize as such. Clinics were scattered and family doctors few. Too many patients got too little care until small problems became big ones. Others who were not very sick went straight to emergency rooms. Cook County could barely begin to handle the need. Faced with soaring budget deficits, it started to cut back on public health services. Medicaid helped, but patients and doctors alike often felt shortchanged. As a result, for tens of thousands of the working poor and the unemployed poorer, the concept of a regular doctor and easy access to affordable care was a fantasy. Beyond the simple fact of limited access were the frustrations of seeking care in a part of town where a trip to the doctor often meant waiting in rough weather for an unreliable bus, waiting at a clinic to see an overstretched doctor, and then waiting again for the bus home. Each unpredictable excursion tested the will of the patient, the employer, and those who looked after the children.

In what would become the largest experiment of its kind in the country, the University of Chicago developed the Urban Health Initiative to attract residents to neighborhood doctors' offices or family clinics—a "medical home," where a primary care doctor saw them at nominal cost and tracked their progress and their needs. Clinic staff attended to many problems, from broken fingers and split lips to allergic reactions and chronic maladies. The theory held that if the clinics were nearby and the care first-rate, patients would return more readily for follow-up visits, checkups, and referrals to community hospitals or specialists. Fewer would show up in emergency rooms. People would be healthier. The cost of their ailments would decline. And at the top of the hierarchy, the university medical center could focus on more cases that demanded specialists.

"We have to create a system where people can go. It doesn't exist and we're trying to build it," said Eric Whitaker, a close friend of the Obamas who departed as director of the Illinois Public Health Department to run the initiative. One partner was the nonprofit Chicago Family Health Center, a group of four clinics where 98 percent of the roughly twenty thousand patients were African American or Hispanic. More than 40 percent were uninsured. The center billed Medicaid and Medicare and collected money from the university, federal grants, and private sources. A sliding-fee scale started at $10 for a visit and lab study. Another partner was the independent Friend Family Health Center, which drew on university money and doctors to expand into the gap created by the new emergency room policy and the closing of two university health clinics. While Friend Family Health, five minutes north of the university hospital, recorded tens of thousands of visits a year, staff members sometimes found it difficult to persuade patients to return for checkups and further care. No-show rates were as high as 50 percent. "People are so used to going to the emergency department. The behavior change is really hard," said Laura Derks, the university's chief liaison to the community clinics.

Michelle increasingly became the face of the project, as well as one of the most high-profile African American figures at the university. She addressed meetings in churches and community centers and spoke with doctors and staff, explaining the university's intentions and plans at a time when skepticism ran deep. "I have seen her in a meeting with the board of trustees, giving a presentation. I have seen her with angry patients and community residents," recalled her friend Susan Sher, the medical center's general counsel.

Reviews of the new urban health project were not entirely positive, and the model was unproven. After Michelle left for Washington, Representative Bobby Rush, who had vanquished Barack in 2000, demanded to know whether the hospital was dumping some of its poorest patients to save money. The Illinois College of Emergency Physicians warned that plans to shrink the emergency department and cut the hospital budget by $100 million would compromise patient safety. In response, the hospital said it was doing no dumping and insisted that time would prove the strategy to be correct.

EARLY IN HIS TENURE as a senator, Barack was already thinking about his next moves. There was really only one, as everybody knew: the presidency. The talk was outlandish, yet also increasingly common. The morning after he was elected to the Senate, reporters in Chicago asked him repeatedly whether he would run for president four years later. As often as they asked, he said no. He called it a "silly question." He declared, "I am not running for president in 2008." He finally said, "Guys, I am a state senator. I was elected *yesterday*. I have never set foot in the U.S. Senate. I have never worked in Washington. And the notion that somehow I am going to start running for higher office, it just doesn't make sense."

The hype never died down, nor did the expectations. He was, plain and simple, a phenomenon. Yet he could always count on Michelle to keep things in perspective. In 2006, his second year in the Senate, he was busy in his three-day-a-week Washington existence and he felt he was making progress on the Senate floor. One day, he called Michelle in Hyde Park after a hearing on an anti-proliferation bill that he was co-sponsoring with Senator Richard Lugar, an Indiana Republican who chaired the Senate Foreign Relations Committee. He launched into an exuberant explanation, but Michelle cut him off. "We have ants," she said. "I found ants in the kitchen. And in the bathroom upstairs." She wanted him to pick up ant traps on his way home from the airport. She would do it herself, she said, but the girls had doctor's appointments after school. "Ant traps. Don't forget, okay, honey? And buy more than one. Listen, I need to go into a meeting. Love you." Barack said he wondered as he hung up whether Ted Kennedy or John McCain ever bought ant traps on the way home from work.

# TEN

# I'm Pretty Convincing

I t was late 2006 when Barack, still not two years into his Senate career, approached his brother-in-law to ask a favor. "He comes out of nowhere, like just says, 'Hey, I think I'm going to do this,'" Craig Robinson recalled of the conversation in the Obamas' kitchen. "I'm thinking, 'Do what?'" Barack said he was planning a presidential race. "Whoa," Craig thought to himself, "you don't grow up on the South Side of Chicago thinking that somebody's going to walk up to you, who you're related to, and say they're going to run for president of the United States." Handicappers put Barack in the mix for 2008 largely on the strength of his Democratic National Convention speech. Truth be told, his early chances registered somewhere between *improbable* and *not gonna happen,* but Barack and his strategists believed that the 2008 election offered as strong a shot at the presidency as he was going to get. "You will never be hotter than you are right now," David Axelrod wrote in a strategy memo. The advisers concluded that they could develop a message that would resonate, an organization that could compete, and a bankroll that would keep Barack in the game. The last hurdle was Michelle. "Have you talked to your wife about this?" Craig asked. Barack said he hadn't, and added, "You've got to do me a favor. You've got to talk to her because she's not going to go for it." As Craig recalled the conversation, "I was like, you're darn right she's not going to go for it."

For all of the popular excitement surrounding Barack's meteoric rise to the Senate and his place on the national stage, his newfound success had done nothing to make Michelle's life easier except in the ways that money could buy. She was working at the university and doing the lion's share of the work of raising Malia and Sasha, who were then eight and five. Surrounded though she was by friends and relatives, there were days when she felt lonely. Barack was commuting to Washington and somehow had made time to write *The Audacity of Hope,* released in 2006 to strong reviews and stronger sales. Greeted in some places like a rock star, he embarked on a book tour that started to resemble the early stages of a campaign. He was in constant demand on the national lecture and fundraising circuit.

On the plus side, Barack's job appeared secure and he was learning the ropes as Michelle continued her successful run at the University of Chicago medical center. At home, the girls were settled into the routine of a top-notch private school and the embrace of a close group of friends. Marian had retired from the bank to spend afternoons with them. Michelle would later describe the advantages of working down the street from the Lab School: "I've got great access to them, which, you know, you need when you're basically doing it all." As Michelle saw it, a presidential campaign would disrupt even this unsatisfying equilibrium in ways she could barely predict.

Following through on Barack's request, Craig decided to try Marian first, borrowing liberally from the lessons that she and Fraser had imparted to their children. "They talked about passion, talked about doing what's best for everyone. Mom and Dad said you never know when an opportunity is going to arise." Like Michelle, who turned her back on the big money prospects of corporate law because it did not make her happy, Craig had quit investment banking in his late-30s. "I had a Porsche 944 Turbo. I had a BMW station wagon. Who gets a BMW station wagon? It's the dumbest car in the world. Why would you buy a $75,000 station wagon?" Instead, he became a basketball coach and was soon running the program at Brown University. In his pitch to Marian, he asked her to imagine that he had suddenly received an offer from Kentucky, one of the country's most storied hoops programs. Outlandish, yes, but he would accept in a heartbeat, he told her. And here was Barack, a junior senator with huge promise who had a shot at becoming the most powerful man in the world. You shouldn't penalize him, Craig said, for being good at what he does. "Well that's fine," Marian replied, "but I don't think you're going to get your sister to go for it."

MICHELLE WAS at the table when Barack and a small team of advisers gathered in David Axelrod's Chicago office on November 8, 2006, to discuss his prospects. The working theory of his candidacy was developed by Axelrod, a wordsmith and former *Chicago Tribune* political reporter who had done much to propel Barack out of the pack in the 2004 Democratic Senate primary. Amid growing dissatisfaction with George W. Bush's handling of the Iraq War, Axelrod spotted a narrow path to victory for an unconventional presidential candidate who could run against the establishment. The candidate needed to be perceived as a unifier, a problem solver, a change maker, a leader from a new generation. The establishment, in this case, would include Senator Hillary Rodham Clinton, a Wellesley and Yale graduate and former first lady whose husband had developed the richest and deepest Democratic network in modern times. She was trying to make history as the first woman elected president. To compete against an aspiring Republican successor to Bush, Barack would first have to stop the Clintons, and it was clear from the start that this would be the harder task. But Axelrod, David Plouffe, Steve Hildebrand, and other members of Barack's team reasoned that if they could outwork Clinton in the four early states—especially neighboring Iowa, which was rural, midwestern, and 95 percent white—well, anything would be possible. It would be Cassius Clay standing over Sonny Liston, the champion flat on his back on the canvas, stunned by the upstart who trained harder, fought smarter, and performed best when the pressure was on. During his longshot Senate campaign, Barack bought a poster-sized photograph of that very scene and hung it on his office wall.

In Axelrod's conference room, Michelle listened and asked questions, just as she had when Barack launched his Senate campaign after the Bobby Rush debacle. "She was interested in whether it was a crazy, harebrained idea," Axelrod said, "because she's not into crazy, hare-brained ideas." She wanted to know about the finances, about the logistics, about the schedule in a typical campaign week, about what it would mean to their home life and to Barack's relationship to the girls. It was not so long ago that they had struggled to mesh their lives. Now this? Plouffe, who would run the campaign, was meeting Michelle for the first time. "I was impressed by her directness and the no-nonsense focus of her questioning," he said. "She clearly wanted all the facts and I could tell that running was not going to be solely Barack's decision. They would decide together."

When Michelle asked whether Barack could be home every week-end and take Sundays off, Hildebrand nodded his head yes, only to be corrected by Plouffe. "No one had good news for Michelle. There could be no shortcuts," Plouffe recalled. "It would be grueling and then more grueling. The candidate would only be home for snatches of time and when he was, there would be calls to make and speeches to review." During the meeting, Michelle wanted to make sure that Barack, too, knew what was coming. The stakes were high. When he tried to explain something to the advisers, she interrupted to declare, "We're talking about you right now," and he said no more. On his way to the airport, Plouffe called Axelrod, who said he thought Barack wanted to run, "but he's drawn more to the idea of running than actually running. We'll see how he processes the reality of what this will mean, how hard it is, and how long the odds are. Michelle is the wild card. If she is opposed, there is no way this is going to happen. And I can't read yet where she'll come down."

MICHELLE WAS METHODICAL in making decisions. She made lists. She tracked every question, considered every permutation, mapped every-thing that could go wrong. She inclined toward worry. To describe their differences, Valerie Jarrett said Barack was "the kind of person who, the day before the final exam, would open the book, read it and get an A." Michelle, on the other hand, was "the kind of person who, the first day of class when they were discussing dissertations, would plot out how to finish hers." Michelle had said in 1996, when Barack went into politics, that she was trying to learn to be more comfortable with risk, to relinquish some of her need for control. Yet there are no political risks quite like a presidential campaign. An Obama '08 campaign would be a maelstrom and victory would mean giving up her career for four years, maybe eight. It would mean, far more thoroughly than before, seeing her identity attached to Barack's. And, to put it bluntly, it would mean accepting a heightened chance that her husband would be assassinated. "I took myself down every dark road you could go on," she said, "just to prepare myself before we jumped out there."

Michelle had veto power. "The person who was most important in that decision was Michelle," Jarrett said. She framed her exploration of the possibility in two parts. One was logistical. "Okay, how are we going to do this?" she asked herself. "How's this going to look? What am I going to do about my job? How will we manage the kids? What's our financial position going to be? How do we make sure we're still contributing to the college fund? Once I got a sense of how this could work not just for me or him but for our family and the people in our lives, once I had that vision in my head, then I could say, 'Okay, we can do this, I can manage this.' I know what I need things to look like and what resources I need to make sure that all bases are covered."

The other part, more complicated, was the grand conundrum of what would be right for her partner, her family, herself, and—this being the presidency—the country. She saw immediately that running for president was something Barack needed to do or else forever wonder what might have been. And a determination to make a progressive difference had been an essential component of their relationship and their choices from the start. "I've never doubted the mission," she said early in the campaign, "and I've never doubted Barack's ability to carry out the mission." It was the White House, it was his ambition, it was his life. And yet it was her life, too, and the lives of their daughters, their family and friends. "The selfish part of me says, 'Run away! Just say no!' because my life would be better," she said. "But that's the problem we face as a society, we have to stop making the *me* decision and we have to make the *we* and *us* decision." She was in.

"It had taken a little convincing to persuade me that this whole running-for-president thing was a good idea," Michelle explained in late 2007, with the campaign in full swing. "And by 'a little convincing,' I mean it was a lot of convincing, because we had two very young daughters at home, I had a full time job that I loved, and I worried about what it would mean for our family. So it took me a while to get out of my own head, and to set aside my own fears and self interest, and focus on all the good that I believed a man like my husband could do as president." Further, a campaign role for her would not only be expected, but required. "To tell you the truth, I was scared. I was worried that I'd say the wrong thing. I was nervous that someone might ask a question that I didn't know the answer to. And I have a tendency to do that thing a lot of women do, where you get 99 things right, but then you stress and beat yourself up over the one thing you mess up."

The choice Michelle made for her husband was a familiar one, especially to working spouses. Connie Schultz, a sharp-witted *Cleveland Plain Dealer* columnist and winner of the Pulitzer Prize, was in her late forties when she met and married Representative Sherrod Brown, a Democrat from Cleveland. Soon after, he told her that he wanted to run for the U.S. Senate. It was sure to be a brutal race, but he thought he had a chance. She had doubts. "I was really the holdout," Schultz said. "We were in a very new marriage. I was not a political spouse. I knew how you could blow a marriage." As they talked, she came to see that Brown needed to run or forever regret it. As she put it, "The stars had aligned, and I was going to be the big, fat moon in the way." Once Brown entered the 2006 Ohio Senate race, it was only a question of time before Schultz would give up her column, for reasons of ethics, especially, but also of logistics. She made appearances for him, and made sure there were mango slices and carrots in his campaign car. On the bright side, she figured they would share the ride. It would be an adventure, and weren't the best adventures always a bit frightening? She was frightened. After she told her editors that she was relinquishing her column for the duration of the campaign, she opened her journal and wrote in big block letters, "WHAT IS TO BECOME OF ME?"

In Michelle's case, there was one other thing. She insisted, in return for her support, that Barack quit smoking. He was an inveterate smoker and he had tried to quit before. Michelle declared that, this time, it would be for keeps. The results during the campaign would be mixed, but it was not for Michelle's lack of trying. Asked if Barack used a nicotine patch, Craig Robinson laughed and said, "Michelle Obama! That's one hell of a patch right there!" Or, as Barack later joked in a conversation caught on an open microphone, he had a good reason to quit: "I'm scared of my wife."

ON FEBRUARY 10, 2007, the campaign began in brilliant sunshine on the steps of the Old State Capitol in Springfield, where Abraham Lincoln had delivered his "House Divided" speech 149 years earlier. The symbolism was intentional for Barack, who looked for strength and inspiration to the sixteenth president and his struggle for a more perfect union. Michelle stood by his side, bundled against temperatures barely in double digits. Stretching out in front of them, filling the square and flowing into the side streets, was a crowd fifteen-thousand-strong that considered Barack the man who would restore compassion and good judgment to the White House and a measure of humility to American actions abroad. From Springfield, the Obama caravan rolled west across the Mississippi to Iowa, the corn-fed state that more than any other would determine the success or failure of the entire Obama '08 enterprise.

It was difficult to overstate the challenges that Barack faced in becoming a credible candidate, much less a winning one. He was not a polished campaigner during the early going. Energized at first, the candidate was in a funk after only a couple of months on the trail. "Meandering, unmotivated, and hesitant," Plouffe said. He did not like political combat or the shallow necessities of winning the daily news cycle. He needed to build a national organization capable of raising vast sums of money, yet he disliked the care and feeding essential to doing so. He missed the solitary time when he did his best thinking. He missed his family. Arrayed against him, meanwhile, was a deep field led by Clinton, whose political organization had done nothing but win, and former vice presidential nominee John Edwards, a North Carolina trial lawyer who threatened to emerge as Clinton's chief rival. Another obstacle was the perception fueled by much of the national media that Clinton, heir to the best parts of her husband's legacy and beneficiary of his political mind, was a lock to win the Democratic nomination. Viewed through a national lens, it was hard to disagree. For months on end, even after the Obama campaign showed it could raise startling sums, national polls showed Clinton ahead by a cool thirty percentage points.

But Team Obama was making a very different bet, one that required a persistent effort to tune out the doubters, the pundits, and the polls. The Obama forces calculated that they could slow Clinton nationally by beating her locally, in Iowa's first-in-the-nation caucus on January 3, 2008. If they could do that, then deliver strong showings in New Hampshire, South Carolina, and Nevada, they might weaken Clinton's candidacy significantly, possibly fatally, before almost half the country voted on Super Tuesday—the day in early February when her campaign confidently expected to claim the crown. The strategy was audacious, even quixotic, to use words more polite than the ones Barack and his strategists were hearing. One afternoon in October 2007, when Clinton appeared to be lapping the field and Barack's chances looked bleak, one of his most faithful supporters was worried. Abner Mikva, who had served Bill Clinton as White House counsel but wholeheartedly backed Barack for president, had been hearing from friends that the upstart candidacy was doomed. Mikva suspected they might be right, but did not want to believe it. As he discussed the race over lunch at the Cliff Dwellers, his Chicago club, he held out hope on two counts. "Barack is the luckiest politician in America," Mikva said, "and the Clintons always make a mistake."

IOWA, AS IT HAPPENED, all but perfectly fit the needs of the Obama forces. For one thing, the state chose its nominees by caucus, a quirky and complex process that rewarded candidates who cultivated the grassroots and thought two steps ahead—in other words, a community organizer's dream. For another, Iowa caucusgoers were accustomed to giving candidates a good, long look in coffee shops, living rooms, and high school gyms, where they listened and questioned, chewed things over, and questioned some more. In contrast to later primaries, where voters mostly got their information from advertising or the news, Iowans had months to study candidates who offered themselves for close inspection. One October afternoon, Michelle spent more than an hour in an Iowa Falls bookstore, the Book Cellar and Coffee Attic. She delivered remarks, gave interviews to local reporters, and talked with every prospective voter who wanted a word with her. One middle-aged voter, who lived on a farm outside of town, said she was impressed. Asked whether she would caucus for Barack, she said, "Well, I would have to meet him first."

Barack was a senator from neighboring Illinois, which helped with name recognition, knowledge of regional issues, and the logistics of shuttling staff and volunteers into the state. He came across as a fresh voice, and unlike Clinton and the other Democrats, including Senators Joe Biden and Chris Dodd, he had opposed the Iraq War. "I am not opposed to all wars, I am opposed to dumb wars," he said at a Chicago antiwar rally in October 2002, five months before the U.S.-led invasion. The stance earned him a hearing from progressives at a time when the heartland was bearing the brunt of casualties in a war that had cost Republicans control of the Senate in November 2006.

Could a brainy black man become the forty-fourth president of the United States? To do the unthinkable and win Iowa, his advisers believed, Barack would need to show that he was not a one-speech wonder and that he had a sturdy message and a vibrant organization. If he won, he would demonstrate that white voters in middle America would support a black candidate named Barack Hussein Obama. It would be his Good Housekeeping Seal of Approval, helping him not just with many whites who had never backed a minority candidate for president, but with many African Americans disinclined to spend a vote on a black candidate unlikely to win enough white support to become a contender. In other words, a victory in overwhelmingly white Iowa, especially if he could draw a smattering of Republicans and independents, could deliver exactly the validation he needed.

MICHELLE SET OUT to demystify Barack, "to introduce the Obamas the people, not the Obamas the résumés," as she put it. She strode into unfamiliar settings in dozens of cities and towns and returned the questioning gaze of strangers. She urged them to look deeply at her husband, the one who was not white and was not named Washington or Adams or Johnson or Ford or Clinton. Speaking without notes or evident nervousness, she gave her listeners license to share her initial doubts by relating her initial impressions of Barack at Sidley & Austin eighteen years earlier: "I've got nothing in common with this guy. He grew up in Hawaii! Who grows up in Hawaii? He was biracial. I was like, okay, what's that about?" Her stump speech resembled a narrated short story, describing how she learned of their very different upbringings and very similar values, a discovery confirmed one summer afternoon in a sweltering church basement in one of Chicago's poorest neighborhoods. She said it was there, as he spoke with people who felt the world was failing them, that he made plain an individual's obligation to act purposefully in a society too often mean-spirited and unfair. He urged his audience not to settle for the world as it is, but to strive for the world as it should be. "What I saw in him on that day was authenticity and truth and principle," Michelle told her invariably rapt listeners. "That's who I fell in love with, that man." She was saying, *Yes, I know what you're thinking. I know. But hear me out. This is the kind of candidate you said you wanted. He's ready. Are you?* She telegraphed confidence. "I guarantee you," she said one afternoon in the basement of the Rockwell City Public Library, "if I could talk to everybody in this state, they would vote for Barack Obama. I'm pretty convincing."

What began as Barack's quest soon became her own. Everything she said was defined by the goal of getting Barack to the White House, yet Michelle made certain that the message was true to herself and her convictions. She told a story not just of Barack's life, but of her own, always against the daily hum of Chicago's South Side and the people she knew there. To appeal to varied audiences in Iowa, South Carolina, and New Hampshire, she took themes familiar to urban voters and broadened them into conundrums faced by families of modest means across the land. She said people weren't asking for much, just a fair shot at a steady job, affordable health care, good schools, and a secure retirement. The archetype was her father, the blue-collar Chicago water plant worker with multiple sclerosis who managed to support a stay-at-home wife and see his two children reach Princeton. Even the most elemental ambitions seemed increasingly remote to ordinary people, she said, and the decline had come in her lifetime. She pointed to politicians too often cynical and a government and society too often cold. She said, "You can't just tell a family of four to suck it up and make it work."

As for the candidate himself, Michelle declared at a June 2007 women's rally in Harlem, "I am married to the answer!" To her depictions of Barack's achievements at Harvard and his bipartisan efforts in the Illinois legislature, she added the occasional putdown, a familiar tactic from the Senate campaign that hinted at her sense of humor, so often under wraps, and helped show his ordinary-man side. "There's Barack Obama the phenomenon," she said at a Beverly Hills fundraiser in February 2007. "And then there's the Barack Obama that lives with me in my house, and that guy's a little less impressive. For some reason this guy still can't manage to put the butter up when he makes toast, secure the bread so that it doesn't get stale, and his five-year-old is still better at making the bed than he is." She described heart-to-heart talks with Malia and Sasha, often on mornings when Barack was not home, and said, "He's too snorey and stinky, they don't want to ever get into bed with him." *New York Times* columnist Maureen Dowd said such revelations made her "wince a bit." She wrote after the Beverly Hills event, "Many people I talked to afterward found Michelle wondrous. But others worried that her chiding was emasculating, casting her husband—under fire for lacking experience—as an undisciplined child." A reporter asked Michelle about that later. "Barack and I laugh about that," she said. "It's just sort of like, do you think anyone could emasculate Barack Obama? Really now."

As their lives became ever more public, and publicly dissected, Michelle and Barack talked about each other in interviews and on the campaign trail. This was not uncharted territory. Each had discussed their relationship with interviewers and, in Barack's case, shared details in *The Audacity of Hope*. For all of their professional success and their emerging celebrity, they painted themselves as essentially ordinary on the home front, their marriage intact and the two of them feeling good about each other. "She's smart. She's funny. She's honest. She's tough. I think of her as my best friend," Barack said, allowing that maybe he was becoming a better partner. "What I realize as I get older is that Michelle is less concerned about me giving her flowers than she is that I'm doing things that are hard for me—carving out time. That to her is proof, evidence, that I'm thinking about her. She appreciates the flowers, but to her, romance is that I'm actually paying attention to the things that she cares about. And time is always an important factor."

TIME SEEMED in ever shorter supply. Michelle carried two Black-Berry mobile phones, symbols of her split existence. One was for the campaign and one for her job at the University of Chicago, where she worked part-time on urban health issues until she was sucked into the vortex of the presidential race. She began an unpaid leave of absence in January 2008. The job had kept her tethered to a professional pursuit outside of politics, but it was the girls who most thoroughly occupied her thoughts. "I am going to be the person who is providing them with the stability," she said in December 2006. "So that means my role with the kids becomes even more important. What I am not willing to do is hand my kids over to my mom and say, 'We'll see you in two years.' . . . There has to be a balance and there will be a balance."

Michelle took to telling campaign audiences that it was Malia and Sasha whom she thought of first when she woke up and last before she fell asleep. The girls were doing fine, she would say, occupied by school and play dates and the typical busyness of childhood. To keep it that way, Michelle strived mightily for normalcy in a life that was becoming anything but. She instructed the campaign staff to mark certain days as off-limits. When she traveled, roughly once a week, her schedulers tried to place the first speaking engagement in the middle of the day, to give her time to get the girls fed, dressed, and off to school before she hopped a private jet at Chicago's Midway Airport. She kept trips as short as possible and tried to avoid spending the night on the road. When she was away, she relied on her mother and Eleanor Kaye Wilson, fondly called "Mama Kaye," the girls' much-loved godmother. A consultant to nonprofit organizations, Wilson had spent a significant part of her career developing urban education projects, from a welfare-to-work training program to an anti-delinquency project for elementary school children in Chicago housing projects. Wilson was also Marian Robinson's yoga partner. Their instructor was often Marian's youngest brother, Stephen Shields, who ran a studio on the North Side.

Central to Michelle's sanity was the group of friends who, over the years, had become her support group and safety net. Professionals and mothers, they had careers whose fates and fortunes tended to be far removed from the vicissitudes of national politics. Michelle had always had close girlfriends, in high school, at Princeton and Harvard, at City Hall. Linked principally by motherhood, the early gatherings, ostensibly for the benefit of the children, "were for us," Michelle said. "We just shared all those things. And those friendships continued because our girls continued to be friends. Many of those women are still the women that I count on to kick ideas around with, to let my hair down, to vent, to laugh. It's been so important. And I think I had to learn that because Barack traveled. I just realized having some kind of support around, whether it was my mom or a set of friends, was essential to keeping me whole and not so angry or frustrated. Because I could always pick up the phone and somebody would come over with a pizza or we'd just go and have dinner at a friend's and we wouldn't have to cook. And you just share the load."

One of the friends was Sandy Matthews, a children's advocacy group executive married to former Chicago Cubs left fielder Gary Matthews Sr. Another was Yvonne Davila, a publicist and onetime City Hall colleague who lived near the Obamas. She sometimes hosted Malia and Sasha on weekend sleepovers. "We're co-parenting our children. Her kids have toothbrushes at my house," Davila said during the campaign. She described a day when she had felt sure Michelle could use a break. Davila drove over to the house on Greenwood Avenue and swept the girls into the car for an outing. "It's just a silent thing that we as her friends know and do. We've all seen each other through all kinds of things." Good and bad alike, she said.

In the group of friends, Michelle probably spent the most time with

Anita Blanchard and Cheryl Rucker Whitaker, women who rose from modest means to become doctors. Blanchard was an obstetrician; she delivered Malia and Sasha, served on the University of Chicago faculty, and led annual South Side seminars for black girls and their mothers about preparing for adolescence, including matters of reproductive health. Whitaker, a medical doctor from Georgia with a Harvard public health degree, conducted research on hypertension and other chronic illnesses in African American communities. They had children of similar ages to Malia and Sasha, and all attended the University of Chicago Laboratory Schools. The families lived close to one another and the husbands were close friends, as well. While the kids took tennis lessons, the fathers sometimes lolled near the courts, reading the morning papers and shooting the breeze. The group vacationed in Hawaii and on Martha's Vineyard, often joined by Valerie Jarrett, divorced years earlier after a short marriage.

The connections could seem dizzying. Blanchard's husband, Marty Nesbitt, the businessman in the group, chaired the Chicago Housing Authority and worked closely with members of the Pritzker family, later becoming treasurer of the 2008 presidential campaign. Eric Whitaker, raised on the South Side, had run a men's health clinic in nearby Woodlawn and led the Illinois public health department before Michelle and Jarrett recruited him to lead the Urban Health Initiative. Whitaker knew Barack from the basketball courts at Harvard. Nesbitt met Craig Robinson on a basketball recruiting trip, when Princeton coach Pete Carril invited him to watch the Tigers play Ohio State. The two met again in business school, and Nesbitt met Barack while playing basketball at Chicago's East Bank Club. Finally, as medical students at the University of Chicago, Anita Blanchard and Eric Whitaker were mentored by James Bowman, Jarrett's father.

Smart, funny, loyal, down-to-earth, and discreet, they supported one another as they rose to prominence and prosperity. When the campaign began, Cheryl Whitaker asked Barack what he and Michelle needed from the group. "We need you all to be the same," he replied. "I just need to know that if all of this goes south, our friends are still there and that we can still come over and sit in your backyard and we can still come over for dinner." Whenever they could, the friends got together, away from the fray. But it was true that "this running for president thing," as Michelle called it, was altogether different. It astonished them to think that Barack, so recently a state senator, so typically the guy they saw playing Scrabble or basketball or watching ESPN, so essentially a black man in a contest that no black man had ever won, was a genuine contender capturing the nation's attention. "I believe [he] will be president," Jarrett said in July 2007. "It gives me goose bumps and if we continue talking, I'll probably start to cry."

STARTING WITH his first trip to Cedar Rapids on February 10, 2007, Barack had a little more than ten months to win the Iowa caucuses and give himself a chance to claim the Democratic nomination. He assembled an experienced campaign staff that understood Iowa's dynamics in a way that the Clinton team never did. Bill Clinton, deferring to the favorite son candidacy of Senator Tom Harkin in 1992, had not competed in Iowa, while much of Hillary's Washington-based senior staff was slow to recognize the peril. By contrast, virtually every ranking member of Team Obama knew how the first-in-the-nation Iowa contests were won, starting with a willingness to indulge voters their long moment in the spotlight. The needs of the campaign also conveniently dovetailed with the community organizing techniques that Barack and Michelle had studied and adopted—the purposeful personal stories, the one-on-one connections, the principle that grassroots volunteers and voters should not just be asked to follow, but inspired to lead. "Paint the fence!" was one Iowa staff motto, recalling Tom Sawyer's strategy to entice his friends to pitch in, do his work for him, and feel happy about doing it.

Michelle, ever the disciplined student, spent hours reading briefing books, aiming to speak fluently about the Iraq War and the Earned Income Tax Credit, and the contours of the Iowa landscape. On Michelle's first overnight trip to the state, chief of staff Melissa Winter said, "She takes this so seriously because every day not with the girls has to be validated." In a period of thirty-six hours, she traveled to Davenport, Ottumwa, Centerville, Corydon, Lamoni, Indianola, Waterloo, Iowa Falls, Rockwell City, and Fort Dodge. Shaken, she also made an unscheduled stop in Mason City to offer support to a reckless motorcyclist who crashed at high speed into her campaign van and was lucky to be alive.

As the appearances piled up, the staff discovered that Michelle possessed political skills her husband lacked. When a precinct captain in an Iowa town was wavering, many campaign workers preferred Michelle, not Barack, to make the final sale. More than one aide recalled watching as she backed an Iowan against a wall in a high school gym and pressed to know what would seal the deal. They started calling her "the closer." Pete Giangreco, a Chicago political strategist who had worked with the Obamas for years, said of the couple, "He has natural political gifts and he's not a natural politician. She has natural gifts and she's a natural politician. He's rootless, all over the place. She's grounded. People think she's very real. They get where she comes from." This was particularly true of women, the campaign learned, making her role in the duel against Hillary Clinton that much more important. "She connects with women in a really, really powerful way," Giangreco said, "because it wasn't too long ago that 'she was me.'" Jobi Petersen Cates, Michelle's Public Allies recruit and colleague, took the thought one step further. "If you had asked me which one of them would have been in the White House, I'd have said Michelle," Cates said. "Why? Heart. She's a badass."

To succeed in Iowa, the Obama campaign sought to bring thousands of first-time caucusgoers into the mix. They moved beyond the Democratic Party regulars, many of whom had been sewn up by Clinton and Edwards, to court newcomers. They learned their issues, their passions, the names of their children and their dogs. They sat alongside them in church, talked high school sports at the local diner, and invited them to the busy Obama offices that popped up in dozens of storefronts across the state. In that spirit, Michelle put black pen to white notepaper, laboriously writing thank-you notes to Iowa supporters in her neat and unadorned cursive. In the same spirit, far from the spotlight, Barack spoke six times to Douglas Burns, columnist for the *Daily Times*

*Herald,* circulation six thousand, in Carroll, Iowa. Through Burns and his small-town colleagues across the state, the campaign aimed to reach Iowans whom no number of column inches on the front page of *The New York Times* could persuade. Iowans were the ones who counted most. They were the golden ticket. "It's Iowa or bust," David Axelrod said privately, and for many months in 2007, the smart money was on bust.

Then came the biggest event on the political calendar before caucus night: the Jefferson Jackson Dinner, held November 10 in a downtown Des Moines arena. On his way there, Barack calmly reassured Emily Parcell, the campaign's worried Iowa political director, "I'm a fourth-quarter player. I've got this." Required by house rules to speak without notes, he had been rehearsing. He delivered a fast-paced, energetic performance, painting Clinton as the status quo candidate. "We are in a defining moment in our history," he declared. "Our nation is at war. The planet is in peril. The dream that so many generations fought for feels as if it's slowly slipping away. We are working harder for less. We've never paid more for health care or for college. It's harder to save, and it's harder to retire. And most of all, we've lost faith that our leaders can or will do anything about it." As he worked his way through his campaign pledges, the crowd roared. The media took notice, as did voters.

TEN DAYS LATER, Michelle made her way to Orangeburg, South Carolina, where her singular mission was to persuade skeptical black voters to believe in Barack and his chances. A CBS poll in late 2007 showed that 40 percent of the state's African American voters thought the country was not "ready to elect a black president." Their doubts mattered because the early road to the White House passed through the heart of the old Confederacy. Black voters were likely to cast half of the ballots in the South Carolina primary, sixteen days after Iowa and ten days before Super Tuesday, and Barack needed them. The campaign asked Michelle to make the sale. No one was closer to Barack or had stronger bona fides in the black community. No one told a better story.

To many African American voters, especially women, Michelle herself was a sign that Barack was all right. He had dated white women, but he married a black woman from Chicago. "Had he married a white woman, he would have signaled that he had chosen whiteness, a consistent visual reminder that he was not on the African American side. Michelle anchored him," said Melissa Harris-Perry, who knew the Obamas in Chicago and authored *Sister Citizen: Shame, Stereotypes, and Black Women in America.* "Part of what we as African Americans like about Barack is the visual image of him in the White House, and it would have been stunningly different without Michelle and those brown-skinned girls." As writer Allison Samuels put it, "Michelle is not only African American, but brown. Real brown."

Amid a campaign that had tacked away from explicit talk about race, Michelle's Orangeburg speech could not have been a more direct appeal. The setting itself made a statement: South Carolina State University, a historically black college that made news for lunch counter sit-ins and a 1968 protest against segregation at a bowling alley, a demonstration that ended with three students shot dead by state police. Drawing on themes and convictions that had long animated her, she placed herself, and Barack, firmly in a historical narrative about racism and racial politics in America. She said she stood on the shoulders of Sojourner Truth and Harriet Tubman, Rosa Parks and Mary McLeod Bethune, an honor roll of women "who knew what it meant to overcome." She owed her own opportunities, she said, to "their courage and sacrifice all those years ago" and to the voices of parents, pastors, and elders "who taught me to work hard, dream big and then bring my blessings and my knowledge back to my community." She spoke of her grandfather Fraser, raised just two hours up the road in Georgetown, who taught her that her destiny had not been written before she was born.

Michelle's own success had not been assured, she told her audience, for she, too, had experienced naysaying that could have sapped her soul had she surrendered to it. "From classmates who thought a black girl with a book was acting white. From teachers who told me not to reach too high because my test scores were too low. And from well-meaning but misguided folks who said . . . 'Success isn't meant for little black girls from the South Side of Chicago.'" She had made it, but her life remained out of reach for "too many women, too many little black girls." Reciting details of disparities, Michelle said pay discrimination resulted in black women being paid 67 cents for every dollar a white man earned for doing the same job. Forty-five percent of children from black middle-class families were ending up "near poor," compared with 16 percent from comparable white families. She said, "We know that millions of women over the past decades have been dropped from the welfare rolls and left to fend for themselves without adequate child care. We know that too many black women don't have quality, afford-able health care. That we are more likely to die than white women of a whole host of diseases. That we are dying too young, too needlessly. That our babies are dying, too. . . . And we are learning that the dream of giving our children a better life is slipping further out of reach."

Then came the pivot to Barack, first to his story, then to his candi-dacy and a tribute to those in generations past who "stood up when it was risky, stood up when it was hard." She was asking her audience to do the same, to see Barack in a long line of civil rights luminaries, to trust him and to believe that he would not be defeated and he would not be shot. Months before, uncommonly early in the election cycle, he had started receiving around-the-clock Secret Service protection. "Now I know folks talk in the barber shops and beauty salons," Michelle said, "and I've heard some folks say, 'That Barack, he seems like a nice guy, but I'm not sure America's ready for a black president.' Well, all I can say is we've heard those voices before. . . . Voices that focus on what might go wrong, rather than what's possible. And I understand it. I know where it comes from. . . . It's the bitter legacy of racism and dis-crimination and oppression in this country. A legacy that hurts us all."

She asked the crowd to overcome the fear—remove the old plastic protecting Grandma's living room furniture, as she put it—and elect her husband. "Ask yourselves, of all the candidates, who will fight to lift black men up so we don't have to keep locking them up? Who will confront the racial profiling and Jena justice that continues to afflict this nation, the voter disenfranchisement that rears its ugly head every few years and the redlining that persists in our communities, keeping prosperity out and hopelessness in? Who will use the bully pulpit of the presidency to call on black men to accept their responsibility and raise their children? Who will refuse to tolerate Corridors of Shame in this country, of all countries? The answer is clear: Barack Obama. . . . So I'm asking you to believe in Barack, but most of all, I'm asking you to believe in yourselves. I'm asking you to stop settling for the world as it is and to help us make the world as it should be."

More immediately, she was inviting black voters—essential, if he were to win—to abandon the Clintons and join them. The next step was up to Barack. If he could win in Iowa six weeks later, these voters might just conclude he had a chance to become president and turn his way for good.

MICHELLE AND THE GIRLS DESCENDED on Des Moines for the final push with an army of relatives, friends, and babysitters. The adults spread out and campaigned while the kids frolicked. It was Michelle's seventeenth trip to Iowa since March. She was bone-tired and on edge. "Exhausted," said Jackie Norris, a campaign aide who often staffed her. "There's an emotional exhaustion that you can never know until your spouse runs for office." Michelle worried that Barack might lose. And yet as the day drew nearer and the odds grew brighter, she worried even more that he might win. What if he did win, she wondered. What would happen to her then?

The night of January 3, 2008, was bitterly cold. Given a chance to see a caucus, the peculiarly democratic phenomenon that had defined the last ten months of his life, Barack headed to a high school in suburban Ankeny. With a Secret Service agent at the wheel, he was accompanied by Plouffe, Jarrett, and two aides. They pulled into the parking lot and were elated to see throngs of people, varying in age and party, ethnicity and class. Barack thought of his late mother, and how she would have appreciated the human tapestry. Afterward, he joined Michelle and Craig, family and friends, at dinner in West Des Moines. He told Plouffe not to call with predictions, only when the results were clear. When the news did arrive, Barack's victory was assured. He would gather 37 percent of the caucus vote, with Clinton slipping into third, a fraction of a point behind Edwards. He won decisively, by eight percentage points, in a state where one year earlier no one had given him a chance. He took the stage, all smiles, at the Hy-Vee Center, with Michelle, Malia, and Sasha beside him, their fashion choices coordinated, a striking family tableau that would soon become familiar.

"Thank you, Iowa!" he called out. "You know, they said this day would never come. They said our sights were set too high. They said this country was too divided, too disillusioned to ever come together around a common purpose. But on this January night, at this defining moment in history, you have done what the cynics said we couldn't do." He thanked the precinct captains, the volunteers, and the campaign staff. He thanked one person by name: "The love of my life, the rock of the Obama family and the closer on the campaign trail. Give it up for Michelle Obama." Thousands of supporters cheered and shouted and grinned from ear to ear. For the Obamas and their growing legion of believers, the moment was electrifying. Tougher days were yet to come, starting five days later in New Hampshire, but there would always be some magic to Iowa.

# ELEVEN

# Veil of Impossibility

Barack's campaign rocketed into New Hampshire on a high and came crashing down nearly as fast, a victim of its own hubris and a comeback that surprised even his opponents. Hillary Clinton won. The margin was just 7,589 votes, 39.1 percent to Barack's 36.5 percent, and the two candidates each earned nine delegates. But the result reset the narrative and erased the possibility that Barack could knock her quickly out of the race. Amid the gloom in a Concord hotel, it was Michelle who moved among the staff, embraced them one by one, and told them to buck up. Never too high, never too low, was a family mantra. Barack felt blue, but he came to consider the defeat one of the most useful things to happen to his unseasoned campaign. In a long march to the nomination that would toughen them all, Barack faced a political pummeling that was new to him, while Michelle found herself labeled "Mrs. Grievance" on the cover of the *National Review*. Hope might have triumphed over fear in Iowa, but it faced a few other opponents down the road. Washington news reporter Gwen Ifill had been right the year before when she wrote, "The Obamas could not possibly have any idea what awaits them."

In Nevada, eleven days after her New Hampshire victory, Clinton won more votes—if fewer delegates—than Barack, setting the stage for South Carolina, the pivotal battle before Super Tuesday. The pressure was growing and both sides felt increasingly testy. In New Hampshire, where Barack staged large rallies with a triumphant feel, the Clinton troops painted him as condescending during the final debate. During a discussion about likability, he glanced up from his notes and cracked, "You're likable enough, Hillary." Three days later, Bill Clinton disparaged Barack's efforts to distinguish his Iraq War record from Hillary's as "the biggest fairy tale I've ever seen." Spinning the upcoming South Carolina contest, the former president said the candidates were getting votes "because of their race or gender, and that's why people tell me that Hillary doesn't have a chance of winning here." In a state with a sorry history of racially coded language, many African Americans found Clinton's assertion dismissive, at best. "The Clintons are disturbing, telling half-truths and being fearmongers. They're trying to scare white voters away," DeDe Mays, a fifty-nine-year-old black woman, said after attending a multiracial Michelle rally in Hilton Head. "If the Obama camp doesn't do something to counter it, it will probably work."

Michelle did not take kindly to the political punishment that Barack was enduring and she did set out to counter it. She started by lending her name to an unusually pithy fundraising letter. It began, "In the past week or two, another candidate's spouse has been getting an awful lot of attention. We knew getting into this race that Barack would be competing with Senator Clinton and President Clinton at the same time. We expected that Bill Clinton would tout his record from the nineties and talk about Hillary's role in his past success. That's a fair approach and a challenge we are prepared to face. What we didn't expect, at least not from our fellow Democrats, are the win-at-all-costs tactics we've seen recently. We didn't expect misleading accusations that willfully distort Barack's record."

For all of her public protestations that she wanted no seat at the strategy table, Michelle was not shy about speaking up when she believed the Obama campaign was falling short. "If she thinks we're being treated unfairly or doesn't think we're being aggressive enough in debunking attacks, she will say so," strategist David Axelrod said in early 2008. "She does not fold up in the lotus position and start chanting Kumbaya. She's against gratuitous attacks but she's not against defending our position and making sure we don't get punked." Michelle shared this trait with her brother, Craig, who was talked down by campaign manager David Plouffe when he wanted to fight back harder. As Michelle's chief of staff, Melissa Winter, said in South Carolina, recalling times when Michelle was more keen than Barack to go on the attack, "My girl's tough."

INCONGRUOUS AS IT MIGHT SEEM, Michelle Obama and Bill Clinton were increasingly measured against one another. She was a recent political recruit—"a conscript," Axelrod said—matched against one of the most gifted politicians in modern times. Clinton was the commander in chief while Michelle was still a young lawyer trying to divine her future. Seventeen years apart in age and vastly different in experience, they were the history-making spouses of history-making Democratic presidential candidates, stating their case the best way they knew how. Both were confident and funny, opinionated and very smart. Both were Ivy League lawyers with working-class roots. Both had formidable identities independent of their formidable partners. They shared an ability to please a crowd, although in styles as different as the instruments they played, saxophone and piano. His riffs were showy and wide-ranging, often roaming exuberantly through complex material; hers were typically smooth and tart, usually understated, always controlled. His speeches often resembled a State of the Union address as he ricocheted through Pell grants, health care reform, stem-cell research, green-collar jobs, Medicare, Iran, the Geneva Conventions, and the tax code. Hers were more focused, befitting a person who prepared carefully, wasted no words and took her time with the ones she used.

To Michelle, the personal was political. "It isn't just about hope and inspiration. It is about character, quite frankly," she said in South Carolina, drawing an implicit contrast with the tumult of the Clinton White House, whose echoes she heard in the attacks on her husband. "I am here, away from my kids, talking like this all over the country because Barack is different. It is about character." Often asked how she and Barack were handling the rough-and-tumble, she said nothing surprised her. "Power concedes nothing without a struggle," she said. The line alluded to Frederick Douglass, who said in 1857, "Power concedes nothing without a demand. It never did, and it never will. Find out just what any people will submit to, and you have found out the exact amount of injustice and wrong which will be imposed upon them."

"My fear is that we don't know what truth looks like anymore," Michelle said the day before the January 26 primary, as Bill Clinton campaigned an hour away. "I desperately want change, personally. A change in tone, a change in the tone that creates division and separates us, that makes us live in isolation from one another. Sometimes our politics uses that division as a tool and a crutch. We think we can mend it all up after all the dirt has been thrown, but we can't." Later that day, she directly addressed the former president's allegation about Barack's position on the Iraq War. As a U.S. senator, Hillary Clinton had voted to give President Bush the authority to wage war, while Barack as a state senator had given a speech opposing a U.S. military role. "Well, let me tell you something, I live with the man," Michelle said, her tone combining authority and incredulity. She said Barack had always opposed the war and spoke against it at a risky time for him, when he was launching his run for the U.S. Senate, a detail that "his opponents won't tell you."

Barack walloped the field in South Carolina, taking 55 percent of the vote and beating all projections. Clinton was second with 27 percent. John Edwards, son of a North Carolina millworker, won four in ten white votes, but just 18 percent overall. Barack earned 78 percent of the black vote and 24 percent of the white vote. "Race doesn't matter! Race doesn't matter!" supporters chanted at his victory party. When Bill Clinton commented archly that Jesse Jackson, too, had won South Carolina primaries, a host of pundits and politicians quickly called him out. The January skirmishes made plain that race was bound to surface more widely as the campaign churned onward. Sooner or later, the topic was going to burst into the open, however ebullient the victory party chants.

.   .   .

BARACK'S CANDIDACY CAPTURED the hearts of his Democratic supporters in ways unseen since Robert F. Kennedy ran for president forty years earlier. Ally Carragher, a young organizer who joined the campaign in Carroll, Iowa, grew up hearing about Kennedy from her mother, whose eyes sparkled as she told stories from the 1960s. "I know what I will be telling my kids about, and it will be about Obama," Carragher said of the candidate on the eve of Super Tuesday. "What I saw in her eyes is what I feel." A music video capturing that spirit cascaded from giant video screens at Obama rallies and went viral on the Internet when going viral was a relatively new concept. Known as "Yes We Can," the video spliced together Barack's New Hampshire election night speech with scenes of actors and musicians singing the same lines. Its creator was Will.i.am, frontman for the Black Eyed Peas. He said he came up with the concept and the tune because the speech made him think of "freedom . . . equality . . . and truth . . . and that's not what we have today."

The campaign's upbeat call for "change we can believe in" was, in fact, undergirded by a measure of truth telling, and one of the principal tellers was Michelle. Often the more direct of the two Obamas, Michelle did not hesitate to describe the inequities she perceived in the United States at the end of the Bush years, when the Census Bureau estimated that 39.8 million people lived below the poverty line. That meant an individual who earned less than $211 a week or a family of four that collected less than $425. The poverty rate was at an eleven-year high and half the households in the country earned less than $50,303 annually, with corresponding constraints on their access to education and opportunity. The Obamas had recently become wealthy—they reported income of $4.2 million in 2007, almost entirely from book royalties. But Michelle knew the stories behind the numbers through her work on the South Side, her years at Public Allies, and the lives of her own extended family, many of whom were still in the working class or just a decade or two beyond it.

"I look at my life since I was a little girl and things have gotten harder, progressively harder, for regular people. The struggle has been getting worse, not better," she told supporters in Hilton Head, South

Carolina. "And we're still a nation that's a little too mean. I wish mean worked, because we're good at it. Our tone is bad and we've grown to believe that somehow mean talk is tough talk . . . and we reward it. Not just in politics, but we reward it in every sliver of our culture."

The same day, up the road in rural Estill, Michelle carried her message to more than 100 black voters in a storefront office of Obama for America. "This nation is broken," she said. "Our souls are broken and we've lost our way. We have lost our will and the understanding that we have to sacrifice and compromise for one another." Ordinary people were being thwarted again and again, she said, even when their goals were clear and the bar was set. "You reach the bar and they move it. This is true regardless of the color of your skin. This is true regardless of your gender. This is the truth of living in America."

The image of the moving bar, which she used for months, suggested a faceless establishment and a rigged game. In September 2007, she counseled the National Conference of Black Women "to understand what we are up against. You see, for so long, we've been asked to compete in a game where we are given few of the rules and none of the resources to win. And when we do the impossible, when we beat the odds and we play the game better than those who made up the rules, then they do what they do. They change the rules, they move the bar and too many are left behind." *They* were faceless leaders, privileged, unconcerned, or out of touch. The result, she said, was often fear and uncertainty that created a "veil of impossibility." Change would come only when voters became "frustrated and a little angry about the way things are going." In an appeal that could have been pulled from a community organizing handbook, she said "regular folks" needed to talk up Barack's candidacy. They needed to vote their interests and not their fears.

As she toggled between conundrums of race and class, Michelle's campaign message contained both ends of Barack's elemental equation of the world as it is and the world as it should be, the first representing need, the second signifying purpose. For all of the gloom, she always tacked back optimistically to Barack and what he could do for the country. It was Barack Obama, she said, who best represented a step toward fairness, integrity, decency, and dignity—and most represented a break with the established ways. Not Hillary Clinton, not a Republican. "I'm here right now," she said in Hilton Head, "because I think that the only person in this race who has an honest chance of changing the game—not playing it better than those who have played it, but changing the game—is my husband, Barack Obama." She took to ending her speeches with a story about a ten-year-old black girl who approached her in a barber shop in Newberry, South Carolina, birthplace of nineteenth-century AME Church leader Henry McNeal Turner. The girl told Michelle, "If Barack Obama becomes the next president of the United States, it will be historical." Michelle asked what that meant to her. "It means that I can dream of being anything I imagine," the girl replied and began to sob.

"That little girl started to cry, see, because she's 10 and she gets it," Michelle told her audience. "She knows what happens when that veil of impossibility suffocates you, when you live in a country that tells you what you can't do and who you can't be before you even get a chance, when you live in a country that gives education to some and not to all, when you live in a country where politics trumps all reason. That's what's at stake in this election."

KATIE MCCORMICK LELYVELD's phone rang. It was February 18, 2008, and the young press secretary was in Wisconsin on a campaign swing with Michelle, her boss. At the other end of the line were Bill Burton and Dan Pfeiffer, senior members of the campaign's communications staff, calling from Chicago. They had seen the reports and they wanted to know what had gone wrong. Lelyveld, too, had seen the news reports, but did not think anything was amiss. "It's her normal sort of thing," Lelyveld recalled saying. "She doesn't speak in sound bites. She was getting to a bigger point that everybody understood. There's not time in a short broadcast to get there." The Chicago men, already fielding calls from reporters, were worried. When Lelyveld hung up, she flipped the Play button on her ubiquitous pocket recorder and began to transcribe the offending part of the speech.

"Hope is making a comeback," Michelle had said that morning in

Milwaukee, "and, let me tell you, for the first time in my adult life, I am proud of my country. Not just because Barack is doing well, but I think people are hungry for change." *For the first time in my adult life, I am proud of my country.* Fourteen words that would be repeated over and over on the airwaves, dissected by commentators and held aloft by Republican critics as proof positive that Michelle was not the good and decent American patriot that she pretended to be.

The next day, Cindy McCain, wife of Republican candidate John McCain, volunteered, "I'm proud of my country. I don't know about you, if you heard those words earlier. I'm very proud of my country." On Fox News, anti-Obama commentator Sean Hannity told his audience, "To think your country is mean and you have nothing to be proud of, I think that's a big issue." Some critics read into her remarks the idea that she was only proud because Barack, whom she had publicly called "the answer," was winning. Others demanded to know how she could not be proud of a country where she could graduate from Princeton and Harvard, earn a small fortune, and stand a decent chance of taking up residence in the White House. "We've grown up and lived in the same era. And yet her self-absorbed attitude is completely foreign to me," wrote conservative columnist Michelle Malkin, the Oberlin-educated daughter of parents from the Philippines. "What planet is she living on?"

Michelle Obama's remarks that day were not accidental or ad-libbed. She made the same point twice, using nearly identical language several hours apart. Moving from Milwaukee to Madison, the state capital, she said, "Hope is making a comeback. And let me tell you something. For the first time in my adult lifetime, I'm really proud of my country. And not just because Barack has done well, but because I think people are hungry for change. And I have been desperate to see our country moving in that direction and just not feeling so alone in my frustration and disappointment. I've seen people who are hungry to be unified around some basic, common issues and it's made me proud. I feel privileged to be a part of even witnessing this, traveling around states all over this country and being reminded that there is more that unites us than divides us, that the struggles of a farmer in Iowa are no different than what's happening on the South Side of Chicago, that people are feeling the same pain and wanting the same things for their families."

To Michelle's staff and many in her audience, what she said was a commonplace—not remarkable, not meriting the firestorm that followed. What, they wondered, was the big deal? No less respected a figure than Colin Powell, the first African American chairman of the Joint Chiefs of Staff, had written in his autobiography, *My American Journey,* a dozen years earlier, "The army made it easier for me to love my country, with all its flaws." Paul Schmitz, Michelle's former Public Allies colleague, happened to be in the front row in Milwaukee, his video camera rolling. "No one who was there thought they had heard a gaffe. No one leaving there thought, 'Oh, boy, we've got a problem,'" said Schmitz, a white man. "It all made absolute sense. I could have said the same thing. How many people do you know who said, 'A guy with the name Barack Hussein Obama? There's no way. It can't happen.' That was a normal conversation at that time. I think that was common knowledge, that the country really had shown that it had grown up."

Back in Chicago, historian Timuel Black thought nothing of it, certain that Michelle was "expressing a feeling that millions and millions of African Americans feel." Lawyer James Montgomery, who like Black had tasted prejudice, did not think Michelle had misspoken. "That was vintage truth: 'Here I am, my husband is running for president. He is black. And Iowa has just given him a resounding victory,'" said the former civil rights attorney, who lived two doors north of the Obamas in Hyde Park. "I think it really says that deep down in her innards, she had doubts about whether or not a white majority would elect a black president. In her day, she has seen a lot of reasons in Chicago not to be proud of her country."

Inside Chicago headquarters, however, the campaign leadership uttered a collective "Uh-oh." They focused on a broad electorate needing to be persuaded that Barack was safe and sufficiently mainstream. Seen through that prism, Michelle's remarks were unhelpful, to say the least. The damage control started quickly. "What she meant," Burton wrote to reporters, "is that she's really proud at this moment." Barack came to his wife's defense, pointing out her longtime skepticism about politics. He said the comment was misunderstood. "What she meant was, this is the first time that she's been proud of the politics of America. Because she's pretty cynical about the political process, and with good reason, and she's not alone," he said.

At her next public event, two days later in Rhode Island, Michelle herself tried to explain. "I'm proud in how Americans are engaging in the political process," she said. "For the first time in my lifetime, I'm seeing people rolling up their sleeves in a way that I haven't seen." A reporter asked whether she had, in fact, always been proud of her country. "Absolutely," she said. Reflecting on the episode after the caravan had moved on, adviser Robert Gibbs said he was just glad the moment had occurred early in the campaign, and not on the eve of the November election.

REACTIONS TO MICHELLE'S REMARKS exposed a divide in what people were prepared to believe about her. To her fans, she was speaking truth to power, being authentic, keeping it real. She saw problems and identified solutions, using her own narrative of renewed hope to reassure the skeptical and rally the tuned-out. To her foes, she was a naysayer, an ingrate, and a snob who failed to appreciate what the country had done for her and her black Icarus of a husband. The budding anti-Michelle narrative suggested that she was not only divisive, but quite possibly dangerous, maybe treasonous. Her Princeton thesis would be invoked to support that view and so would her membership in Trinity United Church of Christ, with its "unashamedly black and unapologetically Christian" credo. Juan Williams, a black commentator for Fox News, would say later that Michelle has "this Stokely Carmichael in a designer dress thing going." When Michelle greeted Barack onstage at campaign events with a fist bump, a Fox personality asked rhetorically if it was a "terrorist fist jab." Unfounded reports lit up the right-wing blogosphere that Michelle had said bad things about a country run by "whitey."

Michelle dismissed the increasingly fantastical allegations as preposterous, and *The New Yorker* spoofed the emerging caricature on its cover. The cartoon depicted Michelle as an Afro-wearing jihadist in combat boots, a Kalashnikov slung over her shoulder, fist-bumping Barack in the Oval Office. The artist, Barry Blitt, said he was trying to reveal the criticism "as the fear-mongering ridiculousness that it is." The line of attack reached the ears of Malia, who turned ten on July 4, 2008. She asked Barack one day, when Michelle was within earshot, why people on the news were saying that "Mom doesn't love her country." Barack explained that sometimes people in politics say mean things. Malia replied, "Yeah, that's nuts."

Looking for explanations, Michelle's law school friend Verna Williams pointed to the relative novelty in national politics of an accomplished, assertive, professional black woman. She said the critics, so quick to turn to stereotypes, were essentially asking, "How can Michelle Obama be First Lady when she's no lady at all?" Through generations of American history, ladyhood was the province of white women alone. The model political wife in popular memory was obsequious, not to mention white. Making news for anything other than glowing encomiums directed toward the candidate was never the goal. As Marjorie Williams once wrote of Barbara Bush, the tart-tongued wife of George H. W. Bush, "It is one of the chief requirements of her job that she say as few genuinely memorable things as possible." Wives were not expected to say, as Michelle had said already, that the country had gone to war in Iraq because U.S. leaders "were not willing to tell us the truth," or that it would be nice to have someone in the White House "who understands the Constitution, particularly as we have seen it obliterated." In Michelle's case, partisan pushback that might have greeted any assertive political spouse was reinforced by disdain grounded in racial prejudice. The vitriol pooled and eddied in countless Internet comments sections, demonstrating that Michelle was becoming a target in her own right. "You are amazed sometimes at how deep the lies can be," she told *The New York Times.* "I mean, 'whitey'? . . . Anyone who says that doesn't know me. They don't know the life I've lived. They don't know anything about me."

With decisive victories in Wisconsin and Hawaii on February 19, Barack had won ten contests in a row by an average margin of thirty-four percentage points, leaving Clinton ever further behind in the delegate chase. But as she steered toward friendlier ground in Texas and Ohio, the New York senator showed no inclination to quit, telling voters that she was the known quantity, the one who had been close to power, the one they could trust. "This is the choice we face," she said. "One of us is ready to be commander in chief in a dangerous world. One of us has faced serious Republican opposition in the past. And one of us is ready to do it again." Indeed, Clinton would win the Texas and Ohio popular vote, sending the Obamas and much of Barack's high command into a funk as they trudged toward certain defeat seven weeks later in Pennsylvania. Before the Pennsylvania vote, things would get worse, in the shape of the Reverend Jeremiah A. Wright Jr. and the sound of his sermons looping through the mediaplex. The eruption prompted Barack to give his most explicit speech yet on race and racism in American society, a shoal his political strategists had hoped to skirt.

WHO WAS Jeremiah Wright? Barack described him as an inspirational and insightful South Side figure, a deep-thinking pastor who "helped bring me to Jesus and helped bring me to church." He cared about social justice, supported the HIV/AIDS community, developed a church mission in Africa, and delivered the sermon that inspired the title of Barack's second book, *The Audacity of Hope*. Something of a mentor to Barack during his early Chicago years, Wright married Barack and Michelle and baptized Malia and Sasha. On the campaign trail, Michelle would often begin her remarks to African American church audiences by offering greetings from Pastor Wright. But the theatrical, dashiki-wearing character who emerged during the campaign hardly resembled Barack's early portrait. Even allowing for the speedy reduction of Wright to media caricature, it was hard to square Barack's initial description with the shotgun sprays of anti-establishment, anti-government bombast in Wright's sermons.

The campaign staff knew in February 2007 that Wright's presence in the Obama camp created a quandary. He was due to deliver the invocation at Barack's presidential announcement in Springfield, but advisers argued that newly published details of a Wright sermon could swamp coverage of the speech. "Fact number one, we've got more black men in prison than there are in college," Wright preached, according to *Rolling Stone*. "Fact number two: Racism is how this country was founded and how this country is still run! We are deeply involved in the importing of drugs, the exporting of guns and the training of professional killers. . . . We believe in white supremacy and black inferiority and believe it more than we believe in God." Alerted to the magazine article, Barack reluctantly informed Wright that he would not have a speaking part on announcement day. He invited the minister to pray beforehand with the family, which he did.

It was on March 13, 2008, nine days after Barack's draining loss in Texas and Ohio, that Wright emerged as a full-blown campaign problem. The source was an ABC News report, three minutes, twenty-five seconds long, that juxtaposed short excerpts from Wright's sermons with supportive comments from Barack about his twenty years in the Trinity congregation. In a 2003 clip, Wright blamed American authorities for imprisoning excessive numbers of African Americans and expecting citizens "to sing 'God *Bless* America.' No, no, no! God *damn* America! That's in the Bible for killing innocent people. God *damn* America for treating our citizens as less than human! God *damn* America for as long as she acts like she is God and she is supreme."

In another sermon, from September 16, 2001, five raw days after the terrorist attacks on the World Trade Center and the Pentagon, Wright suggested that the attacks were payback for American violence and misdeeds abroad. He pointed out that far more people had died when the United States dropped a pair of atomic bombs on Japan in an effort to end World War II. "America's chickens," he declared, "are coming home to roost." The ABC piece quoted Barack likening his pastor, who had recently retired, to "an old uncle who sometimes says things I don't agree with." It also included Trinity members coming to Wright's defense. "No, I wouldn't call it radical," one woman told the camera crew. "I'd call it being black in America."

The news about Wright—propelled by the video images that became ubiquitous—prompted a new wave of scrutiny of Barack's identity and intentions. At a time when the Clinton campaign was trying to paint him as callow and unelectable, skeptics were asking whether a candidate with a preacher like Wright could be trusted with the keys to the White House. Barack had lost white voters by a large margin in Ohio, and now, as the nomination fight dragged on, Pennsylvania was looming, followed by Indiana and North Carolina. Fresh controversy the campaign did not need. Barack released a statement calling Wright's statements "inflammatory and appalling." But the statement only took him so far. "What you had was a moment where all the suspicions and misunderstandings that are embedded in our racial history were suddenly laid bare," Barack later told Dan Balz of *The Washington Post.* "If we had not handled the Reverend Wright episode properly, I think we could have lost."

MARTY NESBITT WAS in Chicago when he got a call from Barack, who was campaigning in Indiana. Barack reported that he was sitting with Eric Whitaker and Valerie Jarrett and they were holding an empty chair for him. Nesbitt had intended to take that campaign swing, but his wife was about to give birth. He had been following the news. "This Jeremiah Wright thing is a blessing in disguise," he said into the phone. Barack burst out laughing and reported to the others what Nesbitt had said. Nesbitt explained that Wright had created an obstacle, for sure, but one that Barack could remove. He could do it with a speech, often considered by Barack but never delivered, about race in America. Only Barack could give that address, Nesbitt went on, not simply because he identified himself as a black man, but because he had a white mother and a white grandmother and had thought deeply about racial issues for much of his adult life. Nesbitt said that if Barack gave the powerful speech that everyone knew he could give—and that Clinton, as a white woman, could not—it would be "game over." Barack, who had already alerted his advisers, said, "I guess I have to give the speech, then."

Michelle, too, saw the Wright conflagration as a moment when Barack needed to step forward. "The conversation that Barack and I had was, 'This is the opportunity. This is the reason why you're here.

This is why you're in this race, because there is a perspective, a voice, that you can bring to this conversation that is needed and that no one else can do or say," Michelle explained. "What I said to Barack was, 'I know you have it in your head. I know exactly what you want to say to the American people about this and how complex it is.' And this is what leadership is all about. This is the opportunity, and this is just one example of how Barack will have to lead."

Once the decision was made to give the speech in Philadelphia, Michelle made a rare call to campaign manager David Plouffe to ask whether an arena with perhaps a hundred seats for spectators, apart from the media, was big enough. "We need energy and fight and passion, not something that will come across as a dry lecture," Plouffe recalled Michelle telling him. She said Barack needed "to see supportive faces and be boosted." Plouffe reviewed the situation with his colleagues. The campaign stuck with its plan to hold the event at the National Constitution Center. He explained the reasoning to Michelle, who would travel to Philadelphia for moral support, as would Nesbitt, Jarrett, and Eric Holder, the future attorney general. "Michelle was very good in moments like this," Plouffe said. "She didn't raise many questions about the campaign broadly, but when she did, it was with good reason. Once she determined we had worked things through thoroughly, she was generally satisfied, and that was the case now."

AFTER LABORING DEEP into the night to get the words right, Barack delivered the speech on March 18 against a backdrop of American flags stationed onstage like sentinels. With nods toward Abraham Lincoln, the Constitution, and the guiding purpose of his own political quest, he titled the address "A More Perfect Union." It was, in many ways, a speech of translation, the work of a thinking man with a window into many worlds, describing black and white to each other. More significantly, it was a speech of explanation, the product of a politician born with brown skin feeling obligated to describe to a white audience what he was not, and what he was. Barack wove his personal history, and Michelle's, through an account of American history informed by the undeniable fact that an African American man married to a descendant of slaves stood on the threshold of the presidency. The thirty-eight-minute address contained elements of their familiar depiction of the world as it is and the world as it should be, but he added an intermediate step: the world as it was becoming.

There was no doubt, Barack said, that black bitterness and white resentment persisted, fueling mutual anger and a sense of "racial stalemate." But Wright's "profound mistake," he said, was to portray U.S. society as static, as being just as racist as it was when the preacher was coming of age in the 1950s and 1960s, when "segregation was still the law of the land and opportunity was systematically constricted." Those were the times of Jim Crow, Barack reminded his audience, when black people were excluded from labor unions, police departments, and certain neighborhoods, when banks denied loans to black business owners, and the fabric of black families eroded, partly due to the shame and frustration that flowed from the lack of economic opportunity. Those profound injustices weighed black people down, he said, and still informed the views of men and women of Wright's generation—a generation that included, not incidentally, Fraser and Marian Robinson. But where Wright went wrong, Barack said, was in his failure to credit evidence "that America can change."

Barack told worried campaign advisers that he had attended Trinity much less frequently in recent years and did not recall hearing the most inflammatory statements. He nonetheless attempted to explain them, describing Wright's performances as bits of set-piece theater familiar to black congregants across the country. From the pews, he said, worshippers felt free to pick and choose from the rhetorical offerings, just as the faithful do in any religious denomination. "The fact that so many people are surprised to hear that anger in some of Reverend Wright's sermons," Barack said, "simply reminds us of the old truism that the most segregated hour in American life occurs on Sunday morning."

Despite the uproar and the pain, Barack said in Philadelphia that he would not dissociate himself from his pastor. "I can no more disown him than I can disown the black community," he said. "I can no more disown him than I can my white grandmother—a woman who helped raise me, a woman who sacrificed again and again for me, a woman who loves me as much as she loves anything in this world. But a woman who once confessed her fear of black men who passed her by on the street, and who on more than one occasion has uttered racial or ethnic stereotypes that made me cringe. These people are a part of me and they are a part of America, this country that I love." Looking ahead, he counseled the African American community to accept "the burdens of our past without becoming victims of our past." He urged the white community to acknowledge that "what ails the African American community does not just exist in the minds of black people, that the legacy of discrimination, and current incidents of discrimination, while less overt than in the past, are real and must be addressed."

The speech was widely viewed as a political success. It stanched the bleeding caused by the Wright sermons and, for voters willing to be reassured, it offered reason to be so. In Barack's circle, Nesbitt was photographed in the audience, watching silently, a tear trickling down his cheek. Michelle said what Barack "did in his speech was give voice to every emotion I have." She knew better than anyone how Barack had lived the words he spoke, and how he had arrived at them. "I was incredibly proud of what he said. Everything he said spoke to me in so many ways. Every word that he uttered was clarifying and wise and kind and unifying." She predicted that the speech was "only the beginning of a long dialogue that we have to have," and that Barack would lead it, "unlike many before who have just shied away from it because it's hard." Her own view, she made clear: "I'm not afraid of the conversation. I'm desperate for us to have it so that we can move beyond it."

THE OBAMA CAMPAIGN WHEEZED its way, exhausted and disheartened, through the predicted loss in Pennsylvania. The night after the defeat, the high command met around the dinner table at the Obamas' Hyde Park house to focus anew. Still leading in the Democratic delegate count, they saw a new chance in North Carolina and Indiana to do what they had repeatedly failed to do, all the way back to New Hampshire, and put Clinton away. Just as they were building momentum, however, Wright resurfaced with a batch of virulent statements bordering on the bizarre. Barack realized he needed to say something more. He called the performance "appalling" and a "spectacle." It "contradicts everything I'm about and who I am," he said. "I have spent my entire adult life trying to bridge the gap between different kinds of people. That's in my DNA, trying to promote mutual understanding." He said Michelle was "similarly angered." Feeling wounded, betrayed, and mystified, they resigned from Trinity. Barack continued to campaign intently through the firestorm, as did Michelle, who finished a punishing stretch of solo appearances with a speech lasting nearly an hour in Gary, Indiana, late on the night before polls opened. She then jetted to Indianapolis for a final rally with Barack that included a morale-boosting appearance by Stevie Wonder, whose music she had first cherished as a young girl, more than thirty-five years earlier.

Voters in North Carolina broke Barack's way, as did enough Indiana voters to put him within a whisker of a victory there. He did particularly well among African American voters and young people, many of them newly registered. At the end of the night, NBC newsman Tim Russert declared, "We now know who the Democratic nominee will be." The remaining half-dozen primaries were a formality. Clinton had won an estimated 18 million votes and pushed the Obama campaign to the limit, but she could not catch up. On June 3, with voters going to the polls in South Dakota and Montana and so-called super delegates flocking to his candidacy, Barack clinched the nomination. He spoke from a stage in Minnesota, clearly moved by the victory and, he said later, a dawning sense of obligation to win in November.

After the celebration, Michelle flew back to Chicago to be home when Malia and Sasha woke up. The girls were half asleep the next morning when they crawled into bed with her and learned that Barack was going to be the Democratic nominee. "And they're like, 'Ooh, this is a big night for Dad!'" Michelle recalled. "I said, 'Well, do you guys realize what a big deal this is? Do you realize there has never been an African American that has been a presidential nominee?'" Malia answered, "Well, yeah, I can believe that. Because black people were slaves and they couldn't vote for such a long time and of *course* this is a big deal.'"

TRIUMPH ASIDE, the months after the "proud" comments were difficult for Michelle. For all of the accolades from friends and supporters as she emerged on the national stage, she felt misunderstood, at best. "A lot of sleepless nights," she said. The tone of the debate was hurtful and at times hateful. It frustrated her and shook her confidence. More than anything, she told friends and staff, she could not bear the thought that she might be harming Barack's chances. A bevy of reports emerged, fueled by her Wisconsin remarks, that Michelle's campaign trail tone was too negative, too edgy—that she appeared to be, as the simplistic and pernicious stereotype would have it, an angry black woman. Her natural style, some members of the campaign staff thought, was becoming a liability to a black candidate who would need white swing voters to win in November. Strategists concluded that she needed to modify her delivery, but no one wanted to be the bearer of that news. "They were afraid they were going to be shot," said Forrest Claypool, a political adviser involved in the discussions. In the end, several staff members talked things over with her. She was furious, but not for the reasons they had anticipated. If her delivery was a problem, she demanded to know, why hadn't someone told her *sooner*? "She was angry that everyone was tiptoeing around the candidate's wife," Claypool said, recalling that she told them, "I can adapt. I want to be an asset to the campaign."

The end of the grueling primary season gave the campaign time to reconsider Michelle's approach, with an eye toward an August relaunch on the grand stage of the Democratic National Convention in Denver. Michelle worked hard at it, following through on her promise. She had never been asked to perform on a stage this big in a moment this important, but her ability to nail a performance had already impressed campaign consultants. Earlier in the primary season, Claypool and John Kupper coached Michelle as she worked through her stump speech. They met in the conference room of the Axelrod firm's headquarters at 730 North Franklin in Chicago. After she delivered the speech, they suggested perhaps two dozen specific improvements in her delivery, such as slowing down in one place or adding emphasis to a particular syllable. "I know that's a lot to absorb. We'll break it out into pieces and we'll go through it," Claypool told her reassuringly. "Okay, let me try it again," Michelle replied. When she finished, Claypool was stunned by how thoroughly she had absorbed the critique and incorporated the changes. "It was flawless. John and I just looked at each other and said, 'I think we're done here.' I've never seen anything like it, ever. She's a pro's pro."

DURING THE LULL after the primaries, Michelle spent more time back in Hyde Park, where the girls finished their year at Lab School and went to after-school activities and sleepovers as Michelle fought to retain a sense of normalcy. Slipping into the rhythms of ordinary family life was next to impossible, not only because of her fame and the demands on her time, but also because of the Secret Service agents who shadowed her around the clock. They set up a command post outside the house. They stationed themselves at school. They organized caravans to ballet classes and soccer matches and kept outsiders at bay. Sasha, who turned seven that year, called them "the secret people."

Michelle had long feared that Barack's prominence could make him a target. Medgar Evers, Malcolm X, and the Reverend Martin Luther King Jr. all fell to assassins' bullets. "It only takes one person and it only takes one incident. I mean, I know history, too," she said. She had met King's widow, Coretta Scott King, a few years earlier. "What I remember most was that she told me not to be afraid because God was with us—Barack and me—and that she would always keep us in her prayers." In agreeing to the presidential race, Michelle made clear to Barack that she expected him to get Secret Service protection. She also wanted to maintain her income and her professional reputation in case he died, given that national politics put him in what she called a position of "high-risk." While there would be "great sympathy and out-pouring if something were to happen, I don't want to be in a position one day where I am vulnerable with my children," she told writer David

Mendell. "I need to be in a position for my kids where, if they lose their father, they don't lose everything."

Early in the campaign, Barack's staff printed a sheaf of incendiary material that was circulating on the Internet and delivered it to Senator Richard Durbin, an Illinois Democrat and member of the Senate leadership. Durbin relayed the information to Senate majority leader Harry Reid, starting the process that would establish the Secret Service presence. In May 2007, eighteen months before the general election, Barack began operating behind the cordon, yet it was hard not to fret. He was the target of hatred—sometimes threatening, sometimes merely vile. Many African American supporters, especially, shuddered to think of the instant they would learn that he had been shot. Television newsman Steve Kroft asked Michelle whether she had considered the possibility. "I don't lose sleep over it because the realities are that, as a black man, Barack can get shot going to the gas station," she said. "So, you can't make decisions based on fear and the possibility of what might happen. We just weren't raised that way." The Secret Service became part of the Obamas' lives. Barack's code name was Renegade. Michelle's was Renaissance.

DESPITE THE BARRICADES and restrictions, Hyde Park was a haven, the community where the Obamas felt most at home during the never-ending campaign. The neighborhood spoke to their desires and their values. It also, perhaps inevitably, became a symbol to Republican critics of what was wrong with them. No American president had been elected from a place quite like Hyde Park, home to a university famous for intellectualism, a pair of 1960s Weather Underground radicals famous for being unrepentant, and a bloc of voters famous for choosing John Kerry over the victorious George W. Bush by 19 to 1. Judging by the demonization, the Obamas might as well have lived at the corner of Liberal and Kumbaya. Republican strategist Karl Rove placed Hyde Park alongside Cambridge and San Francisco in a triad of leftist tomfoolery. *The Weekly Standard* recalled Barack's description of former Weatherman Bill Ayers as merely "a guy who lives in my neighborhood" and asked who lives in a neighborhood like that.

In real life, the area more properly described as Hyde Park–Kenwood could not be so easily typecast. The political ethic was proudly progressive on matters of race and social justice, yet the community was anchored by the University of Chicago, an incubator of some of the nation's most prominent conservatives, from Supreme Court justice Antonin Scalia to Nobel Prize–winning free marketeer Milton Friedman. Nation of Islam leader Louis Farrakhan lived within four blocks of the Obamas' $1.6 million home, as did Ayers and his wife, Bernardine Dohrn, a fellow former radical. Yet so did Richard Epstein, a prominent libertarian law professor quick to say that he was friends with Scalia and Ayers and had once tried to hire Dohrn.

To be a Hyde Parker, dozens of residents explained, was to choose to live in a community that considered variations of race, creed, wealth, and politics to be a neighborhood selling point, like bicycle paths or broadband. "I grew up playing with the children of welfare families and the children of Nobel Prize winners and you don't think anything of it," said Arne Duncan, superintendent of Chicago Public Schools and later U.S. secretary of education. "You grow up very comfortable and confident around people who don't look like you and are from very different backgrounds." Mainstream, as mainstream was commonly defined in statistical terms, was not Hyde Park. The average white metropolitan resident in the United States lived in a neighborhood 80 percent white and only 7 percent black. Census tracts in the exurbs and the countryside were often even whiter. By contrast, the 2000 census found that 43.5 percent of the 29,000 residents of Hyde Park proper called themselves white, 37.7 percent black, 11.3 percent Asian, and 4.1 percent Hispanic. Another 3.4 percent answered "other." In economic terms, there was an abundance of six-figure earners, yet one in six residents lived in poverty. The median household income was about $45,000, roughly 10 percent lower than the national average. It was also surely the rare place in the country where an academic and his wife, going through a divorce, would include a clause splitting future winnings if he won the Nobel Prize in economics. One professor and his ex-wife did just that. He won, and sent her $500,000.

The house on Greenwood Avenue that Barack and Michelle bought in 2005 had a lineage that suited the community's modern-day reputation. For seven years in the mid-twentieth century, it was owned by the Hebrew Theological Academy, which ran a Jewish day school there. In 1954, the Hyde Park Lutheran Church purchased the mansion with its four fireplaces and made it the local headquarters of the Lutheran Human Relations Association of America. The Reverend George Hrbek called it home from 1966 to 1971, directing a project designed to counteract racism, principally by raising the consciousness of young white people who visited the house or lived there. At any given time, as many as twenty people bunked in the building, some for weeks, some for years. Hrbek estimated that three thousand people, including waves of divinity students, took part in the training. "If you wanted to deal with racism," he said, "you had to deal with the white community." During the 1968 Democratic National Convention, members of the Chicago Seven stayed in the house. In 1971, four firebombs did minor damage to the outside of the building. When Hrbek learned after the 2008 election that Barack and Michelle owned it, he sent the president a letter saying that their house was "filled with good spirits."

It was nonetheless true that Hyde Park's twentieth-century history had an ugly side even before the University of Chicago's investment in white neighborhood committees and urban renewal. Phoebe Moten Johnson, mother of LaVaughn Robinson and great-grandmother of Michelle, lived in Hyde Park during a paroxysm of harassment and violence intended to terrorize black residents. Between 1917 and 1921, when Phoebe and her family lived at 5470 South Kenwood—six blocks from where Michelle and Barack would live ninety years later—bombs struck fifty-eight homes owned by black families or the white men who sold homes to black people. One week when violence struck her neighborhood, Phoebe was frantic. She mixed water and lye in a kettle and heated it on a wood-burning stove, ready to throw it in the eyes of any white marauders who broke down her door. Friction continued. In the 1940s, it was restrictive covenants. In the 1950s, it was urban renewal. By the 1960s, when some people actually did sing "Kumbaya," the economic divide in Hyde Park prompted a joke that the community, for all of its pride in racial integration, was really a case of "black and white together, standing shoulder to shoulder against the poor."

Author Blue Balliett based her inquisitive, multicultural twelve-year-old protagonists in *Chasing Vermeer* on students at Lab School, where she had taught. Supreme Court Justice John Paul Stevens earned his high school degree there and Langston Hughes had once been artist in residence. "It's a place where you can be who you are and bring any kind of diversity to the table and be celebrated for it," Balliett said of the community. "Kids really can grow up in Hyde Park and never hear a negative conversation about those differences. My son used to say, 'How come we aren't at least Jewish and Christian?'" When he was a boy, social activist Jamie Kalven lived in a third-floor apartment in a home owned by Manhattan Project chemist Harold Urey. At various times, the house was also owned by prizefighter Sonny Liston and jazz pianist Ahmad Jamal. Muhammad Ali once lived nearby. In an outdoor cage, he kept a pair of lions given to him by Mobutu Sese Seko, the corrupt ruler of Zaire. Kalven spoke of the presence in Hyde Park of a roughly equal number of blacks and whites "for whom the fact of living together is no big deal." Which was, in a sense, the big deal.

For Barack, who wanted to be seen during the campaign as distinctive but unthreatening, his chosen turf represented political eclecticism and a sense of possibility that came to be called, with insufficient reflection, post-racial. But the narrative cut both ways as Republicans pushed the argument that the erudite Barack was overly exotic, elitist, and naive. He bodysurfed in Hawaii, he ordered green tea ice cream in Oregon, he wrote his own books, and his name was Barack Hussein Obama. "This is not a man who sees America as you and I do, as the greatest force for good in the world," said Alaska governor Sarah Palin after she became the Republican vice presidential nominee. Valerie Jarrett, who had lived much of her life in the community, begged to differ. "Hyde Park is the real world as it should be," she said. "If we could take Hyde Park and we could help make more Hyde Parks around our country, I think we would be a much stronger country."

THE DEMOCRATIC NATIONAL CONVENTION opened in Denver on August 25, 2008, with Michelle as the keynote speaker on the tone-setting first night. The campaign knew it had work to do to introduce not only Barack but Michelle, whose unfavorability numbers were uncomfortably high. Earlier that month, 29 percent of respondents to an NBC News/Wall Street Journal poll viewed Michelle negatively, including 18 percent who described their feelings as "very negative." Only 38 percent viewed her positively, while 28 percent were neutral and 5 percent did not know her name or were unsure. "It's scary," an undecided voter told the *St. Petersburg Times* after connecting her "proud of my country" comments with her Princeton thesis, which was circulating on the Web. "To think she's going to be whispering in the president's ear when he's in bed."

The campaign saw Denver as a chance to hit the reset button. "It was important to us for a whole range of reasons for her to do well and to address some of these questions that were lingering about her," Axelrod said. "And it was important to us for her to do what she did to explain Barack to people." For Michelle herself, it was a chance to regain her confidence and demonstrate her value on the biggest stage yet. The criticism "really hurt her," Axelrod said, especially as someone accustomed to "excelling and always being prepared and always being able to do the right thing. I think it also gave her a sense of just how exposed she was . . . in this hair-trigger environment." She asked for a draft of her speech more than a month before the curtain went up, then spent weeks refining and practicing it until she knew the words nearly by heart. Her share of the evening began with a six-minute campaign video titled "South Side Girl," borrowing the regular folks frame that she had adopted on the trail. Enveloped by soft voices and soothing music, the film emphasized the themes of family and community and a commitment to give back. Marian served as narrator and Craig and Barack made cameos. No character, however, figured more prominently than her father, Fraser, who had died seventeen years before.

MARIAN: Michelle was especially close to her daddy.
CRAIG: My father was in his 50s and my sister would still sit on his lap and put her head on his shoulder, as she used to do when she was a kid. And that sort of one picture epitomizes their relationship.

BARACK: Her dad was just a sweet man, a kind-hearted man and somebody who thought everybody should be treated with dignity and respect. And I think that carried over to Michelle.

MARIAN: Michelle has always reached out to others. It was something I loved about my husband, too.

CRAIG: Michelle's compassion came from my father and people came to him with their problems and he always managed to have people go away feeling better than they did when they came to talk to him. I'm certain that that's where Michelle gets her compassion from.

MICHELLE: I think about him every day when I think about how I raise my kids, because I remember his compassion. I remember the words, his advice, the way he lived life. And I am trying each and every day to apply that to how I raise my kids. I want his legacy to live through them, and hopefully it will affect the kind of First Lady that I will become, because it's his compassion and his view of the world that really inspires who I am, who I want my girls to be, and what I hope for the country.

Michelle's speech, which followed the video and an introduction by Craig, featured references to Fraser early and late in the narrative. Three sentences in, she said, "I can feel my dad looking down on us, just as I've felt his presence in every grace-filled moment of my life." She declared that she stood on the podium as a sister, a wife, a daughter, and a "mom." She called her father "our rock" and ended by asking her audience to devote themselves to Barack's election, "in honor of my father's memory and my daughters' future," as well as everyone who labored to build the world as it should be. Beyond telling a story of their lives that emphasized uplift and hard work, she recognized the eighty-eighth anniversary of women winning the right to vote and the forty-fifth anniversary of Martin Luther King's "I Have a Dream" speech. "I stand here today," she said, breaking through the applause, "at the crosscurrents of that history, knowing that my piece of the American dream is a blessing hard won by those who came before me, all of them driven by the same conviction that drove my dad to get up an hour early each day to painstakingly dress himself for work, the same con-

viction that drives the men and women I've met all across this country."
She folded into the speech a declaration that she loved her country. The
crowd cheered.

The address was the opening success in what proved to be a happy
week for Democrats, launching the Obamas toward November and
the battle against John McCain, U.S. senator from Arizona, and Palin,
the idiosyncratic governor of Alaska, who wowed the Republican base
but left many others cold. Michelle's poll numbers immediately shot
skyward, rising eighteen points in the Obama campaign's overnight
tracking polls, and they stayed aloft. By October, she drew crowds of
two thousand in Columbus, seven thousand in Pensacola, and eleven
thousand in Gainesville. "Surreal is almost like an understatement,"
her brother, Craig, said. "It's magical is what it is. I mean, it's like going
to sleep and waking up and you're Tinkerbell."

In Akron, eleven days before election day, Michelle no longer mentioned in her stump speech her Ivy League education or Barack's. She
made no reference to his work as a professor of constitutional law, his
eight years in the Illinois senate, or his three-plus years in Washington.
Nor did she mention the stacked deck or the moving bar. What she
said was "We're just regular folks." Before the rally, Michelle dropped
by the local campaign office, where a dozen volunteers were dialing
for voters. Taking a telephone from a supporter, she said cheerily,
"How are you! You're still undecided? That's okay. What can I tell you
about my husband?" In the next few minutes, she did some listening
and some answering, offering a careful rationale for an Obama presidency. "We've been doing the same thing for the last eight years and it
hasn't worked," she said, describing her husband as "a fighter for regular folks, and that's our background." She described her upbringing
as the daughter of working-class parents who did not attend college.
She mentioned Marian, who had retired and was living on a pension,
and Barack's sister Maya, a teacher. She also mentioned Barack's ailing
grandmother Toot, who had long been unable to travel and would die
within a fortnight, two days before her grandson was elected president.
"We're living close to the issues," said Michelle. She added as she hung
up, "That's my pitch. Thank you for letting me go on and on."

. . .

ON ELECTION DAY, Barack and Michelle, joined by Malia and Sasha, voted early at Beulah Shoesmith Elementary in Hyde Park. Michelle went to have her hair done, taking the girls with her, and Barack made the quickest of campaign trips to neighboring Indiana, where a win would be icing and a loss forgettable. He returned in time for an afternoon game of pickup basketball with friends and relatives, then retreated to the house on Greenwood to await results. As polls began to close and votes were counted, Michelle, Barack, Marian, and the girls sat down to dinner with Craig and his family—his second wife, Kelly, and his two children, Avery and Leslie. Marian asked the kids about school, their teachers, their favorite subjects. The television was off, although Michelle and Barack each kept a BlackBerry on the table in front of them. Every so often, one phone or the other would buzz. They would read the message and make no comment. When the pace of buzzing picked up, Barack walked into the kitchen and turned on a small TV. "Well," he said, "looks like we're going to win this thing." Soon after, Michelle answered a call, turned to Barack, and said, "Congratulations, Mr. President."

Barack gave his victory speech in Grant Park, best known until that night as the place where Chicago police battered protesters outside the 1968 Democratic National Convention. As the motorcade headed north along Lake Shore Drive through an unseasonably warm November night, Malia said, "Hey, how come there are no other cars?" Police had stopped traffic in both directions. At that moment, Craig said, it registered with him that voters had actually chosen Barack to be the next president of the United States. As he rode through the city toward the Hyatt hotel where they would await the official results, he told himself that an unfulfilled promise in the Declaration of Independence had finally been borne out, the line that said, "We hold these truths to be self-evident, that all men are created equal."

The crowd in Grant Park, more than 100,000 strong, was delirious with joy when the networks called the election for Barack at 10 p.m. Central Time as polls closed on the West Coast. MyKela Loury wept.

A black woman, she stood alone on a sidewalk within earshot of the cheering throngs. She put her hand to her mouth, then both hands to her temples, her mouth open in a silent gasp. "I'm thinking justice, finally. Fairness, finally," Loury said. "Oh, gosh." The tears came again. "Oh, Jesus." Car horns blared. Supporters shouted and laughed and screamed and hugged one another and laughed some more. So many of Barack's followers had wanted this outcome so badly and yet had dared not believe it would happen. It seemed just possible, in that crystalline instant, that more good things would follow. "We're finally free," Tracy Boykin declared as she headed toward the park with her friend Caron Warnsby, a surgeon. "I'm a doctor, and I don't have to walk in anymore and be a black doctor. She's not the black surgeon, anymore. She's the surgeon. Everything is different." And for that one glorious moment, it was.

Michelle, Barack, and the girls strode onto the stage. As Barack spoke, his family and friends in the wings pinched themselves. Cameras caught Jesse Jackson with tears streaming down his face. He later said he was thinking of Emmett Till, Rosa Parks, Martin Luther King, and the march in Selma. Capers Funnye, one of Fraser's cousins, found Marian and hugged her. "We cried together for her dad, we cried for her granddad, for my mom and all of her siblings who've gone on," Funnye said. "It was a powerful, profound moment. It was an extraordinary moment. There were no words. What could you say?"

Michelle's mother, Marian Robinson, as a young woman in Chicago, where her parents settled after moving from the South.

Michelle's father, Fraser C. Robinson III, shown here in a high school yearbook photo, took classes at the Art Institute of Chicago.

Michelle and her brother, Craig, twenty-one months older, who said they had the "Shangri-La of upbringings" in working-class Chicago.

Kindergarten at Bryn Mawr Elementary in 1970. Michelle is second from the right in the second row from the top.

Michelle as a first-grader on the South Side of Chicago.

Michelle commuted across town to Whitney Young High School, a diverse magnet school, where she was a class officer and a member of the honor society.

Michelle, seventeen years old when she reached Princeton in 1981, struggled at first.

**Michelle L. Robinson**
7436 S. Euclid Ave.
Chicago, IL 60649
Whitney Young H.S.
January 17, 1964

7436 South Euclid Avenue
Chicago, IL 60649

January 17, 1964

Sociology

Stevenson Hall; Third World Center — Work Study; Third World Center — Governance Board Member; Organization of Black Unity; Third World Center After School Program — Coordinator

## Michelle LaVaughn Robinson

There is nothing in this world more valuable than friendships. Without them you have nothing.

Thank-you Mom, Dad and Craig. You all are the most important things in my life.

Majoring in sociology, Michelle said white students often perceived her as "Black first and a student second."

Michelle dated Stanley Stocker-Edwards, a fellow Harvard Law student. She said later, "My family swore I would never find a man that would put up with me."

Michelle and Harvard Law friend Susan Page, appointed U.S. ambassador to South Sudan in the Obama administration.

Michelle visited Barack's family in Hawaii in 1989, the year they met at a Chicago law firm.

Michelle and Barack were married in 1992, by the Reverend Jeremiah A. Wright Jr. at Trinity United Church of Christ in Chicago.

Barack and Michelle visited Kenya, the home country of Barack's father.

"I was never happier in my life," Michelle said, than when building a leadership program at Public Allies in Chicago in the mid-1990s.

In the first apartment she and Barack owned in Chicago, Michelle stands beside a photograph of Judith Jamison dancing Alvin Ailey's iconic work "Cry."

Barack, Michelle, and Malia on election day in 2000. Barack lost the congressional primary to Representative Bobby Rush by thirty points and entered what an aide called his "morose period."

With Sasha in Oskaloosa, Iowa, on July 4, 2007. Michelle curtailed campaign time and her White House schedule to be home for her daughters.

Michelle and Barack strolling down Pennsylvania Avenue during Barack's first inaugural. Designer Isabel Toledo said Michelle made it safe for women to take fashion risks.

Michelle, wearing a Jason Wu gown later donated to the Smithsonian, shares a moment with Barack after dancing at the 2009 inaugural ball.

Michelle in her first official White House photograph, beneath the gaze of Thomas Jefferson.

Delighting in fashion, Michelle took advantage of public occasions to showcase designers and an ever-changing array of styles.

Michelle saw progress when Jacob Philadelphia, age five, told the first African American president, "I want to know if my hair is just like yours." Barack invited him to see for himself.

After she launched Let's Move!, Michelle said, "I'm pretty much willing to make a complete fool out of myself to get our kids moving."

Michelle made the rounds at federal agencies, drawing crowds armed with cell phone cameras. In October 2011, she visited Secret Service headquarters.

Calling Washington her new hometown, Michelle hoped to set an example for disadvantaged children, here visiting Ferebee Hope Elementary School.

After Barack's November 2012 reelection, Michelle launched Reach Higher to expand higher education and training, particularly for low-income students.

Hugs became Michelle's signature gesture, intended as a symbol that the first lady cared. As part of her Joining Forces initiative, she met military families in Minnesota in March 2012.

Michelle increasingly used social media to spread her message. In 2014, she spoke up for Nigerian girls kidnapped by the extremist group Boko Haram.

Michelle, Barack, and Malia at a Team USA basketball game.

Local schoolchildren and White House staff helped Michelle plant the first vegetable garden on the White House grounds since Eleanor Roosevelt's time.

Michelle, in a tug-of-war with Jimmy Fallon, did spoofs and comedy sketches to advance childhood fitness and nutrition.

Posing here with Sesame Street characters in October 2013. Michelle developed partnerships to draw attention to her initiatives, including Joining Forces.

When Barack congratulated the Miami Heat on their latest NBA championship, stars LeBron James and Dwyane Wade did a video about healthy eating with Michelle.

Applause for Michelle at Barack's State of the Union address to a joint session of Congress in 2015.

Marian Robinson, standing beside Michelle, moved into the third floor of the White House. "I can always go up to her room and cry, complain, argue," Michelle said. "And she just says, 'Go on back down there and do what you're supposed to do.'"

Michelle and Barack shooting an ad for the 2012 campaign. The win gave them four more years and a greater sense of freedom. Shortly before turning fifty, Michelle said, "I have never felt more confident in myself, more clear on who I am as a woman."

# TWELVE

# Nothing Would Have Predicted

Michelle never had any doubt that her ascendance to the White House as first lady of the United States—FLOTUS, in Secret Service parlance—was groundbreaking. This was the executive mansion that slaves had helped build and African Americans had helped run, but it had never sheltered a black president or first family. The symbolism alone was stunning. It was evident on the November day, six days after the election, when George and Laura Bush posed with the Obamas outside the White House. And at the inauguration eve concert on the steps of the Lincoln Memorial, where Martin Luther King had delivered his "I Have a Dream" speech. And in Barack's inaugural address on January 20, 2009, in front of an estimated two million people on the National Mall, when he spoke of being the son of a father who, two generations earlier, "might not have been served in a local restaurant." After the swearing-in, where Barack rested his left hand on the velvet-bound Bible used by Abraham Lincoln at his 1861 inaugural, crowds cheered and called out as Michelle and Barack stepped out of their bulletproof limousine to walk hand in hand in the winter sunshine down Pennsylvania Avenue.

Inside the White House, the largely black staff of butlers, housekeepers, and cooks gathered to meet the new first family. "They could not have been kinder to us and warmer to us," Barack said. "And part of it, I suspect, is they look at Malia and Sasha and they say, 'Well, this looks like my grandbaby or this looks like my daughter.' And I think for them to have a sense that we've come this far was a powerful moment for them—and certainly a powerful moment for us." The first night in the mansion, dozens of friends and relatives gathered for a party, no one quite believing what had come to pass. Barack, after asking how to get there, headed upstairs to the residence at 2:30 a.m., following Michelle, who had retired earlier. A signed copy of the Gettysburg Address lay under glass in the Lincoln Bedroom, once Lincoln's office, where Craig and Kelly slept in an elegant eight-by-six-foot rosewood bed after receiving a house tour. One stop was the Truman Balcony and its view south toward the Washington Monument. "My wife and I were just shaking our heads," Craig said.

Not two weeks later, Michelle was speaking at the White House about equal pay for women. Soon, she addressed cheering workers at the Department of Housing and Urban Development and urged them to find "a new level of passion and vigor." A few days after that, she told teenagers at a Washington community health center that she and Barack were "kids like you who figured out one day that our fate was in our own hands." In April, she made a trip to the Capitol to unveil a bust of Sojourner Truth, a freed slave who became a prominent abolitionist and activist for women's suffrage. Born Isabella Baumfree in the late eighteenth century, Truth was sold several times before escaping with one of her children in 1826. She delivered her famous "Ain't I a Woman" speech in 1851. More than a century and a half later, she was the first black woman to be honored with a bust in the Capitol. By her very presence at the ceremony, Michelle demonstrated the distance that African Americans had traveled since Martha Washington, accompanied by seven house slaves, took up residence in New York as the wife of the country's first president. Noting that she herself was a descendant of slaves, Michelle called Sojourner Truth "an outspoken, tell-it-like-it-is kind of woman. And we all know a little something about that, right?" She urged her audience, which included Nancy Pelosi, the first female speaker of the House, Hillary Clinton, the new secretary of state, and a bevy of Republican leaders, to reflect on the moment.

"Now," she said, "many young boys and girls, like my own daughters, will come to Emancipation Hall and see the face of a woman who looks like them." Just as no one who looked like the Obamas had graced Emancipation Hall, no one who looked like them had occupied the White House, either, a fact that would influence what Barack and Michelle would do and say, even as they set out unambiguously to be the president and first lady of all Americans.

VIRTUALLY OVERNIGHT, Michelle had become one of the most prominent women in America. Hopes soared among some of her most ardent fans that she would become a White House force in her own right. Her new staff was deluged with invitations to lunches and launches and an endless skein of worthy and not-so-worthy events. The screen was blank and she was free, if one could call it that, to define a role for herself. Yet she soon discovered that her freedom was defined by a tangle of often conflicting expectations and options. What was true for any first lady was doubly so for the first African American first lady, one who carried a significant résumé into the position. She had told delegates to the Democratic National Convention that she stood "at the crosscurrents" of the history of race and gender. Her friend Verna Williams said "in the crosshairs" was more like it. "People are going to be watching every move you make. They're watching you—it's like the Police song."

That first year in the White House, Michelle said later, was about "figuring out the job." There were aides to hire, a household staff to manage, a web of rules—written and otherwise—about how to conduct her affairs. She no longer drove, she no longer went anywhere alone, and even her home was not her own. Meanwhile, she was determined to settle Malia and Sasha into their new lives and support Barack as he confronted two wars and the most serious economic crisis since the Great Depression. Accustomed to control, at times she felt at sea. "It wasn't smooth," said Jackie Norris, her first chief of staff. "It's not smooth for any first lady. It's a hard process."

Michelle had made time, during a campaign that had lasted the better part of two years, to think about the role she might play as first lady. Before reaching Washington, she convened small groups to consider what the job could mean, but she intentionally left the contours vague. When asked in 2007 whether she saw herself more as Laura Bush or as Hillary Clinton, she ducked the comparison. "It is so hard to project out realistically what life will be like for me as a woman, for me as a mother, when Barack becomes president. It's hard to know. What I do know is that given the many skills that I have on so many different levels, I will be what I have to be at the time." The answer was an honest one. It made clear her strong sense of obligation to Malia, Sasha, and Barack. It conveyed flexibility and it also bought her some time. Once she moved into 1600 Pennsylvania Avenue, Michelle's prominent place in the history books was assured by the color of her skin. Surely there was more, much more. But what?

Michelle started out as "risk-averse," in one staffer's words, wrestling with unfamiliar conditions and wary of a misstep. As self-described "mom-in-chief," a term that set some supporters' teeth on edge when they considered her education and skills, Michelle telegraphed that she would leap into no issue or cause before she was ready. She instructed her staff to confine her official working schedule to two days a week at first, later raising it to three. She labored informally on other days while focusing on her family. She operated from the East Wing, the president from the West Wing. Privately, she made clear to her staff that once she chose her course, she would be disciplined about it, conserving political capital while protecting her family time. She said from the outset that her role would be collaborative and measured, always in service to the member of the couple who had been elected—in other words, Barack, who had official duties, constitutional powers, a $400,000 salary, and his sights set on winning a second term. Michelle's first goal, as she had learned the hard way during the campaign, was to do no harm.

Which is not to say that she felt no stress or sense of obligation. Her role may have been unpaid, but she was the same i-dotting, t-crossing Michelle who had stayed up late to finish her high school homework and hated to fall short at anything. "I have a huge responsibility to use this platform in a way that's going to make a difference," she told a student questioner in 2011. "In a way that I feel like I don't want to disappoint my parents, I wouldn't want to disappoint the country. Sheesh, that's a burden. . . . I want to be good at what I do. . . . I want to look back and say I did something good for a bunch of people because I was in this position." The student had asked whether being an African American first lady added to the pressure. Michelle replied that her feelings about the job were "not unique to me because of my race" and reported that other first ladies saw the job in similar terms. "None of us chose the position. You get it because of who you're married to and you don't get a paycheck or a title, but you feel like you want to make the most of it and do some good things." She concluded, to laughter, "Thank you for that question. It's like a therapy session."

IT WAS A TRICKY ROLE, being first lady. There was no script, although there were certainly many models. Modern first ladies were as different in style and substance as their husbands. The woman she succeeded, Laura Bush, had cut a gracious, amiable, and sure-footed figure. She spoke up for the No Child Left Behind education policy and traveled to sixty-seven countries in her husband's second term, playing substantive roles on such issues as political freedom in Burma, women's rights in Afghanistan, and AIDS in Africa. A former school librarian, she was steady and low-key in an administration famous for swashbuckling, her position fortified by the knowledge that she had pushed her husband to stop drinking and save his career. "I'm not here for me, I'm here for George," she told Anita McBride when interviewing her for the job of East Wing chief of staff. "Whatever I do here is to help the president's goals for the country."

An earlier White House occupant, Barbara Bush, Laura's mother-in-law, kept order and fired the occasional verbal dagger on her husband's behalf, while Nancy Reagan combined a steely loyalty and a passion for palace intrigue with a fashion sense that sometimes clashed with the zeitgeist of the 1980s. First ladies were variously known for White House portfolios, real or imagined, and their causes. Lady Bird Johnson had beautification and the War on Poverty, Laura Bush had literacy, Nancy Reagan had the "Just Say No" anti-drugs campaign. Rosalynn Carter attended high-level meetings, taking notes quietly.

"There's no way I could discuss things with Jimmy in an intelligent way if I didn't attend Cabinet meetings," she once said. In the margins of policy papers and memos, the president would sometimes write, "Ros. What think?" The pressure of the White House, meanwhile, weighed on Betty Ford, who had been popping pills and drinking heavily long before the summer day when Richard Nixon resigned and made her husband, former Michigan congressman Gerald Ford, the president. Her poll numbers rose when she discussed on national television an earlier mental breakdown and spoke up for abortion rights, calling *Roe v. Wade* a "great, great decision." She revealed a bout with breast cancer and wore a political button in 1975 urging passage of the Equal Rights Amendment. She said her children probably had smoked marijuana: "It's the type of thing that young people have to experience, like your first beer or your first cigarette." Betty Ford bridged the gap between the presidential cocoon and the rest of the country, wrote author Kati Marton. Americans "saw an open, honest woman talking about issues they were dealing with every day."

As Michelle prepared for the move to the White House, she found herself compared with first ladies from three separate eras, each with a distinctive style. The three—Jackie Kennedy, Hillary Clinton, and Eleanor Roosevelt—could hardly have been more different, illustrating the dilemmas Michelle would face in crafting the style and substance of her own role. Each came to be known best by her first name. Jackie Kennedy was just thirty-one years old when her husband was elected and thirty-four when he died. Her public face was all about style, the arts, and the gauzy image of a new Camelot, fueled by a media bored with the stolid Eisenhower era. John Kennedy himself was only forty-three when he entered the White House, a dashing and philandering father whose two young children would become known to the world in joy and mourning. Hillary Clinton came of age in the tumultuous years after John Kennedy died. A politically minded child of the Chicago suburbs, she was elected president of the Young Republicans before moving to the left in the late 1960s. She graduated from Yale Law School and worked as a lawyer in Little Rock, Arkansas, as her husband climbed the political ranks. Her reputation was rooted in her formidable intellect, her independent career, and her early tendency to speak her mind, or something close to it. She landed in the briar patch with her campaign trail assertion that she was not the type of woman to stay home and bake cookies and, later, with her stewardship of a botched health care overhaul—a policymaking role that Michelle and her team made a conscious decision not to emulate. When she took a more traditional tack and stood by her feckless husband after his most recent sexual affair, this one with White House intern Monica Lewinsky, her popularity grew. Whether due to admiration or sympathy or a combination of the two was a matter for debate.

It was Eleanor Roosevelt, however, who provided the most intriguing point of comparison for Michelle, and the most difficult standard to meet. Brave, singular, a progressive force operating before the media spotlight shone so brightly, Roosevelt created an independent identity while working to shape the thirty-second president's agenda, at one point even seeking a federal job. She held press conferences for women reporters and wrote a popular syndicated newspaper column, "My Day." She joined the Washington, D.C., chapter of the NAACP, supported anti-lynching legislation, and resigned her membership in the Daughters of the American Revolution when the organization refused to allow Marian Anderson to sing at Constitution Hall. Not that she was happy when she arrived at the White House. "The turmoil in my heart and mind was rather great," she wrote in 1933. Rather than be called first lady, she said she preferred "Mrs. Roosevelt." Franklin Roosevelt wrote, in verse, of her predicament:

> *Did my Eleanor relate*
> *all the sad and awful fate*
> *of the miserable lives*
> *lived by Washington wives*

Eleanor often left town. She traveled on her own, sometimes setting out by car and reporting back to her husband on what she found. She was a moral, prodding force in the White House, and she was ahead of her husband and party on matters of poverty, racism, and social justice.

In 1943, Chicago publisher John H. Johnson asked if she would contribute a column to his "If I Were a Negro" series in *Negro Digest,* which predated the launch of his glossy magazines, *Ebony* and *Jet.* "If I were a Negro today, I think I would have moments of great bitterness," she wrote. "It would be hard to sustain my faith in democracy and to build up a sense of goodwill toward men of other races." Although African Americans had been "held back by generations of economic inequality," she continued, "I would know that I had to work hard and to go on accomplishing the best that was possible under present conditions. . . . I would not do too much demanding. I would take every chance that came my way to prove my quality."

The column was a huge success. Johnson reported that his circulation spiked by fifty thousand, doubling the usual press run. "She said, 'If I were a Negro, I would have great bitterness,' and all the northern papers picked that up," Johnson recalled. "But she said, 'But I would also have great patience,' and all the southern newspapers picked that up." Three years after her death, writer Claude Brown dedicated his memoir of life in Harlem, *Manchild in the Promised Land,* to Roosevelt. He cited her support of the Wiltwyck School for Boys, a Hudson River reform school that became a refuge for needy and sometimes troubled or delinquent children. It was Wiltwyck, he said, that turned his life around.

MICHELLE TURNED INITIALLY to what spoke to her, just as she had done during the campaign. One of her first public roles was morale booster. Daughter and granddaughter of government workers, she made a tour of federal agencies, thanking federal employees for their anonymous service to the nation. "Everything you do, every piece of blood, sweat and tears you pour into the work is going to make the difference in our nation, in our planet," she told Environmental Protection Agency workers in February. "Just know that we value you, that America values you," she told Transportation Department staff. She mentioned her uncles who had been Pullman porters and praised their labor union as a "trailblazer in civil rights." At the Agriculture Department, she talked up community gardens, renewable energy, and the expansion of the Children's Health Insurance Program. "We are going to need you in the months and years to come," she said. "The challenges that we face are serious and real and it's going to take quite a long time to get this country back on track." More able to get out and about than her husband, Michelle told a packed auditorium of Education Department workers that she aimed "to learn, to listen, to take information back where possible."

Michelle and her team laid out a series of early priorities. Even then, as she was struggling to find her feet, her concerns had a shape familiar to those who knew her biography. In an echo of her work at Public Allies and the University of Chicago, she spoke up for expanded federal funding of national service programs, illustrated by the Serve America Act signed by Barack in April 2009. During a visit to the Corporation for National and Community Service, she recalled that unpaid internships were beyond her reach as a young woman, "a luxury that a working class kid couldn't afford." Everyone, she said, should have a chance to volunteer and benefit, "regardless of their race or their age or their financial ability."

To spotlight diversity in what she called "my new home town," Michelle explored the vibrant and sometimes troubled Washington in the shadows of the federal government and the downtown tourist attractions. She set out to share her story and the president's with fresh audiences, particularly children of color from less-than-elite backgrounds. She saw her younger self in them, and she wanted to play a role in "opening the doors and taking off the veil." The White House, she said, would be the people's house. "You know, there's a playbook in Washington about what you're supposed to do," her friend Sharon Malone said. "Well, she's not following the playbook. She's doing it the way she wants to do it, by being very involved in the community." On March 19, two months into the first term, Michelle drove across the river to Anacostia High School, located in an impoverished African American neighborhood within sight of the Capitol dome. It would take less than an hour to walk there from, say, Emancipation Hall, but the two worlds rarely intersected. "One of those schools that was basically forgotten," said Roscoe Thomas, dean of students, recalling his first impressions. Michelle gathered students around her and explained that when she began to envision her time as first lady, she realized that she wanted to spend "a whole lot of time outside in the D.C. community." The motivation was her own recollection of how distant the University of Chicago felt to her as a working-class black girl, even though the campus was close to her home. "I never set foot on it. I didn't get to attend any classes. And I think the assumption was . . . that place was different," she said. "It was a college, and it was a fancy college, and it didn't have anything to do with me."

At Anacostia, Michelle talked with girls—and a few boys, to whom she said, "You brothers are lucky, because you got to sneak into this." They were chosen to meet her for a reason. "Each of you has struggled with something, but you've overcome it, you've pushed to the next level. And that for me, that was important. I didn't just want the kids who had already arrived, but kids who were pushing to get to the next place," she said in an echo of what she valued when recruiting for Public Allies. She spoke of her own hard work as an adolescent, and how her mother made clear that Michelle needed to take responsibility if she expected to succeed. "I ran into people in my life who told me, 'You can't do it, you're not as smart as that person.' And that never stopped me. That always made me push harder, because I was like, I'm going to prove you wrong." As intended, the event drew news coverage. It caught the eye of Jasmine Williams, a D.C. public charter school senior who had already asked Michelle to speak at her graduation. "She told them how a lot of people told her she spoke like a white girl," Williams said. "I don't know what that means, but I've been told that, too."

Michelle was just one woman of distinction who ventured into D.C.-area schools that day, part of a White House celebration of Women's History Month. In what would become a template, the East Wing deployed an array of accomplished women, sending them to eleven local schools and welcoming them back to the White House to break bread with Michelle and various girls invited to meet them. That day, the guest list ranged from singers Alicia Keys and Sheryl Crow to gymnast Dominique Dawes, former astronaut Mae C. Jemison, and the first female four-star general in the U.S. military, General Ann E. Dunwoody. When the day was over and the guests had gone home, Michelle told her staff that it was their best event yet. The experience would fuel the East Wing's creation of a mentoring program.

To Michelle, mentoring was a pursuit and a philosophy that infused her agenda throughout the White House years. She drew satisfaction from sharing her stories and she found that they resonated with young audiences, especially African American girls. "She really wanted to think about how to engage young people and to engage young people from all walks of life, not just the expected schools," said Jocelyn Frye, a Washington native and Harvard friend who steered the project as Michelle's policy director. The role seemed to come naturally, and it fulfilled her bedrock determination to reach back. "In every phase of my life, whether I was in high school or Princeton or Harvard or working for the city or working at the hospital, I was always looking for somebody to mentor," Michelle said when she took the project to Detroit in 2010. "I was looking for a way to reach out into my neighborhood and my community and pull somebody else along with me, because I thought, 'There but for the grace of God go I.'"

The program paired twenty high school sophomores and juniors with women who worked in the Obama White House. Michelle wanted the students to experience "substance and fun." They saw Air Force One. They went to Anacostia. They went to the Supreme Court. They accompanied Michelle to see the Alvin Ailey dance company. They met Judith Jamison, the powerful and ethereal dancer who was one of Michelle's childhood heroes. The program was small, but its architecture reflected a determination to invest in activities tethered to a clear purpose. In a realm of infinite options and limited time, there would be no tilting at windmills in Michelle Obama's East Wing. "It's not sufficient to say we're going to do an event on childhood obesity. There has to be a reason for it. It has to have a beginning and an end and be part of a broader strategy," explained Frye, who said of the first Anacostia visit, "We didn't want it to be a one-shot deal, where we appear for a photo and not appear again. She wants us to have a plan, so we don't just go from event to event by the seat of our pants."

OVER IN THE WEST WING, it was difficult to exaggerate the calamities that Barack inherited. There were worries about terrorism during preparations for the inaugural festivities, as if the new president and his family needed any reminder of the perils ahead. Just hours before he took the oath of office, aides updated Barack on intelligence reports that Somali extremists might detonate bombs during his address to the nation. The celebration passed without incident, but the demands of the presidency were soon made plain. The economy, in free fall since the collapse of Lehman Brothers in September, lost an estimated 741,000 jobs in January alone. Another 651,000 jobs disappeared in February and 652,000 in March. The housing market was imploding, causing millions of people to lose their homes or a large chunk of the income they had counted on for retirement. The $236 billion budget surplus at the end of the Clinton years had turned into a $1.3 trillion deficit under George W. Bush, thanks to substantial Republican-inspired tax cuts for the wealthy and a pair of wars, in Iraq and Afghanistan, churning along without end. When Barack took office, 144,000 soldiers, marines, sailors, and airmen were deployed to Iraq. Another 34,000 were stationed in Afghanistan, a figure that would nearly triple on Barack's watch. The threat of terrorism, meanwhile, continued to lurk across an unsettled globe. When Barack Hussein Obama placed his hand on the Lincoln Bible and took the oath, wrote Peter Baker of *The New York Times*, he inherited "a nation in crisis at home and abroad."

The rueful joke told by some Obama supporters was that the country was going to hell, so *of course* they gave the job to a black guy. Being president sometimes felt like standing in a vast maze facing an endless sequence of blind turns leading to one set of choices after another. Each decision blended the consequences of the last one with a mind-bending array of considerations about the ones to come. Politics, principle, and practicalities all factored in, as did the inevitable pronouncements of the commentariat. It was no wonder that Barack liked to turn to ESPN, the sports channel, to escape. Michelle sometimes offered her opinions, not least on personnel. Chicago friend Marty Nesbitt called her the most "do what's right" person in Barack's circle, representing true north. "She's just very pragmatic and straightforward. She doesn't sugarcoat her perspective or dance around the issues. She just calls it like she sees it." Valerie Jarrett, who moved into a West Wing office as a presidential adviser, agreed and said Michelle played an essential role.

"She is completely honest. There are very few people you can say that about. She tells the president exactly what she thinks. She doesn't hold back." Susan Sher added that Michelle tended to speak up about public opinion. "She likes to say, 'This is not what people care about. They care about *this.*'"

That said, Michelle chose her moments. She explained that while she was "honest, absolutely," there were times when a talking-to was not what Barack needed. "In a job like this, the last thing a president of the United States needs when he walks in the door to come home is somebody who is drilling him and questioning him about the decisions and choices that he's made. So, there are definitely times when I may feel something, but I'll hold back because I know he'll either get to it on his own or it's just not time." Living a few steps away from the Oval Office did have its advantages in times of turmoil. "Now I can just pop over to his office," Michelle said, "which sometimes I'll do if I know he's having a particularly frustrating day."

Massachusetts governor Deval Patrick said Michelle's personality helped Barack open up emotionally, providing a space "where he lets himself feel the stuff that goes on in the office and not just think about the stuff and evaluate the stuff and consider his options around the stuff." Patrick, who saw Barack in settings public and private, said the president was empathetic and able to show it behind the scenes, when meeting, for example, with wounded soldiers or victims of a tragedy. But in public, Barack was "very careful emotionally. He's uncommonly analytical and self-contained, in the sense that he is going to let things roll off him that just wouldn't roll off of others." Michelle was able to draw him out. "She's more confident about expressing her emotions, whether grief or anger or frustration or what have you," Patrick said. "Not necessarily publicly, but in company with him, and I think that's helpful for him. She makes him better."

WHILE BARACK FACED the recession, the deficit, the wars, and a hundred other problems, Michelle set out to manage the household. In the residence, there were thirty-six rooms, including five bedrooms on the second floor and six on the third, plus sixteen bathrooms. There was a household staff and an office staff. There were new family routines, a new private school for Malia and Sasha, and new duties, from party planning to official correspondence, plus the care and feeding of everyone who wanted a piece of her day. There was even a new dog, a purebred Portuguese water dog named Bo, promised to the girls as a post-campaign reward. Michelle often felt swamped and was not shy about confessing her unhappiness. She had always relied on her girlfriends for support, yet the challenges of Washington were compounded by having few close friends nearby. Sher, her old friend from City Hall and the University of Chicago, was in the White House counsel's office. Desiree Rogers, the former head of Peoples Gas and ex-wife of John Rogers, was her social secretary. Plus she had Jarrett. "Valerie was the counselor. Valerie was the everything," said Jackie Norris, Michelle's first chief of staff.

To help, the Chicago contingent made frequent trips to the nation's capital, offering reassurance. "Do you still recognize me? Do I still feel like Michelle, or are you tripping?" she would ask when checking in with old friends. In search of equilibrium, the "most unexpected and uniform advice" she received from former first ladies was to go early and often to the presidential retreat at Camp David, about sixty miles north in Maryland's Catoctin Mountain Park. "It's one place you can go where you feel some level of freedom and an ability to breathe," Michelle said. "I think every single first lady felt that was an important resource, an important opportunity, an important thing for the health of the family."

To shore up the home front, Michelle asked her seventy-one-year-old mother to move into the White House, where she could live on the third floor of the residence, help with the girls, and support the first lady. Marian was, to say the least, reluctant. "That I can do without. When you move in, you hear just a little bit too much," she once said. Among other drawbacks, she worried that living in the White House would feel like living in a museum and she did not want to give up her car. She liked to drive. Michelle asked her brother to work on her.

"My sister said, 'You've got to talk to Mom. She's not moving,'" said Craig, who knew that Marian prized her independence and had no use for the rarefied White House air or egos inflated by proximity to power. "She doesn't want grand. She doesn't want great. She would much rather stay home." She was close to relatives and friends and had a routine that suited her. There were shopping trips with her sister, yoga at her brother's studio, and a quiet life at home where she read the newspaper, did crossword puzzles, watched home improvement shows, played the piano, and shoveled her own walk. Her means and her needs were modest.

But she relented. Marian locked the door on the Euclid Avenue house and became an integral part of the Obama household. In Washington, after accompanying Malia and Sasha to school in an SUV driven by the Secret Service, she would often return to the residence and, if Michelle were home, chat with her before heading to her third-floor quarters. At a White House tea, Michelle singled her out, declaring that Marian "has pulled me up when I've stumbled. She's pulled me back when I've run out of line, talking a little too much. She'll snap me up. She really does push me to be the best woman that I can be, truly, as a professional and as a mother and as a friend. And she has always, always, always been there for me. Raising our girls in the White House with my mom—oh, not going to do this," Michelle said, starting to choke up, "is a beautiful experience."

As Marian found her way, she had the advantage of relative anonymity, allowing her to walk out the White House gates and stroll through downtown Washington, maybe stopping at the pharmacy, without creating a fuss. Once, when a passerby remarked that she looked just like Mrs. Robinson, she replied, "Oh, yeah, people say that." And she kept walking. She slipped easily out of Washington, traveling to Chicago or to the Pacific Northwest, where she visited Craig and his family at Oregon State University. Of course, she also sat in the president's box at the Kennedy Center, sometimes joined by her friend Bettie Currie, former White House secretary to Bill Clinton. She flew aboard Air Force One to Russia and Ghana. She met Pope Benedict and Queen Elizabeth. Michelle reveled in her presence and said, "I'm pretty sure the president is happy, too." Barack credited Marian for bringing stories back to the

White House from the outside world because, he said, "she escapes the bubble."

THE BUBBLE IS one of the strangest aspects of the modern presidency and a feature the Obamas especially lamented. In physical terms, the bubble is the security cordon that surrounds the president and his immediate family 24 hours a day, 365 days a year. The Obamas could not go anywhere, ever, without being guarded by gun-carrying Secret Service agents. Eighteen months into his presidency, asked what he missed most, Barack answered, "Taking walks." He regretted being unable to sit absently on a bench in a city park or go alone with his kids to get ice cream. Anonymity, he said, is "a profound pleasure that is very hard to experience now." Beyond the physical cordon, the bubble also came to represent the isolation of life in the White House, which Harry Truman called in his 1947 diary "the great white jail." Truman said the executive mansion was "a hell of a place in which to be alone. While I work from early morning until late at night, it is a ghostly place. The floors pop and crack all night long." In the gloom, he saw the specters of his predecessors. "They all walk up and down the halls of this place and moan about what they should have done and didn't."

Sixty years later, an otherwise simple dinner for two at a D.C. restaurant required a security sweep of the premises and a screening of patrons. A decision to spend a few days outside the capital triggered a far more complex and expensive choreography. Even a stroll through the White House and its grounds posed problems, given the presence of news photographers, staff, and guests in a sprawling mansion that served as government office, tourist destination, and private home. It was surreal. Barack left on trips vertically, from the South Lawn. "Once, someone on my staff e-mailed to tell me that the president was on his way," Michelle said. "But you could already hear the helicopter, so it was like, well, no kidding."

During her first spring in Washington, Michelle approached the Secret Service. She wanted to see the city's glorious cherry blossoms, a simple outing in a season that drew tens of thousands of tourists and residents to the Tidal Basin and more secluded spots. Not so simple, it turned out, for a first lady. She put on a baseball cap and met Cindy Moelis, a Chicago friend from their time at City Hall who ran the White House Fellows Program. With an agent at the wheel, they drove to one destination, but the agent decided the crowds were too thick; Michelle would surely be recognized. They drove instead to a less popular place. The trees were in bloom, and they took a walk. Another time, Michelle was delighted to hear that she could walk to an event at the Corcoran Gallery of Art, only to discover that it was barely across the street from the White House complex. When she went to Target one time, a customer, not recognizing Michelle, asked if she would pull something down for her from a high shelf. She obliged. The first lady told friends that some white people simply did not "see" her, a black woman, when she was out in public and trying to be inconspicuous.

Unlike her husband, Michelle was not trailed by a media pool during her private time. Without him, she could escape, albeit driven and escorted by the Secret Service. She discovered restaurants where she could eat unmolested. She went to the theater and ball games. She visited the homes of friends, who were instructed that informal visits were considered "off the grid" by the Secret Service command, for security reasons. No one was to say where Michelle was headed or when. If word leaked, the excursion might be canceled. Michelle did not like it, not one bit, but she adapted even when her staff told her no. "Just give me the rules. Just tell me. I'll live with it," Michelle said, according to Sher, who was struck by the fresh constraints: "Think of the shock to your system, in an incredibly short time."

How little had changed, even as so much had, in the world of first ladies. In 1789, the first year of the first American presidency, Martha Washington said she felt constrained by the role. "I never goe to any public place, indeed, I think I am much more like a state prisoner than anything else," she wrote to her niece from New York, the temporary seat of government. "There is certain bounds set for me which I must not depart from and as I cannot doe as I like I am obstinate and stay at home a great deal." Asked at a public forum with Laura Bush about Washington's "state prisoner" reference, Michelle said, to laughter, "There are prison elements to it, but it's a really nice prison." Bush interjected, "But with a chef!" Michelle continued, "You can't complain, but there are definitely elements that are confining." In some ways, Michelle quickly discovered, the bubble was a fishbowl and she was the one swimming behind glass. Perceptions could be powerful and criticism withering in a life lived in the public eye. But there were advantages. When she wanted to draw attention to an issue, she knew that pens and cameras would be at the ready.

DURING THE CAMPAIGN, Barack promised Michelle a date night in New York. It would be dinner, a show, just the two of them out on the town. But this was their new life and getting to Broadway was, well, a production. The Obamas, dressed in stylish stepping-out clothes, emerged from the White House in bright sunlight on the afternoon of May 30, 2009. As a pool photographer snapped photos, they strolled hand in hand across the South Lawn to a waiting helicopter, where a marine officer crisply saluted. The chopper took them to Andrews Air Force Base in suburban Maryland, where they boarded a small air force jet to New York. A second helicopter was waiting there to fly them to lower Manhattan, where a motorcade was idling. They climbed into the presidential Cadillac limousine, called "The Beast," a rolling fortress that weighed seven and a half tons, thanks to its titanium and steel armor, its bulletproof glass and its doors, as thick as a commercial airliner's. The vehicle could be sealed from the outside air in case of a chemical weapons attack, and in the trunk it carried a supply of blood with the president's type. As Michelle would joke about their attempts at date nights, "Barack has a 20-car motorcade, men with guns, the ambulance is always there. How romantic can you be?"

Dinner in New York that night, reflecting Michelle's foodie interests and tastes, was at Blue Hill, an upscale locavore haven housed in a former Greenwich Village speakeasy. "Perhaps no other restaurant makes as serious and showy an effort to connect diners to the origins of their food," a *New York Times* food critic wrote in 2006. From the restaurant, the Obamas returned to the waiting motorcade, which included a media contingent—reporters, photographers, video teams—and drove to the Belasco Theatre, where New York police and the Secret Service had cordoned off an entire block of West 44th Street hours before the performance of August Wilson's *Joe Turner's Come and Gone*. The play, set in a northern boardinghouse during the Great Migration, depicted a search for livelihood and identity among dislocated black characters. As theatergoers flowed through metal detectors, the 8 p.m. curtain was delayed for forty-five minutes. Afterward, the Obamas passed throngs of people angling for a glimpse or a snapshot, then made their airborne way back to Washington, the South Lawn, and their permanently lighted, staffed, and secured home. Ticket sales for the show doubled the next day. The theater seats they occupied at the Belasco were unbolted from the floor and offered for sale at a charity auction.

Michelle and Barack had not left New York before the Republican National Committee was criticizing the trip as extravagant and insensitive, with the economy in recession and General Motors days away from declaring bankruptcy. "Have a great Saturday evening," RNC spokeswoman Gail Gitcho scoffed to her digital audience, "even if you're not jetting off somewhere at taxpayer expense." The political quandary the Obamas faced, with reporters recording their every move, would recur throughout their White House tenure. The West Wing foresaw trouble with the New York excursion and released a statement to reporters in Barack's name. "I am taking my wife to New York City," he said, "because I promised her during the campaign that I would take her to a Broadway show after it was all finished." As far as he was concerned, that should have been the end of the story.

"IT'S A DERIVATIVE JOB. There's so much there that you're just supposed to do, that everyone's been doing since 1952," Trooper Sanders, an East Wing staff member, said of the role of first lady. To follow the familiar path would be relatively easy, Michelle and her team recognized early on, but it would turn the East Wing into a velvet coffin, comfortable but pointless. A first lady who allowed parties and traditional fare to define her days, Sanders said, would wake up four years or eight years later and say to herself, "I haven't done anything."

Yet Michelle would discover that doing things differently could create its own trouble in hierarchical, tradition-bound Washington. Just as she chose where to play a role, she would choose where not to. Historic preservation, for example, at least in the early going. It was a typical engagement for first ladies, embraced by Hillary Clinton, who created the Save America's Treasures program, and Laura Bush. But Michelle was not particularly interested and felt she brought nothing special to the table, despite a stint on the Chicago Landmarks Commission. When she concluded that it was a cause that could be championed elsewhere in the federal government, she disappointed the leaders of well-connected organizations who had expected more. Similarly, she faced questions about protocol and priorities when she sought to change the tone of the annual Congressional Club First Lady's Luncheon, described by one aide as a "bastion of everything that made us cringe."

The first lady and her staff got a taste of what was to come when a luncheon organizer sent a swatch of fabric from the tablecloths so that Michelle could find a matching dress. Then there was the elevated catwalk, styled like a fashion runway and designed to showcase the guest of honor. Laura Bush walked the catwalk in 2001, her first year in the White House. She "politely declined" thereafter, commenting, "As first lady, I was accustomed to doing almost anything, but this was a bit too much." Bush said the organizers besieged her staff long before the 2002 event, insisting that she use the catwalk. They also asked her to stay for the entire four-hour lunch and honor specific requests about what to say in her remarks. Undeterred, she left the event early that year, hurrying to New Haven to help her daughter Barbara move out of her dormitory room at Yale.

The "constant back-and-forth" over the congressional luncheon invariably reduced someone in her office to tears, said Bush, who reported that in previous years, members of Clinton's staff had cried in frustration, too. Anita McBride sympathized. As Bush's second chief of staff, she alerted Michelle's team to the demands of the social calendar and the choices ahead. She left sample letters for the correspondence office, a list of contacts at every agency, and timelines for all kinds of events, including the annual White House Christmas card, a chore that fell to the first lady's office. She also made sure to mention the challenge of dealing with what Bush called "the Congressional Club ladies." McBride said she told her successors, "This is one of those things that is a have-to-do on the schedule but, you know what, this might be an opportunity to change what the requirements are. There are some have-to-dos, but it doesn't mean the first ladies can't set parameters."

Michelle quickly saw that she was not in Kansas any longer. This was Oz. Or maybe Kafka. Nowhere in her wedding vows did it say "for richer, for poorer, *in the White House* or in health." On the one hand, she wanted to support the political spouses, "because she knows how hard that role is," Norris said. On the other, there was surely a more meaningful option than a fancy lunch. "The one thing that she didn't want to do was just do something because it had been done before." Michelle compromised. She went along with the table linens and the dress, but she also invited the spouses to do a service project. More than 150 wives and husbands joined her on the 100th day of the Obama presidency to fill grocery bags, two thousand in all, at the Capital Area Food Bank.

MICHELLE ARRIVED in London on April 1, 2009, for her first overseas trip as first lady. While Barack held working meetings, she embraced cancer patients at Charing Cross Hospital and took in a ballet at the Royal Opera. Wearing a simple black cardigan and two strands of pearls, she met Queen Elizabeth and promptly broke protocol. Towering above the white-haired monarch, she placed her manicured left hand warmly on Her Majesty's back. It was a natural gesture, but apparently one does not touch the eighty-two-year-old queen, apart from mildly shaking an outstretched hand. The queen did not seem to mind, although gadflies did buzz. It was on a side trip the next day, however, that Michelle unexpectedly found her groove. It happened at the Elizabeth Garrett Anderson School, named for Britain's first female doctor, an advocate of women's suffrage. Ninety percent of the girls came from racial or ethnic minority groups, representing fifty-five languages and count-less challenges overcome. In arranging the event in Islington, Michelle's advisers were looking for a place "the first lady wasn't expected to go," said Trooper Sanders. The team considered what would add value to the president's trip and what would be authentic to Michelle. What they saw at the school was how strongly her own story, anchored in an urban corner of the American Midwest, resonated with teenagers a world away. Michelle saw it, too.

"Nothing in my life ever would have predicted that I would be stand-ing here as the first African-American first lady. I was not raised with wealth or resources or any social standing to speak of. I was raised on the South Side of Chicago. That's the real part of Chicago," she told the girls. "I want you to know that we have very much in common." Echo-ing her remarks at Anacostia High two weeks earlier, she declared that "confidence and fortitude" would win out. "You too, can control your own destiny, please remember that." As she spoke, the girls cheered and Michelle choked up. When she ended her remarks, she surprised them by announcing, "I do hugs." The girls flocked around her and she deliv-ered one embrace after another. Afterward, feeling invigorated, she climbed into her car and said, "I could do that all day."

It was not much of a stretch to say that Michelle had found her métier, in words and gestures. Her story connected with the girls and so did her familiar, affirming embrace. In the White House, a hug would become her signature, natural and abiding, a sign of faith and support. She was not yet certain about the contours of the bully pulpit, nor had she decided which issues to pursue, but a hug was one concrete thing that she could make happen. With a smile, a few words, and an embrace, she would try to convey to thousands of girls and boys that the first lady of the United States believed in them. As for the Elizabeth Garrett Anderson School, she stayed in touch, arranging to meet thirty-five students at Oxford two years later and hosting twelve students at the White House in 2012. On her desk, she kept a photograph of her visit to the school.

Michelle made a point of speaking to young audiences when she visited India, Africa, and Latin America during her first two years in office. East Wing staffers, who asked State Department and National Security Council colleagues how the first lady could be useful, hoped her ability to connect with diverse young people overseas might even deliver a small foreign-policy benefit. At a time when the United States was waging a global competition for hearts and minds, she told university students in Mexico City in April 2010 that the "immense promise" of an Internet-connected generation had persuaded her to make young people the focus of her international efforts. Nearly half of Mexico's population was younger than twenty-five, she noted, while in the Middle East, the figure was 60 percent. She called it a youth bulge and made clear that the status quo would not suffice. "You have an unprecedented ability to organize and to mobilize, and to challenge old assumptions, and to bridge old divides and to find new solutions to our toughest problems," she said. *Organize. Mobilize. Challenge. Bridge.* Through the prism of assets, not deficits. She told her staff, "Don't just put me on a plane, send me someplace and have me smile." She was finding her voice. The challenge was to make it matter.

# THIRTEEN

# Between Politics and Sanity

For all of the glorious trees and flowers on the eighteen acres of the White House grounds, from Andrew Jackson's southern magnolias to roses of more recent vintage, no one had planted a vegetable garden since Eleanor Roosevelt's time. The idea for a garden and a larger project on children's health came to Michelle in 2007. She was in her kitchen in Hyde Park, starting to imagine ways she might make a difference if Barack actually won the presidency. A garden—simple, satisfying, illustrative. Although she arrived in Washington with little experience with seeds and soil, she intended the garden to be more than a garden. She wanted it to be a national conversation starter "about the food we eat, the lives we lead, and how all of that affects our children." Public elementary school children helped with the planting. The raised beds were visible to passersby beyond the White House fence, she said, "because I wanted this to be the 'people's garden,' just as the White House is the 'people's house.'"

The medium was the message. The new garden became a billboard for Michelle's back-to-basics views on nutrition and fitness, a focus of her White House years. Aides invited the media to cover the planting and advertised the use of the garden's harvest, including honey from a swarm of bees, at White House dinners. White House chefs brewed their own Honey Brown Ale and cooked up a veggie pizza for *Tonight Show* host Jay Leno. The garden became the heart of a glossy book,

*American Grown: The Story of the White House Kitchen Garden and Gardens Across America.* Written by Michelle and a ghostwriter, the 2012 volume contained dozens of photographs of the first lady, along with suggestions for helping the needy and tips on establishing a community garden. One of the featured gardens, in fact, was at Chicago's Rainbow Beach, the park on Lake Michigan where Michelle rode her bike and attended summer camp. If all went well, she wrote, schools and communities would follow her example and children who had never grown anything would sow, reap, and learn. "For little kids," she said, "the best part is the compost, where they can dig for worms with their hands. They love the idea that a lot of soil is worm poop."

THE GARDEN CREATED an entry point to Michelle's most ambitious and, it turned out, controversial White House initiative, a nutrition and fitness project launched in February 2010. With nearly one in three American children considered overweight and adult obesity rates rising, her goal was to change children's eating and exercise habits nationwide. Her targets ranged from unhealthy school nutrition standards and urban food deserts to restaurant menus and sweet-toothed marketing messages. Amid energetic photo ops that featured her dancing with students and exercising with sports stars, Michelle picked up a telephone in the White House to urge Congress to pass a $4.5 billion child nutrition bill. She also collaborated with pediatricians and corporate food purveyors, as well as media companies that produced programming for children. She called the project "Let's Move!"

The public health implications of fatness were apparent in the nation's expanding waistlines. In one indication of trouble, excessive weight was by far the biggest medical disqualifier in the U.S. armed forces. Between 1995 and 2008, the military counted 140,000 people who failed their entrance physicals because they were overweight. By 2010, half of all volunteers—46.7 percent of men and 54.6 percent of women—were failing a fitness test that required only sixty seconds of push-ups, sixty seconds of sit-ups, and a one-mile run. Further, many recruits had brittle bones because of a diet containing too many fizzy drinks and sugary foods and too little milk and calcium. Obesity and its effects added an estimated $147 billion to the country's annual health costs, according to the Obama administration, and the problems started young. The U.S. Centers for Disease Control calculated that 16 percent of children in 2010 were obese, with many of them developing habits and ailments that would become costly and debilitating in adulthood. A disproportionate number of overweight children were black or Hispanic. It escaped no one's notice that recess and physical education were increasingly rare in U.S. schools, as a result of budget cuts and changed priorities. The CDC reported that only one in twenty-five elementary schools, one in twelve middle schools, and one in fifty high schools offered daily physical education.

On February 9, 2010, in front of a half-dozen cabinet secretaries and a media contingent, Michelle laid out the problem, suggested solutions, and announced a series of partnerships. The American Academy of Pediatrics would develop procedures for measuring body mass index, or BMI, and devise prescriptions for more healthful living. Suppliers pledged to decrease sugar, fat, and salt in food sold to schools and, over the next ten years, double the amount of fruits and vegetables in school meals. The Food and Drug Administration would work with manufacturers and retailers to make food labels more clear, "so people don't have to spend hours squinting at words they can't pronounce to figure out whether the food they're buying is healthy or not," Michelle said. Media companies, including Disney, Scholastic, Viacom, and Warner Bros., would improve public awareness. In a public signal that the project dovetailed with his agenda, Barack that morning signed an order creating a Task Force on Childhood Obesity to review federal policy on nutrition and physical activity. After the Oval Office signing, he turned to Michelle and said, "It's done, honey."

MICHELLE'S REMARKS at the launch were not glib and glossy. Nor were they brief. In a speech that stretched to 5,800 words, she laid out her reasoning. She made plain that she was not blaming kids for eating too many calories or failing to burn them off. It was the role of adults to decide what schools served for lunch, what was available for dinner, and whether time would be set aside for gym and recess. "Our kids don't choose to make food products with tons of sugar and sodium in super-sized portions and then to have those products marketed to them everywhere they turn," she said. "And no matter how much they beg for pizza, fries and candy, ultimately they are not, and should not, be the ones calling the shots at dinnertime." Standing in the ornate State Dining Room, Michelle recalled mealtime in the cramped kitchen on Euclid Avenue. "There was one simple rule: You ate what was on your plate, good, bad or ugly. Kids had absolutely no say in what they felt like eating. If you didn't like it, you were welcome to go to bed hungry."

Michelle drew on her own experience as a working mother, recalling an alarming visit to a Chicago pediatrician who reported that Malia's and Sasha's weight, measured by body mass index, was too high. (Or, as Barack put it when telling the story, Malia was "a little chubby.") The doctor asked what the family ate, prompting Michelle to consider the way they lived their lives, particularly the pace. They always seemed to be racing from work to school to soccer, from ballet to piano to play dates. The parents had deadlines, the kids had homework, each task dueling with other demands, from maintaining friendships and looking after elders to keeping the house in a semblance of order. Comfortably upper middle class, the Obamas had the money to eat well, but too rarely took the time: "There were some nights when you got home so tired and hungry, and you just wanted to get through the drive-thru because it was quick and it was cheap. Or there were the times when you threw in that less healthy microwave option because it was easy." Her family started eating at home more often. They ate more vegetables and fresh fruit and drank more water and skim milk. They stopped keeping unhealthy food in the pantry and declared, as her parents had done, that desserts would largely be a weekend treat.

To emphasize the difficulties of families at varying economic levels, she spoke of "parents working so hard, longer hours, some cases two jobs" and the cost of fruit and vegetables rising 50 percent more than overall food costs since the 1980s. It did not help, she said, that the nation's cities were dotted with food deserts. These were neighborhoods that lacked a decent grocery store, making it harder for shoppers, especially the unemployed and the working poor, to find fresh food. "So this is where we are. Many parents desperately want to do the right thing, but they feel like the deck is stacked against them."

It may have seemed innocuous for a first lady to advocate fitness and healthy eating, but Michelle anticipated criticism. Hoping to inoculate the effort against allegations of government overreach and the inevitable portrayals of her as nanny-in-chief, she said experts did not think the problem would be solved by the government "telling people what to do." Nor was this about "preparing five-course meals from scratch every night. And it is not about being 100 percent perfect 100 percent of the time because, lord knows, I'm not. There is a place in this life for cookies and ice cream and burgers and fries." Money for fruit and vegetables when the country was on the economic skids and teachers and schoolbooks were in short supply? Funding for parks and sidewalks when the nation could not afford health care for its citizens? "These are false choices," Michelle said, "because if kids aren't given adequate nutrition, even the best books and teachers in the world won't help them get where they want them to be. And if they don't have safe places to run and play and they wind up with obesity-related conditions, those health care costs will just keep rising."

She was right to brace herself. For years to come, critics would call her a hypocrite, and worse.

FASHION BECAME a defining element of Michelle's public profile. She delighted in clothes and developed an admiring and covetous following that crossed lines of class and race. She lit up magazine covers, yet nowhere was the phenomenon more pronounced than in the blogosphere. Bloggers raced to identify every designer and off-the-rack selection, often noting the last time she had worn an outfit or which shoes and accessories accompanied it. For five years on Mrs.-O.com, Mary Tomer offered commentary down to the smallest detail, writing in 2009, "For the event, Mrs. O remixed several familiar pieces from her wardrobe. The black and white stripe blouse, last seen at the President and First

Lady's visit to the Capitol City Charter School. As well as the teal cardigan and royal blue patent leather belt, last seen in combination for the National Day of Service. A gray wool blazer and trousers rounded out the multi-layered ensemble (perhaps a cold weather tactic?)." Michelle's range was striking, from bare feet on the South Lawn to a cardigan at Buckingham Palace to kitten heels everywhere, in part to avoid putting Barack, lean and barely two inches taller, in her shadow.

It had been nearly fifty years since a first lady so captured imaginations with her fashion choices. "She has perhaps even surpassed Jackie O. because the world is bigger now than it was then," said designer Thakoon Panichgul. He admired how Michelle dressed "with such confidence," and conceded that it was refreshing to design clothes for someone with "the body of a modern woman today." A body, in other words, that could not be squeezed into a size 2. Talk of Michelle's body, and there was much talk, usually started with her sculpted arms. She earned them in the gym and bore them with pride, opting for sleeveless looks that caused fans to coo and pundits to bark. "She's made her point. Now she should put away Thunder and Lightning," cracked *New York Times* columnist David Brooks to a colleague. Spotting a trend, magazines ran how-to guides and trainers marketed exercise programs, such as *Totally Toned Arms: Get Michelle Obama Arms in 21 Days.*

Michelle went bare-shouldered at Barack's first State of the Union address. She did the same on the cover of *Vogue.* Perhaps most tellingly, she decided to show off her arms in her first official White House portrait, shot in the Blue Room beneath the watchful eye of Thomas Jefferson. She dressed in a black Michael Kors sheath with a double strand of white pearls, her smile broad, her face and hair impeccably styled, her left fingertips resting on a marble table adorned with flowers. She had just turned forty-five when the photo was taken, in the early days of the first term. The image spoke of youth and fitness, the antithesis of many past first ladies. Her blackness was all the more striking in juxtaposition with the painting of the nation's third president, who owned slaves and fathered as many as six children with one of them, Sally Hemings. In 1781, while professing that all men were created equal, Jefferson wrote that black people had a "much inferior" capacity to reason and were "dull, tasteless, and anomalous" when it came to imagination. "Never yet," wrote one of the most erudite of American presidents, "could I find that a black uttered a thought above the level of plain narration; never see even an elementary trait of painting or sculpture." The contrast in the photograph was unintentional, said her press secretary, Katie McCormick Lelyveld, who staffed Michelle that day. "We tried outside, we tried the Red Room, we tried the Green Room, we tried the Blue Room. We tried sitting, we tried standing. We liked this smile the best. We liked this backdrop the best."

IN HER SARTORIAL CHOICES, Michelle was mindful not only of how she would look, but how the fashions would play. Designers learned they could take risks in color, texture, and style when designing for the first lady. Isabel Toledo, born in Cuba, created the shimmering wool lace dress Michelle wore to the inauguration. She called the color lemongrass. "Fashion is what history looks like. For me, that moment in history was a moment of optimism," explained Toledo, who said admiringly that the first lady is "not just covering herself. She cares about what she looks like. She cares about how people perceive her." Twenty-six-year-old Jason Wu, born in Taiwan, designed the ivory chiffon gown that Michelle wore to the inaugural balls. When she donated it to the Smithsonian, she declared it a "masterpiece." Creations by Panichgul, born in Thailand, and Naeem Khan, born in India, found their way into her closet, along with dresses by Peter Soronen and Narciso Rodriguez.

Michelle had aides who helped shop for her couture, while White House lawyers monitored rules governing gifts and favors. Toledo said Michelle paid "several thousand" dollars for the lemongrass creation, a purchase coordinated by high-end Chicago boutique owner Ikram Goldman. Into a lineup rich with costly designer-made duds, some stitched just for her, she folded off-the-rack choices from the likes of J.Crew, Talbot's, and the Gap. More than once, an outfit sold out swiftly when Michelle wore it on television. The same happened with a unicorn sweater worn by Sasha when she was still in middle school. The populist elements to Michelle's selections multiplied when she added an affordable brooch or a wide belt to enliven a workaday ensemble. Telling *Ebony*, "what you wear is a reflection of who you are," she shunned pantyhose as uncomfortable and urged women to choose clothes that made them feel good. She was neither a fashion model nor a performer, but a woman who had been in the workforce for twenty years, half of that as a working mother. Through her choices—the colors, the combinations, the risks—Michelle "gave women the permission, the liberty, to participate" in fashion, said Isabel Toledo's husband, Ruben, an artist and collaborator. Her fans could relate. New York fashion writer Kate Betts titled her book about Michelle's approach to fashion *Everyday Icon*, crediting her with "helping to liberate a generation of women from the false idea that style and substance are mutually exclusive." Betts connected the first lady's style with a gospel of empowerment "that defines style as knowing who you are and being unafraid to show it to the world."

Together, Michelle and Barack delivered "romantic glamor" said Patricia L. Williams, who wrote about race and society for *The Nation*. "She brings a dignity to it. It's not dressing like Rihanna. It's not the entertainment industry, it's not sports. It underscores *lady*." The attention paid to her clothes demonstrated the array of expectations—gendered and otherwise—still attached to the role of first lady. Everywhere she went, even if only to walk Bo on the White House grounds, Michelle knew she might be photographed and examined for fashion flaws. One summer day, she stepped down the stairs of Air Force One to join her family on a walk at the Grand Canyon. It was 106 degrees and she wore shorts—ordinary shorts that came to mid-thigh. The reaction was swift. The first lady wore shorts? In *public*? After NBC's *Today* show discussed the moment on television, 300,000 viewers offered an opinion. At the *Huffington Post*, nearly 13,000 did the same, with 58.6 percent saying she had "the right to bare legs," 16.8 percent saying no, and 24.6 percent answering, "It's not the end of the world, but maybe she should wear longer shorts next time."

Michelle never forgot. Four years later, she called it her biggest fashion regret. Far more considered was her decision to appear on the cover of the March 2009 issue of *Vogue*. Despite the collective misery of the economic recession, she believed it would send a message to African American girls of many shapes and sizes about who they could be when they grew up. Although Michelle sometimes drew criticism when she veered away from American designers, her choices often drew an excited shiver in the commercial fashion world. "Have you seen someone with his hands down and eyes popped out? That was me for a few seconds. Yesterday, I was the third-most Googled person in America. It is unbelievable," said Naeem Khan after seeing Michelle on television in November 2009, wearing one of his lush creations. Steven Kolb, head of the Council of Fashion Designers of America, called Michelle "an incredible booster. Once Mrs. Obama wears a designer, the pride, the enthusiasm, the boasting is a big moment for a designer, particularly a young designer. You can't build a business based on somebody wearing your clothes, but you can capitalize on it."

Disciplined as she was, Michelle suffered a few self-inflicted wounds. One was the day she wore a $540 pair of Lanvin sneakers to volunteer at a Washington food bank. Fashionistas recognized the brand and located the price tag in an Internet minute. Another was the day she donned a $495 pair of Tory Burch boots to pick pumpkins in the White House garden. When Burch's Facebook page crowed that Michelle was wearing her boots, the response reflected the reigning dichotomy. "Wearing them as she walks through dirt to pick a pumpkin. Yeah, she really understands the plight of the common man," someone posted. Others came to her defense, pointing out that taxpayers were not paying for her footwear and, anyway, she was damned if she did, damned if she didn't. "If she went with her head tied in rags and wearing sweat pants, then folks would say she was not representing her position well," a supporter posted. "Some people will complain about heaven being too sunny!"

FIRST LADIES HAD STAGED concerts in the White House since time immemorial. Jackie Kennedy, in the early 1960s, built a portable stage in the East Room and hosted musical evenings and readings, including events for young people. Yet no previous first lady possessed more eclectic tastes than Michelle, who was determined to showcase a wide range of voices. One emblematic night in May 2009 highlighted jazz, the spoken word, and social justice. James Earl Jones recited a passage from *Othello,* while Chicago poet Mayda del Valle delivered a homage to her late Puerto Rican grandmother: "My tongues are broken needles," she said, "scratching through the grooves of a lost wisdom trying to find a faith that beats like yours. What secrets do your bones hold?" Singer and acoustic bass player Esperanza Spalding took the stage, as did Eric Lewis, a rock-jazz pianist who liked to reach into a piano to pluck the wires. For Lewis, it was sweet validation to play in the East Room as the Obamas and Spike Lee looked on. "I was totally surprised she had that kind of candor and sheer taste for something edgy, fast and hip," said Lewis, whose stage name is ELEW. The audience was similarly varied, by Michelle's design. "I love the notion of having members of Congress sitting in the East Room listening to the spoken word," she said. "It's just those incongruencies, making sure the socialites from D.C. are sitting next to the teachers from Anacostia listening to opera. It's that whole mix. You can get so much done and say so much— without saying anything."

Michelle's broader goal, and one particularly connected to the South Side of her upbringing, was to open the White House to children unlikely to drive past the grounds, much less be invited inside. "If I'm giving those experiences to Malia and Sasha, and I think it's important to them, then I can't pretend it's not important for everyone. If they weren't important, the best high schools and grammar schools in the country wouldn't be fighting to make sure they had music," she told *Washington Post* reporter Robin Givhan in 2010. "The more experiences kids have, the more things that they see, the more things that they know to want." In a twist on the traditional White House concert series, Michelle urged stars scheduled to perform for adults at night to conduct workshops for children during the day. "We want to lift young people up. The country needs to be mindful that we have all these diamonds out there, and it would be a shame not to invest in those talents," she said. What united her projects was her determination to support less fortunate people who did not have access to the polished corridors she now walked. These were people whose lives she understood because they were so familiar to her, the ones living in the world as it was, not as it should be.

On the walls of the White House, too, Michelle made clear her tastes in color, design, and social commentary. The first couple's museum borrowings stretched from Degas and Jasper Johns to Mark Rothko and Josef Albers. A colorful 1940s-era oil-on-plywood painting by William H. Johnson called *Booker T. Washington Legend* showed the educator and author of *Up from Slavery* teaching black students. Also among the borrowings were two canvases by Alma Thomas, a black expressionist painter who taught art in Washington public schools and recalled being turned away from museums because of her race. In the White House residence, Michelle hung a painting by Glenn Ligon titled *Black Like Me #2*. It featured a single phrase repeated over and over as if in typeface, the letters gradually becoming blacker toward the bottom of the piece. The phrase came from *Black Like Me,* John Howard Griffin's memoir of darkening his white skin to experience life as a Negro in the Deep South in 1959. The words in the painting read, "All traces of the Griffin I had been were wiped from existence."

FOR THE FIRST TIME in a dozen years, since before Malia and Sasha were born, Michelle and Barack were consistently at home together under one roof. There were no commutes from Chicago to Springfield or to Washington, D.C. They did not even have to leave the building to get to their offices. From a dressing room window in the residence, Michelle could peer across the Rose Garden into the West Wing and see Barack at work. Laura Bush had showed her the window when Michelle visited the White House in November 2008. Barack's office was not far from the girls' new swing set, the pool, and the tennis court. He was routinely home for dinner at 6:30 p.m. and no one had to cook. Many nights, the president stuck around for bedtime before turning back to his work. The family took turns saying grace, always ending with "We hope we live long and strong." Dinner table conversation tended not to focus on the troubles buffeting the republic, but on Malia and Sasha, "what's going on in their lives, and in ours. Some nights, we discuss issues they've heard about in the news," Michelle said. Asked once whether Barack was helpful around the house, she replied, "Even the president of the United States can handle figuring out whether somebody put their writing assignment in their book bag."

There was plenty of space in the residence for childrens' sleepovers on the third floor, and the family could escape to Camp David, where friends would often join them. On weekends in good weather, Barack played golf, most often with lower-level White House aides, and he sometimes coached Sasha's basketball team, the Vipers. The young players thought of him not as the commander in chief, but as Sasha's dad. "This is what dads are supposed to do," he said. "So they take it for granted." He conceded that he had to discourage Sasha from spending so much time on her three-point shot, rather than perfecting skills closer to the basket. One day, the team's head coach was out of commission, so Barack called for his motorcade and headed up Connecticut Avenue to fill in, even though Sasha was on a Colorado ski trip with Michelle and Malia.

Sports mattered in the family, and not only because Barack loved hoops, watched ESPN, and savored those golf outings. Michelle, who lifted weights, jumped rope, did some kickboxing, and played tennis to keep fit, decreed that the girls would each play two sports. "Because it's good for them," she explained. "It's good to practice teamwork, to understand what it means to suffer a loss, to win with grace." Each girl would choose one sport and Michelle would choose the second one. "I want them to understand what it feels like to do something you don't like and to improve, because in life you don't always get to do the things you want." Her choice for them was tennis, as an activity that could sustain them for a lifetime. "When they started, the racket was bigger than Sasha," Michelle related. "She was frustrated because she couldn't hit the ball. Malia didn't understand why I was making them play. But now they're starting to get better and they actually like it. And I'm like, 'Mom was right!'"

The Obama kids would grow up with their feet on the ground, if their parents had their way. Michelle forbade the housekeepers from making the girls' beds. She expected Malia and Sasha, three years apart in age, to learn how to do laundry and honor limits on screen time. Also, no cell phones before they turned twelve. They attended Sidwell Friends, the celebrated private school in Northwest Washington that Chelsea Clinton attended. "They don't have any excuse not to be outstanding students. We're counting on them to do that," Michelle said. Malia and Sasha were also expected to appreciate lives less privileged than their own. In their teenage years, Barack said, the girls needed to learn about working for minimum wage, "to feel as if going to work and getting a paycheck is not always fun, not always stimulating, not always fair." When Malia lamented one aspect or another of her curious life, Michelle responded, "You want to see hardship? You want to see struggle? You don't have it, kid. Having the president as your father is way down on the list of tough."

The technology had changed and the family lived at a fancier address, but the messages recalled the lessons of Michelle's childhood, even if Marian felt sure that her daughter was a tougher taskmaster than she had been. Michelle, in mom-in-chief mode, instructed the nation's children and her own children alike. "You can't think you can be a jerk and lazy and trifling now and that one day you're going to wake up and just be great, right? . . . I tell my girls this now. 'Make up your bed today so that you know how to make up your bed when you're twenty. Clean up your room now so that when you go to college, you don't live like a pig. Do your homework now, not because you have to, but because you need to be in the practice of sitting down and finishing what you start.'"

By the same token, Michelle worked to preserve kid-friendly routines. The girls often escaped the White House to spend time at their friends' houses, especially as they grew older. They snapped selfies. They went to sleepaway camp. They went on family vacations to Martha's Vineyard in the summer and Hawaii at Christmas. Malia learned to drive. When they had to ride somewhere with their father, they found the presidential motorcade "a complete embarrassment." What they craved was normality, or as much normality as the first family's impossibly rarefied life could deliver. What was true for the children was true for the parents. "I think in our house we don't take ourselves too seriously, and laughter is the best form of unity, I think, in a marriage," Michelle said. "So we still find ways to have fun together, and a lot of it is private and personal. But we keep each other smiling, and that's good." Barack agreed. He spoke of the stress-relieving pleasure of conversations with his daughters. He once said, "What I value most about my marriage is that it is separate and apart from a lot of the silliness of Washington, and Michelle is not a part of that silliness."

In 2010, Barack published a children's book, *Of Thee I Sing,* in the form of a letter to his daughters. It started, "Have I told you lately how wonderful you are?" He interwove their potential with the story of the United States, delivering a notably multicultural portrait of America. He chose thirteen distinctive individuals as models of particular traits. Jane Addams for kindness, Jackie Robinson for bravery, Georgia O'Keeffe for creativity, Martin Luther King for perseverance. He invoked Vietnam memorial designer Maya Lin and farmworkers' organizer Cesar Chavez, as well as George Washington and Abraham Lincoln. To honor differences, he quoted Sitting Bull: "For peace, it is not necessary for eagles to be crows."

BARACK HAD ANOTHER brutal year in 2010. The economy was lagging, job creation was not nearly catching up with the losses of the recession, and unemployment stood at 9.6 percent. On January 19, the eve of his first anniversary as president, Democrats lost the Senate seat that had been occupied by Ted Kennedy for forty-six years before his death in August 2009. With it went the sixtieth vote needed by Democrats to overcome a filibuster. Against the odds, and against the counsel of some of his closest advisers, including chief of staff and future Chicago mayor Rahm Emanuel, Barack pressed ahead with his bid to reform the jury-rigged U.S. health insurance system and expand coverage to millions of Americans who could not afford a quality plan. It was a monumental undertaking and it was messy. Tens of millions of Americans younger than sixty-five, the age when Medicare took effect, had no health coverage. Millions more had coverage that paid for little actual care. Still others, afflicted with illnesses and ailments known in insurance-speak as "preexisting conditions," were unable to change jobs for fear of losing coverage that would be difficult to regain. A single-payer system was not in the cards, not with Republicans in revolt, not with rampant skepticism about the federal government's abilities, not with the private-sector oxen certain to be gored. The House and the Senate found a way forward. The result, which Barack signed with twenty-two pens on March 23, 2010, was sausage. But it was easily the most ambitious expansion of the safety net since the creation of Medicare in 1965. Barack said that day in a raucous East Room ceremony that the law enshrined the principle that everyone should have "some basic security" in tending to their health. If it could survive the Supreme Court and the Republicans—no sure thing—it might just be a step toward the more level playing field that Barack and Michelle were determined to help create.

White House jubilation had barely ebbed when an explosion on the Deepwater Horizon oil platform killed eleven workers and sent oil pouring into the Gulf of Mexico. The calamity showed just how unpredictable the president's job could be. For twelve weeks, the public watched on live video as the underwater well defied public and private efforts to cap it. Barack could do little but watch impotently as an estimated 210 million gallons of oil spilled into the gulf and damaged communities still recovering from Hurricane Katrina. Nationally, the president's approval ratings had dropped to 45 percent, down from 62 percent when he took office less than two years earlier. "The left thinks he did too little; the right too much," wrote *The New York Times* shortly before the November 2010 midterm elections, which could hardly have gone worse for the president. Democrats lost control of the House and surrendered six seats in the Senate, making Barack's legislative ambitions immeasurably harder to achieve. "A shellacking," he conceded at a press conference the next day. He acknowledged that his relationship with the American people had become "rockier and tougher."

It was true that Barack had stirred much of the country when he stood on the Capitol steps as the first African American taking the oath of office. But for many others, the honeymoon was over before it began. A passel of Republicans saw obstructionism as their ticket to Valhalla. Mitch McConnell, a dour Kentucky Republican, said on becoming Senate minority leader in 2011, "The single most important thing we want to achieve is for President Obama to be a one-term president." In rhetorical flights of fancy, opponents painted Barack variously as a socialist, a tyrant, a tribal African, a Muslim. Bugbears all. Most definitely *other*. That was the point. Nor did the disparagement come only from the fledgling Tea Party or the political fringe. Newt Gingrich, former Republican Speaker of the House and future presidential candidate, said Barack suffered from a "Kenyan anti-colonialist mentality." Mike Huckabee, a repeat presidential candidate and Fox News host, said the president's views were shaped by his childhood in Kenya, a country Barack did not visit until after college. John Sununu, a former New Hampshire governor and White House chief of staff to George H. W. Bush, was most succinct of all: "I wish this president would learn how to be an American."

Popular talk radio and television hosts devoted endless airtime to the anti-Barack cause, stoking doubt that morphed into disdain. Forty-five percent of Republicans in 2011 believed the president was born in another country, and they did not mean Hawaii. This was snake oil, the height of ridiculousness. Hawaiian authorities and news organizations had delivered multiple forms of proof that he was, indeed, born in Honolulu. These included his standard birth certificate, the one his fellow Americans used to get a driver's license or a passport, as well as the August 13, 1961, edition of *The Honolulu Advertiser.* On the list of recent births was "Mr. and Mrs. Barack H. Obama, 6085 Kalanianaole Hwy., son, Aug. 4." But the reality-deniers who became known as birthers refused to concede. Like southern state troopers in the Jim Crow era, they demanded to see Barack's papers, in this case his long form Certificate of Live Birth, stored in state files and not ordinarily made public.

On April 27, 2011, Barack strode into the White House press room and announced the release of the long form document. All the information, of course, checked out. "I know that there's going to be a segment of people for which, no matter what we put out, this issue will not be put to rest," he said. "But I'm speaking to the vast majority of the American people, as well as to the press. We do not have time for this kind of silliness." In character, the chairman of the Republican National Committee promptly blasted the president for wasting time on the birther question. "Unfortunately," Reince Priebus said in the tone of mock dudgeon reserved for such occasions, "his campaign politics and talk about birth certificates is distracting him from our No. 1 priority—our economy."

RUNNING FOR PRESIDENT, Barack said he sometimes felt like a Rorschach inkblot because so many voters saw what they chose to see. The same could be said of Michelle. Polls showed that she was quite popular despite the nation's polarization. Her favorability numbers typically ranged from the mid sixties to the low seventies, significantly higher than Barack's, which increasingly ducked into the low forties. She was not easily characterized and yet public reaction was often binary. Adore. *Abhor.* Respect. *Reject.* Warm, wise, and embracing. *Haughty, petty, and disdainful.* Criticism was expectable from anti-Obama partisans who could not bear a Democrat, especially these Democrats, in the White House. Some of the vitriol could be traced to racism and sexism or, at a charitable minimum, a lack of familiarity with a black woman as accomplished and outspoken as Michelle. "Just as an assertive woman is so frequently labeled aggressive, an audacious Black woman runs the risk of appearing, well, there is not another way to say it, uppity," journalist Gwen Ifill wrote in 2007 after traveling with the future first lady.

Criticism also emerged from people who viewed Michelle positively but asked why, given her education, her experience, and her extraordinary platform, she did not speak or act more directly on a host of progressive issues, whether abortion rights, gender inequity, or the structural obstacles facing the urban poor. Where was Michelle the take-charge hospital executive? Where was Michelle the strong-minded advocate who had been so pointed and forceful, so comfortable speaking truth to power, on the campaign trail in 2007 and early 2008? The Michelle, for example, who said of women in April 2007 that "we do what we can, in spite of the fact that we're not getting the kind of support we need from government and society as a whole. . . . We've essentially ignored the plight of women and told them to go figure it out."

The East Wing registered the criticism early, said the chief of staff, Jackie Norris. "We heard it from women's groups. 'You're making her look like eye candy. She's so great, why is it that all we're ever hearing about is fashion?' People wanted us to do more, be out there more, be more aggressive, be more in the community." Through a feminist lens, which often meant white middle-class feminism, "mom-in-chief" sometimes seemed a synonym for copout. Writer Linda Hirshman said Michelle navigated the difficult waters of race and gender with "superbly canny, disciplined perfection," but observed that doing so required Michelle to imitate "a warm and fuzzy, unthreatening, bucolic female from some imaginary era from the past."

There was some truth to the idea that the politics of the job required Michelle to come across as warm and unthreatening, not just because she was the first lady, but because she was the first black first lady. A false step risked death by a thousand tweets. It was also significant, and readily apparent to people who knew her well, that Michelle cared deeply about her responsibilities as a mother. Part of what she meant by mom-in-chief was that Malia and Sasha really did come first. But managing her choices and accounting for the perceptions was like playing a game of three-dimensional chess. Rebecca Traister, author of *Big Girls Don't Cry,* admired Michelle for shattering "all kinds of molds of innocuous, feminine first-ladyhood." Yet she felt Michelle had been forced to surrender much of her identity to White House convention and her husband's career. "The stuff that was hers has been erased. It's not about, 'Does she have a job?' It's about, 'Does she have herself?' It's like somebody in a cage. You know that she knows it all, but what has to be presented to the world is this incredibly reduced version of who she is."

As Traister appreciated, to suggest that Michelle was melting into the White House draperies was to understate what she was doing and saying, and why. It also failed to account for the multiple meanings that Michelle's role tended to hold for African American women. Black women had been in the workforce since slavery, but their experiences were largely ignored in debates about how women should balance career and family. Part of the reason was economic. Until recently, few black women had the combination of financial security and family stability required to consider staying home. In mainstream popular culture, black women had more often been featured raising other people's children—notably, white people's children—than their own. "What's frequently missing from the discussion of black women is their role as loving mothers, beloved wives, valued partners, cherished daughters, cousins, relatives," said Columbia law professor Patricia J. Williams. She recalled long periods when black women were "relentlessly taxonomized as mammy rather than mom." On the other hand, she said, Michelle "defies stereotypes" and "expands the force field of feminism in ecumenical and unsettling ways."

Brittney Cooper, a scholar of black women's history, took similar issue with a critique of Michelle as a "feminist nightmare," in the words of a provocative *Politico Magazine* headline. "My message to white feminists is simple: Lean back. Way back. And take your paws off Michelle Obama," Cooper wrote. "Black women have never been the model for mainstream American womanhood." Michelle, in her view, should be left to decide for herself where to invest her energies. This also happened to be Michelle's opinion. "Part of what we fought for is choice," she said, "not just one definition of what it means to be a woman."

The public debate was mirrored in social media and kitchen table conversations, where a racial divide was similarly evident. In a 2011 poll, nearly eight in ten black women said they personally identified with Michelle. Only 2 percent of black women said she was not a good role model. Eighty-eight percent said she understood their problems, according to the survey by *The Washington Post* and the Kaiser Family Foundation. Eighty-four percent of black men agreed, compared with just 51 percent of white women and 44 percent of white men. One reason that African American women defended Michelle's emphasis on her family, said National Public Radio host Michel Martin, was "a feeling of relief and sympathy that at least one of their community, broadly defined, has the opportunity to protect her children, to cherish her family life, and to even have some personal time to shop and exercise and look good."

AS THE WHITE HOUSE GLARE intensified, friends were as important as ever, maybe more so. "We work hard to make them laugh. Their lives are so serious," said Cheryl Whitaker, who visited from Chicago from time to time and joined Michelle on family vacations. Beyond the friends who visited and those who decamped to Washington, Michelle resumed her friendship with her Princeton roommate, now Angela Kennedy Acree, a senior attorney representing indigent clients in the D.C. public defender's office. At a time when she felt she had few confidants in Washington, she also became close to Sharon Malone, who knew something about the challenge of balancing career, motherhood, and the ambitions of a famous spouse. Malone was a prominent obstetrician-gynecologist married to Eric H. Holder Jr., chosen by Barack as the first African American attorney general of the United States. Malone, who bore the primary responsibility for their household and the daily lives of their three children, did not opt out of her job as Holder moved from assignment to demanding assignment. "I have worked too hard to be where I wanted to be, not to pursue it to the fullest," she said.

Malone was raised in Mobile, Alabama, the youngest of eight children. This was the Deep South during the final paroxysms of Jim Crow. Her father was a farmer, her mother a maid. Neither could vote. In 1963, her older sister Vivian tried to enroll in the all-white University of Alabama and became a central player in a scene that became famous as Governor George Wallace's "stand in the schoolhouse door." As the news media watched on a sweltering June day, deputy U.S. attorney general Nicholas Katzenbach, supported by a federal judge and a commitment from President Kennedy, escorted Malone and James Hood to the Tuscaloosa campus. Wallace yielded, but not before he complained that U.S. government measures to allow African Americans to attend the university were "illegal and unwarranted."

The month that Malone took up her studies, she appeared on the cover of *Newsweek*. Two years later, she became the first black graduate in the university's 134-year history. When Lyndon Johnson signed the landmark Voting Rights Act of 1965 to preserve "the decency of democracy," he invited Malone to the ceremony and presented her with one of the signing pens. Later that year, in Chicago to receive an award from the local NAACP, one of her hosts was the Reverend Carl Fuqua, the organization's executive director, who had presided over Fraser and Marian Robinson's wedding. "Once your sister stands in the face of the governor . . . , it broadens your horizons," Sharon Malone said. "I knew I was going somewhere and wouldn't be sitting on a porch in Mobile, Alabama."

Sharon Malone graduated with honors from Harvard in 1981 and, after a stint at IBM, attended Columbia University Medical School. She considered present-day African Americans to be "survivors of a 300-year legacy" and, like Michelle, gave much credit to her parents. "That's the part that amazes me, that you can grow up where everything negates your humanity and yet you're able to keep intact and impart that to your children. The confidence to be who we are." Malone and Holder married after meeting at a 1989 fundraiser for the Concerned Black Men charity. Holder met Barack at a dinner party hosted by Ann Walker Marchant, a cousin of Valerie Jarrett's, and when Barack decided to run for president, he offered to help. Malone approved, although she counted Barack's chances of victory as zero. "I'm forever colored by my experiences growing up in the segregated South," she said. "I grew up in an era where neither of my parents could vote. And the notion that we would elect an African-American, I honestly didn't believe it."

MICHELLE SOUGHT TO personify vim and vigor. She jumped rope double Dutch and starred in a jumping jack contest with more than four hundred kids. She played flag football in New Orleans and she ran across the lawn while carrying water jugs, an effort to persuade children to drink up. She won a push-up contest on daytime television with Ellen DeGeneres and staged a sack race in the White House with late-night comedian Jimmy Fallon. She did a dance step with middle school kids in Northwest Washington, D.C., showing off the choreography of her friend Beyoncé Knowles. It was a marketing campaign, pure and simple. "As you can see, I'm pretty much willing to make a complete fool out of myself to get our kids moving," Michelle said in late 2011, near the end of the second year of the Let's Move! campaign. "But there is a method to my madness. There's a reason why I've been out there jumping rope and hula hooping and dancing to Beyoncé, whatever it takes. It's because I want kids to see that there are all kinds of ways to be active. And if I can do it, anybody can do it." As she would say in the second term, offering insight into her philosophy of progress, "You have to change attitudes before you can change behavior."

The response could be vicious and personal. "MO is a complete imposter like her husband," one *Washington Post* reader wrote during the Obamas' trip to India in 2010. Others disparaged her clothes, her nutrition efforts, and her now infamous comments about being proud of her country. Sarah Palin mocked and misrepresented her on reality television in 2011 as the former Alaska governor shopped for cookie makings. "Where are the s'mores ingredients?" she asked. "This is in honor of Michelle Obama, who said the other day we should not have dessert." Palin was not finished. She said in a talk show appearance, "Instead of a government thinking that they need to take over and make decisions for us according to some politician or politician's wife's priorities, just leave us alone, get off our back, and allow us as individuals to exercise our own God-given rights to make our own decisions and then our country gets back on the right track."

Representative James Sensenbrenner, a Republican from Wisconsin, was caught discussing Michelle's body in unflattering ways not once, but twice. At a church event, he commented about her "big butt." Soon afterward, he was overheard on his cell phone at an airport saying, "She lectures us on eating right while she has a large posterior herself." He apologized. Meanwhile, one year after the launch of Let's Move!, Rush Limbaugh told his listeners, "It doesn't look like Michelle Obama follows her own nutritionary, dietary advice. . . . I'm trying to say that our first lady does not project the image of women that you might see on the cover of the *Sports Illustrated* swimsuit issue." This would be the portly radio host who sometimes called her "Michelle My Butt."

The criticism got uglier. In the global village that was the Internet, where anyone could be a town crier, Michelle was likened to Dr. Zira, the chimpanzee physician from *Planet of the Apes,* and a Wookiee in the *Star Wars* series. A California rodeo clown joked over the loudspeakers in 2013 that *Playboy* had offered $250,000 to Mitt Romney's wife, Ann, to pose in the magazine. He went on to say that the White House was upset about it because *National Geographic* only offered Michelle Obama $50 to pose for them. A Virginia school board member relayed an email that showed a group of bare-breasted African women doing a tribal dance. The text said it was Michelle's high school reunion. A Republican former chairman of the South Carolina Election Commission posted a comment on Facebook, after a gorilla escaped from the zoo, "I'm sure it's just one of Michelle's ancestors—probably harmless." The Republican speaker of the Kansas House of Representatives forwarded a Christmas email depicting Michelle as the Grinch and alluding to the taxpayer-borne costs of her travel: "I'm sure you'll join me in wishing Mrs. YoMama a wonderful, long Hawaii Christmas vacation—at our expense, of course."

Michelle listened. She heard. She bit her tongue.

# FOURTEEN

# Simple Gifts

There was no fanfare in Michelle's address to the Women's Conference in Long Beach, California, in October 2010. Hers was a solitary voice in a vast arena. The lights were dim and all eyes were trained on her as she quietly explained why American society had an obligation to military families. It was a new interest of hers, one she developed on the campaign trail when she met women whose stories "took my breath away." Michelle considered herself wise about women's concerns. "Reading about, thinking about, talking about and living these issues my entire life," as she put it. But here was a group of women—wives of soldiers, sometimes soldiers themselves—whose experiences were new to her. These were women bearing the weight of wars in Iraq and Afghanistan that would leave more than 6,600 Americans dead, upwards of 50,000 wounded, and an estimated 250,000 bearing the residual effects of traumatic brain injury, principally from roadside bombs. In all, well over two million U.S. military personnel had cycled through the war zones in the decade since 9/11.

While they were away from home, typically for twelve months or more, their families were on their own. Michelle met women whose husbands were on their third, fourth, or fifth deployment. Women who were moving every couple of years, uprooting their children or interrupting their careers and education because of a transfer. Women who struggled to keep a toehold in the middle class. Women who worried that their husbands might die. "A good day," one told her, "is when a military chaplain doesn't knock on my door." It was a revelation. "Many of these women were younger than I was," Michelle said. "They had far less support and far fewer resources than I ever had. And every day, they were confronting challenges that I could barely even imagine."

The speech introduced Joining Forces, an East Wing initiative in support of military families. The launch was still months away, but Michelle and her aides saw the conference, organized by Maria Shriver, wife of California governor Arnold Schwarzenegger, as a chance to get the tone right. They were finding it difficult. "You don't want to preach at people like you're telling them what to do," said Jocelyn Frye, her domestic policy adviser. "And particularly with military families, you want to make sure you're not overdramatizing the issue or pandering." Military families—and wounded soldiers, in particular—too often found themselves treated as victims when what they wanted was awareness and respect. Frye worried that the speech would not go well. The team discussed style as well as substance during the run-throughs. "We were going back and forth. And then she practiced it and virtually every concern I had went away. She just knew how to hit it—to make it lighter where it needed to be lighter, to make it less aggressive where it felt aggressive." It was not the first time that Frye had seen Michelle elevate her game. She said the first lady would set a standard for herself, then exceed it. "Some of it has to do with a very good sense, an almost uncanny sense, of understanding the tone and mood for everything we do," said Frye. She also credited clarity of purpose. "It's an ongoing conversation, not only about the substantive issue, but what her role could be in that issue."

Michelle often saw herself as a woman talking to women about matters that, more often than not, fell to women to accomplish. When she spoke of expanded health insurance, she described it as a benefit to the women who typically bore responsibility for family health care decisions. When she talked about children's nutrition, ditto. And it was the same thing when she appealed to the fourteen thousand female listeners at the Women's Conference, her largest audience since the campaign. She asked them to put themselves in the shoes of military women, wondering aloud how to find balance when one partner is in a dangerous job half a world away, and how to crack the glass ceiling: "Try doing that when you don't live anywhere long enough to get promoted or gain seniority in your job." She pointed to a study that indicated military spouses made $10,500 less annually than their civilian counterparts, yet military families made time for community service at far higher rates than the general population. What she wanted to give military spouses, she said, were opportunities to use their skills "and the support they need to juggle their responsibilities."

Michelle suggested that government could help. But, sounding a note that echoed the Let's Move! approach and the playbook that said officialdom was never the complete answer, she said a little girlfriend-to-girlfriend assist would make a difference. "You see," she said, "this is what we do for each other as women. . . . We show up. We show up at the door with some food. We show up at the door with some chocolate. And if things are really bad, we show up at the door with a bottle of wine, right? We take that shift in the carpool. We say, 'Hey, send the kids over to my house right now. I'll take them off your hands for a day, a night, a weekend, whatever you need.'" The soldiers and their families were doing their part to defend the country and help the world. "It's not enough just to feel grateful," she said, the closest she came to an admonishment. "It's time for each of us to act."

JOINING FORCES WAS NOT glamorous. Much of the early work, in fact, was mundane, a matter of tedious bureaucratic troubleshooting. At the time of its April 2011 launch, for example, one in three military spouses worked in professions that required state licenses, perhaps a nursing or teaching credential. When a soldier was transferred, it often took months before his wife could work. Yet fewer than a dozen states had regulations on the books to correct the problem. Or, when the army moved a soldier from, say, Fort Drum, New York, to Fort Benning, Georgia, would his daughter's new high school grant credit for a history class taken in New York? "At this point, it has affected millions of kids," said navy captain Brad Cooper, imported from the Defense

Department to manage one stage of the project. "There's not a voice for this. It often can't rise above the noise."

Lieutenant Colonel Jason Dempsey, an infantry officer and West Point graduate recently back from Afghanistan, served as something of a coach and translator, explaining military culture to the first lady and a staff largely inexperienced in such matters. "The families just don't have a sense that anybody else understands what they're going through," he said near the end of his assignment as a White House fellow. "They don't want a pity party. They don't want people to just give them a free car." The military community, he knew, was ever watchful for false sincerity, particularly in service to political ambition. Michelle and her partner, Jill Biden, a college English professor, army mother, and wife of the vice president, were willing to do something to help. Yet in the East Wing's eyes, the military bureaucracy was moving too slowly. "Was the first lady frustrated? Absolutely, and rightly so," said Jackie Norris. "She felt like she wanted to do more than a public service announcement that raises visibility. She saw this as 'How can I do something that's more sustainable?'"

Yet Michelle did not want to run the policy herself. That was not her role, and as everyone around her recognized, such a strategy could create as many problems as it might solve. What she could do, she reasoned, was to use her voice and her convening power. Dempsey, in visits to sometimes skeptical Pentagon brass, argued in favor of the project's potential and defended Michelle's authenticity. "Listen," he recalled saying, "you're right that this is not necessarily going to be perfect, it's not going to be all-encompassing, and we're not going to solve all of everybody's problems. But you know what? This is the first and only time that the first lady of the United States has been interested in this issue. . . . Any first lady can come in and choose any issue—autism, hunger. This first lady has decided she's going to dedicate her time to the needs and concerns of the military community, so we've got to take full advantage." He said Michelle was quick to understand the complexities and careful to tread lightly. "Very cognizant that she doesn't have all the answers," he said.

As the program developed, the White House staff labored to understand mental health needs, a significant and growing concern of veterans and their families. They collected pledges from medical schools to improve the training of doctors and nurses in treating veterans. They wrangled promises from American companies to hire veterans returning home to unemployment rates higher than those faced by civilians. Michelle appealed directly to the nation's governors, asking them to make professional credentials more portable and find ways to help soldiers translate their military skills into civilian licenses, and jobs. Little noticed by commentators inclined to dismiss her work as mere mom and apple pie was the fact that many returning military personnel belonged to the nation's hard-pressed working class. In 2012, roughly 80 percent of the nation's active duty military lacked a college degree. Among enlisted men and women, the figure was 93 percent. Joining Forces working groups asked how to help veterans find steady jobs in such roles as drivers or meter readers, then reached out to utilities, delivery companies, and large retailers. "It was in the discussions we had, who we needed to help," said Matthew McGuire, a senior Commerce Department official who had known the Obamas in Chicago. "We cared about everyone who was coming home, of course, but we knew that the gunnery sergeant with just a high school degree was going to need more help reentering the civilian labor market than the commander of a nuclear submarine who went to the Naval Academy."

Michelle took note of the hardships and the country's economic and political divide in remarks in Fort Bragg, North Carolina, six weeks into Barack's presidency: "I think many people were like me, not realizing so many of our military families are living right at the poverty line. Not realizing that it is hard for spouses to get jobs when they move, or that they can't often transfer credits and finish their education, and they're struggling with the high cost of quality and affordable childcare." Barack, echoing the order he issued when Michelle launched Let's Move! the year before, issued a presidential directive to federal agencies demanding coordinated improvements in the way military families were treated. Michelle publicly promised to tell Barack what she learned at roundtables around the country.

For all of the personal connection that Michelle felt to the families, Joining Forces also fulfilled her goal of boosting Barack's agenda. As a U.S. senator, Barack had served on the Veterans Affairs Committee, chairing town hall meetings in Illinois, proposing legislation, and quietly visiting wounded warriors in military hospitals, something he would continue to do as president. During the presidential campaign, he not only criticized the decision to wage a preventive war in Iraq, but blasted the Bush administration for failing to live up to the country's obligation to veterans, especially the wounded. "We've heard rhetoric that hasn't been matched by resources," he told a gathering at a Houston VFW hall in February 2008. In time, the Veterans Administration in Barack's administration would have its own grievous failings, but Michelle worked on the issue, and her focus also served an electoral purpose. Military votes could be helpful against a Republican candidate in 2012. In a toss-up state like Virginia, North Carolina, or Colorado, it could even make the difference between a win and a loss.

ON JANUARY 8, 2011, a wild-eyed shooter named Jared Loughner opened fire at an outdoor political event in Tucson, killing six people, including a federal judge, and piercing the brain of Representative Gabrielle Giffords, a Democratic member of Congress. Giffords, remarkably, survived. While it was not immediately clear why Loughner targeted Giffords at one of her trademark Congress on Your Corner gatherings, the national conversation turned to the bitterness of American political discourse. Four days later, Barack spoke before thousands of people in the University of Arizona field house and, in cadences that echoed the best of his political speeches, urged Americans to listen to one another more carefully and deepen their capacity for empathy. "Let's use this occasion to expand our moral universe," he said in an address that could be filed in the category of Obama essentialism. "We recognize our own mortality and we are reminded that in the fleeting time we have on this earth, what matters is not wealth or status or power or fame. But, rather, how well we have loved and what small part we have played in making the lives of other people better. And that process of reflection, of making sure we align our values with our actions—that,

I believe, is what a tragedy like this requires." Barack quoted scripture as Michelle sat in the front row, next to Giffords's husband, astronaut Mark Kelly. As the president announced that Giffords had opened her eyes for the first time since the shooting, Michelle gripped Kelly's right hand with her left and cupped her right hand reassuringly on his forearm. As the crowd cheered and everyone stood, she gave him a hug. It was a natural gesture, simple and warm.

The shooting got the country's attention only partly because Loughner fired thirty-one shots in less than thirty seconds from a 9mm Glock 19, a semi-automatic handgun widely available for legal purchase. Giffords herself owned one. Other madmen had done the same, and worse. The Tucson case also hit home because of who was shot. The six dead and the 12 wounded offered stories and symbols that would have made Norman Rockwell pull out his palette. The federal judge. The congressional aide. The church volunteer who tried to save his friend. The retired marine, wounded as he tried in vain to shield his wife. And, perhaps most of all, nine-year-old Christina Green, a swimmer, a dancer, a gymnast, an A student recently elected to the student council. Improbably, she was born on September 11, 2001. "She saw all this through the eyes of a child, undimmed by the cynicism or vitriol that we adults all too often just take for granted," Barack said. "I want to live up to her expectations. I want our democracy to be as good as Christina imagined it." After he ended his remarks, a choir sang "Simple Gifts," a nineteenth-century Shaker song also performed during his inauguration.

Michelle and Barack pictured their children in Christina, who was just three months younger than Sasha when she died. Seeing a role for herself as a mother who had a platform as first lady, Michelle wanted to make a public statement. She wrote a letter and taped a video, but the West Wing preferred the president to take the lead, and to be seen as taking it. The video was never released. The day after Barack's speech in Tucson, the White House did release, in Michelle's name, an "open letter to parents." As parents, she said, the assault and its aftermath "makes us think about what an event like this says about the world we live in—and the world in which our children will grow up. . . . The question my daughters have asked are the same ones that many of your children will have—and they don't have easy answers." In echoes of the lessons of her childhood, she urged parents to teach their children "about the values we hold dear, about finding hope at a time when it seems far away." And, too, ways of "assuming the best, rather than the worst, about those around us."

AS SHE CAST her mind over the possibilities for her White House years, Michelle told her staff that the goal was to "move the ball." That meant building something enduring, leaving a legacy. Yet in a role that was forever neither-nor, she had neither a big budget nor a large staff, and turnover was frequent. Anything she wanted to build, the East Wing would have to piece together on its own. "It's not up to her to go from cabinet department to cabinet department saying, 'I'm working on this, I'm doing this, you need to help me.' They don't work for her," said Katie McCormick Lelyveld, her press secretary. Michelle searched for allies and dispatched her aides to do the same. For Let's Move! she wanted support from doctors, business leaders, parents, the president's cabinet—and "certainly, West Wing oomph," Lelyveld said. The staff reached out to federal agencies and courted mayors and governors, inviting them to the White House or onto stages across the country, where they could stand with a first lady consistently more popular than her beleaguered husband. "The power she has," said Norris, "is that most people want to make the first lady happy."

To get the word out, Michelle turned to celebrities, none more prominent than Beyoncé Knowles, a performer with a big voice and a flashy stage presence. With her husband, Shawn Carter, better known as the rapper Jay Z, she was savvy in the ways of music and marketing. Beyoncé reconfigured her song "Get Me Bodied" to create "Move Your Body," a catchy, kid-friendly tune: "A little sweat ain't never hurt nobody. Don't just stand there on the wall! Everybody just move your body." A video staged as if done by a high school flash mob, would register vast numbers of views—more than 30 million by early 2015. Separate videos of Beyoncé doing the dance at P.S. 161 in Harlem and Michelle dancing the Dougie at Alice Deal Middle School in Washington garnered millions more. Soon, schools and public health departments across the country did their own versions. Michelle's staff admitted, somewhat sheepishly, to practicing the dance step in the carpeted confines of the East Wing.

Michelle drew on tennis champion Serena Williams, and other big names from the professional sports ranks. Gymnasts Dominique Dawes and Gabby Douglas. Quarterbacks Drew Brees and Colin Kaepernick. Ice skater Michelle Kwan. Basketball player Grant Hill. Runner Allyson Felix. She also included Cornell McClellan, the Obamas' longtime personal trainer, who moved from Chicago to lead workouts in the White House gym. Barack named McClellan to the revamped president's fitness council, which became the President's Council on Fitness, Sports and Nutrition in honor of Let's Move! Michelle also matched famous chefs with school kitchens and did her own turns on television cooking shows.

Nearly four years into the project, Michelle corralled the Miami Heat into making an irreverent video in praise of healthy eating. When the team visited the White House to celebrate its latest NBA title, head coach Eric Spoelstra staged mock interviews with all-star Heat players Dwyane Wade and Ray Allen, while in the background, LeBron James held up a backboard and hoop. Michelle darted in and dunked, then did a guttural laugh worthy of a preening young street hoops player. Later, Michelle and the players nonchalantly munched apples. This was not Jackie Kennedy's White House. Or Hillary Clinton's. "LOL LOL I love her," one netizen wrote in response to the video, which got big play on television and the Web. Another posted, "That is so funny. . . . Mrs. O is a cool lady." But there were many other reactions, too. Among the more printable ones: "Disgusting is putting it mildly. Not very dignified. She's still got that fat ass." And "Too many monkeys." Plus "God she makes me sick."

THE SECRET SERVICE RECORDED significantly more threats against Barack than against any of his predecessors. The risk accounted for the ubiquity of the security bubble and justified the fact that Barack had received Secret Service protection earlier than any previous presidential candidate. The seriousness of threats was sometimes difficult to assess, but on a November night in 2011, the danger was all too real and the performance of the Secret Service none too impressive. That night, a gunman named Oscar R. Ortega-Hernandez, believing that Barack "had to be stopped," parked his car on Constitution Avenue and fired a Romanian-made semi-automatic rifle at the White House residence, hitting the building at least seven times.

A bullet pierced the antique White House glass but was stopped by a layer of bulletproof glass that protected the residence. Another bullet lodged in a wooden windowsill on the Truman Balcony. When Ortega-Hernandez opened fire at about 8:30 p.m. on a Friday night, only Sasha and Marian were home. Michelle and Barack were away and Malia returned to the residence about an hour later, escorted by her security detail. Although several Secret Service officers felt sure they had heard shots, as did others nearby, a supervisor told his colleagues to stand down, apparently believing a car had backfired. It would be four days before the agency realized that shots had hit the White House. When Michelle learned of the shooting from an assistant White House usher, not the Secret Service, she was "aghast—and then quickly furious," Carol Leonnig of *The Washington Post* reported. Michelle later challenged the Secret Service chief directly. Not only had the Secret Service failed to recognize or stop the attack, but bullets fired from seven hundred yards away had slammed into a part of the residence the Obamas used often. They sat outdoors on the Truman Balcony on warm days and mild nights. They entertained there. And, on the other side of the bulletproof glass, the Yellow Oval Room was Michelle's favorite room in the house.

Not quite three years later, in September 2014, an Iraq War veteran named Omar Gonzalez jumped a White House fence on Pennsylvania Avenue and raced past the North Portico into the building, carrying a knife. He could have run up the stairs to the residence, but darted instead toward the East Room and then the Green Room before he was tackled. An investigation showed that the Secret Service did not release a guard dog and had no swift way to lock the White House doors.

A loud warning alarm had been disconnected at the request of White House ushers, who protested that it often malfunctioned.

PLAYERS FROM THE FOOD, retail, and restaurant industries trekked to the White House to ask what they could do for their overweight country. They heard the same message Michelle delivered to a Grocery Manufacturers Association conference, when she had said, "Step it up." "We need you not just to tweak around the edges, but to entirely rethink the products that you're offering, the information that you provide about these products and how you market those products to our children," Michelle told the conference. The companies needed to reformulate their recipes, she said, and reshape their marketing to tout the benefits. "What it doesn't mean is taking out one problematic ingredient, only to replace it with another. While decreasing fat is certainly a good thing, replacing it with sugar and salt isn't. And it doesn't mean compensating for high amounts of problematic ingredients with small amounts of beneficial ones. For example, adding a little bit of Vitamin C to a product with lots of sugar, or a gram of fiber to a product with tons of fat, doesn't suddenly make those products good for our kids."

Michelle's work led to commitments by the likes of Olive Garden and Red Lobster, restaurant chains that catered to the middle class, to make their meals less salty and more healthy. General Mills and Kraft were among the many companies that promised to reduce calories in their foods. Subway would join the mix, promising to provide healthier options for kids—fruit instead of cookies, skim milk and water instead of soda—while spending $41 million over three years to market the new selections. Walmart, the retailing behemoth working assiduously to reform its image, announced that it would sell more fresh fruit and vegetables, remove trans fats from packaged food, and cut the sodium content of processed foods by 25 percent. The East Wing calculated that Walmart's decision would shape the behavior of its suppliers and spark changes throughout the industry.

Implicit in Michelle's call for better behavior was the fact, welcomed by the industry, that the government would not be imposing new regulations. Her efforts relied on calculations of mutual self-interest, specifically an East Wing bet that voluntary corporate efforts would produce better results than any attempt to mandate rules on, say, nutritional content or marketing to children. The corporate side of the program was coordinated through a new nonprofit, Partnership for a Healthier America (PHA), established alongside Let's Move!, although technically independent. Members of the partnership, including Walgreens, Hyatt, and a bevy of hospitals and health care providers, found it useful to be associated with nutrition and good health—an issue that the first lady described as one of her passions. When announcements were made, Michelle was often on hand with a smile and plenty of praise. The White House saw it as a win-win. "PHA works with the private sector to create meaningful commitments, and ensures that when those commitments are made that credit is given where credit is due," the partnership's website said of its strategy. "PHA has no interest in forcing industry to meet unrealistic benchmarks. The goal is to maximize the potential of the private sector to achieve success. We want the private sector with us because, quite simply, we will not succeed without it."

Nutrition advocates doubted that business conglomerates would move far enough and fast enough without public prodding—in other words, without formal rules and regulations. Research had shown that advertising influenced children's desire for foods high in sugar, salt, and fat. But when Congress developed guidelines designed to limit marketing that targeted children, lobbyists from the food and media industry—some working for companies that publicly backed Let's Move!—killed them. The lobbyists complained that the provisions, although voluntary, were sweeping and unscientific, despite the endorsement of the American Academy of Pediatrics, among others. The White House blamed Congress for backing down. Senator Tom Harkin, an Iowa Democrat, pointed a finger at 1600 Pennsylvania Avenue, although not directly at the East Wing. "The White House got cold feet," Harkin said. "It sort of undermines everything that the first lady was doing."

Popular interest in healthier food was already growing when the Obamas arrived in Washington. Companies had been changing tack for good business reasons. As far back as 2005, McDonald's added salads to its menu. But the first lady's efforts gave the national dialogue a boost. From the White House garden to Let's Move!, from the new nutrition standards to the inspiration for countless school gardens, and even the cajoling of American businesses, the needle was beginning to move.

MICHELLE RECEIVED almost unfailingly positive attention in the mainstream media. One exception was a private trip she took with Sasha to Spain in August 2010—private to the extent that anything could be private, when an air force jet and a Secret Service detail were required. "A Modern-Day Marie Antoinette" blared a headline in the *New York Daily News*. (That would be the Marie Antoinette ever known as having said of starving French peasants, "Let them eat cake," although historians doubt she actually said it.) For Michelle, the trip was a getaway in support of Anita Blanchard, one of her close Chicago friends, whose father had recently died. The genesis of the trip was a birthday promise that Blanchard and her husband, Marty Nesbitt, had made to their children. Each child, upon turning ten, could choose a trip to take. It was Roxanne Nesbitt's turn to celebrate and she picked Spain, where Michelle and her friends would stay in an opulent hotel on the Costa del Sol.

Members of the White House staff spotted trouble. They knew the optics would be bad on a fancy foreign trip in the middle of an economic slump and the tough 2010 election season. Michelle listened, but she said the trip was important to her. She was going. Sure enough, Spanish media were all over the story, and quickly. Photographs appeared of Michelle strolling through Marbella, Ronda, and the Alhambra, later paying a courtesy call with Sasha on King Juan Carlos I and Queen Sofia in Majorca, where she shared an elegant lunch of turbot and gazpacho. The visuals and accompanying stories were instantly troublesome. The Obamas paid hotel expenses and the equivalent of first-class airfare for Michelle and Sasha, an arrangement that predated this presidency, but those costs were minimal next to the share footed by taxpayers, who paid for her traveling staff and the large Secret Service contingent dictated by security concerns. A conservative watchdog group filed a Freedom of Information Act request and estimated later that the four-day vacation cost the federal treasury more than $467,000. Asked about the expense in a time of austerity, White House press secretary Robert Gibbs replied, "The first lady is on a private trip. She is a private citizen and is the mother of a daughter on a private trip. And I think I'd leave it at that."

It was the New York date night all over again, but this time with a considerably higher price tag. There were other trips as well. Skiing with the girls in Colorado, sightseeing and theater with them in New York, a vacation in France, a safari in South Africa. Each time, a scribe or a critic would calculate the cost of operating an air force Boeing 757, which ran to $11,351 an hour, plus other expenses. Traveling with security and being ferried by a U.S. government plane was a fact of first family life, and it had been for many years. George Bush made 77 visits to his ranch in Crawford, Texas, during the eight years of his presidency, spending at least part of 490 days there; he went 187 times to Camp David, where the corresponding number of days was 487. What should a first lady do?

Anita McBride, who wrestled with such questions as Laura Bush's chief of staff, said foreign vacations with hefty price tags might best be left for later in life. When Laura Bush went out of town with her friends, the destination was likely to be a national park. "You have temporary custody of the job," McBride said. "It's probably best to find the least controversial ways to get your down time. . . . It's just not worth it." Michelle's staff, whose job was to deflect the flak, was painfully alert to the dilemma. "She would fly United if she could, but she can't," Lelyveld said. "At a certain point, she just wants to go on an educational trip with her girlfriends and her kids. The question is, should she not make this trip because of the financial and personnel footprint? Where do you draw the line?"

THE SEAS MAY HAVE PARTED to allow Barack to win the first time, but when the reelection campaign got under way in 2011, the tide was high and the waters were rough. Economic growth was barely above flat and the budget deficit seemed stuck on a number with too many zeroes to count. During the summer of 2011, unemployment was running at 9 percent, higher than any incumbent president had faced on election day since before World War II. Six million people had been out of work for twenty-seven weeks or more, according to the Bureau of Labor Statistics. The national unemployment rate was 9.1 percent; for African Americans, it was 16.7 percent. A survey by NBC News and *The Wall Street Journal* fifteen months before the 2012 election concluded that 73 percent of Americans thought the country was on the wrong track. For the first time, a slight majority disapproved of the job Barack was doing overall, while 59 percent disapproved of his handling of the economy. He received higher marks—50 percent approval—on foreign policy. If there were any source of solace, it was that only 13 percent of Americans approved of the performance of Congress, where the House was run by Republicans.

Barack turned fifty on August 4, 2011, dancing with Michelle as Stevie Wonder performed in the East Room. The very next day, credit agencies downgraded U.S. debt for the first time in history, citing political gridlock in Washington. The deficit would drop, of course, when economic activity picked up. Yet Barack and the economists who contended that higher federal spending would speed the recovery—and that austerity would delay it—were stymied by Republicans who insisted that the deficit was too high to justify the outlay. The GOP also had political reasons for thwarting jobs bills and stimulus packages: If the economy improved and more Americans thought the country was moving in the right direction, Barack would get credit. And that would threaten the Republicans' cherished goal of defeating him in November 2012.

The brickbats came from all sides. Barack was rebuffed in his effort to reach a grand bargain on spending and taxes with House Speaker John Boehner, an Ohio Republican saddled with limited vision and an unruly caucus. When word emerged that Barack had offered major concessions and still come up short, growing numbers of Democratic supporters saw the president as callow, particularly after he agreed to extend the Bush-era tax cuts for the wealthiest Americans. Meanwhile, to their consternation, immigration reform had gone nowhere;

the cap-and-trade program to slow climate change was doomed; the Guantánamo prison was still open; and the fate of Barack's signature achievement, the Affordable Care Act, remained in the hands of the Supreme Court and its 5-to-4 conservative majority. The stock market was a bright spot, at least for the 50 percent of Americans with investments, climbing far above its recession lows. But even there, August 2011 provided bad news. The S&P 500 index was down 5.7 percent for the month, its fourth straight decline. The economy added no new jobs in August, raising fears of a double-dip recession.

On the plus side, Barack's unpopular bet on the Detroit auto industry was paying off. He helped bring an end to Muammar Qadhafi's mercurial tenure in Libya without risking American troops. He won the biggest gamble of his presidency when the navy's SEAL Team Six dropped into a compound in Pakistan and killed al Qaeda leader Osama bin Laden, architect of the 9/11 attacks and the most hunted man in the world. As Vice President Joe Biden would say on the campaign trail, arguing for a second Obama term, "Bin Laden is dead and General Motors is alive." And yet August 2011 would also prove to be the deadliest month of the Afghan war, now in its tenth year. Sixty-six American service members died, including thirty aboard a Chinook helicopter shot down by Afghan fighters.

This was not the record that Barack had expected to carry into the 2012 election, when he aimed to become only the second Democrat since Franklin Roosevelt to be elected to two full terms. Bill Clinton was the other. When they returned to Martha's Vineyard for their summer vacation in August, Michelle and Barack discussed the possibility of losing. Barack was determined to persevere. "He felt strongly that he had done a lot of hard work trying to get the economy on track," strategist David Axelrod said. "The notion of surrendering that to the next guy to come in and be the hero, that was not a scenario he was excited about."

Nor did it take an advanced degree to guess whose company Barack would keep in the history books if he lost or quit. It would not be Lincoln or Roosevelt or even Reagan, but the one-termers, Jimmy Carter and George H. W. Bush. A 2012 triumph by a Republican would feel an awful lot like repudiation. What's more, it would threaten Barack's fragile accomplishments, most clearly health care reform. Yes, he was frustrated and worn down, but defeat would not do. Barack and Michelle were nothing if not competitive. Scrabble or the presidency, they hated to lose.

MICHELLE WAS READY again to do her part, maybe more ready than ever. The girls were settled, the household was humming, and her initiatives were gathering speed. As she told a group of reporters in early 2011, "I have better clarity about what my role is going to be. Our agenda is clearer. We know who we are, we know where we're going." She had learned what to expect from the political fray, as well. She was a target, but she was considerably more popular than Barack. In August, as his numbers were drifting toward new lows, an Associated Press poll found that 70 percent of Americans had a favorable impression of Michelle. Even Republican-minded Fox News put her favorability at 62 percent in October, with just 28 percent of respondents viewing her unfavorably. Among Democrats, women, and African Americans, the positives were higher.

One of Michelle's essential political tasks was to energize voters who had backed Barack before. He needed their money, their energy, and their votes. The campaign was positioning him as a defender of the middle class at a time of rising and increasingly visible economic inequality. A new Gilded Age, it sometimes seemed. "A nation cannot prosper long when it favors only the prosperous," Barack had said in his inaugural address. Using every news medium short of smoke signals, Michelle sought to reassure voters that he was worthy and remind them why they should care. Her message echoed her speeches from early in the 2008 campaign and her conversations with Barack about fairness and purpose twenty years earlier in Chicago.

On September 30, 2011, the final day of the fundraising quarter, a lovely autumn day, Michelle spoke to donors dining on lobster in Cape Elizabeth, Maine. On the eve of her visit, the state Republican Party chairman predicted that Barack would lose Maine's four electoral votes. "People who work with their hands are going to vote Republican. They understand the grand experiment didn't work," Charlie Webster told the *Portland Press Herald*. Michelle, who had been raising millions for Obama 2012 and the Democratic Party, recognized the campaign as a political battle. Despite her feelings about the profession, and her less than intensive effort in the 2010 midterm elections, she was all in. She wasted no time before telling her well-heeled audience how the other half lived, and not just people who worked with their hands. She cited stories of "businesses that folks are trying to keep afloat" and "doctor's bills that they cannot pay" and the "mortgage that they can no longer afford." She said, "These struggles aren't new. For decades now, middle-class folks have been squeezed from all sides. The cost of things like gas and groceries and tuition have been rising continuously, but people's paychecks just haven't kept up. And when this economic crisis hit, for so many families the bottom just fell out."

Fairness, a quality she had consistently considered since her youth, lay at the center of the debate and the president's agenda, she said. It was the idea that "everyone, *everyone*, gets a fair shake and does their fair share." Voters choosing between Barack and a Republican would be making a decision between "two very different visions." There was the helping hand from Barack, who she said had a knack for remembering personal stories. And there were the other guys, the GOP candidates, whom she never identified by name or party. "It's about whether we as a country will honor that fundamental promise that we made generations ago, that when times are hard, we don't abandon our fellow citizens. We don't let everything fall apart for struggling families. Instead, we say, 'There but for the grace of God goes my family.' Instead, we remember that we're all in this together."

The language, the tone, the themes; it was vintage Michelle. She offered a pointed defense of Barack's priorities, from the benefits of a jobs bill to the misery that would follow if "folks"—meaning congressional Republicans—repealed the Affordable Care Act. "Today we need to ask ourselves, will we let them succeed? Will we let insurance companies deny us coverage because we have preexisting conditions like breast cancer or diabetes? Or will we stand up and say that in this country, we will not allow folks to go bankrupt because they get sick?

Who are we? Will we let insurance companies refuse to cover basic preventative care, things like cancer screenings and prenatal care, that saves money and saves lives?"

Seven times in the speech, she asked who Americans are as a people. "Will we be a country that tells folks who've done everything right but are struggling, 'Tough luck, you're on your own?' . . . Will we be a country where opportunity is limited to a few at the top? Or will we give every child a chance to succeed, no matter where she's from or what she looks like or how much money her parents have? Who are we?" She ended her speech with a patented call and response. "So, let me ask you one final question: Are you in?" she asked. "Yes!" the audience shouted. "Really, I need to hear this. Are you in?" "*Yes!*"

Ten days later, far from Maine, feminist pioneer Gloria Steinem watched Michelle work an audience of progressive women in Manhattan. Many of them, she said, arrived none too happy. They wished Barack were driving a harder bargain with Republicans. "You can imagine the feeling in a New York room," Steinem said. "Well, by the end of her speech, people were standing and cheering and ready to go to work. It was a transformation." In fact, Michelle became accustomed to pushing back against progressive critics, sometimes in Barack's presence, sometimes not. At a small New York fundraiser in 2012, she told a group of women donors who had paid $20,000 a ticket, "I'm tired of all the complaining. My husband has worked his heart out to get a lot of things done for this country, up against a bunch of folks on the other side who will do anything to get in the way. So just stop it! He needs your help, not your complaints!" After Michelle departed, Axelrod stayed behind to reassure the donors and "make sure everything was okay."

AN ALTOGETHER DIFFERENT CROWD gathered to hear Michelle that year in Woodlawn, on Chicago's South Side, a few blocks from the apartment where she had lived as a baby. The setting was a community room connected to a beauty salon. The neighborhood was dicey— there had been shootings—and it was nighttime. Each time a woman entered, someone made sure the door to the street locked behind her.

Michelle's voice emerged from a speakerphone, rallying women across the country to work for Barack's reelection. The Woodlawn women, all of them African American, were thrilled. "So happy for her and her mother and her children because they are women, black women, in the White House. Living it, eating it, feeling it," said Hope Hundley, an ophthalmic technician. "I never felt that much about a first lady."

Hundley reveled in Michelle's remarks that February night and her big-time role in Washington. "I love him," she said of Barack, "but that's my sister girl." She explained: "We have that fellowship with all the girlfriends we jump rope with, but there's always one sister girl. . . . It's the sister girl connection where they feel you, you feel her. . . . You can pick up the phone and they're already on the phone." Hundley had never met Michelle, yet she loved her confidence, the example she was setting, the mold she was breaking. A few days earlier, Michelle had drawn criticism for taking an expensive ski trip to Aspen, Colorado, something most Americans could not afford. "I was like, 'Girl, go ski. Girl, wear your arms out. Put your stilettos on, on a good day; put your gym shoes on, on a better day. Let your hair down. 'How can you touch Queen Elizabeth?' Guess what? She's gonna do it again." Hundley said Michelle was facing "that hatin' racism" as a black first lady. But she felt sure that she remained a steady force "even in the midnight hours" when Barack was facing obstacles and opponents and demons galore. "I can see her saying, 'Come on, baby, you can do it. Come on. Come on, baby. Just do it one more time. Go back in there tomorrow and get 'em.'"

MICHELLE LIKED CONTROL. She put herself in positions where the chances of mistake or surprise were minimal. When speaking in public, she rehearsed and often used a teleprompter, as Barack did. Her staff was extremely cautious about material dispatched in her name, even though her campaign email appeals brought in more money than Barack's. When two society wannabes crashed the first state dinner, a startling breach of security and protocol, the blame fell partly on the East Wing and social secretary Desiree Rogers, a Chicagoan who was not long for the job. Michelle was upset because the incident embarrassed the White House and drew a spotlight to an avoidable miscue. She made her expectations clear to her aides, who worked fiercely and creatively to avoid unforced errors, target her message, and protect her brand. For media access, White House aides most often chose outlets where the audience was desirable, the questions predictable, and the tone forgiving. They also became expert at winning slots on comedy shows, talk shows, and kids' programs, all the while posting cheerful photographs and videos on White House and campaign social media accounts.

Through the years, the strategy meant granting precious few audiences to the correspondents who covered her for the daily print media, the ones who followed her most closely and knew her work best. Among the group were Robin Givhan, a Pulitzer Prize–winning *Washington Post* culture critic; Krissah Thompson from the *Post*; Darlene Superville from the Associated Press; and *New York Times* correspondent Rachel Swarns, who wrote a serious book about Michelle's ancestry. Beyond limiting interviews and unscripted media sessions with the first lady herself, the East Wing worked hard to limit access to staff members, friends, and former colleagues. This was true even when the prospective sources had positive things to say, which they almost always did. Michelle "frowns on people who speak out of school," said Jackie Norris. "She expects of her friends that they will check in and have conversations and make sure that it's good for her." The people in Michelle's extensive orbit tended toward loyalty, and they toed the line.

Above all, the goal was to promote Michelle's agenda and Barack's reelection. "I'm not a big fan of the press about myself, period, so I can't say there's a huge upside," Michelle said early in her political life. Despite the straight-ahead press she got from reporters who took her seriously—and the professionals did—she often felt that the Michelle Obama portrayed in print bore little resemblance to her actual self. In 2009, she offered praise to a group of African American publishers who visited the White House. "You know our story, our images, our journey," Michelle said as she and Barack welcomed them. "Our paths are not foreign to you and we are reminded of that when we read our story in your stories. It feels different. I often say I finally recognize myself when I read your papers." Not that the experience made her any more willing to talk with Givhan, Thompson, Superville, or Swarns, all of whom were African American.

Michelle's prominence, and the popular fascination with her story, led to news coverage that told her things about her lineage that she had not known. Swarns and colleague Jodi Kantor, working with a genealogist, traced a branch of Michelle's family back to slavery. They reported that she had a white ancestor, a slave owner's son named Charles Marion Shields, who had a child with the family's young slave, Melvinia Shields. The Obamas, who had been hosting a large family Thanksgiving dinner each year at their home in Hyde Park, moved the gathering to the White House in 2009. That year, Michelle handed out copies of the family tree sketched by *The New York Times*. Later, in a rare session with reporters, she reflected on the course of history and her position as the first African American first lady. "My great-great-great-grandmother was actually a slave," she said. "We're still very connected to slavery in a way that's very powerful. . . . That's not very far away. I could have known that woman."

THE OPENING WORDS of a front-page *New York Times* story in January 2012 represented the kind of story Michelle hated. It began, "Michelle Obama was privately fuming, not only at the president's team, but also at her husband." Written by Jodi Kantor, the piece offered an advance look at the reporter's new book, *The Obamas*, billed rather extravagantly as the inside story of a White House marriage. Kantor said in the article that Michelle was "mastering and subtly redefining the role." But the piece also suggested an edgier tale about "strains" and "tensions" between the first lady and the president's advisers. Not necessarily news for the ages, but catnip to a certain Washington audience. By coincidence, Michelle had scheduled a broadcast interview to help Gayle King, a Chicago friend, in her first week as a host of *CBS This Morning*. The CBS show aired the day after Kantor's book appeared. "I never read these books," Michelle told King. But she said she had learned some details and signaled that she thought Kantor had overplayed her material. Her own sensitivities were clear. "I guess it is more interesting to imagine this conflicted situation here, and a strong woman, you know," Michelle said. "But that's been an image that people have tried to paint of me since, you know, the day Barack announced. That I'm some angry black woman." Visibly irritated, she continued, "Who can write about how I feel? Who? What third person can tell me how I feel?"

The East Wing had long known that Kantor's book was coming. She had been granted access to a number of key players, although Michelle declined to be interviewed for the book. Weeks before publication, the White House asked former communications director and Democratic strategist Anita Dunn to evaluate what Kantor was reporting and consider how to respond. Staff members lined up people to defend the first lady. When the book emerged, the West Wing press office pointedly labeled Kantor's work "an overdramatization of old news." Aides worked their phones and keyboards aggressively, telling reporters and producers where they thought the writer had gone wrong. More than a few people in the Obama camp, present and former staff members alike, noted that the generally upbeat book contained neither bombshells nor biting critique and questioned the wisdom of the public relations strategy. If anything, the staff's fusillade drew extra attention to a book that the East Wing would have preferred no one read.

CRITICS ON THE RIGHT were all too eager to add stories, real and invented, to their own Michelle narrative, which bounded wildly down media lane. She was elitist! She was socialist! She was a militant! She was a hypocrite! "We have a name for Michelle: Moochelle," Rush Limbaugh crowed after Michelle returned from Spain. "Mooch, mooch, Moochelle Obama. That will tick 'em off, won't it, Snerdly?" Limbaugh's shtick had earned him a fortune and he was quick to recognize a crowd-pleasing label when he saw it. As used by denizens of the right, "Moochelle" suggested many things. A fat cow, perhaps, or a leech. It encompassed big government, the welfare state, big-spending Democrats, and black people living on the dole. The term harked to the market-worshipping Ayn Rand, whose *Atlas Shrugged* was something of a field guide for the anti-government Tea Party and its mainstream Republican courtiers. Rand disparaged the "moochers," who supposedly lived off the hard work of the producers. Paul Ryan, a Republican congressman from Wisconsin who used to give *Atlas Shrugged* as a Christmas gift, said in 2010 that the United States was developing "a majority of makers versus takers." By 2012, Ryan was the nominee for vice president, and "makers against takers" was a Republican talking point. The man who selected Ryan was Mitt Romney, who reaped great riches largely by putting capital to work for him. Romney finished off his own wounded duck candidacy with comments about "the 47 percent," Americans who, in his view, believed that "government has a responsibility to care for them" and would undoubtedly vote for Barack. Michelle would have pointed things to say about the Romney-Ryan worldview when she addressed the Democratic National Convention in Charlotte in September.

BEFORE MICHELLE REACHED Charlotte, she paid a visit in June to Nashville and the annual African Methodist Episcopal Church national conference to do some tending of black voters. It was Orangeburg 2007 revisited, except this time she was not introducing Barack, but asking her audience not to give up on him. The slaves were not freed nor the vote granted in a day, she said, as she reached into the pantheon to speak of Rosa Parks on a Montgomery bus, Ernest Green at Little Rock's Central High, and Oliver Brown in Topeka, where he gave his name to *Brown v. Board of Education,* the case that ended, as she put it, "the lie of 'separate but equal.'" It was easy to feel "helpless and hopeless," she said, but "history has shown us that there is nothing, *nothing,* more powerful than ordinary citizens coming together for a just cause." Her speech reflected years of conversations with Barack and her friends about the questions she had been asking herself for much of her life. "I mean, what exactly do you do about children who are languishing in crumbling schools, graduating from high schools unprepared for college or a job? And what about the 40 percent of black children who are overweight or obese? . . . What about all those kids growing up in neighborhoods where they don't feel safe, kids who never have opportunities worthy of their promise? What court case do we bring on their behalf? What laws do we pass for them?"

Michelle asked her audience, thousands strong, to start by voting and getting friends and relatives to vote, and then to do more. Follow the news, she said. Start an email list and send people articles about important issues—"and then call them to make sure they've read them." Talk to people in barber shops and church parking lots about political doings in City Hall and Washington. Go to City Hall and "ask what they're doing to fight hunger in their community." Show up at school board meetings. Run for office. It is entirely okay, she assured her listeners, to discuss policy and politics in church: "To anyone who says that church is no place to talk about these issues, you tell them there is no place better. No place better. Because ultimately, these are not just political issues, they are moral issues."

Michelle had always told audiences that she and Barack felt an obligation to reach back, counting themselves among "those to whom much is given," a reference to Luke 12:48, the parable of the faithful servant. In Nashville, she offered a rare look into her religious thinking, drawing connections among faith, politics, and racial uplift. The legacy of Jesus Christ, she said, summons people to do as he did, "fighting injustice and speaking truth to power every single day. He was out there spreading a message of grace and redemption to the least, the last and the lost. And our charge is to find Him everywhere, every day, by how we live our lives."

Creating the world as it should be was not a sporadic thing, she said: "Living out our eternal salvation is not a once a week kind of deal. And in a more literal sense, neither is citizenship. Democracy is also an everyday activity." It is hard to climb the mountain, she continued, when "the problems we face seem so entrenched, so overwhelming that solving them seems nearly impossible. But during those dark moments, I want you to remember that doing the impossible is the root of our faith. It is the history of our people and the lifeblood of this nation."

When Michelle finished, to thunderous applause, churchgoers

thronged to the rope line, hoping to clasp her hand, take a photo, grab a few seconds to wish her God's grace. Once she had retreated to her motorcade and her flight home, a church bishop stepped onstage and announced that the Supreme Court, that very morning, had voted to uphold the Affordable Care Act. He asked for a hallelujah and an amen. The crowd erupted in cheers. Microphone in hand, he called for an organist and started singing a gospel song, "Victory Shall Be Mine."

THE DEMOCRATIC NATIONAL CONVENTION opened on September 4, five days after Mitt Romney accepted the Republican nomination in Tampa. In the months before the Democrats met, Barack's position among voters had strengthened. Even with the economy struggling and unemployment at 8.3 percent, he was running even or better with the enigmatic Romney, who ditched his moderate Massachusetts record in hopes of attracting conservative Republicans, then found himself in an awkward straddle as he tried to move toward the middle. The GOP convention was a muddle, epitomized by the odd sight of eighty-two-year-old actor Clint Eastwood spending eleven excruciating prime-time minutes having a conversation onstage with an empty chair. He said he was talking to an invisible Barack Obama. In the most scripted of events, it was improv and it bombed. More important, the convention failed to dispel the image of Romney as a sheltered son of privilege and the Republican Party as an exceedingly white, overly male bastion, all *noblesse* and no *oblige*. As the curtain fell in Tampa and attention turned to Charlotte, the Democrats could hardly have asked for a better foil. Barack's political luck—"my almost spooky good fortune," he once called it—was holding.

"The way we thought about the convention, the first night was going to be about connecting Obama to the middle-class experience," David Axelrod explained later. The lineup included Deval Patrick, the Massachusetts governor who had spent his boyhood on Chicago's South Side, and keynote speaker Julian Castro, a thirty-seven-year-old San Antonio mayor who said his grandmother "cleaned other people's houses so she could afford to rent her own." There was Tammy Duckworth, a former army helicopter pilot who had been shot out of the sky and grievously wounded in Iraq; and Lilly Ledbetter, whose fight for equal pay made her a progressive symbol. But all were essentially warm-up acts for Michelle, who was tasked with telling Barack's story and making people feel it. "I wanted her to dominate that first night because I knew she would do well. But even I was shocked at how well she did," Axelrod said. "Meryl Streep could not have done it better." He was not alone. On Fox News, Chris Wallace called her delivery "masterful," while Chuck Todd said on NBC that Michelle "owned this convention in a way that no speaker owned the convention in Tampa."

Introduced by Elaine Brye, a science teacher, Air Force ROTC member, and mother of four military children, Michelle touched the stations of the family cross. Her father, climbing the stairs slowly and borrowing money to pay his share of her Princeton bills. Barack's white grandmother, riding the bus to her bank job and training male colleagues who were promoted while she hit the glass ceiling; the men earned "more and more money while Barack's family continued to scrape by." Barack and Michelle in Chicago as young marrieds, paying more toward their student loans than toward their mortgage, "so young, so in love, and so in debt." Barack as father, "strategizing about middle school friendships," and as president, reading letters about hardship. He had been tested "in ways I never could have imagined. I have seen first hand that being president doesn't change who you are. It reveals who you are." For good measure, nearing their twentieth wedding anniversary, she said she loved him more than when they married and more than she had four years earlier.

Threaded through stories designed to make the first family seem modest and recognizable was the idea that Barack, as Michelle liked to say during the 2008 campaign, "gets it." This time, the contrast was with Romney, who once tried to connect with Detroit voters by saying that his wife, Ann, "drives a couple of Cadillacs." Ann had once expressed their sense of economic distress by reporting that they made it through Mitt's college and graduate school years only by selling stocks his auto executive father had given him. The policy contrast was just as stark. "Women," Michelle said, "are more than capable of making our own choices about our bodies and our health care." Helping others is more important than getting ahead yourself and "success doesn't count unless you earn it fair and square." Everyone in the country should have an equal opportunity, she declared, "no matter who we are or where we're from or what we look like or who we love."

Most pointedly, in the context of rugged individualism run amok, Michelle uttered a single, charged line that simultaneously challenged Republican actions and reasserted the principles that had long animated her work: "When you've worked hard and done well and walked through that doorway of opportunity, you do not slam it shut behind you. No. You reach back, and you give other folks the same chances that helped you succeed." By the end, the Democrats in Charlotte were on their feet, cheering and remembering and believing all over again. It was just one speech, but the stakes were high and Michelle was giving people a reason to think. Nielsen reported that 26 million people had watched. The next day, after the positive reviews were in, *New Yorker* humorist Andy Borowitz posted a mock convention schedule:

DEMOCRATS REVISE CONVENTION SCHEDULE

CHARLOTTE (The Borowitz Report)—The Democratic National Convention today released a dramatically revised schedule for the night of Wednesday, September 5th:

8:00: Call to Order by First Lady Michelle Obama

8:10: National Anthem, performed by Branford Marsalis (saxophone), Michelle Obama (vocals)

8:15: Pledge of Allegiance to Michelle

8:20: Former President Bill Clinton introduces video of Michelle Obama

8:25: Video replay of last night's speech by Michelle Obama (on loop until 10:58)

10:58–10:59: Remarks by Vice-President Joe Biden

10:59: Benediction by the Reverend Michelle Obama

. . .

BEFORE THE POLLS OPENED on election day, Michelle and Barack were all but certain they would win. Reports of early votes matched or exceeded the campaign's rigorous projections, and virtually every national poll showed Barack ahead of Romney, who had not been able to capitalize on an awful October 3 debate performance by the president that set Democratic nerves ajangle. The night before the final triumph, Barack and Michelle returned to Iowa one last time, a pilgrimage as much as a rally. By the time she introduced him, after a performance by Bruce Springsteen, twenty thousand people were standing in the cold night air to cheer them. This was where the road to the White House had begun nearly six years before, and they were on the verge of a new triumph. Michelle said it would be the last time they would be onstage together at a campaign rally and recalled the early days, "back when I wasn't so sure about this whole process." She revisited the greatest hits of the first term and introduced "my husband, the love of my life, the president of the United States, Barack Obama."

For Barack, who had poured enormous energy into the campaign, tears came to his tired eyes as he talked about the support Iowa had given him. He threw in a patented wisecrack, too. "You've seen a lot of me these last six years and, you know what? You may not agree with every decision I've made. Michelle doesn't. There may have been times when you've been frustrated at the pace of change. I promise you, so have I." But he said there were fights yet to be won and led the crowd in one last call and response, a refrain from the 2008 campaign: *Fired up? Ready to go! Fired up? Ready to go!* With that, he worked the rope line and headed to Chicago to await the results. The next day, Barack collected 332 electoral votes to Romney's 206. He won the popular vote by five million, swamping his oblivious opponent, who was so sure of victory that he had not prepared a concession speech.

# FIFTEEN

# I Am No Different from You

Nine days after she performed in the 2013 inaugural festivities in Washington, D.C., someone shot Hadiya Pendleton. She was fifteen years old, a cheerful girl sheltering against a Chicago winter rain with a dozen friends less than a mile from the Obamas' house. The young South Side shooter was aiming at someone else, but it didn't matter. A bullet caught Hadiya in the back and killed her, a heartbreakingly random act of violence in a city that had recorded 506 homicides in 2012. Such violence was only the most final of the obstacles that disproportionately afflicted black teenagers, and it revealed the stacked deck. Nearly fifty years after the Civil Rights Act, options for African American young people in Chicago were fewer, schools were worse, and their lives were more perilous than those of their white counterparts, whatever Barack's reelection said about progress. Hadiya was an honor student, a volleyball player, a majorette, and a member of the praise dance ministry at her church. She had good-hearted friends, devoted parents, and a godmother who described her as the kind of kid who had to be told, "Slow down, you can't do everything." Michelle had never met Hadiya, but she flew to Chicago to attend her funeral. She met the slain teenager's mourning friends and wondered what on earth she could say to them. The moment affected her deeply as she considered their future and her remaining years in the public eye. "Hadiya Pendleton was me and I was her," the first lady said later. "Hadiya's family did everything right, but she still didn't have a chance."

Countless children lacked equal chances in the modern-day United States, especially black children. Michelle had always said so. Her views were reflected in her mentoring work, her approach to White House cultural events and the talks she gave in neighborhoods like Anacostia. She sometimes referred to society's responsibility to help young people "fulfill their god-given potential." As she told Valerie Jarrett at Hadiya's funeral, she wanted to reach back and lift up and make a difference, not just an appearance. Entering the second term, with Barack's final election behind them, the Obamas concentrated more directly on issues of fairness. Soon, Michelle would adopt a new mission, aiming to push disadvantaged teenagers like Hadiya's friends toward college, an initiative she called Reach Higher.

Michelle spoke out more in the second term and addressed a greater variety of topics important to her. In addition to the standard tools— a targeted interview or a newspaper column—she often did something short or catchy, perhaps a photograph to her 1.2 million Instagram followers, a video, or a tweet to the million-plus followers of her @FLOTUS Twitter account. In November 2013, she tweeted her support to a group that pushed immigration reform with a public fast on the National Mall. "As families begin to gather for Thanksgiving, I'm thinking of the brave #Fast4Families immigration reform advocates. We're with you.—mo." (A tweet signed "—mo" signified that it came from her, not from her staff.) The day after Thanksgiving, Barack and Michelle visited the protesters and listened to their stories. One critic tweeted back at her, "Michelle Obama thinks she's still occupying the deans office at Harvard." Another typed, "@FLOTUS Politicizing Thanksgiving with your stupid immigration garbage? LMFAO. Pathetic."

In December 2013, Michelle defended the embattled Affordable Care Act and encouraged families, specifically black families, to sign up for health insurance. "We shouldn't live in a country this rich, right, where people are choosing between their rent or their medicine, where kids aren't getting the immunizations they need," she said on the Reverend Al Sharpton's radio show. She joked during an Oval Office publicity session that mothers should "make it a Christmas treat around the table to talk about a little health care. Ring in the New Year with new coverage!" A few months later, the Islamic extremist group Boko

Haram—a phrase loosely translated as "Western education is a sin"—kidnapped more than two hundred girls from a school in northern Nigeria. Amid an unsuccessful international campaign to win the girls' release, Michelle tweeted a photograph that showed her with a sad face holding up a hand-lettered sign that read #BringBackOurGirls.

Abroad, on a 2014 trip to China benignly described by the East Wing as a goodwill tour focused on children and education, Michelle made assertive remarks about Internet freedom, minority rights, and the importance of questioning and criticizing a nation's leaders. In a country where the government heavily censored the Internet and hounded the political opposition, she said at Peking University, "Time and again, we have seen that countries are stronger and more prosperous when the voices and opinions of all their citizens can be heard." She called freedom of worship and open access to information "the birthright of every person on this planet." And she used her own life, and Barack's, as an example of the power of the civil rights movement. She also endeared herself to her Chinese audience by doing tai chi, jumping rope, feeding pandas, and going sightseeing with Marian, Malia, and Sasha, to the Great Wall, the Forbidden City, and Xi'an, home of the terra-cotta warriors. On her last day, she pointedly dined at a Tibetan restaurant in Chengdu to show solidarity with a persecuted ethnic minority. Around her neck, her host draped a *khata*, a ceremonial white scarf. A White House photographer was on hand to ensure that the images went public.

YET, WAS IT ENOUGH? Was Michelle doing all she could? It was a nagging question that came not from the Republican right, which had essentially written her off, but from reasoned voices in her own corner. After she presented the Academy Award for Best Picture to *Argo* by live feed from the White House, Courtland Milloy, a black *Washington Post* columnist, wrote that Michelle "ought to be under consideration for a seat on the Supreme Court, not recruited as a presenter in some Hollywood movie contest." Noting that she often said she was standing on the shoulders of the greats who preceded her, including Sojourner

Truth, he asked whether her own shoulders would be "broad enough for future generations of women and girls to stand on? Or just good to look at?" Milloy said she was frittering away an opportunity. "Enough with the broccoli and Brussels sprouts—to say nothing about all the attention paid to her arms, hair, derriere and designer clothes. Where is that intellectually gifted Princeton graduate, the Harvard-educated lawyer and mentor to the man who would become the first African American president of the United States?"

"I HAVE NEVER FELT more confident in myself, more clear on who I am as a woman," Michelle said a few months before she turned fifty. She had said she intended to live life "with some gusto," and there was evidence she was doing so in public and private, even in the gilded cage of the White House. She pitched Let's Move! by doing a spoof called "The Evolution of Mom Dancing" with Jimmy Fallon, a scene that would be viewed more than 20 million times on YouTube. She and the girls tagged along when Barack visited Ireland and Germany, ducking into a pub one day for lunch with Bono, the charismatic U2 singer and activist. She celebrated her fiftieth birthday in January 2014 with a girl-friends' getaway at Oprah Winfrey's Hawaiian estate and a White House party for hundreds of friends and acquaintances. Beyoncé and Stevie Wonder performed. John Legend sang "Happy Birthday." Barack, who had tweeted on their twentieth anniversary that Michelle was "the love of my life and my best friend," delivered a toast that left guests misty-eyed. Michelle, he said, had made him a better man.

Despite the trappings of Washington and her star turns in designer dresses, Michelle managed to come across to most Americans as authentic. From the self-examination as she answered questions to the humor she showed with a look or an inflection, people felt they could relate to her. High school basketball star Jabari Parker said after volunteering at a Let's Move! event in Chicago, "She's almost like everyday people. She wasn't trying to big-time anybody. She was really cool, down to earth." More than two-thirds of Americans had a favorable impression of the first lady, although conservative Republicans disliked her by a margin of about two to one. Arne Duncan, the education secretary and a longtime friend from Hyde Park, spent family time at the White House and traveled with her to advance an ambitious and controversial schools agenda. After conceding that he was biased, he said, "What you see is what she is. There are no airs, there's no fanciness. She can talk to policymakers, she can talk to parents, she can talk to children. She is absolutely comfortable in every environment. . . . And she just tells the truth."

Support from African American women remained sky-high. Robin Givhan, who graduated from Princeton one year after Michelle and covered her for the *Washington Post,* noted the first lady's ability to win admiration and affection from black people at both ends of the socioeconomic spectrum. She earned working-class respect by paying homage to her forebears, taking pains not to put on airs, and encouraging black young people to excel. "She underscores that she is no different from so many other black folks," said Givhan, who observed that Michelle also earned admiration from more successful African Americans who "know the microscope she's under and admire that she's done it so well. She has made them proud by showing the wider world that their ilk—educated, focused, ambitious, family-oriented—exists."

The reelection helped her confidence and her mission. Together, she and Barack had battled the opposition in a mean, messy, billion-dollar campaign and triumphed straight up. They were happy that the good guys had won, of course, but they also saw the victory as validation of their White House work and evidence that the November 2008 election was not a historical accident. Had they fallen short in 2012, "they thought people would be able to say it was a fluke," said John Rogers, their longtime Chicago ally. Michelle's friend Cheryl Whitaker said the win was something to savor: "He's not the first black president anymore. He's the president. She's the first lady."

Yet in the second term, as in the first, Republican leaders on Capitol Hill practiced obstruction as a savage art, barely bothering to disguise their determination to run out the clock on the Obama presidency. Following the December 2012 rampage that killed twenty schoolchildren and six adults in Newtown, Connecticut, Barack pushed a package of gun measures in Congress that would expand background checks and ban high-capacity magazines. The proposals had overwhelming popular support, and posed no threat to the lawful owners of the roughly 300 million guns in circulation in the United States. Michelle backed them publicly, telling a Chicago audience after Hadiya Pendleton's death, "Right now, my husband is fighting as hard as he can and engaging as many people as he can to pass common-sense reforms to protect our children from gun violence." Despite majority support in the Senate, the rules fell short of the sixty votes needed to break a filibuster and the effort died. "A pretty shameful day for Washington," Barack said in disgust. Not ninety days into the new term, the defeat foretold arduous years ahead. So much for his hope, expressed on the campaign trail, that a November 2012 victory would "break the fever" of the Republican opposition.

NOT LONG AFTER the second term got under way, Michelle made a point of publicly praising the first NBA player to come out as gay: "So proud of you, Jason Collins! This is a huge step forward for our country. We've got your back!—mo." In December 2013, when ABC news reporter Robin Roberts came out, Michelle tweeted, "I am so happy for you and Amber! You continue to make us all proud.—mo." And when University of Missouri defensive end Michael Sam announced in February 2014 that he was gay, she tweeted, "You're an inspiration to all of us, @MikeSamFootball. We couldn't be prouder of your courage both on and off the field.—mo."

Gay rights resonated with the first lady. As Barack struggled to explain what he believed while calculating what he could afford to say, Michelle spoke up for equality for lesbian, gay, bisexual, and transgender people. In 2007, at a California forum, she had spoken of the ways the country was segmented, leaving Americans isolated, "sometimes by fears, sometimes by ignorance, sometimes by resources." She argued that values of decency and honesty united the nation, "I don't care what race, what political party or sexual orientation." Still earlier, in 2004, gay activists in Chicago had been surprised and pleased when she attended a fundraiser for the Lesbian Community Cancer Project. She did not simply greet people and move out the door. She stuck around. "It wasn't like it was busting out with politicians," said Jane Saks, a lesbian friend and occasional workout partner. "I don't think it was, 'Am I for being gay or not?' It was, 'These people are working for progress.' I think she knew a lot of us." In the mid-1990s, Michelle took aside eighteen-year-old Public Allies member Krsna Golden, who considered himself "very homophobic" at the time. When he was assigned a gay roommate at a Public Allies retreat, he chose to sleep on a colleague's couch, instead. Michelle told him calmly that she understood his feelings but felt disappointed. "You have to be more open-minded," she said. "This is something you have to grow past."

Michelle had gay friends and colleagues and paid attention to issues that affected and afflicted the gay community, from parenting and workplace rights to HIV/AIDS. Starting as a teenager in the early 1980s, she spent hours with her Chicago hairdresser, Rahni Flowers, a gay man who was still doing her hair during the 2008 campaign, countless appointments later. He said he told her early about his sexuality because she gave him "that feeling of openness and a very sensible curiosity. She's more concerned with me being a good, kind, giving human being." During Michelle's time at Trinity United Church of Christ, the Reverend Jeremiah A. Wright Jr. endorsed the creation of an HIV ministry, a rare move for a black pastor at a time when many African American churches in Chicago were bitterly anti-gay. Michelle knew people who died of the disease, including a Public Allies colleague, and on a trip to Kenya, she and Barack made a public show of taking HIV tests to reduce the stigma of the test and the illness. In the White House, she considered the Obama administration a force for progress on LGBT rights. She hired as East Wing communications director Kristina Schake, a prominent defender of gay marriage who became an adviser on the issue.

For his part, Barack did an awkward dance, particularly on same-sex marriage. His support could not have been more clear in 1996 when he answered a questionnaire from *Outlines*, an LGBT newspaper in Chicago. On a one-page, typewritten letter that bore his signature, he said, "I favor legalizing same-sex marriages, and would fight efforts to prohibit such marriages." He also said, "I would support and co-sponsor a state civil rights bill for gays and lesbians." Lest there be any doubt, he voiced firm support that year in a separate survey from IMPACT Illinois, a Chicago political action committee. The survey quoted from a proposed resolution that called marriage "a basic human right" and declared that "the state should not interfere with same-gender couples who chose to marry and share fully and equally in the rights, responsibilities and commitment of civil marriage." Barack's handwritten response: "I would support such a resolution."

Those were the most positive public statements Barack would make for sixteen years. In the interim, even as he worked in the Illinois state senate to fight discrimination against the LGBT community, his answers on civil marriage ranged from "undecided" in 1998 to "I am not in favor of gay marriage" in 2007. He said his opinions were "evolving." More than a few aides thought the principal factor in his evolution was the increasingly forgiving political landscape. Finally, in May 2012, pushed by events and reassured by public opinion, Barack told Robin Roberts in a nationally broadcast interview—before she came out publicly as gay—that same-sex couples should be allowed to marry. Recalling dinner table conversations, he said it "doesn't make sense" to Malia and Sasha that the same-sex parents of their friends should be treated differently from other couples. The television moment was "cathartic" for the president, said political adviser David Axelrod. "For as long as I've known him, he has never been comfortable with his position on this." Michelle had always urged Barack's gay supporters to be patient, telling them the moment would come, if more slowly than they wanted. When Barack left the residence for the Roberts interview, Michelle told him, "Enjoy this day. You are free."

Greeting guests in June 2014 at the annual White House Pride celebration, Barack enthusiastically listed his administration's LGBT achievements, including the appointment of eleven openly gay federal judges. He talked about changing attitudes and joked that the marriage of *Modern Family* characters Mitch and Cam in an episode that drew 10 million viewers "caused Michelle and the girls to cry. That was big." Michelle, standing beside him, agreed.

.  .  .

MICHELLE'S STAFF SCHEDULED her for three workdays a week, a practice that dated to 2009, and they tried not to schedule events after roughly 5 p.m. She worked informally on other days, plus times when the demands of her role intervened. On Fridays, at her request, she received her briefing book for the following week and studied it assiduously. She asked for bios and photos of the people she would meet, including notations about their families and interests and whether she had met them before. One of her central goals was to put people at ease. For formal events, she always reviewed her written remarks in advance and often made changes. Unlike Barack, she was not comfortable being handed a speech a few minutes before the lights went up. Her tendency, as ever, was to overprepare. She was an early riser and her predawn emails to her aides, if she felt they had fallen short, could be blistering. She set a high bar for herself and she expected excellence from her staff—and Barack's. "When she thought he was being ill served, that would be communicated. Sometimes through him, sometimes through Valerie Jarrett, and in those unlucky moments when she summoned you to a meeting to explain things," said Axelrod. "When she was unhappy, that pall hung over the West Wing."

Escaping the media pool that followed her husband, Michelle came and went quietly from the White House to see friends and visit restaurants and the gym. Malia and Sasha were teenagers now, and they increasingly had their own plans. They also had Secret Service agents to escort them and Michelle's assistants to help coordinate their schedules. Their parents talked wistfully about how the girls were growing up fast. At home, Michelle and Barack often walked the dogs together—Bo had a new playmate, Sunny—and, in warm weather, the Obamas spent casual time together on the Truman Balcony. "Just kind of hanging out and reading the paper and catching up on the news and all that good stuff," she said. Michelle continued to pay attention to fitness. She was often spotted at a gym outside the White House grounds: "I want to be this really fly 80-, 90-year-old."

Michelle and Barack, who rarely went out to dinner in Washington, started holding private dinners in the White House residence. No motorcade, no hassle, and a limitless pool of prospective guests happy to spend an evening in the residence, with drinks, creative food, lively conversation—and music from Barack's jazz playlists in the background. The unpublicized gatherings included notables from the worlds of art, letters, business, media, and, less often, politics. Not sure what to expect, one couple passed through White House security at 6 p.m., figuring they would be out the gate and on their way home by nine o'clock. It was well after midnight when the gathering ended. A guest who went to dinner on a different night did not make it back to his hotel until 2:30 a.m.

Marian remained a steady and steadying presence. "Not long on pretense," as Michelle put it. "The first one to remind us who we are." Michelle said her mother gave her "endless amounts of time just to talk and talk and talk and talk." Or, as she explained when she hosted the annual White House Mother's Day tea five years into Barack's presidency, "There is no way I would be standing up straight on my feet if it weren't for my mom, who is always there to look after our girls, to love them and be mad at me when I'm disciplining them, which I still don't get. . . . She's like 'Why are you so mean?' But that's what grandmas are for. But, especially, she's been that shoulder for me to lean on. I can always go up to her room and cry, complain, argue. And she just says, 'Go on back down there and do what you're supposed to do.' "


WHERE MICHELLE BELIEVED she could make the greatest difference was in the lives of young people. She spoke to elite audiences from time to time, including the high-profile White House interns, who were already well on their way. When they won seats at the table, she informed them in no uncertain terms, they had a responsibility to speak for people less privileged. And if they were not willing to risk their power, as she put it, they should step aside for someone who would. Far more often, however, Michelle chose to speak to disadvantaged teenagers, particularly from minority communities. Drawing on the narrative of her own upbringing and a cold-eyed assessment of current conditions, she shared tactics and conclusions that flowed from her own experience, all but willing them across the finish line. She implored students on society's bottom rungs to concentrate on the factors they could control. Implicit in her message was the fact that no one, including a well-intentioned president, could remove the vast structural obstacles and equalize the odds any time soon. They should not wait for the cavalry to rescue them, she was saying. There was no cavalry.

"The only reason that I am standing up here today is that back when I was your age, I made a set of choices with my life. Do you hear me? *Choices*," Michelle told several thousand Chicago schoolchildren in March 2013. "Although I am the first lady of the United States of America—listen to this, because this is the truth—I am no different from you. Look, I grew up in the same neighborhoods, went to the same schools, faced the same struggles, shared the same hopes and dreams that all of you share." Her message was fundamentally conservative and it negated the cardboard critique that she and Barack encouraged victimhood, favored government solutions, and played to racial hostility. Nor was she calling for collective action or protest. She was addressing young people as individuals and imploring them to pursue a path to success, one step at a time. Then, if all went well, they could reach back and help others as they climbed. It was a formula that had worked for Michelle, who braced them for the difficulties ahead. "You will get your butts kicked sometimes and you will be disappointed. And you will be knocked down, and you have to get back up. There will be people hating on you. . . . Can you handle that? As you improve your lives, are you going to be afraid? Are you going to be afraid, and then retreat back into what's comfortable?"

Barack, too, used his own story to instruct African American students. Two weeks before Michelle spoke in Chicago, his motorcade pulled up at Hyde Park Academy High School, where Michelle's uncle, Nomenee Robinson, had been a student leader sixty years earlier. To an audience of black teenagers, Barack confessed to getting stoned, getting drunk, neglecting his schoolwork, and being angry about his absent father. He urged them to get serious about their studies and craft "a backup plan in case you don't end up being LeBron or Jay Z." The startling part of his message, in one young man's eyes, was less what

Barack accomplished in high school than what he did wrong. "Are you talking about *you*?" the boy asked uncertainly, unable to reconcile the story with the fact that the storyteller was the president of the United States.

Soon after their Chicago visits, Michelle and Barack delivered graduation speeches two days apart at historically black colleges. Their remarks emphasized personal responsibility, an element of what was sometimes called respectability politics. Michelle spoke on May 17, 2013, at Bowie State University, founded in January 1865 by the Baltimore Association for the Moral and Educational Improvement of Colored People. She told of slaves who risked their lives to read and write. She noted schools burned to the ground and black students jeered, spit upon, and ostracized just for seeking an education. She recalled the Little Rock Nine and six-year-old Ruby Bridges, who integrated a New Orleans school in 1960, then spent the year being taught alone when white parents refused to allow their children to be taught alongside her. (Photographs of the little girl being escorted to school by white federal marshals inspired Norman Rockwell to paint *The Problem We All Live With,* a canvas later displayed in the Obama White House, where Barack welcomed Bridges and paid homage to her.) Each of the protagonists in Michelle's speech had suffered and forged ahead. Yet in modern-day America, she pointed out, only one in five African Americans between the ages of twenty-five and twenty-nine possessed a college degree. Michelle made no more than a glancing reference to the failure of government and society to address the nation's stark inequities. Rather, she focused on individuals and their choices. "When it comes to getting an education, too many of our young people can't be bothered," she said. "Today, instead of walking miles every day to school, they're sitting on couches for hours playing video games, watching TV. Instead of dreaming of being a teacher or a lawyer or a business leader, they're fantasizing about being a baller or a rapper."

Two days later, on May 19, Barack delivered the commencement address at Morehouse College in Atlanta. He spoke of policy in ways that Michelle did not. He described underfunded schools, violent neighborhoods, and the dearth of opportunities for more than the fortunate few. He said society has a collective responsibility "to advocate for an

America where everybody has a fair shot in life." In sync with Michelle, he also invoked the importance of individual decisions. He guessed that each one of the graduates had been told by an elder that "as an African American, you have to work twice as hard as anyone else if you want to get by." He recalled periods in his youth when he dismissed his own failings as "just another example of the world trying to keep a black man down," but he asked the students to look to the tribulations overcome by their black forebears, including some of the greats: "They knew full well the role that racism played in their lives, but when it came to their own accomplishments and sense of purpose, they had no time for excuses."

"THERE'S A LOT WRONG HERE," writer Ta-Nehisi Coates commented after studying the Obamas' speeches that graduation season. Coates believed that the United States had never properly reckoned with the consequences of slavery or the government's role in racial oppression. In his view, Michelle and Barack did not sufficiently acknowledge or address the causes of inequality in low-income, largely segregated neighborhoods. He said Barack was a "remarkable human being" who was "better read on the intersection of racism and American history" than any of his predecessors. Yet he saw the president becoming "the scold of 'black America.'" If the dreams of many black kids did not extend much past LeBron and Jay Z, Coates said, one cause was the limited cultural exposure in "impoverished, segregated neighborhoods. Those neighborhoods are the direct result of American policy."

THE DISCUSSION WAS NOT NEW. The debate over uplift and personal responsibility had a history in the black community that dated to the nineteenth century. What was sometimes painted in shorthand as Booker T. Washington versus W. E. B. Du Bois became by the end of the twentieth century a tangled knot of questions about who was to blame for the problems of the black underclass. The questions persisted—indeed, they intensified—during Barack's presidency. Was black disadvantage a product of institutional racism and the cumulative discrimination suffered by African Americans at the hands of a white-ruled society? Was it modern-day inattention to the grotesque inequality of opportunity in U.S. cities? Was it a failing by a segment of the black community that looked too readily to others for deliverance, or at least a helping hand? To the Obamas, it was pieces of each of these. Barack reported in 2014 that "some thoughtful and sometimes not so thoughtful African-American commentators have gotten on both Michelle and me, suggesting that . . . we're engaging in sort of up-by-the-bootstraps Booker T. Washington messages that let the larger society off the hook." Invoking Malcolm X and the Reverend Martin Luther King Jr., he argued that there is "no contradiction" between calls for greater personal responsibility and an acknowledgment that some troubles in the black community "are a direct result of our history."

To do something meaningful was the challenge. Harvard professor Randall Kennedy asserted in the summer of 2014 that Barack fell woefully short. On "critical matters of racial justice," Kennedy said, "he has posited no agenda, unveiled no vision, set forth no overarching mission to be accomplished." The president "might work on black issues behind the scenes," wrote Kennedy, the brother of Michelle's friend, Angela Kennedy Acree. "But he won't be caught promoting them out front, not even now, when he is free of the burden of seeking reelection." It was Eric Holder, the attorney general, who had spoken most assertively, painting the United States as "a nation of cowards" on racial matters.

During the first term, Barack had confided that he could not talk as openly about race as he wanted. And shortly before he moved into the White House, he had a revealing conversation with Jim Montgomery, a black trial lawyer and Hyde Park neighbor who dropped by with celebratory champagne. As Montgomery recalled it, he told Barack while they were making small talk that he wanted to discuss domestic policy when the president-elect had a moment. Barack asked what he had in mind. Montgomery told him, "'When you get ready to spend these billions of dollars on infrastructure and all this jazz to create jobs, make sure there is a provision in there for some set-asides and some employment for black people.' He says, 'Jim, you ain't gonna ever change. If I did something like that, white folks would go crazy.'" In the same period, a wealthy white woman on Chicago's North Shore shared that very worry with Montgomery: "Jim, I'm concerned. Is he just going to be a president for the black people?" Montgomery replied with a point about electoral math. The onetime civil rights lawyer from the South Side told her, "You will find that Barack is going to be the whitest president you've ever seen."

One year into the second term, Barack launched an effort to help young black and Latino men through a mentoring program called My Brother's Keeper, underwritten by $200 million in starter pledges from foundations and corporate entities. Why young black men? He cited the "plain fact" that there are "groups that have had the odds stacked against them in unique ways that require unique solutions; groups who've seen fewer opportunities that have spanned generations." Earlier, he had argued for expanded Head Start programs and universal preschool, but this was not Great Society 2.0. My Brother's Keeper was a modest public-private partnership that consciously echoed the model of Let's Move! and Joining Forces. In the wake of protests in 2014 against the treatment of African Americans by police and prosecutors, Barack announced that My Brother's Keeper would expand. Adding his name to a project specifically designed to help black people was a second-term sign that Barack felt liberated—in his ever cautious and pragmatic way—to be a president explicitly for African Americans, as well as for all Americans.

THE REUTERS DAYBOOK, a catalog of upcoming events in Washington, announced the screening of a Muppets film at the White House, part of Michelle's effort to draw attention to military families: "Joint Chiefs of Staff Chairman Gen. Martin Dempsey and Kermit the Frog participate." The March 2014 exchange between the frog, the general, and the first lady featured plenty of cornball humor and drew laughs, with Kermit saying to the assembled families, "I may not be a Marine, but I am marine life. I salute you." The media spread the word, boosted by entertaining photos and video, and Michelle notched a small win. Ditto in October 2014, when she did a six-second Vine video, dancing with a purple-and-white turnip in a riff on the song "Turn Down for What." In less than a month, viewers looped through the video more than 34 million times.

Laughs were fewer when Michelle engaged in an unusually public fight over nutrition standards with congressional Republicans who sought to dilute the policy at the heart of Let's Move!. She was not shy about defending the regulations she had lobbied Congress to pass four years earlier and her promise to "fight until the bitter end" showed that the issue was not as benign as some critics suggested. When the House of Representatives approved the Healthy, Hunger-Free Kids Act by a vote of 264–157 in 2010, it started a process designed to promote healthier school meals at a time when 31 million children bought school lunches each day, including 20 million low-income students subsidized by the federal government. The new law expanded access to the program and tightened nutrition regulations to include more whole grains, fruit, and vegetables and less salt, sugar, and fat. The measure also encouraged use of school gardens and locally grown produce, while setting a deadline for improving the healthiness of food sold in school vending machines. When skeptics complained that the costs would weaken school finances, Michelle and a raft of public-interest groups countered that the expenses were manageable and justified, given the stakes. "When we send our kids to school," Michelle said, "we have a right to expect that they won't be eating the kind of fatty, salty, sugary foods that we're trying to keep from them when they're at home."

That brought the wrath of adult naysayers, not to mention an array of students who took to YouTube and Twitter using the hashtag #ThankYouMichelleObama to complain that new meals created by school cooks tasted awful or left them hungry. It was a significant sign of her stature in the national debate that Michelle became the focus of criticism. Never mind that Congress had approved the approach by bipartisan vote or that the Department of Agriculture developed the rules based on independent recommendations from the nonpartisan health arm of the National Academy of Sciences. Michelle was the face of the program, so she took the heat. But backing down unless absolutely necessary was not her style. "I know that kids occasionally grumble about eating healthier food," she said. "But, look, that is to be expected because, frankly, that's what kids do, including my own kids. They want what they want when they want it, regardless of whether it's good for them or not. And when they don't get what they want, they complain. . . . It's our job to say, 'No, you cannot have a candy bar for breakfast.' And, 'Yes, you have to eat some vegetables every day.' And, 'No, you can't sit around playing video games all day. Go outside and run.'"

By 2014, about 90 percent of schools across the country reported being in compliance with the rules, some through gritted teeth. What followed, however, was a revolt among members of Congress, assisted by the School Nutrition Association, a trade organization backed by corporations that did billions of dollars in business with school cafeterias. The battle was already brewing in 2011, when lobbyists persuaded Congress, over the objections of the Obama administration, to count an eighth of a cup of tomato paste in pizza sauce as the equivalent of a half cup of vegetables. Michelle took to the opinion pages of *The New York Times* three years later to defend the nutrition standards. Referring to the pizza squabble, she said, "You don't have to be a nutritionist to know that this doesn't make much sense." She also challenged an effort by the potato lobby and federal legislators to expand access to white potatoes for millions of participants in the Women, Infants and Children program. Potatoes are fine, said the first lady, who often described french fries as her favorite food. But research showed that many women and young children in the supplemental nutrition program were already getting enough starch and potatoes—which they could purchase with food stamps, if they chose—and not enough "nutrient-dense fruits and vegetables."

What really bothered Michelle, however, and prompted her to make repeated calls to individual senators, was the attempt to waive the school nutrition rules. Such efforts, she said, went against science and good sense and did a disservice to parents, who were "working hard to serve their kids balanced meals at home and don't want their efforts undermined during the day at school." Not incidentally, she argued that obesity was now contributing to $190 billion in higher annual health costs. She insisted that the $10 billion spent by taxpayers on school lunches should not pay for "junk food for our children." The heart of her argument rested on the needs of impoverished children. She noted that millions of disadvantaged kids relied on school meals as their main source of nutrition and cited research that well-fed children do better in school. "We simply can't afford to say, 'Oh, well, it's too hard, so let's not do it,'" she said.

MICHELLE CONTINUED to work on Let's Move! and on Joining Forces. She called homelessness among military veterans "a stain on the soul of the nation." She helped enlist local leaders to work on the problem as federal authorities delivered more money for housing vouchers. Drawing attention to women who served in Iraq and Afghanistan, she said it was "just wrong" that their 11.2 percent unemployment rate was five points higher than men from the same wars, and more than double the rate of civilian women. She also took tentative steps to add a new project to her portfolio. Early in the White House years, she had envisioned a larger international role for the second term, but with the girls in school, Barack under pressure, and the optics of foreign travel a potential political liability, she looked for issues closer to home and her heart. Her message was direct and her tone was raw when she spoke up for a $50 million public-private partnership that would deliver after-school programming to urban kids in Chicago. The fate of black teenagers was on her mind. Her voice caught in her throat as she recalled a private scene from Hadiya's funeral, when it was "hard to know what to say to a roomful of teenagers who are about to bury their best friend." She declared that adults have a "moral obligation" to provide children with safe neighborhoods, cultural opportunities, and classrooms without "crumbling ceilings and ripped-up textbooks."

Following the Newtown shootings and Hadiya's death, Michelle discussed gun violence with friends and staff, but did not make urban violence or gun laws or after-school programs a significant part of her agenda. Rather, she turned to higher education and patterns of unequal access to college. In her Chicago speech, she repeated a conviction that had been a constant in her thinking and Barack's. It was the view that disparate outcomes in minority communities had less to do with the young residents' aptitudes than with the disparate opportunities they were afforded. Growing up in South Shore in the 1960s and 1970s, she felt safe, she took part in a range of engaging activities, and she had adults who pushed and supported her. "And that, in the end, was the difference between growing up and becoming a lawyer, a mother and first lady of the United States—and being shot dead at the age of fifteen."

Through a new East Wing project called Reach Higher, she set out to encourage young people from low-income families to attend college or training schools and to persevere long enough to get a degree. The need was clear: Only one in ten young people from low-income backgrounds typically earned a bachelor's degree by age twenty-five, while roughly half from high-income families did. Following the formula of Let's Move! and Joining Forces, the project supported Barack's agenda, in this case his effort to construct a smarter, more skilled workforce. In 1990, the United States ranked first in the world in the percentage of college graduates in the 25-to-34 age group. By 2014, the country had fallen to 12th. Noting that education would influence the nation's economic future and rates of upward mobility, Barack tried to set the nation's sights on regaining the top position by 2020. His project was called North Star.

Michelle and Barack had long talked publicly about the obstacles to higher education for low-income students and the struggles many of them faced when they got there. They saw the disparities during their own climbs through college and, more recently, in the experiences of Malia and Sasha, who attended Sidwell Friends, where the 2014–2015 tuition was $36,264 per student. Students in the girls' circle not only received a first-rate education, but valuable practice in taking college admission exams, which Barack described as standardized tests that are "not standardized." Unequal access to preparation, he said, "tilts the playing field. It's not fair and it's gotten worse."

A few months earlier, Michelle had watched a new film, *The Inevitable Defeat of Mister and Pete.* Partly funded by singer Alicia Keys, it was a story that made her cry not only when she watched it, but when she thought back on its most poignant scenes. The movie depicts the struggles of two young boys largely fending for themselves in a Brooklyn housing project while their mothers are behind bars. By the time the credits rolled, Michelle had decided to screen the film in the White

House to advance the initiative that would become Reach Higher. "Because there are millions of Misters and Petes out there who are just struggling to make it," she said, vowing that the film would be the guidepost for her remaining time as first lady.

At the White House screening in January 2014, on the eve of a gathering of university presidents to discuss ways to improve college access, Michelle spoke soberly and directly, explaining her plan to use her pulpit. She would tell adults that kids needed schools to teach them, programs to support them, and universities "to seek them out and give them a chance and then prepare them and help them finish their degrees once they get in." However much her progressive critics might urge her to play a more active role, Michelle said there was little she could do personally, on the policy or spending front. "The one thing I can bring to this is the message that we can give directly to young people."

To young people all around the country, Michelle set out to be booster, coach, advocate, and role model. She was the mom-in-chief, and she wanted them to see their rocky path through childhood as a strength, not a weakness. Life was tough, sure, but they were still standing. Resilience, as she liked to tell Malia and Sasha, was a response learned through experience. She set out to deliver reassurance and practical advice to teenagers who doubted that they had what it takes, just as she had done at Anacostia High, the Elizabeth Garrett Anderson School, Hadiya Pendleton's funeral, and a hundred other places all the way back to the offices of Public Allies. She had proven that she belonged at one unlikely destination after another, that she *was* supposed to be there. So, too, were they.

MICHELLE FLEW TO Atlanta one day in September 2014 to tell her story and repeat her mantra at Atlanta's Booker T. Washington High School, opened in 1924 as the first public high school in Georgia built for African American children. Standing at a lectern in the school gymnasium as her prepared remarks scrolled through twin teleprompters, Michelle said that she had faced challenges getting her education and she recognized that many Washington High students had confronted worse, from financial hardship and tumult at home to the wounds of drugs and guns. She said their tribulations were "advantages," and their successes demonstrated courage and grit. She urged the ninth and tenth graders to make a plan to advance themselves and instructed the eleventh and twelfth graders to study for college assessment tests. She told them all to ask for help, not once but often. "Are you listening to me?" she asked the hundreds of students who packed the bleachers and stood in front of the stage. "Do you hear what I'm telling you, because I'm giving you some insights that a lot of rich kids all over the country—they know this stuff and I want you to know it, too, because you have got to go and get your education. You have got to!"

MTV personality Sway Calloway flew in from New York to emcee the event. He told the students to look lively because his reports would appear on MTV, BET, and Nickelodeon. He said the first lady "could be anywhere on this planet today, literally, but she chose to come to your high school." Calloway's presence offered evidence of the way that Michelle and her staff had promoted her programs on their own terms, to the audences they coveted. Michelle made no time for questions from news reporters, but she gave risk-free one-on-one backstage interviews to Calloway and LGBT media figure Tyler Oakley, whose upbeat conversation with her registered 1.2 million YouTube views in just ten days.

To the students in the gym, Michelle spoke of racism and Jim Crow. She invoked Booker T. Washington and the school's most famous alumnus, Martin Luther King Jr., who graduated from Morehouse, a ten-minute walk away. She said the two men had bequeathed to the students a legacy of progress and a responsibility to better themselves and their families. "There is absolutely no excuse," she told the teenagers. "If there's anybody telling you that you're not college material—anyone—I want you to brush 'em off. Prove them wrong." She might as easily have been talking about the legacy that her grandparents passed to her parents and that Fraser and Marian Robinson passed to her and to Craig. Ever the South Side girl, Michelle was passing it on, too. "I love you all," she said. "God bless. Keep working hard."

# Epilogue

Nearly six years into her White House life, Michelle took to the campaign trail in late 2014 as Democrats fought to retain their Senate majority. Barack seemed beleaguered, his hair ever grayer and his favorability numbers in the low forties, at least twenty points lower than his wife's. Many candidates calculated that a campaign rally with the president would be a net loss, but coveted a visit from Michelle. In more than a dozen states from Florida to Maine to Colorado and three trips to Iowa, she became Barack's proxy, talking up the things that were going right and criticizing Republican behavior that "just wastes time and wastes taxpayer dollars. In fact, it's gotten so bad, they're even trying to block the work that I do on childhood obesity. And that's really saying something." Barack made a ripe target. Demonized in ever more fantastical ways, he seemed unable to find a response that worked, even to persuade fellow Democrats. In November, the country was in such a sour mood that only 36 percent of voters bothered to cast ballots, the lowest figure since 1942. Republicans surged gleefully into control of the Senate, leaving the forty-fourth president ever more isolated.

Michelle carried on with her projects, but her public and private reflections sometimes took on a valedictory tone. As attention shifted to the election of Barack's successor, she told friends that she intended to stay in Washington until Sasha graduated from high school in 2019, if that's what Sasha wanted. Despite her Chicago roots and the friends and family still living on the South Side, Barack set his sights on New York, at least as one of their future homes. If it came to that, Michelle reckoned that she could be more anonymous there than in Chicago, an appealing thought after the White House fishbowl. She said she looked forward to staying fit, traveling to beautiful places, and, one day, being a grandmother. At an event with Laura Bush, who appeared to be carving a satisfying post-politics life in Dallas, Michelle said she saw in the Bush family "a level of freedom" that comes when the spotlight shifts. "There is more that you're able to do out of office, oftentimes, than you can do when you're in office." Working on a memoir likely to fetch millions of dollars, she told friends that she would have much to say when she no longer had to worry quite so much about the consequences. Privately, she once mused that when she left the White House, she would be just like Barbara Bush. She paused for comic effect as her guests conjured the unlikely image. Because you'll start wearing three strands of pearls? one perplexed friend asked. No, Michelle laughed, because I'll be able to say whatever the hell I want.

Michelle had once called herself a "statistical anomaly," a black woman who had climbed from the Chicago working class into elite American society. Her place in history reflected the distance she and the country had traveled since January 1964. Opportunities had multiplied and paths had grown smoother. And yet she remained, in so many ways, an exception that proved the rule. More than a half century after her birth, the odds remained daunting for the vast majority of the 41 million people in the United States who identified themselves as African American. There were yawning gaps between blacks and whites in household income, home ownership, college completion rates, and net worth, not to mention disparities in incarceration rates and levels of confidence in the legal system. Michelle herself said in May 2014, "We know that in America, too many folks are stopped on the street because of the color of their skin." The idea of the country being post-racial would have been laughable were it not so depressing. Michelle belongs to a generation, said historian Marcia Chatelain, that sees "incredible amounts of change and incredible amounts of stagnation." When the first lady considered the stacked deck and grew impatient, Barack would remind her that they were "playing a long game here, and that change is hard and change is slow and it never happens all at once. But eventually we get there, we always do."

One day in the Oval Office, very quietly, so quietly that Barack had to ask him to repeat it, a five-year-old black boy named Jacob Philadelphia asked the president a question. He said, "I want to know if my hair is just like yours." Barack invited him to see for himself and, standing beside his desk, leaned down. As Jacob reached up to touch his hair, a White House photographer snapped a picture. For more than five years, the photo hung in the West Wing as dozens of others were swapped out. Michelle described the scene to an African American church audience in Nashville, offering it as a sign that progress does come, however glacial, however imperfect. "I want you to think," she said, "about how children who see that photo today think nothing of it because that is all they've ever known, because they have grown up taking for granted that an African American can be president of the United States." She once reflected, while hosting a White House workshop to celebrate the rise of 1960s Motown music, that "something changed when little girls all across the country saw Diana Ross on *The Ed Sullivan Show*." Just maybe, she thought, something was changing, too, as little girls and boys across the country saw Michelle Obama in the White House.

Michelle devoted countless hours to her work on obesity, education, and military families. She hoped her projects, and the messages behind them, would endure. And yet the power that she invoked most often in her public life was the symbolic power of her trajectory—the fact that she made it from Richard J. Daley's unforgiving Chicago all the way to Princeton, to Harvard, to prosperity and a measure of professional fulfillment, and then to the gleaming pulpit that was the White House. That was why she told her story so often to students who felt marginalized and unsure. It was why she emphasized discipline, persistence, and decency—and why she gave out all those hugs. "Maybe if I stay one second longer and ask this little girl what she wants to be, if I tell her that I'm proud of her, if I give her a hug, maybe that one moment will make her go off and be great." One day, explaining "why, as first lady, I do this," she told a high school audience in Washington that she urged them onward "because this is all I can be for you right now, is just this model of an alternative." Could she do more? That was the lingering question of her final stretch in the White House and the years to come.

"WE HAVE A BLACK FAMILY in the White House. Amazing!" said Maya Angelou at a BET awards ceremony after Michelle introduced her. To Michelle, Angelou was a hero and muse whose affirming words "lifted me right out of my own little head." After the poet's death in 2014, the first lady spoke of what she had learned about authenticity and self-worth from the writer, dancer, singer, teacher, and short-order cook from Stamps, Arkansas. She said Angelou, born in 1928, "celebrated black women's beauty like no one had ever dared to before—our curves, our stride, our strength, our grace." In an era when black women faced "stifling constraints," Michelle said, Angelou "serenely disregarded all the rules. . . . She was comfortable in every inch of her glorious brown skin."

In her eulogy, delivered at a memorial service in Winston-Salem, North Carolina, Michelle painted herself anew as "a little black girl from the South Side of Chicago." She described her feelings of loneliness in Ivy League classrooms and "long years on the campaign trail where at times my very womanhood was dissected and questioned." It pleased her when people called her authentic. And when they did, she thought of Angelou. She said the poet's work allowed her and many others "just to be our good old black-woman selves. She showed us that, eventually, if we stayed true to who we are, then the world would embrace us."

# Acknowledgments

This book, much like the Obama presidency, got its start in Iowa. In 2007, Michelle Obama rolled from Davenport to Iowa Falls to Fort Dodge to Rockwell City, telling her story and talking up her husband's candidacy. She spoke of Barack's life and her own, and asked listeners to believe in him the way she did. I followed her through Iowa and, as the campaign gained momentum, I watched her in New York and Texas, South Carolina and Indiana, and, in the final days of the race, Ohio. Before and after the election, I explored Michelle's history and her Chicago career while spending considerable time writing about Barack's own trajectory. For those early forays from *The Washington Post*'s Chicago bureau, I am grateful to the *Post* editors who humored me and to the politics-writing colleagues who made me wiser.

As I watched at close range, it became clear that Michelle merited a book that placed her at the center of her own narrative, not simply as the wife of the famous Barack, nor merely as first lady. When I embarked on the project, two friends at the *Post* steered me to Andrew Wylie and Scott Moyers. After Scott returned to Penguin, Andrew proved savvy and steadfast, the shrewdest ally a writer could want. Thanks to Jacqueline Ko at the Wylie Agency for answering many questions. At Knopf, Erroll McDonald believed in the idea from the start and, through thick and thin, never wavered. I am grateful to Knopf's talented team, who guided the book to the finish, including Nicholas Thomson, Cassandra Pappas, Claire Bradley Ong, and Carol Devine Carson.

At Northwestern University, where I have been fortunate to teach since leaving the *Post,* I gained greatly from the labors of a lively and dedicated team of undergraduate researchers. Rhaina Cohen and Yvonne Kouadjo came to know Michelle's story almost as well as I did, adding details and smart thinking to chapter after chapter. I was fortunate to have Benjamin Purdy's considerable contributions for two years and, in the homestretch, the work of Emily Jan, who paid particular attention to the photographic record; plus Ashley Wood and Yoona Ha. Many thanks to two deans of Northwestern's Medill School of Journalism, Bradley Hamm and John Lavine, and former associate dean Mary Nesbitt. Their support and flexibility contributed mightily to my ability to finish this project in something short of a light-year. As I completed the book, the Hutchins Center for African and African American Research offered a welcome haven and access to Harvard's libraries.

So many colleagues at Northwestern offered conversation and words of encouragement. Heartfelt appreciation to Medill friends Cecilia Vaisman, Ava Greenwell, Rick Tulsky, Jack Doppelt, Judy McCoy, Emily Withrow, Kari Lydersen, Charles Whitaker, and Louise Kiernan. Also Stephan Garnett, Alex Kotlowitz, Beth Bennett, Larry Stuelpnagel, Josh Meyer, Loren Ghiglione, Mei-Ling Hopgood, Karren Thompson, Douglas Foster, and many other terrific colleagues and students. Beyond Medill, I was pleased to be able to turn for guidance on Chicago history and culture to Northwestern professors Henry Binford, Mary Pattillo, and Darlene Clarke Hine.

Dozens of people shared their stories and their wisdom about Michelle and Barack Obama and the world they inhabit. For their reflections and their trust, I thank them. I owe a deep debt to reporters and media figures who asked thoughtful questions of the Obamas, some as long as twenty years ago, others quite recently. Their work enriched the narrative immeasurably. A special shout-out to colleagues who opened their notebooks and shared unpublished interviews, including Michael Powell of *The New York Times,* Scott Helman of *The Boston Globe,* David Mendell and John McCormick, late of the *Chicago Tribune,* and Lauren Collins of *The New Yorker.*

This book would not be the same without the rigor and sage advice of friends who broke into their busy lives to read the manuscript. For that, I thank Robin Givhan, Rachel Swarns, David Remnick, Peter Baker, Kevin Merida, and Dexter Filkins. Each of them not only plowed through the evolving biography but kept up helpful and long-running conversations along the way. Martha Biondi, expert in the history of campus politics, graciously read the Princeton and Harvard chapters. Any errors of fact or interpretation, naturally, are mine alone.

Truth be told, there was never a day when I did not look forward to working on this project and solving one riddle or another. Countless times, a kind word or a generous suggestion from a friend was a welcome balm. I much appreciate support from those who spoke and those who mostly listened, including Bill Hewitt, Krissah Thompson, Geraldine Baum, David Von Drehle, John Rogers, Elizabeth Shogren, Cathy Lasiewicz, Mellody Hobson, Chris Westefeld, John Audley and Andrea Durbin. I am grateful to Russ Canan, Sheryll Cashin, Blaine Harden, Margot Singer, Connie Schultz, Esther Fein, Steve and Rena Reiss, Tom Ricks, Masha Lipman, Joe Day, John Westefeld, John Heilemann, and Steve Mufson. In Evanston, I thank Andrew Johnston—so generous with his expertise about photography—Tracy Van Moorlehem, Deb Turkheimer, Dylan Smith, Dylan Penningroth, Ian Hurd, and all the Lincoln and Nichols friends. Special thanks to Mike Klearman, who always managed to talk of this project with a gleam in his eye.

Every so often, a thick envelope of news clippings would arrive from my mother, Katherine Day Slevin, who first lived in Washington in the 1930s and remembers cutting through the White House grounds to get from Pennsylvania Avenue to the National Mall. Well into her nineties, my mother has a keen eye for details that reveal character, a trait she shared with my late newsman father, Joseph R. Slevin. To the two of them, and their generous spirit, I owe more than I can convey. I thank my siblings, Michael Slevin, Jonathan Slevin, and Ann Peck, for their love and encouragement, and Ann Masur for being a laser-eyed reader of the manuscript and a great support to our family. A bevy of Slevins, Masurs, and their kin offered invariably lively conversation and good cheer.

I recognized how much this project had become part of our family's life when Kate asked a question at dinner one summer evening in 2013: "Does anyone know what's happening July seventeenth?" Without hesitating, six-year-old Milo said, "Michelle Obama's half-birthday?" He was right about the date, although Kate had a different event in mind. Isaac and Milo learned their facts and asked thoughtful questions, even as they surely wondered when I would finally finish. Their older brother, Nik, was unfailingly enthusiastic while cheering from a greater height and distance. Kate Masur contributed a historian's expertise and a scholar's sensibility. Ever smart and stalwart, ever cool under pressure, a great reader and a greater friend, she sharpened my thinking and rallied the troops, staying true to the end.

# Notes

### INTRODUCTION

4  "Maybe you feel like no one has": Michelle Obama, Academies of Anacostia graduation, June 11, 2010.

5  "We live in a nation": Michelle Obama, remarks to the National Congress of Black Women, September 30, 2007.

5  "So the world has": "Running Mates: Michelle Obama One on One," *Good Morning America,* ABC News, May 22, 2007.

5  "So many people have no idea": Verna Williams, interview with author.

5  "the balance between": Michelle Obama, remarks at University of California–Merced, May 16, 2009.

5  "You do not want": Trooper Sanders, interview with author.

6  "I think that girl was": Michelle Obama, *106 and Park,* BET, November 13, 2013.


### 1 | CHICAGO'S PROMISE

7  "The gutsiest guy": Dan Maxime, interview with author.

8  "What would my father think": Michelle Obama, Harlem, June 26, 2007.

8  "the glue": Capers Funnye, interview with author.

8  "I remember his compassion": *South Side Girl,* Democratic National Committee video, August 26, 2008.

9  "I could calculate": Richard Wright, *Black Boy,* p. 252.

9  "depressed and dismayed me": Ibid., p. 261.

9  "I knew that this machine-city was": Ibid., p. 262.

9  overcrowding forced many black schools: St. Clair Drake and Horace R. Cayton, *Black Metropolis: A Study of Negro Life in a Northern City,* p. 202.

10  In one direction was a library named for: Ibid., p. 379; and Adam Green, *Selling the Race: Culture, Community, and Black Chicago, 1940–1955,* pp. 58–59.

10 "The capital of black America": Nicholas Lemann, *The Promised Land: The Great Migration and How It Changed America*, p. 64.

11 "And they risked serious reprisals": John Paul Stevens, "The Court and the Right to Vote: A Dissent," *New York Review of Books*, August 15, 2013.

11 "The whites in power": Rachel L. Swarns, *American Tapestry: The Story of the Black, White, and Multiracial Ancestors of Michelle Obama*, pp. 156–160.

11 "a young man destined for better things": Ibid., p. 79.

11 "He wanted a different kind of life": Ibid., p. 80.

11 He set up pins: Ibid., pp. 92–93.

12 James moved: Ibid., p. 83.

13 The policy, known as redlining: Beryl Satter, *Family Properties: Race, Real Estate, and the Exploitation of Black Urban America*.

13 three-fourths of Chicago's black population: Arnold R. Hirsch, *Making the Second Ghetto: Race & Housing in Chicago, 1940–1960*, pp. 4–5.

13 they charged rents far higher: Ibid., p. 29.

13 Three black infants died: Drake and Cayton, p. 202.

13 By 1945, more than half of the Black Belt: Ibid., p. 206.

13 "They faced what other African American families faced": Barack Obama, speech, Washington, September 18, 2007.

13 LaVaughn again took up housecleaning: Swarns, p. 93.

13 John, who died as a baby: Nomenee Robinson, interview with author.

14 "separated, without dependants [*sic*]": Swarns, p. 97.

14 She relied especially on two older women from Georgetown: Swarns, p. 100.

14 the first African American woman: Scott Young, Moody Bible Institute, email, April 26, 2013.

14 "Everything educational, they got it": Swarns, p. 100.

15 "I just loved that little toy": Nomenee Robinson, interview.

15 "Don't you dare go out there again": Ibid.

15 His mother knew the location: Nomenee Robinson, interview.

16 named for a friendly Italian woman: Swarns, p. 101.

16 "He happened to hear me screaming": Nomenee Robinson, interview.

16 He left that chore to his wife: Craig Robinson, *A Game of Character: A Family Journey from Chicago's Southside to the Ivy League and Beyond*, p. 27.

16 He worked on the horse-drawn cart: Nomenee Robinson, interview; Michelle Obama, *American Grown: The Story of the White House Kitchen Garden and Gardens Across America*, p. 12.

16 "We had to be hustlers": Nomenee Robinson, interview.

16 In the mid-1940s: Ibid.

17 "Her style was very open": Richard Hunt, interview with author.

17 "escaping and coming to the land of the free": Ibid.

17 "The teachers might suggest": Ibid.

17 "You'd hardly know he was around": Reuben Crawford, interview with author.

17 He saw Fraser: Nomenee Robinson, interview; family remembrance prepared for Fraser Robinson's memorial service, Chicago, March 10, 1991.

17 "He was secure with himself.": Nomenee Robinson, interview.

18  "Make your own little list": Nelson Algren, *Chicago: City on the Make*, pp. 45–46.

18  "We were taught the history": Charlie Brown, interview with author.

19  "faced with abhorrence of everything": Margaret T. G. Burroughs, "What Shall I Tell My Children Who Are Black?" Chicago: M.A.A.H. Press, 1968.

19  At first, she thought: Margaret Taylor Burroughs, *Life with Margaret: The Official Autobiography*, pp. 72–73.

19  "An agitator by profession.": Richard Hofstadter, *The American Political Tradition and the Men Who Made It*, p. 135.

19  "When you lived in Chicago back then": Brown, interview.

20  "If one word": Bernard Shaw, interview with author.

20  "You *had* to do better": Crawford, interview.

20  "an absolute conviction": Funnye, interview.

21  He "encouraged striving": Ibid.

21  Eldridge Cleaver and Anne Moody: Adam Green, p. 198.

21  "I couldn't get Emmett Till": "The Murder of Emmett Till," http://www .pbs.org/wgbh/amex/till/sfeature/sf_remember.html.

22  One thought running through her head: The Rev. Jesse Jackson Sr., "Appreciation: Rosa Parks," *Time*, October 30, 2005.

22  once you put money in a bank: Nomenee Robinson, interview.

22  It was an initiative of the Dining Car Workers: National Register of Historic Places registration form, National Park Service, October 2011.

22  In the immediate postwar years: James R. Grossman, Ann Durkin Keating, and Janice L. Reiff, eds., *The Encyclopedia of Chicago*.

22  The complex opened: National Register of Historic Places registration form, National Park Service, October 2011.

23  "the opening of a new frontier": Mary McLeod Bethune, "Chicago's Parkway Gardens Symbol of Growing Economic Unity and Strength," *Chicago Defender*, December 9, 1950.

23  He wanted not only to provide: Richard M. Leeson, *Lorraine Hansberry: A Research and Production Sourcebook*, p. 6.

23  "hellishly hostile": Lorraine Hansberry, *To Be Young, Gifted and Black*, p. 51.

24  "it is a play that tells the truth": Anne Cheney, *Lorraine Hansberry*, p. 55.

24  "We ain't never been that poor": Lorraine Hansberry, *A Raisin in the Sun*, p. 143.

24  "one of America's greatest stories": Scott Feinberg, "Tonys: A Moment in the Sun for 'A Raisin in the Sun' Nominee LaTanya Richardson Jackson," *Hollywood Reporter*, May 27, 2014.

24  Fraser joined the army: Andrew Robinson, interview.

25  "You fell out for formation": Joe Hegedus, interview with author.

25  He was awarded a good conduct medal: U.S. Army records.

25  He would complete his service: U.S. Army records.

25  As African Americans continued to migrate: Christopher Manning, "African Americans," in Grossman, Keating, and Reiff, eds.; Nicholas Lemann, p. 70.

## 2 | SOUTH SIDE

26  They broke up: Marian Robinson, unpublished interview with Scott Helman, 2008.

26  "philosopher in chief": Marian Robinson quoted in Craig Robinson, *A Game of Character: A Family Journey from Chicago's Southside to the Ivy League and Beyond*, p. xi.

26  "If it can be done": Jim Axelrod, "In the Family," *CBS Sunday Morning*, March 1, 2009.

27  "I come from a very articulate": Michelle Obama, "Reaching Out and Reaching Back," *InsideOut*, University of Chicago Office of Community and Government Affairs, September 2005.

27  they would raise seven children: Michelle Obama, remarks to National Council of La Raza, July 23, 2013, New Orleans.

28  As adults, they both learned to read: Rachel Swarns, *American Tapestry: The Story of the Black, White, and Multiracial Ancestors of Michelle Obama*, pp. 150–151.

28  "The women in my family were dressmakers": Scott Helman, unpublished interview with Marian Robinson, 2008.

28  He then found work as a plasterer: Swarns, p. 88.

28  With Purnell and his sister: Ibid., p. 72.

28  "When I finally came to Chicago on May 9, 1930": Dempsey Travis, *An Autobiography of Black Jazz*, p. 240.

29  "You learn to sleep through jazz": Laura Brown, "Michelle Obama: America's Got Talent," *Harper's Bazaar*, October 13, 2010.

29  "By calling a chef, drummer and jazz aficionado": Robinson, p. 16.

29  He was denied better jobs and pay: Susan Saulny, "Michelle Obama Thrives in Campaign Trenches," *New York Times*, February 14, 2008.

29  "I had a father who could be very angry about race": Marian Robinson, unpublished interview with Michael Powell, 2008.

30  "Segregation and poverty have created": National Advisory Commission on Civil Disorders, pp. 1–2.

30  "All of us know what those conditions are": Lyndon Baines Johnson, speech, The White House, July 27, 1967, http://millercenter.org/president/speeches/speech-4040.

31  "This difference has its source": Pierre de Vise, *Chicago's Widening Color Gap*, p. 18.

31  In raw numbers: Ibid., pp. 75–76.

32  "Statistically, Woodlawn had become": John Hall Fish, *Black Power / White Control: The Struggle of the Woodlawn Organization in Chicago* (Princeton, N.J.: Princeton University Press, 1973), p. 13; and interview with author.

32  going "way out south": Timuel Black, interview with author.

32  With no children of their own: Robinson, p. 5.

32  "People here are dedicated": Sel Yackley, "South Shore: Integration Since 1955," *Chicago Tribune*, April 9, 1967.

32  Leonard was a commercial artist: "His Designs on Shower Curtains Led to Success," *Chicago Tribune*, April 14, 1966.

32 "I had the best childhood ever": Leonard Jewell, interview with author.

33 One of the very few stay-at-home mothers: Mariana Cook, interview with Barack and Michelle Obama, 1996.

33 "There were good schools": Ta-Nehisi Coates, "American Girl," *Atlantic,* January 2009.

33 "the Shangri-La of upbringings": Robinson, p. 7.

33 "We are here because the Savings and Loan": Taylor Branch, *At Canaan's Edge: America in the King Years, 1965–68,* p. 516.

34 "I *still* have faith in the future.": Ibid., pp. 501–509.

34 "I wish I were an Alabama trooper": Jeff Kelly Lowenstein, "Resisting the Dream," *Chicago Reporter,* May 2006.

34 "I have never in my life": Branch, pp. 509–511; Lowenstein, "Resisting the Dream."

35 "We should have known better,": Branch, p. 558.

35 "cracked a beguiling": Ibid.

35 "We are all, let us face it": Ibid., p. 523.

35 "Daley had a special weak spot": Leon Despres, *Challenging the Daley Machine: A Chicago Alderman's Memoir,* p. 45.

36 At its height, the Chicago machine: Adam Cohen and Elizabeth Taylor, *American Pharaoh: Mayor Richard M. Daley—His Battle for Chicago and the Nation,* p. 157.

36 "You couldn't cut": Ibid., p. 146.

36 "We gave out jobs": Flynn McRoberts, "Chicago's Black Political Movement: What Happened?," *Chicago Tribune,* July 4, 1999.

36 "blunted by the taste": Ibid.

36 "You went along with things": Mitchell Locin and Joel Kaplan, "'I Never Did Think I Would Ever Be Really Involved in Politics'—Eugene Sawyer," *Chicago Tribune,* February 1, 1989.

37 "There are no virgins": William E. Schmidt, "Chicago Nears Choice for Mayor as Race Issue Flares," *New York Times,* February 27, 1989.

38 "the beginning of the good": Dan Maxime, interview with author.

38 "felt local politics was the most important": Marian Robinson, unpublished interview with Powell, 2008.

38 "a visiting kind": Marian Robinson, unpublished interview with Helman, 2008.

39 "If I had to describe": Craig Robinson, interview with author, 2007.

39 "Everything that I think about": Kristen Gelineau, "Would-be First Lady Drifts into Rock-Star Territory, Tentatively," Associated Press, March 30, 2008.

39 "It was almost": Robinson, p. 12.

39 impossibly contoured blonde Malibu Barbie: Michelle Obama, remarks at a memorial service for Maya Angelou, June 7, 2014.

39 and a black Barbie imitation: Rosalind Rossi, "Obama's Anchor," *Chicago Sun-Times,* January 21, 2007.

39 "I liked everything Barbie": Michelle Obama, North American Aerospace Defense Command, December 24, 2012.

40 "the standard for perfection": Michelle Obama, remarks at memorial service for Maya Angelou, June 7, 2014.

40  "taught me how to throw": Michelle Obama, speech to the International Olympic Committee, Copenhagen, Denmark, October 2, 2009.

40  "kind of a tomboy": Grace Ybarra, "Michelle Obama Gets Kids Moving," *Sports Illustrated Kids,* June 25, 2013.

40  "a gift I shared": Michelle Obama, speech to International Olympic Committee.

40  The children were limited: Saulny, "Michelle Obama Thrives."

40  When the weather: Robinson, p. 11.

40  During football season: Ibid., p. 8.

40  Once earned $7 a day: Barack Obama, presenting the Presidential Medal of Freedom, November 20, 2013.

40  Craig once said: *Chicago Tonight,* WTTW, April 30, 2010.

41  "and after school": Michelle Obama, *American Grown: The Story of the White House Kitchen Garden and Gardens Across America,* p. 15.

41  "I guess she figured": Harriette Cole, "From a Mother's Eyes," *Ebony,* September 2008.

41  "Just like Sasha": Ibid.

41  told a co-worker: Jacquelyn Thomas, interview with author.

41  "Her mom told the teacher": Saulny, "Michelle Obama Thrives."

41  emphasized effort and attitude: Elizabeth Brackett, *Chicago Tonight,* WTTW, October 28, 2004.

42  When they finished: Robinson, p. 70.

42  how much they regretted: Scott Helman, "Holding Down the Obama Family Fort: 'Grandma' Makes the Race Possible," *Boston Globe,* March 30, 2008.

42  "We told the kids": Marian Robinson, interview with Helman, 2008.

42  "written from the black perspective": Robinson, p. 58.

42  "Now, you've got to remember": Craig Robinson, remarks at "Coming Back: Reconnecting Princeton's Black Alumni," Princeton University, October 18, 2014. The Black Panther Party was founded in 1966.

43  He dismissed the 1963 March: Kevin Merida, "A Piece of the Dream," *Washington Post,* January 16, 2008.

43  "I am not advocating": Jackie Robinson column, *Chicago Defender,* March 14, 1964.

43  "Before Malcolm X": Ta-Nehisi Coates, "The Legacy of Malcolm X: Why His Vision Lives On in Barack Obama," *Atlantic,* April 2, 2010.

44  "repeated acts of self-creation": Barack Obama, *Dreams from My Father,* p. 86.

44  "If you think about it": Remnick, *The Bridge,* pp. 233–234.

44  Fraser also spent: Robinson, p. 53.

44  "I liked it because": Robinson, p. 12, and Laura Brown, "Michelle Obama: America's Got Talent."

44  "my mother would not": Ta-Nehisi Coates, "American Girl."

44  Late on a summer night: "Northwestern Dorms Bar Negro Students," *Chicago Defender,* August 14, 1943; "N.U. Keeps Jim Crow in Dorms," *Chicago Defender,* September 11, 1943; "Northwestern Sued for $50,00 in Dorm Ban," *Chicago Defender,* December 11, 1943.

45   "She was friendly, but": Betty Reid, interview with author.

45   Michelle said both sides: Rosemary Ellis, "A Conversation with Michelle Obama," *Good Housekeeping,* November 2008, www.goodhousekeeping .com/family/celebrity-interviews/michelle-obama-interview.

45   She remembered enduring: Michelle Obama, Google+ Hangout with Kelly Ripa, March 4, 2013.

45   "a basic foundation": Rosemary Ellis, "A Conversation with Michelle Obama."

45   "to explore and find": Robinson, p. 77.

46   "about how Fraser": Ibid., p. 155.

46   "That love for one another": Ibid., pp. 6–7.

46   Craig recalled their parents: *A Salute,* p. 68.

46   "a mother who": Michelle Obama, "Be Fearless," in Editors of *Essence* Magazine, *A Salute to Michelle Obama* (New York: Essence Communications, 2012), p. 36.

46   She and her brother: Rosalind Rossi, "Obama's Anchor: As His Career Soars Toward a Presidential Bid, Wife Michelle Keeps His Feet on the Ground," *Chicago Sun-Times,* January 21, 2007.

46   "didn't overdo the praise": Robinson, p. 70.

46   "But there was a whole lot": Elizabeth Brackett, *Chicago Tonight,* WTTW, October 28, 2004.

46   "You follow people": Marian Robinson, unpublished interview with Powell, 2008.

46   "If it sounds like": Cole, "From a Mother's Eyes."

47   She attended: Michelle Obama, remarks in Topeka, Kan., May 17, 2014.

47   "That's where we got": Coates, "American Girl."

47   "resented it when I couldn't say": Ibid.

47   "More important, even": Lauren Collins, "The Other Obama: Michelle Obama and the Politics of Candor," *New Yorker,* March 10, 2008.

47   "by ear, day by day": Cole, "From a Mother's Eyes."

## 3 | DESTINY NOT YET WRITTEN

49   "Thus began a conversation": Craig Robinson, *A Game of Character: A Family Journey from Chicago's Southside to the Ivy League and Beyond,* p. 58.

49   If they experienced animosity: Ibid., p. 59.

49   No one can make: Ibid., pp. 58–60.

49   "When you grow up as a black kid": Craig Robinson, interview with author, 2007.

50   Purnell Shields, Michelle's maternal: Michelle Obama, remarks to National Council of La Raza, July 23, 2013.

50   "They might not like": Grace Hale, interview with author.

50   "Very smart, but very quiet": Ibid.

50   "She had very strong values": Jacquelyn Thomas, interview with author.

51   If he had been born white: William Finnegan, "The Candidate: How the Son of a Kenyan Economist Became an Illinois Everyman," *New Yorker,* May 31, 2004.

51 "a discontent about him": Shailagh Murray, "A Family Tree Rooted in American Soil," *Washington Post*, October 2, 2008.

51 "not always enjoyable": Robinson, pp. 103, 14–15.

51 "On one visit": Ibid., pp. 14–15.

51 "His whole demeanor": Capers Funnye, interview with author.

51 "He was wrestling": Nomenee Robinson, interview with author.

52 "didn't exactly spew love": Andrew Robinson, interview with author.

52 Nomenee went to India: Paul Grimes, "Galbraiths Fete Mrs. Kennedy at Formal Dinner on Her Last Day in India," *New York Times*, March 21, 1962.

52 died a prosperous man: Andrew Robinson and Nomenee Robinson, interviews with author.

53 "veil of impossibility": Michelle Obama, remarks in Orangeburg, S.C., November 20, 2007.

53 "did not let it carry over": Marian Robinson, unpublished interview with Michael Powell, 2008.

53 "An ice house!": Sterling Stuckey, interview with author.

53 "Parents were trying": Rachel Swarns, panel discussion, Northwestern University History Department, October 19, 2012.

53 "We want you to": Rachel Swarns, *American Tapestry: The Story of the Black, White, and Multiracial Ancestors of Michelle Obama*, p. 108.

53 "the mothers and the fathers": Michelle Obama, Whitney Young film screening, White House, August 27, 2013.

54 "We didn't think of it": Deval Patrick, *A Reason to Believe: Lessons from an Improbable Life*, p. 22.

54 "From that position": Ibid., p. 119.

54 "I was surrounded by adults": Ibid., p. 32.

54 "The true gift": Deval Patrick, interview with author.

54 "They did not want": Patrick, p. 17.

55 At that point: Robinson, p. 28.

55 "Lunch on school days": Finnegan, "The Candidate"; Michelle Obama, *American Grown: The Story of the White House Kitchen Garden and Gardens Across America*, p. 13.

55 "If the TV broke": Lauren Collins, "The Other Obama: Michelle Obama and the Politics of Candor," *New Yorker*, March 10, 2008.

55 "Are we rich?": Robinson, pp. 29–30.

56 He would even make time: Craig Robinson, book-tour discussion, Dominican University, April 27, 2010.

56 "A smart man learns": Jim Axelrod, "Craig Robinson, First Coach," CBS, March 1, 2009.

56 "If you disappointed": Craig Robinson, interview with author.

56 "I never had any": Craig Robinson, *Good Morning America*, March 4, 2010.

56 "Unofficial counselor to family": Robinson, p. 147.

56 "Fraser was the type of person": Grace Hale, interview with author.

57 He would shave: Robinson, p. 73.

57 "That's where I went": Nomenee Robinson, interview with author.

57  "Before he got really sick": Laura Brown, "Michelle Obama: America's Got Talent," *Harper's Bazaar,* October 13, 2010.

57  but by 1965: Michelle Obama, speech to Democratic National Convention, August 26, 2008.

57  "I never knew my father": Michelle Obama, remarks in Grinnell, Iowa, December 31, 2007.

58  He took pride: *Rickey Smiley Show,* RadioOne, February 7, 2014.

58  "When you have a parent": Holly Yeager, "The Heart and Mind of Michelle Obama," *O: The Oprah Magazine,* November 2007.

58  "Here's a guy": Dan Maxime, interview with author.

58  "thought he had the greatest": Jim Axelrod, "First Coach."

58  "To have a family": Craig Robinson, interview with author.

58  A favorite destination: Michelle Obama, *American Grown,* p. 15.

59  "I was going through my cursing": Darlene Superville, "First Lady: Not Surprised by Reaction to Oscars," Associated Press, March 1, 2013.

59  One warm day: Robinson, pp. 60–61.

60  "He said, 'You guys can't' ": Leonard Jewell, interview with author.

60  As Michelle propelled herself: Robinson, p. 35.

60  "Michelle works harder": Rebecca Johnson, "The Natural," *Vogue,* September 2007.

60  "strong, strong, strong": Leonard Jewell, interview with author.

61  "We had so much": Ibid.

61  "really does hate to lose": Judy Keen, "Candid and Unscripted, Campaigning Her Way," *USA Today,* May 11, 2007.

61  "She would practice": Karen Springen, *Chicago,* October 2004. Reprinted at www.chicagomag.com as "First Lady in Waiting," June 22, 2007.

61  To soothe Craig's nerves: Robinson, p. 84.

61  If the game was close: Ibid., p. 81.

61  running 50 meters in: Results sheets from Illinois Senior Olympics, per staff member Deborah Staley, Springfield, Ill.

61  "If I can't do it fast": Yeager, "Heart and Mind."

61  put in some time: Grace Ybarra, "Michelle Obama Gets Kids Moving," *Sports Illustrated Kids,* June 25, 2013.

61  "Tall women *can*": Yeager, "Heart and Mind."

62  "represented those women": Judith Jamison, *Dancing Spirit: An Autobiography,* p. 132.

62  "I think to myself": Peter Bailey, "Young: 4th Black Leader to Die Since 1963," *Jet,* April 1, 1971.

62  "drew on his decency": Michelle Obama, Whitney Young film screening, White House, August 27, 2013.

62  "force you outside": Ava Greenwell, interview with author.

62  "probably the finest ever": Chicago Urban League newsletter, May/June 1975.

63  "We are delighted": Ibid.

63  "in such a way that": Bernarr E. Dawson, memorandum, Whitney Young High School archive.

64 "Whitney Young was built": Jeffrey Wilson, interview with author.

64 "It was a grand experiment": Ibid.

65 "I'm fixin' to go": Ibid.

65 Sometimes, to get a seat: Geraldine Brooks, "Michelle Obama and the Roots of Reinvention: How the First Lady Learned to Dream Big," *More*, October 2008.

66 plagued by construction defects: Kathy Burns, "South Shore High: Flaws Mar 'Architect's Jewel,'" *Chicago Tribune*, July 20, 1969. Bernard Judge, "Witness Tells of Vast Waste at School Site," *Chicago Tribune*, March 7, 1970.

66 "the outsider, the racial minority": Robinson, p. 79.

66 "My sister always talked": Craig Robinson, speech to the Democratic National Convention, August 26, 2008.

66 "I signed up for every activity": Michelle Obama, speech to Martin Luther King Jr. Magnet School, Nashville, Tenn., May 18, 2013.

66 She earned extra money: Michelle Obama, Corporation for National and Community Service remarks, May 12, 2009, Washington, D.C.

67 "She badgered and badgered": Yeager, "Heart and Mind."

67 "She sat on his desk": Marian Robinson, unpublished interview with Michael Powell, 2008.

67 In addition to her job: Interview with Grace Hale.

67 "because that's who I saw": Katie Couric, "Michelle Obama: Your First Lady," *Glamour*, November 2009.

67 "I'm sure it was psychological": Richard Wolffe, "Barack's Rock," *Newsweek*, February 25, 2008.

67 "She saw I never studied": Elizabeth Brackett, *Chicago Tonight*, WTTW, October 28, 2004.

67 "She'd study late": Marian Robinson, unpublished interview with Michael Powell, 2008.

68 tasked her with hiring: Aaron Payne papers, University of Illinois–Chicago archives.

68 "They said, 'Go to Spiegel'": Reuben Crawford, interview with author.

68 Another beneficiary was: Murrell Duster, interview with author.

68 She earned two degrees: Teresa Fambro Hooks, "18th Annual Chicago Film Fest Opening Honors the Primos," *Chicago Defender*, August 1, 2012.

68 She was a regular: Grace Hale, interview with author; Murrell Duster, interview with author.

68 a civil rights lawyer: Maureen O'Donnell, "Ida B. Wells' Grandson Took On Machine," *Chicago Sun-Times*, February 17, 2011.

68 "They talked about everything": Murrell Duster, interview with author.

69 "People reacted as if": Robinson, p. 95.

69 "It's like I say": Marian Robinson, unpublished interview with Scott Helman, 2008.

69 Other colleges: *Chicago Tonight*, WTTW, April 30, 2010.

69 "It might as well": Craig Robinson, remarks at "Coming Back: Reconnecting Princeton's Black Alumni," Princeton University, October 18, 2014.

69  His father's offer: Robinson, p. 96.

69  Craig, who later learned: Michelle Obama, speech to Democratic National Convention, September 4, 2012.

70  "It made me mad": Michelle Obama, speech at Booker T. Washington High School, Atlanta, Ga., September 8, 2014.

70  Michelle applied to Princeton: Theresa Fambro Hooks, "Weeklong Drama Festival at Chicago Ensemble Theater," *Chicago Defender,* November 16, 2006.

70  "long, long": Marian Robinson, unpublished interview with Michael Powell, 2008.

## 4 | ORANGE AND BLACKNESS

71  "Of 11,602 aspirants": Alan Sipress, "Class of 1985 Stands as Most Selective Ever," *The Daily Princetonian,* June 4, 1981.

71  "not merely as a means": William Bowen address, September 13, 1981, Princeton archives.

72  "I sometimes feel": Ibid. Former first lady Jacqueline Kennedy Onassis requested that "Ithaka" be read at her 1994 funeral.

72  Michelle Robinson reached: Michelle Obama, remarks at White House, January 16, 2014.

72  "When I first got in": "Obama Speaks with MSNBC's Mika Brzezinski," MSNBC, November 13, 2007.

72  She slept with her: Michelle Obama, remarks, Eastern Kentucky University graduation, May 12, 2013.

72  "I remember being shocked": Rebecca Johnson, "The Natural," *Vogue,* September 2007.

72  Michelle sometimes felt: Michelle Obama, remarks at Bell Multicultural High School, November 12, 2013.

73  "struggling just to keep": Michelle Obama, speech to Martin Luther King Jr. Magnet High School, Nashville, Tenn., May 18, 2013.

73  "a world that existed": Craig Robinson, *A Game of Character: A Family Journey from Chicago's Southside to the Ivy League and Beyond,* p. 105.

73  standing at a pay phone: Ibid., pp. 113–114.

74  He later said that: Ibid., p. 124.

74  "As a freshman": Marvin Bressler, interview with author.

74  "infamous for being racially": Michelle Robinson, "Princeton-Educated Blacks and the Black Community," (senior thesis, Princeton University, 1985), p. 26.

74  "Princeton is actively seeking: Princeton University records.

74  The class of 1985: The class of '85 statistical reference comes from Princeton University records.

75  "double-consciousness": W. E. B. Du Bois, *Souls of Black Folk.*

75  "I grew up around": Hilary Beard, interview with author.

75  "My experiences at Princeton": Michelle LaVaughn Robinson, "Princeton-Educated Blacks and the Black Community," senior thesis, Princeton University, 1985.

76  Brown was horrified: Brian Feagans, "Color of Memory Suddenly Grows Vivid," *Atlanta Journal-Constitution*, April 13, 2008.

76  "one of the funniest": Ibid.

77  "There were those black students who": Ruth Simmons, interview with author.

77  "I didn't want this Third World place": Robin Givhan, interview with author.

77  "I wanted to create a differne social": Sharon Holland, interview with author.

78  "some of the best of times": Ibid.

78  "She took time to talk": Hilary Beard, interview with author.

78  "a program that would": Czerny Brasuell, interview with author.

78  "because of the isolation": Ruth Simmons, interview with author.

78  "You learned about politics": Craig Robinson, remarks at "Coming Back: Reconnecting Princeton's Black Alumni," Princeton University, October 18, 2014.

78  "She was generally": Kenneth Bruce, interview with author.

79  "As a black student:" Lauren Ugorji, interview with author.

79  She was pictured in: *Daily Princetonian*, February 26, 1985.

79  To raise money: Sally Jacobs, "Learning to be Michelle Obama," *Boston Globe*, June 15, 2008.

79  "because she is so tall:" *Daily Princetonian*, February 26, 1985.

79  "If I drove, I would": Hilary Beard, interview with author.

79  "Her thoughts were never": Ibid.

80  "Michelle's always been very vocal": Lauren Collins, "The Other Obama: Michelle Obama and the Politics of Candor," *New Yorker*, March 10, 2008.

80  "You need to make sure": Jodi Kantor, "The Obamas' Marriage," *New York Times Magazine*, October 26, 2009.

80  punched in the stomach: Michelle Obama, remarks to D.C. College Application Program graduates, Washington, D.C., June 21, 2014.

80  "a place of peace and calm": Tamara Jones, "Michelle Obama Gets Personal," *More*, January 31, 2012.

81  "That family more nearly": Marvin Bressler, interview with author.

82  "Across the board": Kenneth Bruce, interview with author.

82  "There were the beginnings": Sharon Holland, interview with author.

82  "The question that bothered me": Lauren Ugorji, interview with author.

83  One year later: William G. Bowen and Derek Bok, *The Shape of the River: Long-Term Consequences of Considering Race in College and University Admissions*, p. 5.

84  But Powell also cited: Ibid., p. 8.

84  "We created a community": Sarah Brown, "Obama '85 Masters a Balancing Act," *Daily Princetonian*, December 7, 2005.

84  "We couldn't afford": Collins, "The Other Obama."

84  "giggled and laughed": Rosalind Rossi, "Obama's Anchor: As His Career Soars Toward a Presidential Bid, Wife Michelle Keeps His Feet on the Ground," *Chicago Sun-Times*, January 21, 2007.

84 "We were three black": Karen Springen and Jonathan Darman, "Ground Support," *Newsweek*, January 29, 2007.

85 "terrorized and humiliated": Randall Kennedy, *The Persistence of the Color Line: Racial Politics and the Obama Presidency*, pp. 182, 16.

85 "My dad reacted": Ibid., p. 183.

85 "We were expected": Mark Bernstein, "Identity Politics: Why Randall Kennedy '77 Writes About Racial Loyalty, Betrayal and Selling Out," *Princeton Alumni Weekly*, April 2, 2008.

86 "They created a family": Randall Kennedy, interview with Brian Lamb, March 3, 2002.

86 "What are the important": Suzanne Alele application file, Princeton University.

87 "Suzanne was the spirit": Czerny Brasuell, interview with author.

87 "always made decisions": Michelle Obama, interview with author, 2007.

87 She was invited: Suzanne Alele obituary, *Princeton Alumni Weekly*, October 24, 1990.

87 valedictorian of her class: Joan Quigley, "Homecoming," *Princeton Alumni Weekly*, December 8, 2010.

88 "I felt guilty to even ask": Michelle Obama, Corporation for National and Community Service remarks, May 12, 2009.

88 "Being in the woods": Eric Schmidt, "Fresh Air Fund Offers Off-Season Adventures," *New York Times*, June 16, 1985.

89 "Average kids with a chance": Geoffrey Canada, newyorktimes.com, video, 2006, https://www.youtube.com/watch?v=Ca9rd4aA_t0&feature =related.

89 "one of my heroes": Michelle Obama, remarks at University of California–Merced graduation, May 16, 2009.

89 "I liked the hayride": "Fresh Air Fund Opens Up New Views of Family and Community," *New York Times*, May 19, 1985.

89 "The first time": "Voices Ring Out at a Fresh Air Camp," *New York Times*, August 11, 1985.

89 "You learn a lot: "Wishes and Goals at Camps for City Children," *New York Times*, August 10, 1986.

90 It was an "illusion": William Julius Wilson, *The Declining Significance of Race: Blacks and Changing American Institutions*, p. 21.

90 Wilson's drives: William Julius Wilson, interview with author.

91 "Before a group can enter": Quoted in Michelle Robinson, "Princeton-Educated Blacks," p. 8.

91 From Andrew Billingsley's: Ibid., p. 7.

91 "They discuss problems": Ibid., pp. 8–9.

91 The "White cultural": Ibid., p. 3.

91 "may be attributed to": Ibid., p. 54.

92 "black underclass": Wilson, p. 2.

92 Black graduates could: Michelle Robinson, "Princeton-Educated Blacks," p. 55.

92 her major conclusion: Ibid., p. 53.

92   Noting that the university: Ibid., p. 62.

92   As for her own views: Ibid., p. 3.

92   "It is conceivable": Ibid., p. 3.

93   Howard Taylor, a sociology: Esther Breger, "All Eyes Turn to Michelle Obama '85," *Daily Princetonian*, November 5, 2008.

93   "Do you become the wealthiest person": Kenneth Bruce, interview with author.

93   "One of the points": Michelle Obama, interview with author, 2007.

93   "It is incumbent on us": Ibid.

94   "We teased them about": *South Side Girl,* Democratic National Convention, August 26, 2008.

## 5 | PROGRESS IN EVERYTHING AND NOTHING

95   pressed ahead: Michelle Obama, remarks to D.C. College Access Program graduation, June 21, 2014.

95   "It is Monday morning": Scott Turow, *One L: The Turbulent True Story of a First Year at Harvard Law School,* p. ix.

96   "feeling like you were": Ibid., p. 277.

96   "I almost didn't apply": Robert Wilkins, interview with author.

96   "The black community": Verna Williams, interview with author.

97   numbering 170 among: *Harvard University Fact Book,* http://oir.harvard .edu/fact-book.

97   It was certainly a contrast: William G. Bowen and Derek Bok, *The Shape of the River: Long-Term Consequences of Considering Race in College and University Admissions,* p. 5.

97   "a lifesaver for me": Verna Williams, interview with author.

97   "'What are you going to do'": Ibid.

97   The 575: Michelle Deakin, spokesperson, Harvard Law School, email exchange with author.

97   "caught up in all that goes": Jocelyn Frye, interview with author.

97   With her friends: Verna Williams, interview with author.

98   "Parents know their children": Kevin Murphy, "Actress Rashad Delivers Cosby's Message," *Capital Times* (Madison, Wisc.), September 19, 2006.

98   "She was not the person": Verna Williams, interview with author.

98   "The thing about law": Jocelyn Frye, interview with author.

99   "She is saying something": Verna Williams, interview with author.

99   "Michelle always, everything she wrote": Charles Ogletree, interview with author.

99   she volunteered as an editor: Michelle Robinson, Harvard Law School yearbook, 1988; *BLJ* 1986 issue.

99   "All the talk and the debates": David Remnick, *The Bridge: The Life and Rise of Barack Obama,* p. 187.

100  The goal was to produce: BLJ document; interview with Ginger Chavers McKnight, a former BLJ editor, with author.

100 "the most race-conscious": Remnick, *The Bridge*, p. 200.

100 "I've worked at the Supreme Court": "Dreams of Obama," *Frontline*, January 2009.

100 "pride in her color and her race": Derrick Bell, "The Civil Rights Chronicles," *Harvard Law Review*, November 1985, p. 13.

101 "defy and transcend": Ibid., p. 14.

101 "We have made progress": Ibid., p. 16.

101 "What is impossible": Ibid., p. 30.

101 "a legal system which": Derrick A. Bell, "Who's Afraid of Critical Race Theory?" *University of Illinois Law Review* 893 (1995): 900.

102 "the spotlighted few": Bell, "Civil Rights Chronicles," p. 11.

102 "the patterns of racial": Wilson, *The Declining Significance of Race*, p. 120.

102 "History gets made through": Fox Butterfield, "Old Rights Campaigner Leads a Harvard Battle," *New York Times*, May 21, 1990.

102 "This is a university": Ibid.

102 "Even liberal white scholars": Vincent Harding, "Equality Is Not Enough," *New York Times*, October 11, 1987.

103 "time for re-evaluation": Victor Bolden, "Black Lawyers Host Constitutional Conference," *Harvard Law Record*, September 18, 1987.

104 "We were trying to search": Robert Wilkins, interview with author.

104 "The absence of minorities": Michael Sudarkasa, "Verna Williams: Providing a Spark, a Light . . . a Beacon," *BLSA Memo*, Summer 1988, p. 7.

105 "In the name of tradition": Michelle Robinson, "Minority and Women Law Professors: A Comparison of Teaching Styles," *BLSA Memo*, Summer 1988, p. 30.

107 "to understand that": Charles Ogletree, interview with author.

107 "Part of the reason why": Michelle Robinson, "Minority and Women Law Professors."

107 "Students come to me": Ibid.

108 "to shake students out": Ibid.

108 "strong on what her opinions": David Wilkins, interview with author.

108 "You can't begin to": Karyn E. Langhorne, "Bureau Commemorates 75 Years of Legal Aid," *Harvard Law Record*, April 29, 1988.

109 "A large number of": Ibid.

109 One was a matter: Harvard Legal Aid Bureau records.

109 "experienced the tactical": 75th Annual Report of the Harvard Legal Aid Bureau, 1988.

109 "a commitment to her father": "Michelle Obama's Commitment to Public Service Began at HLS," *Harvard Law Bulletin*, 2008.

109 "People looked at her": Ilene Seidman, interview with author.

110 "It was less a thoughtful": Mariana Cook, interview with Barack and Michelle Obama, 1996.

110 "There was a real sense": Robert Wilkins, interview with author.

110 "You guys, this is": Areva Bell Martin, interview with author.

111 "We were treated like celebrities": Ibid.

111 "Yes, you're privileged": Ibid.

111 "My personal experience": Karen W. Arenson, "Princeton Honors Ex-Judge Once Turned Away for Race," *New York Times*, June 5, 2001.

112 "There's no other black student": Jocelyn Frye, interview with author.

112 "We had—and we should": Ibid.

113 "something more, not a social club": Verna Williams, interview with author.

114 At least one faculty: Robert Wilkins, interview with author.

114 "The majority of young people": Stefan Fatsis, "Arias Urges 5,500 Harvard Graduates to Help Ease Suffering," Associated Press, June 9, 1988.

114 He lamented the low: "Bok Assails Gap in Pay in Vital Jobs," *New York Times*, June 10, 1988.

115 "Harvard Law School is a hard place": David Wilkins, interview with author.

## 6 | FINDING THE RIGHT THING

116 More money than her parents combined: Michelle Obama, remarks, November 2, 2009, Washington, D.C.

117 "I have been asked": Flynn McRoberts, "Chicago's Black Political Movement: What Happened?," *Chicago Tribune*, July 4, 1999. Metcalfe's words were written for him by Vernon Jarrett, *Chicago Tribune* writer and future father-in-law of Valerie Jarrett, the Obamas' friend and adviser.

117 Washington received just: Andrew H. Malcolm, "A Matter of Blacks and Whites," *New York Times*, March 27, 1983.

118 "His picture was everywhere": Barack Obama, *Dreams from My Father*, p. 147.

119 "so obviously a quality candidate": Alan Greene, interview with author.

120 Michelle's assignments as a young: Lynne Marek, "The 'Other Obama' Honed Her Skills at Sidley Austin," *National Law Journal*, June 23, 2008.

120 for example, reading storyboards: Mary Hutchings Reed, interview with author.

120 "I knew Michelle was frustrated": John Levi, interview with author.

120 "She was very at ease": Mary Hutchings Reed, interview with author.

120 "A lot of people come": Nate Eimer, interview with author.

120 Michelle volunteered: Levi, interview.

121 "There was always a bit": Steven Carlson, interview with author.

121 Despite what she described: Suzanne Malveaux, "The Obamas," CNN, January 1, 2009.

121 For one thing: Barack Obama, "My First Date with Michelle," *O: The Oprah Magazine*, February 2007.

121 It was the ears: Michelle Obama, *The Oprah Winfrey Show*, January 19, 2005.

121 "probably just a black man": Holly Yeager, "The Heart and Mind of Michelle Obama," *O: The Oprah Magazine*, November 2007.

121 "But he walked into": Mariana Cook, interview with Barack and Michelle Obama, 1996.

121 "Well, Barack grew up": Ibid.

122 "I'm going to focus": Cassandra West, "Her Plan Went Awry, but Michelle Obama Doesn't Mind," *Chicago Tribune*, September 1, 2004.

122 a pattern she chose: Michelle Obama, *106 and Park,* BET, November 19, 2013.

122 "My family swore": Michelle Obama, remarks in Harlem, June 26, 2007.

122 the couple quietly married: David Maraniss, *Barack Obama: The Story,* p. 162.

122 At the time, laws prohibiting: Ibid.

122 His younger sister: Michelle Obama, remarks at Maya Angelou memorial service, June 7, 2014.

122 "This is no picnic for": Barack Obama, *Dreams,* pp. 47–48.

123 Madelyn worked: Michelle Obama, speech to Democratic National Convention, September 4, 2012.

123 "too old and too troubled": Barack Obama, *Audacity of Hope,* p. 346.

123 "Well, he ended up pretty": Charles Payne, interview with author.

123 "You know, I got my": Michelle Obama, campaign rally, Akron, Ohio, October 24, 2008.

123 "Indifferent" was how he recalled: Barack Obama, *Dreams,* p. 98.

123 smoked so much pot: Maraniss, *Barack Obama.*

123 "I rebelled," he once said: Barack Obama, speech to Northwestern University commencement, 2006.

124 "She cut me off": Barack Obama, *Dreams,* p. 95.

124 "A few miles from Pasadena": Ibid., p. 98.

124 "leaving your race at the door": Ibid., p. 97.

124 "seemed indistinguishable from": Ibid., p. 98.

124 "We always just thought": Charles Payne, interview with author.

124 "uttered racial or ethnic": Barack Obama, "A More Perfect Union," speech in Philadelphia, April 2008.

125 "a big, dark woman": Barack Obama, *Dreams,* p. 102.

125 When Barack told Regina: Ibid., p. 104.

125 "Oh Barack": Ibid., p. 105.

125 He went to one cloth-napkin lunch: Newton Minow, interview with author.

125 "Barack Obama, One L!": Remnick, *The Bridge,* p. 193.

126 "I was impressed by his": Laurence Tribe, unpublished interview with David Remnick.

126 "in every way you can": Suzanne Malveaux, CNN, January 1, 2009.

126 "When I first met him": Rosemary Ellis, "A Conversation with Michelle Obama," *Good Housekeeping,* November 2008, www.goodhousekeeping .com/family/celebrity-interviews/michelle-obama-interview.

126 "He is very persistent": Ibid.

126 "I said, okay, we'll go": Malveaux, CNN, January 1, 2009.

126 "I was sold": Ibid.

126 "In her eyes": Mariana Cook, interview with the Obamas, 1996.

127 "terrifyingly random": Barack Obama, *Audacity of Hope,* p. 329.

127 He said he would like: Ibid., p. 332.

127 To impress him: Michelle Obama, *Rachael Ray Show,* September 17, 2012.

127 which Fraser and Marian had bought: Cook County property records.

128 "For someone like me": Barack Obama, *Audacity of Hope,* pp. 332–333.

128 "cruddy": Liza Mundy, *Michelle: A Biography,* p. 138.

128 His only pair: Michelle Obama, speech to Democratic National Convention, 2012.

128 "He loved that car": Mundy, p. 138.

128 he considered working: Barack Obama, *Dreams,* p. 142.

128 The project descended: Peter Slevin, "For Clinton and Obama, a Common Ideological Touchstone," *Washington Post,* March 25, 2007.

129 "a basic belief in": Mike Kruglik, interview with author.

129 although his supervisor: Gregory Galluzzo, interview with author; and Slevin, "For Clinton and Obama."

129 he worked with African American: Barack Obama, *Dreams,* p. 170.

129 "this dual sense": Ibid., p. 157.

129 "He said that all too often": Michelle Obama, speech to Democratic National Convention, August 26, 2008.

130 "It was how he felt about": Michelle Obama, speech at Christ Church College, University of Oxford, May 25, 2011.

130 "We gave it a month, tops": Rebecca Johnson, "The Natural," *Vogue,* September 2007.

131 "you sort of felt sorry": M. Charles Bakst, "Brown Coach Robinson a Strong Voice for Brother-in-Law Obama," *Providence Journal,* May 20, 2007.

131 "She's very accomplished": Bill Reynolds, "Welcome to Obama's Family," *Providence Journal,* February 15, 2007.

131 "She found that he never": Suzanne Malveaux, CNN, January 3, 2009.

131 "A little bit": Elizabeth Brackett, *Chicago Tonight,* WTTW, October 28, 2004.

131 "When she asked me": Chuck Klosterman, "First Coach," *Esquire,* February 1, 2009.

131 "Confident without being cocky": Johnson, "The Natural."

132 "The fact that I've been": Fox Butterfield, "First Black Elected to Head Harvard's Law Review," *New York Times,* February 6, 1990.

132 "If Suzanne or I": Amanda Paulson, "Michelle Obama's Story," *Christian Science Monitor,* August 25, 2008.

132 "how I would want to be": Michelle Obama, interview with author, 2007.

133 Doctors at the University: Craig Robinson, *A Game of Character: A Family Journey from Chicago's Southside to the Ivy League and Beyond,* pp. 153–54.

133 "Would you just stop it": Ibid., p. 155.

133 "As the casket was lowered": Barack Obama, *Audacity of Hope,* p. 332.

133 "Can I go to the family reunion": Debra Pickett, "My Parents Weren't College-Educated Folks, So They Didn't Have a Notion of What We Should Want," *Chicago Sun-Times,* September 19, 2004.

133 "Just like that": Michelle Obama, North Carolina A&T commencement, May 12, 2012.

## 7 | ASSETS AND DEFICITS

134 "I don't want to be": Susan Sher, interview with author.

134 Not wanting to let her: Valerie Jarrett, interview with author, 2007.

134 "He wanted to kick": Ibid.

135  "Valerie, put yourself in": Cal Fussman, "Valerie Jarrett: What I've Learned," *Esquire*, May 2013.

135  "Everybody in my mother's": Timuel D. Black Jr., *Bridges of Memory: Chicago's First Wave of Black Migration*, p. 579.

135  Barbara recalled that: Ibid., p. 581.

135  "My grandmother always": Ibid., p. 593.

136  Showing up for work: Valerie Jarrett, remarks at National Medical Fellowships ceremony, Chicago, November 2008.

136  "My wife and I decided": Death notice, University of Chicago, September 29, 2011.

136  "We said, 'Let's look' ": Black, p. 575.

136  "Because she didn't know": Ibid., p. 578.

136  "Because it was so hard": Ibid., p. 592.

136  "In order to compete": Ibid., pp. 581–582.

137  Well into adulthood: Joe Heim, "Just Asking: Valerie Jarrett on Giving Bad Advice, Shyness, and the Value of Loyalty," *Washington Post*, December 7, 2014.

137  "I had a great office": Fussman, "Valerie Jarrett."

137  "there was no reason to be happy": Abner Mikva, interview with author.

137  "She was a political novice": Valerie Jarrett, interview with author, 2007.

138  "before they were married": Ibid.

138  "It just seemed incredible": Jay Newton-Small, "Michelle Obama's Savvy Sacrifice," *Time*, August 25, 2008.

138  "ultimately you're not going": Jim Axelrod, "First Coach," CBS, March 1, 2009.

138  "Don't you want to pay": Newton-Small, "Michelle Obama's Savvy Sacrifice."

138  One was a Coach: Rebecca Johnson, "The Natural," *Vogue*, 2007.

138  "City government, in addition": Michelle Obama, interview with author, 2007.

139  "We all thought Barack": Charles Payne, interview with author.

139  Barack informed Mikva: Abner Mikva, interview with author.

139  In ten years, Barack said: Bruce Orenstein, interview with author.

139  Barack lived with Michelle: Barack Obama, interviewed by *Parade*, June 22, 2014.

140  Barack telephoned Miner: Judson Miner, interview with author.

140  "that would let him": David Remnick, *The Bridge: The Life and Rise of Barack Obama*, p. 220.

140  Barack "knew full well": Judson Miner, interview with author.

141  "The outer limits of minority": *Barnett v. Daley*, 32 F.3d 1196 (1994).

141  Barack also did legal work: Judson Miner, memorandum to author, July 2007.

141  Miner said Barack's efforts: Miner, interview with author.

141  "If this isn't leading to marriage": Debra Pickett, "My Parents Weren't College-Educated Folks, So They Didn't Have a Notion of What We Should Want," *Chicago Sun-Times*, September 19, 2004.

141 "He would sometimes say": "Barack Obama Revealed," CNN, August 20, 2008.

141 Meanwhile, without telling her: Ibid.

142 "That kind of shuts you": Carol Felsenthal, "The Making of a First Lady," *Chicago*, January 16, 2009.

142 first record album: Barack Obama, remarks at the Presidential Medal of Freedom ceremony, Washington, D.C., November 24, 2014.

142 Barack's mother, Ann: Janny Scott, *A Singular Woman: The Untold Story of Barack Obama's Mother*, p. 303.

142 "Everybody was delighted": Charles Payne, interview with author.

143 "We understood that together": Felsenthal, "The Making of a First Lady."

143 "I remember thinking to myself": David Wilkins, interview with author.

143 She worked on business development: Carol Felsenthal, "Yvonne Davila, Close Friend of Michelle Obama, Could Be in Trouble," *Chicago*, December 2012.

143 "whether city government": Cindy Moelis, interview with author.

143 "She was not the type": Sally Duros, interview with author.

144 "I remember a sense of frustration": David Mosena, interview with author.

144 "It still wasn't enough": Geraldine Brooks, "Michelle Obama and the Roots of Reinvention: How the First Lady Learned to Dream Big," *More*, October 2008.

144 "She wanted to be on her": David Mosena, interview with author.

145 "It wasn't part": Sandy Newman, interview with author.

145 "He went around to each": Madeline Talbott, interview with author.

145 the most efficient campaign: Gretchen Reynolds, "Vote of Confidence," *Chicago*, January 1993.

145 "Who knows?": Ibid.

145 "If you have the chance": Veronica Anderson, "Forty Under 40: Here They Are, the Powers to Be," *Crain's Chicago Business*, September 27, 1993.

146 Vanessa Kirsch and Katrina Browne: Wingspread conference agenda, November 1991.

146 On the roster of participants: Wingspread conference participant list, November 1991.

146 But as several participants: Paul Schmitz, *Everyone Leads: Building Leadership from the Community Up*, p. 17.

146 One lawyer did legal: Eric Krol, "Service to Community Helps Pay the Way Toward College Education," *Chicago Tribune*, April 29, 1994.

147 "Boy, she's tall!": Jacky Grimshaw, interview with author.

147 Each Ally received a copy: Leif Elsmo, interview with author.

147 The manual proposed ways: John P. Kretzmann and John L. McKnight, *Building Communities from the Inside Out: A Path Toward Finding and Mobilizing a Community's Assets*, 1993.

148 "My mom and dad would always say": Michelle Obama, speech to Democratic National Convention, 2008.

148 "The first thing that was mine": Geraldine Brooks, "Michelle Obama and the Roots of Reinvention."

148 "It sounded risky and just": Richard Wolffe, "Barack's Rock," *Newsweek*, February 25, 2008.

148 She described her three-year stint as executive: Ibid.

148 In 1995, not two years after: Jeremy Mindich, "AmeriCorps: Young, Spirited and Controversial," *Chicago Tribune*, April 9, 1995.

148 "I was never happier": Michelle Obama, speech to the Corporation for National and Community Service, Washington, D.C., May 12, 2009.

148 "She didn't care": Jobi Petersen Cates, interview with author.

149 "There's nothing funnier": Michelle Obama, speech at a Greater D.C. Cares event, June 16, 2009.

149 "the most powerful thing": Christi Parsons, Bruce Japsen, and Bob Secter, "Barack's Rock," *Chicago Tribune*, April 22, 2007.

149 "who wants to just look": Jobi Petersen Cates, interview with author.

150 "She has a knack": Krsna Golden, interview with author.

150 "where the magic happened": Michelle Obama, speech at a Greater D.C. Cares event, June 16, 2009.

150 "You can't be punching": Leif Elsmo, interview with author.

150 "I hear that": Julie Sullivan, interview with author.

151 "didn't indulge that situation": Jobi Petersen Cates, interview with author.

151 "We'd go from some": Julie Sullivan, interview with author.

151 "That's nice, but we've": Paul Schmitz, interview with author.

152 "It was very focused on": Kelly James, interview with author.

152 "The thrust of our": Hank De Zutter, "What Makes Obama Run?," *Chicago Reader*, December 8, 1995.

153 She viewed her role: Michelle Obama, speech at University of California–Merced commencement, May 16, 2009.

153 "just wasn't big enough": Sunny Fischer, interview with author.

## 8 | A LITTLE TENSION WITH THAT

154 "I grew up five minutes": Holly Yeager, "The Heart and Mind of Michelle Obama," *O: The Oprah Magazine*, November 2007.

154 "As fate would have it": Michelle Obama, speech to University of California–Merced commencement, May 16, 2009.

154 "What I found": Ibid.

155 The university endorsed restrictive covenants: Arnold R. Hirsch, *Making the Second Ghetto: Race and Housing in Chicago, 1940–1960*, pp. 144–145.

155 "The gutters were full": John W. Boyer, *A Hell of a Job Getting It Squared Around: Three Presidents in Times of Change; Ernest D. Burton, Lawrence A. Kimpton, and Edward H. Levi*, p. 112.

155 By one estimate: Ibid., p. 116.

155 "Social engineering on a vast": Ibid., p. 131.

155 "Of those who did not return": Ibid., p. 130.

156 By 1970, the university: James R. Grossman, Ann Durkin Keating, and Janice L. Reiff, eds., *The Encyclopedia of Chicago*, p. 848.

156 "regulate both the number": Hirsch, p. 170.

156  "people like us": John Boyer, interview with author.

156  "I appreciate what you are saying": Timuel D. Black Jr., *Bridges of Memory: Chicago's First Wave of Black Migration,* p. 583.

157  She also had a snapshot: Arthur Sussman, interview with author.

157  "Until you can bridge those": Michelle Obama, interview with author, 2007.

157  Called Summer Links: Summer Links and Jennifer Nanasco, "Close-up on Juvenile Justice: Author Former Offender Among Speakers," *University of Chicago Chronicle* 17, no. 4 (November 6, 1997).

157  "students and faculty explore": Ibid.

158  Improvements in the surrounding communities: Arthur Sussman and John Boyer, interviews with author.

158  In his first year, 15 percent: John Boyer, interview with author.

158  "a broader and more diverse profile": Ibid.

158  "convinced that the university": Ibid.

158  "not just make us into some kind of NGO": Ibid.

159  Many African American students: Melissa Harris-Perry, interview with author.

159  "You cannot do community-based": Samuel Speers, interview with author.

159  "It was possible that other elite schools": Arnold Sussman, interview with author.

159  "We had to fulfill": Paul Schmitz, *Everyone Leads: Building Leadership from the Community Up,* p. 245.

160  A grand total of nine: Robert Draper, "Barack Obama's Work in Progress," *GQ,* November 2009.

160  Many years later: Jeff Zeleny, "As Author, Obama Earns Big Money and a New Deal," *New York Times,* March 20, 2009.

161  "Michael Jordan can come": Thomas Hardy, "Jackson Foe Now Wants Old Job Back," *Chicago Tribune,* December 19, 1995.

161  "She brought elegance and class": David Remnick, *The Bridge: The Life and Rise of Barack Obama,* p. 283.

161  "Because I believe": Michelle Obama, unpublished interview with Scott Helman, 2007.

161  "How can you impact": Scott Helman, "Early Defeat Launched a Rapid Political Climb," *Boston Globe,* October 12, 2007.

161  "We as a family": Liza Mundy, "A Series of Fortunate Events," *Washington Post,* August 12, 2007.

161  "Michelle had a black": Abner Mikva, interview with author.

162  "I don't trust the people": Mariana Cook, interview with Barack and Michelle Obama, May 1996.

162  "When you are involved in politics": Ibid.

162  It was one thing for him to surprise her: Draper, "Barack Obama's Work in Progress."

162  "There is a little tension with that": Cook, interview with the Obamas, May 1996.

163  "He was not any": Remnick, *The Bridge.*

163 "the very real conflicts": Joe Frolik, "A Newcomer to the Business of Politics Has Seen Enough to Reach Some Conclusions About Restoring Voters' Trust," *Cleveland Plain Dealer,* August 3, 1996.

163 Back in Hawaii: Barack Obama, *Dreams from My Father,* p. 97.

163 "What you have been doing": John McKnight, interview with author.

164 "We have no shortage": Hank De Zutter, "What Makes Obama Run?," *Chicago Reader,* December 8, 1995.

164 "What if a politician": Ibid.

164 "I may not be": Madeline Talbott, interview with author.

165 The freshman struck: Emil Jones, interview with author.

165 "He thought you could press": Remnick, *The Bridge,* p. 299

165 "He wasn't a maverick": Cynthia Canary, interview with author.

165 "One night, we were playing": Larry Walsh, interview with author.

165 "sharing the humor": Barack Obama, *Audacity of Hope,* p. 339.

166 "this business is not": Carol Felsenthal, "The Making of a First Lady," *Chicago,* January 16, 2009.

166 "three magical months": Barack Obama, *Audacity of Hope,* p. 339.

166 "It's like, oh": Geraldine Brooks, "Michelle Obama and the Roots of Reinvention: How the First Lady Learned to Dream Big," *More,* October 2008.

166 "The strains in our relationship": Barack Obama, *Audacity of Hope,* p. 339.

166 Money was becoming an increasing: Barack and Michelle Obama, IRS Form 1040, 200.

166 "We didn't pick": Michelle Obama, unpublished interview with Scott Helman, 2007.

166 They paid more: Ibid. See also Michelle Obama, speech to Democratic National Convention, September 4, 2012.

166 Their down payment: Ray Gibson, John McCormick, and Christi Parsons, "How Broke Were the Obamas? Hard to Tell," *Chicago Tribune,* April 20, 2008.

166 with a small assist: Maggie Murphy and Lynn Sherr, "The President and Mrs. Obama on Work, Family and Juggling It All," *Parade,* June 20, 2014.

167 After he was elected: Malik Nevels, interview with author.

167 Barack considered himself: Barack Obama, *Audacity of Hope,* p. 3.

167 he quickly learned: Ibid., p. 105.

168 "went to Harvard and became": Ted Kleine, "Is Bobby Rush in Trouble?," *Chicago Reader,* March 17, 200.

168 "If you so impress white": Ibid.

168 "Barack is viewed": Ibid.

168 "if you're well educated": Ibid.

168 "You talk a certain type": David Mendell, *Obama: From Promise to Power,* pp. 190–191.

169 "Tired and stressed": Barack Obama, *Audacity of Hope,* p. 340.

169 "What a bunch": "Philip, Criminals Win Again," *Chicago Tribune,* December 31, 1999.

169 "a wailing baby in tow": Barack Obama, *Audacity of Hope,* p. 106.

169  "realizing that I would": Ibid.
169  The race, he said: Ibid., p. 354.
170  "it's impossible not to": Ibid., p. 107.
170  "a bit of useful": Ibid., p. 355.
170  "I'm sorry, Mr. Obama": Ibid.
170  "imagine the other person's hopes": Mariana Cook, interview with Barack and Michelle Obama, 1996.
171  "How we approach": Ibid.
171  "I've seen that relationship": Julie Sullivan, interview with author.
171  But as parents: Barack Obama, *Audacity of Hope*, p. 336.
171  "You only think about": Ibid., p. 340.
171  "My wife's anger": Ibid.
171  He had vowed: Ibid., p. 346.
171  Indeed, his role model: Valerie Jarrett, interview with *Frontline*, www.pbs .org/wgbh/pages/frontline/government-elections-politics/choice-2012/the -frontline-interview-valerie-jarrett.
171  "As far as I was": Ibid.
171  "After all, it wasn't as if": Ibid.
172  "We were terrified": Michelle Obama, speech, Dwight D. Eisenhower Executive Office Building, Washington, D.C., September 18, 2009.
172  "not knowing whether": Barack Obama, remarks, Bipartisan Health Care Summit, Washington, D.C., February 25, 2010.
172  "I can't breathe": Valerie Jarrett, interview with *Frontline*, PBS, posted on the show's website, but this comment was not included in the broadcast. See www.pbs.org/wgbh/pages/frontline/government-elections-politics/choice -2012/the-frontline-interview-valerie-jarrett.
172  "narrowed to a single": Barack Obama, *Audacity of Hope*, p. 186.
172  "The bad food and stale air": Ibid., p. 4.
172  "more sensible pursuits": Ibid.
173  Shomon said Barack: Dan Shomon, interview with author.
173  "completely mortified and humiliated": Barack Obama, interviewed by David Remnick, American Magazine Conference, Phoenix, Ariz., November 2006.
173  "For God's sake": Helman, "Early Defeat Launched a Rapid Political Climb."
173  "It's hard to look": Ibid.
173  named for poet Maya Angelou: Michelle Obama, remarks at Maya Angelou memorial service, June 7, 2014.
173  "And at the same time": Helman, "Early Defeat."

## 9 | JUST DON'T SCREW IT UP

174  She walked up: Susan Sher, interview with author.
174  "This is my life": Valerie Jarrett, interview with author, 2007.
175  She told colleagues when: Susan Sher, interview with author.
175  Stepping from a bus: Kenneth Kates and Susan Sher, interviews with author.
175  The heart of her pitch: Rosita Ragin, interview with author.
175  "It's not enough to be": Michelle Obama, "Reaching Out and Reaching

Back," *InsideOut*, University of Chicago Office of Community and Government Affairs, September 2005.

176 "Somebody like me": Michelle Obama, "Reaching Out."

176 "who have jobs to protect": Annah Dumas-Mitchell, "Officials to Contractors: Blacks Won't Be Cheated," *Chicago Defender*, November 29, 2001.

176 In return for his: LaRisa Lynch, "AACA and University of Chicago Hospitals Reach Agreement to Increase Black Participation in Construction Employment Opportunities," *Chicago Defender*, December 6, 2001.

176 Minority contracting was: Chicago Transit Authority documents, obtained through Freedom of Information Act.

176 To strengthen the contracting: Joan Archie, via John Easton, University of Chicago communications department.

176 From the 2002 to 2008: University of Chicago statistics.

177 "She would not shy away": Kenneth Kates, interview with author.

177 "Let's just look at the facts": John Rogers, interview with author.

178 "I saw Barack": Geoffrey Stone, interview with author.

179 "He didn't seem": William Daley, interview with author, 2007.

179 "Walking into that lunch": Valerie Jarrett, interview with author, 2007.

179 "It was, gosh": Michelle Obama, interview with author, 2007.

179 "I'm willing to gamble": Valerie Jarrett, interview with author, 2007.

179 When he added the column: Barack Obama, *Audacity of Hope*, p. 100.

180 roughly what he had raised: Federal Election Commission, campaign finance reports.

180 "more out of pity": Barack Obama, *Audacity of Hope*, p. 5.

180 "I don't like to talk": David Mendell, *Obama: From Promise to Power*, p. 152.

180 On the eve: Scott Fornek, "Barack Obama," *Chicago Sun-Times*, March 1, 2004.

180 "It's hard, and that's why": William Finnegan, "The Candidate: How the Son of a Kenyan Economist Became an Illinois Everyman," *New Yorker*, May 31, 2004.

181 "because she couldn't figure": *New Day*, CNN, June 23, 2014.

181 "the desire to be": Barack Obama, *Audacity of Hope*, p. 341.

181 She was certain: Ibid., p. 341.

181 "Work is rewarding": Rebecca Johnson, "The Natural," *Vogue*, September 2007.

181 He did have a guilty: Dan Shomon, interview with author.

181 "Figuring out how": Cassandra West, "Her Plan Went Awry, but Michelle Obama Doesn't Mind," *Chicago Tribune*, September 1, 2004.

182 "I am sitting there": Holly Yeager, "The Heart and Mind of Michelle Obama," *O: The Oprah Magazine*, November 2007.

182 "it didn't mean he wasn't": Johnson, "The Natural."

182 "The big thing I figured out": Yeager, "Heart and Mind."

182 "Don't sweat the small": Michelle Obama, remarks at the Women's Conference, Long Beach, Calif., October 23, 2007.

182 "I just think that's": Marian Robinson, unpublished interview with Scott Helman, 2008.

183 "no matter how much": Barack Obama, *Audacity of Hope*, p. 340.

183 "Sure, I helped": Ibid., p. 341.

183 "an important period": Yeager, "Heart and Mind."

183 "Michelle's strength, her willingness": Barack Obama, *Audacity of Hope*, p. 341.

183 "We ain't seen no": Barack Obama, remarks at Pleasant Ridge Missionary Baptist Church, 2003. Videotape by Bruce Orenstein and Bill Glader.

184 "Freed from worry": Barack Obama, *Audacity of Hope*, pp. 5–7.

184 "I am tired": Lauren W. Whittington, "Final Days for Fightin' Illini," *Roll Call*, March 9, 2004.

184 In a stroke of good fortune: Frank Main, "Hull's Dirty Laundry on the Line," *Chicago Sun-Times*, February 28, 2004.

185 "She understood": Forrest Claypool, interview with author.

185 "We believe he represents": Monica Davey, "A Surprise Senate Contender Reaches His Biggest Stage Yet," *New York Times*, July 26, 2004.

185 "rhymes uncomfortably": Scott Turow, "The New Face of the Democratic Party—and America," *Salon*, March 30, 2004.

185 "Just don't screw it up": Barack Obama, *Audacity of Hope*, p. 359.

185 "This guy's going": "Dreams of Obama," *Frontline*, January 20, 2009.

185 "Michelle sees this happening": Ibid.

186 a line passed among: Elizabeth Taylor, "There Has Always Been . . . This Hopefulness About the Country," *Chicago Tribune*, October 29, 2006.

186 "It's the hope of slaves": Barack Obama, speech to the Democratic National Convention, July 27, 2004.

187 "Absolutely the messiest": *Oprah Winfrey Show*, January 19, 2005.

187 leaders "who have their feet": Yeager, "Heart and Mind."

187 "Barack is not our savior": Suzanne Bell, "Michelle Obama Speaks at Illinois State U," *Daily Vidette*, October 26, 2004.

188 "a waste of time": Debra Pickett, "My Parents Weren't College-Educated Folks, So They Didn't Have a Notion of What We Should Want," *Chicago Sun-Times*, September 19, 2004.

188 "I didn't believe that politics": Bell, "Michelle Obama Speaks at Illinois State U," 2004.

188 "I'm as black as it gets": Elizabeth Brackett, *Chicago Tonight*, WTTW, October 28, 2004.

188 "Balancing a full-time": Michelle Obama, remarks to Women's Conference, Long Beach, Calif., October 26, 2010.

189 "It was never willy-nilly": Leif Elsmo, interview with author.

189 "The girls came first": Kenneth Kates, interview with author.

189 she put herself: Katie McCormick Lelyveld, interview with author.

189 "What I notice about": Johnson, "The Natural."

189 "If you can, you do": Haroon Rashid, interview with author.

189 "trying to herd these two": Carol Felsenthal, "The Making of a First Lady," *Chicago*, January 16, 2009.

190 "If I did that even": James Grossman, interview with author.

190 "Malia is six years": David Mendell, "Barack Obama: Democrat for U.S. Senate," *Chicago Tribune*, October 22, 2004.

190 In yet another lucky: Rick Pearson and John Chase, "Unusual Match Nears

Wire: Obama, Keyes Faceoff to Have Place in the Books," *Chicago Tribune*, November 2, 2004.

190 "I don't take all the type": Barack Obama, interview with author, 2004.

191 "I'm a big believer": Ibid.

191 "Maybe one day": Jeff Zeleny, "New Man on the Hill," *Chicago Tribune*, March 20, 2005.

191 She also joined the board: Bob Sector, "Obama's 2006 Income Drops," *Chicago Tribune*, April 17, 2007.

192 "There's no doubt": Barack Obama, interview with author, 2006.

192 "tough, smart and connected": Maureen Dowd, "She's Not Buttering Him Up," *New York Times*, April 25, 2007.

193 "The problem is that": Michelle Obama, unpublished interview with John McCormick.

193 "We are going to change": Valerie Jarrett, interview with author, 2007.

193 A family doctor: James Madera, then University of Chicago Hospitals president, interview with author.

194 In what would become: Harlan Krumholz, Yale University, interview with author.

195 "We have to create": Eric Whitaker, interview with author.

195 "People are so used to going": Laura Derks, interview with author.

195 "I have seen her": Yeager, "Heart and Mind."

196 In response, the hospital: James Madera, interview with author.

196 One day, he called: Barack Obama, *Audacity of Hope*, pp. 326–327.

## 10 | I'M PRETTY CONVINCING

197 "He comes out of nowhere": Craig Robinson, book-tour discussion, Dominican University, April 27, 2010.

197 "you don't grow up on": Ibid.

197 "You will never be hotter": Dan Balz and Haynes Johnson, *The Battle for America 2008*, p. 30.

197 "Have you talked to your wife?": Cynthia McFadden, *Nightline*, ABC, October 8, 2012.

198 "I've got great access to them": *Larry King Live*, CNN, February 11, 2008.

198 "They talked about passion": Craig Robinson, Dominican University, April 27, 2010.

198 "I had a Porsche": Pete Thamel, "Coach with a Link to Obama Has Hope for Brown's Future," *New York Times*, February 16, 2007.

199 "Well that's fine": Craig Robinson, Dominican University.

199 "She was interested in whether": Gwen Ifill, "Michelle Obama: Beside Barack," *Essence*, November 5, 2008.

200 "I was impressed by her": David Plouffe, *The Audacity to Win: The Inside Story and Lessons of Barack Obama's Historic Victory*, p. 12.

200 "No one had good news": Ibid.

200 "We're talking about": Jodi Kantor and Jeff Zeleny, "Michelle Obama Adds New Role to Balancing Act," *New York Times*, May 18, 2007.

200 "but he's drawn more": Plouffe, *Audacity to Win*, p. 13.

200  "the kind of person": Cal Fussman, "Valerie Jarrett: What I've Learned," *Esquire,* April 22, 2013.

201  Michelle had said in 1996: Mariana Cook, interview with Barack and Michelle Obama, 1996.

201  "I took myself down": Ifill, "Michelle Obama."

201  Michelle had veto: McFarland, *Nightline.*

201  "The person who was most": Valerie Jarrett, interview with author.

201  "Okay, how are we going to do this?": Michelle Obama, interview with author, 2007.

201  "I've never doubted the mission": Ibid.

201  "The selfish part of me": Ibid.

202  "It had taken a little convincing": Michelle Obama, remarks at the Women's Conference, Long Beach, Calif., October 23, 2007.

202  "I was really the hold out": Connie Schultz, interview with author.

203  "Michelle Obama! That's one": Kantor and Zeleny, "Michelle Obama Adds New Role to Balancing Act."

203  "I'm scared of": "Obama Hasn't Smoked in Years, Scared of My Wife," Associated Press, September 23, 2013.

203  a funk after only: Plouffe, *Audacity to Win,* p. 59.

203  "Meandering, unmotivated, and hesitant": Ibid., p. 138.

204  "Barack is the luckiest": Abner Mikva, interview with author.

205  "Well, I would have to": Author interview with voter.

205  when the heartland was bearing: Peter Slevin, "Midwest Towns Sour on War as Their Tolls Mount," *Washington Post,* July 14, 2007.

206  "I guarantee you": Michelle Obama, remarks in Rockwell City, Iowa, October 9, 2007.

207  "You can't just tell": Robin Roberts, *Good Morning America,* ABC News, May 22, 2007.

207  "I am married to": Michelle Obama, remarks in Harlem, June 26, 2007.

207  "There's Barack Obama the phenomenon": Maureen Dowd, "She's Not Buttering Him Up," *New York Times,* April 25, 2007.

207  "He's too snorey": Tonya Lewis Lee, "Your Next First Lady?" *Glamour,* September 2007.

207  "Many people I talked to afterward": Dowd, "She's Not Buttering Him Up."

207  "Barack and I laugh about that": Raina Kelley, "A Real Wife, In a Real Marriage," *Newsweek,* February 16, 2008.

208  "What I realize as I get older": Lynn Norment, "The Hottest Couple in America," *Ebony,* February 2007.

208  She began an unpaid: John Easton, spokesman, University of Chicago Hospitals, July 17, 2014.

208  "I am going to be the person": David Mendell, *Obama: From Promise to Power,* p. 381.

209  A consultant to nonprofit: President's Commission on White House Fellowships, website.

209  Their instructor was often: Sandra Sobieraj Westfall, "5 Things to Know about Grandma-in-Chief Marian Robinson," *People,* January 20, 2009.

209 "We just shared all": Kelly Wallace, "What's a Hui and Why Michelle Obama Can't Live Without Hers," *iVillage*, November 5, 2012.

209 "It's just a silent thing": Yvonne Davila, interview with author.

210 Blanchard was an obstetrician: "Meet Dr. Anita Blanchard: A Doctor with a Mission," *InsideOut*, University of Chicago, September 2005.

210 Nesbitt met Craig Robinson: Marty Nesbitt, interview with author.

210 He met Barack: Ibid.

210 "We need you all to be": Harriette Cole, "The Real Michelle Obama," *Ebony*, September 2008.

211 "I believe [he] will be president": Valerie Jarrett, interview with author, July 5, 2007.

211 "She takes this so seriously": Melissa Winter, interview with author, 2007.

212 Shaken, she also made: Peter Slevin, "Michelle Obama in Iowa Accident," *Washington Post*, October 9, 2007.

212 "He has natural political": Pete Giangreco, interview with author.

212 "If you had asked me which": Jobi Petersen Cates, interview with author.

213 Through Burns and his small-town: Peter Slevin, "A Tiny Iowa Paper and One Very Big Name: Obama," WashingtonPost.com, January 3, 2008.

213 "It's Iowa or bust": Plouffe, *Audacity to Win*, p. 17.

213 "I'm a fourth-quarter player": Chelsea Kammerer, interview with author.

213 not "ready to elect a black president": Peter Wallsten and Richard Faussett, "For Black Skeptics, Obama Cites Iowa," *Los Angeles Times*, January 7, 2008.

214 "Had he married a": Remnick, *The Bridge*, p. 502.

214 "Michelle is not only African American": Allison Samuels, "What Michelle Means to Us," *Newsweek*, November 21, 2008.

215 "Ask yourselves, of all the candidates": Michelle Obama, speech in Orangeburg, S.C., November 25, 2007. "Jena justice" refers to a sequence of racially charged incidents in Jena, Louisiana. A white prosecutor's decision to charge five black Jena High School students with attempted murder in the December 2006 beating of a white student led to protests by demonstrators who argued that the charges were excessive and represented a pattern of unequal treatment of black residents. Authorities later filed reduced charges. Five students pleaded guilty to misdemeanor simple battery. One student pleaded guilty to second-degree battery and received jail time. Mary Foster, "Jena 6 Case Nears Conclusion," Associated Press, June 25, 2009.

216 "There's an emotional exhaustion": Jackie Norris, interview with author.

## 11 | VEIL OF IMPOSSIBILITY

218 "The Obamas could not possibly": Gwen Ifill, "Michelle Obama: Beside Barack," *Essence*, November 5, 2008.

219 "because of their race or gender": Alec MacGillis, "A Margin That Will Be Hard to Marginalize," *Washington Post*, January 27, 2008.

219 "The Clintons are disturbing": DeDe Mays, interview with author.

219 "In the past week or two": Michelle Obama, Obama campaign letter, January 24, 2008.

219 "If she thinks we're being": Lauren Collins, "The Other Obama: Michelle Obama and the Politics of Candor," *New Yorker,* March 10, 2008.

220 "My girl's tough": Melissa Winter, interview with author, 2008.

220 She was a recent political: David Axelrod, interview with author.

220 "Power concedes nothing": Michelle Obama, speech in Estill, S.C., January 2008.

221 "My fear is that we don't know": Michelle Obama, speech in Hilton Head, S.C., January 2008.

221 "Well, let me tell you something": Ibid.

221 Barack earned 78 percent of black: David Plouffe, *The Audacity to Win,* p. 163.

222 "I know what I will be telling": Ally Carragher, interview with author.

222 "freedom ... equality ...": Will.I.Am, "Why I Recorded 'Yes We Can,'" *Huffington Post,* February 3, 2008.

222 "I look at my life": Michelle Obama, speech in Hilton Head, S.C.

223 "This nation is broken": Michelle Obama, speech in Estill, S.C.

223 "You reach the bar": Ibid.

224 "That little girl started to cry": Michelle Obama, speech in Hilton Head, S.C.

224 Katie McCormick Lelyveld's phone rang: Katie McCormick Lelyveld, interview with author.

225 "To think your country": *Hannity & Colmes,* Fox, March 8, 2008.

225 "We've grown up and lived": Michelle Malkin, "Michelle Obama's America—and Mine," *Augusta Chronicle,* February 21, 2008.

225 "Hope is making a comeback": Michelle Obama, speech in Madison, Wisc., C-SPAN.

226 "The army made it easier": Colin Powell, *My American Journey,* p. 62.

226 "No one who was there": Paul Schmitz, interview with author.

226 "expressing a feeling that": Timuel Black, interview with author.

226 "That was vintage truth": James Montgomery, interview with author.

226 "What she meant" Burton wrote: Michael Cooper, "Comments Bring Wives into Fray in Wisconsin," *New York Times,* February 20, 2008.

227 "What she meant was, this is the first time": "Obama Defends Wife's Remark on Pride in Country," Associated Press, February 20, 2008.

227 "I'm proud in how Americans are": "Michelle Obama Seeks to Clarify 'Proud' Remark," Associated Press, February 21, 2008.

227 Reflecting on the episode: Robert Gibbs, interview with author, 2008.

227 "Stokely Carmichael in a designer dress": *The O'Reilly Factor,* Fox, January 26, 2009.

228 The cartoon depicted Michelle: *New Yorker,* July 21, 2008.

228 "as the fear-mongering": Nico Pitney, "Barry Blitt Defends His New Yorker Cover Art of Obama," *Huffington Post,* July 13, 2008.

228 "Mom doesn't love her country": Rosemary Ellis, "A Conversation with Michelle Obama," *Good Housekeeping,* November 2008.

228 "How can Michelle Obama be": Verna Williams, "The First (Black) Lady," *Denver University Law Review* 86 (June 1, 2009).

228 "It is one of the chief requirements": Marjorie Williams, "Barbara's Backlash!," *Vanity Fair*, August 1992.

228 "who understands the Constitution": Michelle Obama, speech in Iowa, 2007.

228 "You are amazed sometimes": Michael Powell and Jodi Kantor, "After Attacks, Michelle Obama Looks for a New Introduction," *New York Times*, June 18, 2008.

229 "This is the choice we face": Patrick Healy and Jeff Zeleny, "Wisconsin Hands Obama Victory, Ninth in a Row," *New York Times*, February 20, 2008.

229 "helped bring me to Jesus": Obama, Obama for America statement, March 14, 2008.

230 "Fact number one": Ben Wallace-Weld, "Destiny's Child," *Rolling Stone*, February 22, 2007.

230 The source was an ABC News: Brian Ross, ABC, March 13, 2008.

231 "What you had was a moment": Dan Balz and Haynes Johnson, *The Battle for America 2008: The Story of an Extraordinary Election*, p. 201.

231 "This Jeremiah Wright thing": Marty Nesbitt, interview with author.

231 "The conversation that Barack and I had": Cash Michaels, "Wright Episode Was 'Opportunity' to Lead, Says Mrs. Obama," *New York Amsterdam News*, April 18, 2008.

232 "We need energy and fight": Plouffe, *Audacity to Win*, p. 212.

232 "Michelle was very good in moments like": Ibid., p. 213.

233 Barack told worried campaign: Ibid., p. 208.

234 What Barack "did in his speech was give": MacKensie Carpenter, "Michelle Obama Wows Them at CMU," *Pittsburgh Post-Gazette*, April 3, 2008.

234 "I was incredibly proud": Michaels, "Wright Episode."

235 He called the performance "appalling": Barack Obama, remarks in Winston-Salem, N.C., April 29, 2008.

235 "And they're like, 'Ooh, this is a big night' ": Rosemary Ellis, "A Conversation with Michelle Obama," *Good Housekeeping*, November 2008.

236 "A lot of sleepless nights": Michelle Obama, remarks at Tuskegee University, May 9, 2015.

236 It frustrated her and shook: David Axelrod, interview with author.

236 "They were afraid they were going": Forrest Claypool, interview with author.

236 "She was angry that everyone was tiptoeing": Ibid.

237 "Okay, let me try it again": Ibid.

237 "It only takes one": David Mendell, *Obama: From Promise to Power*, p. 382.

237 "What I remember most was": Michelle Obama, speech in Orangeburg, S.C., November 2007.

237 "great sympathy and outpouring": Mendell, p. 382.

238 Durbin relayed the information: Richard Durbin, interview with author.

238 "I don't lose sleep": *60 Minutes*, CBS, February 2007.

239 Yet so did Richard Epstein: Richard Epstein, interview with author.

239 "You grow up very": Arne Duncan, interview with author, 2008.

239 The average white metropolitan resident: Mary Pattillo, interview with author.

239 He won, and sent her: Ellen Warren, "Economist Gets Nobel, but Ex-Wife Is the Real Winner," *Chicago Tribune*, October 20, 1995.

240 During the 1968 Democratic National Convention: George Hrbek, interview with Rhaina Cohen.

240 In 1971, four firebombs: "Firebombs Damage Hyde Park Church," *Chicago Tribune*, June 21, 1971.

240 "filled with good spirits": Hrbek, interview with Rhaina Cohen.

240 She mixed water and lye: Rachel Swarns, *American Tapestry: The Story of the Black, White, and Multiracial Ancestors of Michelle Obama*, p. 63.

240 "black and white together": Comment attributed to comedians Mike Nichols and Elaine May.

241 "It's a place where you can be who you are": Blue Balliett, interview with author.

241 In an outdoor cage: Jamie Kalven, interview with author.

241 "for whom the fact of living together": Ibid.

241 "If we could take Hyde Park": Valerie Jarrett, interview with author, 2008.

242 "It's scary": Alex Leary, "It's Michelle Obama's Time of Opportunity," *St. Petersburg* (Fla.) *Times*, August 25, 2008.

242 It was important to us for a whole range": David Axelrod, interview with author.

244 Michelle's poll numbers: Plouffe, *Audacity to Win*, p. 301.

244 "Surreal is almost like": Kristen Gelineau, "Would-be First Lady Drifts into Rock-Star Status, Tentatively," Associated Press, March 30, 2008.

244 "How are you!": Michelle Obama, campaign office visit, Akron, Ohio.

245 "Congratulations, Mr. President ": Craig Robinson, *A Game of Character: A Family Journey from Chicago's Southside to the Ivy League and Beyond*, p. 243.

245 As he rode through the city: Ibid., p. 244.

246 "I'm thinking justice": MyKela Loury, interview with author.

246 "We're finally free": Tracy Boykin, interview with author.

246 thinking of Emmett Till: David Remnick, *The Bridge: The Life and Rise of Barack Obama*, p. 558.

246 "We cried together": Capers Funnye, interview with author.

## 12 | NOTHING WOULD HAVE PREDICTED

247 "They could not have been kinder": *The Tom Joyner Radio Show*, August 27, 2013.

248 "My wife and I": Craig Robinson, interview with author, 2009.

248 "many young boys and girls": Michelle Obama, remarks at the U.S. Capitol, April 28, 2009.

249 "in the crosshairs": Verna L. Williams, "The First (Black) Lady," *Denver University Law Review* 86 (June 1, 2009).

249 "People are going to be watching": Verna Williams, interview with author.

249 "figuring out the job": Michelle Obama, remarks to reporters, White House, January 13, 2010.

249  "It wasn't smooth": Jackie Norris, interview with author.

250  "It is so hard to project": Robin Roberts, *Good Morning America,* ABC News, May 22, 2007.

250  "I have a huge responsibility": Michelle Obama, remarks at Georgetown University, Washington, D.C., November 11, 2011.

251  "I'm not here for me": Anita McBride, interview with author.

252  "There's no way I could discuss things": Kati Marton, *Hidden Power: Presidential Marriages That Shaped Our Recent History,* p. 232.

252  "It's the type of thing that": Ibid., p. 209

252  "saw an open, honest woman": Ibid.

253  "The turmoil in my heart": Ibid., pp. 61–62.

253  "Did my Eleanor relate": Ibid., p. 64.

254  "If I were a Negro today": Eleanor Roosevelt, "If I Were a Negro," *Negro Digest,* October 1, 1943.

254  "she said, 'If I were'": John Johnson, oral history, TheHistoryMakers .com.

254  "Everything you do, every piece of blood": Katherine Boyle, "EPA: Agency Is at Center of President's 'Highest Priorities,' First Lady Says," *E&E News PM,* February 26, 2009.

254  "trailblazer in civil rights": Michelle Obama, remarks at the U.S. Department of Transportation, February 23, 2009.

254  "We are going to need you": Michelle Obama, remarks at the U.S. Department of Agriculture, February 19, 2009.

255  "to learn, to listen, to take": Michelle Obama, remarks at the U.S. Department of Education, February 2, 2009.

255  "a luxury that a working class kid": Michelle Obama, remarks at the Corporation for National and Community Service, May 12, 2009.

255  "my new home town": Michelle Obama, speech at Washington Mathematics Science Technology High School graduation, June 3, 2009.

255  "opening the doors": Michelle Obama, remarks at Anacostia High School, March 19, 2009.

255  "Well, she's not following": Lois Romano, "White House Rebel," *Newsweek,* June 20, 2011.

255  "One of those schools": Roscoe Thomas, interview with author.

256  "I never set foot on it": Michelle Obama, remarks at Anacostia High School, March 19, 2009.

256  "You brothers are lucky": Ibid.

256  "She told them how a lot of people": Robin Givhan, "Speaking Not of Pomp, but Circumstance," *Washington Post,* June 4, 2009.

256  When the day was over: Michelle Obama, remarks at the White House, November 2, 2009.

257  "She really wanted to think": Jocelyn Frye, interview with author.

257  "In every phase of my life": Michelle Obama, speech at Detroit Institute of Arts, May 27, 2010.

257  "substance and fun": Ibid.

257  "It's not sufficient": Jocelyn Frye, interview with author.

258 Just hours before: Peter Baker, "Inside Obama's War on Terror," *New York Times Magazine,* January 5, 2010.

258 lost an estimated 741,000: "The Employment Situation: March 2009," U.S. Bureau of Labor Statistics.

258 and 652,000 in March: "The Employment Situation: May 2009," U.S. Bureau of Labor Statistics.

258 "a nation in crisis": Peter Baker, "Obama Takes Oath and Nation in Crisis Embraces the Moment," *New York Times,* January 21, 2009.

258 "She's just very pragmatic": Marty Nesbitt, interview with author.

259 "She is completely honest": Valerie Jarrett, interview with author.

259 "She likes to say, 'This is not what people'": Susan Sher, interview with author.

259 "In a job like this": Cynthia McFadden, "The Contenders: Family Ties," *Nightline,* ABC News, October 8, 2012.

259 "Now I can just pop over": Oprah Winfrey, "Oprah Talks to Michelle Obama," *O, The Oprah Magazine,* April 2009.

259 "where he lets himself feel": Deval Patrick, interview with author.

259 In the residence: Details from whitehousemuseum.org.

260 "Valerie was the counselor": Jackie Norris, interview with author.

260 "Do you still recognize me?": Robin Givhan, "One Lady, One Year, a Whole Lot of Firsts," *Washington Post,* January 14, 2010.

260 "It's one place you can go": Michael Scherer and Nancy Gibbs, "Find Your Space, Find Your Spot, Wear What You Love," *Time,* June 1, 2009.

260 "That I can do without": Holly Yeager, "The Heart and Mind of Michelle Obama," *O: The Oprah Magazine,* November 2007.

260 "My sister said": Rachel L. Swarns, "An In-Law Is Finding Washington to Her Liking," *New York Times,* May 4, 2009.

261 There were shopping trips: Eli Saslow, "From the Second City, an Extended First Family," *Washington Post,* February 1, 2009.

261 In Washington, after accompanying Malia: Oprah Winfrey, "Oprah Talks to Michelle Obama," *O: The Magazine,* April 2009.

261 "has pulled me up": Michelle Obama, remarks at Mother's Day tea in White House, May 7, 2010.

261 As Marian found her way: Katherine Skiba, "First Grandma Keeps a Low Profile," *Chicago Tribune,* March 8, 2010.

261 "Oh, yeah, people say that": Susan Sher, interview with author.

261 "I'm pretty sure": Michelle Obama, remarks at Mother's Day tea in the White House, May 7, 2010.

262 "she escapes the bubble": *Oprah Winfrey Show,* May 2, 2011.

262 "A profound pleasure": Michael D. Shear, "Obama Tries Diplomatic Outreach to Israeli Public," *Washington Post,* July 9, 2010.

262 "They all walk up": "Harry S. Truman's Diary Book," January 6, 1947. Truman Presidential Library and Museum, www.trumanlibrary.org/diary/transcript.htm.

262 "Once, someone on my staff": Oprah Winfrey, "Oprah Talks to Michelle Obama," *O, The Oprah Magazine,* April 2009.

263 "Just give me the rules": Susan Sher, interview with author.

263 "I never goe": Peter Henriques, *Realistic Visionary: A Portrait of George Washington,* p. 101.

264 "There are prison elements to it": Michelle Obama and Laura Bush, remarks in Dar es Salaam, Tanzania, July 2, 2013.

264 "Barack has a 20-car motorcade": *Late Night with Jimmy Fallon,* NBC, February 22, 2013.

264 "Perhaps no other restaurant": Frank Bruni, "Food You'd Almost Rather Hug Than Eat," *New York Times,* August 2, 2006.

265 The theater seats they occupied: Randy Kennedy, "The Obamas Sat Here: Theater Seats to Be Auctioned," NewYorkTimes.com, September 25, 2009.

265 "It's a derivative job": Trooper Sanders, interview with author.

266 "bastion of everything": Jackie Norris, interview with author.

266 "As first lady": Laura Bush, *Spoken from the Heart,* p. 288.

266 The "constant back-and-forth": Ibid.

266 She left sample letters: Anita McBride, interview with author.

267 "This is one of those things": Ibid.

267 "because she knows": Jackie Norris, interview with author.

268 "Nothing in my life": Michelle Obama, speech to the Elizabeth Garrett Anderson School, April 2, 2009.

268 "I could do that all day": Trooper Sanders, interview with author.

268 On her desk: Joanna Sugden, " 'She made us all feel that our goals are achievable,' " *Times* (London), January 9, 2012.

269 "You have an unprecedented ability": Michelle Obama, speech in Mexico City, April 14, 2010.

269 "Don't just put me on a plane": Trooper Sanders, interview with author.

## 13 | BETWEEN POLITICS AND SANITY

270 no one had planted: Michelle Obama, *American Grown: The Story of the White House Kitchen Garden and Gardens Across America,* p. 28.

270 She was in her kitchen: Ibid., p. 24.

270 "about the food we eat": Ibid., p. 9.

270 "because I wanted this": Ibid., p. 31.

271 "For little kids": Ibid., p. 107.

271 Amid energetic photo ops: Jocelyn Frye, interview with author.

271 Between 1995 and 2008: "Too Fat to Fight: Retired Military Leaders Want Junk Food Out of America's Schools," www.missionreadiness.org/2010/too -fat-to-fight.

271 Further, many recruits: Michelle Obama, *American Grown,* p. 174.

272 Obesity and its effects: U.S. Department of Agriculture news release, February 9, 2010.

272 The CDC reported: Mark Fainaru-Wada, "Critical Mass Crisis: Child Obesity," ESPN.com, March 26, 2009.

272 "It's done, honey": Sheryl Gay Stolberg, "Childhood Obesity Battle Is Taken Up by First Lady," *New York Times,* February 10, 2010.

273 "Our kids don't choose to make": Michelle Obama, speech at the White House, February 9, 2010.

273 "a little chubby": *Parents,* March 2008.

273 "There were some nights when you got home": Michelle Obama, speech at the White House, February 9, 2010.

273 Her family started eating: Michelle Obama, *American Grown,* p. 17.

274 "For the event, Mrs. O": Mary Tomer, www.Mrs-O.com, March 3, 2009.

275 "She has perhaps even surpassed": Kate Betts, *Everyday Icon: Michelle Obama and the Power of Style,* p. 107.

275 "She's made her point": Maureen Dowd, "Should Michelle Cover Up?," *New York Times,* March 8, 2009.

275 trainers marketed: Rylan Duggan, *Totally Toned Arms: Get Michelle Obama Arms in 21 Days* (New York: Grand Central Life & Style, 2010).

276 "Never yet": Thomas Jefferson, *Notes on the State of Virginia,* 1781.

276 "We tried outside": Katie McCormick Lelyveld, interview with author.

276 "Fashion is what history looks like": Isabel Toledo, interview with author.

276 Toledo said Michelle paid: Ibid.

276 The same thing happened: Rheana Murray, "ASOS to Restock Sasha Obama's Beloved Unicorn Sweater," *New York Daily News,* November 21, 2013.

277 "what you wear": "First-Lady Style," *Ebony,* September 2008.

277 "gave women the permission": Ruben Toledo, interview with author.

277 "helping to liberate": Betts, p. x

277 "that defines style": Ibid., p. xiii.

277 "romantic glamor": Patricia J. Williams, interview with author.

277 After NBC's *Today* show: Lisa Orkin Emmanuel, "Michelle Obama's Shorts Are Latest Style Flap," Associated Press, August 20, 2009.

277 "It's not the end of the world": Ann Strzemien, "Michelle Obama's Shorts: Does the First Lady Have the Right to Bare Legs?," *Huffington Post,* September 13, 2009.

277 Four years later: Michelle Obama, *106 and Park,* BET, November 19, 2009.

278 she believed it would send: Katie McCormick Lelyveld, interview with author.

278 "Have you seen someone": Rachel Dodes, "Naeem Khan on Designing Michelle Obama's 'Priceless' First State Dinner Dress," *Wall Street Journal,* November 25, 2009.

278 "an incredible booster": Steven Kolb, interview with author.

279 "I was totally surprised": Robin Givhan, "To Showcase Nation's Arts, First Lady Isn't Afraid to Spotlight the Unexpected," *Washington Post,* July 21, 2010.

279 "I love the notion of having members": Givhan, "To Showcase Nation's Arts."

279 "If I'm giving those experiences": Ibid.

279 "We want to lift young people up": Laura Brown, "Michelle Obama: America's Got Talent," *Harper's Bazaar,* October 13, 2010.

280 The first couple's museum: Carol Vogel, "A Bold and Modern White House," *New York Times,* October 7, 2009.

280 Also among the borrowings: Holland Carter, "White House Art: Colors from a World of Black and White," *New York Times*, October 10, 2009.

280 Laura Bush had showed: Laura Bush, *Spoken from the Heart*, p. 426. Barbara Bush had shown the window to Hillary Clinton, who showed it to Laura Bush, p. 166.

281 "what's going on in their lives": Michelle Obama, *American Grown*, pp. 213–214.

281 "Even the president": Yungi de Nies, *Good Morning America*, ABC, April 15, 2010.

281 "This is what dads are": Andy Katz, interview with Barack Obama, *Good Morning America*, ABC, March 12, 2012.

281 did some kickboxing: Oprah Winfrey, "Oprah Talks to Michelle Obama," *O: The Oprah Magazine*, April 2009.

281 When they started: Sally Lee, "Michelle Obama's New Mission," *Ladies' Home Journal*, August 2010.

282 "They don't have any excuse": Michelle Obama, *106 and Park*, BET, November 19, 2013.

282 "to feel as if going to work": Maggie Murphy and Lynn Sherr, "The President and Michelle Obama on Work, Family, and Juggling It All," *Parade*, June 22, 2014.

282 "You want to see hardship?": *Nightline*, ABC News, October 8, 2012.

282 "You can't think you can be a jerk": "The First Lady Mentors in Denver," video, www.whitehouse.gov, January 10, 2010.

282 "a complete embarrassment": *Larry King Live*, CNN, February 9, 2010.

282 What they craved was normality: Michelle Obama, appearance with Jimmy Fallon, *Tonight Show*, NBC, February 2014.

283 "I think in our house": Nia-Malika Henderson, "Michelle Obama's Unfolding Legacy," *Washington Post*, February 9, 2011.

283 "What I value most": Jodi Kantor, "The First Marriage," *New York Times*, November 1, 2009.

283 "Have I told you lately": Barack Obama, *Of Thee I Sing: A Letter to My Daughters*, 2010.

284 signed with twenty-two: Sheryl Gay Stolberg and Robert Pear, "Obama Signs Health Care Overhaul Bill, with a Flourish," *New York Times*, March 23, 2010.

284 "The left thinks he did too little": Peter Baker, "The Education of President Obama," *New York Times*, October 17, 2010.

285 "The single most important": Major Garrett, "Top GOP Priority: Make Obama a One-Term President," *National Journal*, October 23, 2010.

285 "Kenyan anti-colonialist": Robert Costa, "Gingrich: Obama's 'Kenyan, Anti-Colonial Worldview,'" *National Review*, September 11, 2010.

285 "I wish this president": Richard A. Oppel Jr., "After Pressing Attacks on Obama, Romney Surrogate Later Apologizes," The Caucus blog, *New York Times*, July 17, 2012.

285 Forty-five percent of Republicans: Michael D. Shear, "Citing 'Silliness,' Obama Shows Birth Certificate," *New York Times*, April 28, 2011.

286 "Just as an assertive woman": Gwen Ifill, "Michelle Obama: Beside Barack," *Essence,* November 5, 2008.

286 "we do what we can": Kate M. Grossman, "Michelle in the Game: 1st Fundraiser adds $750k Fundraiser to Husband's Campaign," *Chicago Sun-Times,* April 17, 2007.

287 "We heard it from women's groups": Jackie Norris, interview with author.

287 "superbly canny, disciplined": Michelle Cottle, "Leaning Out: How Michelle Obama Became a Feminist Nightmare," *Politico,* November 21, 2013.

287 "all kinds of molds of innocuous": Rebecca Traister, interview with author.

288 "What's frequently missing:" Patricia J. Williams, interview with author.

288 "My message to white feminists": Brittney Cooper, "Lay Off Michelle Obama: Why White Feminists Need to Lean Back," *Salon.com,* November 29, 2013.

288 "Part of what we fought for": Jesse Washington, "Michelle Obama: The Person and the Persona," Associated Press, August 18, 2012. See also Michelle Obama, remarks at Tuskegee University, May 9, 2015.

288 In a 2011 poll: Krissah Thompson and Vanessa Williams, "Kindred Spirits," *Washington Post,* January 24, 2012.

288 "a feeling of relief": Michel Martin, "What I've Left Unsaid: On Balancing Career and Family as a Woman of Color," *National Journal Magazine,* July 26, 2014.

289 "We work hard to make": Cheryl Whitaker, interview with author.

289 "I have worked too hard": "Sharon Malone: The First Lady of Justice," *Essence,* December 16, 2009.

289 "illegal and unwarranted": George Wallace, speech, June 11, 1963, Alabama State Archives, www.archives.state.al.us/govs_list/schooldoor.html.

290 Later that year: "Women's Benefit Council Honors Pretty Vivian Malone," *Chicago Defender,* October 2, 1965.

290 "Once your sister stands": Toni Locy, "D.C. Politics Beckons, Repels Holder; Racial Tensions Have Chilling Effect on Prosecutor's Ambitions," *Washington Post,* December 21, 1996.

290 "That's the part that amazes me": Isabel Wilkerson, "Holding Fast," *Essence,* September 2012.

290 Malone and Holder: Ibid.

290 "I'm forever colored by my": "Sharon Malone: The First Lady of Justice," *Essence,* December 16, 2009.

291 "As you can see": Michelle Obama, speech to Partnership for a Healthier America in Washington, D.C., November 30, 2011.

291 "You have to change": Michelle Obama, remarks in conversation with Laura Bush and Cokie Roberts, August 6, 2014, Washington, D.C.

291 "MO is a complete imposter": Comments on Washingtonpost.com following an article by Emily Wax, "Michelle Shakes It Up During Visit to India," *Washington Post,* November 9, 2010.

291 "Instead of a government thinking": Neil Katz, "Sarah Palin: Americans Have 'God-Given Right' to Be Fat?" CBSnews.com, November 30, 2010.

291 At a church: Daniel Bice, "Sensenbrenner Apologizes to First Lady over 'Big Butt' Remark," *Milwaukee Journal-Sentinel,* December 22, 2011.

291 "It doesn't look like Michelle Obama": Dana Milbank, "Limbaugh's Anti-Michelle Binge," *Washington Post,* February 27, 2011.

292 "The White House is upset": Cynthia Lambert and Sarah Linn, "Rodeo Clown Apologizes for Racist Joke About Michelle Obama," *San Luis Obispo Tribune,* September 18, 2012.

292 The text said it was Michelle's: Jenee Desmond-Harris, "More Nat'l Geographic First Lady Jokes: School Board Member Fired," Theroot.com, May 31, 2013.

292 A Republican former chairman: Katrina A. Goggins, "Ex-SC Official Apologizes for Roast Remark," Associated Press, June 17, 2009.

292 "I'm sure you'll join me": Scott Rothschild, "Speaker O'Neal apologizes for Forwarding an Email That Calls Michelle Obama 'Mrs. YoMama,'" *Lawrence Journal-World,* January 5, 2012.

## 14 | SIMPLE GIFTS

293 "more than 6,600 Americans dead: Hannah Fischer, "U.S. Military Casualty Statistics," Congressional Research Service, February 5, 2012.

294 "A good day": Michelle Obama, the Women's Conference, Long Beach, Calif., October 26, 2010.

294 "You don't want to preach": Jocelyn Frye, interview with author.

294 "We were going back": Ibid.

294 When she spoke of expanded health insurance: Michelle Obama, *Keepin' It Real with Reverend Al Sharpton,* December 19, 2013.

295 "It's not enough just": Michelle Obama, Women's Conference, 2010.

295 "At this point": Bradley Cooper, interview with author.

296 "The families just don't": Jason Dempsey, interview with author.

296 "She felt like she wanted to": Jackie Norris, interview with author.

296 "you're right that": Jason Dempsey, interview with author.

297 Michelle appealed directly: Michelle Obama, remarks to National Governors Association, February 25, 2013.

297 roughly 80 percent: "2012 Demographics: Profile of the Military Community," Department of Defense, pp. 40–41.

297 "It was in the discussions": Matthew McGuire, interview with author.

297 "I think many people were": Reginald Rogers, "First Lady Visits Fort Bragg, Vows Support for Military Families," American Forces Press Service, March 13, 2009.

298 "We've heard rhetoric that": Barack Obama, Houston, February 29, 2008.

298 "Let's use this occasion to expand": Barack Obama, Tucson, January 12, 2011.

299 She wrote a letter: Susan Sher, interview with author.

299 "makes us think": Michelle Obama, open letter to parents, January 13, 2011.

300 "move the ball": Sheryl Gay Stolberg, "After a Year of Learning, the First Lady Seeks Out a Legacy," *New York Times,* January 14, 2010.

300 "It's not up to her": Katie McCormick Lelyveld, interview with author.

300 "The power she has": Jackie Norris, interview with author.

301 Michelle's staff admitted: Jocelyn Frye, interview with author.

301 "LOL LOL": "The Miami Heat at the White House: Healthy Tips from NBA Champions," YouTube, comments section, 2014.

301 The Secret Service recorded: Carol D. Leonnig, "Secret Service Fumbled Response After Gunman Hit White House Residence in 2011," *Washington Post*, September 28, 2014.

302 When Michelle learned: Ibid.

303 A loud warning alarm: Carol D. Leonnig, "White House Fence-Jumper Made It Far Deeper into Building Than Previously Known," *Washington Post*, September 29, 2014.

303 "We need you not just to tweak around": Michelle Obama, remarks to Grocery Manufacturers Association, March 16, 2010.

303 The East Wing calculated: Katie McCormick Lelyveld, interview with author.

304 "PHA works with": Partnership for a Healthier America, 2014 website.

304 "The White House got cold feet": Matea Gold and Kathleen Hennessey, "First Lady's Food Effort Stumbles," *Los Angeles Times*, July 21, 2013.

306 A conservative watchdog group: Dave Boyer, "First Lady's Spanish Vacation Cost Taxpayers $467K, Critics Estimate," *Washington Times*, April 27, 2012.

306 "The first lady is on a private": Lynn Sweet, "Michelle Obama at Luxury Spanish Resort: Gibbs Asked About 'the Appearance' of Trip," *Chicago Sun-Times*, August 5, 2010.

306 George Bush made 77 visits: Brian Montopoli, "487 Days at Camp David for Bush," CBSnews.com, January 16, 2009.

306 "You have temporary custody": Anita McBride, interview with author.

306 "She would fly United": Katie McCormick Lelyveld, interview with author.

307 The national unemployment rate: Shaila Dewan, "Zero Job Growth Latest Bleak Sign for Economy," *New York Times*, September 2, 2011.

307 If there were any source of solace: NBC/Wall Street Journal poll, August 2011.

308 "He felt strongly that he had done": David Axelrod, interview with author.

309 "I have better clarity": Nia-Malika Henderson, "Legacy in the Making," *Washington Post*, February 9, 2011.

309 In August, as his numbers were drifting: Katherine Skiba, "First Lady Set for Big Campaign Role," *Chicago Tribune*, September 1, 2011.

309 Even Republican-minded: Fox News poll, August 2011.

310 "People who work with their hands": Tom Bell, "First Lady Visits Maine Today," *Portland Press Herald*, September 30, 2011.

310 "These struggles aren't new": Michelle Obama, remarks in Portland, Maine, White House transcript, September 30, 2011.

311 "You can imagine the feeling": Nancy Benac, "First Lady a Not So Secret Campaign Weapon," Associated Press, September 29, 2011.

311 At a small New York fundraiser: David Axelrod, *The Believer*, p. 5.

311 Axelrod stayed behind: David Axelrod, interview with author.

312 "I love him": Hope Hundley, interview with author, February 22, 2012.

312 brought in more money: Mark Halperin and John Heilemann, *Double Down: Game Change 2012*, p. 35.

313 "frowns on people": Jackie Norris, interview with author.

313 "I'm not a big fan of the press": Rosemary Ellis, "A Conversation with Michelle Obama," *Good Housekeeping,* November 2008, www.goodhouse keeping.com/family/celebrity-interviews/michelle-obama-interview.

313 "Our paths are not foreign to you": Hazel Trice Edney, "White House Celebrates Black Press Week," *Washington Informer,* March 26, 2009.

314 That year, Michelle handed out copies: Capers Funnye, interview with author.

314 "My great-great-great grandmother": Robin Givhan, "We've Gotten a Lot Done, Michelle Obama Says of Year One as First Lady," *Washington Post,* January 14, 2010.

314 "Michelle Obama was privately fuming": Jodi Kantor, "First Lady's Fraught White House Journey to Greater Fulfillment," *New York Times,* January 7, 2012.

315 "I guess it is more interesting": Gayle King, *This Morning,* CBS, January, 11, 2012.

315 "We have a name for": "Obama Tells You to Sacrifice While Moochelle Vacations in Spain," *Rush Limbaugh Show,* August 10, 2010.

316 who used to give: Katherine Mangu-Ward, "Young, Wonky and Proud of It: Wisconsin Republican Paul Ryan Makes Waves," *Weekly Standard,* March 2003.

316 "the 47 percent": David Corn, "Romney Tells Millionaire Donors What He REALLY Thinks of Obama Voters,"*Mother Jones,* September 17, 2012.

316 "she paid a visit in June": Michelle Obama, remarks to African Methodist Episcopal Church General Conference, June 28, 2012.

318 "my almost spooky": Barack Obama, *Audacity of Hope,* p. 118.

318 "cleaned other people's houses": Julian Castro, Democratic National Convention, September 4, 2012.

319 "I wanted her to dominate": David Axelrod, interview with author.

319 "drives a couple of Cadillacs": Felicia Sonmez, "Romney: Wife Ann Drives a Couple of Cadillacs," Washingtonpost.com, February 24, 2012.

319 Ann had once expressed: Jack Thomas, "Ann Romney's Sweetheart Deal," *Boston Globe,* October 20, 1994.

321 "back when I wasn't so sure": Michelle Obama, remarks in Des Moines, Iowa, November 5, 2012.

## 15 | I AM NO DIFFERENT FROM YOU

322 "Slow down, you can't": Jennifer Delgado, Bridget Doyle, and Jeremy Gorner, "Teen's Killing Ignites Widespread Outrage," *Chicago Tribune,* January 31, 2013.

322 "Hadiya Pendleton was": Michelle Obama, remarks in Chicago, April 10, 2013.

323 "fulfill their god-given potential": Michelle Obama, remarks at Michelle Nunn for Senate rally, Atlanta, Georgia, September 8, 2014.

323 she wanted to reach back: Ari Shapiro, "We Have to Do More: Michelle Obama's Next Four Years," NPR, April 12, 2013; Philip Rucker and Krissah

Thompson, "An Increasingly Activist Michelle Obama?," *Washington Post,* April 10, 2013.

323 "We shouldn't live in a country this rich": Michelle Obama, *Keepin' It Real with Reverend Al Sharpton,* December 19, 2013.

323 "make it a Christmas treat": Michelle Obama, remarks at the White House, December 18, 2013.

324 "ought to be under consideration": Courtland Milloy, "Michelle Obama's Oscars Appearance Was an Unbecoming Frivolity," *Washington Post,* February 27, 2013.

325 "I have never felt more confident": Maggie Murphy and Lynn Sherr, "Michelle Obama on the Move," *Parade,* August 15, 2013.

325 "with some gusto": "Oprah Talks to Michelle Obama," *O: The Oprah Magazine,* April 2009.

325 Michelle, he said, had made him: Katherine Skiba, "Michelle Obama's 50th: 'Such a Fun, Fun Party,'" *Chicago Tribune,* January 19, 2014.

325 "She's almost like": Colleen Kane, "Parker Meets Michelle Obama, Speaks to Youth During Busy Week," *Chicago Tribune,* February 28, 2013.

325 More than two-thirds of Americans: Bruce Drake and Seth Motel, "Americans Like Michelle Obama, Except for Conservative Republicans," Pew Research Center, February 10, 2014.

326 "What you see is what": Arne Duncan, interview with author.

326 "She underscores that she is no": Linton Weeks, "The Cultish Appeal of Michelle Obama," NPR.org. February 19, 2014.

326 "they thought people": John Rogers, interview with author.

326 "He's not the first black president": Cheryl Whitaker, interview with author.

327 "Right now, my husband:" Michelle Obama, remarks in Chicago, April 10, 2013.

327 "A pretty shameful day": Barack Obama, remarks in the Rose Garden, April 17, 2013.

327 As Barack struggled to explain: Michelle Obama, "The World as It Should Be," *The Advocate,* August 27, 2008; Michelle Obama, remarks to the Gay and Lesbian Leadership Council, Democratic National Committee, New York, June 26, 2008.

327 "sometimes by fears": Michelle Obama, Women's Conference, October 23, 2007, Long Beach, Calif.

328 "It wasn't like it was busting out": Jane M. Saks, interview with author.

328 "You have to be more open-minded": Krsna Golden, interview with author.

328 "that feeling of openness": Kerry Eleveld, "It's Not Just About the Hair," *The Advocate,* August 27, 2008.

328 On a one-page, typewritten: Tracy Baim, "Obama Changed Views on Gay Marriage," *Windy City Times,* January 14, 2009.

329 "in a separate survey from IMPACT Illinois": Ibid.

329 same-sex couples should be allowed to marry: Barack Obama, interview with Robin Roberts, ABC News, May 9, 2012.

329 "For as long as I've known him": Jo Becker, *Forcing the Spring: Inside the Fight for Marriage Equality* (New York: Penguin, 2014), p. 296.

329 "Enjoy this day": Ibid.

329 "caused Michelle and the girls": Barack Obama, remarks, White House Pride Celebration, June 30, 2014.

330 "When she thought he was:" David Axelrod, interview with author.

330 "Just kind of hanging": Michelle Obama, *Live with Kelly and Michael,* April 21, 2014.

330 "I want to be this really fly": Maggie Murphy and Lynn Sherr, "Michelle Obama on the Move," *Parade,* August 15, 2013.

331 "Not long on pretense": Jonathan Van Meter, "Leading by Example," *Vogue,* April 2013.

331 "endless amounts of time": Michelle Obama, remarks at Mother's Day Tea, White House, May 9, 2013.

331 "There is no way": Michelle Obama, remarks at Mother's Day Tea, White House, May 12, 2014.

332 "The only reason that I am standing": Michelle Obama, remarks in Chicago, April 10, 2013.

332 "You will get your butts": Michelle Obama, remarks at Georgetown University, November 8, 2011.

333 "Are you talking about": David Remnick, "Going the Distance: On and Off the Road with Barack Obama," *New Yorker,* January 27, 2014.

333 a canvas later displayed: DeNeen L. Brown, "Iconic Moment Finds a Space at White House," *Washington Post,* August 29, 2011.

333 "When it comes to getting an education": Michelle Obama, speech at Bowie State University commencement, May 17, 2013.

334 "just another example": Barack Obama, speech at Morehouse College commencement, May 19, 2013.

334 "There's a lot wrong here": Ta-Nehisi Coates, "How the Obama Administration Talks to Black America," *Atlantic,* May 20, 2013.

335 "some thoughtful and sometimes not so thoughtful": Remnick, "Going the Distance."

335 "critical matters of racial justice": Randall Kennedy, "Did Obama Fail Black America?," *Politico Magazine,* July/August 2014.

335 "nation of cowards": Eric Holder, remarks on Black History Month, Washington, D.C., February 18, 2009.

335 " 'When you get ready to spend' ": Jim Montgomery, interview with author.

336 "plain fact": Barack Obama, remarks on My Brother's Keeper, February 27, 2014.

336 "I may not be a Marine": White House transcript, March 12, 2014.

337 Representatives approved: Food Resource and Action Center, October 2011, http://frac.org/about.

337 "When we send our kids": Michelle Obama, remarks in Alexandria, Va., January 25, 2012.

337 "I know that kids": Michelle Obama, remarks in Washington, D.C., September 12, 2013.

338 "You don't have to be": Michelle Obama, "The Campaign for Junk Food," *New York Times,* May 28, 2014.

338 "working hard to serve": Ibid.

339 "We simply can't afford": Michelle Obama, remarks at the White House, June 12, 2014.

339 "a stain on the soul": Kathleen Curthoys, "Helping Homeless Vets," *Army Times*, August 11, 2014.

339 "just wrong": Michelle Obama, remarks at Women's Veterans Care Development Forum, Arlington, Va., November 10, 2014.

339 "hard to know what to say": Michelle Obama, remarks in Chicago, April 10, 2013.

340 "And that, in the end": Ibid.

340 The need was clear: Martha J. Bailey and Susan M. Dynarsk, cited in White House fact sheet, "Increasing College Access for Low-Income Students," January 2014.

340 By 2014, the country: "Education at a Glance 2013," Organization for Economic Cooperation and Development.

340 where the 2014–2015 tuition: Sidwell Friends School, website.

340 "tilts the playing field": Barack Obama, remarks on higher education, White House, January 16, 2014.

341 "Because there are millions": Michelle Obama, remarks, White House, January 15, 2014.

341 "to seek them out and give them": Ibid.

342 "Are you listening": Michelle Obama, remarks, Atlanta, September 8, 2014.

EPILOGUE

343 "just wastes time": Michelle Obama, remarks, Atlanta, September 8, 2014.

343 only 36 percent: Editorial, "The Worst Voter Turnout in 72 Years," *New York Times*, November 11, 2014.

344 yawning gaps: Pew Research Center, "King's Dream Remains an Elusive Goal," August 22, 2013.

344 Michelle herself said: Michelle Obama, remarks in Topeka, Kan., May 17, 2014.

344 "incredible amounts of change": Marcia Chatelain, interview with author.

345 "playing a long game": Michelle Obama, speech, Democratic National Convention, September 5, 2012.

345 "I want to know": Jackie Calmes, "When a Boy Found a Familiar Feel in a Pat of the Head of State," *New York Times*, May 24, 2012.

345 "I want you to think": Michelle Obama, remarks to African Methodist Episcopal Church General Conference, Nashville, Tenn., June 28, 2012.

345 "something changed when": Michelle Obama, remarks at the White House, February 25, 2011.

345 "Maybe if I stay": "Power. Passions. Work. Mothers. And Sting." *More*, July/August 2015.

345 "why, as first lady, I do this": Michelle Obama, remarks at Georgetown University, November 8, 2011.

346 "We have a black family": BET Honors, January 14, 2012.

346 "celebrated black women's": Michelle Obama, remarks in Winston-Salem, N.C., June 7, 2014.

# Bibliography

Algren, Nelson. *Chicago: City on the Make*. Chicago: University of Chicago Press, 2011.

Axelrod, David. *The Believer: My Forty Years in Politics*. New York: Penguin Press, 2015.

Balz, Dan, and Haynes Johnson. *The Battle for America 2008: The Story of an Extraordinary Election*. New York: Viking, 2009.

Bell, Geneva. *My Rose: An African American Mother's Story of AIDS*. Cleveland: United Church Press, 1997.

Betts, Kate. *Everyday Icon: Michelle Obama and the Power of Style*. New York: Clarkson Potter, 2011.

Black, Timuel D., Jr. *Bridges of Memory: Chicago's First Wave of Black Migration*. Evanston, Ill: Northwestern University Press, 2005.

Bowen, William G., and Derek Bok. *The Shape of the River: Long-Term Consequences of Considering Race in College and University Admissions*. Princeton, N.J.: Princeton University Press, 1998.

Boyer, John W. *A Hell of a Job Getting It Squared Around: Three Presidents in Times of Change; Ernest D. Burton, Lawrence A. Kimpton, and Edward H. Levi*. Chicago: University of Chicago Press, 2013.

Branch, Taylor. *At Canaan's Edge: America in the King Years, 1965–68*. New York: Simon & Schuster, 2006.

Burroughs, Margaret Taylor. *Life with Margaret: The Official Autobiography*. Chicago: In Time Pub and Media Group, 2003.

Bush, Laura. *Spoken from the Heart*. New York: Scribner, 2010.

Cheney, Anne. *Lorraine Hansberry*. Boston: Twayne, 1984.

Cohen, Adam, and Elizabeth Taylor. *American Pharaoh: Mayor Richard J. Daley—His Battle for Chicago and the Nation*. Boston: Little, Brown, 2000.

Despres, Leon M., with Kenan Heise. *Challenging the Daley Machine: A Chicago Alderman's Memoir*. Evanston, Ill.: Northwestern University Press, 2005.

de Vise, Pierre. *Chicago's Widening Color Gap*. Chicago: Community and Family Study Center, University of Chicago, 1967.

Drake, St. Clair, and Horace R. Cayton. *Black Metropolis: A Study of Negro Life in a Northern City.* Chicago: University of Chicago Press, 1993.

Du Bois, W. E. B. *The Souls of Black Folk.* New York: Oxford University Press, 2007.

Givhan, Robin. *Michelle Obama: Her First Year as First Lady.* Chicago: Triumph Books, 2010.

Green, Adam. *Selling the Race: Culture, Community, and Black Chicago, 1940–1955.* Chicago: University of Chicago Press, 2007.

Grimshaw, William L. *Bitter Fruit: Black Politics and the Chicago Machine, 1931–1991.* Chicago: University of Chicago Press, 1992.

Grossman, James R. *Land of Hope: Chicago, Black Southerners, and the Great Migration.* Chicago: University of Chicago Press, 1989.

Grossman, James R., Ann Durkin Keating, and Janice L. Reiff, eds. *The Encyclopedia of Chicago.* Chicago: University of Chicago Press, 2004.

Halperin, Mark, and John Heilemann. *Double Down: Game Change 2012.* New York: Penguin, 2013.

Hansberry, Lorraine. *A Raisin in the Sun.* New York: Vintage Books, 1994.

———. *To Be Young, Gifted and Black,* New York, Signet Classics, 2011.

Henriques, Peter R. *Realistic Visionary: A Portrait of George Washington.* Charlottesville: University of Virginia Press, 2006.

Hirsch, Arnold R. *Making the Second Ghetto: Race & Housing in Chicago, 1940–1960.* Chicago: University of Chicago Press, 1998.

Hofstadter, Richard. *The American Political Tradition and the Men Who Made It.* New York: Alfred A. Knopf, 1973.

Jamison, Judith, with Howard Kaplan. *Dancing Spirit: An Autobiography.* New York: Doubleday, 1993.

Kantor, Jodi. *The Obamas.* New York: Little, Brown, 2012.

Kennedy, Randall. *The Persistence of the Color Line: Racial Politics and the Obama Presidency.* New York: Pantheon, 2011.

Kretzmann, John P., and John L. McKnight. *Building Communities from the Inside Out: A Path Toward Finding and Mobilizing a Community's Assets.* Skokie, Ill.: ACTA Publications, 1993.

Leeson, Richard M. *Lorraine Hansberry: A Research and Production Sourcebook.* Westport, Conn.: Greenwood Press, 1997.

Lemann, Nicholas. *The Promised Land: The Great Black Migration and How It Changed America.* New York: Vintage Books, 1992.

Maraniss, David. *Barack Obama: The Story.* New York: Simon & Schuster, 2012.

Marton, Kati. *Hidden Power: Presidential Marriages That Shaped Our Recent History.* New York: Pantheon Books, 2001.

McClain, Leanita. *A Foot in Each World: Essays and Articles by Leanita McClain.* Evanston, Ill., Northwestern University Press, 1986.

Mendell, David. *Obama: From Promise to Power.* New York: Amistad, 2007.

Mundy, Liza. *Michelle: A Biography.* New York: Simon & Schuster, 2009.

Obama, Barack. *The Audacity of Hope: Thoughts on Reclaiming the American Dream.* New York: Crown Publishers, 2006.

———. *Dreams from My Father: A Story of Race and Inheritance.* New York: Three Rivers Press, 2004.

———. *Of Thee I Sing: A Letter to My Daughters.* New York: Alfred A. Knopf, 2010.

Obama, Michelle. *American Grown: The Story of the White House Kitchen Garden and Gardens Across America.* New York: Crown Publishers, 2012.

Patrick, Deval. *A Reason to Believe: Lessons from an Improbable Life.* New York: Broadway, 2011.

Plouffe, David. *The Audacity to Win: The Inside Story and Lessons of Barack Obama's Historic Victory.* New York: Viking, 2009.

Powell, Colin L., with Joseph E. Persico. *My American Journey.* New York: Random House, 1995.

Remnick, David. *The Bridge: The Life and Rise of Barack Obama.* New York: Alfred A. Knopf, 2010.

———. *King of the World: Muhammad Ali and the Rise of an American Hero.* New York: Random House, 1998.

Robinson, Craig. *A Game of Character: A Family Journey from Chicago's Southside to the Ivy League and Beyond.* New York: Gotham Books, 2010.

Royko, Mike. *Boss: Richard J. Daley of Chicago.* New York: Plume, 1971.

Satter, Beryl. *Family Properties: Race, Real Estate, and the Exploitation of Black Urban America.* New York: Metropolitan Books, 2009.

Schmitz, Paul. *Everyone Leads: Building Leadership from the Community Up.* San Francisco: Jossey-Bass, 2012.

Scott, Janny. *A Singular Woman: The Untold Story of Barack Obama's Mother.* New York: Riverhead Books, 2011.

Sugrue, Thomas J. *Not Even Past: Barack Obama and the Burden of Race.* Princeton, N.J.: Princeton University Press, 2010.

Swarns, Rachel L. *American Tapestry: The Story of the Black, White, and Multiracial Ancestors of Michelle Obama.* New York: Amistad, 2012.

Tomer, Mary. *Mrs. O: The Face of Fashion Democracy.* New York: Center Street, 2009.

Travis, Dempsey J. *An Autobiography of Black Chicago.* Chicago: Urban Research Institute, 1981.

———. *An Autobiography of Black Jazz.* Chicago: Urban Research Institute, 1983.

———. *An Autobiography of Black Politics.* Chicago: Urban Research Press, 1987.

Tufankjian, Scout. *Yes We Can: Barack Obama's History-Making Presidential Campaign.* New York: powerHouse Books, 2008.

Turow, Scott. *One L: The Turbulent True Story of a First Year at Harvard Law School.* New York: Penguin, 2010.

Williams, Marjorie. *The Woman at the Washington Zoo: Writings on Politics, Family, and Fate.* New York: Public Affairs, 2005.

Willis, Deborah, and Kevin Merida. *Obama: The Historic Campaign in Photographs.* New York: Amistad, 2008.

Wilson, August. *Joe Turner's Come and Gone.* New York: Theater Communications Group, 2007.

Wilson, William Julius. *The Declining Significance of Race: Blacks and Changing American Institutions.* Chicago: University of Chicago Press, 1980.

Wright, Bruce. *Black Robes, White Justice.* Secaucus, N.J.: Lyle Stuart, 1987.

Wright, Richard. *Black Boy.* New York: Harper Perennial, 1993.

# Index

## ILLUSTRATION CREDITS

Marian Robinson: Obama campaign photo

Fraser Robinson: DuSable High School yearbook

Michelle and Craig: Obama campaign photo

Kindergarten photo: Theodore Ford

Michelle as a first-grader: Obama campaign photo

In high-school modern dance: Whitney Young High School

Michelle as a college freshman: Princeton University

Princeton University yearbook photo: Princeton University

With Stanley Stocker-Edwards: Kimberly M. Talley

With Susan Page: Kimberly M. Talley

With Barack in Hawaii: Obama campaign photo

Wedding: Courtesy of Obama campaign

In Kenya: OFA

At home in Chicago: *Chicago Tribune*, Zbigniew Bzdak

Public Allies: Courtesy of Public Allies

Election Day, 2000: AP Photo/*Chicago Sun-Times*, Scott Stewart

Iowa, 2007: AP Photo/Charlie Neibergall

Inaugural parade: Scout Tufankjian/Polaris

After inaugural ball: White House photo

Official photo: White House photo

Fashion bangle: White House photo

Jacob Philadelphia: White House photo

Hula hoop: White House photo

Secret Service headquarters: AP Photo / Pablo Martinez Monsivais

Ferebee Hope Elementary: White House photo

Reach Higher: White House photo

Minnesota, 2012: Elizabeth Schulze

#BringBackOurGirls: White House photo

Basketball game: AP Photo/Alex Brandon

Gardening: *The Washington Post*

Tug-of-war: White House photo

Elmo: AP Photo/Pablo Martinez Monsivais

LeBron James and Dwayne Wade: White House photo

State of the Union: AP Photo/Jacquelyn Martin

Marian Robinson with Michelle: Scout Tufankjian/Polaris

Ad shoot: Scout Tufankjian/Polaris